God bless me and
very one that thinks about
me. God see him as his
loving child

888 - 0005
3 47 - 33 14

376:17 How to heal or demonstrate
417:4, 28. p485:4. 339:7. 340:12 444:11
19:29 p [422 chemicalization]
401:16

Science and Health

WITH KEY
TO THE SCRIPTURES

Works of Mary Baker Eddy

Science and Health with Key to the Scriptures
Manual of The Mother Church
Miscellaneous Writings
Retrospection and Introspection
Unity of Good
Pulpit and Press
Rudimental Divine Science
No and Yes
Christian Science versus Pantheism
Message to The Mother Church, 1900
Message to The Mother Church, 1901
Message to The Mother Church, 1902
Christian Healing
The People's Idea of God
Poems
Christ and Christmas
*The First Church of Christ, Scientist,
and Miscellany*

Science and Health

WITH KEY TO THE SCRIPTURES

by MARY BAKER EDDY

*President of Massachusetts Metaphysical College
and Pastor Emeritus of The First Church of Christ, Scientist
Boston, Massachusetts*

Marcas Registradas

Published by The First Church of Christ, Scientist, in Boston, Massachusetts, U.S.A.

Ye shall know the truth,
and the truth shall make you free.
— JOHN viii. 32

There is nothing either good or bad,
but thinking makes it so.
— SHAKESPEARE

Oh! Thou hast heard my prayer;
And I am blest!
This is Thy high behest: —
Thou here, and *everywhere*.
— MARY BAKER G. EDDY

Contents

Preface

TO those leaning on the sustaining infinite, to-day is 1
big with blessings. The wakeful shepherd beholds
the first faint morning beams, ere cometh the full radiance 3
of a risen day. So shone the pale star to the prophet-
shepherds; yet it traversed the night, and came where, in
cradled obscurity, lay the Bethlehem babe, the human 6
herald of Christ, Truth, who would make plain to be-
nighted understanding the way of salvation through Christ
Jesus, till across a night of error should dawn the morn- 9
ing beams and shine the guiding star of being. The Wisemen were led to behold and to follow this daystar of
divine Science, lighting the way to eternal harmony. 12

The time for thinkers has come. Truth, independent
of doctrines and time-honored systems, knocks at the
portal of humanity. Contentment with the past and 15
the cold conventionality of materialism are crumbling
away. Ignorance of God is no longer the stepping-
stone to faith. The only guarantee of obedience is a 18
right apprehension of Him whom to know aright is
Life eternal. Though empires fall, "the Lord shall
reign forever." 21

A book introduces new thoughts, but it cannot make
them speedily understood. It is the task of the sturdy
pioneer to hew the tall oak and to cut the rough 24
granite. Future ages must declare what the pioneer
has accomplished.

Since the author's discovery of the might of Truth in 27

1 the treatment of disease as well as of sin, her system has
been fully tested and has not been found wanting; but
3 to reach the heights of Christian Science, man must live
in obedience to its divine Principle. To develop the full
might of this Science, the discords of corporeal sense
6 must yield to the harmony of spiritual sense, even as the
science of music corrects false tones and gives sweet concord to sound.

9   Theology and physics teach that both Spirit and
matter are real and good, whereas the fact is that
Spirit is good and real, and matter is Spirit's oppo-
12 site. The question, What is Truth, is answered by
demonstration, — by healing both disease and sin; and
this demonstration shows that Christian healing con-
15 fers the most health and makes the best men. On this
basis Christian Science will have a fair fight. Sickness
has been combated for centuries by doctors using ma-
18 terial remedies; but the question arises, Is there less
sickness because of these practitioners? A vigorous
"No" is the response deducible from two connate
21 facts, — the reputed longevity of the Antediluvians,
and the rapid multiplication and increased violence of
diseases since the flood.

24   In the author's work, RETROSPECTION AND INTROSPEC-
TION, may be found a biographical sketch, narrating
experiences which led her, in the year 1866, to the dis-
27 covery of the system that she denominated Christian
Science. As early as 1862 she began to write down and
give to friends the results of her Scriptural study, for
30 the Bible was her sole teacher; but these compositions
were crude, — the first steps of a child in the newly discovered world of Spirit.

She also began to jot down her thoughts on the 1
main subject, but these jottings were only infantile
lispings of Truth.   A child drinks in the outward world 3
through the eyes and rejoices in the draught.   He is
as sure of the world's existence as he is of his own; yet
he cannot describe the world.   He finds a few words, 6
and with these he stammeringly attempts to convey his
feeling.   Later, the tongue voices the more definite
thought, though still imperfectly.   9
So was it with the author.   As a certain poet says of
himself, she "lisped in numbers, for the numbers
came."   Certain essays written at that early date are 12
still in circulation among her first pupils; but they are
feeble attempts to state the Principle and practice of
Christian healing, and are not complete nor satisfac- 15
tory expositions of Truth.   To-day, though rejoicing
in some progress, she still finds herself a willing disciple at the heavenly gate, waiting for the Mind of 18
Christ.

Her first pamphlet on Christian Science was copyrighted in 1870; but it did not appear in print until 21
1876, as she had learned that this Science must be
demonstrated by healing, before a work on the subject
could be profitably studied.   From 1867 until 1875, 24
copies were, however, in friendly circulation.

Before writing this work, SCIENCE AND HEALTH, she
made copious notes of Scriptural exposition, which 27
have never been published.   This was during the years
1867 and 1868.   These efforts show her comparative
ignorance of the stupendous Life-problem up to that 30
time, and the degrees by which she came at length
to its solution; but she values them as a parent

1 may treasure the memorials of a child's growth, and
she would not have them changed.

3   The first edition of SCIENCE AND HEALTH was published in 1875. Various books on mental healing have
since been issued, most of them incorrect in theory
6 and filled with plagiarisms from SCIENCE AND HEALTH.
They regard the human mind as a healing agent,
whereas this mind is not a factor in the Principle of
9 Christian Science. A few books, however, which are
based on this book, are useful.

    The author has not compromised conscience to suit
12 the general drift of thought, but has bluntly and honestly given the text of Truth. She has made no effort
to embellish, elaborate, or treat in full detail so in-
15 finite a theme. By thousands of well-authenticated
cases of healing, she and her students have proved the
worth of her teachings. These cases for the most part
18 have been abandoned as hopeless by regular medical
attendants. Few invalids will turn to God till all
physical supports have failed, because there is so little
21 faith in His disposition and power to heal disease.

    The divine Principle of healing is proved in the
personal experience of any sincere seeker of Truth. Its
24 purpose is good, and its practice is safer and more potent than that of any other sanitary method. The un-
biased Christian thought is soonest touched by Truth,
27 and convinced of it. Only those quarrel with her
method who do not understand her meaning, or discerning the truth, come not to the light lest their
30 works be reproved. No intellectual proficiency is requisite in the learner, but sound morals are most desirable.

Many imagine that the phenomena of physical heal- 1
ing in Christian Science present only a phase of the
action of the human mind, which action in some unex- 3
plained way results in the cure of disease. On the contrary, Christian Science rationally explains that all
other pathological methods are the fruits of human 6
faith in matter, — faith in the workings, not of Spirit,
but of the fleshly mind which must yield to Science.

The physical healing of Christian Science results 9
now, as in Jesus' time, from the operation of divine
Principle, before which sin and disease lose their reality in human consciousness and disappear as naturally 12
and as necessarily as darkness gives place to light and
sin to reformation. Now, as then, these mighty works
are not supernatural, but supremely natural. They are 15
the sign of Immanuel, or "God with us," — a divine
influence ever present in human consciousness and repeating itself, coming now as was promised aforetime,   18

> To preach deliverance to the captives [of sense],
> And recovering of sight to the blind,
> To set at liberty them that are bruised.   21

When God called the author to proclaim His Gospel
to this age, there came also the charge to plant and
water His vineyard.   24

The first school of Christian Science Mind-healing
was started by the author with only one student in
Lynn, Massachusetts, about the year 1867. In 1881, 27
she opened the Massachusetts Metaphysical College in
Boston, under the seal of the Commonwealth, a law
relative to colleges having been passed, which enabled 30
her to get this institution chartered for medical pur-

poses. No charters were granted to Christian Scientists for such institutions after 1883, and up to that date, hers was the only College of this character which had been established in the United States, where Christian Science was first introduced.

During seven years over four thousand students were taught by the author in this College. Meanwhile she was pastor of the first established Church of Christ, Scientist; President of the first Christian Scientist Association, convening monthly; publisher of her own works; and (for a portion of this time) sole editor and publisher of the Christian Science Journal, the first periodical issued by Christian Scientists. She closed her College, October 29, 1889, in the height of its prosperity with a deep-lying conviction that the next two years of her life should be given to the preparation of the revision of SCIENCE AND HEALTH, which was published in 1891. She retained her charter, and as its President, reopened the College in 1899 as auxiliary to her church. Until June 10, 1907, she had never read this book throughout consecutively in order to elucidate her idealism.

In the spirit of Christ's charity, — as one who "hopeth all things, endureth all things," and is joyful to bear consolation to the sorrowing and healing to the sick, — she commits these pages to honest seekers for Truth.

MARY BAKER EDDY

Science and Health

CHAPTER I
Prayer

11 - 20 - 84

For verily I say unto you, That whosoever shall say unto this moun-
tain, Be thou removed, and be thou cast into the sea; and shall not doubt
in his heart, but shall believe that those things which he saith shall come
to pass; he shall have whatsoever he saith. Therefore I say unto you,
What things soever ye desire when ye pray, believe that ye receive them,
and ye shall have them.
Your Father knoweth what things ye have need of, before ye ask Him.
— CHRIST JESUS.

THE prayer that reforms the sinner and heals the 1
sick is an absolute faith that all things are
possible to God, — a spiritual understanding of Him, 3
an unselfed love. Regardless of what another may say
or think on this subject, I speak from experience.
Prayer, watching, and working, combined with self-im- 6
molation, are God's gracious means for accomplishing
whatever has been successfully done for the Christianization and health of mankind. 9
Thoughts unspoken are not unknown to the divine
Mind. Desire is prayer; and no loss can occur from
trusting God with our desires, that they may be 12
moulded and exalted before they take form in words
and in deeds.

1

1   What are the motives for prayer? Do we pray to
make ourselves better or to benefit those who hear us,
3   **Right**   to enlighten the infinite or to be heard of
     motives   men? Are we benefited by praying? Yes,
the desire which goes forth hungering after righteous-
6 ness is blessed of our Father, and it does not return
unto us void.

       God is not moved by the breath of praise to do more
9 than He has already done, nor can the infinite do less
       Deity   than bestow all good, since He is unchang-
   unchangeable ing wisdom and Love. We can do more for
12 ourselves by humble fervent petitions, but the All-loving does not grant them simply on the ground of lip-
service, for He already knows all.

15   Prayer cannot change the Science of being, but it
tends to bring us into harmony with it. Goodness at-
tains the demonstration of Truth. A request that
18 God will save us is not all that is required. The mere
habit of pleading with the divine Mind, as one pleads
with a human being, perpetuates the belief in God as
21 humanly circumscribed, — an error which impedes spiritual growth.

       God is Love. Can we ask Him to be more? God is
24 intelligence. Can we inform the infinite Mind of any-
       God's   thing He does not already comprehend?
       standard   Do we expect to change perfection? Shall
27 we plead for more at the open fount, which is pour-
ing forth more than we accept? The unspoken desire
does bring us nearer the source of all existence and
30 blessedness.

       Asking God to *be* God is a vain repetition. God is
"the same yesterday, and to-day, and forever;" and

He who is immutably right will do right without being 1
reminded of His province. The wisdom of man is not
sufficient to warrant him in advising God. 3
Who would stand before a blackboard, and pray the
principle of mathematics to solve the problem? The
rule is already established, and it is our The spiritual 6
task to work out the solution. Shall we mathematics
ask the divine Principle of all goodness to do His own
work? His work is done, and we have only to avail 9
ourselves of God's rule in order to receive His blessing, which enables us to work out our own salvation.
The Divine Being must be reflected by man, — else 12
man is not the image and likeness of the patient,
tender, and true, the One "altogether lovely;" but to
understand God is the work of eternity, and demands 15
absolute consecration of thought, energy, and desire.
How empty are our conceptions of Deity! We admit
theoretically that God is good, omnipotent, omni- 18
present, infinite, and then we try to give Prayerful
information to this infinite Mind. We plead ingratitude
for unmerited pardon and for a liberal outpouring of 21
benefactions. Are we really grateful for the good
already received? Then we shall avail ourselves of the
blessings we have, and thus be fitted to receive more. 24
Gratitude is much more than a verbal expression of
thanks. Action expresses more gratitude than speech.
If we are ungrateful for Life, Truth, and Love, and 27
yet return thanks to God for all blessings, we are insincere and incur the sharp censure our Master pro-
nounces on hypocrites. In such a case, the only 30
acceptable prayer is to put the finger on the lips and
remember our blessings. While the heart is far from

1 divine Truth and Love, we cannot conceal the ingratitude of barren lives.

3   What we most need is the prayer of fervent desire
for growth in grace, expressed in patience, meekness,
    Efficacious love, and good deeds. To keep the com-
6   petitions mandments of our Master and follow his
example, is our proper debt to him and the only
worthy evidence of our gratitude for all that he has
9 done. Outward worship is not of itself sufficient to
express loyal and heartfelt gratitude, since he has
said: "If ye love me, keep my commandments."

12   The habitual struggle to be always good is unceas-
ing prayer. Its motives are made manifest in the
blessings they bring, — blessings which, even if not
15 acknowledged in audible words, attest our worthiness
to be partakers of Love.

Simply asking that we may love God will never
18 make us love Him; but the longing to be better
    Watchfulness and holier, expressed in daily watchful-
    requisite ness and in striving to assimilate more of
21 the divine character, will mould and fashion us
anew, until we awake in His likeness. We reach the
Science of Christianity through demonstration of the
24 divine nature; but in this wicked world goodness
will "be evil spoken of," and patience must bring
experience.

27   Audible prayer can never do the works of spiritual
understanding, which regenerates; but silent prayer,
    Veritable watchfulness, and devout obedience enable
30   devotion us to follow Jesus' example. Long prayers,
superstition, and creeds clip the strong pinions of love,
and clothe religion in human forms. Whatever mate-

rializes worship hinders man's spiritual growth and keeps 1
him from demonstrating his power over error.

Sorrow for wrong-doing is but one step towards reform 3
and the very easiest step. The next and great step required by wisdom is the test of our sincerity, Sorrow and reformation
— namely, reformation. To this end we are 6
placed under the stress of circumstances. Temptation
bids us repeat the offence, and woe comes in return for
what is done. So it will ever be, till we learn that there 9
is no discount in the law of justice and that we must pay
"the uttermost farthing." The measure ye mete "shall
be measured to you again," and it will be full "and run- 12
ning over."

Saints and sinners get their full award, but not always
in this world. The followers of Christ drank his cup. 15
Ingratitude and persecution filled it to the brim; but God
pours the riches of His love into the understanding and
affections, giving us strength according to our day. Sin- 18
ners flourish "like a green bay tree;" but, looking farther,
the Psalmist could see their end, — the destruction of sin
through suffering. 21

Prayer is not to be used as a confessional to cancel sin.
Such an error would impede true religion. Sin is forgiven
only as it is destroyed by Christ, — Truth and Cancellation of human sin 24
Life. If prayer nourishes the belief that sin is
cancelled, and that man is made better merely by praying,
prayer is an evil. He grows worse who continues in sin 27
because he fancies himself forgiven.

An apostle says that the Son of God [Christ] came to
"destroy the *works* of the devil." We should Diabolism destroyed 30
follow our divine Exemplar, and seek the destruction of all evil works, error and disease included.

1 We cannot escape the penalty due for sin. The Scriptures say, that if we deny Christ, "he also will deny us."
3   Divine Love corrects and governs man. Men may
pardon, but this divine Principle alone reforms the
     Pardon and   sinner. God is not separate from the wis-
6   amendment   dom He bestows. The talents He gives we
must improve. Calling on Him to forgive our work
badly done or left undone, implies the vain supposition
9 that we have nothing to do but to ask pardon, and
that afterwards we shall be free to repeat the offence.
     To cause suffering as the result of sin, is the means
12 of destroying sin. Every supposed pleasure in sin
will furnish more than its equivalent of pain, until belief in material life and sin is destroyed. To reach
15 heaven, the harmony of being, we must understand
the divine Principle of being.
     "God is Love." More than this we cannot ask,
18 higher we cannot look, farther we cannot go. To
     Mercy without   suppose that God forgives or punishes sin
     partiality   according as His mercy is sought or un-
21 sought, is to misunderstand Love and to make prayer
the safety-valve for wrong-doing.
     Jesus uncovered and rebuked sin before he cast it
24 out. Of a sick woman he said that Satan had bound
     Divine   her, and to Peter he said, "Thou art an of-
     severity   fence unto me." He came teaching and
27 showing men how to destroy sin, sickness, and death.
He said of the fruitless tree, "[It] is hewn down."
     It is believed by many that a certain magistrate,
30 who lived in the time of Jesus, left this record: "His
rebuke is fearful." The strong language of our Master confirms this description.

The only civil sentence which he had for error was, 1
"Get thee behind me, Satan." Still stronger evidence
that Jesus' reproof was pointed and pungent is found 3
in his own words, — showing the necessity for such
forcible utterance, when he cast out devils and healed
the sick and sinning. The relinquishment of error de- 6
prives material sense of its false claims.

Audible prayer is impressive; it gives momentary
solemnity and elevation to thought. But does it pro- 9
duce any lasting benefit? Looking deeply *Audible
praying*
into these things, we find that "a zeal . . .
not according to knowledge" gives occasion for reac- 12
tion unfavorable to spiritual growth, sober resolve, and
wholesome perception of God's requirements. The motives for verbal prayer may embrace too much love of 15
applause to induce or encourage Christian sentiment.

Physical sensation, not Soul, produces material ecstasy and emotion. If spiritual sense always guided 18
men, there would grow out of ecstatic mo- *Emotional
utterances*
ments a higher experience and a better life
with more devout self-abnegation and purity. A self- 21
satisfied ventilation of fervent sentiments never makes
a Christian. God is not influenced by man. The "divine ear" is not an auditory nerve. It is the all-hearing 24
and all-knowing Mind, to whom each need of man is
always known and by whom it will be supplied.

The danger from prayer is that it may lead us into temp- 27
tation. By it we may become involuntary hypocrites, uttering desires which are not real and consoling
*Danger
from audible
prayer*
ourselves in the midst of sin with the recollection 30
that we have prayed over it or mean to ask forgiveness at some later day. Hypocrisy is fatal to religion.

1   A wordy prayer may afford a quiet sense of self-
justification, though it makes the sinner a hypocrite.
3 We never need to despair of an honest heart; but
there is little hope for those who come only spasmodi-
cally face to face with their wickedness and then seek to
6 hide it. Their prayers are indexes which do not correspond
with their character. They hold secret fellowship with
sin, and such externals are spoken of by Jesus as "like
9 unto whited sepulchres . . . full . . . of all uncleanness."
     If a man, though apparently fervent and prayerful,
is impure and therefore insincere, what (must) be the
12   Aspiration   comment upon him?   If he reached the
     and love   loftiness of his prayer, there would be no
occasion for comment.   If we feel the aspiration, hu-
15 mility, gratitude, and love which our words express, —
this God accepts; and it is wise not to try to deceive
ourselves or others, for "there is nothing covered that
18 shall not be revealed."   Professions and audible prayers are like charity in one respect, — they "cover the
multitude of sins."   Praying for humility with what-
21 ever fervency of expression does not always mean a
desire for it.   If we turn away from the poor, we are
not ready to receive the reward of Him who blesses
24 the poor.   We confess to having a very wicked heart
and ask that it may be laid bare before us, but do
we not already know more of this heart than we are
27 willing to have our neighbor see?
     We should examine ourselves and learn what is the
affection and purpose of the heart, for in this way
30   Searching   only can we learn what we honestly are.   If a
     the heart   friend informs us of a fault, do we listen pa-
tiently to the rebuke and credit what is said?   Do we not

rather give thanks that we are "not as other men"? 1
During many years the author has been most grateful
for merited rebuke. The wrong lies in unmerited cen- 3
sure, — in the falsehood which does no one any good.

The test of all prayer lies in the answer to these
questions: Do we love our neighbor better because of 6
this asking? Do we pursue the old selfish-   Summit of
ness, satisfied with having prayed for some-   aspiration
thing better, though we give no evidence of the sin- 9
cerity of our requests by living consistently with our
prayer? If selfishness has given place to kindness,
we shall regard our neighbor unselfishly, and bless 12
them that curse us; but we shall never meet this great
duty simply by asking that it may be done. There is
a cross to be taken up before we can enjoy the fruition 15
of our hope and faith.

Dost thou "love the Lord thy God with all thy
heart, and with all thy soul, and with all thy mind"? 18
This command includes much, even the sur-   Practical
render of all merely material sensation, affec-   religion
tion, and worship. This is the El Dorado of Christianity. 21
It involves the Science of Life, and recognizes only the
divine control of Spirit, in which Soul is our master,
and material sense and human will have no place. 24

Are you willing to leave all for Christ, for Truth, and
so be counted among sinners? No! Do you really desire
to attain this point? No! Then why make long   The chalice 27
prayers about it and ask to be Christians,   sacrificial
since you do not care to tread in the footsteps of our
dear Master? If unwilling to follow his example, why 30
pray with the lips that you may be partakers of his
nature? Consistent prayer is the desire to do right.

1 Prayer means that we desire to walk and will walk in
the light so far as we receive it, even though with bleed-
3 ing footsteps, and that waiting patiently on the Lord,
we will leave our real desires to be rewarded by Him.

The world must grow to the spiritual understanding
6 of prayer. If good enough to profit by Jesus' cup of
earthly sorrows, God will sustain us under these sorrows. Until we are thus divinely qualified and are
9 willing to drink his cup, millions of vain repetitions
will never pour into prayer the unction of Spirit in
demonstration of power and "with signs following."
12 Christian Science reveals a necessity for overcoming the
world, the flesh, and evil, and thus destroying all error.

Seeking is not sufficient. It is striving that enables
15 us to enter. Spiritual attainments open the door to a
higher understanding of the divine Life.

One of the forms of worship in Thibet is to carry a
18 praying-machine through the streets, and stop at the
Perfunctory doors to earn a penny by grinding out a
prayers prayer. But the advance guard of progress has
21 paid for the privilege of prayer the price of persecution.

Experience teaches us that we do not always receive
the blessings we ask for in prayer. There is some mis-
24   Asking   apprehension of the source and means of
amiss all goodness and blessedness, or we should
certainly receive that for which we ask. The Scrip-
27 tures say: "Ye ask, and receive not, because ye ask
amiss, that ye may consume it upon your lusts." That
which we desire and for which we ask, it is not always
30 best for us to receive. In this case infinite Love will
not grant the request. Do you ask wisdom to be merciful and not to punish sin? Then "ye ask amiss."

Without punishment, sin would multiply. Jesus' prayer, 1
"Forgive us our debts," specified also the terms of
forgiveness. When forgiving the adulterous woman he 3
said, "Go, and sin no more."

A magistrate sometimes remits the penalty, but this
may be no moral benefit to the criminal, and at best, it 6
only saves the criminal from one form of   Remission
punishment. The moral law, which has the   of penalty
right to acquit or condemn, always demands restitu- 9
tion before mortals can "go up higher." Broken law
brings penalty in order to compel this progress.

Mere legal pardon (and there is no other, for divine 12
Principle never pardons our sins or mistakes till they
are corrected) leaves the offender free to re-   Truth anni-
peat the offence, if indeed, he has not already   hilates error   15
suffered sufficiently from vice to make him turn from it
with loathing. Truth bestows no pardon upon error, but
wipes it out in the most effectual manner. Jesus suffered 18
for our sins, not to annul the divine sentence for an individual's sin, but because sin brings inevitable suffering.

Petitions bring to mortals only the results of mor- 21
tals' own faith. We know that a desire for holiness is
requisite in order to gain holiness; but if we   Desire for
desire holiness above all else, we shall sac-   holiness   24
rifice everything for it. We must be willing to do this,
that we may walk securely in the only practical road
to holiness. Prayer cannot change the unalterable 27
Truth, nor can prayer alone give us an understanding
of Truth; but prayer, coupled with a fervent habitual
desire to know and do the will of God, will bring us 30
into all Truth. Such a desire has little need of audible
expression. It is best expressed in thought and in life.

1 √ "The prayer of faith shall save the sick," says the
Scripture. What is this healing prayer? A mere re-
3   Prayer for   quest that God will heal the sick has no
   the sick   power to gain more of the divine presence
than is always at hand. The beneficial effect of
6 such prayer for the sick is on the human mind, making it act more powerfully on the body through a blind
faith in God. This, however, is one belief casting out
9 another, — a belief in the unknown casting out a belief
in sickness. It is neither Science nor Truth which
acts through blind belief, nor is it the human under-
12 standing of the divine healing Principle as manifested
in Jesus, whose humble prayers were deep and conscientious protests of Truth, — of man's likeness to
15 God and of man's unity with Truth and Love.

Prayer to a corporeal God affects the sick like a
drug, which has no efficacy of its own but borrows its
18 power from human faith and belief. The drug does
nothing, because it has no intelligence. It is a mortal
belief, not divine Principle or Love, which causes a
21 drug to be apparently either poisonous or sanative.

The common custom of praying for the recovery of the
sick finds help in blind belief, whereas help should come
24 from the enlightened understanding. Changes in belief
may go on indefinitely, but they are the merchandise of
human thought and not the outgrowth of divine Science.
27 Does Deity interpose in behalf of one worshipper,
and not help another who offers the same measure of
  Love impartial   prayer? If the sick recover because they
30 and universal pray or are prayed for audibly, only peti-
tioners (*per se* or by proxy) should get well. In divine
Science, where prayers are mental, *all* may avail them-

selves of God as "a very present help in trouble." 1
Love is impartial and universal in its adaptation and
bestowals.   It is the open fount which cries, "Ho, 3
every one that thirsteth, come ye to the waters."

In public prayer we often go beyond our convictions,
beyond the honest standpoint of fervent desire.   If we 6
are not secretly yearning and openly striv-   Public
ing for the accomplishment of all we ask,   exaggerations
our prayers are "vain repetitions," such as the heathen 9
use.   If our petitions are sincere, we labor for what we
ask; and our Father, who seeth in secret, will reward
us openly.   Can the mere public expression of our de- 12
sires increase them?   Do we gain the omnipotent ear
sooner by words than by thoughts?   Even if prayer is
sincere, God knows our need before we tell Him or our 15
fellow-beings about it.   If we cherish the desire honestly and silently and humbly, God will bless it, and
we shall incur less risk of overwhelming our real 18
wishes with a torrent of words.

If we pray to God as a corporeal person, this will
prevent us from relinquishing the human doubts and 21
fears which attend such a belief, and so we   Corporeal
cannot grasp the wonders wrought by infi-   ignorance
nite, incorporeal Love, to whom all things are possible. 24
Because of human ignorance of the divine Principle,
Love, the Father of all is represented as a corporeal
creator;   hence men recognize themselves as merely 27
physical, and are ignorant of man as God's image or reflection and of man's eternal incorporeal existence.   The
world of error is ignorant of the world of Truth, — blind 30
to the reality of man's existence, — for the world of sensation is not cognizant of life in Soul, not in body.

1   If we are sensibly with the body and regard omnipotence as a corporeal, material person, whose ear we
3   Bodily   would gain, we are not "absent from the
    presence   body" and "present with the Lord" in the
demonstration of Spirit. We cannot "serve two mas-
6   ters." To be "present with the Lord" is to have, not
mere emotional ecstasy or faith, but the actual demonstration and understanding of Life as revealed in
9   Christian Science. To be "with the Lord" is to be in
obedience to the law of God, to be absolutely governed
by divine Love, — by Spirit, not by matter.
12 Become conscious for a single moment that Life and
intelligence are purely spiritual, — neither in nor of
    Spiritualized matter, — and the body will then utter no
15 consciousness complaints. If suffering from a belief in
sickness, you will find yourself suddenly well. Sorrow
is turned into joy when the body is controlled by spir-
18 itual Life, Truth, and Love. Hence the hope of the
promise Jesus bestows: "He that believeth on me,
the works that I do shall he do also; . . . because I
21 go unto my Father," — [because the Ego is absent from
the body, and present with Truth and Love.] The
Lord's Prayer is the prayer of Soul, not of material
24 sense.
    Entirely separate from the belief and dream of mate-
rial living, is the Life divine, revealing spiritual under-
27 standing and the consciousness of man's dominion
over the whole earth. This understanding casts out
error and heals the sick, and with it you can speak
30 "as one having authority."
    "When thou prayest, enter into thy closet, and,
when thou hast shut thy door, pray to thy Father

which is in secret; and thy Father, which seeth in 1
secret, shall reward thee openly."

So spake Jesus. The closet typifies the sanctuary of 3
Spirit, the door of which shuts out sinful sense but
lets in Truth, Life, and Love. Closed to   Spiritual
error, it is open to Truth, and *vice versa.* sanctuary   6
The Father in secret is unseen to the physical senses,
but He knows all things and rewards according to
motives, not according to speech. To enter into the 9
heart of prayer, the door of the erring senses must be
closed. Lips must be mute and materialism silent,
that man may have audience with Spirit, the divine 12
Principle, Love, which destroys all error.

In order to pray aright, we must enter into the
closet and shut the door. We must close the lips and 15
silence the material senses. In the quiet   Effectual
sanctuary of earnest longings, we must   invocation
deny sin and plead God's allness. We must resolve to 18
take up the cross, and go forth with honest hearts to
work and watch for wisdom, Truth, and Love. We
must "pray without ceasing." Such prayer is an- 21
swered, in so far as we put our desires into practice.
The Master's injunction is, that we pray in secret and
let our lives attest our sincerity.   24

Christians rejoice in secret beauty and bounty, hidden
from the world, but known to God. Self-forgetfulness,
purity, and affection are constant prayers. Trustworthy 27
Practice not profession, understanding not   beneficence
belief, gain the ear and right hand of omnipotence and
they assuredly call down infinite blessings. Trustworthi- 30
ness is the foundation of enlightened faith. Without a
fitness for holiness, we cannot receive holiness.

1   A great sacrifice of material things must precede this
advanced spiritual understanding. The highest prayer
3   *Loftiest*   is not one of faith merely; it is demonstra-
    adoration   tion. Such prayer heals sickness, and must
destroy sin and death. It distinguishes between Truth
6 that is sinless and the falsity of sinful sense.

Our Master taught his disciples one brief prayer,
which we name after him the Lord's Prayer. Our Mas-
9   *The prayer of*   ter said, "After this manner therefore pray
    Jesus Christ   ye," and then he gave that prayer which
covers all human needs. There is indeed some doubt
12 among Bible scholars, whether the last line is not an
addition to the prayer by a later copyist; but this does
not affect the meaning of the prayer itself.

15   In the phrase, "Deliver us from evil," the original
properly reads, "Deliver us from the evil one." This
reading strengthens our scientific apprehension of the peti-
18 tion, for Christian Science teaches us that "the evil one," or
one evil, is but another name for the first lie and all liars.

Only as we rise above all material sensuousness and
21 sin, can we reach the heaven-born aspiration and spiritual consciousness, which is indicated in the Lord's
Prayer and which instantaneously heals the sick.

24   Here let me give what I understand to be the spiritual sense of the Lord's Prayer:

Our Father which art in heaven,
27   *Our Father-Mother God, all-harmonious,*

Hallowed be Thy name.
    Adorable One.

30 Thy kingdom come.
    Thy kingdom is come; Thou art ever-present.

Thy will be done in earth, as it is in heaven. 1
Enable us to know, — as in heaven, so on earth, — God is
omnipotent, supreme. 3

Give us this day our daily bread;
Give us grace for to-day; feed the famished affections;

And forgive us our debts, as we forgive our debtors. 6
And Love is reflected in love;

And lead us not into temptation, but deliver us from
evil; 9
And God leadeth us not into temptation, but delivereth
us from sin, disease, and death.

For Thine is the kingdom, and the power, and the 12
glory, forever.
For God is infinite, all-power, all Life, Truth, Love, over
all, and All. 15

CHAPTER II

Atonement and Eucharist

And they that are Christ's have crucified the flesh with the affections and lusts. — PAUL.

For Christ sent me not to baptize, but to preach the gospel. — PAUL.

For I say unto you, I will not drink of the fruit of the vine, until the kingdom of God shall come. — JESUS.

1 ATONEMENT is the exemplification of man's unity with God, whereby man reflects divine Truth, Life, 3 and Love. Jesus of Nazareth taught and demonstrated man's oneness with the Father, and for this we owe him
Divine endless homage. His mission was both in-
6 oneness dividual and collective. He did life's work aright not only in justice to himself, but in mercy to mortals, — to show them how to do theirs, but not to do 9 it for them nor to relieve them of a single responsibility. Jesus acted boldly, against the accredited evidence of the senses, against Pharisaical creeds and practices, and he 12 refuted all opponents with his healing power.

The atonement of Christ reconciles man to God, not God to man; for the divine Principle of Christ is God, 15 Human and how can God propitiate Himself? Christ reconciliation is Truth, which reaches no higher than itself. The fountain can rise no higher than its source. Christ, 18 Truth, could conciliate no nature above his own, derived

18

from the eternal Love. It was therefore Christ's purpose 1
to reconcile man to God, not God to man. Love and
Truth are not at war with God's image and likeness. 3
Man cannot exceed divine Love, and so atone for himself. Even Christ cannot reconcile Truth to error, for
Truth and error are irreconcilable. Jesus aided in recon- 6
ciling man to God by giving man a truer sense of Love,
the divine Principle of Jesus' teachings, and this truer
sense of Love redeems man from the law of matter, 9
sin, and death by the law of Spirit, — the law of divine
Love.

The Master forbore not to speak the whole truth, de- 12
claring precisely what would destroy sickness, sin, and
death, although his teaching set households at variance,
and brought to material beliefs not peace, but a 15
sword.

Every pang of repentance and suffering, every effort
for reform, every good thought and deed, will help us to 18
understand Jesus' atonement for sin and aid   *Efficacious*
its efficacy; but if the sinner continues to pray   *repentance*
and repent, sin and be sorry, he has little part in the atone- 21
ment, — in the *at-one-ment* with God, — for he lacks the
practical repentance, which reforms the heart and enables
man to do the will of wisdom. Those who cannot dem- 24
onstrate, at least in part, the divine Principle of the teachings and practice of our Master have no part in God. If
living in disobedience to Him, we ought to feel no secur- 27
ity, although God is good.

Jesus urged the commandment, "Thou shalt have no
other gods before me," which may be ren-   *Jesus'*   30
dered: Thou shalt have no belief of Life as   *sinless career*
mortal; thou shalt not know evil, for there is one Life, —

1 even God, good. He rendered "unto Cæsar the things
which are Cæsar's; and unto God the things that are
3 God's." He at last paid no homage to forms of doctrine
or to theories of man, but acted and spake as he was moved,
not by spirits but by Spirit.

6   To the ritualistic priest and hypocritical Pharisee
Jesus said, "The publicans and the harlots go into the
kingdom of God before you." Jesus' history made a
9 new calendar, which we call the Christian era; but he
established no ritualistic worship. He knew that men
can be baptized, partake of the Eucharist, support the
12 clergy, observe the Sabbath, make long prayers, and yet
be sensual and sinful.

Jesus bore our infirmities; he knew the error of mortal
15 belief, and "with his stripes [the rejection of error] we are
Perfect   healed." "Despised and rejected of men,"
example   returning blessing for cursing, he taught mor-
18 tals the opposite of themselves, even the nature of God;
and when error felt the power of Truth, the scourge and
the cross awaited the great Teacher. Yet he swerved not,
21 well knowing that to obey the divine order and trust God,
saves retracing and traversing anew the path from sin to
holiness.

24   Material belief is slow to acknowledge what the
spiritual fact implies. The truth is the centre of all
Behest of   religion. It commands sure entrance into
27 the cross   the realm of Love. St. Paul wrote, "Let us
lay aside every weight, and the sin which doth so
easily beset us, and let us run with patience the race that
30 is set before us;" that is, let us put aside material self
and sense, and seek the divine Principle and Science of
all healing.

If Truth is overcoming error in your daily walk and 1
conversation, you can finally say, "I have fought a
good fight . . . I have kept the faith," be-   Moral   3
cause you are a better man. This is having   victory
our part in the at-one-ment with Truth and Love.
Christians do not continue to labor and pray, expecting 6
because of another's goodness, suffering, and triumph,
that they shall reach his harmony and reward.

If the disciple is advancing spiritually, he is striv- 9
ing to enter in. He constantly turns away from material sense, and looks towards the imperishable things
of Spirit. If honest, he will be in earnest from the 12
start, and gain a little each day in the right direction,
till at last he finishes his course with joy.

If my friends are going to Europe, while I am *en* 15
route for California, we are not journeying together.
We have separate time-tables to consult, Inharmonious
different routes to pursue. Our paths have   travellers   18
diverged at the very outset, and we have little opportunity to help each other. On the contrary, if my
friends pursue my course, we have the same railroad 21
guides, and our mutual interests are identical; or, if I
take up their line of travel, they help me on, and our
companionship may continue.   24

Being in sympathy with matter, the worldly man is at
the beck and call of error, and will be attracted thither-
ward. He is like a traveller going westward   Zigzag   27
for a pleasure-trip. The company is alluring   course
and the pleasures exciting. After following the sun for
six days, he turns east on the seventh, satisfied if he can 30
only imagine himself drifting in the right direction. By-
and-by, ashamed of his zigzag course, he would borrow

1 the passport of some wiser pilgrim, thinking with the aid
of this to find and follow the right road.

3   Vibrating like a pendulum between sin and the hope
of forgiveness, — selfishness and sensuality causing con-
Moral   stant retrogression, — our moral progress will
6 retrogression be slow. Waking to Christ's demand, mortals
experience suffering. This causes them, even as drowning men, to make vigorous efforts to save themselves; and
9 through Christ's precious love these efforts are crowned
with success.

"Work out your own salvation," is the demand of
12 Life and Love, for to this end God worketh with you.
Wait for   "Occupy till I come!" Wait for your re-
reward   ward, and "be not weary in well doing." If
15 your endeavors are beset by fearful odds, and you receive
no present reward, go not back to error, nor become a
sluggard in the race.

18   When the smoke of battle clears away, you will discern the good you have done, and receive according to
your deserving. Love is not hasty to deliver us from
21 temptation, for Love means that we shall be tried and
purified.

Final deliverance from error, whereby we rejoice in
24 immortality, boundless freedom, and sinless sense, is not
Deliverance reached through paths of flowers nor by pinning
not vicarious one's faith without works to another's vicarious
27 effort. Whosoever believeth that wrath is righteous or
that divinity is appeased by human suffering, does not
understand God.

30   Justice requires reformation of the sinner. Mercy
cancels the debt only when justice approves. Revenge
is inadmissible. Wrath which is only appeased is not

destroyed, but partially indulged. Wisdom and Love 1
may require many sacrifices of self to save us from sin.
One sacrifice, however great, is insufficient to   Justice and   3
pay the debt of sin. The atonement requires   substitution
constant self-immolation on the sinner's part. That
God's wrath should be vented upon His beloved Son, is 6
divinely unnatural. Such a theory is man-made. The
atonement is a hard problem in theology, but its scientific explanation is, that suffering is an error of sinful sense 9
which Truth destroys, and that eventually both sin and suffering will fall at the feet of everlasting Love.

Rabbinical lore said: "He that taketh one doctrine, 12
firm in faith, has the Holy Ghost dwelling in him."
This preaching receives a strong rebuke in   Doctrines
the Scripture, "Faith without works is dead."   and faith   15
Faith, if it be mere belief, is as a pendulum swinging between nothing and something, having no fixity. Faith,
advanced to spiritual understanding, is the evidence gained 18
from Spirit, which rebukes sin of every kind and establishes the claims of God.

In Hebrew, Greek, Latin, and English, *faith* and the 21
words corresponding thereto have these two definitions, *trustfulness* and *trustworthiness*. One   Self-reliance
kind of faith trusts one's welfare to others.   and confidence 24
Another kind of faith understands divine Love and how
to work out one's "own salvation, with fear and trembling." "Lord, I believe; help thou mine unbelief!" 27
expresses the helplessness of a blind faith; whereas the
injunction, "Believe . . . and thou shalt be saved!"
demands self-reliant trustworthiness, which includes spir- 30
itual understanding and confides all to God.

The Hebrew verb *to believe* means also *to be firm* or

1 *to be constant.* This certainly applies to Truth and Love
understood and practised. Firmness in error will never
3 save from sin, disease, and death.

Acquaintance with the original texts, and willingness
to give up human beliefs (established by hierarchies, and
6 Life's healing instigated sometimes by the worst passions of
currents men), open the way for Christian Science to be
understood, and make the Bible the chart of life, where
9 the buoys and healing currents of Truth are pointed
out.

He to whom "the arm of the Lord" is revealed will
12 believe our report, and rise into newness of life with re-
Radical generation. This is having part in the atone-
changes ment; this is the understanding, in which
15 Jesus suffered and triumphed. The time is not distant
when the ordinary theological views of atonement will
undergo a great change, — a change as radical as that
18 which has come over popular opinions in regard to predestination and future punishment.

Does erudite theology regard the crucifixion of Jesus
21 chiefly as providing a ready pardon for all sinners who
Purpose of ask for it and are willing to be forgiven?
crucifixion Does spiritualism find Jesus' death necessary
24 only for the presentation, after death, of the material
Jesus, as a proof that spirits can return to earth? Then
we must differ from them both.

27 The efficacy of the crucifixion lay in the practical affection and goodness it demonstrated for mankind. The
truth had been lived among men; but until they saw that
30 it enabled their Master to triumph over the grave, his own
disciples could not admit such an event to be possible.
After the resurrection, even the unbelieving Thomas was

forced to acknowledge how complete was the great proof of   1
Truth and Love.

The spiritual essence of blood is sacrifice. The effi-   3
cacy of Jesus' spiritual offering is infinitely greater than
can be expressed by our sense of human   True flesh
blood. The material blood of Jesus was no   and blood   6
more efficacious to cleanse from sin when it was shed
upon "the accursed tree," than when it was flowing in
his veins as he went daily about his Father's business.   9
His true flesh and blood were his Life; and they truly eat
his flesh and drink his blood, who partake of that divine
Life.   12

Jesus taught the way of Life by demonstration, that
we may understand how this divine Principle heals
the sick, casts out error, and triumphs over   Effective   15
death. Jesus presented the ideal of God better   triumph
than could any man whose origin was less spiritual. By
his obedience to God, he demonstrated more spiritu-   18
ally than all others the Principle of being. Hence the
force of his admonition, "If ye love me, keep my commandments."   21

Though demonstrating his control over sin and disease,
the great Teacher by no means relieved others from giving
the requisite proofs of their own piety. He worked for   24
their guidance, that they might demonstrate this power as
he did and understand its divine Principle. Implicit faith
in the Teacher and all the emotional love we can bestow   27
on him, will never alone make us imitators of him. We
must go and do likewise, else we are not improving the
great blessings which our Master worked and suffered to   30
bestow upon us. The divinity of the Christ was made
manifest in the humanity of Jesus.

1 While we adore Jesus, and the heart overflows with
gratitude for what he did for mortals, — treading alone
3 Individual his loving pathway up to the throne of
experience glory, in speechless agony exploring the way
for us, — yet Jesus spares us not one individual expe-
6 rience, if we follow his commands faithfully; and all
have the cup of sorrowful effort to drink in proportion
to their demonstration of his love, till all are redeemed
9 through divine Love.

The Christ was the Spirit which Jesus implied in his
own statements: "I am the way, the truth, and the life;"
12 Christ's "I and my Father are one." This Christ,
demonstration or divinity of the man Jesus, was his divine
nature, the godliness which animated him. Divine Truth,
15 Life, and Love gave Jesus authority over sin, sickness,
and death. His mission was to reveal the Science of
celestial being, to prove what God is and what He does
18 for man.

A musician demonstrates the beauty of the music he
teaches in order to show the learner the way by prac-
21 Proof in tice as well as precept. Jesus' teaching and
practice practice of Truth involved such a sacrifice
as makes us admit its Principle to be Love. This was
24 the precious import of our Master's sinless career and
of his demonstration of power over death. He proved
by his deeds that Christian Science destroys sickness, sin,
27 and death.

Our Master taught no mere theory, doctrine, or belief.
It was the divine Principle of all real being which he
30 taught and practised. His proof of Christianity was no
form or system of religion and worship, but Christian
Science, working out the harmony of Life and Love.

Jesus sent a message to John the Baptist, which was in- 1
tended to prove beyond a question that the Christ had
come: "Go your way, and tell John what things ye have 3
seen and heard; how that the blind see, the lame walk,
the lepers are cleansed, the deaf hear, the dead are raised,
to the poor the gospel is preached." In other words: 6
Tell John what the demonstration of divine power is,
and he will at once perceive that God is the power in
the Messianic work. 9

That Life is God, Jesus proved by his reappearance
after the crucifixion in strict accordance with his scientific statement: "Destroy this temple [body],   Living 12
and in three days I [Spirit] will raise it up."   temple
It is as if he had said: The I — the Life, substance,
and intelligence of the universe — is not in matter to 15
be destroyed.

Jesus' parables explain Life as never mingling with
sin and death. He laid the axe of Science at the root 18
of material knowledge, that it might be ready to cut
down the false doctrine of pantheism, — that God, or
Life, is in or of matter. 21

Jesus sent forth seventy students at one time, but only
eleven left a desirable historic record. Tradition credits
him with two or three hundred other disciples   Recreant 24
who have left no name. "Many are called,   disciples
but few are chosen." They fell away from grace because
they never truly understood their Master's instruction. 27

Why do those who profess to follow Christ reject the
essential religion he came to establish? Jesus' persecutors made their strongest attack upon this very point. 30
They endeavored to hold him at the mercy of matter and
to kill him according to certain assumed material laws.

1   The Pharisees claimed to know and to teach the divine will, but they only hindered the success of Jesus'
3   Help and   mission. Even many of his students stood
    hindrance in his way. If the Master had not taken a
student and taught the unseen verities of God, he would
6 not have been crucified. The determination to hold Spirit
in the grasp of matter is the persecutor of Truth and
Love.

9   While respecting all that is good in the Church or out
of it, one's consecration to Christ is more on the ground
of demonstration than of profession. In conscience, we
12 cannot hold to beliefs outgrown; and by understanding
more of the divine Principle of the deathless Christ, we
are enabled to heal the sick and to triumph over sin.

15 Neither the origin, the character, nor the work of
Jesus was generally understood. Not a single compo-
    Misleading nent part of his nature did the material
18 conceptions world measure aright. Even his righteousness and purity did not hinder men from saying: He
is a glutton and a friend of the impure, and Beelzebub is
21 his patron.

Remember, thou Christian martyr, it is enough if
thou art found worthy to unloose the sandals of thy
24 Persecution Master's feet! To suppose that persecution
    prolonged for righteousness' sake belongs to the past,
and that Christianity to-day is at peace with the world
27 because it is honored by sects and societies, is to mistake the very nature of religion. Error repeats itself.
The trials encountered by prophet, disciple, and apostle,
30 "of whom the world was not worthy," await, in some
form, every pioneer of truth.

There is too much animal courage in society and not

sufficient moral courage. Christians must take up arms 1
against error at home and abroad. They must grapple
with sin in themselves and in others, and Christian 3
continue this warfare until they have finished warfare
their course. If they keep the faith, they will have the
crown of rejoicing.   6

Christian experience teaches faith in the right and disbelief in the wrong. It bids us work the more earnestly
in times of persecution, because then our labor is more 9
needed. Great is the reward of self-sacrifice, though we
may never receive it in this world.

There is a tradition that Publius Lentulus wrote to 12
the authorities at Rome: "The disciples of Jesus believe him the Son of God." Those instructed The Father-
in Christian Science have reached the glori- hood of God 15
ous perception that God is the only author of man.
The Virgin-mother conceived this idea of God, and
gave to her ideal the name of Jesus — that is, Joshua, 18
or Saviour.

The illumination of Mary's spiritual sense put to
silence material law and its order of generation, and 21
brought forth her child by the revelation of Spiritual
Truth, demonstrating God as the Father of conception
men. The Holy Ghost, or divine Spirit, overshadowed 24
the pure sense of the Virgin-mother with the full recognition that being is Spirit. The Christ dwelt forever
an idea in the bosom of God, the divine Principle of the 27
man Jesus, and woman perceived this spiritual idea,
though at first faintly developed.

Man as the offspring of God, as the idea of Spirit, 30
is the immortal evidence that Spirit is harmonious and
man eternal. Jesus was the offspring of Mary's self-

1 conscious communion with God. Hence he could give
a more spiritual idea of life than other men, and could
3 demonstrate the Science of Love — his Father or divine
Principle.

Born of a woman, Jesus' advent in the flesh partook
6 partly of Mary's earthly condition, although he was en-
   Jesus the   dowed with the Christ, the divine Spirit, with-
   way-shower   out measure. This accounts for his struggles
9 in Gethsemane and on Calvary, and this enabled him to
be the mediator, or *way-shower*, between God and men.
Had his origin and birth been wholly apart from mortal
12 usage, Jesus would not have been appreciable to mortal
mind as "the way."

Rabbi and priest taught the Mosaic law, which said:
15 "An eye for an eye," and "Whoso sheddeth man's blood,
by man shall his blood be shed." Not so did Jesus, the
new executor for God, present the divine law of Love,
18 which blesses even those that curse it.

As the individual ideal of Truth, Christ Jesus came to
rebuke rabbinical error and all sin, sickness, and death, —
21   Rebukes   to point out the way of Truth and Life. This
   helpful   ideal was demonstrated throughout the whole
earthly career of Jesus, showing the difference between
24 the offspring of Soul and of material sense, of Truth and
of error.

If we have triumphed sufficiently over the errors of
27 material sense to allow Soul to hold the control, we
shall loathe sin and rebuke it under every mask. Only
in this way can we bless our enemies, though they
30 may not so construe our words. We cannot choose for
ourselves, but must work out our salvation in the way
Jesus taught. In meekness and might, he was found

preaching the gospel to the poor. Pride and fear are unfit 1
to bear the standard of Truth, and God will never place
it in such hands. 3

Jesus acknowledged no ties of the flesh. He said: "Call
no man your father upon the earth: for one is your Father,
which is in heaven." Again he asked: "Who   Fleshly ties 6
is my mother, and who are my brethren," im-   temporal
plying that it is they who do the will of his Father. We
have no record of his calling any man by the name of 9
father. He recognized Spirit, God, as the only creator, and
therefore as the Father of all.

First in the list of Christian duties, he taught his fol- 12
lowers the healing power of Truth and Love. He attached
no importance to dead ceremonies. It is the   Healing
living Christ, the practical Truth, which makes   primary 15
Jesus "the resurrection and the life" to all who follow him
in deed. Obeying his precious precepts, — following his
demonstration so far as we apprehend it, — we drink of 18
his cup, partake of his bread, are baptized with his purity; and at last we shall rest, sit down with him, in a full
understanding of the divine Principle which triumphs 21
over death. For what says Paul? "As often as ye eat
this bread, and drink this cup, ye do show the Lord's
death till he come." 24

Referring to the materiality of the age, Jesus said:
"The hour cometh, and now is, when the true worshippers shall worship the Father in spirit   Painful 27
and in truth." Again, foreseeing the perse-   prospect
cution which would attend the Science of Spirit, Jesus
said: "They shall put you out of the synagogues; yea, 30
the time cometh, that whosoever killeth you will think
that he doeth God service; and these things will they

1 do unto you, because they have not known the Father
nor me."

3   In ancient Rome a soldier was required to swear
allegiance to his general. The Latin word for this oath
        Sacred   was *sacramentum,* and our English word
6   sacrament   *sacrament* is derived from it. Among the
Jews it was an ancient custom for the master of a
feast to pass each guest a cup of wine. But the
9 Eucharist does not commemorate a Roman soldier's
oath, nor was the wine, used on convivial occasions and
in Jewish rites, the cup of our Lord. The cup shows
12 forth his bitter experience, — the cup which he prayed
might pass from him, though he bowed in holy submission to the divine decree.

15   "As they were eating, Jesus took bread, and blessed
it and brake it, and gave it to the disciples, and said,
Take, eat; this is my body. And he took the cup, and
18 gave thanks, and gave it to them saying, Drink ye all
of it."

The true sense is spiritually lost, if the sacrament is
21 confined to the use of bread and wine. The disciples
        Spiritual   had eaten, yet Jesus prayed and gave them
        refreshment bread. This would have been foolish in a
24 literal sense; but in its spiritual signification, it was natural and beautiful. Jesus prayed; he withdrew from the
material senses to refresh his heart with brighter, with
27 spiritual views.

The Passover, which Jesus ate with his disciples in
the month Nisan on the night before his crucifixion,
30   Jesus' sad was a mournful occasion, a sad supper taken
        repast   at the close of day, in the twilight of a
glorious career with shadows fast falling around; and

this supper closed forever Jesus' ritualism or concessions 1
to matter.

His followers, sorrowful and silent, anticipating the hour 3
of their Master's betrayal, partook of the heavenly manna,
which of old had fed in the wilderness the Heavenly
persecuted followers of Truth. Their bread supplies   6
indeed came down from heaven. It was the great truth
of spiritual being, healing the sick and casting out error.
Their Master had explained it all before, and now this 9
bread was feeding and sustaining them. They had borne
this bread from house to house, *breaking* (explaining) it to
others, and now it comforted themselves.   12

For this truth of spiritual being, their Master was about
to suffer violence and drain to the dregs his cup of sorrow.
He must leave them. With the great glory of an everlast- 15
ing victory overshadowing him, he gave thanks and said,
"Drink ye all of it."

When the human element in him struggled with the 18
divine, our great Teacher said: "Not my will, but
Thine, be done!" — that is, Let not the flesh, The holy
but the Spirit, be represented in me. This struggle   21
is the new understanding of spiritual Love. It gives all
for Christ, or Truth. It blesses its enemies, heals the
sick, casts out error, raises the dead from trespasses 24
and sins, and preaches the gospel to the poor, the meek
in heart.

Christians, are you drinking his cup? Have you 27
shared the blood of the New Covenant, the persecutions
which attend a new and higher understand- Incisive
ing of God? If not, can you then say that questions   30
you have commemorated Jesus in his cup? Are all
who eat bread and drink wine in memory of Jesus willing

1 truly to drink his cup, take his cross, and leave all for
the Christ-principle?   Then why ascribe this inspira-
3 tion to a dead rite, instead of showing, by casting out
error and making the body "holy, acceptable unto God,"
that Truth has come to the understanding?   If Christ,
6 Truth, has come to us in demonstration, no other commemoration is requisite, for demonstration is Immanuel,
or *God with us;* and if a friend be with us, why need we
9 memorials of that friend?

If all who ever partook of the sacrament had really
commemorated the sufferings of Jesus and drunk of
12   Millennial   his cup, they would have revolutionized the
glory   world.   If all who seek his commemoration
through material symbols will take up the cross, heal
15 the sick, cast out evils, and preach Christ, or Truth,
to the poor, — the receptive thought, — they will bring
in the millennium.

18   Through all the disciples experienced, they became more
spiritual and understood better what the Master had
Fellowship   taught. His resurrection was also their resur-
21   with Christ   rection.   It helped them to raise themselves and
others from spiritual dulness and blind belief in God into
the perception of infinite possibilities.   They needed this
24 quickening, for soon their dear Master would rise again
in the spiritual realm of reality, and ascend far above
their apprehension.   As the reward for his faithfulness,
27 he would disappear to material sense in that change which
has since been called the ascension.

What a contrast between our Lord's last supper and
30   The last   his last spiritual breakfast with his disciples
breakfast   in the bright morning hours at the joyful
meeting on the shore of the Galilean Sea!   His gloom

had passed into glory, and his disciples' grief into repent- 1
ance, — hearts chastened and pride rebuked. Convinced
of the fruitlessness of their toil in the dark and wakened 3
by their Master's voice, they changed their methods, turned
away from material things, and cast their net on the right
side. Discerning Christ, Truth, anew on the shore of 6
time, they were enabled to rise somewhat from mortal
sensuousness, or the burial of mind in matter, into newness of life as Spirit. 9

This spiritual meeting with our Lord in the dawn of a
new light is the morning meal which Christian Scientists
commemorate. They bow before Christ, Truth, to re- 12
ceive more of his reappearing and silently to commune
with the divine Principle, Love. They celebrate their
Lord's victory over death, his probation in the flesh 15
after death, its exemplification of human probation, and
his spiritual and final ascension above matter, or the flesh,
when he rose out of material sight. 18

Our baptism is a purification from all error. Our
church is built on the divine Principle, Love. We can
unite with this church only as we are new-   Spiritual   21
born of Spirit, as we reach the Life which   Eucharist
is Truth and the Truth which is Life by bringing forth
the fruits of Love, — casting out error and healing the 24
sick. Our Eucharist is spiritual communion with the one
God. Our bread, "which cometh down from heaven,"
is Truth. Our cup is the cross. Our wine the inspira- 27
tion of Love, the draught our Master drank and com-
mended to his followers.

The design of Love is to reform the sinner. If the 30
sinner's punishment here has been insufficient to reform him, the good man's heaven would be a hell to

1 the sinner. They, who know not purity and affection by
experience, can never find bliss in the blessed company of
3   Final   Truth and Love simply through translation
purpose   into another sphere. Divine Science reveals
the necessity of sufficient suffering, either before or after
6 death, to quench the love of sin. To remit the penalty
due for sin, would be for Truth to pardon error. Escape
from punishment is not in accordance with God's govern-
9 ment, since justice is the handmaid of mercy.

Jesus endured the shame, that he might pour his
dear-bought bounty into barren lives. What was his
12 earthly reward? He was forsaken by all save John,
the beloved disciple, and a few women who bowed in
silent woe beneath the shadow of his cross. The earthly
15 price of spirituality in a material age and the great moral
distance between Christianity and sensualism preclude
Christian Science from finding favor with the worldly-
18 minded.

A selfish and limited mind may be unjust, but the unlimited and divine Mind is the immortal law of justice as
21   Righteous   well as of mercy. It is quite as impossible for
retribution   sinners to receive their full punishment this
side of the grave as for this world to bestow on the right-
24 eous their full reward. It is useless to suppose that the
wicked can gloat over their offences to the last moment
and then be suddenly pardoned and pushed into heaven,
27 or that the hand of Love is satisfied with giving us only
toil, sacrifice, cross-bearing, multiplied trials, and mockery of our motives in return for our efforts at well doing.
30   Vicarious   Religious history repeats itself in the suf-
suffering   fering of the just for the unjust. Can God
therefore overlook the law of righteousness which de-

stroys the belief called sin? Does not Science show that 1
sin brings suffering as much to-day as yesterday? They
who sin must suffer. "With what measure ye mete, it 3
shall be measured to you again."
    History is full of records of suffering. "The blood of
the martyrs is the seed of the Church." Mortals try in 6
vain to slay Truth with the steel or the stake,   Martyrs
but error falls only before the sword of Spirit. inevitable
Martyrs are the human links which connect one stage with 9
another in the history of religion. They are earth's lumi-
naries, which serve to cleanse and rarefy the atmosphere of
material sense and to permeate humanity with purer ideals. 12
Consciousness of right-doing brings its own reward; but
not amid the smoke of battle is merit seen and appreciated
by lookers-on.   15
    When will Jesus' professed followers learn to emulate
him in *all* his ways and to imitate his mighty works?
Those who procured the martyrdom of that   Complete   18
righteous man would gladly have turned his   emulation
sacred career into a mutilated doctrinal platform. May
the Christians of to-day take up the more practical im- 21
port of that career! It is possible, — yea, it is the duty
and privilege of every child, man, and woman, — to follow
in some degree the example of the Master by the demon- 24
stration of Truth and Life, of health and holiness. Christians claim to be his followers, but do they follow him in
the way that he commanded? Hear these imperative com- 27
mands: "Be ye therefore perfect, even as your Father
which is in heaven is perfect!" "Go ye into all the world,
and preach the gospel to every creature!" "*Heal the* 30
sick!"
    Why has this Christian demand so little inspiration

1 to stir mankind to Christian effort?　Because men are
assured that this command was intended only for a par-
3 Jesus' teaching ticular period and for a select number of fol-
belittled 　lowers.　This teaching is even more pernicious
than the old doctrine of foreordination, — the election of a
6 few to be saved, while the rest are damned; and so it will
be considered, when the lethargy of mortals, produced
by man-made doctrines, is broken by the demands of
9 divine Science.

Jesus said: "These signs shall follow them that believe; . . . they shall lay hands on the sick, and they
12 shall recover."　Who believes him?　He was addressing
his disciples, yet he did not say, "These signs shall follow
you," but *them* — "them that believe" in all time to come.
15 Here the word *hands* is used metaphorically, as in the text,
"The right hand of the Lord is exalted."　It expresses
spiritual power; otherwise the healing could not have
18 been done spiritually.　At another time Jesus prayed, not
for the twelve only, but for as many as should believe
"through their word."

21 　Jesus experienced few of the pleasures of the physical
senses, but his sufferings were the fruits of other peo-
Material ple's sins, not of his own.　The eternal Christ,
24 pleasures his spiritual selfhood, never suffered.　Jesus
mapped out the path for others.　He unveiled the Christ,
the spiritual idea of divine Love.　To those buried in the
27 belief of sin and self, living only for pleasure or the grati-
fication of the senses, he said in substance: Having eyes
ye see not, and having ears ye hear not; lest ye should un-
30 derstand and be converted, and I might heal you.　He
taught that the material senses shut out Truth and its
healing power.

Meekly our Master met the mockery of his unrecog- 1
nized grandeur. Such indignities as he received, his followers will endure until Christianity's last 3
triumph. He won eternal honors. He over-
came the world, the flesh, and all error, thus proving
their nothingness. He wrought a full salvation from sin, 6
sickness, and death. We need "Christ, and him crucified." We must have trials and self-denials, as well as
joys and victories, until all error is destroyed. 9

Mockery of truth

The educated belief that Soul is in the body causes
mortals to regard death as a friend, as a stepping-stone
out of mortality into immortality and bliss. 12
The Bible calls death an enemy, and Jesus
overcame death and the grave instead of yielding to them.
He was "the way." To him, therefore, death was not 15
the threshold over which he must pass into living
glory.

A belief suicidal

"*Now*," cried the apostle, "is the accepted time; be- 18
hold, *now* is the day of salvation," — meaning, not that
now men must prepare for a future-world salvation, or safety, but that now is the time in which 21
to experience that salvation in spirit and in life. Now is
the time for so-called material pains and material pleasures to pass away, for both are unreal, because impossible 24
in Science. To break this earthly spell, mortals must get
the true idea and divine Principle of all that really exists
and governs the universe harmoniously. This thought is 27
apprehended slowly, and the interval before its attainment is attended with doubts and defeats as well as
triumphs. 30

Present salvation

Who will stop the practice of sin so long as he believes
in the pleasures of sin? When mortals once admit that

1 evil confers no pleasure, they turn from it. Remove error
from thought, and it will not appear in effect. The ad-
3   Sin and   vanced thinker and devout Christian, perceiv-
  penalty   ing the scope and tendency of Christian healing
and its Science, will support them. Another will say:
6 "Go thy way for this time; when I have a convenient
season I will call for thee."
Divine Science adjusts the balance as Jesus adjusted
9 it. Science removes the penalty only by first removing
the sin which incurs the penalty. This is my sense of
divine pardon, which I understand to mean God's method
12 of destroying sin. If the saying is true, "While there's
life there's hope," its opposite is also true, While there's
sin there's doom. Another's suffering cannot lessen our
15 own liability. Did the martyrdom of Savonarola make
the crimes of his implacable enemies less criminal?
Was it just for Jesus to suffer? No; but it was
18 inevitable, for not otherwise could he show us the way
  Suffering   and the power of Truth. If a career so great
  inevitable   and good as that of Jesus could not avert a
21 felon's fate, lesser apostles of Truth may endure human
brutality without murmuring, rejoicing to enter into
fellowship with him through the triumphal arch of
24 Truth and Love.
Our heavenly Father, divine Love, demands that all
men should follow the example of our Master and his
27   Service and   apostles and not merely worship his personal-
  worship   ity. It is sad that the phrase *divine service*
has come so generally to mean public worship instead of
30 daily deeds.
The nature of Christianity is peaceful and blessed,
but in order to enter into the kingdom, the anchor of

hope (must) be cast beyond the veil of matter into the 1
Shekinah into which Jesus has passed before us; and
this advance beyond matter must come   Within   3
through the joys and triumphs of the right-   the veil
eous as well as through their sorrows and afflictions.
Like our Master, we must depart from material sense 6
into the spiritual sense of being.

The God-inspired walk calmly on though it be with
bleeding footprints, and in the hereafter they will reap 9
what they now sow. The pampered hypo-   The thorns
crite may have a flowery pathway here, but   and flowers
he cannot forever break the Golden Rule and escape the 12
penalty due.

The proofs of Truth, Life, and Love, which Jesus gave
by casting out error and healing the sick, completed his 15
earthly mission; but in the Christian Church   Healing
this demonstration of healing was early lost,   early lost
about three centuries after the crucifixion. No ancient 18
school of philosophy, *materia medica,* or scholastic theology ever taught or demonstrated the divine healing of
absolute Science.   21

Jesus foresaw the reception Christian Science would have
before it was understood, but this foreknowledge hindered
him not. He fulfilled his God-mission, and   Immortal 24
then sat down at the right hand of the Father.   achieval
Persecuted from city to city, his apostles still went about
doing good deeds, for which they were maligned and 27
stoned. The truth taught by Jesus, the elders scoffed at.
Why? Because it demanded more than they were willing
to practise. It was enough for them to believe in a national 30
Deity; but that belief, from their time to ours, has never
made a disciple who could cast out evils and heal the sick.

1 Jesus' life proved, divinely and scientifically, that God
is Love, whereas priest and rabbi affirmed God to be a
3 mighty potentate, who loves and hates. The Jewish theology gave no hint of the unchanging love of God.
The universal belief in death is of no advantage. It
6   A belief   cannot make Life or Truth apparent. Death
   in death   will be found at length to be a mortal dream,
which comes in darkness and disappears with the light.
9 The "man of sorrows" was in no peril from salary or
popularity. Though entitled to the homage of the world
      Cruel   and endorsed pre-eminently by the approval
12   desertion   of God, his brief triumphal entry into Jerusalem was followed by the desertion of all save a few friends,
who sadly followed him to the foot of the cross.
15 The resurrection of the great demonstrator of God's
power was the proof of his final triumph over body
      Death   and matter, and gave full evidence of divine
18   outdone   Science, — evidence so important to mortals.
The belief that man has existence or mind separate from
God is a dying error. This error Jesus met with divine
21 Science and proved its nothingness. Because of the won-
drous glory which God bestowed on His anointed, temptation, sin, sickness, and death had no terror for Jesus.
24 Let men think they had killed the body! Afterwards he
would show it to them unchanged. This demonstrates
that in Christian Science the true man is governed by
27 God — by good, not evil — and is therefore not a mortal
but an immortal. Jesus had taught his disciples the
Science of this proof. He was here to enable them to
30 test his still uncomprehended saying, "He that believeth on me, the works that I do shall he do also." They
must understand more fully his Life-principle by casting

out error, healing the sick, and raising the dead, even as 1
they did understand it after his bodily departure.

The magnitude of Jesus' work, his material disappear- 3
ance before their eyes and his reappearance, all enabled
the disciples to understand what Jesus had *Pentecost*
said. Heretofore they had only believed; *repeated* 6
now they understood. The advent of this understanding
is what is meant by the descent of the Holy Ghost, — that
influx of divine Science which so illuminated the Pentecos- 9
tal Day and is now repeating its ancient history.

Jesus' last proof was the highest, the most convincing,
the most profitable to his students. The malignity of 12
brutal persecutors, the treason and suicide of *Convincing*
his betrayer, were overruled by divine Love to *evidence*
the glorification of the man and of the true idea of God, 15
which Jesus' persecutors had mocked and tried to slay.
The final demonstration of the truth which Jesus taught,
and for which he was crucified, opened a new era for the 18
world. Those who slew him to stay his influence perpetuated and extended it.

Jesus rose higher in demonstration because of the cup 21
of bitterness he drank. Human law had condemned
him, but he was demonstrating divine Science. *Divine*
Out of reach of the barbarity of his enemies, *victory* 24
he was acting under spiritual law in defiance of matter and mortality, and that spiritual law sustained him.
The divine must overcome the human at every point. 27
The Science Jesus taught and lived must triumph over
all material beliefs about life, substance, and intelligence, and the multitudinous errors growing from such 30
beliefs.

Love must triumph over hate. Truth and Life must

1 seal the victory over error and death, before the thorns
can be laid aside for a crown, the benediction follow,
3 "Well done, good and faithful servant," and the supremacy of Spirit be demonstrated.

The lonely precincts of the tomb gave Jesus a refuge
6 from his foes, a place in which to solve the great
Jesus in   problem of being. His three days' work in
the tomb   the sepulchre set the seal of eternity on time.
9 He proved Life to be deathless and Love to be the master of hate. He met and mastered on the basis of Christian Science, the power of Mind over matter, all the claims
12 of medicine, surgery, and hygiene.

He took no drugs to allay inflammation. He did not
depend upon food or pure air to resuscitate wasted
15 energies. He did not require the skill of a surgeon to
heal the torn palms and bind up the wounded side and
lacerated feet, that he might use those hands to remove
18 the napkin and winding-sheet, and that he might employ
his feet as before.

Could it be called supernatural for the God of nature
21 to sustain Jesus in his proof of man's truly derived power?
The deific   It was a method of surgery beyond material
naturalism   art, but it was not a supernatural act. On
24 the contrary, it was a divinely natural act, whereby divinity
brought to humanity the understanding of the Christ-
healing and revealed a method infinitely above that of
27 human invention.

His disciples believed Jesus to be dead while he was
hidden in the sepulchre, whereas he was alive, demon-
30 Obstacles   strating within the narrow tomb the power
overcome   of Spirit to overrule mortal, material sense.
There were rock-ribbed walls in the way, and a great

stone (must) be rolled from the cave's mouth; but Jesus 1
vanquished every material obstacle, overcame every law
of matter, and stepped forth from his gloomy resting-place, 3
crowned with the glory of a sublime success, an everlasting
victory.

Our Master fully and finally demonstrated divine Sci- 6
ence in his victory over death and the grave. Jesus'
deed was for the enlightenment of men and   Victory over
for the salvation of the whole world from sin,   the grave   9
sickness, and death. Paul writes: "For if, when we were
enemies, we were reconciled to God by the [seeming] death
of His Son, much more, being reconciled, we shall be saved 12
by his life." Three days after his bodily burial he talked
with his disciples. The persecutors had failed to hide immortal Truth and Love in a sepulchre.   15

Glory be to God, and peace to the struggling hearts!
Christ hath rolled away the stone from the door of human hope and faith, and through the reve-   The stone   18
lation and demonstration of life in God, hath   rolled away
elevated them to possible at-one-ment with the spiritual
idea of man and his divine Principle, Love.   21

They who earliest saw Jesus after the resurrection
and beheld the final proof of all that he had taught,
misconstrued that event. Even his disciples   After the   24
at first called him a spirit, ghost, or spectre,   resurrection
for they believed his body to be dead. His reply was:
"Spirit hath not flesh and bones, as ye see me have." 27
The reappearing of Jesus was not the return of a spirit.
He presented the same body that he had before his crucifixion, and so glorified the supremacy of Mind over 30
matter.

Jesus' students, not sufficiently advanced fully to un-

1 derstand their Master's triumph, did not perform many
wonderful works, until they saw him after his crucifixion
3 and learned that he had not died. This convinced them
of the truthfulness of all that he had taught.

In the walk to Emmaus, Jesus was known to his friends
6 by the words, which made their hearts burn within them,
Spiritual   and by the breaking of bread. The divine
interpretation Spirit, which identified Jesus thus centuries
9 ago, has spoken through the inspired Word and will speak
through it in every age and clime. It is revealed to the
receptive heart, and is again seen casting out evil and
12 healing the sick.

The Master said plainly that physique was not Spirit,
and after his resurrection he proved to the physical senses
15 Corporeality that his body was not changed until he himself
and Spirit   ascended, — or, in other words, rose even
higher in the understanding of Spirit, God. To convince
18 Thomas of this, Jesus caused him to examine the nail-
prints and the spear-wound.

Jesus' unchanged physical condition after what seemed
21 to be death was followed by his exaltation above all ma-
Spiritual   terial conditions; and this exaltation explained
ascension   his ascension, and revealed unmistakably a
24 probationary and progressive state beyond the grave.
Jesus was "the way;" that is, he marked the way for
all men. In his final demonstration, called the ascen-
27 sion, which closed the earthly record of Jesus, he rose
above the physical knowledge of his disciples, and the
material senses saw him no more.

30   His students then received the Holy Ghost. By this is
meant, that by all they had witnessed and suffered, they
were roused to an enlarged understanding of divine Sci-

ence, even to the spiritual interpretation and discernment 1
of Jesus' teachings and demonstrations, which gave them
a faint conception of the Life which is God. Pentecostal 3
They no longer measured man by material *power*
sense. After gaining the true idea of their glorified Master,
they became better healers, leaning no longer on matter, 6
but on the divine Principle of their work. The influx of
light was sudden. It was sometimes an overwhelming
power as on the Day of Pentecost. 9

Judas conspired against Jesus. The world's ingratitude
and hatred towards that just man effected his betrayal.
The traitor's price was thirty pieces of silver *The traitor's* 12
and the smiles of the Pharisees. He chose his *conspiracy*
time, when the people were in doubt concerning Jesus'
teachings. 15

A period was approaching which would reveal the infinite distance between Judas and his Master. Judas
Iscariot knew this. He knew that the great goodness of 18
that Master placed a gulf between Jesus and his betrayer,
and this spiritual distance inflamed Judas' envy. The
greed for gold strengthened his ingratitude, and for a time 21
quieted his remorse. He knew that the world generally
loves a lie better than Truth; and so he plotted the betrayal of Jesus in order to raise himself in popular esti- 24
mation. His dark plot fell to the ground, and the
traitor fell with it.

The disciples' desertion of their Master in his last 27
earthly struggle was punished; each one came to a violent death except St. John, of whose death we have no
record. 30

During his night of gloom and glory in the garden,
Jesus realized the utter error of a belief in any possi-

48 Science and Health

ble material intelligence. The pangs of neglect and the
staves of bigoted ignorance smote him sorely. His students slept. He said unto them: "Could ye
not watch with me one hour?" Could they
not watch with him who, waiting and struggling in voice-
less agony, held uncomplaining guard over a world?
There was no response to that human yearning, and so
Jesus turned forever away from earth to heaven, from
sense to Soul.

Gethsemane glorified

Remembering the sweat of agony which fell in holy
benediction on the grass of Gethsemane, shall the hum-
blest or mightiest disciple murmur when he drinks from the
same cup, and think, or even wish, to escape the exalting ordeal of sin's revenge on its destroyer? Truth and
Love bestow few palms until the consummation of a
life-work.

Judas had the world's weapons. Jesus had not one
of them, and chose not the world's means of defence.
"He opened not his mouth." The great demonstrator of Truth and Love was silent before
envy and hate. Peter would have smitten the enemies of
his Master, but Jesus forbade him, thus rebuking re-
sentment or animal courage. He said: "Put up thy
sword."

Defensive weapons

Pale in the presence of his own momentous question,
"What is Truth," Pilate was drawn into acquiescence
with the demands of Jesus' enemies. Pilate
was ignorant of the consequences of his awful
decision against human rights and divine Love, knowing
not that he was hastening the final demonstration of what
life is and of what the true knowledge of God can do for
man.

Pilate's question

The women at the cross could have answered Pilate's 1
question. They knew what had inspired their devotion,
winged their faith, opened the eyes of their understand- 3
ing, healed the sick, cast out evil, and caused the disciples
to say to their Master: "Even the devils are subject
unto us through thy name."   6

Where were the seventy whom Jesus sent forth? Were
all conspirators save eleven? Had they forgotten the
great exponent of God? Had they so soon lost   Students'   9
sight of his mighty works, his toils, privations,   ingratitude
sacrifices, his divine patience, sublime courage, and unre-
quited affection? O, why did they not gratify his last 12
human yearning with one sign of fidelity?

The meek demonstrator of good, the highest instruc-
tor and friend of man, met his earthly fate alone with 15
God. No human eye was there to pity, no   Heaven's
arm to save. Forsaken by all whom he had   sentinel
blessed, this faithful sentinel of God at the highest 18
post of power, charged with the grandest trust of
heaven, was ready to be transformed by the renewing
of the infinite Spirit. He was to prove that the Christ 21
is not subject to material conditions, but is above the
reach of human wrath, and is able, through Truth,
Life, and Love, to triumph over sin, sickness, death, and 24
the grave.

The priests and rabbis, before whom he had meekly
walked, and those to whom he had given the highest 27
proofs of divine power, mocked him on the   Cruel
cross, saying derisively, "He saved others;   contumely
himself he cannot save." These scoffers, who turned 30
"aside the right of a man before the face of the Most
High," esteemed Jesus as "stricken, smitten of God."

1 "He is brought as a lamb to the slaughter, and as a sheep
before her shearers is dumb, so he openeth not his mouth."
3 "Who shall declare his generation?" Who shall decide
what truth and love are?

The last supreme moment of mockery, desertion, tor-
6 ture, added to an overwhelming sense of the magnitude

A cry of   of his work, wrung from Jesus' lips the awful
despair   cry, "My God, why hast Thou forsaken me?"

9 This despairing appeal, if made to a human parent, would
impugn the justice and love of a father who could withhold a clear token of his presence to sustain and bless so
12 faithful a son. The appeal of Jesus was made both to
his divine Principle, the God who is Love, and to himself,
Love's pure idea. Had Life, Truth, and Love forsaken
15 him in his highest demonstration? This was a startling
question. No! They must abide in him and he in them,
or that hour would be shorn of its mighty blessing for the
18 human race.

If his full recognition of eternal Life had for a moment given way before the evidence of the bodily senses,
21   what would his accusers have said? Even
Divine
Science mis- what they did say, — that Jesus' teachings
understood   were false, and that all evidence of their cor-
24 rectness was destroyed by his death. But this saying
could not make it so.

The burden of that hour was terrible beyond human
27 conception. The distrust of mortal minds, disbelieving

The real   the purpose of his mission, was a million
pillory   times sharper than the thorns which pierced
30 his flesh. The real cross, which Jesus bore up the hill
of grief, was the world's hatred of Truth and Love. Not
the spear nor the material cross wrung from his faithful

lips the plaintive cry, *"Eloi, Eloi, lama sabachthani?"* It 1
was the possible loss of something more important than
human life which moved him, — the possible misappre- 3
hension of the sublimest influence of his career. This
dread added the drop of gall to his cup.

    Jesus could have withdrawn himself from his enemies. 6
He had power to lay down a human sense of life for his
spiritual identity in the likeness of the divine; Life-power
but he allowed men to attempt the destruc- indestructible 9
tion of the mortal body in order that he might furnish
the proof of immortal life. Nothing could kill this Life
of man. Jesus could give his temporal life into his 12
enemies' hands; but when his earth-mission was accomplished, his spiritual life, indestructible and eternal,
was found forever the same. He knew that matter had 15
no life and that real Life is God; therefore he could no
more be separated from his spiritual Life than God could
be extinguished. 18

    His consummate example was for the salvation of us
all, but only through doing the works which he did and
taught others to do. His purpose in healing Example for 21
was not alone to restore health, but to demon- our salvation
strate his divine Principle. He was inspired by God, by
Truth and Love, in all that he said and did. The motives 24
of his persecutors were pride, envy, cruelty, and vengeance,
inflicted on the physical Jesus, but aimed at the divine Principle, Love, which rebuked their sensuality. 27

    Jesus was unselfish. His spirituality separated him
from sensuousness, and caused the selfish materialist
to hate him; but it was this spirituality which enabled 30
Jesus to heal the sick, cast out evil, and raise the
dead.

1 From early boyhood he was about his "Father's business." His pursuits lay far apart from theirs. His mas-
3 Master's ter was Spirit; their master was matter. He
business served God; they served mammon. His affections were pure; theirs were carnal. His senses drank in
6 the spiritual evidence of health, holiness, and life; their
senses testified oppositely, and absorbed the material evidence of sin, sickness, and death.

9 Their imperfections and impurity felt the ever-present
rebuke of his perfection and purity. Hence the world's
Purity's hatred of the just and perfect Jesus, and the
12 rebuke prophet's foresight of the reception error would
give him. "Despised and rejected of men," was Isaiah's
graphic word concerning the coming Prince of Peace.
15 Herod and Pilate laid aside old feuds in order to unite
in putting to shame and death the best man that ever
trod the globe. To-day, as of old, error and evil again
18 make common cause against the exponents of truth.

The "man of sorrows" best understood the nothingness of material life and intelligence and the mighty ac-
21 Saviour's tuality of all-inclusive God, good. These were
prediction the two cardinal points of Mind-healing, or
Christian Science, which armed him with Love. The high-
24 est earthly representative of God, speaking of human
ability to reflect divine power, prophetically said to his
disciples, speaking not for their day only but for all time:
27 "He that believeth on me, the works that I do shall he do
also;" and "These signs shall follow them that believe."

The accusations of the Pharisees were as self-contra-
30 Defamatory dictory as their religion. The bigot, the deb-
accusations auchee, the hypocrite, called Jesus a glutton
and a wine-bibber. They said: "He casteth out devils

through Beelzebub," and is the "friend of publicans and 1
sinners." The latter accusation was true, but not in their
meaning. Jesus was no ascetic. He did not fast as did 3
the Baptist's disciples; yet there never lived a man so far
removed from appetites and passions as the Nazarene.
He rebuked sinners pointedly and unflinchingly, because 6
he was their friend; hence the cup he drank.

The reputation of Jesus was the very opposite of his
character. Why? Because the divine Principle and 9
practice of Jesus were misunderstood. He   Reputation
was at work in divine Science. His words   and character
and works were unknown to the world because above 12
and contrary to the world's religious sense. Mortals believed in God as humanly mighty, rather than as divine,
infinite Love. 15

The world could not interpret aright the discomfort
which Jesus inspired and the spiritual blessings which
might flow from such discomfort. Science   Inspiring   18
shows the cause of the shock so often pro-   discontent
duced by the truth, — namely, that this shock arises from
the great distance between the individual and Truth. 21
Like Peter, we should weep over the warning, instead of
denying the truth or mocking the lifelong sacrifice which
goodness makes for the destruction of evil. 24

Jesus bore our sins in his body. He knew the
mortal errors which constitute the material body, and
could destroy those errors; but at the time   Bearing   27
when Jesus felt our infirmities, he had not   our sins
conquered all the beliefs of the flesh or his sense of material life, nor had he risen to his final demonstration of 30
spiritual power.

Had he shared the sinful beliefs of others, he would

have been less sensitive to those beliefs. Through the
magnitude of his human life, he demonstrated the divine
Life. Out of the amplitude of his pure affection, he defined Love. With the affluence of Truth, he vanquished
error. The world acknowledged not his righteousness,
seeing it not; but earth received the harmony his glorified
example introduced.

Who is ready to follow his teaching and example? All
must sooner or later plant themselves in Christ, the true
Inspiration of sacrifice idea of God. That he might liberally pour
his dear-bought treasures into empty or sin-
filled human storehouses, was the inspiration of Jesus'
intense human sacrifice. In witness of his divine commission, he presented the proof that Life, Truth, and
Love heal the sick and the sinning, and triumph over
death through Mind, not matter. This was the highest
proof he could have offered of divine Love. His hearers
understood neither his words nor his works. They
would not accept his meek interpretation of life nor
follow his example.

His earthly cup of bitterness was drained to the
dregs. There adhered to him only a few unpretentious
Spiritual friendship friends, whose religion was something more
than a name. It was so vital, that it en-
abled them to understand the Nazarene and to share
the glory of eternal life. He said that those who followed him should drink of his cup, and history has confirmed the prediction.

If that Godlike and glorified man were physically on
Injustice to the Saviour earth to-day, would not some, who now profess to love him, reject him? Would they
not deny him even the rights of humanity, if he enter-

tained any other sense of being and religion than theirs? 1
The advancing century, from a deadened sense of the
invisible God, to-day subjects to unchristian comment and 3
usage the idea of Christian healing enjoined by Jesus; but
this does not affect the invincible facts.

Perhaps the early Christian era did Jesus no more 6
injustice than the later centuries have bestowed upon
the healing Christ and spiritual idea of being. Now
that the gospel of healing is again preached by the 9
wayside, does not the pulpit sometimes scorn it? But
that curative mission, which presents the Saviour in a
clearer light than mere words can possibly do, cannot be 12
left out of Christianity, although it is again ruled out of
the synagogue.

Truth's immortal idea is sweeping down the centuries, 15
gathering beneath its wings the sick and sinning. My
weary hope tries to realize that happy day, when man shall
recognize the Science of Christ and love his neighbor as 18
himself, — when he shall realize God's omnipotence and
the healing power of the divine Love in what it has done
and is doing for mankind. The promises will be ful- 21
filled. The time for the reappearing of the divine healing
is throughout all time; and whosoever layeth his earthly
all on the altar of divine Science, drinketh of Christ's 24
cup now, and is endued with the spirit and power of
Christian healing.

In the words of St. John: "He shall give you another 27
Comforter, that he may abide with you *forever*." This
Comforter I understand to be Divine Science.

CHAPTER III

Marriage

What therefore God hath joined together, let not man put asunder.
In the resurrection they neither marry, nor are given in marriage, but
are as the angels of God in heaven. — JESUS.

1 WHEN our great Teacher came to him for baptism,
John was astounded. Reading his thoughts, Jesus
3 added: "Suffer it to be so now: for thus it becometh us
to fulfil all righteousness." Jesus' concessions (in certain
cases) to material methods were for the advancement of
6 spiritual good.

Marriage is the legal and moral provision for generation among human kind. Until the spiritual creation
9   Marriage   is discerned intact, is apprehended and under-
  temporal   stood, and His kingdom is come as in the vision
of the Apocalypse, — where the corporeal sense of crea-
12 tion was cast out, and its spiritual sense was revealed from
heaven, — marriage will continue, subject to such moral
regulations as will secure increasing virtue.

15   Infidelity to the marriage covenant is the social scourge
of all races, "the pestilence that walketh in darkness,
  Fidelity   . . . the destruction that wasteth at noonday."
18   required   The commandment, "Thou shalt not commit adultery," is no less imperative than the one, "Thou
shalt not kill."

Chastity is the cement of civilization and progress. 1
Without it there is no stability in society, and without it
one cannot attain the Science of Life.   3
Union of the masculine and feminine qualities constitutes completeness.   The masculine mind reaches a
higher tone through certain elements of the   Mental   6
feminine, while the feminine mind gains cour-   elements
age and strength through masculine qualities. These
different elements conjoin naturally with each other, and 9
their true harmony is in spiritual oneness. Both sexes
should be loving, pure, tender, and strong. The attraction between native qualities will be perpetual only as it 12
is pure and true, bringing sweet seasons of renewal like
the returning spring.

Beauty, wealth, or fame is incompetent to meet the 15
demands of the affections, and should never weigh
against the better claims of intellect, good-   Affection's
ness, and virtue. Happiness is spiritual,   demands   18
born of Truth and Love. It is unselfish; therefore
it cannot exist alone, but requires all mankind to
share it.   21

Human affection is not poured forth vainly, even
though it meet no return. Love enriches the nature, en-
larging, purifying, and elevating it. The wintry   Help and   24
blasts of earth may uproot the flowers of affec-   discipline
tion, and scatter them to the winds; but this severance
of fleshly ties serves to unite thought more closely to 27
God, for Love supports the struggling heart until it ceases
to sigh over the world and begins to unfold its wings for
heaven.   30

Marriage is unblest or blest, according to the disappointments it involves or the hopes it fulfils. To happify

1 existence by constant intercourse with those adapted to
elevate it, should be the motive of society. Unity of
3 spirit gives new pinions to joy, or else joy's drooping
wings trail in dust.

Ill-arranged notes produce discord. Tones of the
6 human mind may be different, but they should be con-
Chord and   cordant in order to blend properly. Unselfish
discord   ambition, noble life-motives, and purity, —
9 these constituents of thought, mingling, constitute individually and collectively true happiness, strength, and
permanence.

12   There is moral freedom in Soul. Never contract the
horizon of a worthy outlook by the selfish exaction of
Mutual   all another's time and thoughts. With ad-
15 freedom   ditional joys, benevolence should grow more
diffusive. The narrowness and jealousy, which would
confine a wife or a husband forever within four walls, will
18 not promote the sweet interchange of confidence and love;
but on the other hand, a wandering desire for incessant
amusement outside the home circle is a poor augury for
21 the happiness of wedlock. Home is the dearest spot on
earth, and it should be the centre, though not the boundary, of the affections.

24   Said the peasant bride to her lover: "Two eat no more
together than they eat separately." This is a hint that
A useful   a wife ought not to court vulgar extravagance
27 suggestion   or stupid ease, because another supplies her
wants. Wealth may obviate the necessity for toil or the
chance for ill-nature in the marriage relation, but noth-
30 ing can abolish the cares of marriage.

"She that is married careth . . . how she may please
her husband," says the Bible; and this is the pleasantest

thing to do. Matrimony should never be entered into 1
without a full recognition of its enduring obligations on
both sides. There should be the most tender   Differing   3
solicitude for each other's happiness, and mu-   duties
tual attention and approbation should wait on all the years
of married life.   6
Mutual compromises will often maintain a compact
which might otherwise become unbearable. Man should
not be required to participate in all the annoyances and 9
cares of domestic economy, nor should woman be expected to understand political economy. Fulfilling the
different demands of their united spheres, their sympa- 12
thies should blend in sweet confidence and cheer, each
partner sustaining the other, — thus hallowing the union
of interests and affections, in which the heart finds peace 15
and home.

Tender words and unselfish care in what promotes the
welfare and happiness of your wife will prove more salutary 18
in prolonging her health and smiles than stolid   Trysting
indifference or jealousy. Husbands, hear this   renewed
and remember how slight a word or deed may renew the 21
old trysting-times.

After marriage, it is too late to grumble over incompati-
bility of disposition. A mutual understanding should 24
exist before this union and continue ever after, for decep-
tion is fatal to happiness.

The nuptial vow should never be annulled, so long as 27
its moral obligations are kept intact; but the frequency
of divorce shows that the sacredness of this re-   Permanent
lationship is losing its influence, and that fatal   obligation   30
mistakes are undermining its foundations. Separation
never should take place, and it never would, if both

1 husband and wife were genuine Christian Scientists.
Science inevitably lifts one's being higher in the scale of
3 harmony and happiness.

Kindred tastes, motives, and aspirations are necessary
to the formation of a happy and permanent companion-
6 Permanent ship. The beautiful in character is also the
affection good, welding indissolubly the links of affection. A mother's affection cannot be weaned from her
9 child, because the mother-love includes purity and constancy, both of which are immortal. Therefore maternal
affection lives on under whatever difficulties.

12 From the logic of events we learn that selfishness
and impurity alone are fleeting, and that wisdom will
ultimately put asunder what she hath not joined
15 together.

Marriage should improve the human species, becoming
a barrier against vice, a protection to woman, strength to
18 Centre for man, and a centre for the affections. This,
affections however, in a majority of cases, is not its
present tendency, and why? Because the education of
21 the higher nature is neglected, and other considerations,
— passion, frivolous amusements, personal adornment,
display, and pride, — occupy thought.

24 An ill-attuned ear calls discord harmony, not appreciat-
ing concord. So physical sense, not discerning the true
Spiritual happiness of being, places it on a false basis.
27 concord Science will correct the discord, and teach us
life's sweeter harmonies.

Soul has infinite resources with which to bless mankind,
30 and happiness would be more readily attained and would
be more secure in our keeping, if sought in Soul. Higher
enjoyments alone can satisfy the cravings of immortal

man. We cannot circumscribe happiness within the 1
limits of personal sense. The senses confer no real
enjoyment. 3

The good in human affections must have ascendency
over the evil and the spiritual over the animal, or happiness will never be won. The attainment of Ascendency 6
this celestial condition would improve our of good
progeny, diminish crime, and give higher aims to ambition. Every valley of sin (must) be exalted, and every 9
mountain of selfishness be brought low, that the highway
of our God may be prepared in Science. The offspring
of heavenly-minded parents inherit more intellect, better 12
balanced minds, and sounder constitutions.

If some fortuitous circumstance places promising children in the arms of gross parents, often these beautiful 15
children early droop and die, like tropical Propensities
flowers born amid Alpine snows. If perchance inherited
they live to become parents in their turn, they may re- 18
produce in their own helpless little ones the grosser traits
of their ancestors. What hope of happiness, what noble
ambition, can inspire the child who inherits propensities 21
that must either be overcome or reduce him to a loathsome wreck?

Is not the propagation of the human species a greater 24
responsibility, a more solemn charge, than the culture of
your garden or the raising of stock to increase your flocks
and herds? Nothing unworthy of perpetuity should be 27
transmitted to children.

The formation of mortals must greatly improve to
advance mankind. The scientific *morale* of marriage is 30
spiritual unity. If the propagation of a higher human
species is requisite to reach this goal, then its material con-

1 ditions can only be permitted for the purpose of gener-
ating. The fœtus must be kept mentally pure and the
3 period of gestation have the sanctity of virginity.

The entire education of children should be such as to
form habits of obedience to the moral and spiritual law,
6 with which the child can meet and master the belief in so-
called physical laws, a belief which breeds disease.

If parents create in their babes a desire for incessant
9 amusement, to be always fed, rocked, tossed, or talked
Inheritance heeded to, those parents should not, in after years,
complain of their children's fretfulness or fri-
12 volity, which the parents themselves have occasioned.

Taking less "thought for your life, what ye shall eat, or
what ye shall drink"; less thought "for your body what
15 ye shall put on," will do much more for the health of the
rising generation than you dream. Children should be
allowed to remain children in knowledge, and should
18 become men and women only through growth in the
understanding of man's higher nature.

We must not attribute more and more intelligence
21 to matter, but less and less, if we would be wise and
The Mind creative healthy. The divine Mind, which forms the
bud and blossom, will care for the human
24 body, even as it clothes the lily; but let no mortal interfere with God's government by thrusting in the laws of
erring, human concepts.

27 The higher nature of man is not governed by the lower;
if it were, the order of wisdom would be reversed.
Superior law of Soul Our false views of life hide eternal harmony,
30 and produce the ills of which we complain.

Because mortals believe in material laws and reject the
Science of Mind, this does not make materiality first and

the superior law of Soul last. You would never think 1
that flannel was better for warding off pulmonary disease
than the controlling Mind, if you understood the Science 3
of being.

In Science man is the offspring of Spirit. The beautiful, good, and pure constitute his ancestry. His origin is 6
not, like that of mortals, in brute instinct, nor   Spiritual
does he pass through material conditions prior   origin
to reaching intelligence. Spirit is his primitive and ulti- 9
mate source of being; God is his Father, and Life is the
law of his being.

Civil law establishes very unfair differences between the 12
rights of the two sexes. Christian Science furnishes no
precedent for such injustice, and civilization   The rights
mitigates it in some measure. Still, it is a   of woman 15
marvel why usage should accord woman less rights than
does either Christian Science or civilization.

Our laws are not impartial, to say the least, in their 18
discrimination as to the person, property, and parental
claims of the two sexes. If the elective franchise   Unfair dis-
chise for women will remedy the evil with-   crimination 21
out encouraging difficulties of greater magnitude, let us
hope it will be granted. A feasible as well as rational
means of improvement at present is the elevation of 24
society in general and the achievement of a nobler
race for legislation, — a race having higher aims and
motives. 27

If a dissolute husband deserts his wife, certainly the
wronged, and perchance impoverished, woman should be
allowed to collect her own wages, enter into business 30
agreements, hold real estate, deposit funds, and own her
children free from interference.

1 Want of uniform justice is a crying evil caused by the
selfishness and inhumanity of man. Our forefathers
3 exercised their faith in the direction taught by the Apostle
James, when he said: "Pure religion and undefiled before
God and the Father, is this, To visit the fatherless and
6 widows in their affliction, and to keep himself unspotted
from the world."

Pride, envy, or jealousy seems on most occasions to
9 be the master of ceremonies, ruling out primitive Chris-

Benevolence   tianity. When a man lends a helping hand
hindered   to some noble woman, struggling alone with
12 adversity, his wife should not say, "It is never well to
interfere with your neighbor's business." A wife is
sometimes debarred by a covetous domestic tyrant from
15 giving the ready aid her sympathy and charity would
afford.

Marriage should signify a union of hearts. Further-
18 more, the time cometh of which Jesus spake, when he

Progressive   declared that in the resurrection there should
development   be no more marrying nor giving in marriage,
21 but man would be as the angels. Then shall Soul rejoice in its own, in which passion has no part. Then
white-robed purity will unite in one person masculine wis-
24 dom and feminine love, spiritual understanding and perpetual peace.

Until it is learned that God is the Father of all, mar-
27 riage will continue. Let not mortals permit a disregard
of law which might lead to a worse state of society than
now exists. Honesty and virtue ensure the stability of
30 the marriage covenant. Spirit will ultimately claim its
own, — all that really is, — and the voices of physical
sense will be forever hushed.

Experience should be the school of virtue, and human 1
happiness should proceed from man's highest nature.
May Christ, Truth, be present at every bridal   Blessing   3
altar to turn the water into wine and to give to   of Christ
human life an inspiration by which man's spiritual and
eternal existence may be discerned.   6

If the foundations of human affection are consistent
with progress, they will be strong and enduring. Divorces
should warn the age of some fundamental error   Righteous   9
in the marriage state. The union of the sexes   foundations
suffers fearful discord. To gain Christian Science and its
harmony, life should be more metaphysically regarded. 12

The broadcast powers of evil so conspicuous to-day
show themselves in the materialism and sensualism of
the age, struggling against the advancing   Powerless   15
spiritual era. Beholding the world's lack of   promises
Christianity and the powerlessness of vows to make home
happy, the human mind will at length demand a higher 18
affection.

There will ensue a fermentation over this as over many
other reforms, until we get at last the clear straining of 21
truth, and impurity and error are left among   Transition
the lees. The fermentation even of fluids is   and reform
not pleasant. An unsettled, transitional stage is never 24
desirable on its own account. Matrimony, which was once
a fixed fact among us, must lose its present slippery foot-
ing, and man must find permanence and peace in a more 27
spiritual adherence.

The mental chemicalization, which has brought conjugal infidelity to the surface, will assuredly throw off 30
this evil, and marriage will become purer when the scum
is gone.

1 Thou art right, immortal Shakespeare, great poet of
humanity:

3 Sweet are the uses of adversity;
Which, like the toad, ugly and venomous,
Wears yet a precious jewel in his head.

6 Trials teach mortals not to lean on a material staff, —
a broken reed, which pierces the heart. We do not
Salutary half remember this in the sunshine of joy
9 sorrow and prosperity. Sorrow is salutary. Through
great tribulation we enter the kingdom. Trials are
proofs of God's care. Spiritual development germi-
12 nates not from seed sown in the soil of material hopes,
but when these decay, Love propagates anew the higher
joys of Spirit, which have no taint of earth. Each suc-
15 cessive stage of experience unfolds new views of divine
goodness and love.

Amidst gratitude for conjugal felicity, it is well to re-
18 member how fleeting are human joys. Amidst conjugal
infelicity, it is well to hope, pray, and wait patiently on
divine wisdom to point out the path.

21 Husbands and wives should never separate if there
is no Christian demand for it. It is better to await the
Patience logic of events than for a wife precipitately
24 is wisdom to leave her husband or for a husband to
leave his wife. If one is better than the other, as must
always be the case, the other pre-eminently needs good
27 company. Socrates considered patience salutary under
such circumstances, making his Xantippe a discipline for
his philosophy.

30 The gold Sorrow has its reward. It never leaves us
and dross where it found us. The furnace separates
the gold from the dross that the precious metal may

be graven with the image of God. The cup our Father 1
hath given, shall we not drink it and learn the lessons
He teaches? 3

When the ocean is stirred by a storm, then the clouds
lower, the wind shrieks through the tightened shrouds,
and the waves lift themselves into mountains. Weathering 6
We ask the helmsman: "Do you know your the storm
course? Can you steer safely amid the storm?" He
answers bravely, but even the dauntless seaman is not 9
sure of his safety; nautical science is not equal to the
Science of Mind. Yet, acting up to his highest understanding, firm at the post of duty, the mariner works on 12
and awaits the issue. Thus should we deport ourselves
on the seething ocean of sorrow. Hoping and working, one should stick to the wreck, until an irresistible 15
propulsion precipitates his doom or sunshine gladdens
the troubled sea.

The notion that animal natures can possibly give force 18
to character is too absurd for consideration, when we
remember that through spiritual ascendency Spiritual
our Lord and Master healed the sick, raised power 21
the dead, and commanded even the winds and waves to
obey him. Grace and Truth are potent beyond all other
means and methods. 24

The lack of spiritual power in the limited demonstration
of popular Christianity does not put to silence the labor
of centuries. Spiritual, not corporeal, consciousness is 27
needed. Man delivered from sin, disease, and death
presents the true likeness or spiritual ideal.

Systems of religion and medicine treat of physical pains 30
and pleasures, but Jesus rebuked the suffering from any
such cause or effect. The epoch approaches when the

1 understanding of the truth of being will be the basis of
true religion. At present mortals progress slowly for
3 Basis of true fear of being thought ridiculous. They are
religion slaves to fashion, pride, and sense. Sometime we shall learn how Spirit, the great architect, has
6 created men and women in Science. We ought to weary
of the fleeting and false and to cherish nothing which
hinders our highest selfhood.

9 Jealousy is the grave of affection. The presence of
mistrust, where confidence is due, withers the flowers
of Eden and scatters love's petals to decay. Be not
12 in haste to take the vow "until death do us part."
Consider its obligations, its responsibilities, its relations to your growth and to your influence on other
15 lives.

I never knew more than one individual who believed
in agamogenesis; she was unmarried, a lovely charac-
18 Insanity and ter, was suffering from incipient insanity, and
agamogenesis a Christian Scientist cured her. I have named
her case to individuals, when casting my bread upon
21 the waters, and it may have caused the good to ponder
and the evil to hatch their silly innuendoes and lies, since
salutary causes sometimes incur these effects. The per-
24 petuation of the floral species by bud or cell-division is
evident, but I discredit the belief that agamogenesis
applies to the human species.

27 Christian Science presents unfoldment, not accretion;
it manifests no material growth from molecule to mind,
God's but an impartation of the divine Mind to man
30 creation intact and the universe. Proportionately as human
generation ceases, the unbroken links of eternal, harmonious being will be spiritually discerned; and man,

not of the earth earthly but coexistent with God, will 1
appear. The scientific fact that man and the universe
are evolved from Spirit, and so are spiritual, is as fixed in 3
divine Science as is the proof that mortals gain the sense
of health only as they lose the sense of sin and disease.
Mortals can never understand God's creation while believ- 6
ing that man is a creator. God's children already created
will be cognized only as man finds the truth of being.
Thus it is that the real, ideal man appears in proportion 9
as the false and material disappears. No longer to marry
or to be "given in marriage" neither closes man's continuity nor his sense of increasing number in God's in- 12
finite plan. Spiritually to understand that there is but
one creator, God, unfolds all creation, confirms the Scriptures, brings the sweet assurance of no parting, no pain, 15
and of man deathless and perfect and eternal.

If Christian Scientists educate their own offspring
spiritually, they can educate others spiritually and not 18
conflict with the scientific sense of God's creation. Some
day the child will ask his parent: "Do you keep the First
Commandment? Do you have one God and creator, or 21
is man a creator?" If the father replies, "God creates
man through man," the child may ask, "Do you teach
that Spirit creates materially, or do you declare that 24
Spirit is infinite, therefore matter is out of the question?" Jesus said, "The children of this world marry,
and are given in marriage: But they which shall be ac- 27
counted worthy to obtain that world, and the resurrection from the dead, neither marry, nor are given in
marriage." 30

CHAPTER IV

Christian Science versus Spiritualism

And when they shall say unto you,
Seek unto them that have familiar spirits,
And unto wizards that peep and that mutter;
Should not a people seek unto their God? — ISAIAH.

Verily, verily, I say unto you, If a man keep my saying, he shall never see death. Then said the Jews unto him, Now we know that thou hast a devil. — JOHN.

1 MORTAL existence is an enigma. Every day is a mystery. The testimony of the corporeal senses
3 cannot inform us what is real and what is delusive, but the revelations of Christian Science unlock the treasures
The infinite of Truth. Whatever is false or sinful can
6 one Spirit never enter the atmosphere of Spirit. There is but one Spirit. Man is never God, but spiritual man, made in God's likeness, reflects God. In this scientific
9 reflection the Ego and the Father are inseparable. The supposition that corporeal beings are spirits, or that there are good and evil spirits, is a mistake.
12 The divine Mind maintains all identities, from a blade
Real and of grass to a star, as distinct and eternal. The
unreal identity questions are: What are God's identities?
15 What is Soul? Does life or soul exist in the thing formed?

Nothing is real and eternal, — nothing is Spirit, — but 1
God and His idea. Evil has no reality. It is neither
person, place, nor thing, but is simply a belief, an illusion 3
of material sense.

The identity, or idea, of all reality continues forever;
but Spirit, or the divine Principle of all, is not *in* Spirit's 6
formations. Soul is synonymous with Spirit, God, the
creative, governing, infinite Principle outside of finite form,
which forms only reflect.   9

Close your eyes, and you may dream that you see a
flower, — that you touch and smell it. Thus you learn
that the flower is a product of the so-called   Dream-   12
mind, a formation of thought rather than of   lessons
matter. Close your eyes again, and you may see land-
scapes, men, and women. Thus you learn that these 15
also are images, which mortal mind holds and evolves
and which simulate mind, life, and intelligence. From
dreams also you learn that neither mortal mind nor 18
matter is the image or likeness of God, and that immortal Mind is not in matter.

When the Science of Mind is understood, spiritualism 21
will be found mainly erroneous, having no scientific basis
nor origin, no proof nor power outside of   Found
human testimony. It is the offspring of the   wanting   24
physical senses. There is no sensuality in Spirit. I never
could believe in spiritualism.

The basis and structure of spiritualism are alike ma- 27
terial and physical. Its spirits are so many corporealities,
limited and finite in character and quality. Spiritualism
therefore presupposes Spirit, which is ever infinite, to be 30
a corporeal being, a finite form, — a theory contrary to
Christian Science.

1   There is but one spiritual existence, — the Life of
which corporeal sense can take no cognizance. The
3 divine Principle of man speaks through immortal sense.
If a material body — in other words, mortal, material
sense — were permeated by Spirit, that body would
6 disappear to mortal sense, would be deathless. A condition precedent to communion with Spirit is the gain of
spiritual life.

9   So-called *spirits* are but corporeal communicators. As
light destroys darkness and in the place of darkness all

Spirits is light, so (in absolute Science) Soul, or God,
12 obsolete is the only truth-giver to man. Truth destroys mortality, and brings to light immortality. Mortal
belief (the material sense of life) and immortal Truth
15 (the spiritual sense) are the tares and the wheat, which
are not united by progress, but separated.

Perfection is not expressed through imperfection.
18 Spirit is not made manifest through matter, the antipode of Spirit. Error is not a convenient sieve through
which truth can be strained.

21   God, good, being ever present, it follows in divine
logic that evil, the suppositional opposite of good, is never

Scientific present. In Science, individual good derived
24 phenomena from God, the infinite All-in-all, may flow
from the departed to mortals; but evil is neither communicable nor scientific. A sinning, earthly mortal is
27 not the reality of Life nor the medium through which
truth passes to earth. The joy of intercourse becomes
the jest of sin, when evil and suffering are communicable.
30 Not personal intercommunion but divine law is the communicator of truth, health, and harmony to earth and
humanity. As readily can you mingle fire and frost as

Spirit and matter. In either case, one does not support 1
the other.

Spiritualism calls one person, living in this world, *ma-* 3
terial, but another, who has died to-day a sinner and supposedly will return to earth to-morrow, it terms a *spirit*.
The fact is that neither the one nor the other is infinite 6
Spirit, for Spirit is God, and man is His likeness.

The belief that one man, as spirit, can control another man, as matter, upsets both the individuality and 9
the Science of man, for man is image. God   One
controls man, and God is the only Spirit. Any   government
other control or attraction of so-called spirit is a mortal 12
belief, which ought to be known by its fruit, — the repetition of evil.

If Spirit, or God, communed with mortals or controlled 15
them through electricity or any other form of matter, the
divine order and the Science of omnipotent, omnipresent
Spirit would be destroyed.   18

The belief that material bodies return to dust, hereafter
to rise up as spiritual bodies with material sensations and
desires, is incorrect. Equally incorrect is the   Incorrect   21
belief that spirit is confined in a finite, ma-   theories
terial body, from which it is freed by death, and that, when
it is freed from the material body, spirit retains the sensa- 24
tions belonging to that body.

It is a grave mistake to suppose that matter is any part
of the reality of intelligent existence, or that Spirit and 27
matter, intelligence and non-intelligence, can   No
commune together. This error Science will   mediumship
destroy. The sensual cannot be made the mouthpiece of 30
the spiritual, nor can the finite become the channel of
the infinite. There is no communication between so-

1 called material existence and spiritual life which is not
subject to death.

3   To be on communicable terms with Spirit, persons must
be free from organic bodies; and their return to a mate-
Opposing   rial condition, after having once left it, would
6 conditions   be as impossible as would be the restoration
to its original condition of the acorn, already absorbed
into a sprout which has risen above the soil. The seed
9 which has germinated has a new form and state of existence. When here or hereafter the belief of life in matter
is extinct, the error which has held the belief dissolves
12 with the belief, and never returns to the old condition.

No correspondence nor communion can exist between
persons in such opposite dreams as the belief of having
15 died and left a material body and the belief of still living
in an organic, material body.

The caterpillar, transformed into a beautiful insect,
18 is no longer a worm, nor does the insect return to
Bridgeless   fraternize with or control the worm. Such
division   a backward transformation is impossible in
21 Science. Darkness and light, infancy and manhood,
sickness and health, are opposites, — different beliefs,
which never blend. Who will say that infancy can utter
24 the ideas of manhood, that darkness can represent light,
that we are in Europe when we are in the opposite hemi-
sphere? There is no bridge across the gulf which divides
27 two such opposite conditions as the spiritual, or incorporeal, and the physical, or corporeal.

In Christian Science there is never a retrograde step,
30 never a return to positions outgrown. The so-called dead
and living cannot commune together, for they are in
separate states of existence, or consciousness.

This simple truth lays bare the mistaken assumption 1
that man dies as matter but comes to life as spirit.   The
so-called dead, in order to reappear to those   Unscientific   3
still in the existence cognized by the physical   investiture
senses, would need to be tangible and material, — to have
a material investiture, — or the material senses could take 6
no cognizance of the so-called dead.

Spiritualism would transfer men from the spiritual sense
of existence back into its material sense.   This gross mate- 9
rialism is scientifically impossible, since to infinite Spirit
there can be no matter.

Jesus said of Lazarus: "Our friend Lazarus sleepeth; 12
but I go, that I may awake him out of sleep."   Jesus
restored Lazarus by the understanding that   Raising
Lazarus had never died, not by an admis-   the dead   15
sion that his body had died and then lived again.   Had
Jesus believed that Lazarus had lived or died in his
body, the Master would have stood on the same plane of 18
belief as those who buried the body, and he could not have
resuscitated it.

When you can waken yourself or others out of the belief 21
that all must die, you can then exercise Jesus' spiritual
power to reproduce the presence of those who have thought
they died, — but not otherwise.   24

There is one possible moment, when those living on the
earth and those called dead, can commune together, and
that is the moment previous to the transition,   Vision of   27
— the moment when the link between their op-   the dying
posite beliefs is being sundered.   In the vestibule through
which we pass from one dream to another dream, or 30
when we awake from earth's sleep to the grand verities
of Life, the departing may hear the glad welcome of those

1 who have gone before. The ones departing may whisper
this vision, name the face that smiles on them and the
3 hand which beckons them, as one at Niagara, with eyes
open only to that wonder, forgets all else and breathes
aloud his rapture.

6   When being is understood, Life will be recognized 'as
neither material nor finite, but as infinite, — as God,
Real Life   universal good; and the belief that life, or
9 is God   mind, was ever in a finite form, or good in
evil, will be destroyed. Then it will be understood that
Spirit never entered matter and was therefore never
12 raised from matter. When advanced to spiritual being
and the understanding of God, man can no longer commune with matter; neither can he return to it, any more
15 than a tree can return to its seed. Neither will man seem
to be corporeal, but he will be an individual consciousness, characterized by the divine Spirit as idea, not matter.
18   Suffering, sinning, dying beliefs are unreal. When
divine Science is universally understood, they will have
no power over man, for man is immortal and lives by
21 divine authority.

The sinless joy, — the perfect harmony and immortality
of Life, possessing unlimited divine beauty and goodness
24 Immaterial without a single bodily pleasure or pain, —
pleasure   constitutes the only veritable, indestructible
man, whose being is spiritual. This state of existence
27 is scientific and intact, — a perfection discernible only
by those who have the final understanding of Christ in
divine Science. Death can never hasten this state of
30 existence, for death must be overcome, not submitted to,
before immortality appears.

The recognition of Spirit and of infinity comes not

suddenly here or hereafter. The pious Polycarp said: 1
"I cannot turn at once from good to evil." Neither do
other mortals accomplish the change from error to truth 3
at a single bound.

Existence continues to be a belief of corporeal sense
until the Science of being is reached. Error brings its 6
own self-destruction both here and hereafter,   Second
for mortal mind creates its own physical con-   death
ditions. Death will occur on the next plane of existence 9
as on this, until the spiritual understanding of Life is
reached. Then, and not until then, will it be demonstrated that "the second death hath no power."   12

The period required for this dream of material life,
embracing its so-called pleasures and pains, to vanish
from consciousness, "knoweth no man . . .   A dream   15
neither the Son, but the Father." This period   vanishing
will be of longer or shorter duration according to the
tenacity of error. Of what advantage, then, would it be 18
to us, or to the departed, to prolong the material state and
so prolong the illusion either of a soul inert or of a sinning,
suffering sense, — a so-called mind fettered to matter.   21

Even if communications from spirits to mortal consciousness were possible, such communications would
grow beautifully less with every advanced stage   Progress and   24
of existence. The departed would gradually   purgatory
rise above ignorance and materiality, and Spiritualists
would outgrow their beliefs in material spiritualism. 27
Spiritism consigns the so-called dead to a state resembling
that of blighted buds, — to a wretched purgatory, where
the chances of the departed for improvement narrow 30
into nothing and they return to their old standpoints of
matter.

1   The decaying flower, the blighted bud, the gnarled oak,
the ferocious beast, — like the discords of disease, sin,
3   Unnatural and death, — are unnatural. They are the fal-
deflections sities of sense, the changing deflections of mortal mind; they are not the eternal realities of Mind.

6   How unreasonable is the belief that we are wearing
out life and hastening to death, and that at the same
Absurd time we are communing with immortality!
9   oracles If the departed are in rapport with mortality, or matter, they are not spiritual, but must still
be mortal, sinning, suffering, and dying. Then why
12 look to them — even were communication possible — for
proofs of immortality, and accept them as oracles? Communications gathered from ignorance are pernicious in
15 tendency.

Spiritualism with its material accompaniments would
destroy the supremacy of Spirit. If Spirit pervades all
18 space, it needs no material method for the transmission
of messages. Spirit needs no wires nor electricity in order
to be omnipresent.

21   Spirit is not materially tangible. How then can it
communicate with man through electric, material effects?
Spirit How can the majesty and omnipotence of
24 intangible Spirit be lost? God is not in the medley
where matter cares for matter, where spiritism makes
many gods, and hypnotism and electricity are claimed
27 to be the agents of God's government.

Spirit blesses man, but man cannot "tell whence
it cometh." By it the sick are healed, the sorrowing are
30 comforted, and the sinning are reformed. These are the
effects of one universal God, the invisible good dwelling
in eternal Science.

The act of describing disease — its symptoms, locality, 1
and fatality — is not scientific. Warning people against
death is an error that tends to frighten into   Thought   3
death those who are ignorant of Life as God. regarding death
Thousands of instances could be cited of health restored
by changing the patient's thoughts regarding death.   6

A scientific mental method is more sanitary than the
use of drugs, and such a mental method produces permanent health. Science must go over the whole   Fallacious   9
ground, and dig up every seed of error's sow-   hypotheses
ing. Spiritualism relies upon human beliefs and hypotheses. Christian Science removes these beliefs and 12
hypotheses through the higher understanding of God, for
Christian Science, resting on divine Principle, not on material personalities, in its revelation of immortality, intro- 15
duces the harmony of being.

Jesus cast out evil spirits, or false beliefs. The Apostle
Paul bade men have the Mind that was in the Christ. 18
Jesus did his own work by the one Spirit. He said: "My
Father worketh hitherto, and I work." He never de-
scribed disease, so far as can be learned from the Gospels, 21
but he healed disease.

The unscientific practitioner says: "You are ill. Your
brain is overtaxed, and you must rest. Your body is 24
weak, and it must be strengthened. You have   Mistaken
nervous prostration, and must be treated for it."   methods
Science objects to all this, contending for the rights of in- 27
telligence and asserting that Mind controls body and brain.

Mind-science teaches that mortals need "not be weary
in well doing." It dissipates fatigue in doing   Divine   30
good. Giving does not impoverish us in the   strength
service of our Maker, neither does withholding enrich us.

1 We have strength in proportion to our apprehension of
the truth, and our strength is not lessened by giving
3 utterance to truth. A cup of coffee or tea is not the equal
of truth, whether for the inspiration of a sermon or for
the support of bodily endurance.

6   A communication purporting to come from the late
Theodore Parker reads as follows: "There never was,
      A denial of   and there never will be, an immortal spirit."
9   immortality Yet the very periodical containing this sentence repeats weekly the assertion that spirit-communica-
tions are our only proofs of immortality.

12   I entertain no doubt of the humanity and philanthropy
of many Spiritualists, but I cannot coincide with their
      Mysticism   views. It is mysticism which gives spiritual-
15   unscientific ism its force. Science dispels mystery and
explains extraordinary phenomena; but Science never
removes phenomena from the domain of reason into the
18 realm of mysticism.

It should not seem mysterious that mind, without the
aid of hands, can move a table, when we already know
21   Physical   that it is mind-power which moves both table
      falsities   and hand. Even planchette — the French toy
which years ago pleased so many people — attested the con-
24 trol of mortal mind over its substratum, called matter.

It is mortal mind which convulses its substratum, matter.
These movements arise from the volition of human belief,
27 but they are neither scientific nor rational. Mortal mind
produces table-tipping as certainly as table-setting, and
believes that this wonder emanates from spirits and elec-
30 tricity. This belief rests on the common conviction that
mind and matter cooperate both visibly and invisibly,
hence that matter is intelligent.

There is not so much evidence to prove intercommuni- 1
cation between the so-called dead and the living, as there
is to show the sick that matter suffers and has   3
sensation; yet this latter evidence is destroyed by *Poor post-mortem evidence*
Mind-science. If Spiritualists understood the
Science of being, their belief in mediumship would vanish. 6
At the very best and on its own theories, spiritualism
can only prove that certain individuals have a continued
existence after death and maintain their affili- *No proof of immortality*   9
ation with mortal flesh; but this fact affords
no certainty of everlasting life. A man's assertion that
he is immortal no more proves him to be so, than the op- 12
posite assertion, that he is mortal, would prove immortality a lie. Nor is the case improved when alleged spirits
teach immortality. Life, Love, Truth, is the only proof 15
of immortality.

Man in the likeness of God as revealed in Science cannot help being immortal. Though the grass seemeth to 18
wither and the flower to fade, they reappear. *Mind's manifestations immortal*
Erase the figures which express number, silence
the tones of music, give to the worms the body   21
called man, and yet the producing, governing, divine
Principle lives on, — in the case of man as truly as in
the case of numbers and of music, — despite the so-called 24
laws of matter, which define man as mortal. Though
the inharmony resulting from material sense hides the
harmony of Science, inharmony cannot destroy the divine 27
Principle of Science. In Science, man's immortality depends upon that of God, good, and follows as a necessary
consequence of the immortality of good.   30

That somebody, somewhere, must have known the
deceased person, supposed to be the communicator, is

1 evident, and it is as easy to read distant thoughts as near.
We think of an absent friend as easily as we do of one
3 Reading present. It is no more difficult to read the
thoughts absent mind than it is to read the present.
Chaucer wrote centuries ago, yet we still read his thought
6 in his verse. What is classic study, but discernment of
the minds of Homer and Virgil, of whose personal existence we may be in doubt?

9 If spiritual life has been won by the departed, they
cannot return to material existence, because different
states of consciousness are involved, and one
Impossible
12 intercom- person cannot exist in two different states of
munion consciousness at the same time. In sleep we
do not communicate with the dreamer by our side despite
15 his physical proximity, because both of us are either unconscious or are wandering in our dreams through different mazes of consciousness.

18 In like manner it would follow, even if our departed
friends were near us and were in as conscious a state of
existence as before the change we call death, that their
21 state of consciousness must be different from ours. We
are not in their state, nor are they in the mental realm
in which we dwell. Communion between them and
24 ourselves would be prevented by this difference. The
mental states are so unlike, that intercommunion is as
impossible as it would be between a mole and a human
27 being. Different dreams and different awakenings be-
token a differing consciousness. When wandering in
Australia, do we look for help to the Esquimaux in their
30 snow huts?

In a world of sin and sensuality hastening to a
greater development of power, it is wise earnestly to

consider whether it is the human mind or the divine 1
Mind which is influencing one.   What the prophets of
Jehovah did, the worshippers of Baal failed to do; yet 3
artifice and delusion claimed that they could equal the
work of wisdom.

Science only can explain the incredible good and evil 6
elements now coming to the surface.   Mortals must find
refuge in Truth in order to escape the error of these latter
days.   Nothing is more antagonistic to Christian Science 9
than a blind belief without understanding, for such a
belief hides Truth and builds on error.

Miracles are impossible in Science, and here Science 12
takes issue with popular religions.   The scientific manifestation of power is from the divine nature   Natural
and is not supernatural, since Science is an   wonders   15
explication of nature.   The belief that the universe, including man, is governed in general by material laws, but
that occasionally Spirit sets aside these laws, — this be- 18
lief belittles omnipotent wisdom, and gives to matter the
precedence over Spirit.

It is contrary to Christian Science to suppose that life 21
is either material or organically spiritual.   Between
Christian Science and all forms of superstition   Conflicting
a great gulf is fixed, as impassable as that be-   standpoints   24
tween Dives and Lazarus.   There is mortal mind-reading
and immortal Mind-reading.   The latter is a revelation
of divine purpose through spiritual understanding, by 27
which man gains the divine Principle and explanation of
all things.   Mortal mind-reading and immortal Mind-
reading are distinctly opposite standpoints, from which 30
cause and effect are interpreted.   The act of reading
mortal mind investigates and touches only human beliefs.

1 Science is immortal and coordinate neither with the
premises nor with the conclusions of mortal beliefs.

3   The ancient prophets gained their foresight from a
spiritual, incorporeal standpoint, not by foreshadowing

Scientific evil and mistaking fact for fiction, — predict-
6 *foreseeing* ing the future from a groundwork of corporeality and human belief. When sufficiently advanced
in Science to be in harmony with the truth of being, men
9 become seers and prophets involuntarily, controlled not
by demons, spirits, or demigods, but by the one Spirit.
It is the prerogative of the ever-present, divine Mind, and
12 of thought which is in rapport with this Mind, to know
the past, the present, and the future.

Acquaintance with the Science of being enables us to
15 commune more largely with the divine Mind, to foresee
and foretell events which concern the universal welfare,
to be divinely inspired,— yea, to reach the range of fetter-
18 less Mind.

To understand that Mind is infinite, not bounded by
corporeality, not dependent upon the ear and eye for
21 *The Mind* sound or sight nor upon muscles and bones
unbounded for locomotion, is a step towards the Mind-
science by which we discern man's nature and existence.
24 This true conception of being destroys the belief of spiritualism at its very inception, for without the concession of
material personalities called spirits, spiritualism has no
27 basis upon which to build.

All we correctly know of Spirit comes from God, divine
Principle, and is learned through Christ and Christian
30 *Scientific* Science. If this Science has been thoroughly
foreknowing learned and properly digested, we can know
the truth more accurately than the astronomer can read

the stars or calculate an eclipse. This Mind-reading 1
is the opposite of clairvoyance. It is the illumination of
the spiritual understanding which demonstrates the ca- 3
pacity of Soul, not of material sense. This Soul-sense
comes to the human mind when the latter yields to the
divine Mind.   6

Such intuitions reveal whatever constitutes and perpetuates harmony, enabling one to do good, but not
evil. You will reach the perfect Science of   Value of   9
healing when you are able to read the human   intuition
mind after this manner and discern the error you would
destroy. The Samaritan woman said: "Come, see a 12
man, which told me all things that ever I did: is not this
the Christ?"

It is recorded that Jesus, as he once journeyed with his 15
students, "knew their thoughts," — read them scientifically. In like manner he discerned disease and healed
the sick. After the same method, events of great mo- 18
ment were foretold by the Hebrew prophets. Our
Master rebuked the lack of this power when he said:
"O ye hypocrites! ye can discern the face of the sky; 21
but can ye not discern the signs of the times?"

Both Jew and Gentile may have had acute corporeal
senses, but mortals need spiritual sense. Jesus knew the 24
generation to be wicked and adulterous, seek-   Hypocrisy
ing the material more than the spiritual. His   condemned
thrusts at materialism were sharp, but needed. He never 27
spared hypocrisy the sternest condemnation. He said:
"These ought ye to have done, and not to leave the other
undone." The great Teacher knew both cause and 30
effect, knew that truth communicates itself but never
imparts error.

1 Jesus once asked, "Who touched me?" Supposing this inquiry to be occasioned by physical contact alone,

3 Mental contact his disciples answered, "The multitude throng thee." Jesus knew, as others did not, that it was not matter, but mortal mind, whose touch called 6 for aid. Repeating his inquiry, he was answered by the faith of a sick woman. His quick apprehension of this mental call illustrated his spirituality. The disciples' 9 misconception of it uncovered their materiality. Jesus possessed more spiritual susceptibility than the disciples. Opposites come from contrary directions, and produce 12 unlike results.

Mortals evolve images of thought. These may appear to the ignorant to be apparitions; but they are myste-

15 Images of thought rious only because it is unusual to see thoughts, though we can always feel their influence. Haunted houses, ghostly voices, unusual 18 noises, and apparitions brought out in dark seances either involve feats by tricksters, or they are images and sounds evolved involuntarily by mortal mind. Seeing 21 is no less a quality of physical sense than feeling. Then why is it more difficult to see a thought than to feel one? Education alone determines the difference. In reality 24 there is none.

Portraits, landscape-paintings, fac-similes of penman-ship, peculiarities of expression, recollected sentences,

27 Phenomena explained can all be taken from pictorial thought and memory as readily as from objects cognizable by the senses. Mortal mind sees what it believes as 30 certainly as it believes what it sees. It feels, hears, and sees its own thoughts. Pictures are mentally formed before the artist can convey them to canvas. So is it

with all material conceptions. Mind-readers perceive 1
these pictures of thought. They copy or reproduce
them, even when they are lost to the memory of the mind 3
in which they are discoverable.

It is needless for the thought or for the person holding the transferred picture to be individually and con- 6
sciously present. Though individuals have   Mental
passed away, their mental environment re- environment
mains to be discerned, described, and transmitted. Though 9
bodies are leagues apart and their associations forgotten,
their associations float in the general atmosphere of human
mind.   12

The Scotch call such vision "second sight," when
really it is first sight instead of second, for it presents
primal facts to mortal mind. Science enables   Second 15
one to read the human mind, but not as a   sight
clairvoyant. It enables one to heal through Mind, but
not as a mesmerist.   18

The mine knows naught of the emeralds within its
rocks; the sea is ignorant of the gems within its caverns,
of the corals, of its sharp reefs, of the tall ships   Buried 21
that float on its bosom, or of the bodies which   secrets
lie buried in its sands: yet these are all there. Do not
suppose that any mental concept is gone because you do 24
not think of it. The true concept is never lost. The
strong impressions produced on mortal mind by friendship or by any intense feeling are lasting, and mind- 27
readers can perceive and reproduce these impressions.

Memory may reproduce voices long ago silent. We
have but to close the eyes, and forms rise   Recollected 30
before us, which are thousands of miles away   friends
or altogether gone from physical sight and sense, and

1 this not in dreamy sleep. In our day-dreams we can
recall that for which the poet Tennyson expressed the
3 heart's desire, —

the touch of a vanished hand,
And the sound of a voice that is still.

6 The mind may even be cognizant of a present flavor and
odor, when no viand touches the palate and no scent
salutes the nostrils.

9   How are veritable ideas to be distinguished from illusions? By learning the origin of each. Ideas are
Illusions   emanations from the divine Mind. Thoughts,
12 not ideas   proceeding from the brain or from matter, are
offshoots of mortal mind; they are mortal material beliefs. Ideas are spiritual, harmonious, and eternal. Beliefs
15 proceed from the so-called material senses, which at one
time are supposed to be substance-matter and at another
are called spirits.

18   To love one's neighbor as one's self, is a divine idea;
but this idea can never be seen, felt, nor understood
through the physical senses. Excite the organ of ven-
21 eration or religious faith, and the individual manifests
profound adoration. Excite the opposite development,
and he blasphemes. These effects, however, do not pro-
24 ceed from Christianity, nor are they spiritual phenomena,
for both arise from mortal belief.

Eloquence re-echoes the strains of Truth and Love.
27 It is due to inspiration rather than to erudition. It shows
the possibilities derived from divine Mind,
Trance
speaking   though it is said to be a gift whose endowment
illusion
30   is obtained from books or received from the
impulsion of departed spirits. When eloquence proceeds
from the belief that a departed spirit is speaking, who

can tell what the unaided medium is incapable of know- 1
ing or uttering? This phenomenon only shows that the
beliefs of mortal mind are loosed. Forgetting her igno- 3
rance in the belief that another mind is speaking through
her, the devotee may become unwontedly eloquent. Having more faith in others than in herself, and believing 6
that somebody else possesses her tongue and mind, she
talks freely.

Destroy her belief in outside aid, and her eloquence 9
disappears. The former limits of her belief return. She
says, "I am incapable of words that glow, for I am un-
educated." This familiar instance reaffirms the Scrip- 12
tural word concerning a man, "As he thinketh in his heart,
so is he." If one believes that he cannot be an orator without study or a superinduced condition, the body responds 15
to this belief, and the tongue grows mute which before
was eloquent.

Mind is not necessarily dependent upon educational 18
processes. It possesses of itself all beauty and poetry,
and the power of expressing them. Spirit, Scientific
God, is heard when the senses are silent. We improvisation 21
are all capable of more than we do. The influence or
action of Soul confers a freedom, which explains the phenomena of improvisation and the fervor of untutored lips. 24

Matter is neither intelligent nor creative. The tree is
not the author of itself. Sound is not the originator of
music, and man is not the father of man. Cain Divine 27
very naturally concluded that if life was in the origination
body, and man gave it, man had the right to take it away.
This incident shows that the belief of life in matter was 30
"a murderer from the beginning."

If seed is necessary to produce wheat, and wheat to

1 produce flour, or if one animal can originate another,
how then can we account for their primal origin? How
3 were the loaves and fishes multiplied on the shores of
Galilee, — and that, too, without meal or monad from
which loaf or fish could come?

6   The earth's orbit and the imaginary line called the
equator are not substance. The earth's motion and

Mind is   position are sustained by Mind alone. Divest
9 substance   yourself of the thought that there can be substance in matter, and the movements and transitions now
possible for mortal mind will be found to be equally
12 possible for the body. Then being will be recognized
as spiritual, and death will be obsolete, though now
some insist that death is the necessary prelude to
15 immortality.

In dreams we fly to Europe and meet a far-off friend.
The looker-on sees the body in bed, but the supposed
18   Mortal   inhabitant of that body carries it through
delusions   the air and over the ocean. This shows the
possibilities of thought. Opium and hashish eaters men-
21 tally travel far and work wonders, yet their bodies stay
in one place. This shows what mortal mentality and
knowledge are.

24   The admission to one's self that man is God's own likeness sets man free to master the infinite idea. This con-

Scientific   viction shuts the door on death, and opens it
27 finalities   wide towards immortality. The understanding
and recognition of Spirit must finally come, and we may
as well improve our time in solving the mysteries of being
30 through an apprehension of divine Principle. At present
we know not what man is, but we certainly shall know
this when man reflects God.

The Revelator tells us of "a new heaven and a   1
new earth." Have you ever pictured this heaven and
earth, inhabited by beings under the control of supreme   3
wisdom?

Let us rid ourselves of the belief that man is separated
from God, and obey only the divine Principle, Life and   6
Love. Here is the great point of departure for all true
spiritual growth.

It is difficult for the sinner to accept divine Science,   9
because Science exposes his nothingness; but the sooner
error is reduced to its native nothingness, the Man's genuine
sooner man's great reality will appear and his   being   12
genuine being will be understood. The destruction of
error is by no means the destruction of Truth or Life, but
is the acknowledgment of them.   15

Absorbed in material selfhood we discern and reflect
but faintly the substance of Life or Mind. The denial of
material selfhood aids the discernment of man's spirit-   18
ual and eternal individuality, and destroys the erroneous
knowledge gained from matter or through what are termed
the material senses.   21

Certain erroneous postulates should be here considered
in order that the spiritual facts may be better   Erroneous
apprehended.   postulates   24

The first erroneous postulate of belief is, that substance,
life, and intelligence are something apart from God.

The second erroneous postulate is, that man is both   27
mental and material.

The third erroneous postulate is, that mind is both evil
and good; whereas the real Mind cannot be evil nor the   30
medium of evil, for Mind is God.

The fourth erroneous postulate is, that matter is in-

1 telligent, and that man has a material body which is part
of himself.

3   The fifth erroneous postulate is, that matter holds in
itself the issues of life and death, — that matter is not
only capable of experiencing pleasure and pain, but also
6 capable of imparting these sensations. From the illusion
implied in this last postulate arises the decomposition of
mortal bodies in what is termed death.

9   Mind is not an entity within the cranium with the power
of sinning now and forever.

In old Scriptural pictures we see a serpent coiled around
12 the tree of knowledge and speaking to Adam and Eve.
Knowledge of This represents the serpent in the act of
good and evil commending to our first parents the knowl-
15 edge of good and evil, a knowledge gained from matter,
or evil, instead of from Spirit. The portrayal is still
graphically accurate, for the common conception of mor-
18 tal man — a burlesque of God's man — is an outgrowth
of human knowledge or sensuality, a mere offshoot of
material sense.

21   Uncover error, and it turns the lie upon you. Until
the fact concerning error — namely, its nothingness —
Opposing appears, the moral demand will not be met,
24 power and the ability to make nothing of error will
be wanting. We should blush to call that real which is
only a mistake. The foundation of evil is laid on a belief
27 in something besides God. This belief tends to support
two opposite powers, instead of urging the claims of Truth
alone. The mistake of thinking that error can be real,
30 when it is merely the absence of truth, leads to belief in
the superiority of error.

Do you say the time has not yet come in which to

recognize Soul as substantial and able to control the 1
body? Remember Jesus, who nearly nineteen centuries
ago demonstrated the power of Spirit and said,   The age's   3
"He that believeth on me, the works that I   privilege
do shall he do also," and who also said, "But the hour
cometh, and *now is,* when the true worshippers shall 6
worship the Father in spirit and in truth." "Behold,
now is the accepted time; behold, *now* is the day of salvation," said Paul.   9
  Divine logic and revelation coincide. If we believe
otherwise, we may be sure that either our   Logic and
logic is at fault or that we have misinterpreted   revelation   12
revelation. Good never causes evil, nor creates aught
that can cause evil.
  Good does not create a mind susceptible of causing 15
evil, for evil is the opposing error and not the truth of
creation. Destructive electricity is not the offspring of infinite good. Whatever contradicts the real nature of the 18
divine *Esse,* though human faith may clothe it with angelic
vestments, is without foundation.
  The belief that Spirit is finite as well as infinite has 21
darkened all history. In Christian Science, Spirit, as a
proper noun, is the name of the Supreme Being.   Derivatives
It means quantity and quality, and applies ex-   of spirit   24
clusively to God. The modifying derivatives of the word
spirit refer only to quality, not to God. Man is spiritual.
He is not God, Spirit. If man were Spirit, then men 27
would be spirits, gods. Finite spirit would be mortal,
and this is the error embodied in the belief that the infinite can be contained in the finite. This belief tends to 30
becloud our apprehension of the kingdom of heaven and
of the reign of harmony in the Science of being.

1 Jesus taught but one God, one Spirit, who makes man
in the image and likeness of Himself, — of Spirit, not of

3 Scientific   matter. Man reflects infinite Truth, Life, and
man   Love. The nature of man, thus understood,
includes all that is implied by the terms "image" and

6 "likeness" as used in Scripture. The truly Christian
and scientific statement of personality and of the relation
of man to God, with the demonstration which accompa-

9 nied it, incensed the rabbis, and they said: "Crucify him,
crucify him . . . by our law he ought to die, because he
made himself the Son of God."

12 The eastern empires and nations owe their false government to the misconceptions of Deity there prevalent.
Tyranny, intolerance, and bloodshed, wherever found,

15 arise from the belief that the infinite is formed after the
pattern of mortal personality, passion, and impulse.
The progress of truth confirms its claims, and our

18 Master confirmed his words by his works. His healing-
Ingratitude   power evoked denial, ingratitude, and be-
and denial   trayal, arising from sensuality. Of the ten

21 lepers whom Jesus healed, but one returned to give God
thanks, — that is, to acknowledge the divine Principle
which had healed him.

24 Our Master easily read the thoughts of mankind, and
this insight better enabled him to direct those thoughts
aright; but what would be said at this period of an in-

27 fidel blasphemer who should hint that Jesus used his incisive power injuriously? Our Master read mortal mind
on a scientific basis, that of the omnipresence of Mind.

30 An approximation of this discernment indicates spiritual
growth and union with the infinite capacities of the one
Mind. Jesus could injure no one by his Mind-reading.

The effect of his Mind was always to heal and to save, 1
and this is the only genuine Science of reading mortal
mind.   His holy motives and aims were tra-   Spiritual   3
duced by the sinners of that period, as they   insight
would be to-day if Jesus were personally present.   Paul
said, "To be spiritually minded is life."   We approach 6
God, or Life, in proportion to our spirituality, our fidelity to Truth and Love; and in that ratio we know all
human need and are able to discern the thought of the 9
sick and the sinning for the purpose of healing them.
Error of any kind cannot hide from the law of God.

Whoever reaches this point of moral culture and good- 12
ness cannot injure others, and must do them good.   The
greater or lesser ability of a Christian Scientist to discern
thought scientifically, depends upon his genuine spirit- 15
uality.   This kind of mind-reading is not clairvoyance,
but it is important to success in healing, and is one of the
special characteristics thereof.   18

We welcome the increase of knowledge and the end
of error, because even human invention must have its
day, and we want that day to be succeeded   Christ's   21
by Christian Science, by divine reality.   Mid-   reappearance
night foretells the dawn.   Led by a solitary star amid
the darkness, the Magi of old foretold the Messiahship 24
of Truth.   Is the wise man of to-day believed, when he
beholds the light which heralds Christ's eternal dawn
and describes its effulgence?   27

Lulled by stupefying illusions, the world is asleep
in the cradle of infancy, dreaming away the hours.
Material sense does not unfold the facts of   Spiritual   30
existence; but spiritual sense lifts human   awakening
consciousness into eternal Truth.   Humanity advances

disturbances till the end of error [handwritten annotation] *5, 12* [handwritten]

1 slowly out of sinning sense into spiritual understanding;
unwillingness to learn all things rightly, binds Christen-
3 dom with chains.

Love will finally mark the hour of harmony, and spiritualization will follow, for Love is Spirit. Before error
6 The darkest is wholly destroyed, there will be interrup-
hours of all tions of the general material routine. Earth
will become dreary and desolate, but summer and winter,
9 seedtime and harvest (though in changed forms), will
continue unto the end, — until the final spiritualization of
all things. "The darkest hour precedes the dawn."

12 This material world is even now becoming the arena
for conflicting forces. On one side there will be discord
Arena of and dismay; on the other side there will be
15 contest Science and peace. The breaking up of material beliefs may seem to be famine and pestilence, want
and woe, sin, sickness, and death, which assume new
18 phases until their nothingness appears. These disturbances will continue until the end of error, when all
discord will be swallowed up in spiritual Truth.

21 Mortal error will vanish in a moral chemicalization.
This mental fermentation has begun, and will continue
until all errors of belief yield to understanding. Belief is
24 changeable, but spiritual understanding is changeless.

As this consummation draws nearer, he who has
shaped his course in accordance with divine Science
27 Millennial will endure to the end. As material knowl-
glory edge diminishes and spiritual understanding
increases, real objects will be apprehended mentally
30 instead of materially.

During this final conflict, wicked minds will endeavor
to find means by which to accomplish more evil; but

those who discern Christian Science will hold crime in 1
check. They will aid in the ejection of error. They
will maintain law and order, and cheerfully await the 3
certainty of ultimate perfection.

In reality, the more closely error simulates truth and
so-called matter resembles its essence, mortal mind, the 6
more impotent error becomes as a belief. Ac- Dangerous
cording to human belief, the lightning is fierce resemblances
and the electric current swift, yet in Christian Science 9
the flight of one and the blow of the other will become
harmless. The more destructive matter becomes, the
more its nothingness will appear, until matter reaches 12
its mortal zenith in illusion and forever disappears. The
nearer a false belief approaches truth without passing
the boundary where, having been destroyed by divine 15
Love, it ceases to be even an illusion, the riper it becomes
for destruction. The more material the belief, the more
obvious its error, until divine Spirit, supreme in its do- 18
main, dominates all matter, and man is found in the likeness of Spirit, his original being.

The broadest facts array the most falsities against 21
themselves, for they bring error from under cover. It
requires courage to utter truth; for the higher Truth
lifts her voice, the louder will error scream, until its in- 24
articulate sound is forever silenced in oblivion.

"He uttered His voice, the earth melted." This Scripture indicates that all matter will disappear before the 27
supremacy of Spirit.

Christianity is again demonstrating the Life that is
Truth, and the Truth that is Life, by the apos- Christianity 30
tolic work of casting out error and healing the still rejected
sick. Earth has no repayment for the persecutions which

recompense - to compensate

1 attend a new step in Christianity; but the spiritual recompense of the persecuted is assured in the elevation of ex-
3 istence above mortal discord and in the gift of divine Love.
The prophet of to-day beholds in the mental horizon
the signs of these times, the reappearance of the Chris-
6 Spiritual fore- tianity which heals the sick and destroys error,
shadowings and no other sign shall be given. Body cannot be saved except through Mind. The Science of Chris-
9 tianity is misinterpreted by a material age, for it is the
healing influence of Spirit (not *spirits*) which the material
senses cannot comprehend, — which can only be spiritu-
12 ally discerned. Creeds, doctrines, and human hypotheses
do not express Christian Science; much less can they
demonstrate it.

15   Beyond the frail premises of human beliefs, above the
loosening grasp of creeds, the demonstration of Christian
   Revelation   Mind-healing stands a revealed and practical
18 of Science   Science. It is imperious throughout all ages
as Christ's revelation of Truth, of Life, and of Love, which
remains inviolate for every man to understand and to
21 practise.
For centuries — yea, always — natural science has not
been considered a part of any religion, Christianity not
24   excepted. Even now multitudes consider that
   Science as
   foreign to   which they call *science* has no proper con-
   all religion nection with faith and piety. Mystery does
27 not enshroud Christ's teachings, and they are not theoretical and fragmentary, but practical and complete; and
being practical and complete, they are not deprived of
30 their essential vitality.
The way through which immortality and life are learned
is not ecclesiastical but Christian, not human but divine,

not physical but metaphysical, not material but scien- 1
tifically spiritual. Human philosophy, ethics, and superstition afford no demonstrable divine Principle   Key to the   3
by which mortals can escape from sin; yet   kingdom
to escape from sin, is what the Bible demands. "Work
out your own salvation with fear and trembling," says 6
the apostle, and he straightway adds: "for it is God
which worketh in you both to will and to do of His good
pleasure" (Philippians ii. 12, 13). Truth has furnished 9
the key to the kingdom, and with this key Christian Science has opened the door of the human understanding.
None may pick the lock nor enter by some other door. 12
The ordinary teachings are material and not spiritual.
Christian Science teaches only that which is spiritual and
divine, and not human. Christian Science is unerring 15
and Divine; the human sense of things errs because it
is human.

Those individuals, who adopt theosophy, spiritualism, 18
or hypnotism, may possess natures above some others
who eschew their false beliefs. Therefore my contest is
not with the individual, but with the false system. I 21
love mankind, and shall continue to labor and to endure.

The calm, strong currents of true spirituality, the
manifestations of which are health, purity, and self- 24
immolation, must deepen human experience, until the
beliefs of material existence are seen to be a bald imposi-
tion, and sin, disease, and death give everlasting place 27
to the scientific demonstration of divine Spirit and to
God's spiritual, perfect man.

CHAPTER V

Animal Magnetism Unmasked

For out of the heart proceed evil thoughts, murders, adulteries, forni-
cations, thefts, false witness, blasphemies: these are the things which
defile a man. — JESUS.

1 MESMERISM or animal magnetism was first brought
into notice by Mesmer in Germany in 1775. Ac-
3 cording to the American Cyclopædia, he regarded this
 Earliest   so-called force, which he said could be ex-
investigations erted by one living organism over another, as
6 a means of alleviating disease. His propositions were
as follows:

"There exists a mutual influence between the celestial
9 bodies, the earth, and animated things. Animal bodies
are susceptible to the influence of this agent, disseminat-
ing itself through the substance of the nerves."

12 In 1784, the French government ordered the medical
faculty of Paris to investigate Mesmer's theory and to
report upon it. Under this order a commission was
15 appointed, and Benjamin Franklin was one of the com-
missioners. This commission reported to the government as follows:

18 "In regard to the existence and utility of animal magnetism, we have come to the unanimous conclusions that
there is no proof of the existence of the animal magnetic

100

fluid; that the violent effects, which are observed in 1
the public practice of magnetism, are due to manipula-
tions, or to the excitement of the imagination and the 3
impressions made upon the senses; and that there is one
more fact to be recorded in the history of the errors of
the human mind, and an important experiment upon 6
the power of the imagination."

In 1837, a committee of nine persons was appointed,
among whom were Roux, Bouillaud, and Clo- Clairvoyance, 9
quet, which tested during several sessions the magnetism
phenomena exhibited by a reputed clairvoyant. Their
report stated the results as follows: 12

"The facts which had been promised by Monsieur
Berna [the magnetizer] as conclusive, and as adapted to
throw light on physiological and therapeutical questions, 15
are certainly not conclusive in favor of the doctrine of
animal magnetism, and have nothing in common with
either physiology or therapeutics." 18

This report was adopted by the Royal Academy of
Medicine in Paris.

The author's own observations of the workings of 21
animal magnetism convince her that it is not Personal
a remedial agent, and that its effects upon conclusions
those who practise it, and upon their subjects who do 24
not rcsist it, lead to moral and to physical death.

If animal magnetism seems to alleviate or to cure disease, this appearance is deceptive, since error cannot 27
remove the effects of error. Discomfort under error is
preferable to comfort. In no instance is the effect of
animal magnetism, recently called hypnotism, other 30
than the effect of illusion. Any seeming benefit derived
from it is proportional to one's faith in esoteric magic.

1 Animal magnetism has no scientific foundation, for
God governs all that is real, harmonious, and eternal, and
3   Mere His power is neither animal nor human. Its
negation basis being a belief and this belief animal, in
Science animal magnetism, mesmerism, or hypnotism is
6 a mere negation, possessing neither intelligence, power,
nor reality, and in sense it is an unreal concept of the so-
called mortal mind.

9 There is but one real attraction, that of Spirit. The
pointing of the needle to the pole symbolizes this all-
embracing power or the attraction of God, divine Mind.
12 The planets have no more power over man than over
his Maker, since God governs the universe; but man,
reflecting God's power, has dominion over all the earth
15 and its hosts.

The mild forms of animal magnetism are disappearing, and its aggressive features are coming to the front.
18   Hidden The looms of crime, hidden in the dark re-
agents cesses of mortal thought, are every hour weav-
ing webs more complicated and subtle. So secret are the
21 present methods of animal magnetism that they ensnare
the age into indolence, and produce the very apathy on
the subject which the criminal desires. The following
24 is an extract from the Boston Herald:

"Mesmerism is a problem not lending itself to an easy
explanation and development. It implies the exercise
27 of despotic control, and is much more likely to be abused
by its possessor, than otherwise employed, for the individual or society."

30 Mankind must learn that evil is not power. Its so-
called despotism is but a phase of nothingness. Christian
Science despoils the kingdom of evil, and pre-eminently

promotes affection and virtue in families and therefore 1
in the community.   The Apostle Paul refers to the
personification of evil as "the god of this   Mental   3
world," and further defines it as dishonesty   despotism
and craftiness.   Sin was the Assyrian moon-god.

The destruction of the claims of mortal mind through 6
Science, by which man can escape from sin
and mortality, blesses the whole human fam-   Liberation
                                                 of mental
ily.   As in the beginning, however, this libera-   powers   9
tion does not scientifically show itself in a knowledge of
both good and evil, for the latter is unreal.

On the other hand, Mind-science is wholly separate 12
from any half-way impertinent knowledge, because Mind-
science is of God and demonstrates the divine Principle,
working out the purposes of good only.   The maximum 15
of good is the infinite God and His idea, the All-in-all.
Evil is a suppositional lie.

As named in Christian Science, animal magnetism or 18
hypnotism is the specific term for error, or mortal mind.
It is the false belief that mind is in matter, and   The genus
                                                        of error
is both evil and good;   that evil is as real as   21
good and more powerful.   This belief has not one quality of Truth.   It is either ignorant or malicious.   The
malicious form of hypnotism ultimates in moral idiocy. 24
The truths of immortal Mind sustain man, and they annihilate the fables of mortal mind, whose flimsy and gaudy
pretensions, like silly moths, singe their own wings and 27
fall into dust.

In reality there is no *mortal* mind, and consequently no transference of mortal thought   Thought-   30
and will-power.   Life and being are of   transference
God.   In Christian Science, man can do no harm, for

1 scientific thoughts are true thoughts, passing from God
to man.

3   When Christian Science and animal magnetism are
both comprehended, as they will be at no distant date,
it will be seen why the author of this book has been
6 so unjustly persecuted and belied by wolves in sheep's
clothing.

Agassiz, the celebrated naturalist and author, has
9 wisely said: "Every great scientific truth goes through
three stages. First, people say it conflicts with the Bible.
Next, they say it has been discovered before. Lastly,
12 they say they have always believed it."

Christian Science goes to the bottom of mental action,
and reveals the theodicy which indicates the rightness of
15   all divine action, as the emanation of divine
Perfection
of divine   Mind, and the consequent wrongness of the
government
opposite so-called action, — evil, occultism,
18 necromancy, mesmerism, animal magnetism, hypnotism.

The medicine of Science is divine Mind; and dishonesty,
sensuality, falsehood, revenge, malice, are animal pro-
21 Adulteration pensities and by no means the mental quali-
of Truth   ties which heal the sick. The hypnotizer
employs one error to destroy another. If he heals sick-
24 ness through a belief, and a belief originally caused the
sickness, it is a case of the greater error overcoming the
lesser. This greater error thereafter occupies the ground,
27 leaving the case worse than before it was grasped by the
stronger error.

Our courts recognize evidence to prove the motive as
30 Motives   well as the commission of a crime. Is it not
considered clear that the human mind must move the
body to a wicked act? Is not mortal mind the mur-

derer? The hands, without mortal mind to direct them, 1
could not commit a murder.

Courts and juries judge and sentence mortals in order 3
to restrain crime, to prevent deeds of violence or to punish
them. To say that these tribunals have no   Mental
jurisdiction over the carnal or mortal mind,   crimes   6
would be to contradict precedent and to admit that the
power of human law is restricted to matter, while mortal
mind, evil, which is the real outlaw, defies justice and is 9
recommended to mercy. Can matter commit a crime?
Can matter be punished? Can you separate the mentality from the body over which courts hold jurisdiction? 12
Mortal mind, not matter, is the criminal in every case;
and human law rightly estimates crime, and courts reasonably pass sentence, according to the motive.   15

When our laws eventually take cognizance of mental
crime and no longer apply legal rulings wholly to physical
offences, these words of Judge Parmenter of   Important   18
Boston will become historic: "I see no reason   decision
why metaphysics is not as important to medicine as to
mechanics or mathematics."   21

Whoever uses his developed mental powers like an es-
caped felon to commit fresh atrocities as opportunity occurs is never safe. God will arrest him. Di-   Evil let   24
vine justice will manacle him. His sins will   loose
be millstones about his neck, weighing him down to the
depths of ignominy and death. The aggravation of er- 27
ror foretells its doom, and confirms the ancient axiom:
"Whom the gods would destroy, they first make mad."

The distance from ordinary medical prac-   The misuse of   30
tice to Christian Science is full many a league   mental power
in the line of light; but to go in healing from the use of

1 inanimate drugs to the criminal misuse of human will-
power, is to drop from the platform of common manhood
3 into the very mire of iniquity, to work against the free
course of honesty and justice, and to push vainly against
the current running heavenward.

6　Like our nation, Christian Science has its Declaration
of Independence. God has endowed man with inalien-
　　Proper self- able rights, among which are self-government,
9　*government* reason, and conscience. Man is properly self-
governed only when he is guided rightly and governed by
his Maker, divine Truth and Love.

12　Man's rights are invaded when the divine order is in-
terfered with, and the mental trespasser incurs the divine
penalty due this crime.

15　Let this age, which sits in judgment on Christian
Science, sanction only such methods as are demonstrable
　　Right in Truth and known by their fruit, and classify
18　*methods* all others as did St. Paul in his great epistle
to the Galatians, when he wrote as follows:
"Now the works of the flesh are manifest, which are
21 these; Adultery, fornication, uncleanness, lasciviousness,
idolatry, *witchcraft,* hatred, variance, emulations, wrath,
strife, seditions, heresies, envyings, murders, drunkenness,
24 revellings and such like: of the which I tell you before,
as I have also told you in time past, that they which do
such things shall not inherit the kingdom of God. But
27 the fruit of the Spirit is love, joy, peace, longsuffering,
gentleness, goodness, faith, meekness, temperance: against
such there is no law."

CHAPTER VI

Science, Theology, Medicine

*But I certify you, brethren, that the gospel which was preached of me
is not after man. For I neither received it of man, neither was I taught
it, but by the revelation of Jesus Christ.* — PAUL.

*The kingdom of heaven is like unto leaven, which a woman took, and
hid in three measures of meal, till the whole was leavened.* — JESUS.

IN the year 1866, I discovered the Christ Science or 1
divine laws of Life, Truth, and Love, and
named my discovery Christian Science. God   Christian
Science   3
had been graciously preparing me during many   discovered
years for the reception of this final revelation of the absolute divine Principle of scientific mental healing.   6

This apodictical Principle points to the revelation of
Immanuel, "God with us," — the sovereign ever-presence, delivering the children of men from   9
every ill "that flesh is heir to." Through   Mission of
Christian
Christian Science, religion and medicine are   Science
inspired with a diviner nature and essence; fresh pinions 12
are given to faith and understanding, and thoughts acquaint themselves intelligently with God.

Feeling so perpetually the false consciousness that life 15
inheres in the body, yet remembering that in   Discontent
reality God is our Life, we may well tremble   with life
in the prospect of those days in which we must say, "I 18
have no pleasure in them."

107

1 Whence came to me this heavenly conviction, — a conviction antagonistic to the testimony of the physical senses?
3 According to St. Paul, it was "the gift of the grace of
God given unto me by the effectual working of His power."
It was the divine law of Life and Love, unfolding to me
6 the demonstrable fact that matter possesses neither sensation nor life; that human experiences show the falsity
of all material things; and that immortal cravings, "the
9 price of learning love," establish the truism that the
only sufferer is mortal mind, for the divine Mind cannot
suffer.

12 My conclusions were reached by allowing the evidence
of this revelation to multiply with mathematical certainty
Demonstrable and the lesser demonstration to prove the
15 evidence greater, as the product of three multiplied by
three, equalling nine, proves conclusively that three times
three duodecillions must be nine duodecillions, — not
18 a fraction more, not a unit less.

When apparently near the confines of mortal existence,
standing already within the shadow of the death-valley,
21 Light shining I learned these truths in divine Science: that
in darkness all real being is in God, the divine Mind, and
that Life, Truth, and Love are all-powerful and ever-
24 present; that the opposite of Truth, — called error, sin,
sickness, disease, death, — is the false testimony of false
material sense, of mind in matter; that this false sense
27 evolves, in belief, a subjective state of mortal mind which
this same so-called mind names *matter,* thereby shutting
out the true sense of Spirit.

30 New lines My discovery, that erring, mortal, misnamed
of thought *mind* produces all the organism and action of
the mortal body, set my thoughts to work in new channels,

and led up to my demonstration of the proposition that 1
Mind is All and matter is naught as the leading factor in
Mind-science.   3

Christian Science reveals incontrovertibly that Mind
is All-in-all, that the only realities are the divine Mind
and idea. This great fact is not, however, seen   Scientific   6
to be supported by sensible evidence, until its   evidence
divine Principle is demonstrated by healing the sick and
thus proved absolute and divine. This proof once seen, 9
no other conclusion can be reached.

For three years after my discovery, I sought the solution of this problem of Mind-healing, searched the Scrip- 12
tures and read little else, kept aloof from so-   Solitary
ciety, and devoted time and energies to dis-   research
covering a positive rule. The search was sweet, calm, and 15
buoyant with hope, not selfish nor depressing. I knew
the Principle of all harmonious Mind-action to be God,
and that cures were produced in primitive Christian 18
healing by holy, uplifting faith; but I must know the
Science of this healing, and I won my way to absolute
conclusions through divine revelation, reason, and dem- 21
onstration. The revelation of Truth in the understanding came to me gradually and apparently through divine
power. When a new spiritual idea is borne to earth, the 24
prophetic Scripture of Isaiah is renewedly fulfilled:
"Unto us a child is born, . . . and his name shall be
called Wonderful."   27

Jesus once said of his lessons: "My doctrine is not
mine, but His that sent me. If any man will do His will,
he shall know of the doctrine, whether it be of God, or 30
whether I speak of myself." (John vii. 16, 17.)

The three great verities of Spirit, omnipotence, omni-

1 presence, omniscience, — Spirit possessing all power, filling all space, constituting all Science, — contradict

3 forever the belief that matter can be actual.

God's allness learned

These eternal verities reveal primeval existence as the radiant reality of God's creation,

6 in which all that He has made is pronounced by His wisdom good.

Thus it was that I beheld, as never before, the awful 9 unreality called evil. The equipollence of God brought to light another glorious proposition, — man's perfectibility and the establishment of the kingdom of heaven on 12 earth.

In following these leadings of scientific revelation, the Bible was my only textbook. The Scriptures were

15 *Scriptural foundations* illumined; reason and revelation were reconciled, and afterwards the truth of Christian Science was demonstrated. No human pen nor tongue 18 taught me the Science contained in this book, SCIENCE AND HEALTH; and neither tongue nor pen can overthrow it. This book may be distorted by shallow criti- 21 cism or by careless or malicious students, and its ideas may be temporarily abused and misrepresented; but the Science and truth therein will forever remain to be dis- 24 cerned and demonstrated.

Jesus demonstrated the power of Christian Science to heal mortal minds and bodies. But this power was lost

27 *The demonstration lost and found* sight of, and must again be spiritually discerned, taught, and demonstrated according to Christ's command, with "signs following."

30 Its Science must be apprehended by as many as believe on Christ and spiritually understand Truth.

No analogy exists between the vague hypotheses of

agnosticism, pantheism, theosophy, spiritualism, or 1
millenarianism and the demonstrable truths of Christian Science; and I find the will, or sensuous   Mystical   3
reason of the human mind, to be opposed to   antagonists
the divine Mind as expressed through divine Science.
Christian Science is natural, but not physical. The 6
Science of God and man is no more supernatural than
is the science of numbers, though departing   Optical
from the realm of the physical, as the Science   illustration   9
of God, Spirit, must, some may deny its right to   of Science
the name of Science. The Principle of divine metaphysics
is God; the practice of divine metaphysics is the utiliza- 12
tion of the power of Truth over error; its rules demonstrate its Science. Divine metaphysics reverses perverted
and physical hypotheses as to Deity, even as the ex- 15
planation of optics rejects the incidental or inverted
image and shows what this inverted image is meant to
represent.   18
A prize of one hundred pounds, offered in Oxford University, England, for the best essay on Natural Science,
— an essay calculated to offset the tendency of   Pertinent   21
the age to attribute physical effects to physical   proposal
causes rather than to a final spiritual cause, — is one of
many incidents which show that Christian Science meets 24
a yearning of the human race for spirituality.
After a lengthy examination of my discovery and its
demonstration in healing the sick, this fact became evi- 27
dent to me, — that Mind governs the body, Confirmatory
not partially but wholly. I submitted my   tests
metaphysical system of treating disease to the broad- 30
est practical tests. Since then this system has gradually
gained ground, and has proved itself, whenever scien-

1 tifically employed, to be the most effective curative agent
in medical practice.

3   Is there more than one school of Christian Science?
Christian Science is demonstrable. There can, therefore, be but one method in its teaching. Those who de-
6   One school   part from this method forfeit their claims to
    of Truth   belong to its school, and they become adher-
ents of the Socratic, the Platonic, the Spencerian, or some
9 other school. By this is meant that they adopt and adhere to some particular system of human opinions. Although these opinions may have occasional gleams of
12 divinity, borrowed from that truly divine Science which
eschews man-made systems, they nevertheless remain
wholly human in their origin and tendency and are not
15 scientifically Christian.

From the infinite One in Christian Science comes one
Principle and its infinite idea, and with this infinitude
18   Unchanging   come spiritual rules, laws, and their demon-
    Principle   stration, which, like the great Giver, are "the
same yesterday, and to-day, and forever;" for thus are
21 the divine Principle of healing and the Christ-idea characterized in the epistle to the Hebrews.

Any theory of Christian Science, which departs from
24 what has already been stated and proved to be true, af-
   On sandy   fords no foundation upon which to establish
  foundations   a genuine school of this Science. Also, if any
27 so-called new school claims to be Christian Science, and
yet uses another author's discoveries without giving that
author proper credit, such a school is erroneous, for it
30 inculcates a breach of that divine commandment in the
Hebrew Decalogue, "Thou shalt not steal."

God is the Principle of divine metaphysics. As there

is but one God, there can be but one divine Principle of 1
all Science; and there must be fixed rules for the demonstration of this divine Principle. The letter Principle and 3
of Science plentifully reaches humanity to-day, practice
but its spirit comes only in small degrees. The vital part,
the heart and soul of Christian Science, is Love. With- 6
out this, the letter is but the dead body of Science, —
pulseless, cold, inanimate.

The fundamental propositions of divine metaphysics 9
are summarized in the four following, to me, *self-evident*
propositions. Even if reversed, these proposi- Reversible
tions will be found to agree in statement and propositions 12
proof, showing mathematically their exact relation to
Truth. De Quincey says mathematics has not a foot to
stand upon which is not purely metaphysical. 15

　1. God is All-in-all.
　2. God is good. Good is Mind.
　3. God, Spirit, being all, nothing is matter. 18
　4. Life, God, omnipotent good, deny death, evil, sin,
disease. — Disease, sin, evil, death, deny good, omnipotent God, Life. 21

Which of the denials in proposition four is true? Both
are not, cannot be, true. According to the Scripture,
I find that God is true, "but every [mortal] man a 24
liar."

The divine metaphysics of Christian Science, like the
method in mathematics, proves the rule by inversion. 27
For example: There is no pain in Truth, and Metaphysical
no truth in pain; no nerve in Mind, and no inversions
mind in nerve; no matter in Mind, and no mind in mat- 30
ter; no matter in Life, and no life in matter; no matter
in good, and no good in matter.

1 Usage classes both evil and good together as *mind;*
therefore, to be understood, the author calls sick and sin-
3 Definition of ful humanity *mortal mind,* — meaning by this
mortal mind term the flesh opposed to Spirit, the human
mind and evil in contradistinction to the divine Mind, or
6 Truth and good. The spiritually unscientific definition
of mind is based on the evidence of the physical senses,
which makes minds many and calls *mind* both human and
9 divine.

In Science, Mind is *one,* including noumenon and phenomena, God and His thoughts.
12 Mortal mind is a solecism in language, and involves an
improper use of the word *mind.* As Mind is immortal,
Imperfect the phrase *mortal mind* implies something un-
15 terminology true and therefore unreal; and as the phrase
is used in teaching Christian Science, it is meant to
designate that which has no real existence. Indeed, if
18 a better word or phrase could be suggested, it would
be used; but in expressing the new tongue we must
sometimes recur to the old and imperfect, and the new
21 wine of the Spirit has to be poured into the old bottles of
the letter.

Christian Science explains all cause and effect as men-
24 tal, not physical. It lifts the veil of mystery from Soul and
Causation body. It shows the scientific relation of man
mental to God, disentangles the interlaced ambiguities
27 of being, and sets free the imprisoned thought. In divine
Science, the universe, including man, is spiritual, harmonious, and eternal. Science shows that what is termed *mat-*
30 *ter* is but the subjective state of what is termed by the
author *mortal mind.*

Apart from the usual opposition to everything new,

the one great obstacle to the reception of that spiritual- 1
ity, through which the understanding of Mind-science
comes, is the inadequacy of material terms for Philological 3
metaphysical statements, and the consequent inadequacy
difficulty of so expressing metaphysical ideas as to make
them comprehensible to any reader, who has not person- 6
ally demonstrated Christian Science as brought forth in
my discovery. Job says: "The ear trieth words, as the
mouth tasteth meat." The great difficulty is to give the 9
right impression, when translating material terms back
into the original spiritual tongue.

SCIENTIFIC TRANSLATION OF IMMORTAL MIND 12

GOD: Divine Principle, Life, Truth, Love, Divine
Soul, Spirit, Mind. synonyms
MAN: God's spiritual idea, individual, per- Divine 15
fect, eternal. image
IDEA: An image in Mind; the immediate Divine
object of understanding. — Webster. reflection 18

SCIENTIFIC TRANSLATION OF MORTAL MIND

First Degree: Depravity.

PHYSICAL. Evil beliefs, passions and appetites, fear, 21
depraved will, self-justification, pride, envy, de- Unreality
ceit, hatred, revenge, sin, sickness, disease,
death. 24

Second Degree: Evil beliefs disappearing.

MORAL. Humanity, honesty, affection, com- Transitional
passion, hope, faith, meekness, temperance. qualities 27

1   *Third Degree:* Understanding.

SPIRITUAL.   Wisdom, purity, spiritual understanding,
3   Reality   spiritual power, love, health, holiness.

In the third degree mortal mind disappears, and man as
God's image appears.   Science so reverses the evidence
6   Spiritual   before the corporeal human senses, as to make
universe   this Scriptural testimony true in our hearts,
"The last shall be first, and the first last," so that God
9 and His idea may be to us what divinity really is and
must of necessity be, — all-inclusive.

A correct view of Christian Science and of its adapta-
12 tion to healing includes vastly more than is at first seen.
Aim of   Works on metaphysics leave the grand point
Science   untouched.   They never crown the power of
15 Mind as the Messiah, nor do they carry the day against
physical enemies, — even to the extinction of all belief in
matter, evil, disease, and death, — nor insist upon the fact
18 that God is all, therefore that matter is nothing beyond an
image in mortal mind.

Christian Science strongly emphasizes the thought that
21   Divine   God is not *corporeal,* but *incorporeal,* — that is,
personality   bodiless.   Mortals are corporeal, but God is
incorporeal.

24   As the words *person* and *personal* are commonly and
ignorantly employed, they often lead, when applied to
Deity, to confused and erroneous conceptions of divinity
27 and its distinction from humanity.   If the term personality,
as applied to God, means infinite personality, then God *is*
infinite *Person,* — in the sense of infinite personality, but
30 not in the lower sense.   An infinite Mind in a finite form
is an absolute impossibility.

The term *individuality* is also open to objections, be- 1
cause an individual may be one of a series, one of many,
as an individual man, an individual horse; whereas God 3
is *One*, — not one of a series, but one alone and without
an equal.

God is Spirit; therefore the language of Spirit must 6
be, and is, spiritual. Christian Science attaches no physical nature and significance to the Supreme   Spiritual
Being or His manifestation; mortals alone do language 9
this. God's essential language is spoken of in the last
chapter of Mark's Gospel as the new tongue, the spiritual meaning of which is attained through "signs 12
following."

Ear hath not heard, nor hath lip spoken, the pure language of Spirit. Our Master taught spirituality by simili- 15
tudes and parables. As a divine student he The miracles
unfolded God to man, illustrating and demon-   of Jesus
strating Life and Truth in himself and by his power over 18
the sick and sinning. Human theories are inadequate to
interpret the divine Principle involved in the miracles
(marvels) wrought by Jesus and especially in his mighty, 21
crowning, unparalleled, and triumphant exit from the
flesh.

Evidence drawn from the five physical senses relates 24
solely to human reason; and because of opaci-   Opacity of
ty to the true light, human reason dimly re-   the senses
flects and feebly transmits Jesus' works and words. Truth 27
is a revelation.

Jesus bade his disciples beware of the leaven of the
Pharisees and of the Sadducees, which he de-   Leaven   30
fined as human doctrines. His parable of the   of Truth
"leaven, which a woman took, and hid in three measures

1 of meal, till the whole was leavened," impels the inference that the spiritual leaven signifies the Science of Christ
3 and its spiritual interpretation, — an inference far above
the merely ecclesiastical and formal applications of the
illustration.

6   Did not this parable point a moral with a prophecy,
foretelling the second appearing in the flesh of the
Christ, Truth, hidden in sacred secrecy from the visi-
9 ble world?

Ages pass, but this leaven of Truth is ever at work. It
must destroy the entire mass of error, and so be eternally
12 glorified in man's spiritual freedom.

In their spiritual significance, Science, Theology, and
Medicine are means of divine thought, which include spirit-
15   ual laws emanating from the invisible and in-
*The divine
and human*   finite power and grace. The parable may
contrasted   import that these spiritual laws, perverted by
18 a perverse material sense of law, are metaphysically presented as three measures of meal, — that is, three modes
of mortal thought. In all mortal forms of thought, dust
21 is dignified as the natural status of men and things, and
modes of material motion are honored with the name of
laws. This continues until the leaven of Spirit changes
24 the whole of mortal thought, as yeast changes the chemical
properties of meal.

The definitions of material law, as given by natural
27 science, represent a kingdom necessarily divided against
Certain   itself, because these definitions portray law as
contradictions physical, not spiritual. Therefore they con-
30 tradict the divine decrees and violate the law of Love, in
which nature and God are one and the natural order of
heaven comes down to earth.

When we endow matter with vague spiritual power, — 1
that is, when we do so in our theories, for of course we
cannot really endow matter with what it does Unescapable   3
not and cannot possess, — we disown the Al-   dilemma
mighty, for such theories lead to one of two things. They
either presuppose the self-evolution and self-government 6
of matter, or else they assume that matter is the product
of Spirit. To seize the first horn of this dilemma and consider matter as a power in and of itself, is to leave the cre- 9
ator out of His own universe; while to grasp the other
horn of the dilemma and regard God as the creator of
matter, is not only to make Him responsible for all disas- 12
ters, physical and moral, but to announce Him as their
source, thereby making Him guilty of maintaining perpetual misrule in the form and under the name of natural 15
law.

In one sense God is identical with nature, but this nature is spiritual and is not expressed in matter. The law- 18
giver, whose lightning palsies or prostrates in   God and
death the child at prayer, is not the divine ideal   nature
of omnipresent Love. God is natural good, and is repre- 21
sented only by the idea of goodness; while evil should be
regarded as unnatural, because it is opposed to the nature
of Spirit, God.   24

In viewing the sunrise, one finds that it contradicts
the evidence before the senses to believe that the earth
is in motion and the sun at rest. As astron-   The sun   27
omy reverses the human perception of the   and Soul
movement of the solar system, so Christian Science reverses the seeming relation of Soul and body and makes 30
body tributary to Mind. Thus it is with man, who
is but the humble servant of the restful Mind, though it

1 seems otherwise to finite sense. But we shall never und   ..-
stand this while we admit that soul is in body or mind in
3 matter, and that man is included in non-intelligence.
Soul, or Spirit, is God, unchangeable and eternal; and
man coexists with and reflects Soul, God, for man is God's
6 image.

Science reverses the false testimony of the physical
senses, and by this reversal mortals arrive at the funda-
9 Reversal of mental facts of being. Then the question in-
testimony evitably arises: Is a man sick if the material
senses indicate that he is in good health? No! for matter
12 can make no conditions for man. And is he well if the
senses say he is sick? Yes, he is well in Science in which
health is normal and disease is abnormal.

15 Health is not a condition of matter, but of Mind; nor
can the material senses bear reliable testimony on the sub-
Health and ject of health. The Science of Mind-healing
18 the senses shows it to be impossible for aught but Mind
to testify truly or to exhibit the real status of man. Therefore the divine Principle of Science, reversing the testi-
21 mony of the physical senses, reveals man as harmoniously
existent in Truth, which is the only basis of health; and
thus Science denies all disease, heals the sick, overthrows
24 false evidence, and refutes materialistic logic.

Any conclusion *pro* or *con,* deduced from supposed sensation in matter or from matter's supposed consciousness
27 of health or disease, instead of reversing the testimony of
the physical senses, confirms that testimony as legitimate
and so leads to disease.

30 Historic When Columbus gave freer breath to the
illustrations globe, ignorance and superstition chained the
limbs of the brave old navigator, and disgrace and star-

vation stared him in the face; but sterner still would have 1
been his fate, if his discovery had undermined the favorite inclinations of a sensuous philosophy.   3

Copernicus mapped out the stellar system, and before
he spake, astrography was chaotic, and the heavenly fields
were incorrectly explored.   6

The Chaldean Wisemen read in the stars the fate of
empires and the fortunes of men. Though no higher
revelation than the horoscope was to them dis- Perennial 9
played upon the empyrean, earth and heaven   beauty
were bright, and bird and blossom were glad in God's
perennial and happy sunshine, golden with Truth. So 12
we have goodness and beauty to gladden the heart; but
man, left to the hypotheses of material sense unexplained
by Science, is as the wandering comet or the desolate 15
star — "a weary searcher for a viewless home."

The earth's diurnal rotation is invisible to the physical
eye, and the sun seems to move from east to west, instead 18
of the earth from west to east. Until rebuked Astronomic
by clearer views of the everlasting facts, this unfoldings
false testimony of the eye deluded the judgment and in- 21
duced false conclusions. Science shows appearances often
to be erroneous, and corrects these errors by the simple
rule that the greater controls the lesser. The sun is the 24
central stillness, so far as our solar system is concerned,
and the earth revolves about the sun once a year, besides
turning daily on its own axis.   27

As thus indicated, astronomical order imitates the
action of divine Principle; and the universe, the reflection of God, is thus brought nearer the spiritual fact, and 30
is allied to divine Science as displayed in the everlasting
government of the universe.

1   The evidence of the physical senses often reverses the
real Science of being, and so creates a reign of discord, —
3   Opposing   assigning seeming power to sin, sickness, and
    testimony   death; but the great facts of Life, rightly un-
derstood, defeat this triad of errors, contradict their false
6   witnesses, and reveal the kingdom of heaven, — the actual
reign of harmony on earth. The material senses' reversal of the Science of Soul was practically exposed nine-
9   teen hundred years ago by the demonstrations of Jesus;
yet these so-called senses still make mortal mind tributary
to mortal body, and ordain certain sections of matter, such
12 as brain and nerves, as the seats of pain and pleasure,
from which matter reports to this so-called mind its status
of happiness or misery.

15 The optical focus is another proof of the illusion of
material sense. On the eye's retina, sky and tree-tops
    Testimony of   apparently join hands, clouds and ocean meet
18 the senses   and mingle. The barometer, — that little
prophet of storm and sunshine, denying the testimony of
the senses, — points to fair weather in the midst of murky
21 clouds and drenching rain. Experience is full of instances
of similar illusions, which every thinker can recall for
himself.

24 To material sense, the severance of the jugular vein
    Spiritual   takes away life; but to spiritual sense and
    sense of life   in Science, Life goes on unchanged and
27 being is eternal. Temporal life is a false sense of
existence.

Our theories make the same mistake regarding Soul
30 and body that Ptolemy made regarding the solar system.
They insist that soul is in body and mind therefore tributary to matter. Astronomical science has destroyed the

false theory as to the relations of the celestial bodies, and 1
Christian Science will surely destroy the greater error as
to our terrestrial bodies. The true idea and 3
Principle of man will then appear. The Ptole- Ptolemaic
and psychical
error
maic blunder could not affect the harmony of
being as does the error relating to soul and body, which 6
reverses the order of Science and assigns to matter the
power and prerogative of Spirit, so that man becomes
the most absolutely weak and inharmonious creature in 9
the universe.

The verity of Mind shows conclusively how it is that
matter seems to be, but is not. Divine Science, Seeming 12
and being
rising above physical theories, excludes matter,
resolves *things* into *thoughts,* and replaces the objects of
material sense with spiritual ideas. 15

The term CHRISTIAN SCIENCE was introduced by
the author to designate the scientific system of divine
healing. 18

The revelation consists of two parts:

1. The discovery of this divine Science of Mind-
healing, through a spiritual sense of the Scriptures and 21
through the teachings of the Comforter, as promised by
the Master.

2. The proof, by present demonstration, that the so- 24
called miracles of Jesus did not specially belong to a
dispensation now ended, but that they illustrated an
ever-operative divine Principle. The operation of this 27
Principle indicates the eternality of the scientific order
and continuity of being.

Christian Science differs from material sci- Scientific 30
basis
ence, but not on that account is it less scientific. On the contrary, Christian Science is pre-emi-

1 nently scientific, being based on Truth, the Principle of
all science.

3 Physical science (so-called) is human knowledge, — a
law of mortal mind, a blind belief, a Samson shorn of his
strength. When this human belief lacks organ-

Physical
6 science a   izations to support it, its foundations are gone.
blind belief
Having neither moral might, spiritual basis,
nor holy Principle of its own, this belief mistakes effect
9 for cause and seeks to find life and intelligence in matter,
thus limiting Life and holding fast to discord and death.
In a word, human belief is a blind conclusion from material
12 reasoning. This is a mortal, finite sense of things, which
immortal Spirit silences forever.

The universe, like man, is to be interpreted by Science
15 from its divine Principle, God, and then it can be under-

Right   stood; but when explained on the basis of
interpretation physical sense and represented as subject to
18 growth, maturity, and decay, the universe, like man, is,
and must continue to be, an enigma.

Adhesion, cohesion, and attraction are properties of
21 Mind. They belong to divine Principle, and support

All force   the equipoise of that thought-force, which
mental   launched the earth in its orbit and said to the
24 proud wave, "Thus far and no farther."

Spirit is the life, substance, and continuity of all
things. We tread on forces. Withdraw them, and
27 creation must collapse. Human knowledge calls them
forces of matter; but divine Science declares that they
belong wholly to divine Mind, are inherent in this
30 Mind, and so restores them to their rightful home and
classification.

The elements and functions of the physical body and

of the physical world will change as mortal mind changes 1
its beliefs. What is now considered the best condition
for organic and functional health in the human   Corporeal   3
body may no longer be found indispensable   changes
to health. Moral conditions will be found always harmonious and health-giving. Neither organic inaction 6
nor overaction is beyond God's control; and man will
be found normal and natural to changed mortal thought,
and therefore more harmonious in his manifestations than 9
he was in the prior states which human belief created and
sanctioned.

As human thought changes from one stage to an- 12
other of conscious pain and painlessness, sorrow and
joy, — from fear to hope and from faith to understanding, — the visible manifestation will at last be man gov- 15
erned by Soul, not by material sense. Reflecting God's
government, man is self-governed. When subordinate
to the divine Spirit, man cannot be controlled by sin or 18
death, thus proving our material theories about laws of
health to be valueless.

The seasons will come and go with changes of time and 21
tide, cold and heat, latitude and longitude. The agriculturist will find that these changes cannot   The time
affect his crops. "As a vesture shalt Thou   and tide   24
change them and they shall be changed." The mariner
will have dominion over the atmosphere and the great
deep, over the fish of the sea and the fowls of the air. 27
The astronomer will no longer look up to the stars, —
he will look out from them upon the universe; and the
florist will find his flower before its seed.   30
Thus matter will finally be proved nothing more
than a mortal belief, wholly inadequate to affect a man

1 through its supposed organic action or supposed existence. Error will be no longer used in stating truth. The

3 Mortal problem of nothingness, or "dust to dust," will
nothingness be solved, and mortal mind will be without
form and void, for mortality will cease when man beholds
6 himself God's reflection, even as man sees his reflection
in a glass.

All Science is divine. Human thought never pro-
9 jected the least portion of true being. Human belief
A lack of has sought and interpreted in its own way
originality the echo of Spirit, and so seems to have
12 reversed it and repeated it materially; but the human
mind never produced a real tone nor sent forth a positive
sound.

15 The point at issue between Christian Science on the
one hand and popular theology on the other is this: Shall
Antagonistic Science explain cause and effect as being
18 questions both natural and spiritual? Or shall all that
is beyond the cognizance of the material senses be called
supernatural, and be left to the mercy of speculative
21 hypotheses?

I have set forth Christian Science and its application
to the treatment of disease just as I have discovered them.
24 Biblical I have demonstrated through Mind the effects
basis of Truth on the health, longevity, and morals
of men; and I have found nothing in ancient or in modern
27 systems on which to found my own, except the teachings
and demonstrations of our great Master and the lives of
prophets and apostles. The Bible has been my only au-
30 thority. I have had no other guide in "the straight and
narrow way" of Truth.

If Christendom resists the author's application of the

word Science to Christianity, or questions her use of the 1
word Science, she will not therefore lose faith in Christianity, nor will Christianity lose its hold upon   Science and   3
her. If God, the All-in-all, be the creator of   Christianity
the spiritual universe, including man, then everything
entitled to a classification as truth, or Science, must be 6
comprised in a knowledge or understanding of God, for
there can be nothing beyond illimitable divinity.
   The terms Divine Science, Spiritual Science, Christ 9
Science or Christian Science, or Science alone, she employs interchangeably, according to the re-   Scientific
quirements of the context. These synony-   terms   12
mous terms stand for everything relating to God, the infinite, supreme, eternal Mind. It may be said, however,
that the term Christian Science relates especially to 15
Science as applied to humanity. Christian Science reveals God, not as the author of sin, sickness, and death,
but as divine Principle, Supreme Being, Mind, exempt 18
from all evil. It teaches that matter is the falsity, not
the fact, of existence; that nerves, brain, stomach, lungs,
and so forth, have — as matter — no intelligence, life, nor 21
sensation.
   There is no physical science, inasmuch as all truth
proceeds from the divine Mind. Therefore truth is not 24
human, and is not a law of matter, for matter   No physical
is not a lawgiver. Science is an emanation of   science
divine Mind, and is alone able to interpret God aright. 27
It has a spiritual, and not a material origin. It is a divine
utterance, — the Comforter which leadeth into all truth.
   Christian Science eschews what is called natural science, 30
in so far as this is built on the false hypotheses that matter
is its own lawgiver, that law is founded on material con-

1 ditions, and that these are final and overrule the might of
divine Mind. Good is natural and primitive. It is not
3 miraculous to itself.

The term Science, properly understood, refers only to
the laws of God and to His government of the universe,
6   Practical   inclusive of man. From this it follows that
    Science   business men and cultured scholars have found
that Christian Science enhances their endurance and
9 mental powers, enlarges their perception of character,
gives them acuteness and comprehensiveness and an
ability to exceed their ordinary capacity. The human
12 mind, imbued with this spiritual understanding, becomes
more elastic, is capable of greater endurance, escapes
somewhat from itself, and requires less repose. A knowl-
15 edge of the Science of being develops the latent abilities
and possibilities of man. It extends the atmosphere of
thought, giving mortals access to broader and higher
18 realms. It raises the thinker into his native air of insight
and perspicacity.

An odor becomes beneficent and agreeable only in pro-
21 portion to its escape into the surrounding atmosphere.
So it is with our knowledge of Truth. If one would
not quarrel with his fellow-man for waking him from
24 a cataleptic nightmare, he should not resist Truth, which
banishes — yea, forever destroys with the higher testimony of Spirit — the so-called evidence of matter.
27   Science relates to Mind, not matter. It rests on fixed
Principle and not upon the judgment of false sensation.
      Mathematics   The addition of two sums in mathematics must
30 and scientific always bring the same result. So is it with
      logic   logic. If both the major and the minor propo-
sitions of a syllogism are correct, the conclusion, if properly

drawn, cannot be false. So in Christian Science there 1
are no discords nor contradictions, because its logic is as
harmonious as the reasoning of an accurately stated syl- 3
logism or of a properly computed sum in arithmetic.
Truth is ever truthful, and can tolerate no error in
premise or conclusion.   6

If you wish to know the spiritual fact, you can discover it by reversing the material fable, be the   Truth by
fable *pro* or *con*, — be it in accord with your   inversion   9
preconceptions or utterly contrary to them.

Pantheism may be defined as a belief in the intelligence of matter, — a belief which Science overthrows. 12
In those days there will be "great tribulation Antagonistic
such as was not since the beginning of the   theories
world;" and earth will echo the cry, "Art thou [Truth] 15
come hither to torment us before the time?" Animal
magnetism, hypnotism, spiritualism, theosophy, agnosticism, pantheism, and infidelity are antagonistic to true 18
being and fatal to its demonstration; and so are some
other systems.

We must abandon pharmaceutics, and take up ontol- 21
ogy, — "the science of real being." We must look deep
into realism instead of accepting only the out-   Ontology
ward sense of things. Can we gather peaches   needed   24
from a pine-tree, or learn from discord the concord of
being? Yet quite as rational are some of the leading
illusions along the path which Science must tread in its 27
reformatory mission among mortals. The very name,
illusion, points to nothingness.

The generous liver may object to the author's small 30
estimate of the pleasures of the table. The sinner sees,
in the system taught in this book, that the demands of

1 God must be met. The petty intellect is alarmed by constant appeals to Mind. The licentious disposition is dis-
3   *Reluctant* couraged over its slight spiritual prospects.
     guests When all men are bidden to the feast, the excuses come. One has a farm, another has merchandise,
6 and therefore they cannot accept.

It is vain to speak dishonestly of divine Science, which
     Excuses for destroys all discord, when you can demonstrate
9   *ignorance* the actuality of Science. It is unwise to doubt
if reality is in perfect harmony with God, divine Principle,
— if Science, when understood and demonstrated, will
12 destroy all discord, — since you admit that God is omnipotent; for from this premise it follows that good and
its sweet concords have all-power.

15   Christian Science, properly understood, would disabuse the human mind of material beliefs which war
     Children against spiritual facts; and these material
18   *and adults* beliefs must be denied and cast out to make
place for truth. You cannot add to the contents of a
vessel already full. Laboring long to shake the adult's
21 faith in matter and to inculcate a grain of faith in God, —
an inkling of the ability of Spirit to make the body harmonious, — the author has often remembered our Master's
24 love for little children, and understood how truly such as
they belong to the heavenly kingdom.

If thought is startled at the strong claim of Science
27 for the supremacy of God, or Truth, and doubts the su-
     All evil premacy of good, ought we not, contrari-
     unnatural wise, to be astounded at the vigorous claims
30 of evil and doubt them, and no longer think it natural to
love sin and unnatural to forsake it, — no longer imagine
evil to be ever-present and good absent? Truth should

not seem so surprising and unnatural as error, and error 1
should not seem so real as truth. Sickness should not seem
so real as health. There is no error in Science, and our 3
lives must be governed by reality in order to be in harmony with God, the divine Principle of all being.

When once destroyed by divine Science, the false evi- 6
dence before the corporeal senses disappears. Hence the
opposition of sensuous man to the Science of   The error of
Soul and the significance of the Scripture, "The   carnality   9
carnal mind is enmity against God." The central fact of
the Bible is the superiority of spiritual over physical power.

THEOLOGY   12

Must Christian Science come through the Christian
churches as some persons insist? This Science has come
already, after the manner of God's appoint-   Churchly   15
ing, but the churches seem not ready to re-   neglect
ceive it, according to the Scriptural saying, "He came
unto his own, and his own received him not." Jesus once 18
said: "I thank Thee, O Father, Lord of heaven and
earth, that Thou hast hid these things from the wise
and prudent, and hast revealed them unto babes: even 21
so, Father, for so it seemed good in Thy sight." As aforetime, the spirit of the Christ, which taketh away the ceremonies and doctrines of men, is not accepted until the 24
hearts of men are made ready for it.

The mission of Jesus confirmed prophecy, and explained the so-called miracles of olden time as natural 27
demonstrations of the divine power, demonstrations which were not understood. Jesus' works   John the
Baptist, and
established his claim to the Messiahship. In   the Messiah   30
reply to John's inquiry, "Art thou he that should come,"

1 Jesus returned an affirmative reply, recounting his works
instead of referring to his doctrine, confident that this
3 exhibition of the divine power to heal would fully answer the question. Hence his reply: "Go and show
John again those things which ye do hear and see: the
6 blind receive their sight and the lame walk, the lepers
are cleansed, and the deaf hear, the dead are raised up,
and the poor have the gospel preached to them. And
9 blessed is he, whosoever shall not be offended in me." In
other words, he gave his benediction to any one who
should not deny that such effects, coming from divine
12 Mind, prove the unity of God, — the divine Principle
which brings out all harmony.

The Pharisees of old thrust the spiritual idea and the
15 man who lived it out of their synagogues, and retained
their materialistic beliefs about God. Jesus'
Christ rejected system of healing received no aid nor approval
18 from other sanitary or religious systems, from doctrines
of physics or of divinity; and it has not yet been generally accepted. To-day, as of yore, unconscious of the
21 reappearing of the spiritual idea, blind belief shuts the
door upon it, and condemns the cure of the sick and sinning if it is wrought on any but a material and a doctrinal
24 theory. Anticipating this rejection of idealism, of the
true idea of God, — this salvation from all error, physical and mental, — Jesus asked, "When the Son of man
27 cometh, shall he find faith on the earth?"

Did the doctrines of John the Baptist confer healing
power upon him, or endow him with the truest concep-
30 *John's misgivings* tion of the Christ? This righteous preacher
once pointed his disciples to Jesus as "the
Lamb of God;" yet afterwards he seriously questioned

the signs of the Messianic appearing, and sent the inquiry 1
to Jesus, "Art thou he that should come?"

Was John's faith greater than that of the Samaritan 3
woman, who said, "Is not this the Christ?" Faith according
There was also a certain centurion of whose   to works
faith Jesus himself declared, "I have not found so great 6
faith, no, not in Israel."

In Egypt, it was Mind which saved the Israelites from
belief in the plagues. In the wilderness, streams flowed 9
from the rock, and manna fell from the sky. The Israelites
looked upon the brazen serpent, and straightway believed
that they were healed of the poisonous stings of vipers. 12
In national prosperity, miracles attended the successes of
the Hebrews; but when they departed from the true
idea, their demoralization began. Even in captivity 15
among foreign nations, the divine Principle wrought
wonders for the people of God in the fiery furnace and
in kings' palaces.   18

Judaism was the antithesis of Christianity, because
Judaism engendered the limited form of a national or
tribal religion. It was a finite and material   Judaism   21
system, carried out in special theories concern- antipathetic
ing God, man, sanitary methods, and a religious cultus.
That he made "himself equal with God," was one of the 24
Jewish accusations against him who planted Christianity
on the foundation of Spirit, who taught as he was inspired by the Father and would recognize no life, intelli- 27
gence, nor substance outside of God.

The Jewish conception of God, as Yawah, Jehovah,
or only a mighty hero and king, has not quite   Priestly   30
given place to the true knowledge of God.   learning
Creeds and rituals have not cleansed their hands of

1 rabbinical lore. To-day the cry of bygone ages is repeated, "Crucify him!" At every advancing step, truth
3 is still opposed with sword and spear.

The word *martyr*, from the Greek, means *witness;* but
those who testified for Truth were so often persecuted
6 Testimony   unto death, that at length the word *martyr*
of martyrs   was narrowed in its significance and so has
come always to mean one who suffers for his convictions.
9 The new faith in the Christ, Truth, so roused the hatred
of the opponents of Christianity, that the followers of
Christ were burned, crucified, and otherwise persecuted;
12 and so it came about that human rights were hallowed
by the gallows and the cross.

Man-made doctrines are waning. They have not waxed
15 strong in times of trouble. Devoid of the Christ-power,
Absence of   how can they illustrate the doctrines of Christ
Christ-power   or the miracles of grace? Denial of the possi-
18 bility of Christian healing robs Christianity of the very
element, which gave it divine force and its astonishing and
unequalled success in the first century.
21   The true Logos is demonstrably Christian Science, the
natural law of harmony which overcomes discord, — not
Basis of   because this Science is supernatural or pre-
24 miracles   ternatural, nor because it is an infraction of
divine law, but because it is the immutable law of God,
good. Jesus said: "I knew that Thou hearest me al-
27 ways;" and he raised Lazarus from the dead, stilled the
tempest, healed the sick, walked on the water. There
is divine authority for believing in the superiority of
30 spiritual power over material resistance.

A miracle fulfils God's law, but does not violate that
law. This fact at present seems more mysterious than

the miracle itself. The Psalmist sang: "What ailed 1
thee, O thou sea, that thou fleddest? Thou Jordan,
that thou wast driven back? Ye mountains,   Lawful   3
that ye skipped like rams, and ye little hills,   wonders
like lambs? Tremble, thou earth, at the presence of the
Lord, at the presence of the God of Jacob." The miracle 6
introduces no disorder, but unfolds the primal order,
establishing the Science of God's unchangeable law.
Spiritual evolution alone is worthy of the exercise of 9
divine power.

The same power which heals sin heals also sickness.
This is "the beauty of holiness," that when Truth heals 12
the sick, it casts out evils, and when Truth   Fear and
casts out the evil called disease, it heals the   sickness
identical
sick. When Christ cast out the devil of   15
dumbness, "it came to pass, when the devil was gone out,
the dumb spake." There is to-day danger of repeating
the offence of the Jews by limiting the Holy One of Israel 18
and asking: "Can God furnish a table in the wilderness?"
What cannot God do?

It has been said, and truly, that Christianity must be 21
Science, and Science must be Christianity, else one or the
other is false and useless; but neither is unim-   The unity of
portant or untrue, and they are alike in demon-   Science and   24
Christianity
stration. This proves the one to be identical
with the other. Christianity as Jesus taught it was not
a creed, nor a system of ceremonies, nor a special gift 27
from a ritualistic Jehovah; but it was the demonstration
of divine Love casting out error and healing the sick,
not merely in the *name* of Christ, or Truth, but in demon- 30
stration of Truth, as must be the case in the cycles of
divine light.

1 Jesus established his church and maintained his mission
on a spiritual foundation of Christ-healing. He taught

3   The   his followers that his religion had a divine
Christ-mission Principle, which would cast out error and heal
both the sick and the sinning. He claimed no intelli-

6 gence, action, nor life separate from God. Despite the
persecution this brought upon him, he used his divine
power to save men both bodily and spiritually.

9 The question then as now was, How did Jesus heal the
sick? His answer to this question the world rejected.

   Ancient   He appealed to his students: "Whom do
12 spiritualism men say that I, the Son of man, am?" That
is: Who or what is it that is thus identified with casting
out evils and healing the sick? They replied, "Some

15 say that thou art John the Baptist; some, Elias; and
others, Jeremias, or one of the prophets." These prophets
were considered dead, and this reply may indicate that

18 some of the people believed that Jesus was a medium,
controlled by the spirit of John or of Elias.

This ghostly fancy was repeated by Herod himself.
21 That a wicked king and debauched husband should have
no high appreciation of divine Science and the great work
of the Master, was not surprising; for how could such

24 a sinner comprehend what the disciples did not fully
understand? But even Herod doubted if Jesus was controlled by the sainted preacher. Hence Herod's asser-

27 tion: "John have I beheaded: but who is this?" No
wonder Herod desired to see the new Teacher.

The disciples apprehended their Master better than
30   Doubting   did others; but they did not comprehend all
   disciples   that he said and did, or they would not have
questioned him so often. Jesus patiently persisted in

teaching and demonstrating the truth of being. His stu- 1
dents saw this power of Truth heal the sick, cast out evil,
raise the dead; but the ultimate of this wonderful work 3
was not spiritually discerned, even by them, until after the
crucifixion, when their immaculate Teacher stood before
them, the victor over sickness, sin, disease, death, and 6
the grave.

Yearning to be understood, the Master repeated,
"But whom say *ye* that I am?" This renewed inquiry 9
meant: Who or what is it that is able to do the work, so
mysterious to the popular mind? In his rejection of the
answer already given and his renewal of the question, 12
it is plain that Jesus completely eschewed the narrow
opinion implied in their citation of the common report
about him. 15

With his usual impetuosity, Simon replied for his
brethren, and his reply set forth a great fact: "Thou
art the Christ, the Son of the living God!" A divine 18
That is: The Messiah is what thou hast de- response
clared, — Christ, the spirit of God, of Truth, Life, and
Love, which heals mentally. This assertion elicited from 21
Jesus the benediction, "Blessed art thou, Simon Bar-
jona: for flesh and blood hath not revealed it unto thee,
but my Father which is in heaven;" that is, Love hath 24
shown thee the way of Life!

Before this the impetuous disciple had been called
only by his common names, Simon Bar-jona, or son of 27
Jona; but now the Master gave him a spir- The true and
itual name in these words: "And I say also living rock
unto thee, That thou art Peter; and upon this rock [the 30
meaning of the Greek word *petros,* or *stone*] I will build
my church; and the gates of hell [*hades,* the *under-*

1 *world,* or the *grave*] shall not prevail against it." In other words, Jesus purposed founding his society, not
3 on the personal Peter as a mortal, but on the God-power which lay behind Peter's confession of the true Messiah.

6 It was now evident to Peter that divine Life, Truth, and Love, and not a human personality, was the healer of the
       Sublime   sick and a rock, a firm foundation in the realm
9   summary   of harmony. On this spiritually scientific basis Jesus explained his cures, which appeared miraculous to outsiders. He showed that diseases were cast out neither
12 by corporeality, by *materia medica,* nor by hygiene, but by the divine Spirit, casting out the errors of mortal mind. The supremacy of Spirit was the foundation on which
15 Jesus built. His sublime summary points to the religion of Love.

Jesus established in the Christian era the precedent for
18 all Christianity, theology, and healing. Christians are
     New era   under as direct orders now, as they were then,
     in Jesus   to be Christlike, to possess the Christ-spirit, to
21 follow the Christ-example, and to heal the sick as well as the sinning. It is easier for Christianity to cast out sick-ness than sin, for the sick are more willing to part with
24 pain than are sinners to give up the sinful, so-called pleas-ure of the senses. The Christian can prove this to-day as readily as it was proved centuries ago.

27 Our Master said to every follower: "Go ye into all the world, and preach the gospel to every creature! . . .
     Healthful   Heal the sick! . . . Love thy neighbor as
30   theology   thyself!" It was this theology of Jesus which
healed the sick and the sinning. It is his theology in this book and the spiritual meaning of this theology, which

heals the sick and causes the wicked to "forsake his way, 1
and the unrighteous man his thoughts." It was our Master's theology which the impious sought to destroy. 3

From beginning to end, the Scriptures are full of
accounts of the triumph of Spirit, Mind, over matter.
Moses proved the power of Mind by what men   Marvels and 6
called miracles; so did Joshua, Elijah, and   reformations
Elisha. The Christian era was ushered in with signs and
wonders. Reforms have commonly been attended with 9
bloodshed and persecution, even when the end has been
brightness and peace; but the present new, yet old, reform in religious faith will teach men patiently and wisely 12
to stem the tide of sectarian bitterness, whenever it flows
inward.

The decisions by vote of Church Councils as to what 15
should and should not be considered Holy Writ; the manifest mistakes in the ancient versions; the   Science
thirty thousand different readings in the Old   obscured   18
Testament, and the three hundred thousand in the New,
— these facts show how a mortal and material sense stole
into the divine record, with its own hue darkening to some 21
extent the inspired pages. But mistakes could neither
wholly obscure the divine Science of the Scriptures seen
from Genesis to Revelation, mar the demonstration of 24
Jesus, nor annul the healing by the prophets, who foresaw
that "the stone which the builders rejected" would become "the head of the corner." 27

Atheism, pantheism, theosophy, and agnosticism are
opposed to Christian Science, as they are to ordinary religion; but it does not follow that the profane   Opponents   30
or atheistic invalid cannot be healed by Chris-   benefited
tian Science. The moral condition of such a man de-

1 mands the remedy of Truth more than it is needed in most
cases; and Science is more than usually effectual in the
3 treatment of moral ailments.

That God is a corporeal being, nobody can truly affirm.
The Bible represents Him as saying: "Thou canst not
6 God invisible see My face; for there shall no man see Me,
to the senses and live." Not materially but spiritually we
know Him as divine Mind, as Life, Truth, and Love. We
9 shall obey and adore in proportion as we apprehend the
divine nature and love Him understandingly, warring no
more over the corporeality, but rejoicing in the affluence
12 of our God. Religion will then be of the heart and not of
the head. Mankind will no longer be tyrannical and pro-
scriptive from lack of love, — straining out gnats and
15 swallowing camels.

We worship spiritually, only as we cease to worship
materially. Spiritual devoutness is the soul of Chris-
18 The true tianity. Worshipping through the medium of
worship matter is paganism. Judaic and other rituals
are but types and shadows of true worship. "The true
21 worshippers shall worship the Father in spirit and in
truth."

The Jewish tribal Jehovah was a man-projected God,
24 liable to wrath, repentance, and human changeableness.
Anthropo- The Christian Science God is universal, eter-
morphism nal, divine Love, which changeth not and caus-
27 eth no evil, disease, nor death. It is indeed mournfully
true that the older Scripture is reversed. In the beginning God created man in His, God's, image; but mor-
30 tals would procreate man, and make God in their own
human image. What is the god of a mortal, but a mortal
magnified?

This indicates the distance between the theological and ₁
ritualistic religion of the ages and the truth preached by
Jesus.   More than profession is requisite for   More than   3
Christian demonstration.   Few understand or   profession
adhere to Jesus' divine precepts for living and   required
healing.   Why?   Because his precepts require the disci- 6
ple to cut off the right hand and pluck out the right eye,
— that is, to set aside even the most cherished beliefs
and practices, to leave all for Christ.   9

All revelation (such is the popular thought!) must come
from the schools and along the line of scholarly and ecclesiastical descent, as kings are crowned from a   No   12
royal dynasty.   In healing the sick and sinning,   ecclesiastical
Jesus elaborated the fact that the healing effect   monopoly
followed the understanding of the divine Principle and 15
of the Christ-spirit which governed the corporeal Jesus.
For this Principle there is no dynasty, no ecclesiastical
monopoly.   Its only crowned head is immortal sover- 18
eignty.   Its only priest is the spiritualized man.   The
Bible declares that all believers are made "kings and
priests unto God."   The outsiders did not then, and 21
do not now, understand this ruling of the Christ; therefore they cannot demonstrate God's healing power.
Neither can this manifestation of Christ be com- 24
prehended, until its divine Principle is scientifically
understood.

The adoption of scientific religion and of divine heal- 27
ing will ameliorate sin, sickness, and death.   Let our
pulpits do justice to Christian Science.   Let   A change
it have fair representation by the press.   Give   demanded   30
to it the place in our institutions of learning now occupied by scholastic theology and physiology, and it will

1 eradicate sickness and sin in less time than the old systems,
devised for subduing them, have required for self-estab-
3 lishment and propagation.

Anciently the followers of Christ, or Truth, measured
Christianity by its power over sickness, sin, and death;
6 *Two claims* but modern religions generally omit all but one
omitted of these powers, — the power over sin. We
must seek the undivided garment, the whole Christ, as our
9 first proof of Christianity, for Christ, Truth, alone can
furnish us with absolute evidence.

If the soft palm, upturned to a lordly salary, and archi-
12 tectural skill, making dome and spire tremulous with
Selfishness beauty, turn the poor and the stranger from the
and loss gate, they at the same time shut the door on
15 progress. In vain do the manger and the cross tell their
story to pride and fustian. Sensuality palsies the right
hand, and causes the left to let go its grasp on the divine.
18 As in Jesus' time, so to-day, tyranny and pride need to
be whipped out of the temple, and humility and divine Sci-
Temple ence to be welcomed in. The strong cords of
21 *cleansed* scientific demonstration, as twisted and wielded
by Jesus, are still needed to purge the temples of their
vain traffic in worldly worship and to make them meet
24 dwelling-places for the Most High.

MEDICINE

Which was first, Mind or medicine? If Mind was
27 first and self-existent, then Mind, not matter, must have
Question of been the first medicine. God being All-in-
precedence all, He made medicine; but that medicine was
30 Mind. It could not have been matter, which departs
from the nature and character of Mind, God. Truth

is God's remedy for error of every kind, and Truth de- 1
stroys only what is untrue.   Hence the fact that, to-day,
as yesterday, Christ casts out evils and heals the 3
sick.

It is plain that God does not employ drugs or hygiene,
nor provide them for human use; else Jesus would have 6
recommended and employed them in his heal- Methods
ing.   The sick are more deplorably lost than   rejected
the sinning, if the sick cannot rely on God for help and 9
the sinning can.   The divine Mind never called matter
medicine, and matter required a material and human belief before it could be considered as medicine.   12

Sometimes the human mind uses one error to medicine another.   Driven to choose between two difficulties,
the human mind takes the lesser to relieve the   Error not   15
greater.   On this basis it saves from starva-   curative
tion by theft, and quiets pain with anodynes.   You
admit that mind influences the body somewhat, but 18
you conclude that the stomach, blood, nerves, bones,
etc., hold the preponderance of power.   Controlled by
this belief, you continue in the old routine.   You lean on 21
the inert and unintelligent, never discerning how this de-
prives you of the available superiority of divine Mind.
The body is not controlled scientifically by a negative 24
mind.

Mind is the grand creator, and there can be no power
except that which is derived from Mind.   If Mind was 27
first chronologically, is first potentially, and   Impossible
must be first eternally, then give to Mind the   coalescence
glory, honor, dominion, and power everlastingly due its 30
holy name.   Inferior and unspiritual methods of healing
may try to make Mind and drugs coalesce, but the two will

1 not mingle scientifically. Why should we wish to make
them do so, since no good can come of it?

3   If Mind is foremost and superior, let us rely upon Mind,
which needs no cooperation from lower powers, even if
these so-called powers are real.

6   Naught is the squire, when the king is nigh;
        Withdraws the star, when dawns the sun's brave light.

The various mortal beliefs formulated in human philoso-
9 phy, physiology, hygiene, are mainly predicated of matter,
Soul and   and afford faint gleams of God, or Truth.
sense   The more material a belief, the more obstinately
12 tenacious its error; the stronger are the manifestations of
the corporeal senses, the weaker the indications of Soul.
Human will-power is not Science. Human will belongs
15 to the so-called material senses, and its use is to be con-
Will-power   demned. Willing the sick to recover is not the
detrimental   metaphysical practice of Christian Science, but
18 is sheer animal magnetism. Human will-power may infringe the rights of man. It produces evil continually,
and is not a factor in the realism of being. Truth, and
21 not corporeal will, is the divine power which says to
disease, "Peace, be still."

Because divine Science wars with so-called physical
24 science, even as Truth wars with error, the old schools
Conservative   still oppose it. Ignorance, pride, or prejudice
antagonism   closes the door to whatever is not stereotyped.
27 When the Science of being is universally understood,
every man will be his own physician, and Truth will be
the universal panacea.

30   It is a question to-day, whether the ancient inspired
healers understood the Science of Christian healing, or

whether they caught its sweet tones, as the natural 1
musician catches the tones of harmony, without being
able to explain them.   So divinely imbued   Ancient   3
were they with the spirit of Science, that the   healers
lack of the letter could not hinder their work; and that
letter, without the spirit, would have made void their 6
practice.

The struggle for the recovery of invalids goes on, not
between material methods, but between mortal minds 9
and immortal Mind.   The victory will be on The struggle
the patient's side only as immortal Mind   and victory
through Christ, Truth, subdues the human belief in 12
disease.   It matters not what material method one may
adopt, whether faith in drugs, trust in hygiene, or reliance
on some other minor curative.   15

Scientific healing has this advantage over other methods, — that in it Truth controls error.   From this fact
arise its ethical as well as its physical ef- Mystery of   18
fects.   Indeed, its ethical and physical effects godliness
are indissolubly connected.   If there is any mystery
in Christian healing, it is the mystery which godliness 21
always presents to the ungodly, — the mystery always
arising from ignorance of the laws of eternal and unerring Mind.   24

Other methods undertake to oppose error with error,
and thus they increase the antagonism of one form of
matter towards other forms of matter or error,   Matter   27
and the warfare between Spirit and the flesh versus matter
goes on.   By this antagonism mortal mind must continually weaken its own assumed power.   30

The theology of Christian Science includes healing
the sick.   Our Master's first article of faith propounded

1 to his students was healing, and he proved his faith by
his works. The ancient Christians were healers. Why
3 *How healing* has this element of Christianity been lost?
was lost Because our systems of religion are governed
more or less by our systems of medicine. The first idol-
6 atry was faith in matter. The schools have rendered
faith in drugs the fashion, rather than faith in Deity. By
trusting matter to destroy its own discord, health and
9 harmony have been sacrificed. Such systems are barren
of the vitality of spiritual power, by which material sense
is made the servant of Science and religion becomes
12 Christlike.

Material medicine substitutes drugs for the power of
God — even the might of Mind — to heal the body.
15 *Drugs and* Scholasticism clings for salvation to the per-
divinity son, instead of to the divine Principle, of the
man Jesus; and his Science, the curative agent of God,
18 is silenced. Why? Because truth divests material drugs
of their imaginary power, and clothes Spirit with supremacy. Science is the "stranger that is within thy gates,"
21 remembered not, even when its elevating effects practically prove its divine origin and efficacy.

Divine Science derives its sanction from the Bible,
24 and the divine origin of Science is demonstrated through
the holy influence of Truth in healing sick-
Christian
Science as ness and sin. This healing power of Truth
old as God
27 must have been far anterior to the period in
which Jesus lived. It is as ancient as "the Ancient of
days." It lives through all Life, and extends throughout
30 all space.

Divine metaphysics is now reduced to a system, to a
form comprehensible by and adapted to the thought of

the age in which we live. This system enables the 1
learner to demonstrate the divine Principle,   Reduction
upon which Jesus' healing was based, and   to system   3
the sacred rules for its present application to the cure of
disease.

Late in the nineteenth century I demonstrated the divine 6
rules of Christian Science. They were submitted to the
broadest practical test, and everywhere, when honestly applied under circumstances where demonstration was hu- 9
manly possible, this Science showed that Truth had lost
none of its divine and healing efficacy, even though centuries had passed away since Jesus practised these rules 12
on the hills of Judæa and in the valleys of Galilee.

Although this volume contains the complete Science of
Mind-healing, never believe that you can absorb the whole 15
meaning of the Science by a simple *perusal*   Perusal and
of this book. The book needs to be *studied*,   practice
and the demonstration of the rules of scientific healing 18
will plant you firmly on the spiritual groundwork of
Christian Science. This proof lifts you high above the
perishing fossils of theories already antiquated, and en- 21
ables you to grasp the spiritual facts of being hitherto
unattained and seemingly dim.

Our Master healed the sick, practised Christian heal- 24
ing, and taught the generalities of its divine Principle to
his students; but he left no definite rule for   A definite rule
demonstrating this Principle of healing and   discovered   27
preventing disease. This rule remained to be discovered
in Christian Science. A pure affection takes form in goodness, but Science alone reveals the divine Principle of 30
goodness and demonstrates its rules.

Jesus never spoke of disease as dangerous or as difficult

1 to heal. When his students brought to him a case they
had failed to heal, he said to them, "O faithless gen-
3 Jesus' own eration," implying that the requisite power
practice to heal was in Mind. He prescribed no drugs,
urged no obedience to material laws, but acted in direct
6 disobedience to them.

Neither anatomy nor theology has ever described man
as created by Spirit, — as God's man. The former ex-
9   The man of plains the men of *men,* or the "children of
anatomy and men," as created corporeally instead of spir-
of theology itually and as emerging from the lowest, in-
12 stead of from the highest, conception of being. Both
anatomy and theology define man as both physical and
mental, and place mind at the mercy of matter for every
15 function, formation, and manifestation. Anatomy takes
up man at all points materially. It loses Spirit, drops the
true tone, and accepts the discord. Anatomy and the-
18 ology reject the divine Principle which produces harmonious man, and deal — the one wholly, the other primarily
— with matter, calling that *man* which is not the counter-
21 part, but the counterfeit, of God's man. Then theology
tries to explain how to make this man a Christian, — how
from this basis of division and discord to produce the con-
24 cord and unity of Spirit and His likeness.

Physiology exalts matter, dethrones Mind, and claims
to rule man by material law, instead of spiritual. When
27 Physiology physiology fails to give health or life by this
deficient process, it ignores the divine Spirit as unable
or unwilling to render help in time of physical need.
30 When mortals sin, this ruling of the schools leaves them
to the guidance of a theology which admits God to be
the healer of sin but not of sickness, although our great

Master demonstrated that Truth could save from sickness 1
as well as from sin.

Mind as far outweighs drugs in the cure of disease as 3
in the cure of sin. The more excellent way is divine
Science in every case. Is *materia medica* a Blunders and
science or a bundle of speculative human   blunderers   6
theories? The prescription which succeeds in one instance fails in another, and this is owing to the different
mental states of the patient. These states are not com- 9
prehended, and they are left without explanation except
in Christian Science. The rule and its perfection of operation never vary in Science. If you fail to succeed in any 12
case, it is because you have not demonstrated the life of
Christ, Truth, more in your own life, — because you have
not obeyed the rule and proved the Principle of divine 15
Science.

A physician of the old school remarked with great
gravity: "We know that mind affects the body some- 18
what, and advise our patients to be hopeful Old-school
and cheerful and to take as little medicine as   physician
possible; but mind can never cure organic difficulties." 21
The logic is lame, and facts contradict it. The author
has cured what is termed organic disease as readily as she
has cured purely functional disease, and with no power 24
but the divine Mind.

Since God, divine Mind, governs all, not partially but
supremely, predicting disease does not dignify therapeutics. 27
Whatever guides thought spiritually benefits Tests in
mind and body. We need to understand the   our day
affirmations of divine Science, dismiss superstition, and 30
demonstrate truth according to Christ. To-day there
is hardly a city, village, or hamlet, in which are not to

1 be found living witnesses and monuments to the virtue
and power of Truth, as applied through this Christian
3 system of healing disease.

To-day the healing power of Truth is widely demonstrated as an immanent, eternal Science, instead of a
6 **The main** phenomenal exhibition. Its appearing is the
purpose coming anew of the gospel of "on earth peace,
good-will toward men." This coming, as was promised
9 by the Master, is for its establishment as a permanent
dispensation among men; but the mission of Christian
Science now, as in the time of its earlier demonstration,
12 is not primarily one of physical healing. Now, as then,
signs and wonders are wrought in the metaphysical healing of physical disease; but these signs are only to demon-
15 strate its divine origin, — to attest the reality of the higher
mission of the Christ-power to take away the sins of the
world.

18 The science (so-called) of physics would have one believe that both matter and mind are subject to disease,
Exploded and that, too, in spite of the individual's pro-
21 **doctrine** test and contrary to the law of divine Mind.
This human view infringes man's free moral agency; and
it is as evidently erroneous to the author, and will be to
24 all others at some future day, as the practically rejected
doctrine of the predestination of souls to damnation or
salvation. The doctrine that man's harmony is gov-
27 erned by physical conditions all his earthly days, and that
he is then thrust out of his own body by the operation of
matter, — even the doctrine of the superiority of matter
30 over Mind, — is fading out.

The hosts of Æsculapius are flooding the world with
diseases, because they are ignorant that the human mind

and body are myths. To be sure, they sometimes treat 1
the sick as if there was but one factor in the case; but
this one factor they represent to be body, not   Disease   3
mind. Infinite Mind could not possibly create   mental
a remedy outside of itself, but erring, finite, human mind
has an absolute need of something beyond itself for its 6
redemption and healing.

Great respect is due the motives and philanthropy of
the higher class of physicians. We know that if they un- 9
derstood the Science of Mind-healing, and were   Intentions
in possession of the enlarged power it confers   respected
to benefit the race physically and spiritually, they would 12
rejoice with us. Even this one reform in medicine would
ultimately deliver mankind from the awful and oppressive bondage now enforced by false theories, from which 15
multitudes would gladly escape.

Mortal belief says that death has been occasioned by
fright. Fear never stopped being and its action. The 18
blood, heart, lungs, brain, etc., have nothing Man governed
to do with Life, God. Every function of the   by Mind
real man is governed by the divine Mind. The human 21
mind has no power to kill or to cure, and it has no control over God's man. The divine Mind that made man
maintains His own image and likeness. The human 24
mind is opposed to God and must be put off, as St. Paul
declares. All that really exists is the divine Mind and
its idea, and in this Mind the entire being is found har- 27
monious and eternal. The straight and narrow way is to
see and acknowledge this fact, yield to this power, and
follow the leadings of truth.   30

That mortal mind claims to govern every organ of the
mortal body, we have overwhelming proof. But this so-

1 called mind is a myth, and must by its own consent yield
to Truth. It would wield the sceptre of a monarch, but
3 Mortal mind it is powerless. The immortal divine Mind
dethroned takes away all its supposed sovereignty, and
saves mortal mind from itself. The author has endeavored
6 to make this book the Æsculapius of mind as well as of
body, that it may give hope to the sick and heal them,
although they know not how the work is done. Truth
9 has a healing effect, even when not fully understood.

Anatomy describes muscular action as produced by
mind in one instance and not in another. Such errors
12 All activity beset every material theory, in which one
from thought statement contradicts another over and over
again. It is related that Sir Humphry Davy once ap-
15 parently cured a case of paralysis simply by introducing
a thermometer into the patient's mouth. This he did
merely to ascertain the temperature of the patient's body;
18 but the sick man supposed this ceremony was intended
to heal him, and he recovered accordingly. Such a fact
illustrates our theories.

21 The author's medical researches and experiments had
prepared her thought for the metaphysics of Christian
Science. Every material dependence had
The author's
24 experiments failed her in her search for truth; and she can
in medicine
now understand why, and can see the means
by which mortals are divinely driven to a spiritual source
27 for health and happiness.

Her experiments in homœopathy had made her skep-
tical as to material curative methods. Jahr, from
30 Homœopathic *Aconitum* to *Zincum oxydatum,* enumerates
attenuations the general symptoms, the characteristic
signs, which demand different remedies; but the drug

is frequently attenuated to such a degree that not a ves- 1
tige of it remains. Thus we learn that it is not the drug
which expels the disease or changes one of the symptoms 3
of disease.

The author has attenuated *Natrum muriaticum* (common table-salt) until there was not a single saline property 6
left. The salt had "lost his savour;" and yet,   Only salt
with one drop of that attenuation in a goblet of   and water
water, and a teaspoonful of the water administered at in- 9
tervals of three hours, she has cured a patient sinking in
the last stage of typhoid fever. The highest attenuation
of homœopathy and the most potent rises above matter into 12
mind. This discovery leads to more light. From it may
be learned that either human faith or the divine Mind is
the healer and that there is no efficacy in a drug.   15

You say a boil is painful; but that is impossible, for
matter without mind is not painful. The boil simply
manifests, through inflammation and swell-   Origin   18
ing, a belief in pain, and this belief is called a   of pain
boil. Now administer mentally to your patient a high
attenuation of truth, and it will soon cure the boil. The 21
fact that pain cannot exist where there is no mortal mind
to feel it is a proof that this so-called mind makes its
own pain — that is, its own *belief* in pain.   24

We weep because others weep, we yawn because they
yawn, and we have smallpox because others have it; but
mortal mind, not matter, contains and carries   Source of   27
the infection. When this mental contagion is   contagion
understood, we shall be more careful of our mental conditions, and we shall avoid loquacious tattling about 30
disease, as we would avoid advocating crime. Neither
sympathy nor society should ever tempt us to cherish

1 error in any form, and certainly we should not be error's
advocate.

3 Disease arises, like other mental conditions, from association. Since it is a law of mortal mind that certain
diseases should be regarded as contagious, this law ob-
6 tains credit through association, — calling up the fear that
creates the image of disease and its consequent manifestation in the body.

9 This fact in metaphysics is illustrated by the following
incident: A man was made to believe that he occupied a
Imaginary bed where a cholera patient had died. Imme-
12   cholera   diately the symptoms of this disease appeared,
and the man died. The fact was, that he had not caught
the cholera by material contact, because no cholera patient
15 had been in that bed.

If a child is exposed to contagion or infection, the
mother is frightened and says, "My child will be sick."
18 Children's The law of mortal mind and her own fears gov-
ailments   ern her child more than the child's mind governs itself, and they produce the very results which might
21 have been prevented through the opposite understanding.
Then it is believed that exposure to the contagion wrought
the mischief.

24 That mother is not a Christian Scientist, and her affections need better guidance, who says to her child: "You
look sick," "You look tired," "You need rest," or "You
27 need medicine."

Such a mother runs to her little one, who thinks she has
hurt her face by falling on the carpet, and says, moaning
30 more childishly than her child, "Mamma knows you are
hurt." The better and more successful method for any
mother to adopt is to say: "Oh, never mind! You're not

hurt, so don't think you are." Presently the child forgets 1
all about the accident, and is at play.

When the sick recover by the use of drugs, it is the law 3
of a general belief, culminating in individual faith, which
heals; and according to this faith will the effect   Drug-power
be. Even when you take away the individual   mental   6
confidence in the drug, you have not yet divorced the drug
from the general faith. The chemist, the botanist, the
druggist, the doctor, and the nurse equip the medicine 9
with their faith, and the beliefs which are in the majority
rule. When the general belief endorses the inanimate
drug as doing this or that, individual dissent or faith, un- 12
less it rests on Science, is but a belief held by a minority,
and such a belief is governed by the majority.

The universal belief in physics weighs against the high 15
and mighty truths of Christian metaphysics. This erroneous general belief, which sustains medicine and   Belief in
produces all medical results, works against   physics   18
Christian Science; and the percentage of power on the
side of this Science must mightily outweigh the power of
popular belief in order to heal a single case of disease. The 21
human mind acts more powerfully to offset the discords
of matter and the ills of flesh, in proportion as it puts less
weight into the material or fleshly scale and more weight 24
into the spiritual scale. Homœopathy diminishes the
drug, but the potency of the medicine increases as the
drug disappears.   27

Vegetarianism, homœopathy, and hydropathy have
diminished drugging; but if drugs are an antidote to
disease, why lessen the antidote? If drugs   Nature of   30
are good things, is it safe to say that the   drugs
less in quantity you have of them the better? If drugs

1 possess intrinsic virtues or intelligent curative qualities,
these qualities must be mental. Who named drugs, and
3 what made them good or bad for mortals, beneficial or
injurious?

A case of dropsy, given up by the faculty, fell into
6 my hands. It was a terrible case. Tapping had been
Dropsy cured employed, and yet, as she lay in her bed, the
without drugs patient looked like a barrel. I prescribed
9 the fourth attenuation of *Argentum nitratum* with occasional doses of a high attenuation of *Sulphuris*. She improved perceptibly. Believing then somewhat in the
12 ordinary theories of medical practice, and learning that
her former physician had prescribed these remedies, I
began to fear an aggravation of symptoms from their
15 prolonged use, and told the patient so; but she was
unwilling to give up the medicine while she was recovering. It then occurred to me to give her un-
18 medicated pellets and watch the result. I did so, and
she continued to gain. Finally she said that she would
give up her medicine for one day, and risk the
21 effects. After trying this, she informed me that she
could get along two days without globules; but on
the third day she again suffered, and was relieved by
24 taking them. She went on in this way, taking the
unmedicated pellets, — and receiving occasional visits
from me, — but employing no other means, and she was
27 cured.

Metaphysics, as taught in Christian Science, is the
next stately step beyond homœopathy. In metaphysics,
30 A stately matter disappears from the remedy entirely,
advance and Mind takes its rightful and supreme
place. Homœopathy takes mental symptoms largely

into consideration in its diagnosis of disease. Christian 1
Science deals wholly with the mental cause in judging and
destroying disease. It succeeds where homœopathy fails, 3
solely because its one recognized Principle of healing is
Mind, and the whole force of the mental element is employed through the Science of Mind, which never shares 6
its rights with inanimate matter.

Christian Science exterminates the drug, and rests on
Mind alone as the curative Principle, acknowledging that 9
the divine Mind has all power. Homœopathy
mentalizes a drug with such repetition of
thought-attenuations, that the drug becomes
more like the human mind than the substratum of this so-
called mind, which we call matter; and the drug's power
of action is proportionately increased. 15

*The modus
of
homœopathy*

12

If drugs are part of God's creation, which (according
to the narrative in Genesis) He pronounced *good,* then
drugs cannot be poisonous. If He could create drugs intrinsically bad, then they should
never be used. If He creates drugs at all and designs
them for medical use, why did Jesus not employ them 21
and recommend them for the treatment of disease?
Matter is not self-creative, for it is unintelligent. Erring
mortal mind confers the power which the drug seems to 24
possess.

*Drugging
unchristian*

18

Narcotics quiet mortal mind, and so relieve the body;
but they leave both mind and body worse for this sub- 27
mission. Christian Science impresses the entire corporeality, — namely, mind and body, — and brings out the
proof that Life is continuous and harmonious. Science 30
both neutralizes error and destroys it. Mankind is the
better for this spiritual and profound pathology.

1   It is recorded that the profession of medicine originated
in idolatry with pagan priests, who besought the gods to
3   heal the sick and designated Apollo as "the god

Mythology
and materia of medicine." He was supposed to have dic-
medica
tated the first prescription, according to the
6 "History of Four Thousand Years of Medicine." It is
here noticeable that Apollo was also regarded as the sender
of disease, "the god of pestilence." Hippocrates turned
9 from image-gods to vegetable and mineral drugs for healing. This was deemed progress in medicine; but
what we need is the truth which heals both mind and
12 body. The future history of material medicine may
correspond with that of its material god, Apollo, who was
banished from heaven and endured great sufferings
15 upon earth.

Drugs, cataplasms, and whiskey are stupid substitutes
for the dignity and potency of divine Mind and its effi-
18 Footsteps to cacy to heal. It is pitiful to lead men into
intemperance temptation through the byways of this wilderness world, — to victimize the race with intoxicating
21 prescriptions for the sick, until mortal mind acquires an
educated appetite for strong drink, and men and women
become loathsome sots.

24   Evidences of progress and of spiritualization greet us
on every hand. Drug-systems are quitting their hold on
Advancing matter and so letting in matter's higher stra-
27 degrees tum, mortal mind. Homœopathy, a step in
advance of allopathy, is doing this. Matter is going out
of medicine; and mortal mind, of a higher attenuation
30 than the drug, is governing the pellet.

A woman in the city of Lynn, Massachusetts, was
etherized and died in consequence, although her physi-

cians insisted that it would be unsafe to perform a needed 1
surgical operation without the ether. After the autopsy,
her sister testified that the deceased protested   Effects   3
against inhaling the ether and said it would kill   of fear
her, but that she was compelled by her physicians to take
it. Her hands were held, and she was forced into sub- 6
mission. The case was brought to trial. The evidence
was found to be conclusive, and a verdict was returned that
death was occasioned, not by the ether, but by fear of 9
inhaling it.

Is it skilful or scientific surgery to take no heed of mental conditions and to treat the patient as if she were so 12
much mindless matter, and as if matter were   Mental
the only factor to be consulted? Had these   conditions
                                               to be heeded
unscientific surgeons understood metaphysics,   15
they would have considered the woman's state of mind,
and not have risked such treatment. They would either
have allayed her fear or would have performed the opera- 18
tion without ether.

The sequel proved that this Lynn woman died from
effects produced by mortal mind, and not from the disease 21
or the operation.

The medical schools would learn the state of man
from matter instead of from Mind. They examine the 24
lungs, tongue, and pulse to ascertain how False source
much harmony, or health, matter is permit- of knowledge
ting to matter, — how much pain or pleasure, action or 27
stagnation, one form of matter is allowing another form
of matter.

Ignorant of the fact that a man's belief produces dis- 30
ease and all its symptoms, the ordinary physician is
liable to increase disease with his own mind, when he

1 should address himself to the work of destroying it through
the power of the divine Mind.

3   The systems of physics act against metaphysics, and
vice versa. When mortals forsake the material for the
spiritual basis of action, drugs lose their healing force,
6 for they have no innate power. Unsupported by the
faith reposed in it, the inanimate drug becomes
powerless.

9   The motion of the arm is no more dependent upon the
direction of mortal mind, than are the organic action and
Obedient   secretion of the viscera. When this so-called
12 muscles   mind quits the body, the heart becomes as torpid as the hand.

Anatomy finds a necessity for nerves to convey the man-
15 date of mind to muscle and so cause action; but what does
Anatomy   anatomy say when the cords contract and be-
and mind   come immovable? Has mortal mind ceased
18 speaking to them, or has it bidden them to be impotent?
Can muscles, bones, blood, and nerves rebel against mind
in one instance and not in another, and become cramped
21 despite the mental protest?

Unless muscles are self-acting at all times, they are
never so, — never capable of acting contrary to mental
24 direction. If muscles can cease to act and become rigid
of their own preference, — be deformed or symmetrical,
as they please or as disease directs, — they must be self-
27 directing. Why then consult anatomy to learn how mortal mind governs muscle, if we are only to learn from
anatomy that muscle is not so governed?

30 Mind over   Is man a material fungus without Mind
matter   to help him? Is a stiff joint or a contracted
muscle as much a result of law as the supple and

elastic condition of the healthy limb, and is God the 1
lawgiver?

You say, "*I* have burned my finger." This is an 3
exact statement, more exact than you suppose; for mortal mind, and not matter, burns it. Holy inspiration
has created states of mind which have been able to nullify 6
the action of the flames, as in the Bible case of the three
young Hebrew captives, cast into the Babylonian furnace;
while an opposite mental state might produce spontaneous 9
combustion.

In 1880, Massachusetts put her foot on a proposed
tyrannical law, restricting the practice of medicine. If 12
her sister States follow this example in har-   Restrictive
mony with our Constitution and Bill of Rights,   regulations
they will do less violence to that immortal sentiment of the 15
Declaration, "Man is endowed by his Maker with certain
inalienable rights, among which are life, liberty, and the
pursuit of happiness."   18

The oppressive state statutes touching medicine remind one of the words of the famous Madame Roland,
as she knelt before a statue of Liberty, erected near the 21
guillotine: "Liberty, what crimes are committed in thy
name!"

The ordinary practitioner, examining bodily symptoms, 24
telling the patient that he is sick, and treating the case according to his physical diagnosis, would natu-   Metaphysics
rally induce the very disease he is trying to cure,   challenges 27
even if it were not already determined by mor-   physics
tal mind. Such unconscious mistakes would not occur, if
this old class of philanthropists looked as deeply for cause 30
and effect into mind as into matter. The physician agrees
with his "adversary quickly," but upon different terms

1 than does the metaphysician; for the matter-physician
agrees with the disease, while the metaphysician agrees
3 only with health and challenges disease.

Christian Science brings to the body the sunlight of
Truth, which invigorates and purifies. Christian Science
6   Truth an   acts as an alterative, neutralizing error with
  alterative   Truth. It changes the secretions, expels humors, dissolves tumors, relaxes rigid muscles, restores
9 carious bones to soundness. The effect of this Science is
to stir the human mind to a change of base, on which it
may yield to the harmony of the divine Mind.

12   Experiments have favored the fact that Mind governs
the body, not in one instance, but in every instance. The
  Practical   indestructible faculties of Spirit exist without
15   success   the conditions of matter and also without the
false beliefs of a so-called material existence. Working
out the rules of Science in practice, the author has re-
18 stored health in cases of both acute and chronic disease in
their severest forms. Secretions have been changed, the
structure has been renewed, shortened limbs have been
21 elongated, ankylosed joints have been made supple, and
carious bones have been restored to healthy conditions. I
have restored what is called the lost substance of lungs, and
24 healthy organizations have been established where disease
was organic. Christian Science heals organic disease as
surely as it heals what is called functional, for it requires
27 only a fuller understanding of the divine Principle of
Christian Science to demonstrate the higher rule.

  Testimony   With due respect for the faculty, I kindly
30   of medical   quote from Dr. Benjamin Rush, the famous
  teachers   Philadelphia teacher of medical practice. He
declared that "it is impossible to calculate the mischief

which Hippocrates has done, by first marking Nature 1
with his name, and afterward letting her loose upon sick
people." 3
Dr. Benjamin Waterhouse, Professor in Harvard University, declared himself "sick of learned quackery."
Dr. James Johnson, Surgeon to William IV, King of 6
England, said:
"I declare my conscientious opinion, founded on long
observation and reflection, that if there were not a single 9
physician, surgeon, apothecary, man-midwife, chemist,
druggist, or drug on the face of the earth, there would be
less sickness and less mortality." 12
Dr. Mason Good, a learned Professor in London,
said:
"The effects of medicine on the human system are in 15
the highest degree uncertain; except, indeed, that it has
already destroyed more lives than war, pestilence, and
famine, all combined." 18
Dr. Chapman, Professor of the Institutes and Practice
of Physic in the University of Pennsylvania, in a published
essay said: 21
"Consulting the records of our science, we cannot
help being disgusted with the multitude of hypotheses
obtruded upon us at different times. Nowhere is the 24
imagination displayed to a greater extent; and perhaps
so ample an exhibition of human invention might gratify
our vanity, if it were not more than compensated by the 27
humiliating view of so much absurdity, contradiction,
and falsehood. To harmonize the contrarieties of medical doctrines is indeed a task as impracticable as to 30
arrange the fleeting vapors around us, or to reconcile the
fixed and repulsive antipathies of nature. Dark and

1 perplexed, our devious career resembles the groping of
Homer's Cyclops around his cave."
3   Sir John Forbes, M.D., F.R.S., Fellow of the Royal
College of Physicians, London, said:
    "No systematic or theoretical classification of diseases
6 or of therapeutic agents, ever yet promulgated, is true, or
anything like the truth, and none can be adopted as a safe
guidance in practice."
9   It is just to say that generally the cultured class of medical practitioners are grand men and women, therefore
they are more scientific than are false claimants to Chris-
12 tian Science.   But all human systems based on material
premises are minus the unction of divine Science.   Much
yet remains to be said and done before all mankind is
15 saved and all the mental microbes of sin and all diseased
thought-germs are exterminated.
    If you or I should appear to die, we should not be
18 dead.   The seeming decease, caused by a majority of
human beliefs that man must die, or produced by mental
assassins, does not in the least disprove Christian Science;
21 rather does it evidence the truth of its basic proposition
that mortal thoughts in belief rule the materiality miscalled life in the body or in matter.   But the forever fact
24 remains paramount that Life, Truth, and Love save from
sin, disease, and death.   "When this corruptible shall have
put on incorruption, and this mortal shall have put on
27 immortality [divine Science], then shall be brought to pass
the saying that is written, Death is swallowed up in
victory" (St. Paul).

CHAPTER VII

Physiology

Therefore I say unto you, Take no thought for your life, what ye shall eat, or what ye shall drink; nor yet for your body, what ye shall put on. Is not the life more than meat, and the body than raiment? — JESUS.

He sent His word, and healed them, and delivered them from their destructions. — PSALMS.

PHYSIOLOGY is one of the apples from "the tree 1 of knowledge." Evil declared that eating this fruit would open man's eyes and make him as a god. Instead 3 of so doing, it closed the eyes of mortals to man's God-given dominion over the earth.

To measure intellectual capacity by the size of the 6 brain and strength by the exercise of muscle, is to subjugate intelligence, to make mind mor- Man not tal, and to place this so-called mind at the structural 9 mercy of material organization and non-intelligent matter.

Obedience to the so-called physical laws of health has 12 not checked sickness. Diseases have multiplied, since man-made material theories took the place of spiritual truth. 15

You say that indigestion, fatigue, sleeplessness, cause distressed stomachs and aching heads. Then Causes of you consult your brain in order to remember sickness 18 what has hurt you, when your remedy lies in forgetting

165

1 the whole thing; for matter has no sensation of its own, and the human mind is all that can produce pain.

3   As a man thinketh, so is he. Mind is all that feels, acts, or impedes action. Ignorant of this, or shrinking from its implied responsibility, the healing effort is made 6 on the wrong side, and thus the conscious control over the body is lost.

The Mohammedan believes in a pilgrimage to Mecca 9 for the salvation of his soul. The popular doctor believes in his prescription, and the pharmacist believes

Delusions pagan and medical

in the power of his drugs to save a man's 12 life. The Mohammedan's belief is a religious delusion; the doctor's and pharmacist's is a medical mistake.

15   The erring human mind is inharmonious in itself. From it arises the inharmonious body. To ignore God as of little use in sickness is a mistake.

Health from reliance on spirituality

18 Instead of thrusting Him aside in times of bodily trouble, and waiting for the hour of strength in which to acknowledge Him, we should learn 21 that He can do all things for us in sickness as in health.

Failing to recover health through adherence to physi-24 ology and hygiene, the despairing invalid often drops them, and in his extremity and only as a last resort, turns to God. The invalid's faith in the divine Mind is less 27 than in drugs, air, and exercise, or he would have resorted to Mind first. The balance of power is conceded to be with matter by most of the medical systems; but when 30 Mind at last asserts its mastery over sin, disease, and death, then is man found to be harmonious and immortal.

Should we implore a corporeal God to heal the sick 1
out of His personal volition, or should we understand the
infinite divine Principle which heals? If we rise no higher 3
than blind faith, the Science of healing is not attained, and
Soul-existence, in the place of sense-existence, is not comprehended. We apprehend Life in divine Science only 6
as we live above corporeal sense and correct it. Our pro-
portionate admission of the claims of good or of evil determines the harmony of our existence, — our health, our 9
longevity, and our Christianity.

We cannot serve two masters nor perceive divine Science with the material senses. Drugs and hygiene cannot 12
successfully usurp the place and power of the   The two
divine source of all health and perfection. If   masters
God made man both good and evil, man must remain 15
thus. What can improve God's work? Again, an error
in the premise must appear in the conclusion. To have
one God and avail yourself of the power of Spirit, you 18
must love God supremely.

The "flesh lusteth against the Spirit." The flesh and
Spirit can no more unite in action, than good can coin- 21
cide with evil. It is not wise to take a halt-   Half-way
ing and half-way position or to expect to work   success
equally with Spirit and matter, Truth and error. There 24
is but one way — namely, God and His idea — which
leads to spiritual being. The scientific government of the
body must be attained through the divine Mind. It is im- 27
possible to gain control over the body in any other way.
On this fundamental point, timid conservatism is absolutely inadmissible. Only through radical reliance on 30
Truth can scientific healing power be realized.

Substituting good words for a good life, fair seeming

1 for straightforward character, is a poor shift for the weak
and worldly, who think the standard of Christian Science
3 too high for them.

If the scales are evenly adjusted, the removal of a single
weight from either scale gives preponderance to the oppo-
6 Belief on the site. Whatever influence you cast on the side
wrong side of matter, you take away from Mind, which
would otherwise outweigh all else. Your belief militates
9 against your health, when it ought to be enlisted on the
side of health. When sick (according to belief) you rush
after drugs, search out the material so-called laws of
12 health, and depend upon them to heal you, though you
have already brought yourself into the slough of disease
through just this false belief.

15 Because man-made systems insist that man becomes
sick and useless, suffers and dies, all in consonance with
The divine the laws of God, are we to believe it? Are
18 authority we to believe an authority which denies God's
spiritual command relating to perfection, — an authority
which Jesus proved to be false? He did the will of the
21 Father. He healed sickness in defiance of what is called
material law, but in accordance with God's law, the law
of Mind.

24 I have discerned disease in the human mind, and recognized the patient's fear of it, months before the so-called
Disease disease made its appearance in the body. Dis-
27 foreseen ease being a belief, a latent illusion of mortal
mind, the sensation would not appear if the error of belief
was met and destroyed by truth.

30 Changed Here let a word be noticed which will be
mentality better understood hereafter, — *chemicalization.*
By chemicalization I mean the process which mortal

mind and body undergo in the change of belief from a 1
material to a spiritual basis.

Whenever an aggravation of symptoms has occurred 3
through mental chemicalization, I have seen the mental
signs, assuring me that danger was over, before   Scientific
the patient felt the change; and I have said   foresight   6
to the patient, "You are healed," — sometimes to his dis-
comfiture, when he was incredulous. But it always came
about as I had foretold.   9

I name these facts to show that disease has a mental,
mortal origin, — that faith in rules of health or in drugs
begets and fosters disease by attracting the mind to the 12
subject of sickness, by exciting fear of disease, and by dos-
ing the body in order to avoid it. The faith reposed in
these things should find stronger supports and a higher 15
home. If we understood the control of Mind over body,
we should put no faith in material means.

Science not only reveals the origin of all disease as 18
mental, but it also declares that all disease is cured by
divine Mind. There can be no healing ex-   Mind the
cept by this Mind, however much we trust   only healer   21
a drug or any other means towards which human faith
or endeavor is directed. It is mortal mind, not matter, which brings to the sick whatever good they may 24
seem to receive from materiality. But the sick are never
really healed except by means of the divine power.
Only the action of Truth, Life, and Love can give 27
harmony.

Whatever teaches man to have other laws and to
acknowledge other powers than the divine   Modes of   30
Mind, is anti-Christian. The good that a   matter
poisonous drug seems to do is evil, for it robs man of

1 reliance on God, omnipotent Mind, and according to belief, poisons the human system. Truth is not the basis of
3 theogony. Modes of matter form neither a moral nor a
spiritual system. The discord which calls for material
methods is the result of the exercise of faith in material
6 modes, — faith in matter instead of in Spirit.

Did Jesus understand the economy of man less than
Graham or Cutter? Christian ideas certainly present
9 Physiology what human theories exclude — the Principle
unscientific of man's harmony. The text, "Whosoever
liveth and believeth in me shall never die," not only con-
12 tradicts human systems, but points to the self-sustaining
and eternal Truth.

The demands of Truth are spiritual, and reach the
15 body through Mind. The best interpreter of man's needs
said: "Take no thought for your life, what ye shall eat,
or what ye shall drink."

18   If there are material laws which prevent disease, what
then causes it? Not divine law, for Jesus healed the
sick and cast out error, always in opposition, never in
21 obedience, to physics.

Spiritual causation is the one question to be considered,
for more than all others spiritual causation relates to
24 Causation human progress. The age seems ready to
considered approach this subject, to ponder somewhat
the supremacy of Spirit, and at least to touch the hem
27 of Truth's garment.

The description of man as purely physical, or as both
material and spiritual, — but in either case dependent
30 upon his physical organization, — is the Pandora box,
from which all ills have gone forth, especially despair.
Matter, which takes divine power into its own hands and

claims to be a creator, is a fiction, in which paganism and 1
lust are so sanctioned by society that mankind has caught
their moral contagion. 3

Through discernment of the spiritual opposite of materiality, even the way through Christ, Truth, man will
reopen with the key of divine Science the gates   Paradise   6
of Paradise which human beliefs have closed,   regained
and will find himself unfallen, upright, pure, and free,
not needing to consult almanacs for the probabilities either 9
of his life or of the weather, not needing to study brainology to learn how much of a man he is.

Mind's control over the universe, including man, is 12
no longer an open question, but is demonstrable Science.
Jesus illustrated the divine Principle and the   A closed
power of immortal Mind by healing sickness   question   15
and sin and destroying the foundations of death.

Mistaking his origin and nature, man believes himself to
be combined matter and Spirit. He believes that Spirit 18
is sifted through matter, carried on a nerve, ex-   Matter
posed to ejection by the operation of matter.   versus Spirit
The intellectual, the moral, the spiritual, — yea, the image 21
of infinite Mind, — subject to non-intelligence!

No more sympathy exists between the flesh and Spirit
than between Belial and Christ. 24

The so-called laws of matter are nothing but false beliefs that intelligence and life are present where Mind
is not. These false beliefs are the procuring cause of all 27
sin and disease. The opposite truth, that intelligence and
life are spiritual, never material, destroys sin, sickness,
and death. 30

The fundamental error lies in the supposition that man
is a material outgrowth and that the cognizance of good

1 or evil, which he has through the bodily senses, constitutes his happiness or misery.

3   Theorizing about man's development from mushrooms

Godless   to monkeys and from monkeys into men
evolution   amounts to nothing in the right direction and
6 very much in the wrong.
Materialism grades the human species as rising from
matter upward. How then is the material species main-
9 tained, if man passes through what we call death and
death is the Rubicon of spirituality? Spirit can form
no real link in this supposed chain of material being.
12 But divine Science reveals the eternal chain of existence
as uninterrupted and wholly spiritual; yet this can be
realized only as the false sense of being disappears.
15   If man was first a material being, he must have passed
through all the forms of matter in order to become man.

Degrees of   If the material body is man, he is a portion of
18 development   matter, or dust. On the contrary, man is the
image and likeness of Spirit; and the belief that there is
Soul in sense or Life in matter obtains in mortals, *alias*
21 mortal mind, to which the apostle refers when he says
that we must "put off the old man."
What is man? Brain, heart, blood, bones, etc., the
24 material structure? If the real man is in the material

Identity   body, you take away a portion of the man when
not lost   you amputate a limb; the surgeon destroys
27 manhood, and worms annihilate it. But the loss of a limb
or injury to a tissue is sometimes the quickener of manli-
ness; and the unfortunate cripple may present more no-
30 bility than the statuesque athlete, — teaching us by his
very deprivations, that "a man's a man, for a' that."
When we admit that matter (heart, blood, brain, acting

through the five physical senses) constitutes man, we fail 1
to see how anatomy can distinguish between   When man
humanity and the brute, or determine when   is man   3
man is really *man* and has progressed farther than his
animal progenitors.

When the supposition, that Spirit is within what it 6
creates and the potter is subject to the clay,   Individu-
is individualized, Truth is reduced to the level   alization
of error, and the sensible is required to be made manifest 9
through the insensible.

What is termed matter manifests nothing but a material
mentality. Neither the substance nor the manifestation 12
of Spirit is obtainable through matter. Spirit is positive.
Matter is Spirit's contrary, the absence of Spirit. For
positive Spirit to pass through a negative condition 15
would be Spirit's destruction.

Anatomy declares man to be structural. Physiology
continues this explanation, measuring human   Man not   18
strength by bones and sinews, and human life   structural
by material law. Man is spiritual, individual, and eternal; material structure is mortal.   21

Phrenology makes man knavish or honest according to
the development of the cranium; but anatomy, physiology,
phrenology, do not define the image of God, the real im- 24
mortal man.

Human reason and religion come slowly to the recognition of spiritual facts, and so continue to call upon 27
matter to remove the error which the human mind alone
has created.

The idols of civilization are far more fatal to health 30
and longevity than are the idols of barbarism. The idols
of civilization call into action less faith than Buddhism

1 in a supreme governing intelligence. The Esquimaux
restore health by incantations as consciously as do civi-
3 lized practitioners by their more studied methods.

Is civilization only a higher form of idolatry, that
man should bow down to a flesh-brush, to flannels, to
6 baths, diet, exercise, and air? Nothing save divine
power is capable of doing so much for man as he can
do for himself.

9 The footsteps of thought, rising above material standpoints, are slow, and portend a long night to the traveller;
Rise of but the angels of His presence — the spiritual
12 **thought** intuitions that tell us when "the night is far
spent, the day is at hand" — are our guardians in the
gloom. Whoever opens the way in Christian Science is
15 a pilgrim and stranger, marking out the path for generations yet unborn.

The thunder of Sinai and the Sermon on the Mount
18 are pursuing and will overtake the ages, rebuking in
their course all error and proclaiming the kingdom of
heaven on earth. Truth is revealed. It needs only to
21 be practised.

Mortal belief is all that enables a drug to cure mortal
ailments. Anatomy admits that mind is somewhere in
24 **Medical** man, though out of sight. Then, if an indi-
errors vidual is sick, why treat the body alone and
administer a dose of despair to the mind? Why declare
27 that the body is diseased, and picture this disease to the
mind, rolling it under the tongue as a sweet morsel and
holding it before the thought of both physician and pa-
30 tient? We should understand that the cause of disease
obtains in the mortal human mind, and its cure comes
from the immortal divine Mind. We should prevent the

images of disease from taking form in thought, and we 1
should efface the outlines of disease already formulated in
the minds of mortals.   3

When there are fewer prescriptions, and less thought is
given to sanitary subjects, there will be better   Novel
constitutions and less disease. In old times   diseases   6
who ever heard of dyspepsia, cerebro-spinal meningitis,
hay-fever, and rose-cold?

What an abuse of natural beauty to say that a rose, 9
the smile of God, can produce suffering! The joy of its
presence, its beauty and fragrance, should uplift the
thought, and dissuade any sense of fear or fever. It is 12
profane to fancy that the perfume of clover and the breath
of new-mown hay can cause glandular inflammation,
sneezing, and nasal pangs.   15

If a random thought, calling itself dyspepsia, had
tried to tyrannize over our forefathers, it would have
been routed by their independence and in- No ancestral 18
dustry. Then people had less time for self-   dyspepsia
ishness, coddling, and sickly after-dinner talk. The exact amount of food the stomach could digest was not 21
discussed according to Cutter nor referred to sanitary
laws. A man's belief in those days was not so severe
upon the gastric juices. Beaumont's "Medical Experi- 24
ments" did not govern the digestion.

Damp atmosphere and freezing snow empurpled the
plump cheeks of our ancestors, but they never indulged 27
in the refinement of inflamed bronchial tubes. Pulmonary
They were as innocent as Adam, before he ate   misbeliefs
the fruit of false knowledge, of the existence of tubercles 30
and troches, lungs and lozenges.

"Where ignorance is bliss, 't is folly to be wise," says

1 the English poet, and there is truth in his sentiment. The
action of mortal mind on the body was not so injurious
3   Our modern before inquisitive modern Eves took up the
    Eves study of medical works and unmanly Adams
attributed their own downfall and the fate of their off-
6 spring to the weakness of their wives.

The primitive custom of taking no thought about
food left the stomach and bowels free to act in obedi-
9 ence to nature, and gave the gospel a chance to be seen
in its glorious effects upon the body. A ghastly array of
diseases was not paraded before the imagination. There
12 were fewer books on digestion and more "sermons in
stones, and good in everything." When the mechanism
of the human mind gives place to the divine Mind, self-
15 ishness and sin, disease and death, will lose their
foothold.

Human fear of miasma would load with disease the
18 air of Eden, and weigh down mankind with superimposed
and conjectural evils. Mortal mind is the worst foe of
the body, while divine Mind is its best friend.
21 Should all cases of organic disease be treated by a
regular practitioner, and the Christian Scientist try
truth only in cases of hysteria, hypochon-
    Diseases
24   not to be dria, and hallucination? One disease is no
  classified more real than another. All disease is the
result of education, and disease can carry its ill-effects
27 no farther than mortal mind maps out the way. The
human mind, not matter, is supposed to feel, suffer, enjoy. Hence decided types of acute disease are quite as
30 ready to yield to Truth as the less distinct type and chronic
form of disease. Truth handles the most malignant contagion with perfect assurance.

Human mind produces what is termed organic dis- 1
ease as certainly as it produces hysteria, and it must relinquish all its errors, sicknesses, and sins. One basis for 3
I have demonstrated this beyond all cavil. all sickness
The evidence of divine Mind's healing power and absolute control is to me as certain as the evidence of my own 6
existence.

Mortal mind and body are one. Neither exists without
the other, and both must be destroyed by immortal Mind. 9
Matter, or body, is but a false concept of mor- Mental and
tal mind. This so-called mind builds its own physical
oneness
superstructure, of which the material body is 12
the grosser portion; but from first to last, the body is a
sensuous, human concept.

In the Scriptural allegory of the material creation, 15
Adam or error, which represents the erroneous theory
of life and intelligence in matter, had the The effect
naming of all that was material. These names of names 18
indicated matter's properties, qualities, and forms. But
a lie, the opposite of Truth, cannot name the qualities and
effects of what is termed matter, and create the so-called 21
laws of the flesh, nor can a lie hold the preponderance
of power in any direction against God, Spirit and
Truth. 24

If a dose of poison is swallowed through mistake, and
the patient dies even though physician and Poison
patient are expecting favorable results, does defined 27
mentally
human belief, you ask, cause this death? Even
so, and as directly as if the poison had been intentionally
taken. 30

In such cases a few persons believe the potion swallowed by the patient to be harmless, but the vast ma-

1 jority of mankind, though they know nothing of this particular case and this special person, believe the arsenic,
3 the strychnine, or whatever the drug used, to be poisonous, for it is set down as a poison by mortal mind.
Consequently, the result is controlled by the majority of
6 opinions, not by the infinitesimal minority of opinions in
the sick-chamber.

Heredity is not a law.   The remote cause or belief
9 of disease is not dangerous because of its priority and
the connection of past mortal thoughts with present.
The predisposing cause and the exciting cause are
12 mental.

Perhaps an adult has a deformity produced prior to his
birth by the fright of his mother.   When wrested from
15 human belief and based on Science or the divine Mind, to
which all things are possible, that chronic case is not
difficult to cure.

18 Mortal mind, acting from the basis of sensation in
matter, is animal magnetism; but this so-called mind,
from which comes all evil, contradicts itself,
Animal
21 magnetism and must finally yield to the eternal Truth, or
destroyed
the divine Mind, expressed in Science.   In proportion to our understanding of Christian Science, we are
24 freed from the belief of heredity, of mind in matter or animal magnetism; and we disarm sin of its imaginary power
in proportion to our spiritual understanding of the status
27 of immortal being.

Ignorant of the methods and the basis of metaphysical
healing, you may attempt to unite with it hypnotism,
30 spiritualism, electricity; but none of these methods can
be mingled with metaphysical healing.

Whoever reaches the understanding of Christian Science

in its proper signification will perform the sudden cures 1
of which it is capable; but this can be done only by
taking up the cross and following Christ in the daily 3
life.

Science can heal the sick, who are absent from their
healers, as well as those present, since space is no ob- 6
stacle to Mind. Immortal Mind heals what eye   Absent
hath not seen; but the spiritual capacity to ap-   patients
prehend thought and to heal by the Truth-power, is won 9
only as man is found, not in self-righteousness, but reflecting the divine nature.

Every medical method has its advocates. The prefer- 12
ence of mortal mind for a certain method creates a demand
for that method, and the body then seems to re-   Horses
quire such treatment. You can even educate a   mistaught 15
healthy horse so far in physiology that he will take cold
without his blanket, whereas the wild animal, left to his
instincts, sniffs the wind with delight. The epizoötic is 18
a humanly evolved ailment, which a wild horse might
never have.

Treatises on anatomy, physiology, and health, sustained 21
by what is termed material law, are the pro-   Medical works
moters of sickness and disease. It should not   objectionable
be proverbial, that so long as you read medical works you 24
will be sick.

The sedulous matron — studying her Jahr with homœopathic pellet and powder in hand, ready to put you 27
into a sweat, to move the bowels, or to produce sleep —
is unwittingly sowing the seeds of reliance on matter,
and her household may erelong reap the effect of this 30
mistake.

Descriptions of disease given by physicians and adver-

1 tisements of quackery are both prolific sources of sickness.
As mortal mind is the husbandman of error, it should be
3 taught to do the body no harm and to uproot its false
sowing.

The patient sufferer tries to be satisfied when he sees
6 his would-be healers busy, and his faith in their efforts is
The invalid's outlook somewhat helpful to them and to himself; but
in Science one must understand the resusci-
9 tating law of Life. This is the seed within itself bearing
fruit after its kind, spoken of in Genesis.

Physicians should not deport themselves as if Mind
12 were non-existent, nor take the ground that all causation
is matter, instead of Mind. Ignorant that the human
mind governs the body, its phenomenon, the invalid may
15 unwittingly add more fear to the mental reservoir already
overflowing with that emotion.

Doctors should not implant disease in the thoughts of
18 their patients, as they so frequently do, by declaring dis-
Wrong and right way ease to be a fixed fact, even before they go to
work to eradicate the disease through the ma-
21 terial faith which they inspire. Instead of furnishing
thought with fear, they should try to correct this turbulent
element of mortal mind by the influence of divine Love
24 which casteth out fear.

When man is governed by God, the ever-present
Mind who understands all things, man knows that with
27 God all things are possible. The only way to this
living Truth, which heals the sick, is found in the Science
of divine Mind as taught and demonstrated by Christ
30 Jesus.

To reduce inflammation, dissolve a tumor, or cure organic disease, I have found divine Truth more potent than

all lower remedies. And why not, since Mind, God, is 1
the source and condition of all existence? Before decid-
ing that the body, matter, is disordered, one   The 3
should ask, "Who art thou that repliest to important
decision
Spirit? Can matter speak for itself, or does
it hold the issues of life?" Matter, which can neither 6
suffer nor enjoy, has no partnership with pain and pleasure, but mortal belief has such a partnership.

When you manipulate patients, you trust in electricity 9
and magnetism more than in Truth; and for Manipulation
that reason, you employ matter rather than unscientific
Mind. You weaken or destroy your power when you re- 12
sort to any except spiritual means.

It is foolish to declare that you manipulate patients but
that you lay no stress on manipulation. If this be so, why 15
manipulate? In reality you manipulate because you are
ignorant of the baneful effects of magnetism, or are not
sufficiently spiritual to depend on Spirit. In either case 18
you must improve your mental condition till you finally
attain the understanding of Christian Science.

If you are too material to love the Science of Mind and 21
are satisfied with good words instead of effects, if you
adhere to error and are afraid to trust Truth, Not words
the question then recurs, "Adam, where art but deeds 24
thou?" It is unnecessary to resort to aught besides
Mind in order to satisfy the sick that you are doing something for them, for if they are cured, they generally know 27
it and are satisfied.

"Where your treasure is, there will your heart be also."
If you have more faith in drugs than in Truth, this faith 30
will incline you to the side of matter and error. Any
hypnotic power you may exercise will diminish your

1 ability to become a Scientist, and *vice versa*. The act
of healing the sick through divine Mind alone, of casting
3 out error with Truth, shows your position as a Christian
Scientist.

The demands of God appeal to thought only; but the
6 claims of mortality, and what are termed laws of nature,
Physiology   appertain to matter. Which, then, are we to
or Spirit   accept as legitimate and capable of producing
9 the highest human good? We cannot obey both physiology and Spirit, for one absolutely destroys the other,
and one or the other must be supreme in the affections.
12 It is impossible to work from two standpoints. If we
attempt it, we shall presently "hold to the one, and
despise the other."

15 The hypotheses of mortals are antagonistic to Science
and cannot mix with it. This is clear to those who heal
the sick on the basis of Science.

18 Mind's government of the body must supersede the so-
called laws of matter. Obedience to material law pre-
No   vents full obedience to spiritual law, — the law
21 material law   which overcomes material conditions and puts
matter under the feet of Mind. Mortals entreat the divine Mind to heal the sick, and forthwith shut out the aid
24 of Mind by using material means, thus working against
themselves and their prayers and denying man's God-
given ability to demonstrate Mind's sacred power. Pleas
27 for drugs and laws of health come from some sad incident,
or else from ignorance of Christian Science and its transcendent power.

30 To admit that sickness is a condition over which God
has no control, is to presuppose that omnipotent power
is powerless on some occasions. The law of Christ, or

Truth, makes all things possible to Spirit; but the so- 1
called laws of matter would render Spirit of no avail, and
demand obedience to materialistic codes, thus departing 3
from the basis of one God, one lawmaker. To suppose
that God constitutes laws of inharmony is a mistake; discords have no support from nature or divine law, however 6
much is said to the contrary.

Can the agriculturist, according to belief, produce a
crop without sowing the seed and awaiting its germina- 9
tion according to the laws of nature? The answer is no,
and yet the Scriptures inform us that sin, or error, first
caused the condemnation of man to till the ground, and 12
indicate that obedience to God will remove this necessity.
Truth never made error necessary, nor devised a law to
perpetuate error. 15

The supposed laws which result in weariness and disease are not His laws, for the legitimate and only possible
action of Truth is the production of harmony. Laws of 18
Laws of nature are laws of Spirit; but mortals nature spiritual
commonly recognize as law that which hides the power of
Spirit. Divine Mind rightly demands man's entire obe- 21
dience, affection, and strength. No reservation is made
for any lesser loyalty. Obedience to Truth gives man
power and strength. Submission to error superinduces 24
loss of power.

Truth casts out all evils and materialistic methods
with the actual spiritual law, — the law which gives 27
sight to the blind, hearing to the deaf, voice Belief
to the dumb, feet to the lame. If Christian and understanding
Science dishonors human belief, it honors spir- 30
itual understanding; and the one Mind only is entitled to
honor.

1 The so-called laws of health are simply laws of mortal belief. The premises being erroneous, the conclusions 3 are wrong. Truth makes no laws to regulate sickness, sin, and death, for these are unknown to Truth and should not be recognized as reality.

6 Belief produces the results of belief, and the penalties it affixes last so long as the belief and are inseparable from it. The remedy consists in probing the trouble 9 to the bottom, in finding and casting out by denial the error of belief which produces a mortal disorder, never honoring erroneous belief with the title of law nor yielding 12 obedience to it. Truth, Life, and Love are the only legitimate and eternal demands on man, and they are spiritual lawgivers, enforcing obedience through divine 15 statutes.

Controlled by the divine intelligence, man is harmonious and eternal. Whatever is governed by a false belief 18 *Laws of* is discordant and mortal. We say man suffers *human belief* from the effects of cold, heat, fatigue. This is human belief, not the truth of being, for matter cannot 21 suffer. Mortal mind alone suffers, — not because a law of matter has been transgressed, but because a law of this so-called mind has been disobeyed. I have demonstrated 24 this as a rule of divine Science by destroying the delusion of suffering from what is termed a fatally broken physical law.

27 A woman, whom I cured of consumption, always breathed with great difficulty when the wind was from the east. I sat silently by her side a few moments. Her 30 breath came gently. The inspirations were deep and natural. I then requested her to look at the weather-vane. She looked and saw that it pointed due east. The wind

had not changed, but her thought of it had and so her diffi- 1
culty in breathing had gone. The wind had not produced
the difficulty. My metaphysical treatment changed the 3
action of her belief on the lungs, and she never suffered
again from east winds, but was restored to health.

No system of hygiene but Christian Science is purely 6
mental. Before this book was published, other books
were in circulation, which discussed "mental A so-called
medicine" and "mind-cure," operating through mind-cure 9
the power of the earth's magnetic currents to regulate life
and health. Such theories and such systems of so-called
mind-cure, which have sprung up, are as material as the 12
prevailing systems of medicine. They have their birth
in mortal mind, which puts forth a human conception
in the name of Science to match the divine Science of im- 15
mortal Mind, even as the necromancers of Egypt strove
to emulate the wonders wrought by Moses. Such theories
have no relationship to Christian Science, which rests on 18
the conception of God as the only Life, substance, and
intelligence, and excludes the human mind as a spiritual
factor in the healing work. 21

Jesus cast out evil and healed the sick, not only without drugs, but without hypnotism, which is Jesus and
the reverse of ethical and pathological Truth- hypnotism 24
power.

Erroneous mental practice may seem for a time to benefit the sick, but the recovery is not permanent. This is 27
because erroneous methods act on and through the material stratum of the human mind, called brain, which is
but a mortal consolidation of material mentality and its 30
suppositional activities.

A patient under the influence of mortal mind is healed

1 only by removing the influence on him of this mind, by
False stimulus emptying his thought of the false stimulus
3 and reaction of will-power and filling it with
the divine energies of Truth.

Christian Science destroys material beliefs through the
6 understanding of Spirit, and the thoroughness of this work
determines health. Erring human mind-forces can work
only evil under whatever name or pretence they are em-
9 ployed; for Spirit and matter, good and evil, light and
darkness, cannot mingle.

Evil is a negation, because it is the absence of truth.
12 It is nothing, because it is the absence of something. It
Evil negative and self-destructive is unreal, because it presupposes the absence
of God, the omnipotent and omnipresent.
15 Every mortal must learn that there is neither
power nor reality in evil.

Evil is self-assertive. It says: "I am a real entity, over-
18 mastering good." This falsehood should strip evil of all
pretensions. The only power of evil is to destroy itself. It
can never destroy one iota of good. Every attempt of evil
21 to destroy good is a failure, and only aids in peremptorily
punishing the evil-doer. If we concede the same reality to
discord as to harmony, discord has as lasting a claim upon
24 us as has harmony. If evil is as real as good, evil is also as
immortal. If death is as real as Life, immortality is a myth.
If pain is as real as the absence of pain, both must be im-
27 mortal; and if so, harmony cannot be the law of being.

Mortal mind is ignorant of self, or it could never be
self-deceived. If mortal mind knew how to be better, it
30 Ignorant idolatry would be better. Since it must believe in something besides itself, it enthrones matter as deity.
The human mind has been an idolater from the beginning,

having other gods and believing in more than the one 1
Mind.

As mortals do not comprehend even mortal existence, 3
how ignorant must they be of the all-knowing Mind and
of His creations.

Here you may see how so-called material sense creates 6
its own forms of thought, gives them material names, and
then worships and fears them. With pagan blindness,
it attributes to some material god or medicine an ability 9
beyond itself. The beliefs of the human mind rob and
enslave it, and then impute this result to another illusive
personification, named Satan. 12

The valves of the heart, opening and closing for the passage of the blood, obey the mandate of mor- Action of
tal mind as directly as does the hand, ad- mortal mind 15
mittedly moved by the will. Anatomy allows the mental
cause of the latter action, but not of the former.

We say, "My hand hath done it." What is this *my* but 18
mortal mind, the cause of all materialistic action? All
voluntary, as well as miscalled *involuntary*, action of the
mortal body is governed by this so-called mind, not by 21
matter. There is no involuntary action. The divine Mind
includes all action and volition, and man in Science is governed by this Mind. The human mind tries to classify 24
action as voluntary and involuntary, and suffers from the
attempt.

If you take away this erring mind, the mortal material 27
body loses all appearance of life or action, and this so-
called mind then calls itself dead; but the hu- Death and
man mind still holds in belief a body, through the body 30
which it acts and which appears to the human mind to
live, — a body like the one it had before death. This body

1 is put off only as the mortal, erring mind yields to God,
immortal Mind, and man is found in His image.

3   What is termed disease does not exist. It is neither
mind nor matter. The belief of sin, which has grown

Embryonic
sinful
thoughts

terrible in strength and influence, is an uncon-
6   scious error in the beginning, — an embryonic
thought without motive; but afterwards it
governs the so-called man. Passion, depraved appetites,
9 dishonesty, envy, hatred, revenge ripen into action, only to
pass from shame and woe to their final punishment.

Mortal existence is a dream of pain and pleasure in
12 matter, a dream of sin, sickness, and death; and it is like

Disease
a dream

the dream we have in sleep, in which every one
recognizes his condition to be wholly a state of
15 mind. In both the waking and the sleeping dream, the
dreamer thinks that his body is material and the suffering
is in that body.

18   The smile of the sleeper indicates the sensation produced physically by the pleasure of a dream. In the
same way pain and pleasure, sickness and care, are
21 traced upon mortals by unmistakable signs.

Sickness is a growth of error, springing from mortal
ignorance or fear. Error rehearses error. What causes
24 disease cannot cure it. The soil of disease is mortal
mind, and you have an abundant or scanty crop of disease,
according to the seedlings of fear. Sin and the fear of
27 disease must be uprooted and cast out.

When darkness comes over the earth, the physical

Sense
yields to
understanding

senses have no immediate evidence of a sun.
30   The human eye knows not where the orb of
day is, nor if it exists. Astronomy gives the
desired information regarding the sun. The human or

material senses yield to the authority of this science, and 1
they are willing to leave with astronomy the explanation of
the sun's influence over the earth. If the eyes see no sun 3
for a week, we still believe that there is solar light and
heat. Science (in this instance named natural) raises
the human thought above the cruder theories of the 6
human mind, and casts out a fear.

In like manner mortals should no more deny the power
of Christian Science to establish harmony and to explain 9
the effect of mortal mind on the body, though the cause
be unseen, than they should deny the existence of the sunlight when the orb of day disappears, or doubt that the sun 12
will reappear. The sins of others should not make good
men suffer.

We call the body material; but it is as truly mortal 15
mind, according to its degree, as is the material brain
which is supposed to furnish the evidence Ascending
of all mortal thought or things. The human the scale 18
mortal mind, by an inevitable perversion, makes all
things start from the lowest instead of from the highest
mortal thought. The reverse is the case with all the 21
formations of the immortal divine Mind. They proceed
from the divine source; and so, in tracing them, we constantly ascend in infinite being.   24

From mortal mind comes the reproduction of the
species, — first the belief of inanimate, and then of animate matter. According to mortal thought, Human 27
the development of embryonic mortal mind reproduction
commences in the lower, basal portion of the brain, and
goes on in an ascending scale by evolution, keeping always 30
in the direct line of matter, for matter is the subjective
condition of mortal mind.

1 Next we have the formation of so-called embryonic
mortal mind, afterwards mortal men or mortals, — all this
3 while matter is a belief, ignorant of itself, ignorant of what
it is supposed to produce. The mortal says that an inanimate unconscious seedling is producing mortals, both body
6 and mind; and yet neither a mortal mind nor the immortal
Mind is found in brain or elsewhere in matter or in mortals.
This embryonic and materialistic human belief called
9   Human   mortal man in turn fills itself with thoughts
        stature   of pain and pleasure, of life and death, and
arranges itself into five so-called senses, which presently
12 measure mind by the size of a brain and the bulk of a
body, called man.

Human birth, growth, maturity, and decay are as the
15 grass springing from the soil with beautiful green blades,
        Human   afterwards to wither and return to its native
        frailty   nothingness. This mortal seeming is temporal;
18 it never merges into immortal being, but finally disappears, and immortal man, spiritual and eternal, is found
to be the real man.

21 The Hebrew bard, swayed by mortal thoughts, thus
swept his lyre with saddening strains on human existence:

As for man, his days are as grass:
24   As a flower of the field, so he flourisheth.
For the wind passeth over it, and it is gone;
And the place thereof shall know it no more.

27 When hope rose higher in the human heart, he sang:

As for me, I will behold Thy face in righteousness:
I shall be satisfied, when I awake, with Thy likeness.
.   .   .   .
30   For with Thee is the fountain of life;
In Thy light shall we see light.

The brain can give no idea of God's man. It can take 1
no cognizance of Mind. Matter is not the organ of infinite Mind.   3

As mortals give up the delusion that there is more than
one Mind, more than one God, man in God's likeness will
appear, and this eternal man will include in that likeness 6
no material element.

As a material, theoretical life-basis is found to be a
misapprehension of existence, the spiritual and divine 9
Principle of man dawns upon human thought, The immortal
and leads it to "where the young child was,"   birth
— even to the birth of a new-old idea, to the spiritual 12
sense of being and of what Life includes. Thus the whole
earth will be transformed by Truth on its pinions of light,
chasing away the darkness of error.   15

The human thought must free itself from self-imposed
materiality and bondage. It should no longer   Spiritual
ask of the head, heart, or lungs: What are   freedom   18
man's prospects for life? Mind is not helpless. Intelligence is not mute before non-intelligence.

By its own volition, not a blade of grass springs up, not 21
a spray buds within the vale, not a leaf unfolds its fair
outlines, not a flower starts from its cloistered cell.

The Science of being reveals man and immortality as 24
based on Spirit. Physical sense defines mortal man as
based on matter, and from this premise infers the mortality of the body.   27

The illusive senses may fancy affinities with their opposites; but in Christian Science, Truth never mingles
with error. Mind has no affinity with matter, No physical 30
and therefore Truth is able to cast out the ills   affinity
of the flesh. Mind, God, sends forth the aroma of Spirit,

1 the atmosphere of intelligence. The belief that a pulpy
substance under the skull is mind is a mockery of intelli-
3 gence, a mimicry of Mind.

We are Christian Scientists, only as we quit our reliance
upon that which is false and grasp the true. We are not
6 Christian Scientists until we leave all for Christ. Human
opinions are not spiritual. They come from the hearing
of the ear, from corporeality instead of from Principle,
9 and from the mortal instead of from the immortal. Spirit
is not separate from God. Spirit *is* God.

Erring power is a material belief, a blind miscalled force,
12 the offspring of will and not of wisdom, of the mortal mind

Human power and not of the immortal. It is the headlong

a blind force cataract, the devouring flame, the tempest's
15 breath. It is lightning and hurricane, all that is selfish,
wicked, dishonest, and impure.

Moral and spiritual might belong to Spirit, who holds
18 the "wind in His fists;" and this teaching accords with

The one Science and harmony. In Science, you can

real power have no power opposed to God, and the physi-
21 cal senses must give up their false testimony. Your influence for good depends upon the weight you throw into
the right scale. The good you do and embody gives you
24 the only power obtainable. Evil is not power. It is a
mockery of strength, which erelong betrays its weakness
and falls, never to rise.

27 We walk in the footsteps of Truth and Love by following the example of our Master in the understanding of
divine metaphysics. Christianity is the basis of true heal-
30 ing. Whatever holds human thought in line with unselfed
love, receives directly the divine power.

I was called to visit Mr. Clark in Lynn, who had been

confined to his bed six months with hip-disease, caused by 1
a fall upon a wooden spike when quite a boy. On entering the house I met his physician, who said that Mind cures 3
the patient was dying. The physician had just hip-disease
probed the ulcer on the hip, and said the bone was carious
for several inches. He even showed me the probe, which 6
had on it the evidence of this condition of the bone. The
doctor went out. Mr. Clark lay with his eyes fixed and
sightless. The dew of death was on his brow. I went to 9
his bedside. In a few moments his face changed; its
death-pallor gave place to a natural hue. The eyelids
closed gently and the breathing became natural; he was 12
asleep. In about ten minutes he opened his eyes and
said: "I feel like a new man. My suffering is all gone."
It was between three and four o'clock in the afternoon 15
when this took place.

I told him to rise, dress himself, and take supper with
his family. He did so. The next day I saw him in the 18
yard. Since then I have not seen him, but am informed
that he went to work in two weeks. The discharge from
the sore stopped, and the sore was healed. The diseased 21
condition had continued there ever since the injury was
received in boyhood.

Since his recovery I have been informed that his physi- 24
cian claims to have cured him, and that his mother has
been threatened with incarceration in an insane asylum
for saying: "It was none other than God and that woman 27
who healed him." I cannot attest the truth of that
report, but what I saw and did for that man, and what
his physician said of the case, occurred just as I have 30
narrated.

It has been demonstrated to me that Life is God.

1 and that the might of omnipotent Spirit shares not its
strength with matter or with human will. Review-
3 ing this brief experience, I cannot fail to discern the
coincidence of the spiritual idea of man with the divine
Mind.

6   A change in human belief changes all the physical symp-
Change of   toms, and determines a case for better or for
belief   worse. When one's false belief is corrected,
9 Truth sends a report of health over the body.

Destruction of the auditory nerve and paralysis of the
optic nerve are not necessary to ensure deafness and blind-
12 ness; for if mortal mind says, "I am deaf and blind," it
will be so without an injured nerve. Every theory opposed to this fact (as I learned in metaphysics) would
15 presuppose man, who is immortal in spiritual understanding, a mortal in material belief.

The authentic history of Kaspar Hauser is a useful hint
18 as to the frailty and inadequacy of mortal mind. It
Power of   proves beyond a doubt that education consti-
habit   tutes this so-called mind, and that, in turn,
21 mortal mind manifests itself in the body by the false
sense it imparts. Incarcerated in a dungeon, where
neither sight nor sound could reach him, at the age of
24 seventeen Kaspar was still a mental infant, crying and
chattering with no more intelligence than a babe, and
realizing Tennyson's description:

27   An infant crying in the night,
              An infant crying for the light,
              And with no language but a cry.

30   His case proves material sense to be but a belief formed
by education alone. The light which affords us joy gave

him a belief of intense pain. His eyes were inflamed by 1
the light. After the babbling boy had been taught to
speak a few words, he asked to be taken back to his dun- 3
geon, and said that he should never be happy elsewhere.
Outside of dismal darkness and cold silence he found no
peace. Every sound convulsed him with anguish. All 6
that he ate, except his black crust, produced violent
retchings. All that gives pleasure to our educated senses
gave him pain through those very senses, trained in an 9
opposite direction.

The point for each one to decide is, whether it is mortal
mind or immortal Mind that is causative. We   Useful   12
should forsake the basis of matter for meta-   knowledge
physical Science and its divine Principle.

Whatever furnishes the semblance of an idea governed 15
by its Principle, furnishes food for thought. Through astronomy, natural history, chemistry, music, mathematics,
thought passes naturally from effect back to cause.   18

Academics of the right sort are requisite. Observation, invention, study, and original thought are expansive
and should promote the growth of mortal mind out of it- 21
self, out of all that is mortal.

It is the tangled barbarisms of learning which we
deplore, — the mere dogma, the speculative theory, the 24
nauseous fiction. Novels, remarkable only for their
exaggerated pictures, impossible ideals, and specimens
of depravity, fill our young readers with wrong tastes 27
and sentiments. Literary commercialism is lowering the
intellectual standard to accommodate the purse and to
meet a frivolous demand for amusement instead of for 30
improvement. Incorrect views lower the standard of
truth.

1   If materialistic knowledge is power, it is not wisdom.
It is but a blind force. Man has "sought out many inven-
3 tions," but he has not yet found it true that knowledge can
save him from the dire effects of knowledge. The power
of mortal mind over its own body is little understood.

6   Better the suffering which awakens mortal mind from
its fleshly dream, than the false pleasures
Sin destroyed
through   which tend to perpetuate this dream. Sin
suffering
9   alone brings death, for sin is the only element
of destruction.

"Fear him which is able to destroy both soul and body
12 in hell," said Jesus. A careful study of this text shows
that here the word *soul* means a false sense or material
consciousness. The command was a warning to beware,
15 not of Rome, Satan, nor of God, but of sin. Sickness,
sin, and death are not concomitants of Life or Truth.
No law supports them. They have no relation to God
18 wherewith to establish their power. Sin makes its own
hell, and goodness its own heaven.

Such books as will rule disease out of mortal mind, —
21   and so efface the images and thoughts of dis-
Dangerous
shoals   ease, instead of impressing them with forcible
avoided
descriptions and medical details, — will help
24 to abate sickness and to destroy it.

Many a hopeless case of disease is induced by a single
post mortem examination, — not from infection nor from
27 contact with material virus, but from the fear of the
disease and from the image brought before the mind; it
is a mental state, which is afterwards outlined on the
30 body.

The press unwittingly sends forth many sorrows and
diseases among the human family. It does this by giv-

ing names to diseases and by printing long descriptions 1
which mirror images of disease distinctly in thought. A
new name for an ailment affects people like a 3
Parisian name for a novel garment. Every one
hastens to get it. A minutely described disease costs many a man his earthly days of comfort. What 6
a price for human knowledge! But the price does not exceed the original cost. God said of the tree of knowledge,
which bears the fruit of sin, disease, and death, "In the 9
day that thou eatest thereof thou shalt surely die."

The less that is said of physical structure and laws, and
the more that is thought and said about moral 12
and spiritual law, the higher will be the standard of living and the farther mortals will be removed from imbecility or disease. 15

We should master fear, instead of cultivating it. It
was the ignorance of our forefathers in the departments
of knowledge now broadcast in the earth, that made them 18
hardier than our trained physiologists, more honest than
our sleek politicians.

We are told that the simple food our forefathers ate 21
helped to make them healthy, but that is a mistake.
Their diet would not cure dyspepsia at this
period. With rules of health in the head 24
and the most digestible food in the stomach, there would
still be dyspeptics. Many of the effeminate constitutions
of our time will never grow robust until individual opin- 27
ions improve and mortal belief loses some portion of its
error.

The doctor's mind reaches that of his patient. The 30
doctor should suppress his fear of disease, else his belief
in its reality and fatality will harm his patients even more

Marginal notes:
Pangs caused by the press

Higher standard for mortals

Diet and dyspepsia

1 than his calomel and morphine, for the higher stratum of
mortal mind has in belief more power to harm man than
3 Harm done the substratum, matter. A patient hears the
by physicians doctor's verdict as a criminal hears his death-
sentence. The patient may seem calm under it, but he is
6 not. His fortitude may sustain him, but his fear, which
has already developed the disease that is gaining the
mastery, is increased by the physician's words.

9 The materialistic doctor, though humane, is an artist who outlines his thought relative to disease, and then
Disease fills in his delineations with sketches from text-
12 depicted books. It is better to prevent disease from
forming in mortal mind afterwards to appear on the
body; but to do this requires attention. The thought of
15 disease is formed before one sees a doctor and before
the doctor undertakes to dispel it by a counter-irritant,
— perhaps by a blister, by the application of caustic or
18 croton oil, or by a surgical operation. Again, giving another direction to faith, the physician prescribes drugs,
until the elasticity of mortal thought haply causes a
21 vigorous reaction upon itself, and reproduces a picture
of healthy and harmonious formations.

A patient's belief is more or less moulded and formed
24 by his doctor's belief in the case, even though the doctor
says nothing to support his theory. His thoughts and his
patient's commingle, and the stronger thoughts rule the
27 weaker. Hence the importance that doctors be Christian
Scientists.

Because the muscles of the blacksmith's arm are
30 Mind over strongly developed, it does not follow that
matter exercise has produced this result or that a
less used arm must be weak. If matter were the cause

of action, and if muscles, without volition of mortal 1
mind, could lift the hammer and strike the anvil, it
might be thought true that hammering would enlarge 3
the muscles. The trip-hammer is not increased in size
by exercise. Why not, since muscles are as material as
wood and iron? Because nobody believes that mind is 6
producing such a result on the hammer.

Muscles are not self-acting. If mind does not move
them, they are motionless. Hence the great fact that 9
Mind alone enlarges and empowers man through its
mandate, — by reason of its demand for and supply of
power. Not because of muscular exercise, but by rea- 12
son of the blacksmith's faith in exercise, his arm becomes
stronger.

Mortals develop their own bodies or make them sick, 15
according as they influence them through mortal mind.
To know whether this development is produced Latent fear
consciously or unconsciously, is of less impor- subdued 18
tance than a knowledge of the fact. The feats of the gym-
nast prove that latent mental fears are subdued by him.
The devotion of thought to an honest achievement makes 21
the achievement possible. Exceptions only confirm this
rule, proving that failure is occasioned by a too feeble
faith. 24

Had Blondin believed it impossible to walk the rope
over Niagara's abyss of waters, he could never have
done it. His belief that he could do it gave his thought- 27
forces, called muscles, their flexibility and power which
the unscientific might attribute to a lubricating oil. His
fear must have disappeared before his power of putting 30
resolve into action could appear.

When Homer sang of the Grecian gods, Olympus was

1 dark, but through his verse the gods became alive in a
nation's belief. Pagan worship began with muscularity,
3   Homer and   but the law of Sinai lifted thought into the
     Moses   song of David. Moses advanced a nation to
the worship of God in Spirit instead of matter, and il-
6 lustrated the grand human capacities of being bestowed
by immortal Mind.

Whoever is incompetent to explain Soul would be wise
9 not to undertake the explanation of body. Life is, always
     A mortal   has been, and ever will be independent of
     not man   matter; for Life is God, and man is the idea
12 of God, not formed materially but spiritually, and not
subject to decay and dust. The Psalmist said: "Thou
madest him to have dominion over the works of Thy
15 hands. Thou hast put all things under his feet."

The great truth in the Science of being, that the real
man was, is, and ever shall be perfect, is incontrovertible;
18 for if man is the image, reflection, of God, he is neither
inverted nor subverted, but upright and Godlike.

The suppositional antipode of divine infinite Spirit
21 is the so-called human soul or spirit, in other words
the five senses, — the flesh that warreth against Spirit.
These so-called material senses must yield to the infinite
24 Spirit, named God.

St. Paul said: "For I determined not to know anything among you, save Jesus Christ, and him crucified."
27 (I Cor. ii. 2.) Christian Science says: I am determined
not to know anything among you, save Jesus Christ, and
him glorified.

CHAPTER VIII

Footsteps of Truth

Remember, Lord, the reproach of Thy servants; how I do bear in my
bosom the reproach of all the mighty people; wherewith Thine enemies
have reproached, O Lord; wherewith they have reproached the footsteps
of Thine anointed. — PSALMS.

THE best sermon ever preached is Truth practised 1
and demonstrated by the destruction of sin, sickness,
and death. Knowing this and knowing too   Practical   3
that one affection would be supreme in us and   preaching
take the lead in our lives, Jesus said, "No man can serve
two masters."   6
We cannot build safely on false foundations. Truth
makes a new creature, in whom old things pass away
and "all things are become new." Passions, selfishness, 9
false appetites, hatred, fear, all sensuality, yield to spirituality, and the superabundance of being is on the side
of God, good.   12
We cannot fill vessels already full. They must first be
emptied. Let us disrobe error. Then, when   The uses
the winds of God blow, we shall not hug our   of truth   15
tatters close about us.
The way to extract error from mortal mind is to pour
in truth through flood-tides of Love. Christian perfec- 18
tion is won on no other basis.
Grafting holiness upon unholiness, supposing that sin

201

1 can be forgiven when it is not forsaken, is as foolish as
straining out gnats and swallowing camels.

3   The scientific unity which exists between God and man
must be wrought out in life-practice, and God's will must
be universally done.

6   If men would bring to bear upon the study of the
Science of Mind half the faith they bestow upon the so-

Divine   called pains and pleasures of material sense,
9   study   they would not go on from bad to worse,
until disciplined by the prison and the scaffold; but
the whole human family would be redeemed through
12 the merits of Christ, — through the perception and acceptance of Truth. For this glorious result Christian
Science lights the torch of spiritual understanding.

15   Outside of this Science all is mutable; but immortal
man, in accord with the divine Principle of his being,

Harmonious   God, neither sins, suffers, nor dies. The days
18   life-work   of our pilgrimage will multiply instead of diminish, when God's kingdom comes on earth; for the
true way leads to Life instead of to death, and earthly
21 experience discloses the finity of error and the infinite
capacities of Truth, in which God gives man dominion
over all the earth.

24   Our beliefs about a Supreme Being contradict the
practice growing out of them. Error abounds where

Belief and   Truth should "much more abound." We
27   practice   admit that God has almighty power, is "a
very present help in trouble;" and yet we rely on a drug
or hypnotism to heal disease, as if senseless matter or err-
30 ing mortal mind had more power than omnipotent Spirit.

   Common opinion admits that a man may take cold in
the act of doing good, and that this cold may produce

fatal pulmonary disease; as though evil could overbear 1
the law of Love, and check the reward for do-
ing good. In the Science of Christianity, Mind   **Sure
reward of**   3
— omnipotence — has all-power, assigns sure   **righteousness**
rewards to righteousness, and shows that matter can
neither heal nor make sick, create nor destroy.   6

If God were understood instead of being merely believed, this understanding would establish health. The
accusation of the rabbis, "He made himself   9
the Son of God," was really the justification   **Our
belief and
understanding**
of Jesus, for to the Christian the only true
spirit is Godlike. This thought incites to a more exalted 12
worship and self-abnegation. Spiritual perception brings
out the possibilities of being, destroys reliance on aught
but God, and so makes man the image of his Maker in 15
deed and in truth.

We are prone to believe either in more than one Supreme Ruler or in some power less than God. We im- 18
agine that Mind can be imprisoned in a sensuous body.
When the material body has gone to ruin, when evil has
overtaxed the belief of life in matter and destroyed it, 21
then mortals believe that the deathless Principle, or
Soul, escapes from matter and lives on; but this is not
true. Death is not a stepping-stone to Life, immortality, 24
and bliss. The so-called sinner is a suicide.   **Suicide
and sin**
Sin kills the sinner and will continue to kill
him so long as he sins. The foam and fury of illegiti- 27
mate living and of fearful and doleful dying should
disappear on the shore of time; then the waves of sin,
sorrow, and death beat in vain.   30

God, divine good, does not kill a man in order to give
him eternal Life, for God alone is man's life. God is at

1 once the centre and circumference of being. It is evil
that dies; good dies not.

3   All forms of error support the false conclusions that
there is more than one Life; that material history is as
real and living as spiritual history; that mortal
Spirit the only
6   intelligence error is as conclusively mental as immortal
and substance
Truth; and that there are two separate, antagonistic entities and beings, two powers, — namely,
9 Spirit and matter, — resulting in a third person (mortal
man) who carries out the delusions of sin, sickness, and
death.

12   The first power is admitted to be good, an intelligence or
Mind called God. The so-called second power, evil, is the
unlikeness of good. It cannot therefore be mind, though
15 so called. The third power, mortal man, is a supposed
mixture of the first and second antagonistic powers, intelligence and non-intelligence, of Spirit and matter.

18   Such theories are evidently erroneous. They can never
stand the test of Science. Judging them by their fruits,
Unscientific they are corrupt. When will the ages under-
21   theories   stand the Ego, and realize only one God, one
Mind or intelligence?

False and self-assertive theories have given sinners the
24 notion that they can create what God cannot, — namely,
sinful mortals in God's image, thus usurping the name
without the nature of the image or reflection of divine
27 Mind; but in Science it can never be said that man
has a mind of his own, distinct from God, the all
Mind.

30   The belief that God lives in matter is pantheistic. The
error, which says that Soul is in body, Mind is in matter,
and good is in evil, must unsay it and cease from such

utterances; else God will continue to be hidden from hu- 1
manity, and mortals will sin without knowing that they
are sinning, will lean on matter instead of Spirit, stumble 3
with lameness, drop with drunkenness, consume with disease, — all because of their blindness, their false sense
concerning God and man. 6

When will the error of believing that there is life in
matter, and that sin, sickness, and death are creations of
God, be unmasked? When will it be under- Creation 9
stood that matter has neither intelligence, life, perfect
nor sensation, and that the opposite belief is the prolific
source of all suffering? God created all through Mind, 12
and made all perfect and eternal. Where then is the
necessity for recreation or procreation?

Befogged in error (the error of believing that matter 15
can be intelligent for good or evil), we can catch clear
glimpses of God only as the mists disperse,
or as they melt into such thinness that we per- Perceiving the divine 18
ceive the divine image in some word or deed image
which indicates the true idea, — the supremacy and reality of good, the nothingness and unreality of evil. 21

When we realize that there is one Mind, the divine law
of loving our neighbor as ourselves is unfolded;
whereas a belief in many ruling minds hinders Redemption from 24
man's normal drift towards the one Mind, one selfishness
God, and leads human thought into opposite channels
where selfishness reigns. 27

Selfishness tips the beam of human existence towards
the side of error, not towards Truth. Denial of the oneness of Mind throws our weight into the scale, not of 30
Spirit, God, good, but of matter.

When we fully understand our relation to the Divine,

1 we can have no other Mind but His, — no other Love,
wisdom, or Truth, no other sense of Life, and no con-
3 sciousness of the existence of matter or error.

The power of the human will should be exercised only
in subordination to Truth; else it will misguide the judg-

6   Will-power   ment and free the lower propensities. It is the
  unrighteous   province of spiritual sense to govern man.
Material, erring, human thought acts injuriously both
9 upon the body and through it.

Will-power is capable of all evil. It can never heal
the sick, for it is the prayer of the unrighteous; while
12 the exercise of the sentiments — hope, faith, love — is the
prayer of the righteous. This prayer, governed by Science
instead of the senses, heals the sick.

15   In the scientific relation of God to man, we find that
whatever blesses one blesses all, as Jesus showed with
the loaves and the fishes, — Spirit, not matter, being the
18 source of supply.

Does God send sickness, giving the mother her child
for the brief space of a few years and then taking it away
21   Birth and   by death? Is God creating anew what He
  death unreal   has already created? The Scriptures are definite on this point, declaring that His work was *finished*,
24 nothing is new to God, and that it was *good*.

Can there be any birth or death for man, the spiritual
image and likeness of God? Instead of God sending
27 sickness and death, He destroys them, and brings to light
immortality. Omnipotent and infinite Mind made all
and includes all. This Mind does not make mistakes
30 and subsequently correct them. God does not cause man
to sin, to be sick, or to die.

There are evil beliefs, often called evil spirits; but

these evils are not Spirit, for there is no evil in Spirit. 1
Because God is Spirit, evil becomes more apparent and
obnoxious proportionately as we advance spir-   No evil   3
itually, until it disappears from our lives.   in Spirit
This fact proves our position, for every scientific statement in Christianity has its proof. Error of statement 6
leads to error in action.

God is not the creator of an evil mind. Indeed, evil
is not Mind. We must learn that evil is the awful decep- 9
tion and unreality of existence. Evil is not Subordination
supreme; good is not helpless; nor are the   of evil
so-called laws of matter primary, and the law of Spirit 12
secondary. Without this lesson, we lose sight of the perfect Father, or the divine Principle of man.

Body is not first and Soul last, nor is evil mightier than 15
good. The Science of being repudiates self-   Evident
evident impossibilities, such as the amalgama- impossibilities
tion of Truth and error in cause or effect. Science sepa- 18
rates the tares and wheat in time of harvest.

There is but one primal cause. Therefore there can
be no effect from any other cause, and there can be no 21
reality in aught which does not proceed from   One primal
this great and only cause. Sin, sickness, dis-   cause
ease, and death belong not to the Science of being. They 24
are the errors, which presuppose the absence of Truth,
Life, or Love.

The spiritual reality is the scientific fact in all things. 27
The spiritual fact, repeated in the action of man and the
whole universe, is harmonious and is the ideal of Truth.
Spiritual facts are not inverted; the opposite discord, 30
which bears no resemblance to spirituality, is not real.
The only evidence of this inversion is obtained from

1 suppositional error, which affords no proof of God,
Spirit, or of the spiritual creation. Material sense de-
3 fines all things materially, and has a finite sense of the
infinite.

The Scriptures say, "In Him we live, and move, and
6 have our being." What then is this seeming power, independent of God, which causes disease and
Seemingly independent authority cures it? What is it but an error of belief, —
9 a law of mortal mind, wrong in every sense,
embracing sin, sickness, and death? It is the very antipode of immortal Mind, of Truth, and of spiritual law.
12 It is not in accordance with the goodness of God's character that He should make man sick, then leave man to
heal himself; it is absurd to suppose that matter can both
15 cause and cure disease, or that Spirit, God, produces
disease and leaves the remedy to matter.

John Young of Edinburgh writes: "God is the father
18 of mind, and of nothing else." Such an utterance is
"the voice of one crying in the wilderness" of human
beliefs and preparing the way of Science. Let us learn
21 of the real and eternal, and prepare for the reign of
Spirit, the kingdom of heaven, — the reign and rule of
universal harmony, which cannot be lost nor remain
24 forever unseen.

Mind, not matter, is causation. A material body
only expresses a material and mortal mind. A mortal
27 Sickness as only thought man possesses this body, and he makes it
harmonious or discordant according to the
images of thought impressed upon it. You embrace
30 your body in your thought, and you should delineate
upon it thoughts of health, not of sickness. You should
banish all thoughts of disease and sin and of other beliefs

included in matter. Man, being immortal, has a perfect 1
indestructible life. It is the mortal belief which makes
the body discordant and diseased in proportion as igno- 3
rance, *fear,* or human will governs mortals.

Mind, supreme over all its formations and governing
them all, is the central sun of its own systems of ideas, 6
the life and light of all its own vast creation;   Allness of
and man is tributary to divine Mind.√ The   Truth
material and mortal body or mind is not the man.   9

The world would collapse without Mind, without the intelligence which holds the winds in its grasp. Neither
philosophy nor skepticism can hinder the march of the 12
Science which reveals the supremacy of Mind. The immanent sense of Mind-power enhances the glory of Mind.
Nearness, not distance, lends enchantment to this view. 15

The compounded minerals or aggregated substances
composing the earth, the relations which constituent
masses hold to each other, the magnitudes,   Spiritual 18
distances, and revolutions of the celestial   translation
bodies, are of no real importance, when we remember
that they all must give place to the spiritual fact by the 21
translation of man and the universe back into Spirit. In
proportion as this is done, man and the universe will be
found harmonious and eternal.   24

Material substances or mundane formations, astronomical calculations, and all the paraphernalia of speculative theories, based on the hypothesis of material law 27
or life and intelligence resident in matter, will ultimately vanish, swallowed up in the infinite calculus of
Spirit.   30

Spiritual sense is a conscious, constant capacity to understand God. It shows the superiority of faith by works

1 over faith in words. Its ideas are expressed only in "new
tongues;" and these are interpreted by the translation of
3 the spiritual original into the language which human
thought can comprehend.

The Principle and proof of Christianity are discerned
6 by spiritual sense. They are set forth in Jesus' demonstrations, which show — by his healing the
sick, casting out evils, and destroying death,
9 "the last enemy that shall be destroyed," —
his disregard of matter and its so-called laws.

*Jesus'
disregard
of matter*

Knowing that Soul and its attributes were forever
12 manifested through man, the Master healed the sick,
gave sight to the blind, hearing to the deaf, feet to the
lame, thus bringing to light the scientific action of the
15 divine Mind on human minds and bodies and giving
a better understanding of Soul and salvation. Jesus
healed sickness and sin by one and the same metaphysical
18 process.

The expression *mortal mind* is really a solecism, for
Mind is immortal, and Truth pierces the error of mortality
21 as a sunbeam penetrates the cloud. Because,
in obedience to the immutable law of Spirit,
this so-called mind is self-destructive, I name it mortal.
24 Error soweth the wind and reapeth the whirlwind.

*Mind not
mortal*

What is termed matter, being unintelligent, cannot say,
"I suffer, I die, I am sick, or I am well." It is the so-
27 called mortal mind which voices this and appears to itself to make good its claim. To
mortal sense, sin and suffering are real, but immortal
30 sense includes no evil nor pestilence. Because immortal
sense has no error of sense, it has no sense of error; therefore it is without a destructive element.

*Matter
mindless*

If brain, nerves, stomach, are intelligent, — if they talk 1
to us, tell us their condition, and report how they feel, —
then Spirit and matter, Truth and error, commingle 3
and produce sickness and health, good and evil, life and
death; and who shall say whether Truth or error is the
greater?   6

The sensations of the body must either be the sensations of a so-called mortal mind or of matter. Nerves
are not mind. Is it not provable that Mind is   Matter   9
not *mortal* and that matter has no sensation? sensationless
Is it not equally true that matter does not appear in the
spiritual understanding of being?   12

The sensation of sickness and the impulse to sin seem
to obtain in mortal mind. When a tear starts, does not
this so-called mind produce the effect seen in the lachry- 15
mal gland? Without mortal mind, the tear could not
appear; and this action shows the nature of all so-called
material cause and effect.   18

It should no longer be said in Israel that "the fathers
have eaten sour grapes, and the children's teeth are set
on edge." Sympathy with error should disappear. The 21
transfer of the thoughts of one erring mind to another,
Science renders impossible.

If it is true that nerves have sensation, that matter has 24
intelligence, that the material organism causes the eyes to
see and the ears to hear, then, when the body   Nerves
is dematerialized, these faculties must be lost,   painless   27
for their immortality is not in Spirit; whereas the fact
is that only through dematerialization and spiritualization of thought can these faculties be conceived of as 30
immortal.

Nerves are not the source of pain or pleasure. We

1 suffer or enjoy in our dreams, but this pain or pleasure
is not communicated through a nerve. A tooth which has
3 been extracted sometimes aches again in belief, and the
pain seems to be in its old place. A limb which has been
amputated has continued in belief to pain the owner. If
6 the sensation of pain in the limb can return, can be prolonged, why cannot the limb reappear?

Why need pain, rather than pleasure, come to this mor-
9 tal sense? Because the memory of pain is more vivid
than the memory of pleasure. I have seen an unwitting
attempt to scratch the end of a finger which had been cut
12 off for months. When the nerve is gone, which we say
was the occasion of pain, and the pain still remains, it
proves sensation to be in the mortal mind, not in matter.
15 Reverse the process; take away this so-called mind instead
of a piece of the flesh, and the nerves have no sensation.

Mortals have a modus of their own, undirected and un-
18 sustained by God. They produce a rose through seed and

Human
falsities

soil, and bring the rose into contact with the
olfactory nerves that they may smell it. In
21 legerdemain and credulous frenzy, mortals believe that
unseen spirits produce the flowers. God alone makes
and clothes the lilies of the field, and this He does by
24 means of Mind, not matter.

Because all the methods of Mind are not understood,
we say the lips or hands must move in order to convey

27

No miracles
in Mind-
methods

thought, that the undulations of the air convey
sound, and possibly that other methods involve
so-called miracles. The realities of being, its
30 normal action, and the origin of all things are unseen to
mortal sense; whereas the unreal and imitative movements of mortal belief, which would reverse the immortal

modus and action, are styled the real. Whoever con- 1
tradicts this mortal mind supposition of reality is called
a deceiver, or is said to be deceived. Of a man it has 3
been said, "As he thinketh in his heart, so is he;" hence
as a man spiritually *understandeth,* so is he in truth.

Mortal mind conceives of something as either liquid 6
or solid, and then classifies it materially. Immortal and
spiritual facts exist apart from this mortal and   Good
material conception. God, good, is self-exist- indefinable   9
ent and self-expressed, though indefinable as a whole.
Every step towards goodness is a departure from materiality, and is a tendency towards God, Spirit. Material 12
theories partially paralyze this attraction towards infinite
and eternal good by an opposite attraction towards the
finite, temporary, and discordant.   15

Sound is a mental impression made on mortal belief.
The ear does not really hear. Divine Science reveals
sound as communicated through the senses of Soul — 18
through spiritual understanding.

Mozart experienced more than he expressed. The
rapture of his grandest symphonies was never heard. He 21
was a musician beyond what the world knew.   Music,
This was even more strikingly true of Beet- rhythm of
                                              head and
hoven, who was so long hopelessly deaf. Men-   heart   24
tal melodies and strains of sweetest music supersede conscious sound. Music is the rhythm of head and heart.
Mortal mind is the harp of many strings, discoursing 27
either discord or harmony according as the hand, which
sweeps over it, is human or divine.

Before human knowledge dipped to its depths into a 30
false sense of things, — into belief in material origins
which discard the one Mind and true source of being, —

1 it is possible that the impressions from Truth were as
distinct as sound, and that they came as sound to the
3 primitive prophets. If the medium of hearing is wholly
spiritual, it is normal and indestructible.

If Enoch's perception had been confined to the evidence
6 before his material senses, he could never have "walked
with God," nor been guided into the demonstration of
life eternal.

9 Adam, represented in the Scriptures as formed from
dust, is an object-lesson for the human mind. The mate-
Adam and
the senses rial senses, like Adam, originate in matter and
12 return to dust, — are proved non-intelligent.
They go out as they came in, for they are still the error,
not the truth of being. When it is learned that the spirit-
15 ual sense, and not the material, conveys the impressions
of Mind to man, then being will be understood and found
to be harmonious.

18 We bow down to matter, and entertain finite thoughts
of God like the pagan idolater. Mortals are inclined to
Idolatrous
illusions fear and to obey what they consider a material
21 body more than they do a spiritual God. All
material knowledge, like the original "tree of knowledge,"
multiplies their pains, for mortal illusions would rob God,
24 slay man, and meanwhile would spread their table with
cannibal tidbits and give thanks.

How transient a sense is mortal sight, when a wound on
27 the retina may end the power of light and lens! But the
The senses
of Soul real sight or sense is not lost. Neither age nor
accident can interfere with the senses of Soul,
30 and there are no other real senses. It is evident that the
body as matter has no sensation of its own, and there is no
oblivion for Soul and its faculties. Spirit's senses are with-

out pain, and they are forever at peace. Nothing can hide 1
from them the harmony of all things and the might and
permanence of Truth.   3

If Spirit, Soul, could sin or be lost, then being and immortality would be lost, together with all the faculties of
Mind; but being cannot be lost while God ex-   Real being   6
ists. Soul and matter are at variance from the   never lost
very necessity of their opposite natures. Mortals are
unacquainted with the reality of existence, because matter 9
and mortality do not reflect the facts of Spirit.

Spiritual vision is not subordinate to geometric alti-
tudes. Whatever is governed by God, is never for an 12
instant deprived of the light and might of intelligence
and Life.

We are sometimes led to believe that darkness is as real 15
as light; but Science affirms darkness to be only a mortal
sense of the absence of light, at the coming of   Light and
which darkness loses the appearance of reality.   darkness   18
So sin and sorrow, disease and death, are the suppositional
absence of Life, God, and flee as phantoms of error before
truth and love.   21

With its divine proof, Science reverses the evidence of
material sense. Every quality and condition of mortality
is lost, swallowed up in immortality. Mortal man is the 24
antipode of immortal man in origin, in existence, and in his
relation to God.

Because he understood the superiority and immor- 27
tality of good, Socrates feared not the hemlock poison.
Even the faith of his philosophy spurned phys-   Faith of
ical timidity. Having sought man's spiritual   Socrates   30
state, he recognized the immortality of man. The ignorance and malice of the age would have killed the vener-

1 able philosopher because of his faith in Soul and his indifference to the body.

3 Who shall say that man is alive to-day, but may be dead
to-morrow?   What has touched Life, God, to such
The serpent strange issues?   Here theories cease, and Sci-
6 of error ence unveils the mystery and solves the problem of man.   Error bites the heel of truth, but cannot kill
truth.   Truth bruises the head of error — destroys error.
9 Spirituality lays open siege to materialism.   On which
side are we fighting?

The understanding that the Ego is Mind, and that
12 there is but one Mind or intelligence, begins at once to
Servants destroy the errors of mortal sense and to supply
and masters the truth of immortal sense.   This understand-
15 ing makes the body harmonious; it makes the nerves,
bones, brain, etc., servants, instead of masters.   If man
is governed by the law of divine Mind, his body is in sub-
18 mission to everlasting Life and Truth and Love.   The
great mistake of mortals is to suppose that man, God's
image and likeness, is both matter and Spirit, both good
21 and evil.

If the decision were left to the corporeal senses, evil
would appear to be the master of good, and sickness to
24 be the rule of existence, while health would seem the
exception, death the inevitable, and life a paradox.   Paul
asked: "What concord hath Christ with Belial?" (2 Cor-
27 inthians vi. 15.)

When you say, "Man's body is material," I say with
Paul: Be "willing rather to be absent from the body,
30 Personal and to be present with the Lord." Give up
identity your material belief of mind in matter, and
have but one Mind, even God; for this Mind forms its

own likeness. The loss of man's identity through the 1
understanding which Science confers is impossible; and
the notion of such a possibility is more absurd than to 3
conclude that individual musical tones are lost in the
origin of harmony.

Medical schools may inform us that the healing work 6
of Christian Science and Paul's peculiar Christian conversion and experience, — which prove Mind   Paul's
to be scientifically distinct from matter, — are experience 9
indications of unnatural mental and bodily conditions,
even of catalepsy and hysteria; yet if we turn to the Scriptures, what do we read? Why, this: "If a man keep my 12
saying, he shall never see death!" and "Henceforth know
we no man after the flesh!"

That scientific methods are superior to others, is 15
seen by their effects. When you have once conquered
a diseased condition of the body through   Fatigue is
Mind, that condition never recurs, and you   mental   18
have won a point in Science. When mentality gives
rest to the body, the next toil will fatigue you less, for
you are working out the problem of being in divine meta- 21
physics; and in proportion as you understand the control which Mind has over so-called matter, you will be
able to demonstrate this control. The scientific and 24
permanent remedy for fatigue is to learn the power of
Mind over the body or any illusion of physical weariness,
and so destroy this illusion, for matter cannot be weary 27
and heavy-laden.

You say, "Toil fatigues me." But what is this *me?*
Is it muscle or mind? Which is tired and so speaks? 30
Without mind, could the muscles be tired? Do the
muscles talk, or do you talk for them? Matter is non-

1 intelligent. Mortal mind does the false talking, and that
which affirms weariness, made that weariness.

3 You do not say a wheel is fatigued; and yet the body
is as material as the wheel. If it were not for what the
Mind never human mind says of the body, the body, like
6 weary the inanimate wheel, would never be weary.
The consciousness of Truth rests us more than hours of
repose in unconsciousness.

9 The body is supposed to say, "I am ill." The reports
of sickness may form a coalition with the reports of sin,
Coalition and say, "I am malice, lust, appetite, envy,
12 of sin and hate." What renders both sin and sickness
sickness difficult of cure is, that the human mind is the
sinner, disinclined to self-correction, and believing that
15 the body can be sick independently of mortal mind and
that the divine Mind has no jurisdiction over the body.

Why pray for the recovery of the sick, if you are with-
18 out faith in God's willingness and ability to heal them?
Sickness If you do believe in God, why do you sub-
akin to sin stitute drugs for the Almighty's power, and
21 employ means which lead only into material ways of
obtaining help, instead of turning in time of need to
God, divine Love, who is an ever-present help?

24 Treat a belief in sickness as you would sin, with sudden
dismissal. Resist the temptation to believe in matter as
intelligent, as having sensation or power.

27 The Scriptures say, "They that wait upon the Lord
. . . shall run, and not be weary; and they shall walk,
and not faint." The meaning of that passage is not
30 perverted by applying it literally to moments of fatigue,
for the moral and physical are as one in their results.
When we wake to the truth of being, all disease,

pain, weakness, weariness, sorrow, sin, death, will be 1
unknown, and the mortal dream will forever cease. My
method of treating fatigue applies to all bodily ailments, 3
since Mind should be, and is, supreme, absolute, and
final.

In mathematics, we do not multiply when we should 6
subtract, and then say the product is correct. No more
can we say in Science that muscles give strength, Affirmation
that nerves give pain or pleasure, or that matter   and result   9
governs, and then expect that the result will be harmony.
Not muscles, nerves, nor bones, but mortal mind makes
the whole body "sick, and the whole heart faint;" whereas 12
divine Mind heals.

When this is understood, we shall never affirm concerning the body what we do not wish to have manifested. We 15
shall not call the body weak, if we would have it strong;
for the belief in feebleness must obtain in the human
mind before it can be made manifest on the body, and 18
the destruction of the belief will be the removal of its
effects. Science includes no rule of discord, but governs
harmoniously. "The wish," says the poet, "is ever father 21
to the thought."

We may hear a sweet melody, and yet misunderstand
the science that governs it. Those who are healed 24
through metaphysical Science, not compre-   Scientific
hending the Principle of the cure, may misun-   beginning
derstand it, and impute their recovery to change of air or 27
diet, not rendering to God the honor due to Him alone.
Entire immunity from the belief in sin, suffering, and
death may not be reached at this period, but we may look 30
for an abatement of these evils; and this scientific beginning is in the right direction.

1 We hear it said: "I exercise daily in the open air. I take cold baths, in order to overcome a predisposition to 3 **Hygiene ineffectual** take cold; and yet I have continual colds, catarrh, and cough." Such admissions ought to open people's eyes to the inefficacy of material hygiene, 6 and induce sufferers to look in other directions for cause and cure.

Instinct is better than misguided reason, as even na-9 ture declares. The violet lifts her blue eye to greet the early spring. The leaves clap their hands as nature's untired worshippers. The snowbird sings and soars 12 amid the blasts; he has no catarrh from wet feet, and procures a summer residence with more ease than a nabob. The atmosphere of the earth, kinder than the at-15 mosphere of mortal mind, leaves catarrh to the latter. Colds, coughs, and contagion are engendered solely by human theories.

18 Mortal mind produces its own phenomena, and then **The reflex phenomena** charges them to something else, — like a kitten glancing into the mirror at itself and thinking 21 it sees another kitten.

A clergyman once adopted a diet of bread and water to increase his spirituality. Finding his health failing, 24 he gave up his abstinence, and advised others never to try dietetics for growth in grace.

The belief that either fasting or feasting makes men 27 better morally or physically is one of the fruits of "the **Volition far-reaching** tree of the knowledge of good and evil," concerning which God said, "Thou shalt not eat 30 of it." Mortal mind forms all conditions of the mortal body, and controls the stomach, bones, lungs, heart, blood, etc., as directly as the volition or will moves the hand.

I knew a person who when quite a child adopted the 1
Graham system to cure dyspepsia. For many years, he
ate only bread and vegetables, and drank noth- 3
ing but water. His dyspepsia increasing, he
decided that his diet should be more rigid, and
thereafter he partook of but one meal in twenty-four 6
hours, this meal consisting of only a thin slice of bread
without water. His physician also recommended that
he should not wet his parched throat until three hours 9
after eating. He passed many weary years in hunger
and weakness, almost in starvation, and finally made up
his mind to die, having exhausted the skill of the doctors, 12
who kindly informed him that death was indeed his only
alternative. At this point Christian Science saved him,
and he is now in perfect health without a vestige of the 15
old complaint.

Starvation and dyspepsia

He learned that suffering and disease were the self-
imposed beliefs of mortals, and not the facts of being; 18
that God never decreed disease, — never ordained a law
that fasting should be a means of health. Hence semi-
starvation is not acceptable to wisdom, and it is equally 21
far from Science, in which being is sustained by God, Mind.
These truths, opening his eyes, relieved his stomach, and
he ate without suffering, "giving God thanks;" but he 24
never enjoyed his food as he had imagined he would
when, still the slave of matter, he thought of the flesh-
pots of Egypt, feeling childhood's hunger and undisci- 27
plined by self-denial and divine Science.

This new-born understanding, that neither food nor
the stomach, without the consent of mortal 30
mind, can make one suffer, brings with it another lesson, — that gluttony is a sensual illusion, and

Mind and stomach

1 that this phantasm of mortal mind disappears as we better
apprehend our spiritual existence and ascend the ladder
3 of life.

This person learned that food affects the body only
as mortal mind has its material methods of working, one
6 of which is to believe that proper food supplies nutriment
and strength to the human system. He learned also that
mortal mind makes a mortal body, whereas Truth re-
9 generates this fleshly mind and feeds thought with the
bread of Life.

Food had less power to help or to hurt him after he
12 had availed himself of the fact that Mind governs man,
and he also had less faith in the so-called pleasures and
pains of matter. Taking less thought about what he
15 should eat or drink, consulting the stomach less about
the economy of living and God more, he recovered
strength and flesh rapidly. For many years he had
18 been kept alive, as was believed, only by the strictest adherence to hygiene and drugs, and yet he continued ill
all the while. Now he dropped drugs and material
21 hygiene, and was well.

He learned that a dyspeptic was very far from being
the image and likeness of God, — far from having "do-
24 minion over the fish of the sea, and over the fowl of the
air, and over the cattle," if eating a bit of animal flesh
could overpower him. He finally concluded that God
27 never made a dyspeptic, while fear, hygiene, physiology,
and physics had made him one, contrary to His commands.

In seeking a cure for dyspepsia consult matter not at
30 Life only in Spirit   all, and eat what is set before you, "asking
no question for conscience sake." We must
destroy the false belief that life and intelligence are in

matter, and plant ourselves upon what is pure and per- 1
fect. Paul said, "Walk in the Spirit, and ye shall not
fulfil the lust of the flesh." Sooner or later we shall learn 3
that the fetters of man's finite capacity are forged by the
illusion that he lives in body instead of in Soul, in matter
instead of in Spirit.   6

Matter does not express Spirit. God is infinite omnipresent Spirit. If Spirit is *all* and is everywhere, what
and where is matter? Remember that truth   Soul greater 9
is greater than error, and we cannot put the   than body
greater into the less. Soul is Spirit, and Spirit is greater
than body. If Spirit were once within the body, Spirit 12
would be finite, and therefore could not be Spirit.

The question, "What is Truth," convulses the world.
Many are ready to meet this inquiry with the assurance 15
which comes of understanding; but more are   The question
blinded by their old illusions, and try to "give   of the ages
it pause." "If the blind lead the blind, both shall fall into 18
the ditch."

The efforts of error to answer this question by some
ology are vain. Spiritual rationality and free thought ac- 21
company approaching Science, and cannot be put down.
They will emancipate humanity, and supplant unscientific
means and so-called laws.   24

Peals that should startle the slumbering thought from
its erroneous dream are partially unheeded; but the last
trump has not sounded, or this would not be   Heralds of 27
so. Marvels, calamities, and sin will much   Science
more abound as truth urges upon mortals its resisted
claims; but the awful daring of sin destroys sin, and 30
foreshadows the triumph of truth. God will over-
turn, until "He come whose right it is." Longevity

1 is increasing and the power of sin diminishing, for the
world feels the alterative effect of truth through every
3 pore.

As the crude footprints of the past disappear from the
dissolving paths of the present, we shall better understand
6 the Science which governs these changes, and shall plant
our feet on firmer ground. Every sensuous pleasure or
pain is self-destroyed through suffering. There should
9 be painless progress, attended by life and peace instead
of discord and death.

In the record of nineteen centuries, there are sects
12 many but not enough Christianity. Centuries ago re-

Sectarianism
and
opposition

ligionists were ready to hail an anthropomorphic God, and array His vicegerent with pomp
15 and splendor; but this was not the manner
of truth's appearing. Of old the cross was truth's central sign, and it is to-day. The modern lash is less
18 material than the Roman scourge, but it is equally as
cutting. Cold disdain, stubborn resistance, opposition
from church, state laws, and the press, are still the har-
21 bingers of truth's full-orbed appearing.

A higher and more practical Christianity, demonstrating justice and meeting the needs of mortals in sickness
24 and in health, stands at the door of this age, knocking
for admission. Will you open or close the door upon this
angel visitant, who cometh in the quiet of meekness, as he
27 came of old to the patriarch at noonday?

Truth brings the elements of liberty. On its banner
is the Soul-inspired motto, "Slavery is abolished." The
30　　Mental　　power of God brings deliverance to the cap-
emancipation tive. No power can withstand divine Love.
What is this supposed power, which opposes itself to God?

Whence cometh it? What is it that binds man with iron 1
shackles to sin, sickness, and death? Whatever enslaves
man is opposed to the divine government. Truth makes 3
man free.

You may know when first Truth leads by the few-
ness and faithfulness of its followers. Thus it is that 6
the march of time bears onward freedom's   Truth's
banner. The powers of this world will fight,   ordeal
and will command their sentinels not to let truth pass 9
the guard until it subscribes to their systems; but Science,
heeding not the pointed bayonet, marches on. There is
always some tumult, but there is a rallying to truth's 12
standard.

The history of our country, like all history, illustrates
the might of Mind, and shows human power to be propor- 15
tionate to its embodiment of right thinking. A   Immortal
few immortal sentences, breathing the omnipo-   sentences
tence of divine justice, have been potent to break despotic 18
fetters and abolish the whipping-post and slave market;
but oppression neither went down in blood, nor did the
breath of freedom come from the cannon's mouth. Love 21
is the liberator.

Legally to abolish unpaid servitude in the United
States was hard; but the abolition of mental slavery is 24
a more difficult task. The despotic tenden-   Slavery
cies, inherent in mortal mind and always ger-   abolished
minating in new forms of tyranny, must be rooted out 27
through the action of the divine Mind.

Men and women of all climes and races are still in
bondage to material sense, ignorant how to obtain their 30
freedom. The rights of man were vindicated in a single
section and on the lowest plane of human life, when Afri-

1 can slavery was abolished in our land. That was only
prophetic of further steps towards the banishment of a
3 world-wide slavery, found on higher planes of existence
and under more subtle and depraving forms.

The voice of God in behalf of the African slave was
6 still echoing in our land, when the voice of the herald of
Liberty's   this new crusade sounded the keynote of uni-
crusade   versal freedom, asking a fuller acknowledg-
9 ment of the rights of man as a Son of God, demanding
that the fetters of sin, sickness, and death be stricken
from the human mind and that its freedom be won, not
12 through human warfare, not with bayonet and blood, but
through Christ's divine Science.

God has built a higher platform of human rights, and
15 He has built it on diviner claims. These claims are not
Cramping   made through code or creed, but in demonstra-
systems   tion of "on earth peace, good-will toward men."
18 Human codes, scholastic theology, material medicine and
hygiene, fetter faith and spiritual understanding. Divine
Science rends asunder these fetters, and man's birthright
21 of sole allegiance to his Maker asserts itself.

I saw before me the sick, wearing out years of servitude to an unreal master in the belief that the body gov-
24 erned them, rather than Mind.

The lame, the deaf, the dumb, the blind, the sick, the
sensual, the sinner, I wished to save from the slavery of
27 House of   their own beliefs and from the educational
bondage   systems of the Pharaohs, who to-day, as of
yore, hold the children of Israel in bondage. I saw be-
30 fore me the awful conflict, the Red Sea and the wilderness; but I pressed on through faith in God, trusting
Truth, the strong deliverer, to guide me into the land

of Christian Science, where fetters fall and the rights of   1
man are fully known and acknowledged.

I saw that the law of mortal belief included all error,   3
and that, even as oppressive laws are disputed and mortals are taught their right to freedom, so the   Higher law
claims of the enslaving senses must be de-   ends bondage   6
nied and superseded. The law of the divine Mind must
end human bondage, or mortals will continue unaware
of man's inalienable rights and in subjection to hope-   9
less slavery, because some public teachers permit
an ignorance of divine power, — an ignorance that
is the foundation of continued bondage and of human   12
suffering.

Discerning the rights of man, we cannot fail to foresee the doom of all oppression. Slavery is not the legiti-   15
mate state of man. God made man free.   Native
Paul said, "I was free born." All men should   freedom
be free. "Where the Spirit of the Lord is, there is lib-   18
erty." Love and Truth make free, but evil and error
lead into captivity.

Christian Science raises the standard of liberty and   21
cries: "Follow me! Escape from the bondage of sickness, sin, and death!" Jesus marked out the   Standard
way. Citizens of the world, accept the "glori-   of liberty   24
ous liberty of the children of God," and be free! This
is your divine right. The illusion of material sense, not
divine law, has bound you, entangled your free limbs,   27
crippled your capacities, enfeebled your body, and de-
faced the tablet of your being.

If God had instituted material laws to govern man,   30
disobedience to which would have made man ill, Jesus
would not have disregarded those laws by healing in

1 direct opposition to them and in defiance of all material
conditions.

3 The transmission of disease or of certain idiosyncra-
sies of mortal mind would be impossible if this great fact

No fleshly of being were learned, — namely, that nothing
6 heredity inharmonious can enter being, for Life *is* God.
Heredity is a prolific subject for mortal belief to pin theories upon; but if we learn that nothing is real but the
9 right, we shall have no dangerous inheritances, and fleshly
ills will disappear.

The enslavement of man is not legitimate. It will
12 cease when man enters into his heritage of freedom, his

God-given God-given dominion over the material senses.
dominion Mortals will some day assert their freedom in
15 the name of Almighty God. Then they will control their
own bodies through the understanding of divine Science.
Dropping their present beliefs, they will recognize har-
18 mony as the spiritual reality and discord as the material
unreality.

If we follow the command of our Master, "Take no
21 thought for your life," we shall never depend on bodily
conditions, structure, or economy, but we shall be masters
of the body, dictate its terms, and form and control it with
24 Truth.

There is no power apart from God. Omnipotence has
all-power, and to acknowledge any other power is to dis-
27 Priestly pride honor God. The humble Nazarene overthrew
humbled the supposition that sin, sickness, and death
have power. He proved them powerless. It should have
30 humbled the pride of the priests, when they saw the demonstration of Christianity excel the influence of their dead
faith and ceremonies.

If Mind is not the master of sin, sickness, and death, 1
they are immortal, for it is already proved that matter has not destroyed them, but is their basis and 3
support.

We should hesitate to say that Jehovah sins or suffers;
but if sin and suffering are realities of being, whence did 6
they emanate? God made all that was made, No union of
and Mind signifies God, — infinity, not finity. opposites
Not far removed from infidelity is the belief which 9
unites such opposites as sickness and health, holiness
and unholiness, calls both the offspring of spirit, and
at the same time admits that Spirit is God, — vir- 12
tually declaring Him good in one instance and evil in
another.

By universal consent, mortal belief has constituted 15
itself a law to bind mortals to sickness, sin, and death.
This customary belief is misnamed material Self-constituted
law, and the individual who upholds it is mis- law 18
taken in theory and in practice. The so-called law of
mortal mind, conjectural and speculative, is made void
by the law of immortal Mind, and false law should be 21
trampled under foot.

If God causes man to be sick, sickness must be good,
and its opposite, health, must be evil, for all that He 24
makes is good and will stand forever. If the Sickness from
transgression of God's law produces sickness, it mortal mind
is right to be sick; and we cannot if we would, and should 27
not if we could, annul the decrees of wisdom. It is the
transgression of a belief of mortal mind, not of a law of
matter nor of divine Mind, which causes the belief of sick- 30
ness. The remedy is Truth, not matter, — the truth that
disease is *unreal*.

1 If sickness is real, it belongs to immortality; if true,
it is a part of Truth. Would you attempt with drugs,
3 or without, to destroy a quality or condition of Truth?
But if sickness and sin are illusions, the awakening from
this mortal dream, or illusion, will bring us into health,
6 holiness, and immortality. This awakening is the forever coming of Christ, the advanced appearing of Truth,
which casts out error and heals the sick. This is the sal-
9 vation which comes through God, the divine Principle,
Love, as demonstrated by Jesus.

It would be contrary to our highest ideas of God to
12 suppose Him capable of first arranging law and causation
God never   so as to bring about certain evil results, and
inconsistent then punishing the helpless victims of His vo-
15 lition for doing what they could not avoid doing. Good
is not, cannot be, the author of experimental sins. God,
good, can no more produce sickness than goodness can
18 cause evil and health occasion disease.

Does wisdom make blunders which must afterwards
be rectified by man? Does a law of God produce sick-
21   Mental   ness, and can man put that law under his feet
    narcotics   by healing sickness? According to Holy Writ,
the sick are never really healed by drugs, hygiene, or any
24 material method. These merely evade the question.
They are soothing syrups to put children to sleep, satisfy
mortal belief, and quiet fear.

27 We think that we are healed when a disease disappears, though it is liable to reappear; but we are never
The true   thoroughly healed until the liability to be
30 healing   ill is removed. So-called mortal mind or the
mind of mortals being the remote, predisposing, and
the exciting cause of all suffering, the cause of disease

must be obliterated through Christ in divine Science, or 1
the so-called physical senses will get the victory.

Unless an ill is rightly met and fairly overcome by 3
Truth, the ill is never conquered. If God destroys not
sin, sickness, and death, they are not de-   Destruction
stroyed in the mind of mortals, but seem to   of all evil   6
this so-called mind to be immortal. What God cannot
do, man need not attempt. If God heals not the sick,
they are not healed, for no lesser power equals the infinite 9
All-power; but God, Truth, Life, Love, does heal the
sick through the prayer of the righteous.

If God makes sin, if good produces evil, if truth results 12
in error, then Science and Christianity are helpless; but
there are no antagonistic powers nor laws, spiritual or
material, creating and governing man through perpetual 15
warfare. God is not the author of mortal discords.
Therefore we accept the conclusion that discords have
only a fabulous existence, are mortal beliefs which divine 18
Truth and Love destroy.

To hold yourself superior to sin, because God made
you superior to it and governs man, is true wisdom. To 21
fear sin is to misunderstand the power of Love   Superiority
and the divine Science of being in man's rela-   to sickness
                                                  and sin
tion to God, — to doubt His government and   24
distrust His omnipotent care. To hold yourself superior
to sickness and death is equally wise, and is in accordance
with divine Science. To fear them is impossible, when 27
you fully apprehend God and know that they are no part
of His creation.

Man, governed by his Maker, having no other Mind, — 30
planted on the Evangelist's statement that "all things
were made by Him [the Word of God]; and without

1 Him was not anything made that was made," — can
triumph over sin, sickness, and death.

3   Many theories relative to God and man neither make
man harmonious nor God lovable. The beliefs we com-
Denials of monly entertain about happiness and life
6 divine power afford no scatheless and permanent evidence
of either. Security for the claims of harmonious and
eternal being is found only in divine Science.

9   Scripture informs us that "with God all things are
possible," — all good is possible to Spirit; but our prevalent theories practically deny this, and make healing
12 possible only through matter. These theories must be
untrue, for the Scripture is true. Christianity is not
false, but religions which contradict its Principle are
15 false.

In our age Christianity is again demonstrating the
power of divine Principle, as it did over nineteen hun-
18 dred years ago, by healing the sick and triumphing over
death. Jesus never taught that drugs, food, air, and exercise could make a man healthy, or that they could de-
21 stroy human life; nor did he illustrate these errors by his
practice. He referred man's harmony to Mind, not to
matter, and never tried to make of none effect the sen-
24 tence of God, which sealed God's condemnation of sin,
sickness, and death.

In the sacred sanctuary of Truth are voices of sol-
27 emn import, but we heed them not. It is only when the
Signs   so-called pleasures and pains of sense pass
following away in our lives, that we find unquestion-
30 able signs of the burial of error and the resurrection to
spiritual life.

There is neither place nor opportunity in Science for error

of any sort. Every day makes its demands upon us for
higher proofs rather than professions of Christian power.
These proofs consist solely in the destruction   Profession
of sin, sickness, and death by the power of   and proof
Spirit, as Jesus destroyed them. This is an element of
progress, and progress is the law of God, whose law demands of us only what we can certainly fulfil.

In the midst of imperfection, perfection is seen and
acknowledged only by degrees. The ages must slowly
work up to perfection. How long it must be
before we arrive at the demonstration of scien-   Perfection
                                                    gained
tific being, no man knoweth, — not even "the   slowly
Son but the Father;" but the false claim of error continues its delusions until the goal of goodness is assidu-
ously earned and won.

Already the shadow of His right hand rests upon the
hour. Ye who can discern the face of the sky, — the
sign material, — how much more should ye   Christ's
discern the sign mental, and compass the de-   mission
struction of sin and sickness by overcoming the thoughts
which produce them, and by understanding the spiritual
idea which corrects and destroys them. To reveal this
truth was our Master's mission to all mankind, including
the hearts which rejected him.

When numbers have been divided according to a fixed
rule, the quotient is not more unquestionable than the
scientific tests I have made of the effects of   Efficacy
truth upon the sick. The counter fact rela-   of truth
tive to any disease is required to cure it. The utterance
of truth is designed to rebuke and destroy error. Why
should truth not be efficient in sickness, which is solely
the result of inharmony?

1 Spiritual draughts heal, while material lotions interfere
with truth, even as ritualism and creed hamper spirit-
3 uality. If we trust matter, we distrust Spirit.

Whatever inspires with wisdom, Truth, or Love — be
it song, sermon, or Science — blesses the human family

6 Crumbs of with crumbs of comfort from Christ's table,
comfort feeding the hungry and giving living waters to
the thirsty.

9 We should become more familiar with good than with
evil, and guard against false beliefs as watchfully as we
bar our doors against the approach of thieves

Hospitality
12 to health and murderers. We should love our enemies
and good and help them on the basis of the Golden
Rule; but avoid casting pearls before those who trample
15 them under foot, thereby robbing both themselves and
others.

If mortals would keep proper ward over mortal mind,
18 the brood of evils which infest it would be cleared out.

Cleansing We must begin with this so-called mind and
the mind empty it of sin and sickness, or sin and sick-
21 ness will never cease. The present codes of human
systems disappoint the weary searcher after a divine
theology, adequate to the right education of human
24 thought.

Sin and disease must be thought before they can be
manifested. You must control evil thoughts in the first
27 instance, or they will control you in the second. Jesus
declared that to look with desire on forbidden objects was
to break a moral precept. He laid great stress on the
30 action of the human mind, unseen to the senses.

Evil thoughts and aims reach no farther and do no more
harm than one's belief permits. Evil thoughts, lusts, and

malicious purposes cannot go forth, like wandering pollen, 1
from one human mind to another, finding unsuspected
lodgment, if virtue and truth build a strong defence. 3
Better suffer a doctor infected with smallpox to attend
you than to be treated mentally by one who does not obey
the requirements of divine Science.   6

The teachers of schools and the readers in churches
should be selected with as direct reference to their
morals as to their learning or their correct   Teachers'   9
reading. Nurseries of character should be   functions
strongly garrisoned with virtue. School-examinations are
one-sided; it is not so much academic education, as a 12
moral and spiritual culture, which lifts one higher. The
pure and uplifting thoughts of the teacher, constantly
imparted to pupils, will reach higher than the heavens of 15
astronomy; while the debased and unscrupulous mind,
though adorned with gems of scholarly attainment, will
degrade the characters it should inform and elevate.   18

Physicians, whom the sick employ in their helplessness,
should be models of virtue. They should be wise spiritual guides to health and hope. To the trem-   Physicians'   21
blers on the brink of death, who understand   privilege
not the divine Truth which is Life and perpetuates being,
physicians should be able to teach it. Then when the soul 24
is willing and the flesh weak, the patient's feet may be
planted on the rock Christ Jesus, the true idea of spiritual
power.   27

Clergymen, occupying the watchtowers of the world,
should uplift the standard of Truth. They should so raise
their hearers spiritually, that their listeners Clergymen's   30
will love to grapple with a new, right idea   duty
and broaden their concepts. Love of Christianity, rather

1 than love of popularity, should stimulate clerical labor
and progress. Truth should emanate from the pulpit,
3 but never be strangled there. A special privilege is vested
in the ministry. How shall it be used? Sacredly, in the
interests of humanity, not of sect.

6   Is it not professional reputation and emolument rather
than the dignity of God's laws, which many leaders seek?
Do not inferior motives induce the infuriated attacks on
9 individuals, who reiterate Christ's teachings in support
of his proof by example that the divine Mind heals sickness as well as sin?

12   A mother is the strongest educator, either for or
against crime. Her thoughts form the embryo of an-
A mother's   other mortal mind, and unconsciously mould
15 responsibility it, either after a model odious to herself or
through divine influence, "according to the pattern
showed to thee in the mount." Hence the importance
18 of Christian Science, from which we learn of the one
Mind and of the availability of good as the remedy for
every woe.

21   Children should obey their parents; insubordination
is an evil, blighting the buddings of self-government.
Children's   Parents should teach their children at the
24 tractability earliest possible period the truths of health
and holiness. Children are more tractable than adults,
and learn more readily to love the simple verities that will
27 make them happy and good.

Jesus loved little children because of their freedom
from wrong and their receptiveness of right. While
30 age is halting between two opinions or battling with
false beliefs, youth makes easy and rapid strides towards
Truth.

A little girl, who had occasionally listened to my ex- 1
planations, badly wounded her finger. She seemed not
to notice it. On being questioned about it she answered 3
ingenuously, "There is no sensation in matter." Bound-
ing off with laughing eyes, she presently added, "Mamma,
my finger is not a bit sore." 6

It might have been months or years before her parents
would have laid aside their drugs, or reached the mental
height their little daughter so naturally at- Soil and 9
tained. The more stubborn beliefs and theo- seed
ries of parents often choke the good seed in the minds of
themselves and their offspring. Superstition, like "the 12
fowls of the air," snatches away the good seed before it
has sprouted.

Children should be taught the Truth-cure, Christian 15
Science, among their first lessons, and kept from discussing or entertaining theories or thoughts about Teaching
sickness. To prevent the experience of error children 18
and its sufferings, keep out of the minds of your children
either sinful or diseased thoughts. The latter should
be excluded on the same principle as the former. This 21
makes Christian Science early available.

Some invalids are unwilling to know the facts or to
hear about the fallacy of matter and its supposed laws. 24
They devote themselves a little longer to their Deluded
material gods, cling to a belief in the life and invalids
intelligence of matter, and expect this error to do more 27
for them than they are willing to admit the only living and
true God can do. Impatient at your explanation, unwilling to investigate the Science of Mind which would rid 30
them of their complaints, they hug false beliefs and suffer
the delusive consequences.

1   Motives and acts are not rightly valued before they are
understood. It is well to wait till those whom you would
3   Patient   benefit are ready for the blessing, for Science
waiting   is working changes in personal character as
well as in the material universe.

6   To obey the Scriptural command, "Come out from
among them, and be ye separate," is to incur society's
frown; but this frown, more than flatteries, enables one
9 to be Christian. Losing her crucifix, the Roman Catholic
girl said, "I have nothing left but Christ." "If God be
for us, who can be against us?"

12   To fall away from Truth in times of persecution, shows
that we never understood Truth. From out the bridal
Unimproved chamber of wisdom there will come the warn-
15 opportunities ing, "I know you not." Unimproved opportunities will rebuke us when we attempt to claim the
benefits of an experience we have not made our own, try
18 to reap the harvest we have not sown, and wish to enter
unlawfully into the labors of others. Truth often remains
unsought, until we seek this remedy for human woe be-
21 cause we suffer severely from error.

Attempts to conciliate society and so gain dominion over
mankind, arise from worldly weakness. He who leaves
24 all for Christ forsakes popularity and gains Christianity.

Society is a foolish juror, listening only to one side of
the case. Justice often comes too late to secure a verdict.
27 Society and People with mental work before them have
intolerance no time for gossip about false law or testimony.
To reconstruct timid justice and place the fact above the
30 falsehood, is the work of time.

The cross is the central emblem of history. It is the
lodestar in the demonstration of Christian healing, — the

demonstration by which sin and sickness are destroyed. 1
The sects, which endured the lash of their predecessors,
in their turn lay it upon those who are in advance of 3
creeds.

Take away wealth, fame, and social organizations,
which weigh not one jot in the balance of God, and we 6
get clearer views of Principle. Break up *Right views*
cliques, level wealth with honesty, let worth *of humanity*
be judged according to wisdom, and we get better views 9
of humanity.

The wicked man is not the ruler of his upright
neighbor. Let it be understood that success in error is 12
defeat in Truth. The watchword of Christian Science
is Scriptural: "Let the wicked forsake his way, and the
unrighteous man his thoughts." 15

To ascertain our progress, we must learn where our
affections are placed and whom we acknowledge and
obey as God. If divine Love is becoming *Standpoint* 18
nearer, dearer, and more real to us, matter is *revealed*
then submitting to Spirit. The objects we pursue and
the spirit we manifest reveal our standpoint, and show 21
what we are winning.

Mortal mind is the acknowledged seat of human motives. It forms material concepts and produces every 24
discordant action of the body. If action pro- *Antagonistic*
ceeds from the divine Mind, action is harmo- *sources*
nious. If it comes from erring mortal mind, it is discord- 27
ant and ends in sin, sickness, death. Those two opposite
sources never mingle in fount or stream. The perfect
Mind sends forth perfection, for God is Mind. Imper- 30
fect mortal mind sends forth its own resemblances, of
which the wise man said, "All is vanity."

1 Nature voices natural, spiritual law and divine Love,
but human belief misinterprets nature. Arctic regions,
3 Some lessons sunny tropics, giant hills, winged winds,
from nature mighty billows, verdant vales, festive flowers,
and glorious heavens, — all point to Mind, the spiritual
6 intelligence they reflect. The floral apostles are hiero-
glyphs of Deity. Suns and planets teach grand lessons.
The stars make night beautiful, and the leaflet turns nat-
9 urally towards the light.

In the order of Science, in which the Principle is above
what it reflects, all is one grand concord. Change this
12 Perpetual statement, suppose Mind to be governed by
motion matter or Soul in body, and you lose the keynote of being, and there is continual discord. Mind is
15 perpetual motion. Its symbol is the sphere. The rota-
tions and revolutions of the universe of Mind go on
eternally.

18 Mortals move onward towards good or evil as time
glides on. If mortals are not progressive, past failures
Progress will be repeated until all wrong work is ef-
21 demanded faced or rectified. If at present satisfied with
wrong-doing, we must learn to loathe it. If at present
content with idleness, we must become dissatisfied with
24 it. Remember that mankind must sooner or later, either
by suffering or by Science, be convinced of the error that
is to be overcome.

27 In trying to undo the errors of sense one must pay fully
and fairly the utmost farthing, until all error is finally
brought into subjection to Truth. The divine method
30 of paying sin's wages involves unwinding one's snarls,
and learning from experience how to divide between sense
and Soul.

"Whom the Lord loveth He chasteneth." He, who 1
knows God's will or the demands of divine Science and
obeys them, incurs the hostility of envy; and he who 3
refuses obedience to God, is chastened by Love.

Sensual treasures are laid up "where moth and rust
doth corrupt." Mortality is their doom. Sin breaks in 6
upon them, and carries off their fleeting joys. The doom
The sensualist's affections are as imaginary, of sin
whimsical, and unreal as his pleasures. Falsehood, envy, 9
hypocrisy, malice, hate, revenge, and so forth, steal away
the treasures of Truth. Stripped of its coverings, what
a mocking spectacle is sin! 12

The Bible teaches transformation of the body by the
renewal of Spirit. Take away the spiritual signification
of Scripture, and that compilation can do no Spirit 15
more for mortals than can moonbeams to melt transforms
a river of ice. The error of the ages is preaching without
practice. 18

The substance of all devotion is the reflection and
demonstration of divine Love, healing sickness and
destroying sin. Our Master said, "If ye love me, keep 21
my commandments."

One's aim, a point beyond faith, should be to find the
footsteps of Truth, the way to health and holiness. We 24
should strive to reach the Horeb height where God is revealed; and the corner-stone of all spiritual building is
purity. The baptism of Spirit, washing the body of all 27
the impurities of flesh, signifies that the pure in heart
see God and are approaching spiritual Life and its
demonstration. 30

It is "easier for a camel to go through the eye of a
needle," than for sinful beliefs to enter the kingdom of

1 heaven, eternal harmony. Through repentance, spiritual
baptism, and regeneration, mortals put off their material
3   Spiritual   beliefs and false individuality. It is only a
        baptism   question of time when "they shall all know
Me [God], from the least of them unto the greatest."
6 Denial of the claims of matter is a great step towards
the joys of Spirit, towards human freedom and the final
triumph over the body.

9   There is but one way to heaven, harmony, and Christ
in divine Science shows us this way. It is to know no
       The one   other reality — to have no other conscious-
12   only way   ness of life — than good, God and His reflection, and to rise superior to the so-called pain and pleasure
of the senses.

15   Self-love is more opaque than a solid body. In patient obedience to a patient God, let us labor to dissolve with the universal solvent of Love the adamant
18 of error, — self-will, self-justification, and self-love, —
which wars against spirituality and is the law of sin
and death.

21   The vesture of Life is Truth. According to the Bible,
the facts of being are commonly misconstrued, for it is
       Divided   written: "They parted my raiment among
24   vestments   them, and for my vesture they did cast lots."
The divine Science of man is woven into one web of
consistency without seam or rent. Mere speculation or
27 superstition appropriates no part of the divine vesture,
while inspiration restores every part of the Christly garment of righteousness.

30   The finger-posts of divine Science show the way our
Master trod, and require of Christians the proof which
he gave, instead of mere profession. We may hide

spiritual ignorance from the world, but we can never 1
succeed in the Science and demonstration of spiritual
good through ignorance or hypocrisy.   3

The divine Love, which made harmless the poisonous
viper, which delivered men from the boiling oil, from
the fiery furnace, from the jaws of the lion,   Ancient   6
can heal the sick in every age and triumph   and modern
                                               miracles
over sin and death. It crowned the demonstrations of Jesus with unsurpassed power and love. But 9
the same "Mind . . . which was also in Christ Jesus"
must always accompany the letter of Science in order to
confirm and repeat the ancient demonstrations of prophets 12
and apostles. That those wonders are not more commonly repeated to-day, arises not so much from lack of
desire as from lack of spiritual growth.   15

The clay cannot reply to the potter. The head, heart,
lungs, and limbs do not inform us that they are dizzy,
diseased, consumptive, or lame. If this in-   Mental   18
formation is conveyed, mortal mind conveys   telegraphy
it. Neither immortal and unerring Mind nor matter,
the inanimate substratum of mortal mind, can carry 21
on such telegraphy; for God is "of purer eyes than
to behold evil," and matter has neither intelligence nor
sensation.   24

Truth has no consciousness of error. Love has no
sense of hatred. Life has no partnership Annihilation
with death. Truth, Life, and Love are a law   of error   27
of annihilation to everything unlike themselves, because
they declare nothing except God.

Sickness, sin, and death are not the fruits of Life. 30
They are inharmonies which Truth destroys. Perfection
does not animate imperfection. Inasmuch as God is

1 good and the fount of all being, He does not produce
moral or physical deformity; therefore such deformity is
3 not real, but is illusion, the mirage of error.

Deformity
and
perfection

Divine Science reveals these grand facts. On
their basis Jesus demonstrated Life, never
6 fearing nor obeying error in any form.

If we were to derive all our conceptions of man from
what is seen between the cradle and the grave, happi-
9 ness and goodness would have no abiding-place in man,
and the worms would rob him of the flesh; but Paul
writes: "The law of the Spirit of life in Christ Jesus hath
12 made me free from the law of sin and death."

Man undergoing birth, maturity, and decay is like the
beasts and vegetables, — subject to laws of decay. If
15 man were dust in his earliest stage of exist-

Man never
less than
man

ence, we might admit the hypothesis that he
returns eventually to his primitive condition;
18 but man was never more nor less than man.

If man flickers out in death or springs from matter into
being, there must be an instant when God is without His
21 entire manifestation, — when there is no full reflection
of the infinite Mind.

Man in Science is neither young nor old. He has
24 neither birth nor death. He is not a beast, a vegetable,

Man not
evolved

nor a migratory mind. He does not pass from
matter to Mind, from the mortal to the im-
27 mortal, from evil to good, or from good to evil. Such
admissions cast us headlong into darkness and dogma.
Even Shakespeare's poetry pictures age as infancy, as
30 helplessness and decadence, instead of assigning to man
the everlasting grandeur and immortality of development,
power, and prestige.

The error of thinking that we are growing old, and the 1
benefits of destroying that illusion, are illustrated in a
sketch from the history of an English woman, published 3
in the London medical magazine called The Lancet.
Disappointed in love in her early years, she became
insane and lost all account of time. Believing that she 6
was still living in the same hour which parted   Perpetual
her from her lover, taking no note of years,   youth
she stood daily before the window watching for her 9
lover's coming. In this mental state she remained young.
Having no consciousness of time, she literally grew no
older. Some American travellers saw her when she was 12
seventy-four, and supposed her to be a young woman.
She had no care-lined face, no wrinkles nor gray hair, but
youth sat gently on cheek and brow. Asked to guess her 15
age, those unacquainted with her history conjectured that
she must be under twenty.

This instance of youth preserved furnishes a useful 18
hint, upon which a Franklin might work with more certainty than when he coaxed the enamoured lightning
from the clouds. Years had not made her old, because 21
she had taken no cognizance of passing time nor thought
of herself as growing old. The bodily results of her belief
that she was young manifested the influence of such a be- 24
lief. She could not age while believing herself young, for
the mental state governed the physical.

Impossibilities never occur. One instance like the 27
foregoing proves it possible to be young at seventy-four;
and the primary of that illustration makes it plain that
decrepitude is not according to law, nor is it a necessity of 30
nature, but an illusion.

The infinite never began nor will it ever end. Mind

1 and its formations can never be annihilated. Man is not
a pendulum, swinging between evil and good, joy and
3   Man   sorrow, sickness and health, life and death.
reflects God Life and its faculties are not measured by
calendars. The perfect and immortal are the eternal
6 likeness of their Maker. Man is by no means a material
germ rising from the imperfect and endeavoring to reach
Spirit above his origin. The stream rises no higher than
9 its source.

The measurement of life by solar years robs youth and
gives ugliness to age. The radiant sun of virtue and truth
12 coexists with being. Manhood is its eternal noon, un-
dimmed by a declining sun. As the physical and material, the transient sense of beauty fades, the radiance of
15 Spirit should dawn upon the enraptured sense with bright
and imperishable glories.

Never record ages. Chronological data are no part
18 of the vast forever. Time-tables of birth and death are
Undesirable so many conspiracies against manhood and
records   womanhood. Except for the error of meas-
21 uring and limiting all that is good and beautiful, man
would enjoy more than threescore years and ten and
still maintain his vigor, freshness, and promise. Man,
24 governed by immortal Mind, is always beautiful and
grand. Each succeeding year unfolds wisdom, beauty,
and holiness.

27   Life is eternal. We should find this out, and begin the
demonstration thereof. Life and goodness are immortal.
True life   Let us then shape our views of existence into
30   eternal   loveliness, freshness, and continuity, rather
than into age and blight.

Acute and chronic beliefs reproduce their own types.

The acute belief of physical life comes on at a remote 1
period, and is not so disastrous as the chronic belief.

I have seen age regain two of the elements it had lost, 3
sight and teeth. A woman of eighty-five, whom I knew,
had a return of sight. Another woman at   Eyes
ninety had new teeth, incisors, cuspids, bi- and teeth   6
cuspids, and one molar. One man at sixty   renewed
had retained his full set of upper and lower teeth without
a decaying cavity.   9

Beauty, as well as truth, is eternal; but the beauty
of material things passes away, fading and fleeting as
mortal belief. Custom, education, and fashion   Eternal   12
form the transient standards of mortals. Im-   beauty
mortality, exempt from age or decay, has a glory of its
own, — the radiance of Soul. Immortal men and women 15
are models of spiritual sense, drawn by perfect Mind
and reflecting those higher conceptions of loveliness
which transcend all material sense.   18

Comeliness and grace are independent of matter. Being possesses its qualities before they are perceived humanly. Beauty is a thing of life, which   The divine   21
dwells forever in the eternal Mind and re-   loveliness
flects the charms of His goodness in expression, form,
outline, and color. It is Love which paints the petal 24
with myriad hues, glances in the warm sunbeam, arches
the cloud with the bow of beauty, blazons the night with
starry gems, and covers earth with loveliness.   27

The embellishments of the person are poor substitutes
for the charms of being, shining resplendent and eternal
over age and decay.   30

The recipe for beauty is to have less illusion and
more Soul, to retreat from the belief of pain or pleasure

1 in the body into the unchanging calm and glorious freedom of spiritual harmony.

3   Love never loses sight of loveliness. Its halo rests upon
its object. One marvels that a friend can ever seem less

Love's
endowment than beautiful. Men and women of riper
6 years and larger lessons ought to ripen into
health and immortality, instead of lapsing into darkness
or gloom. Immortal Mind feeds the body with supernal
9 freshness and fairness, supplying it with beautiful images
of thought and destroying the woes of sense which each
day brings to a nearer tomb.

12   The sculptor turns from the marble to his model in
order to perfect his conception. We are all sculptors,

Mental
sculpture working at various forms, moulding and chisel-
15 ing thought. What is the model before mortal
mind? Is it imperfection, joy, sorrow, sin, suffering?
Have you accepted the mortal model? Are you repro-
18 ducing it? Then you are haunted in your work by vicious
sculptors and hideous forms. Do you not hear from all
mankind of the imperfect model? The world is holding
21 it before your gaze continually. The result is that you
are liable to follow those lower patterns, limit your life-
work, and adopt into your experience the angular outline
24 and deformity of matter models.

  To remedy this, we must first turn our gaze in the right
direction, and then walk that way. We must form perfect
27 Perfect
models models in thought and look at them continually,
or we shall never carve them out in grand and
noble lives. Let unselfishness, goodness, mercy, justice,
30 health, holiness, love — the kingdom of heaven — reign
within us, and sin, disease, and death will diminish until
they finally disappear.

Let us accept Science, relinquish all theories based on 1
sense-testimony, give up imperfect models and illusive
ideals; and so let us have one God, one Mind, and that 3
one perfect, producing His own models of excellence.
Let the "male and female" of God's creating appear.
Let us feel the divine energy of Spirit, bringing us into 6
newness of life and recognizing no mortal nor   Renewed
material power as able to destroy. Let us re-   selfhood
joice that we are subject to the divine "powers that be." 9
Such is the true Science of being. Any other theory of
Life, or God, is delusive and mythological.

Mind is not the author of matter, and the creator of 12
ideas is not the creator of illusions. Either there is no
omnipotence, or omnipotence is the only power. God is
the infinite, and infinity never began, will never end, and 15
includes nothing unlike God. Whence then is soulless
matter?

Life is, like Christ, "the same yesterday, and to-day, 18
and forever." Organization and time have nothing to do
with Life. You say, "I dreamed last night."   Illusive
What a mistake is that! The I is Spirit. God   dreams   21
never slumbers, and His likeness never dreams. Mortals
are the Adam dreamers.

Sleep and apathy are phases of the dream that life, sub- 24
stance, and intelligence are material. The mortal night-
dream is sometimes nearer the fact of being than are the
thoughts of mortals when awake. The night-dream has 27
less matter as its accompaniment. It throws off some
material fetters. It falls short of the skies, but makes its
mundane flights quite ethereal.   30

Man is the reflection of Soul. He is the direct opposite of material sensation, and there is but one Ego. We

1 run into error when we divide Soul into souls, multiply
Mind into minds and suppose error to be mind, then mind
3 Philosophical to be in matter and matter to be a lawgiver,
blunders unintelligence to act like intelligence, and mortality to be the matrix of immortality.

6 Mortal existence is a dream; mortal existence has no
real entity, but saith "It is I." Spirit is the Ego which
Spirit the never dreams, but understands all things;
9 one Ego which never errs, and is ever conscious; which
never believes, but knows; which is never born and
never dies. Spiritual man is the likeness of this Ego.
12 Man is not God, but like a ray of light which comes from
the sun, man, the outcome of God, reflects God.

Mortal body and mind are one, and that one is called
15 man; but a mortal is not man, for man is immortal. A
Mortal exist- mortal may be weary or pained, enjoy or suffer,
ence a dream according to the dream he entertains in sleep.
18 When that dream vanishes, the mortal finds himself
experiencing none of these dream-sensations. To the
observer, the body lies listless, undisturbed, and sensa-
21 tionless, and the mind seems to be absent.

Now I ask, Is there any more reality in the waking
dream of mortal existence than in the sleeping dream?
24 There cannot be, since whatever appears to be a mortal
man is a mortal dream. Take away the mortal mind,
and matter has no more sense as a man than it has as
27 a tree. But the spiritual, real man is immortal.

Upon this stage of existence goes on the dance of mortal
mind. Mortal thoughts chase one another like snowflakes,
30 and drift to the ground. Science reveals Life as not being
at the mercy of death, nor will Science admit that happiness is ever the sport of circumstance.

Error is not real, hence it is not more imperative 1
as it hastens towards self-destruction. The so-called
belief of mortal mind apparent as an abscess   Error   3
should not grow more painful before it suppu-   self-destroyed
rates, neither should a fever become more severe before
it ends.   6

Fright is so great at certain stages of mortal belief
as to drive belief into new paths. In the illusion of
death, mortals wake to the knowledge of two   Illusion   9
facts: (1) that they are not dead; (2) that   of death
they have but passed the portals of a new belief. Truth
works out the nothingness of error in just these ways. 12
Sickness, as well as sin, is an error that Christ, Truth,
alone can destroy.

We must learn how mankind govern the body, — 15
whether through faith in hygiene, in drugs, or in will-
power. We should learn whether they govern   Mortal
the body through a belief in the necessity of   mind's   18
sickness and death, sin and pardon, or govern   disappearance
it from the higher understanding that the divine Mind
makes perfect, acts upon the so-called human mind 21
through truth, leads the human mind to relinquish all
error, to find the divine Mind to be the only Mind,
and the healer of sin, disease, death. This process of 24
higher spiritual understanding improves mankind until
error disappears, and nothing is left which deserves to
perish or to be punished.   27

Ignorance, like intentional wrong, is not Science.
Ignorance must be seen and corrected before we can attain harmony. Inharmonious beliefs, which   Spiritual   30
rob Mind, calling it matter, and deify their   ignorance
own notions, imprison themselves in what they create.

1 They are at war with Science, and as our Master said,
"If a kingdom be divided against itself, that kingdom
3 cannot stand."

Human ignorance of Mind and of the recuperative
energies of Truth occasions the only skepticism regard-
6 ing the pathology and theology of Christian Science.

When false human beliefs learn even a little of their
own falsity, they begin to disappear. A knowledge of
9 *Eternal man recognized* error and of its operations must precede that
understanding of Truth which destroys error,
until the entire mortal, material error finally disappears,
12 and the eternal verity, man created by and of Spirit,
is understood and recognized as the true likeness of his
Maker.

15 The false evidence of material sense contrasts strikingly
with the testimony of Spirit. Material sense lifts its voice
with the arrogance of reality and says:

18 I am wholly dishonest, and no man knoweth it. I can
cheat, lie, commit adultery, rob, murder, and I elude
Testimony of sense detection by smooth-tongued villainy. Ani-
21 mal in propensity, deceitful in sentiment,
fraudulent in purpose, I mean to make my short span
of life one gala day. What a nice thing is sin! How
24 sin succeeds, where the good purpose waits! The world
is my kingdom. I am enthroned in the gorgeousness
of matter. But a touch, an accident, the law of God,
27 may at any moment annihilate my peace, for all my
fancied joys are fatal. Like bursting lava, I expand but
to my own despair, and shine with the resplendency of
30 consuming fire.

Spirit, bearing opposite testimony, saith:

I am Spirit. Man, whose senses are spiritual, is my

likeness. He reflects the infinite understanding, for I am 1
Infinity. The beauty of holiness, the perfection of being,
imperishable glory, — all are Mine, for I am Testimony 3
God. I give immortality to man, for I am of Soul
Truth. I include and impart all bliss, for I am Love.
I give life, without beginning and without end, for I am 6
Life. I am supreme and give all, for I am Mind. I am
the substance of all, because I AM THAT I AM.

I hope, dear reader, I am leading you into the under- 9
standing of your divine rights, your heaven-bestowed harmony, — that, as you read, you see there is no Heaven-
cause (outside of erring, mortal, material sense bestowed 12
which is not power) able to make you sick or prerogative
sinful; and I hope that you are conquering this false sense.
Knowing the falsity of so-called material sense, you can 15
assert your prerogative to overcome the belief in sin, disease, or death.

If you believe in and practise wrong knowingly, you 18
can at once change your course and do right. Matter can
make no opposition to right endeavors against Right
sin or sickness, for matter is inert, mindless. endeavor 21
Also, if you believe yourself diseased, you can possible
alter this wrong belief and action without hindrance from
the body. 24

Do not believe in any supposed necessity for sin, disease, or death, knowing (as you ought to know) that God
never requires obedience to a so-called material law, for 27
no such law exists. The belief in sin and death is destroyed by the law of God, which is the law of Life instead of death, of harmony instead of discord, of Spirit 30
instead of the flesh.

The divine demand, "Be ye therefore perfect," is sci-

1 entific, and the human footsteps leading to perfection are
indispensable. Individuals are consistent who, watching
3   *Patience* and praying, can "run, and not be weary; . . .
and final walk, and not faint," who gain good rapidly
perfection and hold their position, or attain slowly and
6 yield not to discouragement. God requires perfection,
but not until the battle between Spirit and flesh is fought
and the victory won. To stop eating, drinking, or being
9 clothed materially before the spiritual facts of existence
are gained step by step, is not legitimate. When we wait
patiently on God and seek Truth righteously, He directs
12 our path. Imperfect mortals grasp the ultimate of spiritual perfection slowly; but to *begin* aright and to continue the strife of demonstrating the great problem of
15 being, is doing much.

During the sensual ages, absolute Christian Science
may not be achieved prior to the change called death,
18 for we have not the power to demonstrate what we do
not understand. But the human self must be evangel-
ized. This task God demands us to accept lovingly
21 to-day, and to abandon so fast as practical the material,
and to work out the spiritual which determines the outward and actual.

24   If you venture upon the quiet surface of error and are
in sympathy with error, what is there to disturb the waters?
What is there to strip off error's disguise?

27   If you launch your bark upon the ever-agitated but
healthful waters of truth, you will encounter storms.
The cross Your good will be evil spoken of. This is the
30   *and crown* cross. Take it up and bear it, for through it
you win and wear the crown. Pilgrim on earth, thy home
is heaven; stranger, thou art the guest of God.

Ended 11-84

CHAPTER IX

Creation

Thy throne is established of old:
Thou art from everlasting. — PSALMS.

For we know that the whole creation groaneth and travaileth in pain
together until now. And not only they, but ourselves also, which have
the firstfruits of the Spirit, even we ourselves groan within ourselves,
waiting for the adoption, to wit, the redemption of our body. — PAUL.

ETERNAL Truth is changing the universe. As mor- 1
tals drop off their mental swaddling-clothes, thought
expands into expression. "Let there be light," 3
is the perpetual demand of Truth and Love,   **Inadequate**
   theories of
changing chaos into order and discord into the   **creation**
music of the spheres. The mythical human theories of 6
creation, anciently classified as the higher criticism, sprang
from cultured scholars in Rome and in Greece, but they
afforded no foundation for accurate views of creation by 9
the divine Mind.

Mortal man has made a covenant with his eyes to belittle Deity with human conceptions. In league   **Finite views** 12
with material sense, mortals take limited views   **of Deity**
of all things. That God is corporeal or material, no man
should affirm. 15

The human form, or physical finiteness, cannot be
made the basis of any true idea of the infinite Godhead.
Eye hath not seen Spirit, nor hath ear heard His voice. 18

1 Progress takes off human shackles. The finite must
yield to the infinite. Advancing to a higher plane of ac-
3 No material tion, thought rises from the material sense to
creation the spiritual, from the scholastic to the in-
spirational, and from the mortal to the immortal. All
6 things are created spiritually. Mind, not matter, is the
creator. Love, the divine Principle, is the Father and
Mother of the universe, including man.

9 The theory of three persons in one God (that is, a per-
Tritheism sonal Trinity or Tri-unity) suggests polythe-
impossible ism, rather than the one ever-present I AM.
12 "Hear, O Israel: the Lord our God is one Lord."

The everlasting I AM is not bounded nor compressed
within the narrow limits of physical humanity, nor can
15 No divine He be understood aright through mortal con-
corporeality cepts. The precise form of God must be of
small importance in comparison with the sublime ques-
18 tion, What is infinite Mind or divine Love?

Who is it that demands our obedience? He who, in
the language of Scripture, "doeth according to His will
21 in the army of heaven, and among the inhabitants of the
earth; and none can stay His hand, or say unto Him,
What doest Thou?"

24 No form nor physical combination is adequate to represent infinite Love. A finite and material sense of God
leads to formalism and narrowness; it chills the spirit of
27 Christianity.

A limitless Mind cannot proceed from physical limita-
tions. Finiteness cannot present the idea or the vast-
30 Limitless ness of infinity. A mind originating from a
Mind finite or material source must be limited and
finite. Infinite Mind is the creator, and creation is the

infinite image or idea emanating from this Mind. If 1
Mind is within and without all things, then all is Mind;
and this definition is scientific. 3

If matter, so-called, is substance, then Spirit, matter's
unlikeness, must be shadow; and shadow cannot produce
substance. The theory that Spirit is not the   Matter is not   6
only substance and creator is pantheistic het-   substance
erodoxy, which ultimates in sickness, sin, and death; it is
the belief in a bodily soul and a material mind, a soul 9
governed by the body and a mind in matter. This belief is shallow pantheism.

Mind creates His own likeness in ideas, and the sub- 12
stance of an idea is very far from being the supposed substance of non-intelligent matter. Hence the Father Mind
is not the father of matter. The material senses and 15
human conceptions would translate spiritual ideas into
material beliefs, and would say that an anthropomorphic
God, instead of infinite Principle, — in other words, divine 18
Love, — is the father of the rain, "who hath begotten the
drops of dew," who bringeth "forth Mazzaroth in his season," and guideth "Arcturus with his sons." 21

Finite mind manifests all sorts of errors, and thus
proves the material theory of mind in matter to be the
antipode of Mind. Who hath found finite life   Inexhaustible   24
or love sufficient to meet the demands of human   divine Love
want and woe, — to still the desires, to satisfy the aspirations? Infinite Mind cannot be limited to a finite form, 27
or Mind would lose its infinite character as inexhaustible
Love, eternal Life, omnipotent Truth.

It would require an infinite form to contain infinite 30
Mind. Indeed, the phrase *infinite form* involves a contradiction of terms. Finite man cannot be the image and

1 likeness of the infinite God. A mortal, corporeal, or
finite conception of God cannot embrace the glories of
3   limitless, incorporeal Life and Love. Hence
  Infinite
  physique   the unsatisfied human craving for something
  impossible better, higher, holier, than is afforded by a
6 material belief in a physical God and man. The insuffi-
ciency of this belief to supply the true idea proves the
falsity of material belief.

9   Man is more than a material form with a mind inside,
  Infinity's which must escape from its environments in
  reflection order to be immortal. Man reflects infinity,
12 and this reflection is the true idea of God.
   God expresses in man the infinite idea forever develop-
ing itself, broadening and rising higher and higher from
15 a boundless basis. Mind manifests all that exists in
the infinitude of Truth. We know no more of man as
the true divine image and likeness, than we know of
18 God.
   The infinite Principle is reflected by the infinite idea
and spiritual individuality, but the material so-called senses
21 have no cognizance of either Principle or its idea. The
human capacities are enlarged and perfected in proportion as humanity gains the true conception of man and
24 God.
   Mortals have a very imperfect sense of the spiritual
man and of the infinite range of his thought. To him
27 Individual belongs eternal Life. Never born and
  permanency never dying, it were impossible for man, under
the government of God in eternal Science, to fall from his
30 high estate.
   Through spiritual sense you can discern the heart of
divinity, and thus begin to comprehend in Science the

generic term *man.* Man is not absorbed in Deity, and 1
man cannot lose his individuality, for he re-   God's man
flects eternal Life; nor is he an isolated, soli-   discerned   3
tary idea, for he represents infinite Mind, the sum of all
substance.

In divine Science, man is the true image of God. The 6
divine nature was best expressed in Christ Jesus, who
threw upon mortals the truer reflection of God and lifted
their lives higher than their poor thought-models would 9
allow, — thoughts which presented man as fallen, sick,
sinning, and dying. The Christlike understanding of
scientific being and divine healing includes a perfect Prin- 12
ciple and idea, — perfect God and perfect man, — as the
basis of thought and demonstration.

If man was once perfect but has now lost his perfection, 15
then mortals have never beheld in man the reflex image
of God. The *lost* image is no image. The   The divine
true likeness cannot be lost in divine reflection.   image not   18
                                                       lost
Understanding this, Jesus said: "Be ye therefore perfect, even as your Father which is in heaven is
perfect."   21

Mortal thought transmits its own images, and forms
its offspring after human illusions. God, Spirit, works
spiritually, not materially. Brain or matter   Immortal   24
never formed a human concept. Vibration is   models
not intelligence; hence it is not a creator. Immortal
ideas, pure, perfect, and enduring, are transmitted by 27
the divine Mind through divine Science, which corrects
error with truth and demands spiritual thoughts, divine
concepts, to the end that they may produce harmonious 30
results.

Deducing one's conclusions as to man from imperfec-

1 tion instead of perfection, one can no more arrive at the
true conception or understanding of man, and make him-
3 self like it, than the sculptor can perfect his outlines from
an imperfect model, or the painter can depict the form
and face of Jesus, while holding in thought the character
6 of Judas.

The conceptions of mortal, erring thought must give
way to the ideal of all that is perfect and eternal. Through
9   Spiritual   many generations human beliefs will be attain-
     discovery   ing diviner conceptions, and the immortal and
perfect model of God's creation will finally be seen as
12 the only true conception of being.

Science reveals the possibility of achieving all good,
and sets mortals at work to discover what God has already
15 done; but distrust of one's ability to gain the goodness
desired and to bring out better and higher results, often
hampers the trial of one's wings and ensures failure at the
18 outset.

Mortals must change their ideals in order to improve
            their models. A sick body is evolved from
    Requisite
21   change of   sick thoughts. Sickness, disease, and death
    our ideals
            proceed from fear. Sensualism evolves bad
physical and moral conditions.

24 Selfishness and sensualism are educated in mortal
mind by the thoughts ever recurring to one's self, by
conversation about the body, and by the expectation of
27 perpetual pleasure or pain from it; and this education
is at the expense of spiritual growth. If we array
thought in mortal vestures, it must lose its immortal
30 nature.

If we look to the body for pleasure, we find pain; for
Life, we find death; for Truth, we find error; for Spirit,

we find its opposite, matter. Now reverse this action. 1
Look away from the body into Truth and Love,   Thoughts
the Principle of all happiness, harmony, and   are things   3
immortality. Hold thought steadfastly to the enduring, the good, and the true, and you will bring these
into your experience proportionably to their occupancy 6
of your thoughts.

The effect of mortal mind on health and happiness is
seen in this: If one turns away from the body with such 9
absorbed interest as to forget it, the body   Unreality
experiences no pain. Under the strong im-   of pain
pulse of a desire to perform his part, a noted actor was 12
accustomed night after night to go upon the stage and
sustain his appointed task, walking about as actively
as the youngest member of the company. This old man 15
was so lame that he hobbled every day to the theatre, and
sat aching in his chair till his cue was spoken, — a signal
which made him as oblivious of physical infirmity as if 18
he had inhaled chloroform, though he was in the full possession of his so-called senses.

Detach sense from the body, or matter, which is only 21
a form of human belief, and you may learn the meaning
of God, or good, and the nature of the immu-   Immutable
table and immortal. Breaking away from the   identity   24
mutations of time and sense, you will neither   of man
lose the solid objects and ends of life nor your own identity. Fixing your gaze on the realities supernal, you will 27
rise to the spiritual consciousness of being, even as the bird
which has burst from the egg and preens its wings for a
skyward flight.   30

We should forget our bodies in remembering good and
the human race. Good demands of man every hour, in

1 which to work out the problem of being. Consecration
to good does not lessen man's dependence on God, but
3 Forgetfulness heightens it. Neither does consecration di-
of self minish man's obligations to God, but shows
the paramount necessity of meeting them. Christian
6 Science takes naught from the perfection of God, but it
ascribes to Him the entire glory. By putting "off the old
man with his deeds," mortals "put on immortality."

9   We cannot fathom the nature and quality of God's
creation by diving into the shallows of mortal belief. We
must reverse our feeble flutterings — our efforts to find
12 life and truth in matter — and rise above the testimony
of the material senses, above the mortal to the immortal
idea of God. These clearer, higher views inspire the God-
15 like man to reach the absolute centre and circumference
of his being.

Job said: "I have heard of Thee by the hearing of the
18 ear: but now mine eye seeth Thee." Mortals will echo
The true   Job's thought, when the supposed pain and
sense   pleasure of matter cease to predominate. They
21 will then drop the false estimate of life and happiness, of
joy and sorrow, and attain the bliss of loving unselfishly,
working patiently, and conquering all that is unlike God.
24 Starting from a higher standpoint, one rises spontane-
ously, even as light emits light without effort; for "where
your treasure is, there will your heart be also."

27   The foundation of mortal discord is a false sense of
man's origin. To begin rightly is to end rightly. Every
Mind the   concept which seems to begin with the brain
30 only cause   begins falsely. Divine Mind is the only cause
or Principle of existence. Cause does not exist in matter,
in mortal mind, or in physical forms.

Mortals are egotists. They believe themselves to be 1
independent workers, personal authors, and even privileged originators of something which Deity   Human   3
would not or could not create. The creations   egotism
of mortal mind are material. Immortal spiritual man
alone represents the truth of creation.   6

When mortal man blends his thoughts of existence
with the spiritual and works only as God works,
he will no longer grope in the dark and cling Mortal man   9
to earth because he has not tasted heaven.   a mis-creator
Carnal beliefs defraud us. They make man an involuntary hypocrite, — producing evil when he would create 12
good, forming deformity when he would outline grace
and beauty, injuring those whom he would bless. He
becomes a general mis-creator, who believes he is a 15
semi-god. His "touch turns hope to dust, the dust we
all have trod." He might say in Bible language: "The
good that I would, I do not: but the evil which I would 18
not, *that I do*."

There can be but one creator, who has created all.
Whatever seems to be a new creation, is but the discovery 21
of some distant idea of Truth; else it is a   No new
new multiplication or self-division of mor-   creation
tal thought, as when some finite sense peers from its 24
cloister with amazement and attempts to pattern the
infinite.

The multiplication of a human and mortal sense of per- 27
sons and things is not creation. A sensual thought, like
an atom of dust thrown into the face of spiritual immensity, is dense blindness instead of a scientific eternal 30
consciousness of creation.

The fading forms of matter, the mortal body and ma-

1 terial earth, are the fleeting concepts of the human mind.
They have their day before the permanent facts and their

3 **Mind's true camera** perfection in Spirit appear. The crude creations of mortal thought must finally give place
to the glorious forms which we sometimes behold in the

6 camera of divine Mind, when the mental picture is spiritual and eternal. Mortals must look beyond fading,
finite forms, if they would gain the true sense of things.

9 Where shall the gaze rest but in the unsearchable realm
of Mind? We must look where we would walk, and we
must act as possessing all power from Him in whom we

12 have our being.

As mortals gain more correct views of God and man,
multitudinous objects of creation, which before were

15 **Self-completeness** invisible, will become visible. When we
realize that Life is Spirit, never in nor of
matter, this understanding will expand into self-com-

18 pleteness, finding all in God, good, and needing no other
consciousness.

Spirit and its formations are the only realities of being.

21 Matter disappears under the microscope of Spirit. Sin

Spiritual proofs of existence is unsustained by Truth, and sickness and
death were overcome by Jesus, who proved

24 them to be forms of error. Spiritual living
and blessedness are the only evidences, by which we can
recognize true existence and feel the unspeakable peace

27 which comes from an all-absorbing spiritual love.

When we learn the way in Christian Science and recognize man's spiritual being, we shall behold and under-

30 stand God's creation, — all the glories of earth and heaven
and man.

The universe of Spirit is peopled with spiritual beings,

and its government is divine Science. Man is the off- 1
spring, not of the lowest, but of the highest qualities of
Mind. Man understands spiritual existence   Godward   3
in proportion as his treasures of Truth and   gravitation
Love are enlarged. Mortals must gravitate Godward,
their affections and aims grow spiritual, — they must near 6
the broader interpretations of being, and gain some proper
sense of the infinite, — in order that sin and mortality
may be put off.   9
This scientific sense of being, forsaking matter for
Spirit, by no means suggests man's absorption into Deity
and the loss of his identity, but confers upon man en- 12
larged individuality, a wider sphere of thought and action,
a more expansive love, a higher and more permanent
peace.   15
The senses represent birth as untimely and death as
irresistible, as if man were a weed growing apace or a
flower withered by the sun and nipped by   Mortal birth 18
untimely frosts; but this is true only of a   and death
mortal, not of a man in God's image and likeness. The
truth of being is perennial, and the error is unreal and 21
obsolete.
Who that has felt the loss of human peace has not gained
stronger desires for spiritual joy? The aspiration after 24
heavenly good comes even before we discover   Blessings
what belongs to wisdom and Love. The loss   from pain
of earthly hopes and pleasures brightens the ascending 27
path of many a heart. The pains of sense quickly inform
us that the pleasures of sense are mortal and that joy is
spiritual.   30
The pains of sense are salutary, if they wrench away
false pleasurable beliefs and transplant the affections

6 existence without person... friends

1 from sense to Soul, where the creations of God are good,
     Decapitation   "rejoicing the heart." Such is the sword of
     of error
3   Science, with which Truth decapitates error,
materiality giving place to man's higher individuality and
destiny.

6   Would existence without personal friends be to you
a blank? Then the time will come when you will be
     Uses of   solitary, left without sympathy; but this
9   adversity   seeming vacuum is already filled with divine
Love. When this hour of development comes, even if
you cling to a sense of personal joys, spiritual Love will
12 force you to accept what best promotes your growth.
Friends will betray and enemies will slander, until the
lesson is sufficient to exalt you; for "man's extremity
15 is God's opportunity." The author has experienced the
foregoing prophecy and its blessings. Thus He teaches
mortals to lay down their fleshliness and gain spirituality.
18 This is done through self-abnegation. Universal Love
is the divine way in Christian Science.

    The sinner makes his own hell by doing evil, and the
21 saint his own heaven by doing right. The opposite persecutions of material sense, aiding evil with evil, would
deceive the very elect.

24   Mortals must follow Jesus' sayings and his demonstrations, which dominate the flesh. Perfect and infinite
     Beatific   Mind enthroned is heaven. The evil beliefs
27   presence   which originate in mortals are hell. Man is the
idea of Spirit; he reflects the beatific presence, illuming
the universe with light. Man is deathless, spiritual. He
30 is above sin or frailty. He does not cross the barriers
of time into the vast forever of Life, but he coexists with
God and the universe.

Every object in material thought will be destroyed, but 1
the spiritual idea, whose substance is in Mind, is eternal.
The offspring of God start not from matter The infinitude 3
of God
or ephemeral dust. They are in and of Spirit,
divine Mind, and so forever continue. God is one. The
allness of Deity is His oneness. Generically man is one, 6
and specifically man means all men.

It is generally conceded that God is Father, eternal, self-
created, infinite. If this is so, the forever Father must 9
have had children prior to Adam. The great I AM made
all "that was made." Hence man and the spiritual universe coexist with God. 12

Christian Scientists understand that, in a religious
sense, they have the same authority for the appellative
mother, as for that of brother and sister. Jesus said: 15
"For whosoever shall do the will of my Father which
is in heaven, the same is my brother, and sister, and
mother." 18

When examined in the light of divine Science, mortals
present more than is detected upon the surface, since
inverted thoughts and erroneous beliefs must Waymarks 21
be counterfeits of Truth. Thought is bor- to eternal
Truth
rowed from a higher source than matter, and
by reversal, errors serve as waymarks to the one Mind, 24
in which all error disappears in celestial Truth. The
robes of Spirit are "white and glistering," like the raiment
of Christ. Even in this world, therefore, "let thy gar- 27
ments be always white." "Blessed is the man that endureth [overcometh] temptation: for when he is tried,
[proved faithful], he shall receive the crown of life, 30
which the Lord hath promised to them that love him."
(James i. 12.)

CHAPTER X

Science of Being

That which was from the beginning, which we have heard, which we have seen with our eyes, which we have looked upon, and our hands have handled, of the Word of life, . . . That which we have seen and heard declare we unto you, that ye also may have fellowship with us: and truly our fellowship is with the Father, and with His Son Jesus Christ. — JOHN, First Epistle.

Here I stand. I can do no otherwise; so help me God! Amen! — MARTIN LUTHER.

1 IN the material world, thought has brought to light with great rapidity many useful wonders. With 3 like activity have thought's swift pinions been rising

Materialistic towards the realm of the real, to the spiritual
challenge cause of those lower things which give im-
6 pulse to inquiry. Belief in a material basis, from which may be deduced all rationality, is slowly yielding to the idea of a metaphysical basis, looking away from 9 matter to Mind as the cause of every effect. Materialistic hypotheses challenge metaphysics to meet in final combat. In this revolutionary period, like the shep-12 herd-boy with his sling, woman goes forth to battle with Goliath.

In this final struggle for supremacy, semi-metaphysi-15 cal systems afford no substantial aid to scientific meta-

Confusion physics, for their arguments are based on
confounded the false testimony of the material senses as
18 well as on the facts of Mind. These semi-metaphysical

268

systems are one and all pantheistic, and savor of Pan- 1
demonium, a house divided against itself.

From first to last the supposed coexistence of Mind 3
and matter and the mingling of good and evil have resulted from the philosophy of the serpent. Jesus' demonstrations sift the chaff from the wheat, and unfold the 6
unity and the reality of good, the unreality, the nothingness, of evil.

Human philosophy has made God manlike. Christian 9
Science makes man Godlike. The first is error; the latter
is truth. Metaphysics is above physics, and   Divine
matter does not enter into metaphysical prem- metaphysics 12
ises or conclusions. The categories of metaphysics rest
on one basis, the divine Mind. Metaphysics resolves
things into thoughts, and exchanges the objects of sense 15
for the ideas of Soul.

These ideas are perfectly real and tangible to spiritual
consciousness, and they have this advantage over the ob- 18
jects and thoughts of material sense, — they are good and
eternal.

The testimony of the material senses is neither abso- 21
lute nor divine. I therefore plant myself unreservedly
on the teachings of Jesus, of his apostles, of   Biblical
the prophets, and on the testimony of the   foundations 24
Science of Mind. Other foundations there are none.
All other systems — systems based wholly or partly on
knowledge gained through the material senses — are reeds 27
shaken by the wind, not houses built on the rock.

The theories I combat are these: (1) that all is matter;
(2) that matter originates in Mind, and is as   Rejected 30
real as Mind, possessing intelligence and life.   theories
The first theory, that matter is everything, is quite as

1 reasonable as the second, that Mind and matter coexist
and cooperate. One only of the following statements can
3 be true: (1) that everything is matter; (2) that everything is Mind. Which one is it?

Matter and Mind are opposites. One is contrary to
6 the other in its very nature and essence; hence both cannot be real. If one is real, the other must be unreal. Only
by understanding that there is but one power, — not two
9 powers, matter and Mind, — are scientific and logical
conclusions reached. Few deny the hypothesis that intelligence, apart from man and matter, governs the uni-
12 verse; and it is generally admitted that this intelligence
is the eternal Mind or divine Principle, Love.

The prophets of old looked for something higher than
15 Prophetic   the systems of their times; hence their fore-
ignorance   sight of the new dispensation of Truth. But
they knew not what would be the precise nature of the
18 teaching and demonstration of God, divine Mind, in His
more infinite meanings, — the demonstration which was
to destroy sin, sickness, and death, establish the definition
21 of omnipotence, and maintain the Science of Spirit.

The pride of priesthood is the prince of this world. It
has nothing in Christ. Meekness and charity have divine
24 authority. Mortals think wickedly; consequently they
are wicked. They think sickly thoughts, and so become
sick. If sin makes sinners, Truth and Love alone can
27 unmake them. If a sense of disease produces suffering
and a sense of ease antidotes suffering, disease is mental,
not material. Hence the fact that the human mind alone
30 suffers, is sick, and that the divine Mind alone heals.

The life of Christ Jesus was not miraculous, but it was
indigenous to his spirituality, — the good soil wherein the

27/:7 How to heal with truth. M

Science of Being   271

seed of Truth springs up and bears much fruit. Christ's 1
Christianity is the chain of scientific being reappearing
in all ages, maintaining its obvious correspondence with 3
the Scriptures and uniting all periods in the design of
God. Neither emasculation, illusion, nor insubordination
exists in divine Science.   6

Jesus instructed his disciples whereby to heal the sick
through Mind instead of matter. He knew that the philosophy, Science, and proof of Christianity were in Truth, 9
casting out all inharmony.

In Latin the word rendered *disciple* signifies student;
and the word indicates that the power of healing was not 12
a supernatural gift to those learners, but the   Studious
result of their cultivated spiritual understand-   disciples
ing of the divine Science, which their Master demonstrated 15
by healing the sick and sinning. Hence the universal application of his saying: "Neither pray I for these alone,
but for them also which shall believe on me [understand 18
me] through their word."

Our Master said, "But the Comforter . . . shall
teach you all things." When the Science of Christianity 21
appears, it will lead you into all truth. The New Testament
Sermon on the Mount is the essence of this   basis
Science, and the eternal life, not the death of Jesus, is 24
its outcome.

Those, who are willing to leave their nets or to cast
them on the right side for Truth, have the opportunity 27
now, as aforetime, to learn and to practise   Modern
Christian healing. The Scriptures contain it. evangel
The spiritual import of the Word imparts this power. 30
But, as Paul says, "How shall they hear without a
preacher? and how shall they preach, except they be

1 sent?" If sent, how shall they preach, convert, and heal
multitudes, except the people hear?

3 The spiritual sense of truth must be gained before
Truth can be understood. This sense is assimilated only
Spirituality   as we are honest, unselfish, loving, and meek.
6 of Scripture   In the soil of an "honest and good heart" the
seed must be sown; else it beareth not much fruit, for the
swinish element in human nature uproots it. Jesus said:
9 "Ye do err, not knowing the Scriptures." The spiritual
sense of the Scriptures brings out the scientific sense, and
is the new tongue referred to in the last chapter of Mark's
12 Gospel.

Jesus' parable of "the sower" shows the care our
Master took not to impart to dull ears and gross hearts
15 the spiritual teachings which dulness and grossness could
not accept. Reading the thoughts of the people, he said:
"Give not that which is holy unto the dogs, neither cast
18 ye your pearls before swine."

It is the spiritualization of thought and Christianization
of daily life, in contrast with the results of the ghastly farce
21 Unspiritual   of material existence; it is chastity and purity,
contrasts   in contrast with the downward tendencies
and earthward gravitation of sensualism and impurity,
24 which really attest the divine origin and operation of Christian Science. The triumphs of Christian Science are recorded in the destruction of error and evil, from which are
27 propagated the dismal beliefs of sin, sickness, and death.

The divine Principle of the universe must interpret the
universe. God is the divine Principle of all that repre-
30 God the   sents Him and of all that really exists. Chris-
Principle of all   tian Science, as demonstrated by Jesus, alone
reveals the natural, divine Principle of Science.

Matter and its claims of sin, sickness, and death are 1
contrary to God, and cannot emanate from Him. There
is no *material* truth. The physical senses can take no 3
cognizance of God and spiritual Truth. Human belief
has sought out many inventions, but not one of them
can solve the problem of being without the divine Prin- 6
ciple of divine Science. Deductions from material hypotheses are not scientific. They differ from real Science
because they are not based on the divine law. 9

Divine Science reverses the false testimony of the material senses, and thus tears away the foundations of error. Hence the enmity between   Science
versus   12
Science and the senses, and the impossibility   sense
of attaining perfect understanding till the errors of sense
are eliminated. 15

The so-called laws of matter and of medical science have
never made mortals whole, harmonious, and immortal.
Man is harmonious when governed by Soul. Hence the 18
importance of understanding the truth of being, which
reveals the laws of spiritual existence.

God never ordained a material law to annul the spiritual 21
law. If there were such a material law, it would oppose
the supremacy of Spirit, God, and impugn the   Spiritual law
wisdom of the creator. Jesus walked on the   the only law   24
waves, fed the multitude, healed the sick, and raised the
dead in direct opposition to material laws. His acts were
the demonstration of Science, overcoming the false claims 27
of material sense or law.

Science shows that material, conflicting mortal opinions and beliefs emit the effects of error at all times, but 30
this atmosphere of mortal mind cannot be destructive to
morals and health when it is opposed promptly and per-

1 sistently by Christian Science. Truth and Love antidote
this mental miasma, and thus invigorate and sustain ex-
3   istence. Unnecessary knowledge gained from

*Material
knowledge
illusive* the five senses is only temporal, — the conception of mortal mind, the offspring of sense, not
6 of Soul, Spirit, — and symbolizes all that is evil and
perishable. *Natural science,* as it is commonly called, is
not really natural nor scientific, because it is deduced from
9 the evidence of the material senses. Ideas, on the contrary, are born of Spirit, and are not mere inferences
drawn from material premises.

12   The senses of Spirit abide in Love, and they demonstrate Truth and Life. Hence Christianity and the Sci-

*Five senses
deceptive* ence which expounds it are based on spiritual
15   understanding, and they supersede the so-
called laws of matter. Jesus demonstrated this great
verity. When what we erroneously term the five physical
18 senses are misdirected, they are simply the manifested
beliefs of mortal mind, which affirm that life, substance,
and intelligence are material, instead of spiritual. These
21 false beliefs and their products constitute the flesh, and
the flesh wars against Spirit.

Divine Science is absolute, and permits no half-way
24 position in learning its Principle and rule — establishing

*Impossible
partnership* it by demonstration. The conventional firm,
called matter and mind, God never formed.
27 Science and understanding, governed by the unerring and
eternal Mind, destroy the imaginary copartnership, matter
and mind, formed only to be destroyed in a manner and
30 at a period as yet unknown. This suppositional partnership is already obsolete, for matter, examined in the light
of divine metaphysics, disappears.

Matter has no life to lose, and Spirit never dies. A 1
partnership of mind with matter would ignore omnipresent and omnipotent Mind. This shows that   Spirit the   3
matter did not originate in God, Spirit, and is   starting-point
not eternal. Therefore matter is neither substantial, living,
nor intelligent. The starting-point of divine Science is 6
that God, Spirit, is All-in-all, and that there is no other
might nor Mind, — that God is Love, and therefore He
is divine Principle.   9

To grasp the reality and order of being in its Science,
you must begin by reckoning God as the divine Principle
of all that really is. Spirit, Life, Truth, Love,   Divine   12
combine as one, — and are the Scriptural names   synonyms
for God. All substance, intelligence, wisdom, being, immortality, cause, and effect belong to God. These are 15
His attributes, the eternal manifestations of the infinite
divine Principle, Love. No wisdom is wise but His
wisdom; no truth is true, no love is lovely, no life is Life 18
but the divine; no good is, but the good God bestows.

Divine metaphysics, as revealed to spiritual understanding, shows clearly that all is Mind, and that Mind is 21
God, omnipotence, omnipresence, omniscience,   The divine
— that is, all power, all presence, all Science.   completeness
Hence all is in reality the manifestation of Mind.   24

Our material human theories are destitute of Science.
The true understanding of God is spiritual. It robs the
grave of victory. It destroys the false evidence that mis- 27
leads thought and points to other gods, or other so-called
powers, such as matter, disease, sin, and death, superior
or contrary to the one Spirit.   30

Truth, spiritually discerned, is scientifically understood.
It casts out error and heals the sick.

1 Having one God, one Mind, unfolds the power that
heals the sick, and fulfils these sayings of Scripture, "I

3 Universal　am the Lord that healeth thee," and "I have
brotherhood　found a ransom." When the divine precepts
are understood, they unfold the foundation of fellowship,

6 in which one mind is not at war with another, but all have
one Spirit, God, one intelligent source, in accordance with
the Scriptural command: "Let this Mind be in you,

9 which was also in Christ Jesus." Man and his Maker
are correlated in divine Science, and real consciousness
is cognizant only of the things of God.

12 The realization that all inharmony is unreal brings
objects and thoughts into human view in their true light,
and presents them as beautiful and immortal. Harmony

15 in man is as real and immortal as in music. Discord is
unreal and mortal.

If God is admitted to be the only Mind and Life,

18 there ceases to be any opportunity for sin and death.
Perfection　When we learn in Science how to be perfect
requisite　even as our Father in heaven is perfect,

21 thought is turned into new and healthy channels, —
towards the contemplation of things immortal and away
from materiality to the Principle of the universe, includ-

24 ing harmonious man.
Material beliefs and spiritual understanding never
mingle. The latter destroys the former. Discord is the

27 *nothingness* named error. Harmony is the *somethingness*
named Truth.

Nature and revelation inform us that like produces

30 Like　like. Divine Science does not gather grapes
evolving like　from thorns nor figs from thistles. Intelligence never produces non-intelligence; but matter is

be substance to us, — the erring, changing, and dying, 1
the mutable and mortal, or the unerring, immutable,
and immortal? A New Testament writer plainly de- 3
scribes faith, a quality of mind, as "the *substance* of things
hoped for."

The doom of matter establishes the conclusion that 6
matter, slime, or protoplasm never originated   Material
in the immortal Mind, and is therefore not   mortality
eternal. Matter is neither created by Mind nor for the 9
manifestation and support of Mind.

Ideas are tangible and real to immortal consciousness,
and they have the advantage of being eternal.   Spiritual   12
Spirit and matter can neither coexist nor co-   tangibility
operate, and one can no more create the other than
Truth can create error, or *vice versa*.   15

In proportion as the belief disappears that life and intelligence are in or of matter, the immortal facts of
being are seen, and their only idea or intelligence is 18
in God. Spirit is reached only through the understanding and demonstration of eternal Life and Truth and
Love.   21

Every system of human philosophy, doctrine, and
medicine is more or less infected with the pantheistic
belief that there is mind in matter; but this   Pantheistic   24
belief contradicts alike revelation and right   tendencies
reasoning. A logical and scientific conclusion is reached
only through the knowledge that there are not two 27
bases of being, matter and mind, but one alone, —
Mind.

Pantheism, starting from a material sense of God, 30
seeks cause in effect, Principle in its idea, and life and
intelligence in matter.

1 In the infinitude of Mind, matter must be unknown.
Symbols and elements of discord and decay are not prod-
3   ucts of the infinite, perfect, and eternal *All.*
The things
of God are From Love and from the light and harmony
beautiful
which are the abode of Spirit, only reflections
6 of good can come. All things beautiful and harmless are
ideas of Mind. Mind creates and multiplies them, and
the product must be mental.

9 Finite belief can never do justice to Truth in any direction. Finite belief limits all things, and would compress
Mind, which is infinite, beneath a skull bone. Such be-
12 lief can neither apprehend nor worship the infinite; and
to accommodate its finite sense of the divisibility of Soul
and substance, it seeks to divide the one Spirit into per-
15 sons and souls.

Through this error, human belief comes to have "gods
many and lords many." Moses declared as Jehovah's
18   Belief in   first command of the Ten: "Thou shalt have
many gods   no other gods before me!" But behold the
zeal of belief to establish the opposite error of many
21 minds. The argument of the serpent in the allegory, "Ye
shall be as gods," urges through every avenue the belief
that Soul is in body, and that infinite Spirit, and Life, is
24 in finite forms.

Rightly understood, instead of possessing a sentient
material form, man has a sensationless body; and God,
27 Sensationless the Soul of man and of all existence, being
body   perpetual in His own individuality, harmony,
and immortality, imparts and perpetuates these qualities
30 in man, — through Mind, not matter. The only excuse
for entertaining human opinions and rejecting the Science
of being is our mortal ignorance of Spirit, — ignorance

which yields only to the understanding of divine Science, 1
the understanding by which we enter into the kingdom
of Truth on earth and learn that Spirit is infinite and 3
supreme. Spirit and matter no more commingle than
light and darkness. When one appears, the other disappears.   6

Error presupposes man to be both mind and matter.
Divine Science contradicts the corporeal senses, rebukes
mortal belief, and asks: What is the Ego,   God and   9
whence its origin and what its destiny? The   His image
Ego-man is the reflection of the Ego-God; the Ego-man
is the image and likeness of perfect Mind, Spirit, divine 12
Principle.

The one Ego, the one Mind or Spirit called God, is
infinite individuality, which supplies all form and come- 15
liness and which reflects reality and divinity in individual
spiritual man and things.

The mind supposed to exist in matter or beneath a 18
skull bone is a myth, a misconceived sense and false
conception as to man and Mind. When we put off the
false sense for the true, and see that sin and mortality 21
have neither Principle nor permanency, we shall learn
that sin and mortality are without actual origin or rightful existence. They are native nothingness, out of which 24
error would simulate creation through a man formed from
dust.

Divine Science does not put new wine into old bottles, 27
Soul into matter, nor the infinite into the finite. Our
false views of matter perish as we grasp   The true
the facts of Spirit. The old belief must be   new idea   30
cast out or the new idea will be spilled, and the inspiration, which is to change our standpoint, will be

1 lost. Now, as of old, Truth casts out evils and heals the sick.

3 The real Life, or Mind, and its opposite, the so-called material life and mind, are figured by two geometrical
Figures of **symbols, a circle or sphere and a straight**
6 being **line. The circle represents the infinite with-**
out beginning or end; the straight line represents the finite, which has both beginning and end. The sphere
9 represents good, the self-existent and eternal individuality or Mind; the straight line represents evil, a belief in a self-made and temporary material existence. Eternal
12 Mind and temporary material existence never unite in figure or in fact.

A straight line finds no abiding-place in a curve, and a
15 curve finds no adjustment to a straight line. Similarly,
Opposite **matter has no place in Spirit, and Spirit has**
symbols **no place in matter. Truth has no home in**
18 error, and error has no foothold in Truth. Mind cannot pass into non-intelligence and matter, nor can non-intel-ligence become Soul. At no point can these opposites
21 mingle or unite. Even though they seem to touch, one is still a curve and the other a straight line.

There is no inherent power in matter; for all that is
24 material is a material, human, mortal thought, always governing itself erroneously.

Truth is the intelligence of immortal Mind. Error is
27 the so-called intelligence of mortal mind.

Whatever indicates the fall of man or the opposite of God or God's absence, is the Adam-dream, which is neither
30 Truth is not **Mind nor man, for it is not begotten of the**
inverted **Father. The rule of inversion infers from**
error its opposite, Truth; but Truth is the light which

dispels error. As mortals begin to understand Spirit, 1
they give up the belief that there is any true existence
apart from God. 3

Mind is the source of all movement, and there is no
inertia to retard or check its perpetual and harmonious
action. Mind is the same Life, Love, and wis- 6
dom "yesterday, and to-day, and forever." Source of
all life and action
Matter and its effects — sin, sickness, and
death — are states of mortal mind which act, react, and 9
then come to a stop. They are not facts of Mind. They
are not ideas, but illusions. Principle is absolute. It
admits of no error, but rests upon understanding. 12

But what say prevalent theories? They insist that
Life, or God, is one and the same with material life so-
called. They speak of both Truth and error as *mind,* 15
and of good and evil as *spirit.* They claim that to be
life which is but the objective state of material sense, —
such as the structural life of the tree and of material 18
man, — and deem this the manifestation of the one Life,
God.

This false belief as to what really constitutes life so 21
detracts from God's character and nature, that the true
sense of His power is lost to all who cling to Spiritual
structure
this falsity. The divine Principle, or Life, can- 24
not be practically demonstrated in length of days, as it
was by the patriarchs, unless its Science be accurately
stated. We must receive the divine Principle in the under- 27
standing, and live it in daily life; and unless we so do, we
can no more demonstrate Science, than we can teach and
illustrate geometry by calling a curve a straight line or a 30
straight line a sphere.

Are mentality, immortality, consciousness, resident in

1 matter? It is not rational to say that Mind is infinite,
but dwells in finiteness, — in matter, — or that matter is
3 infinite and the medium of Mind.

If God were limited to man or matter, or if the infinite
could be circumscribed within the finite, God would be
6 Mind never corporeal, and unlimited Mind would seem
limited   to spring from a limited body; but this is an
impossibility. Infinite Mind can have no starting-point,
9 and can return to no limit. It can never be in bonds,
nor be fully manifested through corporeality.

Is God's image or likeness matter, or a mortal, sin,
12 sickness, and death? Can matter recognize Mind?
            Can infinite Mind recognize matter? Can the
Material
recognition infinite dwell in the finite or know aught un-
impossible
15   like the infinite? Can Deity be known through
the material senses? Can the material senses, which receive no direct evidence of Spirit, give correct testimony
18 as to spiritual life, truth, and love?

The answer to all these questions must forever be in
the negative.
21   The physical senses can obtain no proof of God. They
can neither see Spirit through the eye nor hear it through
            the ear, nor can they feel, taste, or smell Spirit.
Our physical
24 insensibility Even the more subtile and misnamed ma-
to Spirit
            terial elements are beyond the cognizance
of these senses, and are known only by the effects com-
27 monly attributed to them.

According to Christian Science, the only real senses
of man are spiritual, emanating from divine Mind.
30 Thought passes from God to man, but neither sensation
nor report goes from material body to Mind. The in-
tercommunication is always from God to His idea, man.

Matter is not sentient and cannot be cognizant of good 1
or of evil, of pleasure or of pain. Man's individuality is not material. This Science of being obtains not 3
alone hereafter in what men call Paradise, but here
and now; it is the great fact of being for time and
eternity.   6

What, then, is the material personality which suffers,
sins, and dies? It is not man, the image and likeness
of God, but man's counterfeit, the inverted The human 9
likeness, the *unlikeness* called sin, sickness, counterfeit
and death. The unreality of the claim that a mortal is
the true image of God is illustrated by the opposite na- 12
tures of Spirit and matter, Mind and body, for one is
intelligence while the other is non-intelligence.

Is God a physical personality? Spirit is not physical. 15
The belief that a material body is man is a false conception of man. The time has come for a Material
finite conception of the infinite and of a ma- miscon- 18
terial body as the seat of Mind to give place ceptions
to a diviner sense of intelligence and its manifestations, —
to the better understanding that Science gives of the 21
Supreme Being, or divine Principle, and idea.

By interpreting God as a corporeal Saviour but not as
the saving Principle, or divine Love, we shall continue 24
to seek salvation through pardon and not Salvation
through reform, and resort to matter instead is through
of Spirit for the cure of the sick. As mortals reform 27
reach, through knowledge of Christian Science, a higher
sense, they will seek to learn, not from matter, but from
the divine Principle, God, how to demonstrate the Christ, 30
Truth, as the healing and saving power.

It is essential to understand, instead of believe, what

1 relates most nearly to the happiness of being. To seek
Truth through belief in a human doctrine is not to un-
3 derstand the infinite. We must not seek the immutable
and immortal through the finite, mutable, and mortal,
and so depend upon belief instead of demonstration, for
6 this is fatal to a knowledge of Science. The understanding of Truth gives full faith in Truth, and spiritual understanding is better than all burnt offerings.

9 The Master said, "No man cometh unto the Father
[the divine Principle of being] but by me," Christ,
Life, Truth, Love; for Christ says, "I am the way."
12 Physical causation was put aside from first to
last by this original man, Jesus. He knew that the
divine Principle, Love, creates and governs all that
15 is real.

In the Saxon and twenty other tongues *good* is the term
for God. The Scriptures declare all that He
made to be good, like Himself, — good in
Principle and in idea. Therefore the spiritual
universe is good, and reflects God as He is.

Goodness a portion of God

18

21 God's thoughts are perfect and eternal, are substance
and Life. Material and temporal thoughts are human,
involving error, and since God, Spirit, is the
only cause, they lack a divine cause. The
temporal and material are not then creations of Spirit.
They are but counterfeits of the spiritual and eternal.
27 Transitory thoughts are the antipodes of everlasting
Truth, though (by the supposition of opposite qualities)
error must also say, "I am true." But by this saying
30 error, the lie, destroys itself.

Spiritual thoughts

24

Sin, sickness, and death are comprised in human material belief, and belong not to the divine Mind. They

are without a real origin or existence. They have neither 1
Principle nor permanence, but belong, with all that is
material and temporal, to the nothingness of error, which 3
simulates the creations of Truth. All creations of Spirit
are eternal; but creations of matter must return to dust.
Error supposes man to be both mental and material. 6
Divine Science contradicts this postulate and maintains
man's spiritual identity.

We call the absence of Truth, *error*. Truth and error 9
are unlike. In Science, Truth is divine, and the *infinite*
God can have no unlikeness. Did God, Truth,   Divine
create error? No! "Doth a fountain send   allness   12
forth at the same place sweet water and bitter?" God
being everywhere and all-inclusive, how can He be absent
or suggest the absence of omnipresence and omnipotence? 15
How can there be more than *all?*

Neither understanding nor truth accompanies error,
nor is error the offshoot of Mind. Evil calls itself some- 18
thing, when it is nothing. It saith, "I am man, but I am
not the image and likeness of God;" whereas the Scriptures declare that man was made in God's likeness. 21

Error is false, mortal belief; it is illusion, without spiritual identity or foundation, and it has no real existence.
The supposition that life, substance, and in-   Error   24
telligence are *in* matter, or *of* it, is an error.   unveiled
Matter is neither a thing nor a person, but merely the
objective supposition of Spirit's opposite. The five mate- 27
rial senses testify to truth and error as united in a mind
both good and evil. Their false evidence will finally
yield to Truth, — to the recognition of Spirit and of the 30
spiritual creation.

Truth cannot be contaminated by error. The state-

1 ment that *Truth is real* necessarily includes the correlated
statement, that *error, Truth's unlikeness, is unreal.*

3 The suppositional warfare between truth and error is
only the mental conflict between the evidence of the spir-

The great
conflict
itual senses and the testimony of the material
6 senses, and this warfare between the Spirit and
flesh will settle all questions through faith in and the understanding of divine Love.

9 Superstition and understanding can never combine.
When the final physical and moral effects of Christian
Science are fully apprehended, the conflict between truth
12 and error, understanding and belief, Science and material
sense, foreshadowed by the prophets and inaugurated
by Jesus, will cease, and spiritual harmony reign. The
15 lightnings and thunderbolts of error may burst and flash
till the cloud is cleared and the tumult dies away in the
distance. Then the raindrops of divinity refresh the
18 earth. As St. Paul says: "There remaineth therefore
a rest to the people of God" (of Spirit).

The chief stones in the temple of Christian Science are
21 to be found in the following postulates: that Life is God,

The chief
stones in
the temple
good, and not evil; that Soul is sinless, not
to be found in the body; that Spirit is not, and
24 cannot be, materialized; that Life is not subject
to death; that the spiritual real man has no birth, no material life, and no death.

27 Science reveals the glorious possibilities of immortal

The
Christ-element
man, forever unlimited by the mortal senses.
The Christ-element in the Messiah made him
30 the Way-shower, Truth and Life.

The eternal Truth destroys what mortals seem to have
learned from error, and man's real existence as a child

of God comes to light. Truth demonstrated is eternal 1
life. Mortal man can never rise from the temporal *débris*
of error, belief in sin, sickness, and death, until he learns 3
that God is the only Life. The belief that life and sensation are in the body should be overcome by the understanding of what constitutes man as the image of God. 6
Then Spirit will have overcome the flesh.

A wicked mortal is not the idea of God. He is little
else than the expression of error. To suppose that sin, 9
lust, hatred, envy, hypocrisy, revenge, have life   *Wickedness*
abiding in them, is a terrible mistake. Life   *is not man*
and Life's idea, Truth and Truth's idea, never make men 12
sick, sinful, or mortal.

The fact that the Christ, or Truth, overcame and still
overcomes death proves the "king of terrors" to be but 15
a mortal belief, or error, which Truth destroys   *Death but*
with the spiritual evidences of Life; and this   *an illusion*
shows that what appears to the senses to be death is but a 18
mortal illusion, for to the real man and the real universe
there is no death-process.

The belief that matter has life results, by the universal 21
law of mortal mind, in a belief in death. So man, tree,
and flower are supposed to die; but the fact remains,
that God's universe is spiritual and immortal.   24

The spiritual fact and the material belief of things are
contradictions; but the spiritual is true, and therefore the
material must be untrue. Life is not in matter.   *Spiritual*   27
Therefore it cannot be said to pass out of mat-   *offspring*
ter. Matter and death are mortal illusions. Spirit and
all things spiritual are the real and eternal.   30

Man is not the offspring of flesh, but of Spirit, — of
Life, not of matter. Because Life is God, Life must be

1 eternal, self-existent. Life is the everlasting I am, the Being who was and is and shall be, whom nothing can erase.

3   If the Principle, rule, and demonstration of man's being
are not in the least understood before what is termed death
      Death no   overtakes mortals, they will rise no higher spir-
6   advantage   itually in the scale of existence on account of
that single experience, but will remain as material as before the transition, still seeking happiness through a ma-
9 terial, instead of through a spiritual sense of life, and from
selfish and inferior motives. That Life or Mind is finite
and physical or is manifested through brain and nerves,
12 is false. Hence Truth comes to destroy this error and
its effects, — sickness, sin, and death. To the spiritual
class, relates the Scripture: "On such the second death
15 hath no power."

If the change called *death* destroyed the belief in sin,
sickness, and death, happiness would be won at the mo-
18   Future   ment of dissolution, and be forever permanent;
    purification but this is not so. Perfection is gained only
by perfection. They who are unrighteous shall be un-
21 righteous still, until in divine Science Christ, Truth, removes all ignorance and sin.

The sin and error which possess us at the instant of
24 death do not cease at that moment, but endure until the
      Sin is   death of these errors. To be wholly spiritual,
    punished   man must be sinless, and he becomes thus only
27 when he reaches perfection. The murderer, though slain
in the act, does not thereby forsake sin. He is no more
spiritual for believing that his body died and learning that
30 his cruel mind died not. His thoughts are no purer until
evil is disarmed by good. His body is as material as his
mind, and *vice versa.*

The suppositions that sin is pardoned while unfor- 1
saken, that happiness can be genuine in the midst of
sin, that the so-called death of the body frees from sin, 3
and that God's pardon is aught but the destruction of
sin, — these are grave mistakes. We know that all will
be changed "in the twinkling of an eye," when the last 6
trump shall sound; but this last call of wisdom cannot
come till mortals have already yielded to each lesser call
in the growth of Christian character. Mortals need not 9
fancy that belief in the experience of death will awaken
them to glorified being.

Universal salvation rests on progression and probation, 12
and is unattainable without them. Heaven is not a locality, but a divine state of Mind in which all the
manifestations of Mind are harmonious and   Salvation
                                                       and   15
immortal, because sin is not there and man is   probation
found having no righteousness of his own, but in possession of "the mind of the Lord," as the Scripture says.   18

"In the place where the tree falleth, there it shall
be." So we read in Ecclesiastes. This text has been
transformed into the popular proverb, "As the tree 21
falls, so it must lie." As man falleth asleep, so shall he
awake. As death findeth mortal man, so shall he be
after death, until probation and growth shall effect the 24
needed change. Mind never becomes dust. No resurrection from the grave awaits Mind or Life, for the grave
has no power over either.   27

No final judgment awaits mortals, for the judgment-
day of wisdom comes hourly and continually,   Day of
even the judgment by which mortal man is di-   judgment   30
vested of all material error. As for spiritual error there
is none.

1 When the last mortal fault is destroyed, then the final
trump will sound which will end the battle of Truth with
3 error and mortality; "but of that day and hour, knoweth
no man." Here prophecy pauses. Divine Science alone
can compass the heights and depths of being and reveal
6 the infinite.

Truth will be to us "the resurrection and the life" only
as it destroys all error and the belief that Mind, the only
9 Primitive immortality of man, can be fettered by the
error body, and Life be controlled by death. A sinful, sick, and dying mortal is not the likeness of God, the
12 perfect and eternal.

Matter is the primitive belief of mortal mind, because
this so-called mind has no cognizance of Spirit. To
15 mortal mind, matter is substantial, and evil is
real. The so-called senses of mortals are material.
Hence the so-called life of mortals is dependent on
18 matter.

Explaining the origin of material man and mortal mind,
Jesus said: "Why do ye not understand my speech?
21 Even because ye cannot hear my word. Ye are of your
father, the devil [evil], and the lusts of your father ye will
do. He was a murderer from the beginning, and abode
24 not in the truth, because there is no truth in him. When
he speaketh a lie, he speaketh of his own: for he is a liar,
and the father of it."

27 This carnal material mentality, misnamed *mind*, is
mortal. Therefore man would be annihilated, were it
Immortal not for the spiritual real man's indissoluble
30 man connection with his God, which Jesus brought
to light. In his resurrection and ascension, Jesus showed
that a mortal man is not the real essence of manhood, and

that this unreal material mortality disappears in presence 1
of the reality.

Electricity is not a vital fluid, but the least material 3
form of illusive consciousness, — the material mindless-
ness, which forms no link between matter and Elementary
Mind, and which destroys itself. Matter and electricity 6
mortal mind are but different strata of human belief. The
grosser substratum is named matter or body; the more
ethereal is called mind. This so-called mind and body 9
is the illusion called a mortal, a mind in matter. In reality
and in Science, both strata, mortal mind and mortal body,
are false representatives of man.   12

The material so-called gases and forces are counterfeits of the spiritual forces of divine Mind, whose potency
is Truth, whose attraction is Love, whose adhesion and 15
cohesion are Life, perpetuating the eternal facts of being.
Electricity is the sharp surplus of materiality which counterfeits the true essence of spirituality or truth, — the 18
great difference being that electricity is not intelligent,
while spiritual truth is Mind.

There is no vapid fury of mortal mind — expressed in 21
earthquake, wind, wave, lightning, fire, bestial ferocity
— and this so-called mind is self-destroyed. The counterfeit
The manifestations of evil, which counterfeit   forces   24
divine justice, are called in the Scriptures, "The anger
of the Lord." In reality, they show the self-destruction
of error or matter and point to matter's opposite, the 27
strength and permanency of Spirit. Christian Science
brings to light Truth and its supremacy, universal harmony, the entireness of God, good, and the nothingness 30
of evil.

The five physical senses are the avenues and instru-

1 ments of human error, and they correspond with error.
  These senses indicate the common human belief, that life,
3 Instruments substance, and intelligence are a unison of
  of error   matter with Spirit. This is pantheism, and
carries within itself the seeds of all error.

6   If man is both mind and matter, the loss of one finger
would take away some quality and quantity of the man,
for matter and man would be one.

9   The belief that matter thinks, sees, or feels is not more
real than the belief that matter enjoys and suffers. This
         Mortal   mortal belief, misnamed *man,* is error, saying:
12   verdict   "Matter has intelligence and sensation. Nerves
feel. Brain thinks and sins. The stomach can make a
man cross. Injury can cripple and matter can kill man."
15 This verdict of the so-called material senses victimizes
mortals, taught, as they are by physiology and pathology,
to revere false testimony, even the errors that are destroyed
18 by Truth through spiritual sense and Science.

The lines of demarcation between immortal man, representing Spirit, and mortal man, representing the error that
21   Mythical   life and intelligence are in matter, show the
      pleasure   pleasures and pains of matter to be myths, and
human belief in them to be the father of mythology, in
24 which matter is represented as divided into intelligent gods.
Man's genuine selfhood is recognizable only in what is
good and true. Man is neither self-made nor made by
27 mortals. God created man.

The inebriate believes that there is pleasure in intoxication. The thief believes that he gains something by steal-
30 ing, and the hypocrite that he is hiding himself. The
Science of Mind corrects such mistakes, for Truth demonstrates the falsity of error.

The belief that a severed limb is aching in the old loca- 1
tion, the sensation seeming to be in nerves which   Severed
are no longer there, is an added proof of the un-   members 3
reliability of physical testimony.

God creates and governs the universe, including man.
The universe is filled with spiritual ideas, which He 6
evolves, and they are obedient to the Mind   Mortals
that makes them. Mortal mind would trans-   unlike
    immortals
form the spiritual into the material, and then 9
recover man's original self in order to escape from the
mortality of this error. Mortals are not like immortals,
created in God's own image; but infinite Spirit being all, 12
mortal consciousness will at last yield to the scientific fact
and disappear, and the real sense of being, perfect and
forever intact, will appear. 15

The manifestation of God through mortals is as light
passing through the window-pane. The light and the
glass never mingle, but as matter, the glass   Goodness 18
is less opaque than the walls. The mortal   transparent
mind through which Truth appears most vividly is that
one which has lost much materiality — much error — in 21
order to become a better transparency for Truth. Then,
like a cloud melting into thin vapor, it no longer hides
the sun. 24

All that is called mortal thought is made up of error.
The theoretical mind is matter, named *brain,* or *mate-*
rial consciousness, the exact opposite of real   Brainology 27
Mind, or Spirit. Brainology teaches that   a myth
mortals are created to suffer and die. It further
teaches that when man is dead, his immortal soul is 30
resurrected from death and mortality. Thus error the-
orizes that spirit is born of matter and returns to mat-

1 ter, and that man has a resurrection from dust; whereas
Science unfolds the eternal verity, that man is the spiritual,
3 eternal reflection of God.

Progress is born of experience. It is the ripening of
mortal man, through which the mortal is dropped for
6   Scientific   the immortal. Either here or hereafter, suf-
   purgation   fering or Science must destroy all illusions
regarding life and mind, and regenerate material sense
9 and self. The old man with his deeds must be put off.
Nothing sensual or sinful is immortal. The death of a
false material sense and of sin, not the death of organic
12 matter, is what reveals man and Life, harmonious, real,
and eternal.

The so-called pleasures and pains of matter perish,
15 and they must go out under the blaze of Truth, spiritual
sense, and the actuality of being. Mortal belief must lose
all satisfaction in error and sin in order to part with
18 them.

Whether mortals will learn this sooner or later, and
how long they will suffer the pangs of destruction, de-
21 pends upon the tenacity of error.

The knowledge obtained from the corporeal senses
leads to sin and death. When the evidence of Spirit
24   Mixed   and matter, Truth and error, seems to com-
   testimony   mingle, it rests upon foundations which time
is wearing away. Mortal mind judges by the testimony
27 of the material senses, until Science obliterates this false
testimony. An improved belief is one step out of error,
and aids in taking the next step and in understanding
30 the situation in Christian Science.

Mortal belief is a liar from the beginning, not deserving
power. It says to mortals, "You are wretched!" and they

think they are so; and nothing can change this state, until 1
the belief changes. Mortal belief says, "You are happy!"
and mortals are so; and no circumstance can   Belief an   3
alter the situation, until the belief on this sub-   autocrat
ject changes. Human belief says to mortals, "You are
sick!" and this testimony manifests itself on the body as 6
sickness. It is as necessary for a health-illusion, as for
an illusion of sickness, to be instructed out of itself into
the understanding of what constitutes health; for a change 9
in either a health-belief or a belief in sickness affects the
physical condition.

Erroneous belief is destroyed by truth. Change the 12
evidence, and that disappears which before seemed real
to this false belief, and the human conscious-   Self-
ness rises higher. Thus the reality of being   improvement   15
is attained and man found to be immortal. The only
fact concerning any material concept is, that it is neither
scientific nor eternal, but subject to change and dis- 18
solution.

Faith is higher and more spiritual than belief. It is
a chrysalis state of human thought, in which spiritual 21
evidence, contradicting the testimony of mate-   Faith higher
rial sense, begins to appear, and Truth, the   than belief
ever-present, is becoming understood. Human thoughts 24
have their degrees of comparison. Some thoughts are
better than others. A belief in Truth is better than a
belief in error, but no mortal testimony is founded on the 27
divine rock. Mortal testimony can be shaken. Until
belief becomes faith, and faith becomes spiritual understanding, human thought has little relation to the actual 30
or divine.

A mortal belief fulfils its own conditions. Sickness,

1 sin, and death are the vague realities of human conclusions. Life, Truth, and Love are the realities of divine
3 Science. They dawn in faith and glow full-orbed in
spiritual understanding. As a cloud hides the sun it
cannot extinguish, so false belief silences for a while the
6 voice of immutable harmony, but false belief cannot destroy Science armed with faith, hope, and fruition.

What is termed material sense can report only a mor-
9 tal temporary sense of things, whereas spiritual sense can
Truth's bear witness only to Truth. To material sense,
witness the unreal is the real until this sense is corrected
12 by Christian Science.

Spiritual sense, contradicting the material senses, involves intuition, hope, faith, understanding, fruition, real-
15 ity. Material sense expresses the belief that mind is in
matter. This human belief, alternating between a sense
of pleasure and pain, hope and fear, life and death, never
18 reaches beyond the boundary of the mortal or the unreal.
When the real is attained, which is announced by Science,
joy is no longer a trembler, nor is hope a cheat. Spirit-
21 ual ideas, like numbers and notes, start from Principle,
and admit no materialistic beliefs. Spiritual ideas lead
up to their divine origin, God, and to the spiritual sense
24 of being.

Angels are not etherealized human beings, evolving
animal qualities in their wings; but they are celestial
27 Thought- visitants, flying on spiritual, not material,
angels   pinions. Angels are pure thoughts from God,
winged with Truth and Love, no matter what their indi-
30 vidualism may be. Human conjecture confers upon angels
its own forms of thought, marked with superstitious outlines, making them human creatures with suggestive

feathers; but this is only fancy. It has behind it no more 1
reality than has the sculptor's thought when he carves
his "Statue of Liberty," which embodies his concep- 3
tion of an unseen quality or condition, but which has
no physical antecedent reality save in the artist's own observation and "chambers of imagery." 6

My angels are exalted thoughts, appearing at the door
of some sepulchre, in which human belief has buried
its fondest earthly hopes. With white fin- Our angelic 9
gers they point upward to a new and glo- messengers
rified trust, to higher ideals of life and its joys. Angels
are God's representatives. These upward-soaring beings 12
never lead towards self, sin, or materiality, but guide to
the divine Principle of all good, whither every real individuality, image, or likeness of God, gathers. By giving 15
earnest heed to these spiritual guides they tarry with us,
and we entertain "angels unawares."

Knowledge gained from material sense is figuratively 18
represented in Scripture as a tree, bearing the fruits of
sin, sickness, and death. Ought we not then Knowledge
to judge the knowledge thus obtained to be and Truth 21
untrue and dangerous, since "the tree is known by his
fruit"?

Truth never destroys God's idea. Truth is spiritual, 24
eternal substance, which cannot destroy the right reflection. Corporeal sense, or error, may seem to hide Truth,
health, harmony, and Science, as the mist obscures the 27
sun or the mountain; but Science, the sunshine of Truth,
will melt away the shadow and reveal the celestial
peaks. 30

If man were solely a creature of the material senses,
he would have no eternal Principle and would be mutable

1 and mortal. Human logic is awry when it attempts
to draw correct spiritual conclusions regarding life from
3 Old and   matter. Finite sense has no true apprecia-
   new man   tion of infinite Principle, God, or of His infinite image or reflection, man. The mirage, which makes
6 trees and cities seem to be where they are not, illustrates
the illusion of material man, who cannot be the image
of God.

9   So far as the scientific statement as to man is understood, it can be proved and will bring to light the true
reflection of God — the real man, or the *new* man (as
12 St. Paul has it).

The temporal and unreal never touch the eternal and
real. The mutable and imperfect never touch the im-
15 The tares   mutable and perfect. The inharmonious and
   and wheat   self-destructive never touch the harmonious
and self-existent. These opposite qualities are the tares
18 and wheat, which never really mingle, though (to mortal
sight) they grow side by side until the harvest; then, Science separates the wheat from the tares, through the real-
21 ization of God as ever present and of man as reflecting
the divine likeness.

Spirit is God, Soul; therefore Soul is not in matter. If
24 Spirit were in matter, God would have no representative,
   The divine   and matter would be identical with God.
   reflection   The theory that soul, spirit, intelligence, in-
27 habits matter is taught by the schools. This theory is
unscientific. The universe reflects and expresses the divine substance or Mind; therefore God is seen only in the
30 spiritual universe and spiritual man, as the sun is seen in
the ray of light which goes out from it. God is revealed only in that which reflects Life, Truth, Love, —

yea, which manifests God's attributes and power, even 1
as the human likeness thrown upon the mirror, repeats
the color, form, and action of the person in front of the 3
mirror.

Few persons comprehend what Christian Science
means by the word *reflection*. To himself, mortal and 6
material man seems to be substance, but his sense of
substance involves error and therefore is material,
temporal.   9

On the other hand, the immortal, spiritual man is really
substantial, and reflects the eternal substance, or Spirit,
which mortals hope for. He reflects the divine, which 12
constitutes the only real and eternal entity. This reflection
seems to mortal sense transcendental, because the spiritual
man's substantiality transcends mortal vision and is re- 15
vealed only through divine Science.

As God is substance and man is the divine image and
likeness, man should wish for, and in reality has, only 18
the substance of good, the substance of Spirit,
not matter. The belief that man has any other   Inverted
substance, or mind, is not spiritual and breaks   images and ideas
                                                    21
the First Commandment, Thou shalt have one God, one
Mind. Mortal man seems to himself to be material substance, while man is "image" (idea). Delusion, sin, dis- 24
ease, and death arise from the false testimony of material
sense, which, from a supposed standpoint outside the
focal distance of infinite Spirit, presents an inverted image 27
of Mind and substance with everything turned upside
down.

This falsity presupposes soul to be an unsubstantial 30
dweller in material forms, and man to be material instead
of spiritual. Immortality is not bounded by mortality.

1 Soul is not compassed by finiteness. Principle is not to
be found in fragmentary ideas.

3   The material body and mind are temporal, but the
real man is spiritual and eternal. The identity of the
      Identity   real man is not lost, but found through this
6   not lost   explanation; for the conscious infinitude of
existence and of all identity is thereby discerned and remains unchanged. It is impossible that man should lose
9 aught that is real, when God is all and eternally his. The
notion that mind is in matter, and that the so-called pleasures and pains, the birth, sin, sickness, and death of
12 matter, are real, is a mortal belief; and this belief is all
that will ever be lost.

    Continuing our definition of *man,* let us remember that
15 harmonious and immortal man has existed forever, and
    Definition   is always beyond and above the mortal illu-
    of man   sion of any life, substance, and intelligence
18 as existent in matter. This statement is based on fact,
not fable. The Science of being reveals man as perfect,
even as the Father is perfect, because the Soul, or Mind,
21 of the spiritual man is God, the divine Principle of all
being, and because this real man is governed by Soul
instead of sense, by the law of Spirit, not by the so-called
24 laws of matter.

    God is Love. He is therefore the divine, infinite Prin-
ciple, called Person or God. Man's true consciousness
27 is in the mental, not in any bodily or personal likeness
to Spirit. Indeed, the body presents no proper likeness
of divinity, though mortal sense would fain have us so
30 believe.

    Even in Christian Science, reproduction by Spirit's
individual ideas is but the reflection of the creative power

of the divine Principle of those ideas. The reflection, 1
through mental manifestation, of the multitudinous
forms of Mind which people the realm of   Mental   3
the real is controlled by Mind, the Principle propagation
governing the reflection. Multiplication of God's children comes from no power of propagation in matter, it 6
is the reflection of Spirit.

The minutiæ of lesser individualities reflect the one divine individuality and are comprehended in and formed 9
by Spirit, not by material sensation. Whatever reflects
Mind, Life, Truth, and Love, is spiritually conceived and
brought forth; but the statement that man is conceived 12
and evolved both spiritually and materially, or by both
God and man, contradicts this eternal truth. All the
vanity of the ages can never make both these contraries 15
true. Divine Science lays the axe at the root of the illusion that life, or mind, is formed by or is in the material
body, and Science will eventually destroy this illusion 18
through the self-destruction of all error and the beatified
understanding of the Science of Life.

The belief that pain and pleasure, life and death, holi- 21
ness and unholiness, mingle in man, — that   Error
mortal, material man is the likeness of God   defined
and is himself a creator, — is a fatal error.   24

God, without the image and likeness of Himself, would
be a nonentity, or Mind unexpressed. He would be
without a witness or proof of His own na-   27
ture. Spiritual man is the image or idea of   Man's
God, an idea which cannot be lost nor sep-   spiritual
arated from its divine Principle. When the evidence 30
before the material senses yielded to spiritual sense, the
apostle declared that nothing could alienate him from

1 God, from the sweet sense and presence of Life and
Truth.

3 It is ignorance and false belief, based on a material
sense of things, which hide spiritual beauty and goodness. Understanding this, Paul said: "Nei-
6 ther death, nor life, . . . nor things present,
nor things to come, nor height, nor depth, nor
any other creature, shall be able to separate us from
9 the love of God." This is the doctrine of Christian
Science: that divine Love cannot be deprived of its
manifestation, or object; that joy cannot be turned into
12 sorrow, for sorrow is not the master of joy; that good can
never produce evil; that matter can never produce mind
nor life result in death. The perfect man — governed
15 by God, his perfect Principle — is sinless and eternal.

Harmony is produced by its Principle, is controlled
by it and abides with it. Divine Principle is the Life
18 of man. Man's happiness is not, therefore, at
the disposal of physical sense. Truth is not
contaminated by error. Harmony in man is as beautiful
21 as in music, and discord is unnatural, unreal.

The science of music governs tones. If mortals caught
harmony through material sense, they would lose har-
24 mony, if time or accident robbed them of material sense.
To be master of chords and discords, the science of
music must be understood. Left to the decisions
27 of material sense, music is liable to be misappre-
hended and lost in confusion. Controlled by belief,
instead of understanding, music is, must be, imper-
30 fectly expressed. So man, not understanding the Science of being, — thrusting aside his divine Principle as
incomprehensible, — is abandoned to conjectures, left in

*Man
inseparable
from Love*

*Harmony
natural*

the hands of ignorance, placed at the disposal of illusions, 1
subjected to material sense which is discord. A discontented, discordant mortal is no more a *man* than discord 3
is music.

A picture in the camera or a face reflected in the mirror
is not the original, though resembling it. Man, in the 6
likeness of his Maker, reflects the central light   Human
of being, the invisible God. As there is no cor-   reflection
poreality in the mirrored form, which is but a reflection, 9
so man, like all things real, reflects God, his divine Principle, not in a mortal body.

Gender also is a quality, not of God, but a character- 12
istic of mortal mind. The verity that God's image is not
a creator, though he reflects the creation of Mind, God,
constitutes the underlying reality of reflection. "Then 15
answered Jesus and said unto them: Verily, verily I say
unto you, the Son can do nothing of himself, but what he
seeth the Father do: for what things soever He doeth, 18
these also doeth the Son likewise."

The inverted images presented by the senses, the deflections of matter as opposed to the Science of spirit- 21
ual reflection, are all unlike Spirit, God. In   Inverted
the illusion of life that is here to-day and   images
gone to-morrow, man would be wholly mortal, were 24
it not that Love, the divine Principle that obtains in
divine Science, destroys all error and brings immortality to light. Because man is the reflection of his 27
Maker, he is not subject to birth, growth, maturity, decay. These mortal dreams are of human origin, not
divine. 30

The Sadducees reasoned falsely about the resurrection, but not so blindly as the Pharisees, who believed

1 error to be as immortal as Truth. The Pharisees thought
that they could raise the spiritual from the material. They
3 Jewish   would first make life result in death, and then
   traditions resort to death to reproduce spiritual life.
Jesus taught them how death was to be overcome by
6 spiritual Life, and demonstrated this beyond cavil.

Life demonstrates Life. The immortality of Soul makes
man immortal. If God, who is Life, were parted for a
9 Divinity not moment from His reflection, man, during that
   childless   moment there would be no divinity reflected.
The Ego would be unexpressed, and the Father would be
12 childless, — no Father.

If Life or Soul and its representative, man, unite for
a period and then are separated as by a law of divorce to
15 be brought together again at some uncertain future time
and in a manner unknown, — and this is the general
religious opinion of mankind, — we are left without a
18 rational proof of immortality. ✓ But man cannot be separated for an instant from God, if man reflects God.
Thus Science proves man's existence to be intact.

21 The myriad forms of mortal thought, made manifest
as matter, are not more distinct nor real to the mate-
   Thought-   rial senses than are the Soul-created forms
24 forms   to spiritual sense, which cognizes Life as permanent. ✓ Undisturbed amid the jarring testimony of the
material senses, Science, still enthroned, is unfolding
27 to mortals the immutable, harmonious, divine Principle,
— is unfolding Life and the universe, ever present and
eternal.

30 God's man, spiritually created, is not material and
mortal.

The parent of all human discord was the Adam-dream,

the deep sleep, in which originated the delusion that life 1
and intelligence proceeded from and passed into matter.
This pantheistic error, or so-called *serpent*, in- The serpent's 3
sists still upon the opposite of Truth, saying, whisper
"Ye shall be as gods;" that is, I will make error as real
and eternal as Truth. 6
Evil still affirms itself to be mind, and declares that
there is more than one intelligence or God. It says:
"There shall be lords and gods many. I declare that God 9
makes evil minds and evil spirits, and that I aid Him.
Truth shall change sides and be unlike Spirit. I will
put spirit into what I call matter, and matter shall seem 12
to have life as much as God, Spirit, who *is* the only Life."
This error has proved itself to be error. Its life is found
to be not Life, but only a transient, false sense of an ex- 15
istence which ends in death. Error charges Bad results
its lie to Truth and says: "The Lord knows from error
it. He has made man mortal and material, out of mat- 18
ter instead of Spirit." Thus error partakes of its own
nature and utters its own falsities. If we regard matter
as intelligent, and Mind as both good and evil, every sin 21
or supposed material pain and pleasure seems normal,
a part of God's creation, and so weighs against our course
Spiritward. 24
Truth has no beginning. The divine Mind is the Soul
of man, and gives man dominion over all things. Man
was not created from a material basis, nor Higher 27
bidden to obey material laws which Spirit never statutes
made; his province is in spiritual statutes, in the higher
law of Mind. 30
Above error's awful din, blackness, and chaos, the voice
of Truth still calls: "Adam, where art thou? Conscious-

1 ness, where art thou? Art thou dwelling in the belief
that mind is in matter, and that evil is mind, or art thou
3   The great   in the living faith that there is and can be but
    question   one God, and keeping His commandment?"
Until the lesson is learned that God is the only Mind gov-
6 erning man, mortal belief will be afraid as it was in the
beginning, and will hide from the demand, "Where art
thou?" This awful demand, "Adam, where art thou?"
9 is met by the admission from the head, heart, stomach,
blood, nerves, etc.: "Lo, here I am, looking for happiness
and life in the body, but finding only an illusion, a blend-
12 ing of false claims, false pleasure, pain, sin, sickness, and
death."

The Soul-inspired patriarchs heard the voice of Truth,
15 and talked with God as consciously as man talks with man.

Jacob was *alone,* wrestling with error, — struggling
with a mortal sense of life, substance, and intelligence
18   Wrestling   as existent in matter with its false pleasures
   of Jacob   and pains, — when an angel, a message from
Truth and Love, appeared to him and smote the sinew,
21 or strength, of his error, till he saw its unreality; and
Truth, being thereby understood, gave him spiritual
strength in this Peniel of divine Science. Then said
24 the spiritual evangel: "Let me go, for the day breaketh;"
that is, the light of Truth and Love dawns upon thee.
But the patriarch, perceiving his error and his need
27 of help, did not loosen his hold upon this glorious light
until his nature was transformed. When Jacob was
asked, "What is thy name?" he straightway answered;
30 and then his name was changed to Israel, for "as a prince"
had he prevailed and had "power with God and with
men." Then Jacob questioned his deliverer, "Tell me,

I pray thee, *thy* name;" but this appellation was withheld, 1
for the messenger was not a corporeal being, but a nameless, incorporeal impartation of divine Love to man, which, 3
to use the word of the Psalmist, *restored* his Soul, — gave
him the spiritual sense of being and rebuked his material
sense.   6

The result of Jacob's struggle thus appeared. He had
conquered material error with the understanding of Spirit
and of spiritual power. This changed the man.   Israel the   9
He was no longer called Jacob, but Israel, —   new name
a prince of God, or a soldier of God, who had fought
a good fight. He was to become the father of those, who 12
through earnest striving followed his demonstration of the
power of Spirit over the material senses; and the children
of earth who followed his example were to be called the 15
children of Israel, until the Messiah should rename them.
If these children should go astray, and forget that Life
is God, good, and that good is not in elements which are 18
not spiritual, — thus losing the divine power which heals
the sick and sinning, — they were to be brought back
through great tribulation, to be renamed in Christian 21
Science and led to deny material sense, or mind in matter,
even as the gospel teaches.

The Science of being shows it to be impossible for in- 24
finite Spirit or Soul to be in a finite body or for man to
have an intelligence separate from his Maker.   Life never
It is a self-evident error to suppose that there   structural   27
can be such a reality as organic animal or vegetable life,
when such so-called life always ends in death. Life is
never for a moment extinct. Therefore it is never struc- 30
tural nor organic, and is never absorbed nor limited by its
own formations.

1 The artist is not in his painting. The picture is the
artist's thought objectified. The human belief fancies
3 Thought seen that it delineates thought on matter, but what
as substance is matter? Did it exist prior to thought?
Matter is made up of supposititious mortal mind-force;
6 but all might is divine Mind. ⸢Thought will finally be
understood and seen in all form, substance, and color, but
without material accompaniments.⸥ The potter is not in
9 the clay; else the clay would have power over the potter.
God is His own infinite Mind, and expresses all.

Day may decline and shadows fall, but darkness flees
12 when the earth has again turned upon its axis. The sun
The central is not affected by the revolution of the earth.
intelligence So Science reveals Soul as God, untouched
15 by sin and death, — as the central Life and intelligence
around which circle harmoniously all things in the systems of Mind.

18 Soul changeth not. We are commonly taught that there
is a human soul which sins and is spiritually lost, — that
Soul soul may be lost, and yet be immortal. If
21 imperishable Soul could sin, Spirit, Soul, would be flesh instead of Spirit. It is the belief of the flesh and of material sense which sins. If Soul sinned, Soul would die.
24 Sin is the element of self-destruction, and spiritual death
is oblivion. If there was sin in Soul, the annihilation of
Spirit would be inevitable. The only Life is Spirit, and
27 if Spirit should lose Life as God, good, then Spirit, which
has no other existence, would be annihilated.

Mind is God, and God is not seen by material sense,
30 because Mind is Spirit, which material sense cannot discern. There is neither growth, maturity, nor decay in
Soul. These changes are the mutations of material sense,

the varying clouds of mortal belief, which hide the truth 1
of being.

What we term mortal mind or carnal mind, dependent 3
on matter for manifestation, is not Mind. God is Mind:
all that Mind, God, is, or hath made, is good, and He
made all. Hence evil is not made and is not real. 6

Soul is immortal because it is Spirit, which has no element of self-destruction. Is man lost spiritually? No,
he can only lose a sense material. All sin is Sin only of 9
of the flesh. It cannot be spiritual. Sin exists the flesh
here or hereafter only so long as the illusion of mind in
matter remains. It is a sense of sin, and not a sinful soul, 12
which is lost. Evil is destroyed by the sense of good.

Through false estimates of soul as dwelling in sense
and of mind as dwelling in matter, belief strays into a 15
sense of temporary loss or absence of soul, spir- Soul
itual truth. This state of error is the mortal impeccable
dream of life and substance as existent in matter, and is 18
directly opposite to the immortal reality of being. So long
as we believe that soul can sin or that immortal Soul is in
mortal body, we can never understand the Science of be- 21
ing. When humanity does understand this Science, it
will become the law of Life to man, — even the higher law
of Soul, which prevails over material sense through har- 24
mony and immortality.

The objects cognized by the physical senses have not
the reality of substance. They are only what mortal 27
belief calls them. Matter, sin, and mortality lose all
supposed consciousness or claim to life or existence, as
mortals lay off a false sense of life, substance, and intelli- 30
gence. But the spiritual, eternal man is not touched by
these phases of mortality.

1 ✓ How true it is that whatever is learned through material
sense must be lost because such so-called knowledge is
3   Sense-   reversed by the spiritual facts of being in
   dreams   Science. That which material sense calls
intangible, is found to be substance. What to material
6 sense seems substance, becomes nothingness, as the sense-
dream vanishes and reality appears.

The senses regard a corpse, not as man, but simply as
9 matter. People say, "Man is dead;" but this death is
the departure of a mortal's mind, not of matter. The
matter is still there. The belief of that mortal that he
12 must die occasioned his departure; yet you say that
matter has caused his death.

People go into ecstasies over the sense of a corporeal
15 Jehovah, though with scarcely a spark of love in their
   Vain   hearts; yet God *is* Love, and without Love,
   ecstasies   God, immortality cannot appear. Mortals try
18 to believe without understanding Truth; yet God *is*
Truth. Mortals claim that death is inevitable; but man's
eternal Principle is ever-present Life. Mortals believe in
21 a finite personal God; while God is infinite Love, which
must be unlimited.

Our theories are based on finite premises, which can-
24 not penetrate beyond matter. A personal sense of God
   Man-made   and of man's capabilities necessarily limits
   theories   faith and hinders spiritual understanding. It
27 divides faith and understanding between matter and Spirit,
the finite and the infinite, and so turns away from the
intelligent and divine healing Principle to the inanimate
30 drug.

Jesus' spiritual origin and his demonstration of divine
Principle richly endowed him and entitled him to sonship

in Science. He was the son of a virgin. The term 1
Christ Jesus, or Jesus the Christ (to give the full and
proper translation of the Greek), may be ren-   The one   3
dered "Jesus the anointed," Jesus the God-   anointed
crowned or the divinely royal man, as it is said of him in
the first chapter of Hebrews: —   6

> Therefore God, even thy God, hath anointed thee
> With the oil of gladness above thy fellows.

With this agrees another passage in the same chapter, 9
which refers to the Son as "the brightness of His [God's]
glory, and the express [expressed] image of His person
[infinite Mind]." It is noteworthy that the phrase "ex- 12
press image" in the Common Version is, in the Greek
Testament, *character*. Using this word in its higher meaning, we may assume that the author of this remarkable 15
epistle regarded Christ as the Son of God, the royal
reflection of the infinite; and the cause given for the exaltation of Jesus, Mary's son, was that he "loved right- 18
eousness and hated iniquity." The passage is made
even clearer in the translation of the late George R.
Noyes, D.D.: "Who, being a brightness from His glory, 21
and an image of His being."

Jesus of Nazareth was the most scientific man that
ever trod the globe. He plunged beneath the material 24
surface of things, and found the spiritual   Jesus the
cause. To accommodate himself to imma-   Scientist
ture ideas of spiritual power, — for spirituality was pos- 27
sessed only in a limited degree even by his disciples, —
Jesus called the body, which by spiritual power he
raised from the grave, "flesh and bones." To show 30
that the substance of himself was Spirit and the body

1 no more perfect because of death and no less material
until the ascension (his further spiritual exaltation),
3 Jesus waited until the mortal or fleshly sense had re-
linquished the belief of substance-matter, and spiritual
sense had quenched all earthly yearnings. Thus he found
6 the eternal Ego, and proved that he and the Father were
inseparable as God and His reflection or spiritual man.
Our Master gained the solution of being, demonstrating
9 the existence of but one Mind without a second or equal.

The Jews, who sought to kill this man of God, showed
plainly that their material views were the parents of their
12   The bodily   wicked deeds. When Jesus spoke of repro-
  resurrection   ducing his body, — knowing, as he did, that
Mind was the builder, — and said, "Destroy this temple,
15 and in three days I will raise it up," they thought that he
meant their material temple instead of his body. To such
materialists, the real man seemed a spectre, unseen and
18 unfamiliar, and the body, which they laid in a sepulchre,
seemed to be substance. This materialism lost sight of
the true Jesus; but the faithful Mary saw him, and he
21 presented to her, more than ever before, the true idea of
Life and substance.

Because of mortals' material and sinful belief, the
24 spiritual Jesus was imperceptible to them. The higher
  Opposition of   his demonstration of divine Science carried
  materialists   the problem of being, and the more dis-
27 tinctly he uttered the demands of its divine Principle,
Truth and Love, the more odious he became to sinners
and to those who, depending on doctrines and material
30 laws to save them from sin and sickness, were submis-
sive to death as being in supposed accord with the
inevitable law of life. Jesus proved them wrong by

his resurrection, and said: "Whosoever liveth and be- 1
lieveth in me shall never die."

That saying of our Master, "I and my Father are one," 3
separated him from the scholastic theology of the rabbis.
His better understanding of God was a rebuke   Hebrew
to them. He knew of but one Mind and laid   theology   6
no claim to any other. He knew that the Ego was Mind
instead of body and that matter, sin, and evil were not
Mind; and his understanding of this divine Science 9
brought upon him the anathemas of the age.

The opposite and false views of the people hid from
their sense Christ's sonship with God. They could not 12
discern his spiritual existence. Their carnal   The true
minds were at enmity with it. Their thoughts   sonship
were filled with mortal error, instead of with God's spirit- 15
ual idea as presented by Christ Jesus. The likeness of
God we lose sight of through sin, which beclouds the spiritual sense of Truth; and we realize this likeness only 18
when we subdue sin and prove man's heritage, the liberty
of the sons of God.

Jesus' spiritual origin and understanding enabled him 21
to demonstrate the facts of being, — to prove irrefutably
how spiritual Truth destroys material error, Immaculate
heals sickness, and overcomes death. The   conception   24
divine conception of Jesus pointed to this truth and presented an illustration of creation. The history of Jesus
shows him to have been more spiritual than all other 27
earthly personalities.

Wearing in part a human form (that is, as it seemed
to mortal view), being conceived by a human mother, 30
Jesus was the mediator between Spirit and the flesh,
between Truth and error. Explaining and demonstrat-

1 ing the way of divine Science, he became the way of
salvation to all who accepted his word. From him mor-
3   Jesus as   tals may learn how to escape from evil. The
   mediator   real man being linked by Science to his Maker,
mortals need only turn from sin and lose sight of mortal
6 selfhood to find Christ, the real man and his relation to
God, and to recognize the divine sonship. Christ, Truth,
was demonstrated through Jesus to prove the power of
9 Spirit over the flesh, — to show that Truth is made
manifest by its effects upon the human mind and body,
healing sickness and destroying sin.
12   Jesus represented Christ, the true idea of God. Hence
the warfare between this spiritual idea and perfunctory
     Spiritual   religion, between spiritual clear-sightedness
15   government   and the blindness of popular belief, which led
to the conclusion that the spiritual idea could be killed
by crucifying the flesh. The Christ-idea, or the Christ-
18 man, rose higher to human view because of the crucifixion,
and thus proved that Truth was the master of death.
Christ presents the indestructible man, whom Spirit cre-
21 ates, constitutes, and governs. Christ illustrates that
blending with God, his divine Principle, which gives man
dominion over all the earth.
24   The spiritual idea of God, as presented by Jesus, was
scourged in person, and its Principle was rejected. That
     Deadness   man was accounted a criminal who could
27   in sin   prove God's divine power by healing the
sick, casting out evils, spiritualizing materialistic beliefs,
and raising the dead, — those dead in trespasses and
30 sins, satisfied with the flesh, resting on the basis of matter, blind to the possibilities of Spirit and its correla-
tive truth.

Jesus uttered things which had been "secret from the 1
foundation of the world," — since material knowledge
usurped the throne of the creative divine Principle, insisted 3
on the might of matter, the force of falsity, the insignificance of spirit, and proclaimed an anthropomorphic God.

Whosoever lives most the life of Jesus in this age 6
and declares best the power of Christian Science, will
drink of his Master's cup. Resistance to   The cup
Truth will haunt his steps, and he will in-   of Jesus   9
cur the hatred of sinners, till "wisdom is justified of
her children." These blessed benedictions rest upon
Jesus' followers: "If the world hate you, ye know that 12
it hated me before it hated you;" "Lo, I am with you
alway," — that is, not only in all time, but in *all ways*
and conditions.   15

The individuality of man is no less tangible because
it is spiritual and because his life is not at the mercy of
matter. The understanding of his spiritual individuality 18
makes man more real, more formidable in truth, and enables him to conquer sin, disease, and death. Our Lord
and Master presented himself to his disciples after his 21
resurrection from the grave, as the self-same Jesus whom
they had loved before the tragedy on Calvary.

To the materialistic Thomas, looking for the ideal 24
Saviour in matter instead of in Spirit and to the testimony of the material senses and the body,   Material
more than to Soul, for an earnest of immor-   skepticism   27
tality, — to him Jesus furnished the proof that he was
unchanged by the crucifixion. To this dull and doubting disciple Jesus remained a fleshly reality, so long as 30
the Master remained an inhabitant of the earth. Nothing but a display of matter could make existence real

1 to Thomas. For him to believe in matter was no task,
but for him to conceive of the substantiality of Spirit —
3 to know that nothing can efface Mind and immortality, in
which Spirit reigns — was more difficult.

Corporeal senses define diseases as realities; but the
6 Scriptures declare that God made all, even while the cor-

What   poreal senses are saying that matter causes
the senses disease and the divine Mind cannot or will
originate
9   not heal it. The material senses originate and
support all that is material, untrue, selfish, or debased.
They would put soul into soil, life into limbo, and doom
12 all things to decay. We must silence this lie of material
sense with the truth of spiritual sense. We must cause
the error to cease that brought the belief of sin and death
15 and would efface the pure sense of omnipotence.

Is the sick man sinful above all others? No! but
so far as he is discordant, he is not the image of God.
18   Sickness   Weary of their material beliefs, from which
as discord   comes so much suffering, invalids grow more
spiritual, as the error — or belief that life is in matter —
21 yields to the reality of spiritual Life.

The Science of Mind denies the error of sensation in
matter, and heals with Truth. Medical science treats
24 disease as though disease were real, therefore right, and
attempts to heal it with matter. If disease is right it is
wrong to heal it. Material methods are temporary, and
27 are not adapted to elevate mankind.

The governor is not subjected to the governed. In
Science man is governed by God, divine Principle, as
30 numbers are controlled and proved by His laws. Intelligence does not originate in numbers, but is manifested
through them. The body does not include soul, but man-

ifests mortality, a false sense of soul. The delusion that 1
there is life in matter has no kinship with the Life supernal.

Science depicts disease as error, as matter *versus* 3
Mind, and error reversed as subserving the facts of
health. To calculate one's life-prospects Unscientific
from a material basis, would infringe upon introspection 6
spiritual law and misguide human hope. Having faith
in the divine Principle of health and spiritually understanding God, sustains man under all circumstances; 9
whereas the lower appeal to the general faith in material
means (commonly called nature) must yield to the all-
might of infinite Spirit.   12

Throughout the infinite cycles of eternal existence,
Spirit and matter neither concur in man nor in the universe.

The varied doctrines and theories which presuppose 15
life and intelligence to exist in matter are so many ancient
and modern mythologies. Mystery, miracle, God the
sin, and death will disappear when it becomes only Mind 18
fairly understood that the divine Mind controls man and
man has no Mind but God.

The divine Science taught in the original language 21
of the Bible came through inspiration, and needs inspiration to be understood. Hence the misapprehension of the spiritual meaning of the Bible, Scriptures
misinter- 24
and the misinterpretation of the Word in preted
some instances by uninspired writers, who only wrote
down what an inspired teacher had said. A misplaced 27
word changes the sense and misstates the Science of
the Scriptures, as, for instance, to name Love as merely
an attribute of God; but we can by special and proper 30
capitalization speak of the love of Love, meaning by that
what the beloved disciple meant in one of his epistles,

1 when he said, "God is love." Likewise we can speak of
the truth of Truth and of the life of Life, for Christ plainly
3 declared, "I am the way, the truth, and the life."

Metaphors abound in the Bible, and names are often
expressive of spiritual ideas. The most distinguished
6 Interior   theologians in Europe and America agree that
  meaning   the Scriptures have both a spiritual and literal meaning. In Smith's Bible Dictionary it is said:
9 "The spiritual interpretation of Scripture must rest
upon both the literal and moral;" and in the learned
article on Noah in the same work, the familiar text,
12 Genesis vi. 3, "And the Lord said, My spirit shall not
always strive with man, for that he also is flesh," is quoted
as follows, from the original Hebrew: "And Jehovah
15 said, My spirit shall not forever rule [or be humbled] in
men, seeing that they are [or, in their error they are]
but flesh." Here the original text declares plainly the
18 spiritual fact of being, even man's eternal and harmonious existence as image, idea, instead of matter (however transcendental such a thought appears), and avers
21 that this fact is not forever to be humbled by the belief
that man is flesh and matter, for according to that error
man is mortal.

24 The one important interpretation of Scripture is the
spiritual. For example, the text, "In my flesh shall I
Job, on the   see God," gives a profound idea of the di-
27 resurrection   vine power to heal the ills of the flesh, and
encourages mortals to hope in Him who healeth all our
diseases; whereas this passage is continually quoted
30 as if Job intended to declare that even if disease and
worms destroyed his body, yet in the latter days he should
stand in celestial perfection before Elohim, still clad

in material flesh, — an interpretation which is just the op- 1
posite of the true, as may be seen by studying the book
of Job.   As Paul says, in his first epistle to the Corin- 3
thians, "Flesh and blood cannot inherit the kingdom of
God."

The Hebrew Lawgiver, slow of speech, despaired of 6
making the people understand what should be revealed
to him. When, led by wisdom to cast down his

Fear of the
serpent
overcome

rod, he saw it become a serpent, Moses fled be- 9
fore it; but wisdom bade him come back and
handle the serpent, and then Moses' fear departed. In
this incident was seen the actuality of Science. Matter 12
was shown to be a belief only. The serpent, evil, under
wisdom's bidding, was destroyed through understanding
divine Science, and this proof was a staff upon which to 15
lean. The illusion of Moses lost its power to alarm him,
when he discovered that what he apparently saw was really
but a phase of mortal belief. 18

It was scientifically demonstrated that leprosy was a
creation of mortal mind and not a condition of matter,
when Moses first put his hand into his bosom

Leprosy
healed

21
and drew it forth white as snow with the dread
disease, and presently restored his hand to its natural condition by the same simple process. God had lessened 24
Moses' fear by this proof in divine Science, and the inward voice became to him the voice of God, which said:
"It shall come to pass, if they will not believe thee, neither 27
hearken to the voice of the first sign, that they will believe
the voice of the latter sign." And so it was in the coming
centuries, when the Science of being was demonstrated 30
by Jesus, who showed his students the power of Mind by
changing water into wine, and taught them how to handle

1 serpents unharmed, to heal the sick and cast out evils in
proof of the supremacy of Mind.

3   When understanding changes the standpoints of life and
intelligence from a material to a spiritual basis, we shall
Standpoints   gain the reality of Life, the control of Soul over
changed
6   sense, and we shall perceive Christianity, or
Truth, in its divine Principle. This must be the climax
before harmonious and immortal man is obtained and his
9 capabilities revealed. It is highly important — in view
of the immense work to be accomplished before this recognition of divine Science can come — to turn our thoughts
12 towards divine Principle, that finite belief may be prepared to relinquish its error.

Man's wisdom finds no satisfaction in sin, since God
15 has sentenced sin to suffer. The necromancy of yester-
Saving the   day foreshadowed the mesmerism and hypno-
inebriate   tism of to-day. The drunkard thinks he enjoys
18 drunkenness, and you cannot make the inebriate leave
his besottedness, until his physical sense of pleasure yields
to a higher sense. Then he turns from his cups, as
21 the startled dreamer who wakens from an incubus in-
curred through the pains of distorted sense. A man who
likes to do wrong — finding pleasure in it and refraining
24 from it only through fear of consequences — is neither
a temperate man nor a reliable religionist.

The sharp experiences of belief in the supposititious life
27 of matter, as well as our disappointments and ceaseless
Uses of   woes, turn us like tired children to the arms
suffering   of divine Love. Then we begin to learn Life
30 in divine Science. Without this process of weaning,
"Canst thou by searching find out God?" It is easier
to desire Truth than to rid one's self of error. Mortals

may seek the understanding of Christian Science, but they 1
will not be able to glean from Christian Science the facts
of being without striving for them.   This strife consists 3
in the endeavor to forsake error of every kind and to possess no other consciousness but good.

Through the wholesome chastisements of Love, we 6
are helped onward in the march towards righteousness,
peace, and purity, which are the landmarks   A bright
of Science.   Beholding the infinite tasks of   outlook   9
truth, we pause, — wait on God.   Then we push onward,
until boundless thought walks enraptured, and conception unconfined is winged to reach the divine glory.   12

In order to apprehend more, we must put into practice what we already know.   We must recollect that
Truth is demonstrable when understood, and   Need and   15
that good is not understood until demonstrated.   supply
If "faithful over a few things," we shall be made rulers
over many; but the one unused talent decays and is lost. 18
When the sick or the sinning awake to realize their need
of what they have not, they will be receptive of divine
Science, which gravitates towards Soul and away from 21
material sense, removes thought from the body, and ele-
vates even mortal mind to the contemplation of something better than disease or sin.   The true idea of God 24
gives the true understanding of Life and Love, robs the
grave of victory, takes away all sin and the delusion that
there are other minds, and destroys mortality.   27

The effects of Christian Science are not so much seen
as felt.   It is the "still, small voice" of Truth   Childlike
uttering itself.   We are either turning away   receptivity   30
from this utterance, or we are listening to it and going
up higher.   Willingness to become as a little child and

1 to leave the old for the new, renders thought receptive of
the advanced idea. Gladness to leave the false landmarks
3 and joy to see them disappear, — this disposition helps
to precipitate the ultimate harmony. The purification
of sense and self is a proof of progress. "Blessed are the
6 pure in heart: for they shall see God."

Unless the harmony and immortality of man are becoming more apparent, we are not gaining the true idea
9   Narrow   of God; and the body will reflect what gov-
  pathway   erns it, whether it be Truth or error,
understanding or belief, Spirit or matter. Therefore
12 "acquaint now thyself with Him, and be at peace."
Be watchful, sober, and vigilant. The way is straight
and narrow, which leads to the understanding that God
15 is the only Life. It is a warfare with the flesh, in which
we must conquer sin, sickness, and death, either here
or hereafter, — certainly before we can reach the goal
18 of Spirit, or life in God.

Paul was not at first a disciple of Jesus but a persecutor of Jesus' followers. When the truth first appeared
21   Paul's   to him in Science, Paul was made blind,
  enlightenment   and his blindness was felt; but spiritual
light soon enabled him to follow the example and teach-
24 ings of Jesus, healing the sick and preaching Christianity throughout Asia Minor, Greece, and even in imperial
Rome.

27 Paul writes, "If Christ [Truth] be not risen, then is
our preaching vain." That is, if the idea of the supremacy of Spirit, which is the true conception of being,
30 come not to your thought, you cannot be benefited by
what I say.

Jesus said substantially, "He that believeth in me

shall not see death." That is, he who perceives the 1
true idea of Life loses his belief in death. He who has
the true idea of good loses all sense of evil,   Abiding   3
and by reason of this is being ushered into the   in Life
undying realities of Spirit. Such a one abideth in Life, —
life obtained not of the body incapable of supporting life, 6
but of Truth, unfolding its own immortal idea. Jesus
gave the true idea of being, which results in infinite blessings to mortals.   9

In Colossians (iii. 4) Paul writes: "When Christ, who
is our life, shall appear [be manifested], then shall ye also
appear [be manifested] with him in glory."   Indestructible 12
When spiritual being is understood in all its   being
perfection, continuity, and might, then shall man be found
in God's image. The absolute meaning of the apostolic 15
words is this: Then shall man be found, in His likeness,
perfect as the Father, indestructible in Life, "hid with
Christ in God," — with Truth in divine Love, where 18
human sense hath not seen man.

Paul had a clear sense of the demands of Truth upon
mortals physically and spiritually, when he said: "Pre- 21
sent your bodies a living sacrifice, holy, ac-   Consecration
ceptable unto God, which is your reasonable   required
service." But he, who is begotten of the beliefs of the 24
flesh and serves them, can never reach in this world the
divine heights of our Lord. The time cometh when
the spiritual origin of man, the divine Science which 27
ushered Jesus into human presence, will be understood
and demonstrated.

When first spoken in any age, Truth, like the light, 30
"shineth in darkness, and the darkness comprehended
it not." A false sense of life, substance, and mind

1 hides the divine possibilities, and conceals scientific
demonstration.

3   If we wish to follow Christ, Truth, it must be in the
way of God's appointing. Jesus said, "He that believeth

Loving God   on me, the works that I do shall he do also."
6 supremely He, who would reach the source and find the
divine remedy for every ill, must not try to climb the hill
of Science by some other road. All nature teaches God's
9 love to man, but man cannot love God supremely and set
his whole affections on spiritual things, while loving the
material or trusting in it more than in the spiritual.

12   We must forsake the foundation of material systems,
however time-honored, if we would gain the Christ as
our only Saviour. Not partially, but fully, the great
15 healer of mortal mind is the healer of the body.

The purpose and motive to live aright can be gained
now. This point won, you have started as you should.
18 You have begun at the numeration-table of Christian
Science, and nothing but wrong intention can hinder your
advancement. Working and praying with true motives,
21 your Father will open the way. "Who did hinder you,
that ye should not obey the truth?"

Saul of Tarsus beheld the way — the Christ, or Truth
24 — only when his uncertain sense of right yielded to a
Conversion   spiritual sense, which is always right. Then
of Saul   the man was changed. Thought assumed a
27 nobler outlook, and his life became more spiritual. He
learned the wrong that he had done in persecuting Christians, whose religion he had not understood, and in hu-
30 mility he took the new name of Paul. He beheld for the
first time the true idea of Love, and learned a lesson in
divine Science.

Reform comes by understanding that there is no abid- 1
ing pleasure in evil, and also by gaining an affection for
good according to Science, which reveals the immortal 3
fact that neither pleasure nor pain, appetite nor passion,
can exist in or of matter, while divine Mind can and does
destroy the false beliefs of pleasure, pain, or fear and all 6
the sinful appetites of the human mind.

What a pitiful sight is malice, finding pleasure in revenge! Evil is sometimes a man's highest conception 9
of right, until his grasp on good grows stronger. Image of
Then he loses pleasure in wickedness, and it the beast
becomes his torment. The way to escape the misery of 12
sin is to cease sinning. There is no other way. Sin is
the image of the beast to be effaced by the sweat of agony.
It is a moral madness which rushes forth to clamor with 15
midnight and tempest.

To the physical senses, the strict demands of Christian
Science seem peremptory; but mortals are has- Peremptory 18
tening to learn that Life is God, good, and that demands
evil has in reality neither place nor power in the human or
the divine economy. 21

Fear of punishment never made man truly honest.
Moral courage is requisite to meet the wrong and to
proclaim the right. But how shall we re- Moral 24
form the man who has more animal than courage
moral courage, and who has not the true idea of good?
Through human consciousness, convince the mortal of 27
his mistake in seeking material means for gaining happiness. Reason is the most active human faculty. Let
that inform the sentiments and awaken the man's dor- 30
mant sense of moral obligation, and by degrees he will
learn the nothingness of the pleasures of human sense

1 and the grandeur and bliss of a spiritual sense, which
silences the material or corporeal. Then he not only will
3 be saved, but *is* saved.

Mortals suppose that they can live without goodness,
when God is good and the only real Life. What is the
6   Final destruc- result? Understanding little about the divine
   tion of error Principle which saves and heals, mortals get
rid of sin, sickness, and death only in belief. These errors
9 are not thus really destroyed, and must therefore cling
to mortals until, here or hereafter, they gain the true understanding of God in the Science which destroys human
12 delusions about Him and reveals the grand realities of
His allness.

This understanding of man's power, when he is
15 equipped by God, has sadly disappeared from Christian
  Promise   history. For centuries it has been dormant, a
  perpetual   lost element of Christianity. Our missionaries
18 carry the Bible to India, but can it be said that they
explain it practically, as Jesus did, when hundreds of
persons die there annually from serpent-bites? Under-
21 standing spiritual law and knowing that there is no material law, Jesus said: "These signs shall follow them that
believe, . . . they shall take up serpents, and if they
24 drink any deadly thing, it shall not hurt them. They
shall lay hands on the sick, and they shall recover." It
were well had Christendom believed and obeyed this
27 sacred saying.

Jesus' promise is perpetual. Had it been given only
to his immediate disciples, the Scriptural passage would
30 read *you*, not *they*. The purpose of his great life-work
extends through time and includes universal humanity.
Its Principle is infinite, reaching beyond the pale of a

leaven 5

single period or of a limited following. As time moves 1
on, the healing elements of pure Christianity will be fairly
dealt with; they will be sought and taught, and will glow 3
in all the grandeur of universal goodness.

A little leaven leavens the whole lump. A little understanding of Christian Science proves the truth of all that 6
I say of it. Because you cannot walk on the   *Imitation
of Jesus*
water and raise the dead, you have no right to
question the great might of divine Science in these direc- 9
tions. Be thankful that Jesus, who was the true demonstrator of Science, did these things, and left his example for
us. In Science we can use only what we understand. We 12
must prove our faith by demonstration.

One should not tarry in the storm if the body is freezing, nor should he remain in the devouring flames. Un- 15
til one is able to prevent bad results, he should avoid their
occasion. To be discouraged, is to resemble a pupil in
addition, who attempts to solve a problem of Euclid, and 18
denies the rule of the problem because he fails in his first
effort.

There is no hypocrisy in Science. Principle is impera- 21
tive. You cannot mock it by human will. Science is a
divine demand, not a human. Always right,   *Error
destroyed,* 24
its divine Principle never repents, but main-   *not pardoned*
tains the claim of Truth by quenching error.
The pardon of divine mercy is the destruction of error. If
men understood their real spiritual source to be all bless- 27
edness, they would struggle for recourse to the spiritual
and be at peace; but the deeper the error into which mortal mind is plunged, the more intense the opposition to 30
spirituality, till error yields to Truth.

Human resistance to divine Science weakens in pro-

1 portion as mortals give up error for Truth and the understanding of being supersedes mere belief. Until the

3 **The hopeful outlook** author of this book learned the vastness of
Christian Science, the fixedness of mortal illu-
sions, and the human hatred of Truth, she cherished

6 sanguine hopes that Christian Science would meet with
immediate and universal acceptance.

When the following platform is understood and the

9 letter and the spirit bear witness, the infallibility of divine
metaphysics will be demonstrated.

I. God is infinite, the only Life, substance, Spirit, or

12 Soul, the only intelligence of the universe, including man.

The deific supremacy Eye hath neither seen God nor His image and
likeness. Neither God nor the perfect man

15 can be discerned by the material senses. The individuality of Spirit, or the infinite, is unknown, and thus a
knowledge of it is left either to human conjecture or to the

18 revelation of divine Science.

II. God is what the Scriptures declare Him to be, —
Life, Truth, Love. Spirit is divine Principle, and divine

21 **The deific definitions** Principle is Love, and Love is Mind, and
Mind is not both good and bad, for God is
Mind; therefore there is in reality one Mind only, be-

24 cause there is one God.

III. The notion that both evil and good are real is a
delusion of material sense, which Science annihilates.

27 **Evil obsolete** Evil is nothing, no thing, mind, nor power.
As manifested by mankind it stands for a lie,
nothing claiming to be something, — for lust, dishonesty,

30 selfishness, envy, hypocrisy, slander, hate, theft, adultery,
murder, dementia, insanity, inanity, devil, hell, with all
the etceteras that word includes.

IV. God is divine Life, and Life is no more confined 1
to the forms which reflect it than substance is in its
shadow. If life were in mortal man or mate- **Life the** 3
rial things, it would be subject to their limi- **creator**
tations and would end in death. Life is Mind, the creator
reflected in His creations. If He dwelt within what He 6
creates, God would not be reflected but absorbed, and the
Science of being would be forever lost through a mortal
sense, which falsely testifies to a beginning and an 9
end.

V. The Scriptures imply that God is All-in-all. From
this it follows that nothing possesses reality nor existence 12
except the divine Mind and His ideas. The **Allness of**
Scriptures also declare that God is Spirit. **Spirit**
Therefore in Spirit all is harmony, and there can be no 15
discord; all is Life, and there is no death. Everything
in God's universe expresses Him.

VI. God is individual, incorporeal. He is divine Prin- 18
ciple, Love, the universal cause, the only creator, and
there is no other self-existence. He is all- **The universal**
inclusive, and is reflected by all that is real **cause** 21
and eternal and by nothing else. He fills all space, and
it is impossible to conceive of such omnipresence and individuality except as infinite Spirit or Mind. Hence all 24
is Spirit and spiritual.

VII. Life, Truth, and Love constitute the triune Person
called God, — that is, the triply divine Principle, Love. 27
They represent a trinity in unity, three in **Divine**
one, — the same in essence, though multi- **trinity**
form in office: God the Father-Mother; Christ the spirit- 30
ual idea of sonship; divine Science or the Holy Comforter.
These three express in divine Science the threefold, essen-

1 tial nature of the infinite. They also indicate the divine
Principle of scientific being, the intelligent relation of God
3 to man and the universe.

VIII. Father-Mother is the name for Deity, which indicates His tender relationship to His spiritual creation.
6   Father-   As the apostle expressed it in words which he
        Mother   quoted with approbation from a classic poet:
"For we are also His offspring."

9   IX. Jesus was born of Mary. Christ is the true idea
voicing good, the divine message from God to men speak-
        The Son   ing to the human consciousness. The Christ
12   of God   is incorporeal, spiritual, — yea, the divine
image and likeness, dispelling the illusions of the senses;
the Way, the Truth, and the Life, healing the sick and
15 casting out evils, destroying sin, disease, and death. As
Paul says: "There is one God, and one mediator between
God and men, the man Christ Jesus." The corporeal
18 man Jesus was human.

X. Jesus demonstrated Christ; he proved that Christ
        Holy Ghost   is the divine idea of God — the Holy Ghost,
21   or Comforter or Comforter, revealing the divine Principle,
Love, and leading into all truth.

XI. Jesus was the son of a virgin. He was appointed
24 to speak God's word and to appear to mortals in such
        Christ   a form of humanity as they could understand
        Jesus   as well as perceive. Mary's conception of
27 him was spiritual, for only purity could reflect Truth
and Love, which were plainly incarnate in the good and
pure Christ Jesus. He expressed the highest type of
30 divinity, which a fleshly form could express in that age.
Into the real and ideal man the fleshly element cannot
enter. Thus it is that Christ illustrates the coincidence,

or spiritual agreement, between God and man in His image.

XII. The word *Christ* is not properly a synonym for Jesus, though it is commonly so used. Jesus was a human name, which belonged to him in common with Messiah other Hebrew boys and men, for it is identical or Christ with the name Joshua, the renowned Hebrew leader. On the other hand, Christ is not a name so much as the divine title of Jesus. Christ expresses God's spiritual, eternal nature. The name is synonymous with Messiah, and alludes to the spirituality which is taught, illustrated, and demonstrated in the life of which Christ Jesus was the embodiment. The proper name of our Master in the Greek was Jesus the Christ; but Christ Jesus better signifies the Godlike.

XIII. The advent of Jesus of Nazareth marked the first century of the Christian era, but the Christ is without beginning of years or end of days. The divine Throughout all generations both before and Principle after the Christian era, the Christ, as the spiritual idea, — the reflection of God, — has come with some measure of power and grace to all prepared to receive Christ, Truth. Abraham, Jacob, Moses, and the prophets caught glorious glimpses of the Messiah, or Christ, which baptized these seers in the divine nature, the essence of Love. The divine image, idea, or Christ was, is, and ever will be inseparable from the divine Principle, God. Jesus referred to this unity of his spiritual identity thus: "Before Abraham was, I am;" "I and my Father are one;" "My Father is greater than I." The one Spirit includes all identities.

XIV. By these sayings Jesus meant, not that the hu-

1 man Jesus was or is eternal, but that the divine idea or
Christ was and is so and therefore antedated Abraham;
3   Spiritual   not that the corporeal Jesus was one with the
    oneness   Father, but that the spiritual idea, Christ,
dwells forever in the bosom of the Father, God, from
6 which it illumines heaven and earth; not that the Father
is greater than Spirit, which is God, but greater, infinitely
greater, than the fleshly Jesus, whose earthly career was
9 brief.

XV. The invisible Christ was imperceptible to the
so-called personal senses, whereas Jesus appeared as a
12   The Son's   bodily existence. This dual personality of the
     duality   unseen and the seen, the spiritual and mate-
rial, the eternal Christ and the corporeal Jesus manifest
15 in flesh, continued until the Master's ascension, when
the human, material concept, or Jesus, disappeared,
while the spiritual self, or Christ, continues to exist in
18 the eternal order of divine Science, taking away the sins
of the world, as the Christ has always done, even before
the human Jesus was incarnate to mortal eyes.

21   XVI. This was "the Lamb slain from the foundation
of the world," — slain, that is, according to the testi-
     Eternity of   mony of the corporeal senses, but undying in
24   the Christ   the deific Mind. The Revelator represents the
Son of man as saying (Revelation i. 17, 18): "I am the
first and the last: I am he that liveth, and was dead
27 [not understood]; and, behold, I am alive for evermore,
[Science has explained me]." This is a mystical statement of the eternity of the Christ, and is also a reference
30 to the human sense of Jesus crucified.

XVII. Spirit being God, there is but one Spirit, for
there can be but one infinite and therefore one God.

There are neither spirits many nor gods many. There 1
is no evil in Spirit, because God is Spirit. The theory,
that Spirit is distinct from matter but must   Infinite   3
pass through it, or into it, to be individualized,   Spirit
would reduce God to dependency on matter, and establish
a basis for pantheism.   6

XVIII. Spirit, God, has created all in and of Himself. Spirit never created matter. There is nothing in
Spirit out of which matter could be made,   The only   9
for, as the Bible declares, without the Logos,   substance
the Æon or Word of God, "was not anything made
that was made." Spirit is the only substance, the in- 12
visible and indivisible infinite God. Things spiritual and
eternal are substantial. Things material and temporal
are insubstantial.   15

XIX. Soul and Spirit being one, God and Soul are
one, and this one never included in a limited mind or a
limited body. Spirit is eternal, divine. Noth-   Soul and   18
ing but Spirit, Soul, can evolve Life, for Spirit   Spirit one
is more than all else. Because Soul is immortal, it does
not exist in mortality. Soul must be incorporeal to be 21
Spirit, for Spirit is not finite. Only by losing the false
sense of Soul can we gain the eternal unfolding of Life as
immortality brought to light.   24

XX. Mind is the divine Principle, Love, and can produce nothing unlike the eternal Father-Mother, God.
Reality is spiritual, harmonious, immutable,   The one   27
immortal, divine, eternal. Nothing unspirit-   divine Mind
ual can be real, harmonious, or eternal. Sin, sickness,
and mortality are the suppositional antipodes of Spirit, 30
and must be contradictions of reality.

XXI. The Ego is deathless and limitless, for limits

1 would imply and impose ignorance. Mind is the I AM,
or infinity. Mind never enters the finite. Intelligence
3   The divine   never passes into non-intelligence, or matter.
      Ego   Good never enters into evil, the unlimited into
the limited, the eternal into the temporal, nor the im-
6 mortal into mortality. The divine Ego, or individuality,
is reflected in all spiritual individuality from the infinitesimal to the infinite.

9   XXII. Immortal man was and is God's image or idea,
even the infinite expression of infinite Mind, and immor-
    The real   tal man is coexistent and coeternal with that
12   manhood   Mind. He has been forever in the eternal
Mind, God; but infinite Mind can never be in man, but
is reflected by man. The spiritual man's consciousness
15 and individuality are reflections of God. They are the
emanations of Him who is Life, Truth, and Love. Immortal man is not and never was material, but always
18 spiritual and eternal.

  XXIII. God is indivisible. A portion of God could
not enter man; neither could God's fulness be reflected
21   Indivisibility   by a single man, else God would be manifestly
  of the infinite   finite, lose the deific character, and become
less than God. Allness is the measure of the infinite, and
24 nothing less can express God.

  XXIV. God, the divine Principle of man, and man in
God's likeness are inseparable, harmonious, and eternal.
27   God the   The Science of being furnishes the rule of per-
  parent Mind   fection, and brings immortality to light. God
and man are not the same, but in the order of divine Sci-
30 ence, God and man coexist and are eternal. God is the
parent Mind, and man is God's spiritual offspring.

  XXV. God is individual and personal in a scientific

sense, but not in any anthropomorphic sense. Therefore 1
man, reflecting God, cannot lose his individuality; but as
material sensation, or a soul in the body, blind   Man reflects 3
mortals do lose sight of spiritual individuality. the perfect
God
Material personality is not realism; it is not
the reflection or likeness of Spirit, the perfect God. Sen- 6
sualism is not bliss, but bondage. For true happiness,
man must harmonize with his Principle, divine Love; the
Son must be in accord with the Father, in conformity with 9
Christ. According to divine Science, man is in a degree
as perfect as the Mind that forms him. The truth of being makes man harmonious and immortal, while error is 12
mortal and discordant.

XXVI. Christian Science demonstrates that none but
the pure in heart can see God, as the gospel   Purity the   15
teaches. In proportion to his purity is man   path to
perfection
perfect; and perfection is the order of celestial
being which demonstrates Life in Christ, Life's spiritual 18
ideal.

XXVII. The true idea of man, as the reflection of the
invisible God, is as incomprehensible to the limited senses 21
as is man's infinite Principle. The visible uni-   True idea
verse and material man are the poor counter-   of man
feits of the invisible universe and spiritual man. Eternal 24
things (verities) are God's thoughts as they exist in the
spiritual realm of the real. Temporal things are the
thoughts of mortals and are the unreal, being the oppo- 27
site of the real or the spiritual and eternal.

XXVIII. Subject sickness, sin, and death to the rule
of health and holiness in Christian Science,   Truth   30
and you ascertain that this Science is demon- demonstrated
strably true, for it heals the sick and sinning as no

1 other system can. Christian Science, rightly understood, leads to eternal harmony. It brings to light the
3 only living and true God and man as made in His likeness; whereas the opposite belief — that man originates
in matter and has beginning and end, that he is both
6 soul and body, both good and evil, both spiritual and
material — terminates in discord and mortality, in the
error which must be destroyed by Truth. The mortality
9 of material man proves that error has been ingrafted
into the premises and conclusions of material and mortal
humanity.

12   XXIX. The word *Adam* is from the Hebrew *adamah*,
signifying the *red color of the ground, dust, nothingness.*
    Adam not   Divide the name Adam into two syllables,
15   ideal man   and it reads, *a dam*, or obstruction. This
suggests the thought of something fluid, of mortal mind
in solution. It further suggests the thought of that
18 "darkness . . . upon the face of the deep," when matter or dust was deemed the agent of Deity in creating
man, — when matter, as that which is accursed, stood
21 opposed to Spirit. Here *a dam* is not a mere play upon
words; it stands for obstruction, error, even the supposed separation of man from God, and the obstacle
24 which the serpent, sin, would impose between man and
his creator. The dissection and definition of words,
aside from their metaphysical derivation, is not scien-
27 tific. Jehovah declared the ground was accursed; and
from this ground, or matter, sprang Adam, notwithstanding God had blessed the earth "for man's sake."
30 From this it follows that Adam was not the ideal man
for whom the earth was blessed. The ideal man was
revealed in due time, and was known as Christ Jesus.

XXX. The destruction of sin is the divine method of 1
pardon. Divine Life destroys death, Truth destroys
error, and Love destroys hate. Being de-   Divine   3
stroyed, sin needs no other form of forgiveness.   pardon
Does not God's pardon, destroying any one sin, prophesy
and involve the final destruction of all sin?   6

XXXI. Since God is All, there is no room for His
unlikeness. God, Spirit, alone created all, and called it
good. Therefore evil, being contrary to good, Evil not pro- 9
is unreal, and cannot be the product of God. duced by God
A sinner can receive no encouragement from the fact that
Science demonstrates the unreality of evil, for the sinner 12
would make a reality of sin, — would make that real
which is unreal, and thus heap up "wrath against the
day of wrath." He is joining in a conspiracy against 15
himself, — against his own awakening to the awful unreality by which he has been deceived. Only those, who
repent of sin and forsake the unreal, can fully understand 18
the unreality of evil.

XXXII. As the mythology of pagan Rome has yielded
to a more spiritual idea of Deity, so will our material 21
theories yield to spiritual ideas, until the finite
gives place to the infinite, sickness to health,   Basis of
                                                    health and
sin to holiness, and God's kingdom comes "in   immortality 24
earth, as it is in heaven." The basis of all health, sinlessness, and immortality is the great fact that God is
the only Mind; and this Mind must be not merely be- 27
lieved, but it must be understood. To get rid of sin
through Science, is to divest sin of any supposed mind
or reality, and never to admit that sin can have intelli- 30
gence or power, pain or pleasure. You conquer error by
denying its verity. Our various theories will never lose

1 their imaginary power for good or evil, until we lose our
faith in them and make life its own proof of harmony
3 and God.

This text in the book of Ecclesiastes conveys the
Christian Science thought, especially when the word
6 *duty*, which is not in the original, is omitted: "Let
us hear the conclusion of the whole matter: Fear God,
and keep His commandments: for this is the whole
9 duty of man." In other words: Let us hear the conclusion of the whole matter: love God and keep His
commandments: for this is the whole of man in His
12 image and likeness. Divine Love is infinite. Therefore
all that really exists is in and of God, and manifests His
love.

15　"Thou shalt have no other gods before me." (Exodus
xx. 3.) The First Commandment is my favorite text.
It demonstrates Christian Science. It inculcates the tri-
18 unity of God, Spirit, Mind; it signifies that man shall
have no other spirit or mind but God, eternal good, and
that all men shall have one Mind. The divine Principle
21 of the First Commandment bases the Science of being, by
which man demonstrates health, holiness, and life eternal.

One infinite God, good, unifies men and nations; con-
24 stitutes the brotherhood of man; ends wars; fulfils the
Scripture, "Love thy neighbor as thyself;" annihilates
pagan and Christian idolatry, — whatever is wrong in
27 social, civil, criminal, political, and religious codes;
equalizes the sexes; annuls the curse on man, and leaves
nothing that can sin, suffer, be punished or destroyed.

CHAPTER XI

Some Objections Answered

And because I tell you the truth, ye believe me not. Which of you convinceth me of sin? And if I say the truth, why do ye not believe me? — JESUS.

But if the spirit of Him that raised up Jesus from the dead dwell in you, He that raised up Christ from the dead shall also quicken your mortal bodies by His spirit that dwelleth in you. — PAUL.

THE strictures on this volume would condemn to 1
oblivion the truth, which is raising up thousands
from helplessness to strength and elevating them from 3
a theoretical to a practical Christianity. These criticisms
are generally based on detached sentences or clauses separated from their context. Even the Scriptures, which 6
grow in beauty and consistency from one grand root, appear contradictory when subjected to such usage. Jesus
said, "Blessed are the pure in heart: for they shall see 9
God" [Truth].

In Christian Science mere opinion is valueless. Proof
is essential to a due estimate of this subject. Sneers at 12
the application of the word *Science* to Christianity cannot prevent that from being scien- Supported by facts
tific which is based on divine Principle, demonstrated according to a divine given rule, and subjected to proof. 15
The facts are so absolute and numerous in support of
Christian Science, that misrepresentation and denuncia- 18

341

1 tion cannot overthrow it.   Paul alludes to "doubtful dis-
putations."   The hour has struck when proof and demon-
3 stration, instead of opinion and dogma, are summoned to
the support of Christianity, "making wise the simple."

In the result of some unqualified condemnations of
6 scientific Mind-healing, one may see with sorrow the sad

Commands
of Jesus

effects on the sick of denying Truth.   He that
decries this Science does it presumptuously,
9 in the face of Bible history and in defiance of the direct
command of Jesus, "Go ye into all the world, and preach
the gospel," to which command was added the promise
12 that his students should cast out evils and heal the sick.
He bade the seventy disciples, as well as the twelve,
heal the sick in any town where they should be hospitably
15 received.

If Christianity is not scientific, and Science is not of
God, then there is no invariable law, and truth becomes
18 Christianity
scientific

an accident.   Shall it be denied that a system
which works according to the Scriptures has
Scriptural authority?
21 Christian Science awakens the sinner, reclaims the
infidel, and raises from the couch of pain the helpless

Argument of
good works

invalid.   It speaks to the dumb the words of
Truth, and they answer with rejoicing.   It
24 causes the deaf to hear, the lame to walk, and the blind
to see.   Who would be the first to disown the Christli-
27 ness of good works, when our Master says, "By their
fruits ye shall know them"?

If Christian Scientists were teaching or practising
30 pharmacy or obstetrics according to the common theories, no denunciations would follow them, even if their
treatment resulted in the death of a patient.   The people

are taught in such cases to say, Amen. Shall I then be 1
smitten for healing and for teaching Truth as the Principle of healing, and for proving my word by my deed? 3
James said: "Show me thy faith without thy works, and
I will show thee my faith by my works."

Is not finite mind ignorant of God's method? This 6
makes it doubly unfair to impugn and misrepresent the
facts, although, without this cross-bearing,   Personal
one might not be able to say with the apostle, experience 9
"None of these things move me." The sick, the halt,
and the blind look up to Christian Science with blessings,
and Truth will not be forever hidden by unjust parody 12
from the quickened sense of the people.

Jesus strips all disguise from error, when his teachings
are fully understood. By parable and argument he ex- 15
plains the impossibility of good producing evil; Proof from
and he also scientifically demonstrates this great   miracles
fact, proving by what are wrongly called miracles, that 18
sin, sickness, and death are beliefs — illusive errors —
which he could and did destroy.

It would sometimes seem as if truth were rejected be- 21
cause meekness and spirituality are the conditions of its
acceptance, while Christendom generally demands so
much less.   24

Anciently those apostles who were Jesus' students,
as well as Paul who was not one of his students, healed
the sick and reformed the sinner by their Example of 27
religion. Hence the mistake which allows the disciples
words, rather than works, to follow such examples!
Whoever is the first meekly and conscientiously to press 30
along the line of gospel-healing, is often accounted a
heretic.

1 It is objected to Christian Science that it claims God
as the only absolute Life and Soul, and man to be His
3 Strong idea, — that is, His image. It should be
position added that this is claimed to represent the
normal, healthful, and sinless condition of man in divine
6 Science, and that this claim is made because the Scriptures say that God has created man in His own image
and after His likeness. Is it sacrilegious to assume that
9 God's likeness is not found in matter, sin, sickness, and
death?

Were it more fully understood that Truth heals and
12 that error causes disease, the opponents of a demonstrable
Efficacy may Science would perhaps mercifully withhold
be attested their misrepresentations, which harm the sick;
15 and until the enemies of Christian Science test its efficacy
according to the rules which disclose its merits or de-
merits, it would be just to observe the Scriptural precept,
18 "Judge not."

There are various methods of treating disease, which
are not included in the commonly accepted systems; but
21 The one there is only one which should be presented
divine method to the whole world, and that is the Christian
Science which Jesus preached and practised and left to us
24 as his rich legacy.

Why should one refuse to investigate this method
of treating disease? Why support the popular systems
27 of medicine, when the physician may perchance be an
infidel and may lose ninety-and-nine patients, while
Christian Science cures its hundred? Is it because
30 allopathy and homœopathy are more fashionable and
less spiritual?

In the Bible the word *Spirit* is so commonly applied

to Deity, that Spirit and God are often regarded as syn- 1
onymous terms; and it is thus they are uniformly used
and understood in Christian Science. As it Omnipotence 3
is evident that the likeness of Spirit cannot be set forth
material, does it not follow that God cannot be in His
unlikeness and work through drugs to heal the sick? 6
When the omnipotence of God is preached and His ab-
soluteness is set forth, Christian sermons will heal the
sick. 9

It is sometimes said, in criticising Christian Science,
that the mind which contradicts itself neither knows
itself nor what it is saying. It is indeed no Contradictions 12
small matter to know one's self; but in this not
found
volume of mine there are no contradictory
statements, — at least none which are apparent to those 15
who understand its propositions well enough to pass
judgment upon them. One who understands Christian
Science can heal the sick on the divine Principle of Chris- 18
tian Science, and this practical proof is the only feasible
evidence that one does understand this Science.

Anybody, who is able to perceive the incongruity be- 21
tween God's idea and poor humanity, ought to be able
to discern the distinction (made by Christian Science)
between God's man, made in His image, and the sinning 24
race of Adam.

The apostle says: "For if a man think himself to be
something, when he is nothing, he deceiveth himself." 27
This thought of human, material nothingness, which
Science inculcates, enrages the carnal mind and is the
main cause of the carnal mind's antagonism. 30

It is not the purpose of Christian Science to "educate
the idea of God, or treat it for disease," as is alleged

1 by one critic. I regret that such criticism confounds *man*
with Adam. When man is spoken of as made in God's
3   God's idea   image, it is not sinful and sickly mortal man
the ideal man who is referred to, but the ideal man, reflecting
God's likeness.

6   It is sometimes said that Christian Science teaches the
nothingness of sin, sickness, and death, and then teaches
Nothingness how this nothingness is to be saved and healed.
9   of error   The nothingness of nothing is plain; but we
need to understand that error *is* nothing, and that its
nothingness is not saved, but must be demonstrated in
12 order to prove the somethingness — yea, the allness —
of Truth. It is self-evident that we are harmonious only
as we cease to manifest evil or the belief that we suffer
15 from the sins of others. Disbelief in error destroys error,
and leads to the discernment of Truth. There are no
vacuums. How then can this demonstration be "fraught
18 with falsities painful to behold"?
We treat error through the understanding of Truth,
because Truth is error's antidote. If a dream ceases, it
21   Truth   is self-destroyed, and the terror is over. When
antidotes error a sufferer is convinced that there is no reality
in his belief of pain, — because matter has no sensation,
24 hence pain in matter is a false belief, — how can he suffer
longer? Do you feel the pain of tooth-pulling, when you
believe that nitrous-oxide gas has made you unconscious?
27 Yet, in your concept, the tooth, the operation, and the
forceps are unchanged.
Material beliefs must be expelled to make room for
30   Serving   spiritual understanding. We cannot serve both
two masters God and mammon at the same time; but is
not this what frail mortals are trying to do? Paul says:

"The flesh lusteth against the Spirit, and the Spirit against 1
the flesh." Who is ready to admit this?

It is said by one critic, that to verify this wonderful 3
philosophy Christian Science declares that whatever is
mortal or discordant has no origin, existence, nor real-
ness. Nothing really has Life but God, who is infinite 6
Life; hence all is Life, and death has no dominion. This
writer infers that if anything needs to be doctored, it
must be the one God, or Mind. Had he stated his syllo- 9
gism correctly, the conclusion would be that there is nothing left to be doctored.

Critics should consider that the so-called mortal man 12
is not the reality of man. Then they would behold the
signs of Christ's coming. Christ, as the spir- Essential
itual or true idea of God, comes now as of   element of   15
old, preaching the gospel to the poor, heal-   Christianity
ing the sick, and casting out evils. Is it error which
is restoring an essential element of Christianity, — 18
namely, apostolic, divine healing? No; it is the Science
of Christianity which is restoring it, and is the light
shining in darkness, which the darkness comprehends 21
not.

If Christian Science takes away the popular gods, —
sin, sickness, and death, — it is Christ, Truth, who de- 24
stroys these evils, and so proves their nothingness.

The dream that matter and error are something
must yield to reason and revelation. Then mortals 27
will behold the nothingness of sickness and sin, and
sin and sickness will disappear from consciousness.
The harmonious will appear real, and the inharmo- 30
nious unreal. These critics will then see that error
is indeed the nothingness, which they chide us for

1 naming nothing and which we desire neither to honor
nor to fear.

3 Medical theories virtually admit the nothingness of
hallucinations, even while treating them as disease; and
who objects to this? Ought we not, then, to approve
6 any cure, which is effected by making the disease appear
to be — what it really is — an illusion?

Here is the difficulty: it is not generally understood how
9 one disease can be just as much a delusion as another. It
All disease is a pity that the medical faculty and clergy
a delusion have not learned this, for Jesus established
12 this foundational fact, when devils, delusions, were cast
out and the dumb spake.

Are we irreverent towards sin, or imputing too much
15 power to God, when we ascribe to Him almighty Life
Elimination and Love? I deny His cooperation with evil,
of sickness because I desire to have no faith in evil or in
18 any power but God, good. Is it not well to eliminate from
so-called mortal mind that which, so long as it remains in
mortal mind, will show itself in forms of sin, sickness, and
21 death? Instead of tenaciously defending the supposed
rights of disease, while complaining of the suffering disease brings, would it not be well to abandon the defence,
24 especially when by so doing our own condition can be improved and that of other persons as well?

I have never supposed the world would immediately
27 witness the full fruitage of Christian Science, or that sin,
Full fruitage disease, and death would not be believed for
yet to come an indefinite time; but this I do aver, that,
30 as a result of teaching Christian Science, ethics and
temperance have received an impulse, health has been
restored, and longevity increased. If such are the pres-

ent fruits, what will the harvest be, when this Science is 1
more generally understood?

As Paul asked of the unfaithful in ancient days, so 3
the rabbis of the present day ask concerning our healing and teaching, "Through breaking the law, Law and
dishonorest thou God?" We have the gospel,   gospel   6
however, and our Master annulled material law by healing contrary to it. We propose to follow the Master's
example. We should subordinate material law to spirit- 9
ual law. Two essential points of Christian Science are,
that neither Life nor man dies, and that God is not the
author of sickness.   12

The chief difficulty in conveying the teachings of divine
Science accurately to human thought lies in this, that like
all other languages, English is inadequate to Language 15
the expression of spiritual conceptions and inadequate
propositions, because one is obliged to use material terms
in dealing with spiritual ideas. The elucidation of Chris- 18
tian Science lies in its spiritual sense, and this sense must
be gained by its disciples in order to grasp the meaning of
this Science. Out of this condition grew the prophecy 21
concerning the Christian apostles, "They shall speak with
new tongues."

Speaking of the things of Spirit while dwelling on 24
a material plane, material terms must be generally employed. Mortal thought does not at once catch the
higher meaning, and can do so only as thought is edu- 27
cated up to spiritual apprehension. To a certain extent
this is equally true of all learning, even that which is
wholly material.   30

In Christian Science, substance is understood to be
Spirit, while the opponents of Christian Science believe

1 substance to be matter. They think of matter as something and almost the only thing, and of the things which
3   Substance   pertain to Spirit as next to nothing, or as very
    spiritual   far removed from daily experience. Christian
Science takes exactly the opposite view.
6   To understand all our Master's sayings as recorded
in the New Testament, sayings infinitely important,
   Both words his followers must grow into that stature of
9   and works   manhood in Christ Jesus which enables them
to interpret his spiritual meaning. Then they know
how Truth casts out error and heals the sick. His
12 words were the offspring of his deeds, both of which
must be understood. Unless the works are comprehended which his words explained, the words are
15 blind.

    The Master often refused to explain his words, because
it was difficult in a material age to apprehend spiritual
18 Truth. He said: "This people's heart is waxed gross,
and their ears are dull of hearing, and their eyes they
have closed; lest at any time they should see with their
21 eyes, and hear with their ears, and should understand
with their heart, and should be converted, and I should
heal them."

24   "The Word was made flesh." Divine Truth must be
known by its effects on the body as well as on the mind,
   The divine before the Science of being can be demon-
27   life-link   strated. Hence its embodiment in the incarnate Jesus, — that life-link forming the connection through
which the real reaches the unreal, Soul rebukes sense, and
30 Truth destroys error.

    In Jewish worship the Word was materially explained,
and the spiritual sense was scarcely perceived. The

religion which sprang from half-hidden Israelitish history 1
was pedantic and void of healing power. When we lose
faith in God's power to heal, we distrust the   Truth a   3
divine Principle which demonstrates Christian   present help
Science, and then we cannot heal the sick. Neither can
we heal through the help of Spirit, if we plant ourselves 6
on a material basis.

The author became a member of the orthodox Con-
gregational Church in early years. Later she learned 9
that her own prayers failed to heal her as did the prayers
of her devout parents and the church; but when the
spiritual sense of the creed was discerned in the Science 12
of Christianity, this spiritual sense was a *present help*. It
was the living, palpitating presence of Christ, Truth, which
healed the sick.   15

We cannot bring out the practical proof of Christianity,
which Jesus required, while error seems as potent and
real to us as Truth, and while we make a per-   Fatal   18
sonal devil and an anthropomorphic God our   premises
starting-points, — especially if we consider Satan as a
being coequal in power with Deity, if not superior to Him. 21
Because such starting-points are neither spiritual nor
scientific, they cannot work out the Spirit-rule of Christian
healing, which proves the nothingness of error, discord, 24
by demonstrating the all-inclusiveness of harmonious
Truth.

The Israelites centred their thoughts on the material 27
in their attempted worship of the spiritual. To them
matter was substance, and Spirit was shadow.   Fruitless
They thought to worship Spirit from a ma-   worship   30
terial standpoint, but this was impossible. They might
appeal to Jehovah, but their prayer brought down no

1 proof that it was heard, because they did not sufficiently
understand God to be able to demonstrate His power
3 to heal, — to make harmony the reality and discord the
unreality.

Our Master declared that his material body was not
6 spirit, evidently considering it a mortal and material be-
Spirit the   lief of flesh and bones, whereas the Jews took
tangible   a diametrically opposite view. To Jesus, not
9 materiality, but spirituality, was the reality of man's existence, while to the rabbis the spiritual was the intangible and uncertain, if not the unreal.

12   Would a mother say to her child, who is frightened at
imaginary ghosts and sick in consequence of the fear:
Ghosts   "I know that ghosts are real. They exist,
15 not realities   and are to be feared; but you must not be
afraid of them"?

Children, like adults, *ought* to fear a reality which
18 can harm them and which they do not understand, for
at any moment they may become its helpless victims;
but instead of increasing children's fears by declaring
21 ghosts to be real, merciless, and powerful, thus water-
ing the very roots of childish timidity, children should
be assured that their fears are groundless, that ghosts
24 are not realities, but traditional beliefs, erroneous and
man-made.

In short, children should be told not to believe in ghosts,
27 because there are no such things. If belief in their reality
is destroyed, terror of ghosts will depart and health be restored. The objects of alarm will then vanish into noth-
30 ingness, no longer seeming worthy of fear or honor. To
accomplish a good result, it is certainly not irrational to
tell the truth about ghosts.

The Christianly scientific real is the sensuous unreal. 1
Sin, disease, whatever seems real to material sense, is unreal in divine Science.   The physical senses   The real and   3
and Science have ever been antagonistic, and   the unreal
they will so continue, till the testimony of the physical
senses yields entirely to Christian Science.   6

How can a Christian, having the stronger evidence of
Truth which contradicts the evidence of error, think of
the latter as real or true, either in the form of sickness or 9
of sin?   All must admit that Christ is "the way, the
truth, and the life," and that omnipotent Truth certainly
does destroy error.   12

The age has not wholly outlived the sense of ghostly
beliefs.   It still holds them more or less.   Time has not
yet reached eternity, immortality, complete   Superstition   15
reality.   All the real is eternal.   Perfection   obsolete
underlies reality.   Without perfection, nothing is wholly
real.   All things will continue to disappear, until per- 18
fection appears and reality is reached.   We must give up
the spectral at all points.   We must not continue to admit
the somethingness of superstition, but we must yield up 21
all belief in it and be wise.   When we learn that error
is not real, we shall be ready for progress, "forgetting
those things which are behind."   24

The grave does not banish the ghost of materiality.
So long as there are supposed limits to Mind, and those
limits are human, so long will ghosts seem to continue. 27
Mind is limitless.   It never was material.   The true idea
of being is spiritual and immortal, and from this it follows
that whatever is laid off is the ghost, some unreal belief. 30
Mortal beliefs can neither demonstrate Christianity nor
apprehend the reality of Life.

1   Are the protests of Christian Science against the notion
that there can be material life, substance, or mind "utter
3   Christian   falsities and absurdities," as some aver? Why
warfare   then do Christians try to obey the Scriptures
and war against "the world, the flesh, and the devil"?
6 Why do they invoke the divine aid to enable them to leave
all for Christ, Truth? Why do they use this phraseology,
and yet deny Christian Science, when it teaches precisely
9 this thought? The words of divine Science find their
immortality in deeds, for their Principle heals the sick
and spiritualizes humanity.

12   On the other hand, the Christian opponents of Christian Science neither give nor offer any proofs that their
Healing   Master's religion can heal the sick. Surely
15   omitted   it is not enough to cleave to barren and desul-
tory dogmas, derived from the traditions of the elders who
thereunto have set their seals.

18   Consistency is seen in example more than in precept.
Inconsistency is shown by words without deeds, which
Scientific   are like clouds without rain. If our words
21   consistency   fail to express our deeds, God will redeem that
weakness, and out of the mouth of babes He will perfect
praise. The night of materiality is far spent, and with
24 the dawn Truth will waken men spiritually to hear and
to speak the new tongue.

Sin should become unreal to every one. It is in itself
27 inconsistent, a divided kingdom. Its supposed realism
has no divine authority, and I rejoice in the apprehension
of this grand verity.

30   Spiritual   The opponents of divine Science must be
meaning   charitable, if they would be Christian. If the
letter of Christian Science appears inconsistent, they should

gain the spiritual meaning of Christian Science, and then 1
the ambiguity will vanish.

The charge of inconsistency in Christianly scientific 3
methods of dealing with sin and disease is met by something practical, — namely, the proof of the   Practical
utility of these methods; and proofs are better   arguments   6
than mere verbal arguments or prayers which evince no
spiritual power to heal.

As for sin and disease, Christian Science says, in the 9
language of the Master, "Follow me; and let the dead
bury their dead." Let discord of every name and nature
be heard no more, and let the harmonious and true sense 12
of Life and being take possession of human consciousness.

What is the relative value of the two conflicting theories regarding Christian healing? One, according to 15
the commands of our Master, heals the sick. The other,
popular religion, declines to admit that Christ's religion
has exercised any systematic healing power since the first 18
century.

The statement that the teachings of Christian Science in this work are "absolutely false, and the most 21
egregious fallacies ever offered for accept-   Conditions
ance," is an opinion wholly due to a misap-   of criticism
prehension both of the divine Principle and practice of 24
Christian Science and to a consequent inability to demonstrate this Science. Without this understanding, no one
is capable of impartial or correct criticism, because demon- 27
stration and spiritual understanding are God's immortal
keynotes, proved to be such by our Master and evidenced
by the sick who are cured and by the sinners who are 30
reformed.

Strangely enough, we ask for material theories in sup-

1 port of spiritual and eternal truths, when the two are so
antagonistic that the material thought must become spir-
3 itualized before the spiritual fact is attained.

Weakness of material theories So-called material existence affords no evidence
of spiritual existence and immortality. Sin,
6 sickness, and death do not prove man's entity or immortality. Discord can never establish the facts of harmony.
Matter is not the vestibule of Spirit.

9 Jesus reasoned on this subject practically, and controlled sickness, sin, and death on the basis of his spirituality. Understanding the nothingness of

Irreconcilable differences material things, he spoke of flesh and Spirit
12 as the two opposites, — as error and Truth, not contrib-
uting in any way to each other's happiness and existence.
15 Jesus knew, "It is the spirit that quickeneth; the flesh
profiteth nothing."

There is neither a present nor an eternal copartner-
18 ship between error and Truth, between flesh and Spirit.

Copartnership impossible God is as incapable of producing sin, sickness, and death as He is of experiencing these
21 errors. How then is it possible for Him to create man
subject to this triad of errors, — man who is made in the
divine likeness?

24 Does God create a material man out of Himself, Spirit?
Does evil proceed from good? Does divine Love commit a fraud on humanity by making man inclined to sin,
27 and then punishing him for it? Would any one call it
wise and good to create the primitive, and then punish its
derivative?

30 Does subsequent follow its antecedent? It does.
Was there original self-creative sin? Then there must
have been more than one creator, more than one God.

In common justice, we must admit that God will not 1
punish man for doing what He created man
capable of doing, and knew from the outset   *Two infinite creators absurd*   3
that man would do. God is "of purer eyes
than to behold evil." We sustain Truth, not by accept-
ing, but by rejecting a lie.   6

Jesus said of personified evil, that it was "a liar, and
the father of it." Truth creates neither a lie, a capacity
to lie, nor a liar. If mankind would relinquish the belief 9
that God makes sickness, sin, and death, or makes man
capable of suffering on account of this malevolent triad,
the foundations of error would be sapped and error's de- 12
struction ensured; but if we theoretically endow mortals
with the creativeness and authority of Deity, how dare we
attempt to destroy what He hath made, or even to deny 15
that God made man evil and made evil good?

History teaches that the popular and false notions
about the Divine Being and character have originated 18
in the human mind. As there is in reality but   *Anthropo-morphism*
one God, one Mind, wrong notions about God
must have originated in a false supposition, not in im- 21
mortal Truth, and they are fading out. They are false
claims, which will eventually disappear, according to the
vision of St. John in the Apocalypse.   24

If what opposes God is real, there must be two
powers, and God is not supreme and infinite. Can
Deity be almighty, if another mighty and   *One supremacy*   27
self-creative cause exists and sways man-
kind? Has the Father "Life in Himself," as the Scriptures say, and, if so, can Life, or God, dwell in evil and 30
create it? Can matter drive Life, Spirit, hence, and so
defeat omnipotence?

1 Is the woodman's axe, which destroys a tree's so-called
life, superior to omnipotence? Can a leaden bullet de-
3 Matter prive a man of Life, — that is, of God, who is
impotent man's Life? If God is at the mercy of matter,
then matter is omnipotent. Such doctrines are "confu-
6 sion worse confounded." If two statements directly contradict each other and one is true, the other must be false.
Is Science thus contradictory?

9 Christian Science, understood, coincides with the
Scriptures, and sustains logically and demonstratively
Scientific and every point it presents. Otherwise it would
12 Biblical facts not be Science, and could not present its
proofs. Christian Science is neither made up of contradictory aphorisms nor of the inventions of those who scoff
15 at God. It presents the calm and clear verdict of Truth
against error, uttered and illustrated by the prophets,
by Jesus, by his apostles, as is recorded throughout the
18 Scriptures.

Why are the words of Jesus more frequently cited
for our instruction than are his remarkable works? Is
21 it not because there are few who have gained a true
knowledge of the great import to Christianity of those
works?

24 Sometimes it is said: "Rest assured that whatever
effect Christian Scientists may have on the sick, comes
Personal through rousing within the sick a belief
27 confidence that in the removal of disease these healers
have wonderful power, derived from the Holy Ghost."
Is it likely that church-members have more faith in
30 some Christian Scientist, whom they have perhaps
never seen and against whom they have been warned,
than they have in their own accredited and orthodox

pastors, whom they have seen and have been taught 1
to love and to trust?

Let any clergyman try to cure his friends by their 3
faith in him. Will that faith heal them? Yet Scientists will take the same cases, and cures will follow.
Is this because the patients have more faith in the Scien- 6
tist than in their pastor? I have healed infidels whose
only objection to this method was, that I as a Christian Scientist believed in the Holy Spirit, while they, the 9
patients, did not.

Even though you aver that the material senses are
indispensable to man's existence or entity, you must 12
change the human concept of life, and must at length
know yourself spiritually and scientifically. The evidence of the existence of Spirit, Soul, is palpable only to 15
spiritual sense, and is not apparent to the material senses,
which cognize only that which is the opposite of Spirit.

True Christianity is to be honored wherever found, 18
but when shall we arrive at the goal which that word
implies? From Puritan parents, the discov-   Author's
erer of Christian Science early received her   parentage   21
religious education. In childhood, she often listened
with joy to these words, falling from the lips of her
saintly mother, "God is able to raise you up from sick- 24
ness;" and she pondered the meaning of that Scripture
she so often quotes: "And these signs shall follow them
that believe; . . . they shall lay hands on the sick, 27
and they shall recover."

A Christian Scientist and an opponent are like two
artists. One says: "I have spiritual ideals, Two different 30
indestructible and glorious. When others see   artists
them as I do, in their true light and loveliness, — and

1 know that these ideals are real and eternal because drawn
from Truth, — they will find that nothing is lost, and all
3 is won, by a right estimate of what is real."

The other artist replies: "You wrong my experience.
I have no mind-ideals except those which are both mental
6 and material. It is true that materiality renders these
ideals imperfect and destructible; yet I would not exchange mine for thine, for mine give me such personal
9 pleasure, and they are not so shockingly transcendental.
They require less self-abnegation, and keep Soul well out
of sight. Moreover, I have no notion of losing my old
12 doctrines or human opinions."

Dear reader, which mind-picture or externalized thought
shall be real to you, — the material or the spiritual?
15 Choose ye Both you cannot have. You are bringing out
to-day your own ideal. This ideal is either temporal
or eternal. Either Spirit or matter is your model. If you
18 try to have two models, then you practically have none.
Like a pendulum in a clock, you will be thrown back and
forth, striking the ribs of matter and swinging between the
21 real and the unreal.

Hear the wisdom of Job, as given in the excellent translation of the late Rev. George R. Noyes, D.D.: —

24　　　Shall mortal man be more just than God?
　　　Shall man be more pure than his Maker?
　　　Behold, He putteth no trust in His ministering spirits,
27　　　And His angels He chargeth with frailty.

Of old, the Jews put to death the Galilean Prophet,
the best Christian on earth, for the truth he spoke and
30 demonstrated, while to-day, Jew and Christian can unite
in doctrine and denomination on the very basis of Jesus'
words and works. The Jew believes that the Messiah or

Christ has not yet come; the Christian believes that 1
Christ is God. Here Christian Science intervenes, explains these doctrinal points, cancels the disagreement, 3
and settles the question. Christ, as the true spiritual idea,
is the ideal of God now and forever, here and everywhere.
The Jew who believes in the First Commandment is a 6
monotheist; he has one omnipresent God. Thus the Jew
unites with the Christian's doctrine that God is come and
is present now and forever. The Christian who believes 9
in the First Commandment is a monotheist. Thus he
virtually unites with the Jew's belief in one God, and
recognizes that Jesus Christ is not God, as Jesus himself 12
declared, but is the Son of God. This declaration of
Jesus, understood, conflicts not at all with another of his
sayings: "I and my Father are one," — that is, one in 15
quality, not in quantity. As a drop of water is one with
the ocean, a ray of light one with the sun, even so God
and man, Father and son, are one in being. The Scrip- 18
ture reads: "For in Him we live, and move, and have
our being."

I have revised SCIENCE AND HEALTH only to give a 21
clearer and fuller expression of its original meaning. √Spir-
itual ideas unfold as we advance. A human perception of
divine Science, however limited, must be correct in order 24
to be Science and subject to demonstration. A germ of infinite Truth, though least in the kingdom of heaven, is the
higher hope on earth, but it will be rejected and reviled 27
until God prepares the soil for the seed. That which
when sown bears immortal fruit, enriches mankind only
when it is understood, — hence the many readings given 30
the Scriptures, and the requisite revisions of SCIENCE AND
HEALTH WITH KEY TO THE SCRIPTURES.

CHAPTER XII

Christian Science Practice

Why art thou cast down, O my soul [sense]?
And why art thou disquieted within me?
Hope thou in God; for I shall yet praise Him,
Who is the health of my countenance and my God. — PSALMS.

And these signs shall follow them that believe: In my name shall they
cast out devils: they shall speak with new tongues; they shall take up
serpents; and if they drink any deadly thing, it shall not hurt them;
they shall lay hands on the sick, and they shall recover. — JESUS.

1 IT is related in the seventh chapter of Luke's Gospel
that Jesus was once the honored guest of a certain
3 Pharisee, by name Simon, though he was quite unlike
Simon the disciple. While they were at meat, an unusual

A gospel
narrative
incident occurred, as if to interrupt the scene
6 of Oriental festivity. A "strange woman"
came in. Heedless of the fact that she was debarred from
such a place and such society, especially under the stern
9 rules of rabbinical law, as positively as if she were a Hindoo pariah intruding upon the household of a high-caste
Brahman, this woman (Mary Magdalene, as she has
12 since been called) approached Jesus. According to the
custom of those days, he reclined on a couch with his
head towards the table and his bare feet away from it.
15 It was therefore easy for the Magdalen to come behind

362

the couch and reach his feet. She bore an alabaster jar 1
containing costly and fragrant oil, — sandal oil perhaps,
which is in such common use in the East. Breaking 3
the sealed jar, she perfumed Jesus' feet with the oil,
wiping them with her long hair, which hung loosely
about her shoulders, as was customary with women of her 6
grade.

Did Jesus spurn the woman? Did he repel her adoration? No! He regarded her compassionately. Nor was 9
this all. Knowing what those around him   Parable of
were saying in their hearts, especially his host,   the creditor
— that they were wondering why, being a prophet, the 12
exalted guest did not at once detect the woman's immoral
status and bid her depart, — knowing this, Jesus rebuked
them with a short story or parable. He described two 15
debtors, one for a large sum and one for a smaller, who
were released from their obligations by their common
creditor. "Which of them will love him most?" was the 18
Master's question to Simon the Pharisee; and Simon replied, "He to whom he forgave most." Jesus approved
the answer, and so brought home the lesson to all, follow- 21
ing it with that remarkable declaration to the woman,
"Thy sins are forgiven."

Why did he thus summarize her debt to divine Love? 24
Had she repented and reformed, and did his insight
detect this unspoken moral uprising? She   Divine
bathed his feet with her tears before she   insight   27
anointed them with the oil. In the absence of other
proofs, was her grief sufficient evidence to warrant the
expectation of her repentance, reformation, and growth 30
in wisdom? Certainly there was encouragement in the
mere fact that she was showing her affection for a man

1 of undoubted goodness and purity, who has since been rightfully regarded as the best man that ever trod this 3 planet. Her reverence was unfeigned, and it was manifested towards one who was soon, though they knew it not, to lay down his mortal existence in behalf of all 6 sinners, that through his word and works they might be redeemed from sensuality and sin.

Which was the higher tribute to such ineffable affec- 9 tion, the hospitality of the Pharisee or the contrition of

Penitence or hospitality the Magdalen? This query Jesus answered by rebuking self-righteousness and declaring 12 the absolution of the penitent. He even said that this poor woman had done what his rich entertainer had neglected to do, — wash and anoint his guest's feet, a special 15 sign of Oriental courtesy.

Here is suggested a solemn question, a question indicated by one of the needs of this age. Do Christian 18 Scientists seek Truth as Simon sought the Saviour, through material conservatism and for personal homage? Jesus told Simon that such seekers as he gave small reward 21 in return for the spiritual purgation which came through the Messiah. If Christian Scientists are like Simon, then it must be said of them also that they *love* 24 little.

On the other hand, do they show their regard for Truth, or Christ, by their genuine repentance, by their 27 Genuine repentance broken hearts, expressed by meekness and human affection, as did this woman? If so, then it may be said of them, as Jesus said of the 30 unwelcome visitor, that they indeed love much, because much is forgiven them.

Did the careless doctor, the nurse, the cook, and the

brusque business visitor sympathetically know the thorns 1
they plant in the pillow of the sick and the heavenly
homesick looking away from earth, — Oh, did Compassion 3
they know! — this knowledge would do much requisite
more towards healing the sick and preparing their helpers
for the "midnight call," than all cries of "Lord, Lord!" 6
The benign thought of Jesus, finding utterance in such
words as "Take no thought for your life," would heal
the sick, and so enable them to rise above the supposed 9
necessity for physical thought-taking and doctoring;
but if the unselfish affections be lacking, and common
sense and common humanity are disregarded, what men- 12
tal quality remains, with which to evoke healing from
the outstretched arm of righteousness?

If the Scientist reaches his patient through divine 15
Love, the healing work will be accomplished at one
visit, and the disease will vanish into its native Speedy
nothingness like dew before the morning sun- healing 18
shine. If the Scientist has enough Christly affection to
win his own pardon, and such commendation as the Magdalen gained from Jesus, then he is Christian enough to 21
practise scientifically and deal with his patients compassionately; and the result will correspond with the spiritual
intent. 24

If hypocrisy, stolidity, inhumanity, or vice finds its
way into the chambers of disease through the would-be
healer, it would, if it were possible, convert Truth 27
into a den of thieves the temple of the Holy desecrated
Ghost, — the patient's spiritual power to resuscitate himself. The unchristian practitioner is not giving to mind 30
or body the joy and strength of Truth. The poor suffering heart needs its rightful nutriment, such as peace,

1 patience in tribulation, and a priceless sense of the dear
Father's loving-kindness.

3 In order to cure his patient, the metaphysician
must first cast moral evils out of himself and thus

Moral evils attain the spiritual freedom which will en-
6 to be cast out able him to cast physical evils out of his
patient; but heal he cannot, while his own spiritual
barrenness debars him from giving drink to the thirsty
9 and hinders him from reaching his patient's thought, —
yea, while mental penury chills his faith and understanding.

12 The physician who lacks sympathy for his fellow-
being is deficient in human affection, and we have the

The true apostolic warrant for asking: "He that loveth
15 physician not his brother whom he hath seen, how can
he love God whom he hath not seen?" Not having this
spiritual affection, the physician lacks faith in the divine
18 Mind and has not that recognition of infinite Love which
alone confers the healing power. Such so-called Scientists will strain out gnats, while they swallow the camels
21 of bigoted pedantry.

The physician must also watch, lest he be over-
whelmed by a sense of the odiousness of sin and by the
24 Source of unveiling of sin in his own thoughts. The
calmness sick are terrified by their sick beliefs, and
sinners should be affrighted by their sinful beliefs; but
27 the Christian Scientist will be calm in the presence of
both sin and disease, knowing, as he does, that Life is
God and God is All.

30 If we would open their prison doors for the sick, we
must first learn to bind up the broken-hearted. If we
would heal by the Spirit, we must not hide the talent

of spiritual healing under the napkin of its form, nor 1
bury the *morale* of Christian Science in the grave-clothes
of its letter.   The tender word and Christian   Genuine   3
encouragement of an invalid, pitiful patience   healing
with his fears and the removal of them, are better than
hecatombs of gushing theories, stereotyped borrowed 6
speeches, and the doling of arguments, which are but so
many parodies on legitimate Christian Science, aflame
with divine Love.   9

This is what is meant by seeking Truth, Christ, not
"for the loaves and fishes," nor, like the Pharisee, with
the arrogance of rank and display of scholar-   Gratitude   12
ship, but like Mary Magdalene, from the sum-   and humility
mit of devout consecration, with the oil of gladness and
the perfume of *gratitude*, with tears of repentance and 15
with those hairs all numbered by the Father.

A Christian Scientist occupies the place at this period
of which Jesus spoke to his disciples, when he said: "Ye 18
are the salt of the earth."   "Ye are the light   The salt of
of the world.   A city that is set on an hill can-   the earth
not be hid."   Let us watch, work, and pray that this salt 21
lose not its saltness, and that this light be not hid, but
radiate and glow into noontide glory.

The infinite Truth of the Christ-cure has come to this 24
age through a "still, small voice," through silent utterances and divine anointing which quicken and increase
the beneficial effects of Christianity.   I long to see the 27
consummation of my hope, namely, the student's higher
attainments in this line of light.

Because Truth is infinite, error should be known as 30
nothing.   Because Truth is omnipotent in goodness,
error, Truth's opposite, has no might.   Evil is but the

1 counterpoise of nothingness. The greatest wrong is but a supposititious opposite of the highest right. The

3 **Real and counterfeit** confidence inspired by Science lies in the fact that Truth is real and error is unreal. Error is a coward before Truth. Divine Science insists that

6 time will prove all this. Both truth and error have come nearer than ever before to the apprehension of mortals, and truth will become still clearer as error is self-

9 destroyed.

Against the fatal beliefs that error is as real as Truth, that evil is equal in power to good if not superior, and that

12 **Results of faith in Truth** discord is as normal as harmony, even the hope of freedom from the bondage of sickness and sin has little inspiration to nerve endeavor. When we

15 come to have more faith in the truth of being than we have in error, more faith in Spirit than in matter, more faith in living than in dying, more faith in God than in man,

18 then no material suppositions can prevent us from healing the sick and destroying error.

That Life is not contingent on bodily conditions is

21 proved, when we learn that life and man survive this **Life independent of matter** body. Neither evil, disease, nor death can be spiritual, and the material belief in them dis-

24 appears in the ratio of one's spiritual growth. Because matter has no consciousness or Ego, it cannot act; its conditions are illusions, and these false conditions are the

27 source of all seeming sickness. Admit the existence of matter, and you admit that mortality (and therefore disease) has a foundation in fact. Deny the existence of

30 matter, and you can destroy the belief in material conditions. When fear disappears, the foundation of disease is gone. Once let the mental physician believe in the

reality of matter, and he is liable to admit also the reality 1
of all discordant conditions, and this hinders his destroying them. Thus he is unfitted for the successful 3
treatment of disease.

In proportion as matter loses to human sense all entity as man, in that proportion does man become its 6
master. He enters into a diviner sense of the   Man's
facts, and comprehends the theology of Jesus   entity
as demonstrated in healing the sick, raising the dead, 9
and walking over the wave. All these deeds manifested
Jesus' control over the belief that matter is substance,
that it can be the arbiter of life or the constructor of any 12
form of existence.

We never read that Luke or Paul made a reality of
disease in order to discover some means of healing it. 15
Jesus never asked if disease were acute or   The Christ
chronic, and he never recommended atten-   treatment
tion to laws of health, never gave drugs, never prayed 18
to know if God were willing that a man should live. He
understood man, whose Life is God, to be immortal, and
knew that man has not two lives, one to be destroyed and 21
the other to be made indestructible.

The prophylactic and therapeutic (that is, the preventive and curative) arts belong emphatically to Christian 24
Science, as would be readily seen, if psychology,   Matter not
or the Science of Spirit, God, was understood.   medicine
Unscientific methods are finding their dead level. Lim- 27
ited to matter by their own law, what have they of the
advantages of Mind and immortality?

No man is physically healed in wilful error or by it, 30
any more than he is morally saved in or by sin. It is
error even to murmur or to be angry over sin. To be

1 every whit whole, man must be better spiritually as well
as physically. To be immortal, we must forsake the
3 No healing mortal sense of things, turn from the lie of false
in sin belief to Truth, and gather the facts of being
from the divine Mind. The body improves under the
6 same regimen which spiritualizes the thought; and if
health is not made manifest under this regimen, this
proves that fear is governing the body. This is the law
9 of cause and effect, or like producing like.

Homœopathy furnishes the evidence to the senses, that
symptoms, which might be produced by a certain drug,
12 Like curing are removed by using the same drug which
like might cause the symptoms. This confirms
my theory that faith in the drug is the sole factor in the
15 cure. The effect, which mortal mind produces through
one belief, it removes through an opposite belief, but it
uses the same medicine in both cases.

18 The moral and spiritual facts of health, whispered
into thought, produce very direct and marked effects on
the body. A physical diagnosis of disease — since mor-
21 tal mind must be the cause of disease — tends to induce
disease.

According to both medical testimony and individual
24 experience, a drug may eventually lose its supposed power
Transient and do no more for the patient. Hygienic
potency treatment also loses its efficacy. Quackery
of drugs
27 likewise fails at length to inspire the credulity
of the sick, and then they cease to improve. These lessons are useful. They should naturally and genuinely
30 change our basis from sensation to Christian Science,
from error to Truth, from matter to Spirit.

Physicians examine the pulse, tongue, lungs, to dis-

cover the condition of matter, when in fact all is 1
Mind. The body is the substratum of mortal mind,
and this so-called mind must finally yield   Diagnosis 3
to the mandate of immortal Mind.   of matter

Disquisitions on disease have a mental effect similar
to that produced on children by telling ghost-stories in 6
the dark. By those uninstructed in Christian   Ghost-stories
Science, nothing is really understood of material   inducing fear
existence. Mortals are believed to be here without their 9
consent and to be removed as involuntarily, not knowing
why nor when. As frightened children look everywhere
for the imaginary ghost, so sick humanity sees danger in 12
every direction, and looks for relief in all ways except the
right one. Darkness induces fear. The adult, in bondage to his beliefs, no more comprehends his real being 15
than does the child; and the adult must be taken out of
his darkness, before he can get rid of the illusive sufferings which throng the gloaming. The way in divine 18
Science is the only way out of this condition.

I would not transform the infant at once into a
man, nor would I keep the suckling a lifelong babe. 21
No impossible thing do I ask when urging   Mind imparts
the claims of Christian Science; but because   purity, health,
this teaching is in advance of the age, we   and beauty 24
should not deny our need of its spiritual unfoldment.
Mankind will improve through Science and Christianity. The necessity for uplifting the race is father to 27
the fact that Mind can do it; for Mind can impart
purity instead of impurity, strength instead of weakness, and health instead of disease. Truth is an altera- 30
tive in the entire system, and can make it "every whit
whole."

1 Remember, brain is not mind. Matter cannot be sick,
and Mind is immortal. The mortal body is only an erro-
3 Brain not   neous mortal belief of mind in matter. What
intelligent   you call matter was originally error in solution, elementary mortal mind, — likened by Milton to
6 "chaos and old night." One theory about this mortal
mind is, that its sensations can reproduce man, can form
blood, flesh, and bones. The Science of being, in which
9 all is divine Mind, or God and His idea, would be clearer
in this age, but for the belief that matter is the medium
of man, or that man can enter his own embodied thought,
12 bind himself with his own beliefs, and then call his bonds
material and name them divine law.

When man demonstrates Christian Science absolutely,
15 he will be perfect. He can neither sin, suffer, be subject
Veritable   to matter, nor disobey the law of God. There-
success   fore he will be as the angels in heaven. Chris-
18 tian Science and Christianity are one. How, then, in
Christianity any more than in Christian Science, can we
believe in the reality and power of both Truth and error,
21 Spirit and matter, and hope to succeed with contraries?
Matter is not self-sustaining. Its false supports fail one
after another. Matter succeeds for a period only by
24 falsely parading in the vestments of law.

"Whosoever shall deny me before men, him will I also
deny before my Father which is in heaven." In Chris-
27 Recognition   tian Science, a denial of Truth is fatal, while
of benefits   a just acknowledgment of Truth and of what
it has done for us is an effectual help. If pride, super-
30 stition, or any error prevents the honest recognition of
benefits received, this will be a hindrance to the recovery
of the sick and the success of the student.

If we are Christians on all moral questions, but are in darkness as to the physical exemption which Christianity includes, then we must have more faith in God on this subject and be more alive to His promises. It is easier to cure the most malignant disease than it is to cure sin. The author has raised up the dying, partly because they were willing to be restored, while she has struggled long, and perhaps in vain, to lift a student out of a chronic sin. Under all modes of pathological treatment, the sick recover more rapidly from disease than does the sinner from his sin. Healing is easier than teaching, if the teaching is faithfully done.

Disease far more docile than iniquity

The fear of disease and the love of sin are the sources of man's enslavement. "The fear of the Lord is the beginning of wisdom," but the Scriptures also declare, through the exalted thought of John, that "perfect Love casteth out fear."

Love frees from fear

The fear occasioned by ignorance can be cured; but to remove the effects of fear produced by sin, you must rise above both fear and sin. Disease is expressed not so much by the lips as in the functions of the body. Establish the scientific sense of health, and you relieve the oppressed organ. The inflammation, decomposition, or deposit will abate, and the disabled organ will resume its healthy functions.

When the blood rushes madly through the veins or languidly creeps along its frozen channels, we call these conditions disease. This is a misconception. Mortal mind is producing the propulsion or the languor, and we prove this to be so when by mental means the circulation is changed, and returns to that standard

Mind circulates blood

1 which mortal mind has decided upon as essential for
health. Anodynes, counter-irritants, and depletion never
3 reduce inflammation scientifically, but the truth of being,
whispered into the ear of mortal mind, will bring relief.

Hatred and its effects on the body are removed by
6 Love. Because mortal mind seems to be conscious, the
Mind can   sick say: "How can my mind cause a disease
destroy all ills   I never thought of and knew nothing about,
9 until it appeared on my body?" The author has answered this question in her explanation of disease as originating in human belief before it is consciously apparent
12 on the body, which is in fact the objective state of mortal
mind, though it is called matter. This mortal blindness
and its sharp consequences show our need of divine meta-
15 physics. Through immortal Mind, or Truth, we can
destroy all ills which proceed from mortal mind.

Ignorance of the cause or approach of disease is no
18 argument against the mental origin of disease. You confess to ignorance of the future and incapacity to preserve
your own existence, and this belief helps rather than
21 hinders disease. Such a state of mind induces sickness.
It is like walking in darkness on the edge of a precipice.
You cannot forget the belief of danger, and your steps
24 are less firm because of your fear, and ignorance of mental
cause and effect.

Heat and cold are products of mortal mind. The body,
27 when bereft of mortal mind, at first cools, and after-
Temperature   wards it is resolved into its primitive mortal
is mental   elements. Nothing that lives ever dies, and
30 vice versa. Mortal mind produces animal heat, and then
expels it through the abandonment of a belief, or increases it to the point of self-destruction. Hence it is

mortal mind, not matter, which says, "I die." Heat 1
would pass from the body as painlessly as gas dissipates
into the air when it evaporates but for the belief that in- 3
flammation and pain must accompany the separation of
heat from the body.

Chills and heat are often the form in which fever mani- 6
fests itself. Change the mental state, and the chills and
fever disappear. The old-school physician   Science
proves this when his patient says, "I am better,"   versus   9
but the patient believes that matter, not mind,   hypnotism
has helped him. The Christian Scientist demonstrates
that divine Mind heals, while the hypnotist dispossesses 12
the patient of his individuality in order to control him.
No person is benefited by yielding his mentality to any
mental despotism or malpractice. All unscientific mental 15
practice is erroneous and powerless, and should be understood and so rendered fruitless. The genuine Christian
Scientist is adding to his patient's mental and moral power, 18
and is increasing his patient's spirituality while restoring
him physically through divine Love.

Palsy is a belief that matter governs mortals, and can 21
paralyze the body, making certain portions of   Cure for
it motionless. Destroy the belief, show mortal   palsy
mind that muscles have no power to be lost, for Mind is 24
supreme, and you cure the palsy.

Consumptive patients always show great hopeful-
ness and courage, even when they are supposed to be in 27
hopeless danger. This state of mind seems   Latent fear
anomalous except to the expert in Christian   diagnosed
Science. This mental state is not understood, simply 30
because it is a stage of fear so excessive that it amounts
to fortitude. The belief in consumption presents to mor-

1 tal thought a hopeless state, an image more terrifying than
that of most other diseases. The patient turns involun-
3 tarily from the contemplation of it, but though unacknowledged, the latent fear and the despair of recovery remain
in thought.

6   Just so is it with the greatest sin. It is the most subtle,
and does its work almost self-deceived. The diseases
Insidious   deemed dangerous sometimes come from the
9 concepts   most hidden, undefined, and insidious beliefs.
The pallid invalid, whom you declare to be wasting away
with consumption of the blood, should be told that blood
12 never gave life and can never take it away, — that Life is
Spirit, and that there is more life and immortality in one
good motive and act, than in all the blood which ever
15 flowed through mortal veins and simulated a corporeal
sense of life.

If the body is material, it cannot, for that very reason,
18 suffer with a fever. Because the so-called material body
Remedy   is a mental concept and governed by mortal
for fever   mind, it manifests only what that so-called
21 mind expresses. Therefore the efficient remedy is to
destroy the patient's false belief by both silently and audibly arguing the true facts in regard to harmonious
24 being, — representing man as healthy instead of diseased,
and showing that it is impossible for matter to suffer, to
feel pain or heat, to be thirsty or sick. Destroy fear,
27 and you end fever. Some people, mistaught as to Mind-
science, inquire when it will be safe to check a fever.
Know that in Science you cannot check a fever after ad-
30 mitting that it must have its course. To fear and admit
the power of disease, is to paralyze mental and scientific
demonstration.

If your patient believes in taking cold, mentally convince him that matter cannot take cold, and that thought governs this liability. If grief causes suffering, convince the sufferer that affliction is often the source of joy, and that he should rejoice always in ever-present Love.

Invalids flee to tropical climates in order to save their lives, but they come back no better than when they went away. Then is the time to cure them through Christian Science, and prove that they can be healthy in all climates, when their fear of climate is exterminated.

Climate harmless

Through different states of mind, the body becomes suddenly weak or abnormally strong, showing mortal mind to be the producer of strength or weakness. A sudden joy or grief has caused what is termed instantaneous death. Because a belief originates unseen, the mental state should be continually watched that it may not produce blindly its bad effects. The author never knew a patient who did not recover when the belief of the disease had gone. Remove the leading error or governing fear of this lower so-called mind, and you remove the cause of all disease as well as the morbid or excited action of any organ. You also remove in this way what are termed organic diseases as readily as functional difficulties.

Mind governs body

The cause of all so-called disease is mental, a mortal fear, a mistaken belief or conviction of the necessity and power of ill-health; also a fear that Mind is helpless to defend the life of man and incompetent to control it. Without this ignorant human belief, any circumstance is of itself powerless to produce suffering. It is latent belief in disease, as well as the fear of disease, which associates sick-

1 ness with certain circumstances and causes the two to
appear conjoined, even as poetry and music are repro-
3 duced in union by human memory. Disease has no intelligence. Unwittingly you sentence yourself to suffer.
The understanding of this will enable you to commute this
6 self-sentence, and meet every circumstance with truth.
Disease is less than mind, and Mind can control it.

Without the so-called human mind, there can be no
9 inflammatory nor torpid action of the system. Remove

Latent power the error, and you destroy its effects. By
looking a tiger fearlessly in the eye, Sir Charles
12 Napier sent it cowering back into the jungle. An animal may infuriate another by looking it in the eye, and
both will fight for nothing. A man's gaze, fastened
15 fearlessly on a ferocious beast, often causes the beast to
retreat in terror. This latter occurrence represents the
power of Truth over error, — the might of intelligence
18 exercised over mortal beliefs to destroy them; whereas
hypnotism and hygienic drilling and drugging, adopted
to cure matter, is represented by two material erroneous
21 bases.

Disease is not an intelligence to dispute the empire of
Mind or to dethrone Mind and take the government into
24 Disease powerless its own hands. Sickness is not a God-given,
nor a self-constituted material power, which
copes astutely with Mind and finally conquers it. God
27 never endowed matter with power to disable Life or to
chill harmony with a long and cold night of discord.
Such a power, without the divine permission, is incon-
30 ceivable; and if such a power could be divinely directed,
it would manifest less wisdom than we usually find displayed in human governments.

If disease can attack and control the body without the consent of mortals, sin can do the same, for both are errors, announced as partners in the be- *Jurisdiction of Mind* ginning. The Christian Scientist finds only effects, where the ordinary physician looks for causes. The real jurisdiction of the world is in Mind, controlling every effect and recognizing all causation as vested in divine Mind.

A felon, on whom certain English students experimented, fancied himself bleeding to death, and died because of that belief, when only a stream of *Power of imagination* warm water was trickling over his arm. Had he known his sense of bleeding was an illusion, he would have risen above the false belief. Let the despairing invalid, inspecting the hue of her blood on a cambric handkerchief, think of the experiment of those Oxford boys, who caused the death of a man, when not a drop of his blood was shed. Then let her learn the opposite statement of Life as taught in Christian Science, and she will understand that she is not dying on account of the state of her blood, but is suffering from her belief that blood is destroying her life. The so-called vital current does not affect the invalid's health, but her belief produces the very results she dreads.

Fevers are errors of various types. The quickened pulse, coated tongue, febrile heat, dry skin, pain in the head and limbs, are pictures drawn on the *Fevers the effect of fear* body by a mortal mind. The images, held in this disturbed mind, frighten conscious thought. Unless the fever-picture, drawn by millions of mortals and imaged on the body through the belief that mind is in matter and discord is as real as harmony, is destroyed through

1 Science, it may rest at length on some receptive thought,
and become a fever case, which ends in a belief called
3 death, which belief must be finally conquered by eternal
Life. Truth is always the victor. Sickness and sin fall
by their own weight. Truth is the rock of ages, the head-
6 stone of the corner, "but on whomsoever it shall fall, it
will grind him to powder."

Contending for the evidence or indulging the demands
9 of sin, disease, or death, we virtually contend against
Misdirected the control of Mind over body, and deny the
contention power of Mind to heal. This false method
12 is as though the defendant should argue for the plaintiff
in favor of a decision which the defendant knows will
be turned against himself.

15 The physical effects of fear illustrate its illusion. Gaz-
ing at a chained lion, crouched for a spring, should not
Benefits of terrify a man. The body is affected only with
18 metaphysics the belief of disease produced by a so-called
mind ignorant of the truth which chains disease. Nothing but the power of Truth can prevent the fear of
21 error, and prove man's dominion over error.

Many years ago the author made a spiritual discovery, the scientific evidence of which has accumulated to
24 A higher prove that the divine Mind produces in man
discovery health, harmony, and immortality. Gradually this evidence will gather momentum and clearness,
27 until it reaches its culmination of scientific statement and
proof. Nothing is more disheartening than to believe
that there is a power opposite to God, or good, and that
30 God endows this opposing power with strength to be used
against Himself, against Life, health, harmony.

Every law of matter or the body, supposed to govern

man, is rendered null and void by the law of Life, God. 1
Ignorant of our God-given rights, we submit to unjust
decrees, and the bias of education enforces   Ignorance   3
this slavery. Be no more willing to suffer the   of our rights
illusion that you are sick or that some disease is develop-
ing in the system, than you are to yield to a sinful temp- 6
tation on the ground that sin has its necessities.

When infringing some supposed law, you say that
there is danger. This fear is the danger and induces the 9
physical effects. We cannot in reality suffer   No laws
from breaking anything except a moral or   of matter
spiritual law. The so-called laws of mortal belief are 12
destroyed by the understanding that Soul is immortal,
and that mortal mind cannot legislate the times, periods,
and types of disease, with which mortals die. God is the 15
lawmaker, but He is not the author of barbarous codes.
In infinite Life and Love there is no sickness, sin, nor
death, and the Scriptures declare that we live, move, and 18
have our being in the infinite God.

Think less of the enactments of mortal mind, and you
will sooner grasp man's God-given dominion. You must 21
understand your way out of human theories   God-given
relating to health, or you will never believe   dominion
that you are quite free from some ailment. The har- 24
mony and immortality of man will never be reached
without the understanding that Mind is not in matter.
Let us banish sickness as an outlaw, and abide by the 27
rule of perpetual harmony, — God's law. It is man's
moral right to annul an unjust sentence, a sentence never
inflicted by divine authority.   30

Christ Jesus overruled the error which would impose
penalties for transgressions of the physical laws of

1 health; he annulled supposed laws of matter, opposed
      Begin   to the harmonies of Spirit, lacking divine au-
3   rightly   thority and having only human approval for
their sanction.

If half the attention given to hygiene were given to the
6 study of Christian Science and to the spiritualization of
      Hygiene   thought, this alone would usher in the millen-
      excessive   nium. Constant bathing and rubbing to alter
9 the secretions or to remove unhealthy exhalations from
the cuticle receive a useful rebuke from Jesus' precept,
"Take no thought . . . for the body." We must beware
12 of making clean merely the outside of the platter.

He, who is ignorant of what is termed hygienic law, is
more receptive of spiritual power and of faith in one
15   Blissful   God, than is the devotee of supposed hygienic
      ignorance   law, who comes to teach the so-called igno-
rant one. Must we not then consider the so-called law
18 of matter a canon "more honored in the breach than
the observance"? A patient thoroughly booked in medical theories is more difficult to heal through Mind than
21 one who is not. This verifies the saying of our Master:
"Whosoever shall not receive the kingdom of God as a
little child, shall in no wise enter therein."

24   One whom I rescued from seeming spiritual oblivion,
in which the senses had engulfed him, wrote to me: "I
should have died, but for the glorious Principle you teach,
27 — supporting the power of Mind over the body and showing me the nothingness of the so-called pleasures and pains
of sense. The treatises I had read and the medicines I
30 had taken only abandoned me to more hopeless suffering
and despair. Adherence to hygiene was useless. Mortal
mind needed to be set right. The ailment was not bodily,

but mental, and I was cured when I learned my way in 1
Christian Science."

We need a clean body and a clean mind, — a body 3
rendered pure by Mind as well as washed by water.
One says: "I take good care of my body." A clean mind
To do this, the pure and exalting influence of   and body   6
the divine Mind on the body is requisite, and the Christian
Scientist takes the best care of his body when he leaves
it most out of his thought, and, like the Apostle Paul, is 9
"willing rather to be absent from the body, and to be present with the Lord."

A hint may be taken from the emigrant, whose filth 12
does not affect his happiness, because mind and body
rest on the same basis.   To the mind equally gross, dirt
gives no uneasiness.   It is the native element of such a 15
mind, which is symbolized, and not chafed, by its surroundings; but impurity and uncleanliness, which do
not trouble the gross, could not be borne by the refined. 18
This shows that the mind must be clean to keep the body
in proper condition.

The tobacco-user, eating or smoking poison for half a 21
century, sometimes tells you that the weed preserves
his health, but does this make it so? Does his   Beliefs
assertion prove the use of tobacco to be a salu-   illusive   24
brious habit, and man to be the better for it? Such instances only prove the illusive physical effect of a false
belief, confirming the Scriptural conclusion concerning a 27
man, "As he thinketh in his heart, so is he."

The movement-cure — pinching and pounding the poor
body, to make it sensibly well when it ought to be in- 30
sensibly so — is another medical mistake, resulting from
the common notion that health depends on inert matter

1 instead of on Mind. Can matter, or what is termed
matter, either feel or act without mind?

3   We should relieve our minds from the depressing thought
that we have transgressed a material law and must of

Corporeal   necessity pay the penalty. Let us reassure
6   penalties   ourselves with the law of Love. God never
punishes man for doing right, for honest labor, or for
deeds of kindness, though they expose him to fatigue,
9 cold, heat, contagion. If man seems to incur the penalty
through matter, this is but a belief of mortal mind, not
an enactment of wisdom, and man has only to enter his
12 protest against this belief in order to annul it. Through
this action of thought and its results upon the body, the
student will prove to himself, by small beginnings, the
15 grand verities of Christian Science.

If exposure to a draught of air while in a state of
perspiration is followed by chills, dry cough, influenza,
18 Not matter,   congestive symptoms in the lungs, or hints of
but Mind   inflammatory rheumatism, your Mind-remedy
is safe and sure. If you are a Christian Scientist, such
21 symptoms are not apt to follow exposure; but if you
believe in laws of matter and their fatal effects when
transgressed, you are not fit to conduct your own case or
24 to destroy the bad effects of your belief. When the fear
subsides and the conviction abides that you have broken
no law, neither rheumatism, consumption, nor any other
27 disease will ever result from exposure to the weather. In
Science this is an established fact which all the evidence
before the senses can never overrule.

30   Sickness, sin, and death must at length quail before
the divine rights of intelligence, and then the power
of Mind over the entire functions and organs of the

human system will be acknowledged. It is proverbial 1
that Florence Nightingale and other philanthropists en-
gaged in humane labors have been able to   Benefit of   3
undergo without sinking fatigues and expo- philanthropy
sures which ordinary people could not endure. The explanation lies in the support which they derived from 6
the divine law, rising above the human. The spiritual
demand, quelling the material, supplies energy and endurance surpassing all other aids, and forestalls the 9
penalty which our beliefs would attach to our best
deeds. Let us remember that the eternal law of right,
though it can never annul the law which makes sin its 12
own executioner, exempts man from all penalties but
those due for wrong-doing.

Constant toil, deprivations, exposures, and all untow- 15
ard conditions, *if without sin,* can be experienced without suffering. Whatever it is your duty to do,   Honest toil
you can do without harm to yourself. If you   has no   18
sprain the muscles or wound the flesh, your   penalty
remedy is at hand. Mind decides whether or not the
flesh shall be discolored, painful, swollen, and inflamed. 21

You say that you have not slept well or have overeaten.
You are a law unto yourself. Saying this and believing
it, you will suffer in proportion to your belief   Our sleep   24
and fear. Your sufferings are not the penalty   and food
for having broken a law of matter, for it is a law of mortal
mind which you have disobeyed. You say or think, be- 27
cause you have partaken of salt fish, that you must be
thirsty, and you are thirsty accordingly, while the opposite belief would produce the opposite result.   30

Any supposed information, coming from the body or
from inert matter as if either were intelligent, is an illu-

1 sion of mortal mind, — one of its dreams. Realize that
Doubtful   the evidence of the senses is not to be accepted
3 evidence   in the case of sickness, any more than it is in
the case of sin.

Expose the body to certain temperatures, and belief
6 says that you may catch cold and have catarrh; but no
Climate   such result occurs without mind to demand
and belief   it and produce it. So long as mortals declare
9 that certain states of the atmosphere produce catarrh,
fever, rheumatism, or consumption, those effects will
follow, — not because of the climate, but on account of
12 the belief. The author has in too many instances healed
disease through the action of Truth on the minds of mortals, and the corresponding effects of Truth on the body,
15 not to know that this is so.

A blundering despatch, mistakenly announcing the
death of a friend, occasions the same grief that the friend's
18 Erroneous   real death would bring. You think that your
despatch   anguish is occasioned by your loss. Another
despatch, correcting the mistake, heals your grief, and
21 you learn that your suffering was merely the result of
your belief. Thus it is with all sorrow, sickness, and
death. You will learn at length that there is no cause
24 for grief, and divine wisdom will then be understood.
Error, not Truth, produces all the suffering on earth.

If a Christian Scientist had said, while you were labor-
27 ing under the influence of the belief of grief, "Your sor-
Mourning   row is without cause," you would not have
causeless   understood him, although the correctness of
30 the assertion might afterwards be proved to you. So,
when our friends pass from our sight and we lament,
that lamentation is needless and causeless. We shall

perceive this to be true when we grow into the under- 1
standing of Life, and know that there is no death.

Because mortal mind is kept active, must it pay the 3
penalty in a softened brain? Who dares to say that actual
Mind can be overworked? When we reach   *Mind heals*
our limits of mental endurance, we conclude *brain-disease* 6
that intellectual labor has been carried sufficiently far;
but when we realize that immortal Mind is ever active,
and that spiritual energies can neither wear out nor can 9
so-called material law trespass upon God-given powers
and resources, we are able to rest in Truth, refreshed by
the assurances of immortality, opposed to mortality.   12

Our thinkers do not die early because they faithfully
perform the natural functions of being. If printers and
authors have the shortest span of earthly ex- *Right never* 15
istence, it is not because they occupy the most *punishable*
important posts and perform the most vital functions in
society. That man does not pay the severest penalty 18
who does the most good. By adhering to the realities of
eternal existence, — instead of reading disquisitions on
the inconsistent supposition that death comes in obedience 21
to the law of life, and that God punishes man for doing
good, — one cannot suffer as the result of any labor of
love, but grows stronger because of it. It is a law of so- 24
called mortal mind, misnamed matter, which causes all
things discordant.

The history of Christianity furnishes sublime proofs 27
of the supporting influence and protecting power bestowed
on man by his heavenly Father, omnipotent *Christian*
Mind, who gives man faith and understanding *history* 30
whereby to defend himself, not only from temptation, but
from bodily suffering.

1   The Christian martyrs were prophets of Christian
Science. Through the uplifting and consecrating power
3 of divine Truth, they obtained a victory over the corporeal senses, a victory which Science alone can explain.
Stolidity, which is a resisting state of mortal mind, suffers
6 less, only because it knows less of material law.

The Apostle John testified to the divine basis of Christian Science, when dire inflictions failed to destroy his
9 body. Idolaters, believing in more than one mind, had
"gods many," and thought that they could kill the body
with matter, independently of mind.

12   Admit the common hypothesis that food is the nutriment of life, and there follows the necessity for another
Sustenance admission in the opposite direction, — that
15   spiritual   food has power to destroy Life, God, through
a deficiency or an excess, a quality or a quantity. This
is a specimen of the ambiguous nature of all material
18 health-theories. They are self-contradictory and self-destructive, constituting a "kingdom divided against itself,"
which is "brought to desolation." If food was prepared
21 by Jesus for his disciples, it cannot destroy life.

The fact is, food does not affect the absolute Life of
man, and this becomes self-evident, when we learn that
24   God   God is our Life. Because sin and sickness are
sustains man not qualities of Soul, or Life, we have hope in
immortality; but it would be foolish to venture beyond
27 our present understanding, foolish to stop eating until
we gain perfection and a clear comprehension of the living
Spirit. In that perfect day of understanding, we shall
30 neither eat to live nor live to eat.

If mortals think that food disturbs the harmonious
functions of mind and body, either the food or this thought

must be dispensed with, for the penalty is coupled with 1
the belief. Which shall it be? If this decision be left
to Christian Science, it will be given in behalf   Diet and   3
of the control of Mind over this belief and every   digestion
erroneous belief, or material condition. The less we
know or think about hygiene, the less we are predisposed 6
to sickness. Recollect that it is not the nerves, not matter, but mortal mind, which reports food as undigested.
Matter does not inform you of bodily derangements; it 9
is supposed to do so. This pseudo-mental testimony can
be destroyed only by the better results of Mind's opposite evidence.   12

Our dietetic theories first admit that food sustains the
life of man, and then discuss the certainty that food can
kill man. This false reasoning is rebuked in   Scripture   15
Scripture by the metaphors about the fount   rebukes
and stream, the tree and its fruit, and the kingdom divided against itself. If God has, as prevalent theories 18
maintain, instituted laws that food shall support human
life, He cannot annul these regulations by an opposite
law that food shall be inimical to existence.   21

Materialists contradict their own statements. Their
belief in material laws and in penalties for their infraction is the ancient error that there is fraternity   Ancient   24
between pain and pleasure, good and evil, God   confusion
and Satan. This belief totters to its falling before the
battle-axe of Science.   27

A case of convulsions, produced by indigestion, came
under my observation. In her belief the woman had
chronic liver-complaint, and was then suffering from a 30
complication of symptoms connected with this belief. I
cured her in a few minutes. One instant she spoke de-

1 spairingly of herself. The next minute she said, "My
food is all digested, and I should like something more
3 to eat."

We cannot deny that Life is self-sustained, and we
should never deny the everlasting harmony of Soul, sim-
6   Ultimate   ply because, to the mortal senses, there is seem-
      harmony   ing discord. It is our ignorance of God, the
divine Principle, which produces apparent discord, and
9 the right understanding of Him restores harmony. Truth
will at length compel us all to exchange the pleasures and
pains of sense for the joys of Soul.

12   When the first symptoms of disease appear, dispute the
testimony of the material senses with divine Science. Let
      Unnecessary   your higher sense of justice destroy the false
15   prostration   process of mortal opinions which you name
law, and then you will not be confined to a sick-room nor
laid upon a bed of suffering in payment of the last far-
18 thing, the last penalty demanded by error. "Agree with
thine adversary quickly, whiles thou art in the way with
him." Suffer no claim of sin or of sickness to grow upon
21 the thought. Dismiss it with an abiding conviction that
it is illegitimate, because you know that God is no more
the author of sickness than He is of sin. You have no
24 law of His to support the necessity either of sin or sickness, but you have divine authority for denying that necessity and healing the sick.

27   "Agree to disagree" with approaching symptoms of
chronic or acute disease, whether it is cancer, consump-
      Treatment   tion, or smallpox. Meet the incipient stages
30   of disease   of disease with as powerful mental opposition as a legislator would employ to defeat the passage of
an inhuman law. Rise in the conscious strength of the

spirit of Truth to overthrow the plea of mortal mind, 1
alias matter, arrayed against the supremacy of Spirit.
Blot out the images of mortal thought and its beliefs in 3
sickness and sin. Then, when thou art delivered to the
judgment of Truth, Christ, the judge will say, "Thou
art whole!" 6

Instead of blind and calm submission to the incipient
or advanced stages of disease, rise in rebellion against
them. Banish the belief that you can possi-   Righteous 9
bly entertain a single intruding pain which can-   rebellion
not be ruled out by the might of Mind, and in this way
you can prevent the development of pain in the body. 12
No law of God hinders this result. It is error to suffer
for aught but your own sins. Christ, or Truth, will destroy all other supposed suffering, and real suffering for 15
your own sins will cease in proportion as the sin ceases.

Justice is the moral signification of law. Injustice declares the absence of law. When the body is supposed 18
to say, "I am sick," never plead guilty. Since   Contradict
matter cannot talk, it must be mortal mind   error
which speaks; therefore meet the intimation with a pro- 21
test. If you say, "I am sick," you plead guilty. Then
your adversary will deliver you to the judge (mortal
mind), and the judge will sentence you. Disease has 24
no intelligence to declare itself something and announce
its name. Mortal mind alone sentences itself. Therefore
make your own terms with sickness, and be just to yourself 27
and to others.

Mentally contradict every complaint from the body,
and rise to the true consciousness of Life as   Sin to be 30
Love, — as all that is pure, and bearing the   overcome
fruits of Spirit. Fear is the fountain of sickness,

1 and you master fear and sin through divine Mind; hence
it is through divine Mind that you overcome disease.
3 Only while fear or sin remains can it bring forth death.
To cure a bodily ailment, every broken moral law should
be taken into account and the error be rebuked. Fear,
6 which is an element of all disease, must be cast out to
readjust the balance for God. Casting out evil and fear
enables truth to outweigh error. The only course is to
9 take antagonistic grounds against all that is opposed to
the health, holiness, and harmony of man, God's image.
The physical affirmation of disease should always be
12 met with the mental negation. Whatever benefit is pro-
   Illusions   duced on the body, must be expressed men-
  about nerves tally, and thought should be held fast to this
15 ideal. If you believe in inflamed and weak nerves, you
are liable to an attack from that source. You will call it
neuralgia, but we call it a belief. If you think that con-
18 sumption is hereditary in your family, you are liable to
the development of that thought in the form of what is
termed pulmonary disease, unless Science shows you
21 otherwise. If you decide that climate or atmosphere is
unhealthy, it will be so to you. Your decisions will master you, whichever direction they take.
24   Reverse the case. Stand porter at the door of thought.
Admitting only such conclusions as you wish realized in
   Guarding   bodily results, you will control yourself har-
27   the door   moniously. When the condition is present
which you say induces disease, whether it be air, exercise,
heredity, contagion, or accident, then perform your office
30 as porter and shut out these unhealthy thoughts and fears.
Exclude from mortal mind the offending errors; then the
body cannot suffer from them. The issues of pain or

pleasure must come through mind, and like a watchman 1
forsaking his post, we admit the intruding belief, forgetting that through divine help we can forbid this entrance. 3
    The body seems to be self-acting, only because mortal
mind is ignorant of itself, of its own actions, and of their
results, — ignorant that the predisposing, re- The strength   6
mote, and exciting cause of all bad effects is a   of Spirit
law of so-called mortal mind, not of matter. Mind is the
master of the corporeal senses, and can conquer sickness, 9
sin, and death. Exercise this God-given authority. Take
possession of your body, and govern its feeling and action.
Rise in the strength of Spirit to resist all that is unlike 12
good. God has made man capable of this, and nothing
can vitiate the ability and power divinely bestowed on
man.   15
    Be firm in your understanding that the divine Mind
governs, and that in Science man reflects God's government. Have no fear that matter can ache,   No pain   18
swell, and be inflamed as the result of a law   in matter
of any kind, when it is self-evident that matter can have
no pain nor inflammation. Your body would suffer no 21
more from tension or wounds than the trunk of a tree
which you gash or the electric wire which you stretch,
were it not for mortal mind.   24
    When Jesus declares that "the light of the body is the
eye," he certainly means that light depends upon Mind,
not upon the complex humors, lenses, muscles, the iris 27
and pupil, constituting the visual organism.
    Man is never sick, for Mind is not sick and matter
cannot be. A false belief is both the tempter   No real   30
and the tempted, the sin and the sinner, the   disease
disease and its cause. It is well to be calm in sickness;

1 to be hopeful is still better; but to understand that sickness is not real and that Truth can destroy its seeming
3 reality, is best of all, for this understanding is the universal and perfect remedy.

By conceding power to discord, a large majority of
6 doctors depress mental energy, which is the only real
Recuperation recuperative power. Knowledge that we
mental can accomplish the good we hope for, stimu-
9 lates the system to act in the direction which Mind points
out. The admission that any bodily condition is beyond
the control of Mind disarms man, prevents him from
12 helping himself, and enthrones matter through error. To
those struggling with sickness, such admissions are discouraging, — as much so as would be the advice to a man
15 who is down in the world, that he should not try to rise
above his difficulties.

Experience has proved to the author the fallacy of
18 material systems in general, — that their theories are
sometimes pernicious, and that their denials are better
than their affirmations. Will you bid a man let evils
21 overcome him, assuring him that all misfortunes are from
God, against whom mortals should not contend? Will
you tell the sick that their condition is hopeless, unless it
24 can be aided by a drug or climate? Are material means
the only refuge from fatal chances? Is there no divine
permission to conquer discord of every kind with harmony,
27 with Truth and Love?

We should remember that Life is God, and that God
Arguing is omnipotent. Not understanding Christian
30 wrongly Science, the sick usually have little faith in
it till they feel its beneficent influence. This shows
that faith is not the healer in such cases. The sick

unconsciously argue for suffering, instead of against it. 1
They admit its reality, whereas they should deny it.
They should plead in opposition to the testimony of the 3
deceitful senses, and maintain man's immortality and
eternal likeness to God.

Like the great Exemplar, the healer should speak to 6
disease as one having authority over it, leaving Soul to
master the false evidences of the corporeal Divine
senses and to assert its claims over mortal- authority 9
ity and disease. The same Principle cures both sin and
sickness. When divine Science overcomes faith in a carnal mind, and faith in God destroys all faith in sin and in 12
material methods of healing, then sin, disease, and death
will disappear.

Prayers, in which God is not asked to heal but is be- 15
sought to take the patient to Himself, do not benefit the
sick. An ill-tempered, complaining, or deceit- Aids in
ful person should not be a nurse. The nurse sickness 18
should be cheerful, orderly, punctual, patient, full of
faith, — receptive to Truth and Love.

It is mental quackery to make disease a reality — to 21
hold it as something seen and felt — and then to attempt
its cure through Mind. It is no less erroneous Mental
to believe in the real existence of a tumor, a quackery 24
cancer, or decayed lungs, while you argue against their
reality, than it is for your patient to feel these ills in
physical belief. Mental practice, which holds disease 27
as a reality, fastens disease on the patient, and it may
appear in a more alarming form.

The knowledge that brain-lobes cannot kill a man nor 30
affect the functions of mind would prevent the brain from
becoming diseased, though a moral offence is indeed the

1 worst of diseases. One should never hold in mind
the thought of disease, but should efface from

Effacing images of disease

3 thought all forms and types of disease, both for
one's own sake and for that of the patient.

Avoid talking illness to the patient. Make no unne-
6 cessary inquiries relative to feelings or disease. Never

Avoid talking disease

startle with a discouraging remark about recovery, nor draw attention to certain symp-
9 toms as unfavorable, avoid speaking aloud the name of
the disease. Never say beforehand how much you have
to contend with in a case, nor encourage in the patient's
12 thought the expectation of growing worse before a crisis
is passed.

The refutation of the testimony of material sense is
15 not a difficult task in view of the conceded falsity of this

False testimony refuted

testimony. The refutation becomes arduous,
not because the testimony of sin or disease is
18 true, but solely on account of the tenacity of belief in its
truth, due to the force of education and the overwhelming weight of opinions on the wrong side, — all teaching
21 that the body suffers, as if matter could have sensation.

At the right time explain to the sick the power which
their beliefs exercise over their bodies. Give them divine

24 **Healthful explanation**

and wholesome understanding, with which to
combat their erroneous sense, and so efface the
images of sickness from mortal mind. Keep distinctly in
27 thought that man is the offspring of God, not of man;
that man is spiritual, not material; that Soul is Spirit,
outside of matter, never in it, never giving the body life
30 and sensation. It breaks the dream of disease to understand that sickness is formed by the human mind, not by
matter nor by the divine Mind.

By not perceiving vital metaphysical points, not seeing 1
how mortal mind affects the body, — acting beneficially
or injuriously on the health, as well as on the   Misleading   3
morals and the happiness of mortals, — we are   methods
misled in our conclusions and methods. We throw the
mental influence on the wrong side, thereby actually in- 6
juring those whom we mean to bless.

Suffering is no less a mental condition than is enjoyment. You cause bodily sufferings and increase them 9
by admitting their reality and continuance,   Remedy for
as directly as you enhance your joys by be-   accidents
lieving them to be real and continuous. When an ac- 12
cident happens, you think or exclaim, "I am hurt!"
Your thought is more powerful than your words, more
powerful than the accident itself, to make the injury 15
real.

Now reverse the process. Declare that you are not hurt
and understand the reason why, and you will find the 18
ensuing good effects to be in exact proportion to your
disbelief in physics, and your fidelity to divine metaphysics, confidence in God as All, which the Scriptures 21
declare Him to be.

To heal the sick, one must be familiar with the great
verities of being. Mortals are no more material in their 24
waking hours than when they act, walk, see,   Independent
hear, enjoy, or suffer in dreams. We can   mentality
never treat mortal mind and matter separately, because 27
they combine as one. Give up the belief that mind
is, even temporarily, compressed within the skull, and
you will quickly become more manly or womanly. You 30
will understand yourself and your Maker better than
before.

1   Sometimes Jesus called a disease by name, as when he
said to the epileptic boy, "Thou dumb and deaf spirit, I
3   Naming   charge thee, come out of him, and enter no
maladies   more into him." It is added that "the spirit
[error] cried, and rent him sore and came out of him, and
6 he was as one dead," — clear evidence that the malady
was not material. These instances show the concessions
which Jesus was willing to make to the popular ignorance
9 of spiritual Life-laws. Often he gave no name to the
distemper he cured. To the synagogue ruler's daughter,
whom they called dead but of whom he said, "she is not
12 dead, but sleepeth," he simply said, "Damsel, I say unto
thee, arise!" To the sufferer with the withered hand
he said, "Stretch forth thine hand," and it "was restored
15 whole, like as the other."

Homœopathic remedies, sometimes not containing a
particle of medicine, are known to relieve the symptoms
18   The action   of disease. What produces the change? It is
of faith   the faith of the doctor and the patient, which
reduces self-inflicted sufferings and produces a new effect
21 upon the body. In like manner destroy the illusion of
pleasure in intoxication, and the desire for strong drink
is gone. Appetite and disease reside in mortal mind, not
24 in matter.

So also faith, cooperating with a belief in the healing
effects of time and medication, will soothe fear and change
27 the belief of disease to a belief of health. Even a blind
faith removes bodily ailments for a season, but hypnotism
changes such ills into new and more difficult forms of dis-
30 ease. The Science of Mind must come to the rescue,
to work a radical cure. Then we understand the process.
The great fact remains that evil is not mind. Evil has

no power, no intelligence, for God is good, and therefore 1
good is infinite, is All.

   You say that certain material combinations produce 3
disease; but if the material body causes disease, can
matter cure what matter has caused? Mortal   Corporeal
mind prescribes the drug, and administers it. combinations   6
Mortal mind plans the exercise, and puts the body through
certain motions. No gastric gas accumulates, not a secretion nor combination can operate, apart from the 9
action of mortal thought, *alias* mortal mind.

   So-called mortal mind sends its despatches over its
body, but this so-called mind is both the service and 12
message of this telegraphy. Nerves are un-   Automatic
able to talk, and matter can return no an-   mechanism
swer to immortal Mind. If Mind is the only actor, how 15
can mechanism be automatic? Mortal mind perpetuates
its own thought. It constructs a machine, manages it,
and then calls it material. A mill at work or the action 18
of a water-wheel is but a derivative from, and continua-
tion of, the primitive mortal mind. Without this force
the body is devoid of action, and this deadness shows 21
that so-called mortal life is mortal mind, not matter.

   Scientifically speaking, there is no mortal mind out of
which to make material beliefs, springing from illusion. 24
This misnamed mind is not an entity. It is   Mental
only a false sense of matter, since matter is not   strength
sensible. The one Mind, God, contains no mortal opin- 27
ions. All that is real is included in this immortal Mind.

   Our Master asked: "How can one enter into a strong
man's house and spoil his goods, except he first Confirmation   30
bind the strong man?" In other words: How   in a parable
can I heal the body, without beginning with so-called

1 mortal mind, which directly controls the body? When
disease is once destroyed in this so-called mind, the fear
3 of disease is gone, and therefore the disease is thoroughly cured. Mortal mind is "the strong man," which
must be held in subjection before its influence upon health
6 and morals can be removed. This error conquered, we
can despoil "the strong man" of his goods, — namely, of
sin and disease.

9   Mortals obtain the harmony of health, only as they
forsake discord, acknowledge the supremacy of divine

            Mind, and abandon their material beliefs.

Eradicate error from thought
12   Eradicate the image of disease from the perturbed thought before it has taken tangible
shape in conscious thought, *alias* the body, and you pre-
15 vent the development of disease. This task becomes easy,
if you understand that every disease is an error, and has
no character nor type, except what mortal mind assigns to
18 it. By lifting thought above error, or disease, and contending persistently for truth, you destroy error.

   When we remove disease by addressing the disturbed
21 mind, giving no heed to the body, we prove that thought

Mortal mind controlled
alone creates the suffering. Mortal mind
rules all that is mortal. We see in the body
24 the images of this mind, even as in optics we see painted
on the retina the image which becomes visible to the
senses. The action of so-called mortal mind must be
27 destroyed by the divine Mind to bring out the harmony
of being. Without divine control there is discord, manifest as sin, sickness, and death.

30   The Scriptures plainly declare the baneful influence of
sinful thought on the body. Even our Master felt this.
It is recorded that in certain localities he did not many

mighty works "because of their unbelief" in Truth. Any 1
human error is its own enemy, and works against itself;
it does nothing in the right direction and much Mortal mind   3
in the wrong. If so-called mind is cherishing not a healer
evil passions and malicious purposes, it is not a healer,
but it engenders disease and death.   6

If faith in the truth of being, which you impart mentally while destroying error, causes chemicalization (as
when an alkali is destroying an acid), it is be-   Effect of   9
cause the truth of being must transform the   opposites
error to the end of producing a higher manifestation.
This fermentation should not aggravate the disease, but 12
should be as painless to man as to a fluid, since matter
has no sensation and mortal mind only feels and sees
materially.   15

What I term *chemicalization* is the upheaval produced
when immortal Truth is destroying erroneous mortal belief. Mental chemicalization brings sin and sickness to 18
the surface, forcing impurities to pass away, as is the case
with a fermenting fluid.

The only effect produced by medicine is dependent upon 21
mental action. If the mind were parted from the body,
could you produce any effect upon the brain   Medicine
or body by applying the drug to either? Would   and brain   24
the drug remove paralysis, affect organization, or restore
will and action to cerebrum and cerebellum?

Until the advancing age admits the efficacy and suprem- 27
acy of Mind, it is better for Christian Scientists to leave
surgery and the adjustment of broken bones   Skilful
and dislocations to the fingers of a surgeon,   surgery   30
while the mental healer confines himself chiefly to mental
reconstruction and to the prevention of inflammation.

1 Christian Science is always the most skilful surgeon, but surgery is the branch of its healing which will be last 3 acknowledged. However, it is but just to say that the author has already in her possession well-authenticated records of the cure, by herself and her students through 6 mental surgery alone, of broken bones, dislocated joints, and spinal vertebræ.

The time approaches when mortal mind will forsake 9 its corporeal, structural, and material basis, when im-

Indestructible mortal Mind and its formations will be appre-
life of man hended in Science, and material beliefs will 12 not interfere with spiritual facts. Man is indestructible and eternal. Sometime it will be learned that mortal mind constructs the mortal body with this mind's own 15 mortal materials. In Science, no breakage nor dislocation can really occur. You say that accidents, injuries, and disease kill man, but this is not true. The life of man is 18 Mind. The material body manifests only what mortal mind believes, whether it be a broken bone, disease, or sin.

We say that one human mind can influence another and 21 in this way affect the body, but we rarely remember that

The evil of we govern our own bodies. The error, mes-
mesmerism merism — or hypnotism, to use the recent term 24 — illustrates the fact just stated. The operator would make his subjects believe that they cannot act voluntarily and handle themselves as they should do. If they yield 27 to this influence, it is because their belief is not better instructed by spiritual understanding. Hence the proof that hypnotism is not scientific; Science cannot produce 30 both disorder and order. The involuntary pleasure or pain of the person under hypnotic control is proved to be a belief without a real cause.

So the sick through their beliefs have induced their own 1
diseased conditions. The great difference between voluntary and involuntary mesmerism is that vol- Wrong-doer 3
untary mesmerism is induced consciously and should suffer
should and does cause the perpetrator to suffer, while self-
mesmerism is induced unconsciously and by his mistake 6
a man is often instructed. In the first instance it is understood that the difficulty is a mental illusion, while in the
second it is believed that the misfortune is a material effect. 9
The human mind is employed to remove the illusion in
one case, but matter is appealed to in the other. In reality, both have their origin in the human mind, and can be 12
healed only by the divine Mind.

You command the situation if you understand that
mortal existence is a state of self-deception and not the 15
truth of being. Mortal mind is constantly Error's power
producing on mortal body the results of false imaginary
opinions; and it will continue to do so, until mortal 18
error is deprived of its imaginary powers by Truth,
which sweeps away the gossamer web of mortal illusion.
The most Christian state is one of rectitude and spir- 21
itual understanding, and this is best adapted for healing the sick. Never conjure up some new discovery from
dark forebodings regarding disease and then acquaint 24
your patient with it.

The mortal so-called mind produces all that is unlike
the immortal Mind. The human mind determines the 27
nature of a case, and the practitioner improves Disease-
or injures the case in proportion to the truth production
or error which influences his conclusions. The mental 30
conception and development of disease are not understood by the patient, but the physician should be familiar

1 with mental action and its effect in order to judge the case
according to Christian Science.

3   If a man is an inebriate, a slave to tobacco, or the special
servant of any one of the myriad forms of sin, meet and
Appetites to destroy these errors with the truth of being, —
6 *be abandoned* by exhibiting to the wrong-doer the suffering
which his submission to such habits brings, and by convincing him that there is no real pleasure in false appe-
9 tites. A corrupt mind is manifested in a corrupt body.
Lust, malice, and all sorts of evil are diseased beliefs, and
you can destroy them only by destroying the wicked
12 motives which produce them. If the evil is over in the
repentant mortal mind, while its effects still remain on the
individual, you can remove this disorder as God's law is
15 fulfilled and reformation cancels the crime. The healthy
sinner is the hardened sinner.

The temperance reform, felt all over our land, results
18 from metaphysical healing, which cuts down every tree
Temperance that brings not forth good fruit. This con-
reform viction, that there is no real pleasure in sin,
21 is one of the most important points in the theology of
Christian Science. Arouse the sinner to this new and
true view of sin, show him that sin confers no pleasure,
24 and this knowledge strengthens his moral courage and
increases his ability to master evil and to love good.

Healing the sick and reforming the sinner are one and
27 the same thing in Christian Science. Both cures require
the same method and are inseparable in Truth.
Sin or fear
the root of Hatred, envy, dishonesty, fear, and so forth,
sickness
30 make a man sick, and neither material medicine nor Mind can help him permanently, even in body,
unless it makes him better mentally, and so delivers him

from his destroyers. The basic error is mortal mind. 1
Hatred inflames the brutal propensities. The indulgence
of evil motives and aims makes any man, who is above the 3
lowest type of manhood, a hopeless sufferer.

Christian Science commands man to master the propensities, — to hold hatred in abeyance with kindness, 6
to conquer lust with chastity, revenge with   Mental
charity, and to overcome deceit with hon-   conspirators
esty. Choke these errors in their early stages, if you 9
would not cherish an army of conspirators against
health, happiness, and success. They will deliver you
to the judge, the arbiter of truth against error. The 12
judge will deliver you to justice, and the sentence of
the moral law will be executed upon mortal mind and
body. Both will be manacled until the last farthing 15
is paid, — until you have balanced your account with
God. "Whatsoever a man soweth, that shall he also
reap." The good man finally can overcome his fear of 18
sin. This is sin's necessity, — to destroy itself. Immortal man demonstrates the government of God, good,
in which is no power to sin.   21

It were better to be exposed to every plague on earth
than to endure the cumulative effects of a guilty conscience. The abiding consciousness of wrong- Cumulative 24
doing tends to destroy the ability to do right. repentance
If sin is not regretted and is not lessening, then it is
hastening on to physical and moral doom. You are con- 27
quered by the moral penalties you incur and the ills they
bring. The pains of sinful sense are less harmful than its
pleasures. Belief in material suffering causes mortals to 30
retreat from their error, to flee from body to Spirit, and
to appeal to divine sources outside of themselves.

1   The Bible contains the recipe for all healing. "The
leaves of the tree were for the healing of the nations."
3   The leaves   Sin and sickness are both healed by the same
of healing   Principle. The tree is typical of man's divine
Principle, which is equal to every emergency, offering
6 full salvation from sin, sickness, and death. Sin will
submit to Christian Science when, in place of modes and
forms, the power of God is understood and demonstrated
9 in the healing of mortals, both mind and body. "Perfect Love casteth out fear."

The Science of being unveils the errors of sense, and
12 spiritual perception, aided by Science, reaches Truth.
Sickness   Then error disappears. Sin and sickness will
will abate   abate and seem less real as we approach the
15 scientific period, in which mortal sense is subdued and
all that is unlike the true likeness disappears. The moral
man has no fear that he will commit a murder, and he
18 should be as fearless on the question of disease.

Resist evil — error of every sort — and it will flee from
you. Error is opposed to Life. We can, and ultimately
21   Resist to   shall, so rise as to avail ourselves in every direc-
the end   tion of the supremacy of Truth over error, Life
over death, and good over evil, and this growth will go
24 on until we arrive at the fulness of God's idea, and no
more fear that we shall be sick and die. Inharmony of
any kind involves weakness and suffering, — a loss of
27 control over the body.

The depraved appetite for alcoholic drinks, tobacco,
tea, coffee, opium, is destroyed only by Mind's mastery
30   Morbid   of the body. This normal control is gained
cravings   through divine strength and understanding.
There is no enjoyment in getting drunk, in becoming a

fool or an object of loathing; but there is a very sharp 1
remembrance of it, a suffering inconceivably terrible to
man's self-respect. Puffing the obnoxious fumes of to- 3
bacco, or chewing a leaf naturally attractive to no creature except a loathsome worm, is at least disgusting.

Man's enslavement to the most relentless masters — 6
passion, selfishness, envy, hatred, and revenge — is conquered only by a mighty struggle. Every   Universal
hour of delay makes the struggle more severe.   panacea   9
If man is not victorious over the passions, they crush
out happiness, health, and manhood. Here Christian
Science is the sovereign panacea, giving strength to the 12
weakness of mortal mind, — strength from the immortal
and omnipotent Mind, — and lifting humanity above
itself into purer desires, even into spiritual power and 15
good-will to man.

Let the slave of wrong desire learn the lessons of Christian Science, and he will get the better of that desire, 18
and ascend a degree in the scale of health, happiness,
and existence.

If delusion says, "I have lost my memory," contra- 21
dict it. No faculty of Mind is lost. In Science, all
being is eternal, spiritual, perfect, harmoni-   Immortal
ous in every action. Let the perfect model be   memory   24
present in your thoughts instead of its demoralized opposite. This spiritualization of thought lets in the light,
and brings the divine Mind, Life not death, into your 27
consciousness.

There are many species of insanity. All sin is insanity in different degrees. Sin is spared from   Sin a form   30
this classification, only because its method of   of insanity
madness is in consonance with common mortal belief.

1 Every sort of sickness is error, — that is, sickness is
loss of harmony. This view is not altered by the fact
3 that sin is worse than sickness, and sickness is not acknowledged nor discovered to be error by many who are
sick.

6   There is a universal insanity of so-called health, which
mistakes fable for fact throughout the entire round of the
material senses, but this general craze cannot, in a scien-
9 tific diagnosis, shield the individual case from the special
name of insanity. Those unfortunate people who are
committed to insane asylums are only so many distinctly
12 defined instances of the baneful effects of illusion on mortal minds and bodies.

The supposition that we can correct insanity by the use
15 of purgatives and narcotics is in itself a mild species of
Drugs and   insanity. Can drugs go of their own accord
brain-lobes to the brain and destroy the so-called inflam-
18 mation of disordered functions, thus reaching mortal
mind through matter? Drugs do not affect a corpse, and
Truth does not distribute drugs through the blood, and
21 from them derive a supposed effect on intelligence and sentiment. A dislocation of the tarsal joint would produce
insanity as perceptibly as would congestion of the brain,
24 were it not that mortal mind thinks that the tarsal joint is
less intimately connected with the mind than is the brain.
Reverse the belief, and the results would be perceptibly
27 different.

The unconscious thought in the corporeal substratum of brain produces no effect, and that condition of
30 Matter and   the body which we call sensation in matter
animate error is unreal. Mortal mind is ignorant of itself, — ignorant of the errors it includes and of their

effects. Intelligent matter is an impossibility. You 1
may say: "But if disease obtains in matter, why do
you insist that disease is formed by mortal mind and 3
not by matter?" *Mortal mind* and body combine as
one, and the nearer matter approaches its final statement, — animate error called nerves, brain, mind, — the 6
more prolific it is likely to become in sin and disease-
beliefs.

Unconscious mortal mind — *alias* matter, brain — can- 9
not dictate terms to consciousness nor say, "I am sick."
The belief, that the unconscious substratum   Dictation
of mortal mind, termed the body, suffers and   of error   12
reports disease independently of this so-called conscious
mind, is the error which prevents mortals from knowing
how to govern their bodies.   15

The so-called conscious mortal mind is believed to be
superior to its unconscious substratum, matter, and
the stronger never yields to the weaker, ex-   So-called   18
cept through fear or choice. The animate   superiority
should be governed by God alone. The real man is
spiritual and immortal, but the mortal and imperfect 21
so-called "children of men" are counterfeits from the
beginning, to be laid aside for the pure reality. This
mortal is put off, and the new man or real man is put 24
on, in proportion as mortals realize the Science of man
and seek the true model.

We have no right to say that life depends on matter 27
now, but will not depend on it after death. We cannot
spend our days here in ignorance of the Science   Death no
of Life, and expect to find beyond the grave   benefactor   30
a reward for this ignorance. Death will not make us
harmonious and immortal as a recompense for ignorance.

1 If here we give no heed to Christian Science, which is
spiritual and eternal, we shall not be ready for spiritual
3 Life hereafter.

"This is life eternal," says Jesus, — is, not *shall be;*
and then he defines everlasting life as a present knowledge
6   Life eternal   of his Father and of himself, — the knowledge
and present   of Love, Truth, and Life. "This is life eternal, that they might know Thee, the only true God, and
9 Jesus Christ, whom Thou hast sent." The Scriptures
say, "Man shall not live by bread *alone,* but by every
word that proceedeth out of the mouth of God," show-
12 ing that Truth is the actual life of man; but mankind
objects to making this teaching practical.

Every trial of our faith in God makes us stronger.
15 The more difficult seems the material condition to be
Love casteth   overcome by Spirit, the stronger should be our
out fear   faith and the purer our love. The Apostle
18 John says: "There is no fear in Love, but perfect Love
casteth out fear. . . . He that feareth is not made perfect in Love." Here is a definite and inspired proclama-
21 tion of Christian Science.

MENTAL TREATMENT ILLUSTRATED

The Science of mental practice is susceptible of no
24 misuse. Selfishness does not appear in the practice of
Be not   Truth or Christian Science. If mental prac-
afraid   tice is abused or is used in any way except to
27 promote right thinking and doing, the power to heal
mentally will diminish, until the practitioner's healing
ability is wholly lost. Christian scientific practice be-
30 gins with Christ's keynote of harmony, "Be not afraid!"

Said Job: "The thing which I greatly feared is come 1
upon me."

My first discovery in the student's practice was this: 3
If the student silently called the disease by name, when
he argued against it, as a general rule the body   Naming
would respond more quickly, — just as a per-   diseases   6
son replies more readily when his name is spoken; but
this was because the student was not perfectly attuned to
divine Science, and needed the arguments of truth for 9
reminders.   If Spirit or the power of divine Love bear
witness to the truth, this is the ultimatum, the scientific
way, and the healing is instantaneous.   12

It is recorded that once Jesus asked the name of a disease, — a disease which moderns would call *dementia.*
The demon, or evil, replied that his name was   Evils cast   15
Legion.   Thereupon Jesus cast out the evil,   out
and the insane man was changed and straightway became whole.   The Scripture seems to import that Jesus 18
caused the evil to be self-seen and so destroyed.

The procuring cause and foundation of all sickness is
fear, ignorance, or sin.   Disease is always induced by a 21
false sense mentally entertained, not destroyed.   Fear as the
Disease is an image of thought externalized.   foundation
The mental state is called a material state.   Whatever 24
is cherished in mortal mind as the physical condition is
imaged forth on the body.

Always begin your treatment by allaying the fear 27
of patients.   Silently reassure them as to their exemption from disease and danger.   Watch the re-   Unspoken
sult of this simple rule of Christian Science,   pleading   30
and you will find that it alleviates the symptoms of every
disease.   If you succeed in wholly removing the fear,

1 your patient is healed. The great fact that God lovingly
governs all, never punishing aught but sin, is your stand-
3 point, from which to advance and destroy the human fear
of sickness. Mentally and silently plead the case scientifically for Truth. You may vary the arguments to meet
6 the peculiar or general symptoms of the case you treat,
but be thoroughly persuaded in your own mind concerning the truth which you think or speak, and you will be
9 the victor.

You may call the disease by name when you mentally
deny it; but by naming it audibly, you are liable under
12   Eloquent   some circumstances to impress it upon the
silence   thought. The power of Christian Science and
divine Love is omnipotent. It is indeed adequate to un-
15 clasp the hold and to destroy disease, sin, and death.

To prevent disease or to cure it, the power of Truth,
of divine Spirit, must break the dream of the material
18   Insistence   senses. To heal by argument, find the type
requisite   of the ailment, get its name, and array your
mental plea against the physical. Argue at first men-
21 tally, not audibly, that the patient has no disease, and
conform the argument so as to destroy the evidence of
disease. Mentally insist that harmony is the fact, and
24 that sickness is a temporal dream. Realize the presence
of health and the fact of harmonious being, until the
body corresponds with the normal conditions of health
27 and harmony.

If the case is that of a young child or an infant, it needs
to be met mainly through the parent's thought, silently
30   The cure   or audibly on the aforesaid basis of Christian
of infants   Science. The Scientist knows that there can
be no hereditary disease, since matter is not intelligent

and cannot transmit good or evil intelligence to man, and 1
God, the only Mind, does not produce pain in matter.
The act of yielding one's thoughts to the undue contem- 3
plation of physical wants or conditions induces those very
conditions. A single requirement, beyond what is necessary to meet the simplest needs of the babe is harmful. 6
Mind regulates the condition of the stomach, bowels, and
food, the temperature of children and of men, and matter
does not. The wise or unwise views of parents and other 9
persons on these subjects produce good or bad effects on
the health of children.

The daily ablutions of an infant are no more natural 12
nor necessary than would be the process of taking a fish
out of water every day and covering it with dirt Ablutions for
in order to make it thrive more vigorously in its cleanliness 15
own element. "Cleanliness is next to godliness," but
washing should be only for the purpose of keeping the
body clean, and this can be effected without scrubbing the 18
whole surface daily. Water is not the natural habitat of
humanity. I insist on bodily cleanliness within and without. I am not patient with a speck of dirt; but in caring 21
for an infant one need not wash his little body all over each
day in order to keep it sweet as the new-blown flower.

Giving drugs to infants, noticing every symptom of 24
flatulency, and constantly directing the mind to such
signs, — that mind being laden with illusions Juvenile
about disease, health-laws, and death, — these ailments 27
actions convey mental images to children's budding
thoughts, and often stamp them there, making it probable
at any time that such ills may be reproduced in the very 30
ailments feared. A child may have worms, if you say so,
or any other malady, timorously held in the beliefs con-

1 cerning his body. Thus are laid the foundations of the
belief in disease and death, and thus are children educated
3 into discord.

The treatment of insanity is especially interesting.
However obstinate the case, it yields more readily than
6   Cure of   do most diseases to the salutary action of
insanity   truth, which counteracts error. The arguments to be used in curing insanity are the same as in
9 other diseases: namely, the impossibility that matter,
brain, can control or derange mind, can suffer or cause
suffering; also the fact that truth and love will establish
12 a healthy state, guide and govern mortal mind or the
thought of the patient, and destroy all error, whether it is
called dementia, hatred, or any other discord.

15 To fix truth steadfastly in your patients' thoughts, explain Christian Science to them, but not too soon, — not
until your patients are prepared for the explanation, —
18 lest you array the sick against their own interests by troub-
ling and perplexing their thought. The Christian Scientist's argument rests on the Christianly scientific basis of
21 being. The Scripture declares, "The Lord He is God
[good]; there is none else beside Him." Even so, harmony
is universal, and discord is unreal. Christian Science de-
24 clares that Mind is substance, also that matter neither
feels, suffers, nor enjoys. Hold these points strongly in
view. Keep in mind the verity of being, — that man is
27 the image and likeness of God, in whom all being is
painless and permanent. Remember that man's perfection is real and unimpeachable, whereas imperfection is
30 blameworthy, unreal, and is not brought about by divine
Love.

Matter cannot be inflamed. Inflammation is fear, an

excited state of mortals which is not normal. Immor- 1
tal Mind is the only cause; therefore disease is neither a
cause nor an effect. Mind in every case is the   Matter is   3
eternal God, good. Sin, disease, and death   not inflamed
have no foundations in Truth. Inflammation as a mortal belief quickens or impedes the action of the system, 6
because thought moves quickly or slowly, leaps or halts
when it contemplates unpleasant things, or when the individual looks upon some object which he dreads. In- 9
flammation never appears in a part which mortal thought
does not reach. That is why opiates relieve inflammation.
They quiet the thought by inducing stupefaction and by 12
resorting to matter instead of to Mind. Opiates do not
remove the pain in any scientific sense. They only render mortal mind temporarily less fearful, till it can master 15
an erroneous belief.

Note how thought makes the face pallid. It either re-
tards the circulation or quickens it, causing a pale or 18
flushed cheek. In the same way thought in-   Truth calms
creases or diminishes the secretions, the action   the thought
of the lungs, of the bowels, and of the heart. The mus- 21
cles, moving quickly or slowly and impelled or palsied by
thought, represent the action of all the organs of the human system, including brain and viscera. To remove 24
the error producing disorder, you must calm and instruct
mortal mind with immortal Truth.

Etherization will apparently cause the body to dis- 27
appear. Before the thoughts are fully at rest, the limbs
will vanish from consciousness. Indeed, the   Effects of
whole frame will sink from sight along with   etherization   30
surrounding objects, leaving the pain standing forth as
distinctly as a mountain-peak, as if it were a separate

1 bodily member. At last the agony also vanishes. This
process shows the pain to be in the mind, for the inflam-
3 mation is not suppressed; and the belief of pain will
presently return, unless the mental image occasioning
the pain be removed by recognizing the truth of being.

6   A hypodermic injection of morphine is administered
to a patient, and in twenty minutes the sufferer is qui-
Sedatives etly asleep. To him there is no longer any
9 valueless pain. Yet any physician — allopathic, homœopathic, botanic, eclectic — will tell you that the trouble-
some material cause is unremoved, and that when the
12 soporific influence of the opium is exhausted, the patient will find himself in the same pain, unless the belief
which occasions the pain has meanwhile been changed.
15 Where is the pain while the patient sleeps?

The material body, which you call *me,* is mortal mind,
and this mind is material in sensation, even as the body,
18 The so-called which has originated from this material sense
physical ego and been developed according to it, is material. This materialism of parent and child is only in
21 mortal mind, as the dead body proves; for when the
mortal has resigned his body to dust, the body is no
longer the parent, even in appearance.

24   The sick know nothing of the mental process by
which they are depleted, and next to nothing of the
Evil thought metaphysical method by which they can be
27 depletes healed. If they ask about their disease, tell
them only what is best for them to know. Assure them
that they think too much about their ailments, and
30 have already heard too much on that subject. Turn
their thoughts away from their bodies to higher objects. Teach them that their being is sustained by

Spirit, not by matter, and that they find health, peace, 1
and harmony in God, divine Love.

Give sick people credit for sometimes knowing more 3
than their doctors. Always support their trust in the
power of Mind to sustain the body. Never Helpful en-
tell the sick that they have more courage couragement 6
than strength. Tell them rather, that their strength
is in proportion to their courage. If you make the sick
realize this great truism, there will be no reaction from 9
over-exertion or from excited conditions. Maintain
the facts of Christian Science, — that Spirit is God, and
therefore cannot be sick; that what is termed matter 12
cannot be sick; that all causation is Mind, acting
through spiritual law. Then hold your ground with
the unshaken understanding of Truth and Love, and 15
you will win. When you silence the witness against your
plea, you destroy the evidence, for the disease disappears. The evidence before the corporeal senses is not 18
the Science of immortal man.

To the Christian Science healer, sickness is a dream
from which the patient needs to be awakened. Dis- 21
ease should not appear real to the physician, since it is demonstrable that the way to Disease to be made unreal
cure the patient is to make disease unreal to him. To 24
do this, the physician must understand the unreality
of disease in Science.

Explain audibly to your patients, as soon as they can 27
bear it, the complete control which Mind holds over the
body. Show them how mortal mind seems to induce
disease by certain fears and false conclusions, and how 30
divine Mind can cure by opposite thoughts. Give your
patients an underlying understanding to support them

1 and to shield them from the baneful effects of their own conclusions. Show them that the conquest over sickness, 3 as well as over sin, depends on mentally destroying all belief in material pleasure or pain.

Stick to the truth of being in contradistinction to the 6 error that life, substance, or intelligence can be in matter.

Christian pleading Plead with an honest conviction of truth and a clear perception of the unchanging, unerr- 9 ing, and certain effect of divine Science. Then, if your fidelity is half equal to the truth of your plea, you will heal the sick.

12 It must be clear to you that sickness is no more the reality of being than is sin. This mortal dream

Truthful arguments of sickness, sin, and death should cease 15 through Christian Science. Then one dis- ease would be as readily destroyed as another. What- ever the belief is, if arguments are used to destroy it, 18 the belief must be repudiated, and the negation must ex- tend to the supposed disease and to whatever decides its type and symptoms. Truth is affirmative, and confers 21 harmony. All metaphysical logic is inspired by this sim- ple rule of Truth, which governs all reality. By the truthful arguments you employ, and especially by the 24 spirit of Truth and Love which you entertain, you will heal the sick.

Include moral as well as physical belief in your efforts 27 to destroy error. Cast out all manner of evil. "Preach

Morality required the gospel to every creature." Speak the truth to every form of error. Tumors, ulcers, 30 tubercles, inflammation, pain, deformed joints, are wak- ing dream-shadows, dark images of mortal thought, which flee before the light of Truth.

A moral question may hinder the recovery of the sick. 1
Lurking error, lust, envy, revenge, malice, or hate will
perpetuate or even create the belief in disease. Errors 3
of all sorts tend in this direction. Your true course is
to destroy the foe, and leave the field to God, Life, Truth,
and Love, remembering that God and His ideas alone 6
are real and harmonious.

If your patient from any cause suffers a relapse, meet
the cause mentally and courageously, knowing that 9
there can be no reaction in Truth. Neither   Relapse
disease itself, sin, nor fear has the power to   unnecessary
cause disease or a relapse. Disease has no intelligence 12
with which to move itself about or to change itself from
one form to another. If disease moves, mind, not matter, moves it; therefore be sure that you move it off. 15
Meet every adverse circumstance as its master. Observe mind instead of body, lest aught unfit for development enter thought. Think less of material conditions 18
and more of spiritual.

Mind produces all action. If the action proceeds from
Truth, from immortal Mind, there is harmony; but mor- 21
tal mind is liable to any phase of belief. A   Conquer
relapse cannot in reality occur in mortals or   beliefs
so-called mortal minds, for there is but one   and fears 24
Mind, one God. Never fear the mental malpractitioner,
the mental assassin, who, in attempting to rule mankind,
tramples upon the divine Principle of metaphysics, for God 27
is the only power. To succeed in healing, you must conquer your own fears as well as those of your patients, and
rise into higher and holier consciousness.   30

If it is found necessary to treat against relapse, know
that disease or its symptoms cannot change forms, nor

1 go from one part to another, for Truth destroys disease.
There is no metastasis, no stoppage of harmonious
3 True government action, no paralysis. Truth not error, Love
of man not hate, Spirit not matter, governs man. If
students do not readily heal themselves, they should
6 early call an experienced Christian Scientist to aid
them. If they are unwilling to do this for themselves,
they need only to know that error cannot produce this
9 unnatural reluctance.

Instruct the sick that they are not helpless victims,
for if they will only accept Truth, they can resist disease
12 Positive and ward it off, as positively as they can the
reassurance temptation to sin. This fact of Christian Science should be explained to invalids when they are in a
15 fit mood to receive it, — when they will not array themselves against it, but are ready to become receptive to the
new idea. The fact that Truth overcomes both disease
18 and sin reassures depressed hope. It imparts a healthy
stimulus to the body, and regulates the system. It increases or diminishes the action, as the case may require,
21 better than any drug, alterative, or tonic.

Mind is the natural stimulus of the body, but erroneous belief, taken at its best, is not promotive of health
24 Proper or happiness. Tell the sick that they can
stimulus meet disease fearlessly, if they only realize
that divine Love gives them all power over every physical
27 action and condition.

If it becomes necessary to startle mortal mind to break
its dream of suffering, vehemently tell your patient that
30 Awaken the he must awake. Turn his gaze from the false
patient evidence of the senses to the harmonious facts
of Soul and immortal being. Tell him that he suffers

only as the insane suffer, from false beliefs. The only 1
difference is, that insanity implies belief in a diseased
brain, while physical ailments (so-called) arise from the 3
belief that other portions of the body are deranged. De-
rangement, or *disarrangement*, is a word which conveys
the true definition of all human belief in ill-health, or dis- 6
turbed harmony. Should you thus startle mortal mind
in order to remove its beliefs, afterwards make known
to the patient your motive for this shock, showing him 9
that it was to facilitate recovery.

If a crisis occurs in your treatment, you must treat
the patient less for the disease and more for the mental 12
disturbance or fermentation, and subdue the   How to
symptoms by removing the belief that this   treat a crisis
chemicalization produces pain or disease.   Insist vehe- 15
mently on the great fact which covers the whole ground,
that God, Spirit, is all, and that there is none beside
Him. There is *no disease*. When the supposed suffer- 18
ing is gone from mortal mind, there can be no pain; and
when the fear is destroyed, the inflammation will sub-
side. Calm the excitement sometimes induced by chemi- 21
calization, which is the alterative effect produced by
Truth upon error, and sometimes explain the symptoms
and their cause to the patient.   24

It is no more Christianly scientific to see disease than
it is to experience it. If you would destroy the sense
of disease, you should not build it up by   No   27
wishing to see the forms it assumes or by   perversion of
employing a single material application for   Mind-science
its relief. The perversion of Mind-science is like as- 30
serting that the products of eight multiplied by five, and
of seven by ten, are both forty, and that their combined

1 sum is fifty, and then calling the process mathematics.
Wiser than his persecutors, Jesus said: "If I by Beelze-
3 bub cast out devils, by whom do your children cast them
out?"

If the reader of this book observes a great stir through-
6 out his whole system, and certain moral and physical
Effect of   symptoms seem aggravated, these indications
this book   are favorable. Continue to read, and the book
9 will become the physician, allaying the tremor which
Truth often brings to error when destroying it.

Patients, unfamiliar with the cause of this commotion
12 and ignorant that it is a favorable omen, may be alarmed.
Disease   If such be the case, explain to them the law
neutralized   of this action. As when an acid and alkali
15 meet and bring out a third quality, so mental and moral
chemistry changes the material base of thought, giving
more spirituality to consciousness and causing it to depend
18 less on material evidence. These changes which go on
in mortal mind serve to reconstruct the body. Thus
Christian Science, by the alchemy of Spirit, destroys sin
21 and death.

Let us suppose two parallel cases of bone-disease, both
similarly produced and attended by the same symptoms.
24 Bone-healing A surgeon is employed in one case, and a
by surgery   Christian Scientist in the other. The surgeon, holding that matter forms its own conditions and
27 renders them fatal at certain points, entertains fears and
doubts as to the ultimate outcome of the injury. Not
holding the reins of government in his own hands, he
30 believes that something stronger than Mind — namely,
matter — governs the case. His treatment is therefore
tentative. This mental state invites defeat. The belief

that he has met his master in matter and may not be 1
able to mend the bone, increases his fear; yet this belief
should not be communicated to the patient, either ver- 3
bally or otherwise, for this fear greatly diminishes the
tendency towards a favorable result. Remember that the
unexpressed belief oftentimes affects a sensitive patient 6
more strongly than the expressed thought.

The Christian Scientist, understanding scientifically
that all is Mind, commences with mental causation, the 9
truth of being, to destroy the error. This cor- *Scientific*
rective is an alterative, reaching to every part *corrective*
of the human system. According to Scripture, it searches 12
"the joints and marrow," and it restores the harmony of
man.

The matter-physician deals with matter as both his foe 15
and his remedy. He regards the ailment as weakened or
strengthened according to the evidence which *Coping with*
matter presents. The metaphysician, making *difficulties* 18
Mind his basis of operation irrespective of matter and
regarding the truth and harmony of being as superior to
error and discord, has rendered himself strong, instead 21
of weak, to cope with the case; and he proportionately
strengthens his patient with the stimulus of courage and
conscious power. Both Science and consciousness are 24
now at work in the economy of being according to the law
of Mind, which ultimately asserts its absolute supremacy.

Ossification or any abnormal condition or derange- 27
ment of the body is as directly the action of mortal
mind as is dementia or insanity. Bones have *Formation*
only the substance of thought which forms *from thought* 30
them. They are only phenomena of the mind of mortals. The so-called substance of bone is formed first

1 by the parent's mind, through self-division. Soon the
child becomes a separate, individualized mortal mind,
3 which takes possession of itself and its own thoughts of
bones.

Accidents are unknown to God, or immortal Mind,
6   and we must leave the mortal basis of belief
Accidents
unknown   and unite with the one Mind, in order to
to God
      change the notion of chance to the proper sense
9 of God's unerring direction and thus bring out harmony.

Under divine Providence there can be no accidents,
since there is no room for imperfection in perfection.

12   In medical practice objections would be raised if one
doctor should administer a drug to counteract the work-
      Opposing   ing of a remedy prescribed by another doctor.
15 mentality   It is equally important in metaphysical practice that the *minds* which surround your patient should
not act against your influence by continually expressing
18 such opinions as may alarm or discourage, — either by
giving antagonistic advice or through unspoken thoughts
resting on your patient. While it is certain that the
21 divine Mind can remove any obstacle, still you need the
ear of your auditor. It is not more difficult to make yourself heard mentally while others are thinking about your
24 patients or conversing with them, if you understand
Christian Science — the oneness and the allness of divine
Love; but it is well to be alone with God and the sick
27 when treating disease.

To prevent or to cure scrofula and other so-called hereditary diseases, you must destroy the belief in these ills
30 Mind removes and the faith in the possibility of their trans-
      scrofula   mission. The patient may tell you that he
has a humor in the blood, a scrofulous diathesis. His

parents or some of his progenitors farther back have so 1
believed. Mortal mind, not matter, induces this conclusion and its results. You will have humors, just so 3
long as you believe them to be safety-valves or to be
ineradicable.

If the case to be mentally treated is consumption, take 6
up the leading points included (according to belief) in
this disease. Show that it is not inherited; Nothing to
that inflammation, tubercles, hemorrhage, and consume 9
decomposition are beliefs, images of mortal thought superimposed upon the body; that they are not the truth
of man; that they should be treated as error and put out 12
of thought. Then these ills will disappear.

If the body is diseased, this is but one of the beliefs of
mortal mind. Mortal man will be less mortal, when he 15
learns that matter never sustained existence The lungs
and can never destroy God, who is man's Life. re-formed
When this is understood, mankind will be more spiritual 18
and know that there is nothing to consume, since Spirit,
God, is All-in-all. What if the belief is consumption?
God is more to a man than his belief, and the less we ac- 21
knowledge matter or its laws, the more immortality we
possess. Consciousness constructs a better body when
faith in matter has been conquered. Correct material 24
belief by spiritual understanding, and Spirit will form
you anew. You will never fear again except to offend
God, and you will never believe that heart or any por- 27
tion of the body can destroy you.

If you have sound and capacious lungs and want
them to remain so, be always ready with the Soundness 30
mental protest against the opposite belief in maintained
heredity. Discard all notions about lungs, tubercles, in-

1 herited consumption, or disease arising from any circumstance, and you will find that mortal mind, when
3 instructed by Truth, yields to divine power, which steers
the body into health.

The discoverer of Christian Science finds the path less
6 difficult when she has the high goal always before her
Our footsteps thoughts, than when she counts her footsteps
heavenward in endeavoring to reach it. When the desti-
9 nation is desirable, expectation speeds our progress. The
struggle for Truth makes one strong instead of weak,
resting instead of wearying one. If the belief in death
12 were obliterated, and the understanding obtained that
there is no death, this would be a "tree of life," known
by its fruits. Man should renew his energies and en-
15 deavors, and see the folly of hypocrisy, while also learning the necessity of working out his own salvation. When
it is learned that disease cannot destroy life, and that
18 mortals are not saved from sin or sickness by death, this
understanding will quicken into newness of life. It will
master either a desire to die or a dread of the grave,
21 and thus destroy the great fear that besets mortal
existence.

The relinquishment of all faith in death and also of
24 the fear of its sting would raise the standard of health
Christian and morals far beyond its present elevation,
standard and would enable us to hold the banner of
27 Christianity aloft with unflinching faith in God, in Life
eternal. Sin brought death, and death will disappear
with the disappearance of sin. Man is immortal, and
30 the body cannot die, because matter has no life to sur-
render. The human concepts named matter, death, disease, sickness, and sin are all that can be destroyed.

If it is true that man lives, this fact can never change 1
in Science to the opposite belief that man dies. Life is
the law of Soul, even the law of the spirit of   3
Truth, and Soul is never without its represent-   Life not
                                                    contingent
ative. Man's individual being can no more   on matter
die nor disappear in unconsciousness than can Soul, for 6
both are immortal. If man believes in death now, he
must disbelieve in it when learning that there is no reality
in death, since the truth of being is deathless. The be- 9
lief that existence is contingent on matter must be met
and mastered by Science, before Life can be understood
and harmony obtained.   12
Death is but another phase of the dream that existence can be material. Nothing can interfere with the
harmony of being nor end the existence of   Mortality   15
man in Science. Man is the same after as   vanquished
before a bone is broken or the body guillotined. If man
is never to overcome death, why do the Scriptures say, 18
"The last enemy that shall be destroyed is death"? The
tenor of the Word shows that we shall obtain the victory
over death in proportion as we overcome sin. The great 21
difficulty lies in ignorance of what God is. God, Life,
Truth, and Love make man undying. Immortal Mind,
governing all, must be acknowledged as supreme in the 24
physical realm, so-called, as well as in the spiritual.
Called to the bed of death, what material remedy has
man when all such remedies have failed? Spirit is his 27
last resort, but it should have been his first No death
and only resort. The dream of death must   nor inaction
be mastered by Mind here or hereafter. Thought 30
will waken from its own material declaration, "I am
dead," to catch this trumpet-word of Truth, "There

1 is no death, no inaction, diseased action, overaction, nor
reaction."

3 Life is real, and death is the illusion. A demonstration of the facts of Soul in Jesus' way resolves the dark

Vision visions of material sense into harmony and
6 opening immortality. Man's privilege at this supreme
moment is to prove the words of our Master: "If a man
keep my saying, he shall never see death." To divest
9 thought of false trusts and material evidences in order
that the spiritual facts of being may appear, — this is
the great attainment by means of which we shall sweep
12 away the false and give place to the true. Thus we may
establish in truth the temple, or body, "whose builder
and maker is God."

15 We should consecrate existence, not "to the unknown
God" whom we "ignorantly worship," but to the eternal

Intelligent builder, the everlasting Father, to the Life
18 consecration which mortal sense cannot impair nor mortal
belief destroy. We must realize the ability of mental
might to offset human misconceptions and to replace them
21 with the life which is spiritual, not material.

The great spiritual fact must be brought out that man
is, not *shall be,* perfect and immortal. We must hold
24 The present forever the consciousness of existence, and
immortality sooner or later, through Christ and Christian
Science, we must master sin and death. The evidence
27 of man's immortality will become more apparent, as material beliefs are given up and the immortal facts of being
are admitted.

30 The author has healed hopeless organic disease, and
raised the dying to life and health through the understanding of God as the only Life. It is a sin to believe

that aught can overpower omnipotent and eternal Life, 1
and this Life must be brought to light by the understanding that there is no death, as well as by other   Careful   3
graces of Spirit. We must begin, however,   guidance
with the more simple demonstrations of control, and
the sooner we begin the better. The final demonstration 6
takes time for its accomplishment. When walking, we
are guided by the eye. We look before our feet, and if
we are wise, we look beyond a single step in the line of 9
spiritual advancement.

The corpse, deserted by thought, is cold and decays,
but it never suffers. Science declares that man is sub- 12
ject to Mind. Mortal mind affirms that mind   Clay
is subordinate to the body, that the body is   replying to
                                                    the potter
dying, that it must be buried and decomposed   15
into dust; but mortal mind's affirmation is not true.
Mortals waken from the dream of death with bodies unseen by those who think that they bury the body.   18

If man did not exist before the material organization
began, he could not exist after the body is disintegrated.
If we live after death and are immortal, we   Continuity   21
must have lived before birth, for if Life ever   of existence
had any beginning, it must also have an ending, even according to the calculations of natural science. Do you 24
believe this? No! Do you understand it? No! This
is why you doubt the statement and do not demonstrate
the facts it involves. We must have faith in all the say- 27
ings of our Master, though they are not included in the
teachings of the schools, and are not understood generally by our ethical instructors.   30

Jesus said (John viii. 51), "If a man keep my saying,
he shall never see death." That statement is not con-

1 fined to spiritual life, but includes all the phenomena of
existence. Jesus demonstrated this, healing the dying
3   Life   and raising the dead. Mortal mind must part
  all-inclusive with error, must put off itself with its deeds,
and immortal manhood, the Christ ideal, will appear.
6 Faith should enlarge its borders and strengthen its base
by resting upon Spirit instead of matter. When man
gives up his belief in death, he will advance more rapidly
9 towards God, Life, and Love. Belief in sickness and
death, as certainly as belief in sin, tends to shut out the
true sense of Life and health. When will mankind wake
12 to this great fact in Science?

I here present to my readers an allegory illustrative
of the law of divine Mind and of the supposed laws of mat-
15 ter and hygiene, an allegory in which the plea of Christian
Science heals the sick.

— Suppose a mental case to be on trial, as cases are tried
18 in court. A man is charged with having committed liver-
    A mental   complaint. The patient feels ill, ruminates,
    court case and the trial commences. Personal Sense is
21 the plaintiff. Mortal Man is the defendant. False Belief
is the attorney for Personal Sense. Mortal Minds, Materia Medica, Anatomy, Physiology, Hypnotism, Envy,
24 Greed and Ingratitude, constitute the jury. The court-
room is filled with interested spectators, and Judge
Medicine is on the bench.

27   The evidence for the prosecution being called for, a
witness testifies thus: —

I represent Health-laws. I was present on certain nights
30 when the prisoner, or patient, watched with a sick friend.
Although I have the superintendence of human affairs, I
was personally abused on those occasions. I was told that

I must remain silent until called for at this trial, when I would be allowed to testify in the case. Notwithstanding my rules to the contrary, the prisoner watched with the sick every night in the week. When the sick mortal was thirsty, the prisoner gave him drink. During all this time the prisoner attended to his daily labors, partaking of food at irregular intervals, sometimes going to sleep immediately after a heavy meal. At last he committed liver-complaint, which I considered criminal, inasmuch as this offence is deemed punishable with death. Therefore I arrested Mortal Man in behalf of the state (namely, the body) and cast him into prison.

At the time of the arrest the prisoner summoned Physiology, Materia Medica, and Hypnotism to prevent his punishment. The struggle on their part was long. Materia Medica held out the longest, but at length all these assistants resigned to me, Health-laws, and I succeeded in getting Mortal Man into close confinement until I should release him.

The next witness is called: —

I am Coated Tongue. I am covered with a foul fur, placed on me the night of the liver-attack. Morbid Secretion hypnotized the prisoner and took control of his mind, making him despondent.

Another witness takes the stand and testifies: —

I am Sallow Skin. I have been dry, hot, and chilled by turns since the night of the liver-attack. I have lost my healthy hue and become unsightly, although nothing on my part has occasioned this change. I practise daily ablutions and perform my functions as usual, but I am robbed of my good looks.

1   The next witness testifies: —

I am Nerve, the State Commissioner for Mortal Man.
3 I am intimately acquainted with the plaintiff, Personal
Sense, and know him to be truthful and upright, whereas
Mortal Man, the prisoner at the bar, is capable of false-
6 hood. I was witness to the crime of liver-complaint. I
knew the prisoner would commit it, for I convey messages
from my residence in matter, *alias* brain, to body.

9   Another witness is called for by the Court of Error
and says: —

I am Mortality, Governor of the Province of Body, in
12 which Mortal Man resides. In this province there is a statute regarding disease, — namely, that he upon whose person disease is found shall be treated as a criminal and
15 punished with death.

The Judge asks if by doing good to his neighbor, it is
possible for man to become diseased, transgress the laws,
18 and merit punishment, and Governor Mortality replies in
the affirmative.
Another witness takes the stand and testifies: —

21   I am Death. I was called for, shortly after the report of
the crime, by the officer of the Board of Health, who protested that the prisoner had abused him, and that my pres-
24 ence was required to confirm his testimony. One of the
prisoner's friends, Materia Medica, was present when I
arrived, endeavoring to assist the prisoner to escape from
27 the hands of justice, *alias* nature's so-called law; but my
appearance with a message from the Board of Health
changed the purpose of Materia Medica, and he decided at
30 once that the prisoner should die.

The testimony for the plaintiff, Personal Sense, being 1
closed, Judge Medicine arises, and with great solemnity
addresses the jury of Mortal Minds. He an- Judge Medi- 3
alyzes the offence, reviews the testimony, and cine charges
explains the law relating to liver-complaint. the jury
His conclusion is, that laws of nature render disease 6
homicidal. In compliance with a stern duty, his Honor,
Judge Medicine, urges the jury not to allow their judgment to be warped by the irrational, unchristian sugges- 9
tions of Christian Science. The jury must regard in such
cases only the evidence of Personal Sense against Mortal
Man.   12

As the Judge proceeds, the prisoner grows restless. His
sallow face blanches with fear, and a look of despair and
death settles upon it. The case is given to the jury. A 15
brief consultation ensues, and the jury returns a verdict
of "Guilty of liver-complaint in the first degree."

Judge Medicine then proceeds to pronounce the solemn 18
sentence of death upon the prisoner. Because he has
loved his neighbor as himself, Mortal Man has Mortal Man
been guilty of benevolence in the first degree, sentenced 21
and this has led him into the commission of the second
crime, liver-complaint, which material laws condemn as
homicide. For this crime Mortal Man is sentenced to 24
be tortured until he is dead. "May God have mercy on
your soul," is the Judge's solemn peroration.

The prisoner is then remanded to his cell (sick-bed), 27
and Scholastic Theology is sent for to prepare the frightened sense of Life, God, — which sense must be immortal,
— for *death*.   30

Ah! but Christ, Truth, the spirit of Life and the
friend of Mortal Man, can open wide those prison doors

1 and set the captive free. Swift on the wings of divine
Love, there comes a despatch: "Delay the execution;
3 **Appeal to a higher tribunal** the prisoner is not guilty." Consternation fills
the prison-yard. Some exclaim, "It is con-
trary to law and justice." Others say,
6 "The law of Christ supersedes *our* laws; let us follow
Christ."

After much debate and opposition, permission is ob-
9 tained for a trial in the Court of Spirit, where Christian
Counsel for defence Science is allowed to appear as counsel for
the unfortunate prisoner. Witnesses, judges,
12 and jurors, who were at the previous Court of Error,
are now summoned to appear before the bar of Justice
and eternal Truth.

15 When the case for Mortal Man *versus* Personal Sense
is opened, Mortal Man's counsel regards the prisoner
with the utmost tenderness. The counsel's earnest,
18 solemn eyes, kindling with hope and triumph, look upward. Then Christian Science turns suddenly to the
supreme tribunal, and opens the argument for the
21 defence: —

The prisoner at the bar has been unjustly sentenced.
His trial was a tragedy, and is morally illegal. Mortal
24 Man has had no proper counsel in the case. All the testimony has been on the side of Personal Sense, and we shall
unearth this foul conspiracy against the liberty and life of
27 Man. The only valid testimony in the case shows the
alleged crime never to have been committed. The prisoner is not proved "worthy of death, or of bonds."
30 Your Honor, the lower court has sentenced Mortal Man
to die, but God made Man immortal and amenable to
Spirit only. Denying justice to the body, that court com-

mended man's immortal Spirit to heavenly mercy, — Spirit 1
which is God Himself and Man's only lawgiver! Who or
what has sinned? Has the body or has Mortal Mind 3
committed a criminal deed? Counsellor False Belief has
argued that the body should die, while Reverend Theology
would console conscious Mortal Mind, which alone is capa- 6
ble of sin and suffering. The body committed no offence.
Mortal Man, in obedience to higher law, helped his fellow-
man, an act which should result in good to himself as well 9
as to others.

The law of our Supreme Court decrees that whosoever
sinneth shall die; but good deeds are immortal, bringing 12
joy instead of grief, pleasure instead of pain, and life
instead of death. If liver-complaint was committed by
trampling on Laws of Health, this was a good deed, for the 15
agent of those laws is an outlaw, a destroyer of Mortal
Man's liberty and rights. Laws of Health should be sentenced to die.   18

Watching beside the couch of pain in the exercise of a
love that "is the fulfilling of the law," — doing "unto
others as ye would that they should do unto you," — this 21
is no infringement of law, for no demand, human or divine,
renders it just to punish a man for acting justly. If mortals sin, our Supreme Judge in equity decides what penalty 24
is due for the sin, and Mortal Man can suffer only for his
sin. For naught else can he be punished, according to the
law of Spirit, God.   27

Then what jurisdiction had his Honor, Judge Medicine,
in this case? To him I might say, in Bible language, "Sit-
test thou to judge . . . after the law, and commandest . . . 30
to be smitten contrary to the law?" The only jurisdiction
to which the prisoner can submit is that of Truth, Life, and
Love. If they condemn him not, neither shall Judge Medi- 33
cine condemn him; and I ask that the prisoner be restored
to the liberty of which he has been unjustly deprived.

1   The principal witness (the officer of the Health-laws)
deposed that he was an eye-witness to the good deeds for
3 which Mortal Man is under sentence of death. After be-
traying him into the hands of your law, the Health-agent
disappeared, to reappear however at the trial as a witness
6 against Mortal Man and in the interest of Personal Sense,
a murderer. Your Supreme Court must find the prisoner on the night of the alleged offence to have been acting
9 within the limits of the divine law, and in obedience
thereto. Upon this statute hangs all the law and testimony.
Giving a cup of cold water in Christ's name, is a Christian
12 service. Laying down his life for a good deed, Mortal Man
should find it again. Such acts bear their own justification, and are under the protection of the Most High.
15   Prior to the night of his arrest, the prisoner summoned
two professed friends, Materia Medica and Physiology, to
prevent his committing liver-complaint, and thus save him
18 from arrest. But they brought with them Fear, the sheriff,
to precipitate the result which they were called to prevent.
It was Fear who handcuffed Mortal Man and would now
21 punish him. You have left Mortal Man no alternative.
He must obey your law, fear its consequences, and be punished for his fear. His friends struggled hard to rescue the
24 prisoner from the penalty they considered justly due, but
they were compelled to let him be taken into custody, tried,
and condemned. Thereupon Judge Medicine sat in judg-
27 ment on the case, and substantially charged the jury, twelve
Mortal Minds, to find the prisoner guilty. His Honor sentenced Mortal Man to die for the very deeds which the di-
30 vine law compels man to commit. Thus the Court of Error
construed obedience to the law of divine Love as disobedience to the law of Life. Claiming to protect Mortal Man
33 in right-doing, that court pronounced a sentence of death
for doing right.
One of the principal witnesses, Nerve, testified that he

was a ruler of Body, in which province Mortal Man resides. 1
He also testified that he was on intimate terms with the
plaintiff, and knew Personal Sense to be truthful; that he 3
knew Man, and that Man was made in the image of God,
but was a criminal. This is a foul aspersion on man's
Maker. It blots the fair escutcheon of omnipotence. It in- 6
dicates malice aforethought, a determination to condemn
Man in the interest of Personal Sense. At the bar of Truth,
in the presence of divine Justice, before the Judge of our 9
higher tribunal, the Supreme Court of Spirit, and before
its jurors, the Spiritual Senses, I proclaim this witness,
Nerve, to be destitute of intelligence and truth and to be 12
a false witness.

Man self-destroyed; the testimony of matter respected;
Spirit not allowed a hearing; Soul a criminal though 15
recommended to mercy; the helpless innocent body tortured, — these are the terrible records of your Court of
Error, and I ask that the Supreme Court of Spirit reverse 18
this decision.

Here the opposing counsel, False Belief, called Christian Science to order for contempt of court. Various 21
notables — Materia Medica, Anatomy, Physiology, Scholastic Theology, and Jurisprudence — rose to the question of expelling Christian Science from the bar, for such 24
high-handed illegality. They declared that Christian Science was overthrowing the judicial proceedings of a regu-
larly constituted court. 27

But Judge Justice of the Supreme Court of Spirit overruled their motions on the ground that unjust usages
were not allowed at the bar of Truth, which ranks above 30
the lower Court of Error.

The attorney, Christian Science, then read from the
supreme statute-book, the Bible, certain extracts on the 33

1 Rights of Man, remarking that the Bible was better authority than Blackstone: —

3   Let us make man in our image, after our likeness; and
let them have dominion.
    Behold, I give unto you power . . . over all the power
6 of the enemy: and nothing shall by any means hurt you.
    If a man keep my saying, he shall never see death.

Then Christian Science proved the witness, Nerve, to
9 be a perjurer. Instead of being a ruler in the Province
of Body, in which Mortal Man was reported to reside,
Nerve was an insubordinate citizen, putting in false
12 claims to office and bearing false witness against Man.
Turning suddenly to Personal Sense, by this time silent,
Christian Science continued: —

15   I ask your arrest in the name of Almighty God on three
distinct charges of crime, to wit: perjury, treason, and conspiracy against the rights and life of man.

18   Then Christian Science continued: —

    Another witness, equally inadequate, said that on the
night of the crime a garment of foul fur was spread over
21 him by Morbid Secretion, while the facts in the case show
that this fur is a foreign substance, imported by False Belief, the attorney for Personal Sense, who is in partnership
24 with Error and smuggles Error's goods into market without the inspection of Soul's government officers. When
the Court of Truth summoned Furred Tongue for examina-
27 tion, he disappeared and was never heard of more.
    Morbid Secretion is not an importer or dealer in fur, but
we have heard Materia Medica explain how this fur is
30 manufactured, and we know Morbid Secretion to be on
friendly terms with the firm of Personal Sense, Error, &

Co., receiving pay from them and introducing their goods 1
into the market. Also, be it known that False Belief, the
counsel for the plaintiff, Personal Sense, is a buyer for this 3
firm. He manufactures for it, keeps a furnishing store,
and advertises largely for his employers.

Death testified that he was absent from the Province of 6
Body, when a message came from False Belief, commanding him to take part in the homicide. At this request
Death repaired to the spot where the liver-complaint was 9
in process, frightening away Materia Medica, who was then
manacling the prisoner in the attempt to save him. True,
Materia Medica was a misguided participant in the misdeed 12
for which the Health-officer had Mortal Man in custody,
though Mortal Man was innocent.

Christian Science turned from the abashed witnesses, 15
his words flashing as lightning in the perturbed faces
of these worthies, Scholastic Theology, Materia Medica,
Physiology, the blind Hypnotism, and the masked Per- 18
sonal Sense, and said: —

God will smite you, O whited walls, for injuring in your
ignorance the unfortunate Mortal Man who sought your 21
aid in his struggles against liver-complaint and Death.
You came to his rescue, only to fasten upon him an offence
of which he was innocent. You aided and abetted Fear 24
and Health-laws. You betrayed Mortal Man, meanwhile
declaring Disease to be God's servant and the righteous
executor of His laws. Our higher statutes declare you all, 27
witnesses, jurors, and judges, to be offenders, awaiting the
sentence which General Progress and Divine Love will
pronounce. 30

We send our best detectives to whatever locality is reported to be haunted by Disease, but on visiting the spot,
they learn that Disease was never there, for he could not 33

1 possibly elude their search. Your Material Court of Errors,
when it condemned Mortal Man on the ground of hygienic
3 disobedience, was manipulated by the oleaginous machina-
tions of the counsel, False Belief, whom Truth arraigns
before the supreme bar of Spirit to answer for his crime.
6 Morbid Secretion is taught how to make sleep befool reason
before sacrificing mortals to their false gods.

Mortal Minds were deceived by your attorney, False Be-
9 lief, and were influenced to give a verdict delivering Mortal
Man to Death. Good deeds are transformed into crimes,
to which you attach penalties; but no warping of justice
12 can render disobedience to the so-called laws of Matter
disobedience to God, or an act of homicide. Even penal
law holds homicide, under stress of circumstances, to be
15 justifiable. Now what greater justification can any deed
have, than that it is for the good of one's neighbor? Wherefore, then, in the name of outraged justice, do you sentence
18 Mortal Man for ministering to the wants of his fellow-man
in obedience to divine law? You cannot trample upon the
decree of the Supreme Bench. Mortal Man has his appeal
21 to Spirit, God, who sentences only for sin.

The false and unjust beliefs of your human mental legis-
lators compel them to enact wicked laws of sickness and so
24 forth, and then render obedience to these laws punishable
as crime. In the presence of the Supreme Lawgiver, standing at the bar of Truth, and in accordance with the divine
27 statutes, I repudiate the false testimony of Personal Sense.
I ask that he be forbidden to enter against Mortal Man
any more suits to be tried at the Court of Material Error.
30 I appeal to the just and equitable decisions of divine Spirit
to restore to Mortal Man the rights of which he has been
deprived.

33   Here the counsel for the defence closed, and the Chief
Justice of the Supreme Court, with benign and imposing

presence, comprehending and defining all law and evi- 1
dence, explained from his statute-book, the Charge of the
Bible, that any so-called law, which under- Chief Justice   3
takes to punish aught but sin, is null and void.

He also decided that the plaintiff, Personal Sense, be
not permitted to enter any suits at the bar of Soul, but 6
be enjoined to keep perpetual silence, and in case of
temptation, to give heavy bonds for good behavior. He
concluded his charge thus: —   9

The plea of False Belief we deem unworthy of a hearing.
Let what False Belief utters, now and forever, fall into
oblivion, "unknelled, uncoffined, and unknown." Accord- 12
ing to our statute, Material Law is a liar who cannot bear
witness against Mortal Man, neither can Fear arrest Mortal
Man nor can Disease cast him into prison. Our law refuses 15
to recognize Man as sick or dying, but holds him to be forever in the image and likeness of his Maker. Reversing the
testimony of Personal Sense and the decrees of the Court of 18
Error in favor of Matter, Spirit decides in favor of Man
and against Matter. We further recommend that Materia
Medica adopt Christian Science and that Health-laws, 21
Mesmerism, Hypnotism, Oriental Witchcraft, and Esoteric
Magic be publicly executed at the hands of our sheriff,
Progress.   24

The Supreme Bench decides in favor of intelligence, that
no law outside of divine Mind can punish or reward Mortal
Man. Your personal jurors in the Court of Error are 27
myths. Your attorney, False Belief, is an impostor, per-
suading Mortal Minds to return a verdict contrary to law
and gospel. The plaintiff, Personal Sense, is recorded in 30
our Book of books as a liar. Our great Teacher of mental
jurisprudence speaks of him also as "a murderer from the
beginning." We have no trials for sickness before the tri- 33

1 bunal of divine Spirit. There, Man is adjudged innocent
of transgressing physical laws, because there are no such
3 laws. Our statute is spiritual, our Government is divine.
"Shall not the Judge of all the earth do right?"

The Jury of Spiritual Senses agreed at once upon a
6 verdict, and there resounded throughout the vast audience-
Divine   chamber of Spirit the cry, Not guilty. Then
verdict   the prisoner rose up regenerated, strong, free.
9 We noticed, as he shook hands with his counsel, Christian Science, that all sallowness and debility had disappeared. His form was erect and commanding, his
12 countenance beaming with health and happiness. Divine
Love had cast out fear. Mortal Man, no longer sick
and in prison, walked forth, his feet "beautiful upon the
15 mountains," as of one "that bringeth good tidings."

Neither animal magnetism nor hypnotism enters into
the practice of Christian Science, in which truth cannot
18   be reversed, but the reverse of error is true.
Christ
the great An improved belief cannot retrograde. When
physician
Christ changes a belief of sin or of sickness into
21 a better belief, then belief melts into spiritual understanding, and sin, disease, and death disappear. Christ, Truth,
gives mortals temporary food and clothing until the ma-
24 terial, transformed with the ideal, disappears, and man
is clothed and fed spiritually. St. Paul says, "Work
out your own salvation with fear and trembling:" Jesus
27 said, "Fear not, little flock; for it is your Father's good
pleasure to give you the kingdom." This truth is
Christian Science.
30   Christian Scientists, be a law to yourselves that mental
malpractice cannot harm you either when asleep or when
awake.

CHAPTER XIII

Teaching Christian Science

Give instruction to a wise man, and he will be yet wiser: teach a just man, and he will increase in learning. — PROVERBS.

W HEN the discoverer of Christian Science is con- 1
sulted by her followers as to the propriety, advantage, and consistency of systematic medical   Study of   3
study, she tries to show them that under ordi-   medicine
nary circumstances a resort to faith in corporeal means
tends to deter those, who make such a compromise, from 6
entire confidence in omnipotent Mind as really possessing
all power.   While a course of medical study is at times
severely condemned by some Scientists, she feels, as she 9
always has felt, that all are privileged to work out their
own salvation according to their light, and that our motto
should be the Master's counsel, "Judge not, that ye be 12
not judged."

If patients fail to experience the healing power of
Christian Science, and think they can be benefited by 15
certain ordinary physical methods of medical   Failure's
treatment, then the Mind-physician should   lessons
give up such cases, and leave invalids free to resort to 18
whatever other systems they fancy will afford relief.
Thus such invalids may learn the value of the apostolic
precept: "Reprove, rebuke, exhort with all longsuffering 21
and doctrine."   If the sick find these material expedients

1 unsatisfactory, and they receive no help from them, these
very failures may open their blind eyes. In some way,
3 sooner or later, all must rise superior to materiality, and
suffering is oft the divine agent in this elevation. "All
things work together for good to them that love God," is
6 the dictum of Scripture.

If Christian Scientists ever fail to receive aid from
other Scientists, — their brethren upon whom they may
9 Refuge and call, — God will still guide them into the right
strength use of temporary and eternal means. Step by
step will those who trust Him find that "God is our refuge
12 and strength, a very present help in trouble."

Students are advised by the author to be charitable
and kind, not only towards differing forms of religion
15 Charity and medicine, but to those who hold these dif-
to those fering opinions. Let us be faithful in pointing
opposed the way through Christ, as we understand it,
18 but let us also be careful always to "judge righteous judgment," and never to condemn rashly. "Whosoever shall
smite thee on thy right cheek, turn to him the other also."
21 That is, Fear not that he will smite thee again for thy for-
bearance. If ecclesiastical sects or medical schools turn
a deaf ear to the teachings of Christian Science, then part
24 from these opponents as did Abraham when he parted
from Lot, and say in thy heart: "Let there be no strife, I
pray thee, between me and thee, and between my herd-
27 men and thy herdmen; for we be brethren." Immortals,
or God's children in divine Science, are one harmonious
family; but mortals, or the "children of men" in material
30 sense, are discordant and ofttimes false brethren.

The teacher must make clear to students the Science
of healing, especially its ethics, — that all is Mind, and

that the Scientist must conform to God's requirements. 1
Also the teacher must thoroughly fit his students to defend
themselves against sin, and to guard against the 3
attacks of the would-be *mental assassin*, who
attempts to kill morally and physically. No
hypothesis as to the existence of another power should 6
interpose a doubt or fear to hinder the demonstration of
Christian Science. Unfold the latent energies and capacities for good in your pupil. Teach the great possibilities 9
of man endued with divine Science. Teach the dangerous
possibility of dwarfing the spiritual understanding and
demonstration of Truth by sin, or by recourse to material 12
means for healing. Teach the meekness and might of life
"hid with Christ in God," and there will be no desire for
other healing methods. You render the divine law of 15
healing obscure and void, when you weigh the human in
the scale with the divine, or limit in any direction of
thought the omnipresence and omnipotence of God. 18
Christian Science silences human will, quiets fear with
Truth and Love, and illustrates the unlabored motion
of the divine energy in healing the sick. Self- 21
seeking, envy, passion, pride, hatred, and
revenge are cast out by the divine Mind which heals
disease. The human will which maketh and worketh a lie, 24
hiding the divine Principle of harmony, is destructive to
health, and is the cause of disease rather than its cure.

There is great danger in teaching Mind-healing indis- 27
criminately, thus disregarding the morals of the student
and caring only for the fees. Recalling Jeffer- 30
son's words about slavery, "I tremble, when I
remember that God is just," the author trembles whenever
she sees a man, for the petty consideration of money,

Marginal notes:
Conforming to explicit rules

Divine energy

Blight of avarice

1 teaching his slight knowledge of Mind-power, — perhaps communicating his own bad morals, and in this way
3 dealing pitilessly with a community unprepared for self-defence.

A thorough perusal of the author's publications heals
6 sickness. If patients sometimes seem worse while reading this book, the change may either arise from the alarm of the physician, or it may mark the crisis of the disease.
9 Perseverance in the perusal of the book has generally completely healed such cases.

Whoever practises the Science the author teaches,
12 through which Mind pours light and healing upon this
Exclusion of generation, can practise on no one from sin-
malpractice ister or malicious motives without destroying
15 his own power to heal and his own health. Good must dominate in the thoughts of the healer, or his demonstration is protracted, dangerous, and impossible in Sci-
18 ence. A wrong motive involves defeat. In the Science of Mind-healing, it is imperative to be honest, for victory rests on the side of immutable right. To understand
21 God strengthens hope, enthrones faith in Truth, and verifies Jesus' word: "Lo, I am with you alway, even unto the end of the world."

24 Resisting evil, you overcome it and prove its nothingness. Not human platitudes, but divine beatitudes, re-
Iniquity flect the spiritual light and might which heal
27 overcome the sick. The exercise of will brings on a hypnotic state, detrimental to health and integrity of thought. This must therefore be watched and guarded
30 against. Covering iniquity will prevent prosperity and the ultimate triumph of any cause. Ignorance of the error to be eradicated oftentimes subjects you to its abuse.

The heavenly law is broken by trespassing upon 1
man's individual right of self-government. We have no
authority in Christian Science and no moral 3
right to attempt to influence the thoughts of
others, except it be to benefit them. In mental practice you must not forget that erring human opin- 6
ions, conflicting selfish motives, and ignorant attempts
to do good may render you incapable of knowing or
judging accurately the need of your fellow-men. There- 9
fore the rule is, heal the sick when called upon for aid,
and save the victims of the mental assassins.

No trespass
on human
rights

Ignorance, subtlety, or false charity does not for- 12
ever conceal error; evil will in time disclose and punish itself. The recuperative action of the
system, when mentally sustained by Truth, 15
goes on naturally. When sin or sickness —
the reverse of harmony — seems true to material sense,
impart without frightening or discouraging the pa- 18
tient the truth and spiritual understanding, which destroy disease. Expose and denounce the claims of
evil and disease in all their forms, but realize no 21
reality in them. A sinner is not reformed merely
by assuring him that he cannot be a sinner because
there is no sin. To put down the claim of sin, 24
you must detect it, remove the mask, point out the
illusion, and thus get the victory over sin and so prove
its unreality. The sick are not healed merely by 27
declaring there is no sickness, but by knowing that
there is none.

Expose sin
without
believing in it

A sinner is afraid to cast the first stone. He may 30
say, as a subterfuge, that evil is unreal, but to know it,
he must demonstrate his statement. To assume that

1 there are no claims of evil and yet to indulge them, is
a moral offence. Blindness and self-righteousness cling
3 Wicked fast to iniquity. When the Publican's wail
evasions went out to the great heart of Love, it won his
humble desire. Evil which obtains in the bodily senses,
6 but which the heart condemns, has no foundation; but if
evil is uncondemned, it is undenied and nurtured. Under
such circumstances, to say that there is no evil, is an evil
9 in itself. When needed tell the truth concerning the lie.
Evasion of Truth cripples integrity, and casts thee down
from the pinnacle.

12   Christian Science rises above the evidence of the corporeal senses; but if you have not risen above sin your-
Truth's self, do not congratulate yourself upon your
15 grand results blindness to evil or upon the good you know
and *do* not. A dishonest position is far from Christianly
scientific. "He that covereth his sins shall not prosper:
18 but whoso confesseth and forsaketh them shall have
mercy." Try to leave on every student's mind the strong
impress of divine Science, a high sense of the moral and
21 spiritual qualifications requisite for healing, well knowing
it to be impossible for error, evil, and hate to accomplish
the grand results of Truth and Love. The reception or
24 pursuit of instructions opposite to absolute Christian
Science must always hinder scientific demonstration.

If the student adheres strictly to the teachings of Chris-
27 tian Science and ventures not to break its rules, he can-
Adherence to not fail of success in healing. It is Christian
righteousness Science to do right, and nothing short of right-
30 doing has any claim to the name. To talk the right and
live the wrong is foolish deceit, doing one's self the most
harm. Fettered by sin yourself, it is difficult to free

another from the fetters of disease. With your own wrists 1
manacled, it is hard to break another's chains. A little
leaven causes the whole mass to ferment. A grain of 3
Christian Science does wonders for mortals, so omnipotent is Truth, but more of Christian Science must be
gained in order to continue in well doing. 6
The wrong done another reacts most heavily against
one's self. Right adjusts the balance sooner or later.
Think it "easier for a camel to go through Right adjusts 9
the eye of a needle," than for you to benefit the balance
yourself by injuring others. Man's moral mercury, rising or falling, registers his healing ability and fitness to 12
teach. You should practise well what you know, and
you will then advance in proportion to your honesty
and fidelity, — qualities which insure success in this 15
Science; but it requires a higher understanding to teach
this subject properly and correctly than it does to heal
the most difficult case. 18
The baneful effect of evil associates is less seen than
felt. The inoculation of evil human thoughts ought to
be understood and guarded against. The Inoculation 21
first impression, made on a mind which is of thought
attracted or repelled according to personal merit or de-
merit, is a good detective of individual character. Cer- 24
tain minds meet only to separate through simultaneous
repulsion. They are enemies without the preliminary
offence. The impure are at peace with the impure. 27
Only virtue is a rebuke to vice. A proper teacher of Christian Science improves the health and the morals of his
student if the student practises what he is taught, and 30
unless this result follows, the teacher is a Scientist only
in name.

1 There is a large class of thinkers whose bigotry and
conceit twist every fact to suit themselves. Their creed
3 Three classes teaches belief in a mysterious, supernatural
of neophytes God, and in a natural, all-powerful devil. Another class, still more unfortunate, are so depraved that
6 they appear to be innocent. They utter a falsehood,
while looking you blandly in the face, and they never
fail to stab their benefactor in the back. A third class
9 of thinkers build with solid masonry. They are sincere,
generous, noble, and are therefore open to the approach
and recognition of Truth. To teach Christian Science
12 to such as these is no task. They do not incline long-
ingly to error, whine over the demands of Truth, nor
play the traitor for place and power.

15 Some people yield slowly to the touch of Truth. Few
yield without a struggle, and many are reluctant to ac-
Touchstone knowledge that they have yielded; but un-
18 of Science less this admission is made, evil will boast
itself above good. The Christian Scientist has enlisted
to lessen evil, disease, and death; and he will overcome
21 them by understanding their nothingness and the allness
of God, or good. Sickness to him is no less a temptation
than is sin, and he heals them both by understanding
24 God's power over them. The Christian Scientist knows
that they are errors of belief, which Truth can and will
destroy.

27 Who, that has felt the perilous beliefs in life, substance,
and intelligence separated from God, can say that there
False claims is no error of belief? Knowing the claim of
30 annihilated animal magnetism, that all evil combines in
the belief of life, substance, and intelligence in matter,
electricity, animal nature, and organic life, who will deny

that these are the errors which Truth must and will an- 1
nihilate? Christian Scientists must live under the constant pressure of the apostolic command to come out from 3
the material world and be separate. They must re-
nounce aggression, oppression and the pride of power.
Christianity, with the crown of Love upon her brow, 6
must be their queen of life.

Students of Christian Science, who start with its letter
and think to succeed without the spirit, will either make 9
shipwreck of their faith or be turned sadly   Treasure
awry. They must not only seek, but strive,   in heaven
to enter the narrow path of Life, for "wide is the gate, 12
and broad is the way, that leadeth to destruction, and
many there be which go in thereat." Man walks in the
direction towards which he looks, and where his treasure 15
is, there will his heart be also. If our hopes and affections are spiritual, they come from above, not from beneath, and they bear as of old the fruits of the Spirit.   18

Every Christian Scientist, every conscientious teacher
of the Science of Mind-healing, knows that human will
is not Christian Science, and he must recog-   Obligations   21
nize this in order to defend himself from the   of teachers
influence of human will. He feels morally obligated to
open the eyes of his students that they may perceive the 24
nature and methods of error of every sort, especially any
subtle degree of evil, deceived and deceiving. All mental
malpractice arises from ignorance or malice aforethought. 27
It is the injurious action of one mortal mind controlling
another from wrong motives, and it is practised either
with a mistaken or a wicked purpose.   30

Show your student that mental malpractice tends to
blast moral sense, health, and the human life. Instruct

1 him how to bar the door of his thought against this
seeming power, — a task not difficult, when one under-
3 Indispensable stands that evil has in reality no power.
defence   Incorrect reasoning leads to practical error.
The wrong thought should be arrested before it has a
6 chance to manifest itself.

Walking in the light, we are accustomed to the light
and require it; we cannot see in darkness. But eyes ac-
9 Egotistic   customed to darkness are pained by the light.
darkness   When outgrowing the old, you should not fear
to put on the new. Your advancing course may pro-
12 voke envy, but it will also attract respect. When error
confronts you, withhold not the rebuke or the explanation which destroys error. Never breathe an immoral
15 atmosphere, unless in the attempt to purify it. Better is
the frugal intellectual repast with contentment and virtue,
than the luxury of learning with egotism and vice.
18 Right is radical. The teacher must know the truth
himself. He must live it and love it, or he cannot impart
Unwarranted it to others. We soil our garments with con-
21 expectations servatism, and afterwards we must wash them
clean. When the spiritual sense of Truth unfolds its
harmonies, you take no risks in the policy of error. Ex-
24 pect to heal simply by repeating the author's words, by
right talking and wrong acting, and you will be disappointed. Such a practice does not demonstrate the
27 Science by which divine Mind heals the sick.

Acting from sinful motives destroys your power of
healing from the right motive. On the other hand, if
30 Reliable   you had the inclination or power to practise
authority   wrongly and then should adopt Christian
Science, the wrong power would be destroyed. You do

not deny the mathematician's right to distinguish the cor- 1
rect from the incorrect among the examples on the blackboard, nor disbelieve the musician when he distinguishes 3
concord from discord. In like manner it should be granted
that the author understands what she is saying.

Right and wrong, truth and error, will be at strife in 6
the minds of students, until victory rests on the side of
invincible truth. Mental chemicalization fol- Winning
lows the explanation of Truth, and a higher the field 9
basis is thus won; but with some individuals the morbid
moral or physical symptoms constantly reappear. I
have never witnessed so decided effects from the use of 12
material remedies as from the use of spiritual.

Teach your student that he must know himself before he can know others and minister to human needs. 15
Honesty is spiritual power. Dishonesty is Knowledge
human weakness, which forfeits divine help. and honesty
You uncover sin, not in order to injure, but in order 18
to bless the corporeal man; and a right motive has
its reward. Hidden sin is spiritual wickedness in high
places. The masquerader in this Science thanks God 21
that there is no evil, yet serves evil in the name of
good.

You should treat sickness mentally just as you would 24
sin, except that you must not tell the patient that he is
sick nor give names to diseases, for such a Metaphysical
course increases fear, the foundation of dis- treatment 27
ease, and impresses more deeply the wrong mind-picture.
A Christian Scientist's medicine is Mind, the divine Truth
that makes man free. A Christian Scientist never recom- 30
mends material hygiene, never manipulates. He does
not trespass on the rights of mind nor can he practise

1 animal magnetism or hypnotism. It need not be added
that the use of tobacco or intoxicating drinks is not in
3 harmony with Christian Science.

Teach your students the omnipotence of Truth, which
illustrates the impotence of error. The understanding,
6   Impotence   even in a degree, of the divine All-power de-
   of hate   stroys fear, and plants the feet in the true path,
— the path which leads to the house built without hands
9 "eternal in the heavens." Human hate has no legitimate mandate and no kingdom. Love is enthroned.
That evil or matter has neither intelligence nor power,
12 is the doctrine of absolute Christian Science, and this is
the great truth which strips all disguise from error.

He, who understands in a sufficient degree the Princi-
15 ple of Mind-healing, points out to his student error as
  Love the   well as truth, the wrong as well as the right
  incentive   practice. Love for God and man is the true
18 incentive in both healing and teaching. Love inspires,
illumines, designates, and leads the way. Right motives
give pinions to thought, and strength and freedom to
21 speech and action. Love is priestess at the altar of
Truth. Wait patiently for divine Love to move upon the
waters of mortal mind, and form the perfect concept.
24 Patience must "have her perfect work."

Do not dismiss students at the close of a class term,
feeling that you have no more to do for them. Let your
27   Continuity   loving care and counsel support all their feeble
  of interest   footsteps, until your students tread firmly in
the straight and narrow way. The superiority of spir-
30 itual power over sensuous is the central point of Christian Science. Remember that the letter and mental
argument are only human auxiliaries to aid in bringing

thought into accord with the spirit of Truth and Love, 1
which heals the sick and the sinner.

A mental state of self-condemnation and guilt or a 3
faltering and doubting trust in Truth are unsuitable
conditions for healing the sick. Such mental   Weakness
states indicate weakness instead of strength.   and guilt   6
Hence the necessity of being right yourself in order to
teach this Science of healing. You must utilize the moral
might of Mind in order to walk over the waves of error 9
and support your claims by demonstration. If you are
yourself lost in the belief and fear of disease or sin, and
if, knowing the remedy, you fail to use the energies of 12
Mind in your own behalf, you can exercise little or no
power for others' help. "First cast out the beam out
of thine own eye; and then shalt thou see clearly to cast 15
out the mote out of thy brother's eye."

The student, who receives his knowledge of Christian
Science, or metaphysical healing, from a human teacher, 18
may be mistaken in judgment and demonstra-   The trust of
tion, but God cannot mistake. God selects   the All-wise
for the highest service one who has grown into such a 21
fitness for it as renders any abuse of the mission an impossibility. The All-wise does not bestow His highest
trusts upon the unworthy. When He commissions a mes- 24
senger, it is one who is spiritually near Himself. No person can misuse this mental power, if he is taught of God
to discern it.   27

This strong point in Christian Science is not to be
overlooked, — that the same fountain cannot send forth
both sweet waters and bitter. The higher   Integrity   30
your attainment in the Science of mental   assured
healing and teaching, the more impossible it will be-

1 come for you intentionally to influence mankind adverse
to its highest hope and achievement.

3 Teaching or practising in the name of Truth, but contrary to its spirit or rules, is most dangerous quackery.
Chicanery Strict adherence to the divine Principle and
6 impossible rules of the scientific method has secured
the only success of the students of Christian Science.
This alone entitles them to the high standing which
9 most of them hold in the community, a reputation ex-
perimentally justified by their efforts. Whoever affirms that there is more than one Principle and method
12 of demonstrating Christian Science greatly errs, ignorantly or intentionally, and separates himself from the
true conception of Christian Science healing and from
15 its possible demonstration.

Any dishonesty in your theory and practice betrays a
gross ignorance of the method of the Christ-cure. Science
18 No dishonest makes no concessions to persons or opinions.
concessions One must abide in the *morale* of truth or he
cannot demonstrate the divine Principle. So long as
21 matter is the basis of practice, illness cannot be effica-
ciously treated by the metaphysical process. Truth does
the work, and you must both understand and abide by the
24 divine Principle of your demonstration.

A Christian Scientist requires my work SCIENCE AND
HEALTH for his textbook, and so do all his students and
27 This volume patients. Why? *First:* Because it is the voice
indispensable of Truth to this age, and contains the full
statement of Christian Science, or the Science of healing
30 through Mind. *Second:* Because it was the first book
known, containing a thorough statement of Christian
Science. Hence it gave the first rules for demonstrating

this Science, and registered the revealed Truth uncon- 1
taminated by human hypotheses. Other works, which
have borrowed from this book without giving it credit, 3
have adulterated the Science. *Third:* Because this book
has done more for teacher and student, for healer and
patient, than has been accomplished by other books.   6

Since the divine light of Christian Science first dawned
upon the author, she has never used this newly discovered
power in any direction which she fears to have   Purity of   9
fairly understood. Her prime object, since   science
entering this field of labor, has been to prevent suffering,
not to produce it. That we cannot scientifically both 12
cure and cause disease is self-evident. In the legend of
the shield, which led to a quarrel between two knights
because each of them could see but one face of it, both 15
sides were beautiful according to their degree; but to
mental malpractice, prolific of evil, there is no good as-
pect, either silvern or golden.   18

Christian Science is not an exception to the general
rule, that there is no excellence without labor in a direct
line. One cannot scatter his fire, and at the   Backsliders   21
same time hit the mark. To pursue other   and mistakes
vocations and advance rapidly in the demonstration of
this Science, is not possible. Departing from Christian 24
Science, some learners commend diet and hygiene.
They even practise these, intending thereby to initiate
the cure which they mean to complete with Mind, as if 27
the non-intelligent could aid Mind! The Scientist's
demonstration rests on one Principle, and there must
and can be no opposite rule. Let this Principle be ap- 30
plied to the cure of disease without exploiting other
means.

1 Mental quackery rests on the same platform as all
other quackery. The chief plank in this platform is the
3 Mental   doctrine that Science has two principles in
charlatanism partnership, one good and the other evil, —
one spiritual, the other material, — and that these two
6 may be simultaneously at work on the sick. This
theory is supposed to favor practice from both a mental
and a material standpoint. Another plank in the plat-
9 form is this, that error will finally have the same effect
as truth.

It is anything but scientifically Christian to think of
12 aiding the divine Principle of healing or of trying to sus-
Divinity   tain the human body until the divine Mind
ever ready is ready to take the case. Divinity is always
15 ready. *Semper paratus* is Truth's motto. Having seen
so much suffering from quackery, the author desires to
keep it out of Christian Science. The two-edged sword
18 of Truth must turn in every direction to guard "the tree
of life."

Sin makes deadly thrusts at the Christian Scientist as
21 ritualism and creed are summoned to give place to higher
The panoply law, but Science will ameliorate mortal malice.
of wisdom   The Christianly scientific man reflects the
24 divine law, thus becoming a law unto himself. He does
violence to no man. Neither is he a false accuser. The
Christian Scientist wisely shapes his course, and is hon-
27 est and consistent in following the leadings of divine
Mind. He must prove, through living as well as healing and teaching, that Christ's way is the only one
30 by which mortals are radically saved from sin and
sickness.

Christianity causes men to turn naturally from matter

to Spirit, as the flower turns from darkness to light. 1
Man then appropriates those things which "eye hath
not seen nor ear heard." Paul and John $\quad$ Advancement 3
had a clear apprehension that, as mortal man $\quad$ by
$\qquad\qquad\qquad\qquad\qquad\qquad\qquad\quad$ sacrifice
achieves no worldly honors except by sacrifice,
so he must gain heavenly riches by forsaking all worldli- 6
ness. Then he will have nothing in common with the
worldling's affections, motives, and aims. Judge not the
future advancement of Christian Science by the steps 9
already taken, lest you yourself be condemned for failing to take the first step.

Any attempt to heal mortals with erring mortal mind, 12
instead of resting on the omnipotence of the divine
Mind, must prove abortive. Committing the $\quad$ Dangerous
bare process of mental healing to frail mor- $\quad$ knowledge $\quad$ 15
tals, untaught and unrestrained by Christian Science,
is like putting a sharp knife into the hands of a blind
man or a raging maniac, and turning him loose in 18
the crowded streets of a city. Whether animated by
malice or ignorance, a false practitioner will work mischief, and ignorance is more harmful than wilful wicked- 21
ness, when the latter is distrusted and thwarted in its
incipiency.

To mortal sense Christian Science seems abstract, but 24
the process is simple and the results are sure if the Science
is understood. The tree must be good, which $\quad$ Certainty
produces good fruit. Guided by divine Truth $\quad$ of results $\quad$ 27
and not guesswork, the *theologus* (that is, the student —
the Christian and scientific expounder — of the divine
law) treats disease with more certain results than any 30
other healer on the globe. The Christian Scientist should
understand and adhere strictly to the rules of divine meta-

1 physics as laid down in this work, and rest his demonstration on this sure basis.

3   Ontology is defined as "the science of the necessary constituents and relations of all beings," and it under-

Ontology defined — lies all metaphysical practice. Our system of
6   Mind-healing rests on the apprehension of the nature and essence of all being, — on the divine Mind and Love's essential qualities. Its pharmacy is moral, 9 and its medicine is intellectual and spiritual, though used for physical healing. Yet this most fundamental part of metaphysics is the one most difficult to understand and 12 demonstrate, for to the material thought all is material, till such thought is rectified by Spirit.

Sickness is neither imaginary nor unreal, — that is, 15 to the frightened, false sense of the patient. Sickness

Mischievous imagination — is more than fancy; it is solid conviction. It is therefore to be dealt with through right ap-
18 prehension of the truth of being. If Christian healing is abused by mere smatterers in Science, it becomes a tedious mischief-maker. Instead of scientifically effect-
21 ing a cure, it starts a petty crossfire over every cripple and invalid, buffeting them with the superficial and cold assertion, "Nothing ails you."

24   When the Science of Mind was a fresh revelation to the author, she had to impart, while teaching its grand

Author's early instructions — facts, the hue of spiritual ideas from her own
27   spiritual condition, and she had to do this orally through the meagre channel afforded by language and by her manuscript circulated among the students. As for-
30 mer beliefs were gradually expelled from her thought, the teaching became clearer, until finally the shadow of old errors was no longer cast upon divine Science.

I do not maintain that anyone can exist in the flesh 1
without food and raiment; but I do believe that the
real man is immortal and that he lives in   Proof by   3
Spirit, not matter. Christian Science must induction
be accepted at this period by induction. We admit the
whole, because a part is proved and that part illustrates 6
and proves the entire Principle. Christian Science can
be taught only by those who are morally advanced and
spiritually endowed, for it is not superficial, nor is it 9
discerned from the standpoint of the human senses.
Only by the illumination of the spiritual sense, can
the light of understanding be thrown upon this Science, 12
because Science reverses the evidence before the material
senses and furnishes the eternal interpretation of God and
man.   15

If you believe that you are sick, should you say, "I am
sick"? No, but you should tell your belief sometimes,
if this be requisite to protect others. If you commit a 18
crime, should you acknowledge to yourself that you are
a criminal? Yes. Your responses should differ because
of the different effects they produce. Usually to admit 21
that you are sick, renders your case less curable, while
to recognize your sin, aids in destroying it. Both sin and
sickness are error, and Truth is their remedy. The truth 24
regarding error is, that error is not true, hence it is unreal.
To prove scientifically the error or unreality of sin, you
must first see the claim of sin, and then destroy it. 27
Whereas, to prove scientifically the error or unreality of
disease, you must mentally unsee the disease; then you
will not feel it, and it is destroyed.   30

Systematic teaching and the student's spiritual growth
and experience in practice are requisite for a thorough

1 comprehension of Christian Science. Some individuals assimilate truth more readily than others, but any

3 Rapidity of assimilation student, who adheres to the divine rules of Christian Science and imbibes the spirit of Christ, can demonstrate Christian Science, cast out

6 error, heal the sick, and add continually to his store of spiritual understanding, potency, enlightenment, and success.

9 If the student goes away to practise Truth's teachings only in part, dividing his interests between God and

Divided loyalty mammon and substituting his own views for

12 Truth, he will inevitably reap the error he sows. Whoever would demonstrate the healing of Christian Science must abide strictly by its rules, heed every state-

15 ment, and advance from the rudiments laid down. There is nothing difficult nor toilsome in this task, when the way is pointed out; but self-denial, sincerity, Christianity, and

18 persistence alone win the prize, as they usually do in every department of life.

Anatomy, when conceived of spiritually, is mental self-

21 knowledge, and consists in the dissection of thoughts to

Anatomy defined discover their quality, quantity, and origin. Are thoughts divine or human? That is the

24 important question. This branch of study is indispensable to the excision of error. The anatomy of Christian Science teaches when and how to probe the self-in-

27 flicted wounds of selfishness, malice, envy, and hate. It teaches the control of mad ambition. It unfolds the hallowed influences of unselfishness, philanthropy, spir-

30 itual love. It urges the government of the body both in health and in sickness. The Christian Scientist, through understanding mental anatomy, discerns and

deals with the real cause of disease. The material physi- 1
cian gropes among phenomena, which fluctuate every instant under influences not embraced in his diagnosis, and 3
so he may stumble and fall in the darkness.

Teacher and student should also be familiar with the
obstetrics taught by this Science. To attend properly 6
the birth of the new child, or divine idea,   Scientific
you should so detach mortal thought from its   obstetrics
material conceptions, that the birth will be natural and 9
safe. Though gathering new energy, this idea cannot
injure its useful surroundings in the travail of spiritual
birth. A spiritual idea has not a single element of error, 12
and this truth removes properly whatever is offensive.
The new idea, conceived and born of Truth and Love, is
clad in white garments. Its beginning will be meek, its 15
growth sturdy, and its maturity undecaying. When
this new birth takes place, the Christian Science infant
is born of the Spirit, born of God, and can cause the 18
mother no more suffering. By this we know that Truth
is here and has fulfilled its perfect work.

To decide quickly as to the proper treatment of error — 21
whether error is manifested in forms of sickness, sin,
or death — is the first step towards destroy- Unhesitating
ing error. Our Master treated error through   decision   24
Mind. He never enjoined obedience to the laws of nature,
if by these are meant laws of matter, nor did he use drugs.
There is a law of God applicable to healing, and it is a 27
spiritual law instead of material. The sick are not healed
by inanimate matter or drugs, as they believe that they
are. Such seeming medical effect or action is that of so- 30
called mortal mind.

It has been said to the author, "The world is bene-

1 fited by you, but it feels your influence without seeing
you. Why do you not make yourself more widely
3 **Seclusion of** known?" Could her friends know how little
the author time the author has had, in which to make
herself outwardly known except through her laborious
6 publications, — and how much time and toil are still required to establish the stately operations of Christian
Science, — they would understand why she is so secluded.
9 Others could not take her place, even if willing so to do.
She therefore remains unseen at her post, seeking no self-
aggrandizement but praying, watching, and working for
12 the redemption of mankind.

If from an injury or from any cause, a Christian Scientist were seized with pain so violent that he could not
15 treat himself mentally, — and the Scientists had failed
to relieve him, — the sufferer could call a surgeon, who
would give him a hypodermic injection, then, when the
18 belief of pain was lulled, he could handle his own case
mentally. Thus it is that we "prove all things; [and]
hold fast that which is good."

21   In founding a pathological system of Christianity, the
author has labored to expound divine Principle, and not
The right to exalt personality. The weapons of bigotry,
24 **motive and** ignorance, envy, fall before an honest heart.
its reward Adulterating Christian Science, makes it void.
Falsity has no foundation. "The hireling fleeth, because
27 he is an hireling, and careth not for the sheep." Neither
dishonesty nor ignorance ever founded, nor can they overthrow a scientific system of ethics.

CHAPTER XIV

Recapitulation

*For precept must be upon precept, precept upon precept; line upon
line, line upon line; here a little, and there a little.* — ISAIAH.

THIS chapter is from the first edition of the author's 1
class-book, copyrighted in 1870. After much labor
and increased spiritual understanding, she revised that 3
treatise for this volume in 1875. Absolute Christian
Science pervades its statements, to elucidate scientific
metaphysics. 6

QUESTIONS AND ANSWERS

Question. — What is God?
Answer. — God is incorporeal, divine, supreme, infinite 9
Mind, Spirit, Soul, Principle, Life, Truth, Love.

Question. — Are these terms synonymous?
Answer. — They are. They refer to one absolute God. 12
They are also intended to express the nature, essence, and
wholeness of Deity. The attributes of God are justice,
mercy, wisdom, goodness, and so on. 15

Question. — Is there more than one God or Principle?
Answer. — There is not. Principle and its idea is one,
and this one is God, omnipotent, omniscient, and omni- 18

465

1 present Being, and His reflection is man and the universe.
Omni is adopted from the Latin adjective signifying *all.*
3 Hence God combines all-power or potency, all-science
or true knowledge, all-presence. The varied manifestations of Christian Science indicate Mind, never matter,
6 and have one Principle.

Question. — What are spirits and souls?

Answer. — To human belief, they are personalities
9 constituted of mind and matter, life and death, truth and
Real versus unreal error, good and evil; but these contrasting
pairs of terms represent contraries, as Chris-
12 tian Science reveals, which neither dwell together nor
assimilate. Truth is immortal; error is mortal. Truth
is limitless; error is limited. Truth is intelligent; error
15 is non-intelligent. Moreover, Truth is real, and error is
unreal. This last statement contains the point you will
most reluctantly admit, although first and last it is the
18 most important to understand.

The term *souls* or *spirits* is as improper as the term
gods. Soul or Spirit signifies Deity and nothing else.
21 Mankind redeemed There is no finite soul nor spirit. Soul or
Spirit means only one Mind, and cannot be
rendered in the plural. Heathen mythology and Jewish
24 theology have perpetuated the fallacy that intelligence,
soul, and life can be in matter; and idolatry and ritualism
are the outcome of all man-made beliefs. The Science
27 of Christianity comes with fan in hand to separate the
chaff from the wheat. Science will declare God aright,
and Christianity will demonstrate this declaration and
30 its divine Principle, making mankind better physically,
morally, and spiritually.

Question. — What are the demands of the Science of 1
Soul?

Answer. — The first demand of this Science is, "Thou 3
shalt have no other gods before me." This *me* is Spirit.
Therefore the command means this: Thou shalt   Two chief
have no intelligence, no life, no substance, no   commands 6
truth, no love, but that which is spiritual. The second
is like unto it, "Thou shalt love thy neighbor as thyself."
It should be thoroughly understood that all men have one 9
Mind, one God and Father, one Life, Truth, and Love.
Mankind will become perfect in proportion as this fact
becomes apparent, war will cease and the true brother- 12
hood of man will be established. Having no other gods,
turning to no other but the one perfect Mind to guide
him, man is the likeness of God, pure and eternal, hav- 15
ing that Mind which was also in Christ.

Science reveals Spirit, Soul, as not in the body, and
God as not in man but as reflected by man. The greater 18
cannot be in the lesser. The belief that the   Soul not con-
greater can be in the lesser is an error that   fined in body
works ill. This is a leading point in the Science of Soul, 21
that Principle is not in its idea. Spirit, Soul, is not
confined in man, and is never in matter. We reason imperfectly from effect to cause, when we conclude that 24
matter is the effect of Spirit; but *a priori* reasoning
shows material existence to be enigmatical. Spirit gives
the true mental idea. We cannot interpret Spirit, Mind, 27
through matter. Matter neither sees, hears, nor feels.

Reasoning from cause to effect in the Science of Mind,
we begin with Mind, which must be under-   Sinlessness of 30
stood through the idea which expresses it and   Mind, Soul
cannot be learned from its opposite, matter. Thus we

1 arrive at Truth, or intelligence, which evolves its own
unerring idea and never can be coordinate with human
3 illusions. If Soul sinned, it would be mortal, for sin is
mortality's self, because it kills itself. If Truth is immortal, error must be mortal, because error is unlike
6 Truth. Because Soul is immortal, Soul cannot sin, for
sin is not the eternal verity of being.

Question. — What is the scientific statement of being?
9   *Answer.* — There is no life, truth, intelligence, nor substance in matter. All is infinite Mind and its infinite
manifestation, for God is All-in-all. Spirit is immortal
12 Truth; matter is mortal error. Spirit is the real and
eternal; matter is the unreal and temporal. Spirit is
God, and man is His image and likeness. Therefore
15 man is not material; he is spiritual.

Question. — What is substance?
Answer. — Substance is that which is eternal and inca-
18 pable of discord and decay. Truth, Life, and Love are
   Spiritual   substance, as the Scriptures use this word in
   synonyms   Hebrews: "The substance of things hoped
21 for, the evidence of things not seen." Spirit, the synonym
of Mind, Soul, or God, is the only real substance. The
spiritual universe, including individual man, is a com-
24 pound idea, reflecting the divine substance of Spirit.

Question. — What is Life?
Answer. — Life is divine Principle, Mind, Soul, Spirit.
27   Eternity   Life is without beginning and without end.
   of Life   Eternity, not time, expresses the thought of
Life, and time is no part of eternity. One ceases in
30 proportion as the other is recognized. Time is finite;

eternity is forever infinite.   Life is neither in nor of mat- 1
ter.   What is termed matter is unknown to Spirit, which
includes in itself all substance and is Life eternal.   Mat- 3
ter is a human concept.   Life is divine Mind.   Life is not
limited.   Death and finiteness are unknown to Life.   If
Life ever had a beginning, it would also have an ending. 6

Question. — What is intelligence?
Answer. — Intelligence is omniscience, omnipresence,
and omnipotence.   It is the primal and eternal quality 9
of infinite Mind, of the triune Principle, — Life, Truth,
and Love, — named God.

Question. — What is Mind?   12
Answer. — Mind is God.   The exterminator of error
is the great truth that God, good, is the *only* Mind, and
that the supposititious opposite of infinite Mind True sense of 15
— called *devil* or evil — is not Mind, is not   infinitude
Truth, but error, without intelligence or reality.   There
can be but one Mind, because there is but one God; and 18
if mortals claimed no other Mind and accepted no other,
sin would be unknown.   We can have but one Mind, if
that one is infinite.   We bury the sense of infinitude, 21
when we admit that, although God is infinite, evil has a
place in this infinity, for evil can have no place, where all
space is filled with God.   24
We lose the high signification of omnipotence, when
after admitting that God, or good, is omnipresent and
has all-power, we still believe there is another   The sole 27
power, named *evil*.   This belief that there   governor
is more than one mind is as pernicious to divine theology
as are ancient mythology and pagan idolatry.   With 30

1 one Father, even God, the whole family of man would
be brethren; and with one Mind and that God, or good,
3 the brotherhood of man would consist of Love and Truth,
and have unity of Principle and spiritual power which
constitute divine Science. The supposed existence of
6 more than one mind was the basic error of idolatry. This
error assumed the loss of spiritual power, the loss of the
spiritual presence of Life as infinite Truth without an
9 unlikeness, and the loss of Love as ever present and
universal.

Divine Science explains the abstract statement that
12 there is one Mind by the following self-evident propo-

The divine
standard of
perfection

sition: If God, or good, is real, then evil, the
unlikeness of God, is unreal. And evil can
15 only seem to be real by giving reality to the
unreal. The children of God have but one Mind. How
can good lapse into evil, when God, the Mind of man,
18 never sins? The standard of perfection was originally
God and man. Has God taken down His own standard,
and has man fallen?

21 God is the creator of man, and, the divine Principle
of man remaining perfect, the divine idea or reflection,
man, remains perfect. Man is the expression

Indestructible
relationship

24 of God's being. If there ever was a moment
when man did not express the divine perfection, then there was a moment when man did not express
27 God, and consequently a time when Deity was unexpressed — that is, without entity. If man has lost perfection, then he has lost his perfect Principle, the divine
30 Mind. If man ever existed without this perfect Principle
or Mind, then man's existence was a myth.

The relations of God and man, divine Principle and

idea, are indestructible in Science; and Science knows 1
no lapse from nor return to harmony, but holds the divine
order or spiritual law, in which God and all that He cre- 3
ates are perfect and eternal, to have remained unchanged
in its eternal history.

The unlikeness of Truth, — named *error*, — the op- 6
posite of Science, and the evidence before the five corporeal senses, afford no indication of the grand   Celestial
facts of being; even as these so-called senses   evidence   9
receive no intimation of the earth's motions or of the
science of astronomy, but yield assent to astronomical
propositions on the authority of natural science.   12

The facts of divine Science should be admitted, —
although the evidence as to these facts is not supported
by evil, by matter, or by material sense, — because the 15
evidence that God and man coexist is fully sustained by
spiritual sense. Man is, and forever has been, God's reflection. God is infinite, therefore ever present, and 18
there is no other power nor presence. Hence the spirituality of the universe is the only fact of creation. "Let
God be true, but every [material] man a liar."   21

Question. — Are doctrines and creeds a benefit to man?
Answer. — The author subscribed to an orthodox
creed in early youth, and tried to adhere to it until she 24
caught the first gleam of that which inter-   The test of
prets God as above mortal sense. This   experience
view rebuked human beliefs, and gave the spiritual im- 27
port, expressed through Science, of all that proceeds
from the divine Mind. Since then her highest creed has
been divine Science, which, reduced to human apprehen- 30
sion, she has named Christian Science. This Science

1 teaches man that God is the only Life, and that this Life
is Truth and Love; that God is to be understood, adored,
3 and demonstrated; that divine Truth casts out suppositional error and heals the sick.

The way which leads to Christian Science is straight
6 and narrow. God has set His signet upon Science, mak-

God's law   ing it coordinate with all that is real and only
destroys evil   with that which is harmonious and eternal.
9 Sickness, sin, and death, being inharmonious, do not
originate in God nor belong to His government. His
law, rightly understood, destroys them. Jesus furnished
12 proofs of these statements.

Question. — What is error?
Answer. — Error is a supposition that pleasure and
15 pain, that intelligence, substance, life, are existent in mat-

Evanescent   ter. Error is neither Mind nor one of Mind's
materiality   faculties. Error is the contradiction of Truth.
18 Error is a belief without understanding. Error is unreal
because untrue. It is that which seemeth to be and is not.
If error were true, its truth would be error, and we should
21 have a self-evident absurdity — namely, *erroneous truth.*
Thus we should continue to lose the standard of Truth.

Question. — Is there no sin?
24 *Answer.* — All reality is in God and His creation, harmonious and eternal. That which He creates is good,

Unrealities   and He makes all that is made. Therefore
27 that seem real   the only reality of sin, sickness, or death is
the awful fact that unrealities seem real to human, erring
belief, until God strips off their disguise. They are not
30 true, because they are not of God. We learn in Christian

Science that all inharmony of mortal mind or body is illu- 1
sion, possessing neither reality nor identity though seeming
to be real and identical.   3
The Science of Mind disposes of all evil. Truth, God,
is not the father of error. Sin, sickness, and death are
to be classified as effects of error. Christ Christ the 6
came to destroy the belief of sin. The God-   ideal Truth
principle is omnipresent and omnipotent. God is everywhere, and nothing apart from Him is present or has 9
power. Christ is the ideal Truth, that comes to heal
sickness and sin through Christian Science, and attributes
all power to God. Jesus is the name of the man who, 12
more than all other men, has presented Christ, the true
idea of God, healing the sick and the sinning and destroying the power of death. Jesus is the human man, and 15
Christ is the divine idea; hence the duality of Jesus the
Christ.

In an age of ecclesiastical despotism, Jesus introduced 18
the teaching and practice of Christianity, affording the
proof of Christianity's truth and love; but to Jesus not
reach his example and to test its unerring Sci-   God   21
ence according to his rule, healing sickness, sin, and
death, a better understanding of God as divine Principle, Love, rather than personality or the man Jesus, is 24
required.

Jesus established what he said by demonstration,
thus making his acts of higher importance than his 27
words. He proved what he taught. This Jesus not
is the Science of Christianity. Jesus *proved* understood
the Principle, which heals the sick and casts out error, 30
to be divine. Few, however, except his students understood in the least his teachings and their glorious

1 proofs, — namely, that Life, Truth, and Love (the Principle of this unacknowledged Science) destroy all error,
3 evil, disease, and death.

The reception accorded to Truth in the early Christian era is repeated to-day. Whoever introduces the
6   Miracles   Science of Christianity will be scoffed at and
   rejected   scourged with worse cords than those which
cut the flesh. To the ignorant age in which it first
9 appears, Science seems to be a mistake, — hence the
misinterpretation and consequent maltreatment which
it receives. Christian marvels (and *marvel* is the sim-
12 ple meaning of the Greek word rendered *miracle* in the
New Testament) will be misunderstood and misused
by many, until the glorious Principle of these marvels is
15 gained.

If sin, sickness, and death are as real as Life, Truth,
and Love, then they must all be from the same source;
18   Divine   God must be their author. Now Jesus came
   fulfilment   to destroy sin, sickness, and death; yet the
Scriptures aver, "I am not come to destroy, but to fulfil."
21 Is it possible, then, to believe that the evils which Jesus
lived to destroy are real or the offspring of the divine
will?

24   Despite the hallowing influence of Truth in the destruction of error, must error still be immortal? Truth
   Truth   spares all that is true. If evil is real, Truth
27 destroys falsity must make it so; but error, not Truth, is
the author of the unreal, and the unreal vanishes,
while all that is real is eternal. The apostle says that
30 the mission of Christ is to "destroy the works of the
devil." Truth destroys falsity and error, for light and
darkness cannot dwell together. Light extinguishes the

darkness, and the Scripture declares that there is "no 1
night there." To Truth there is no error, — all is Truth.
To infinite Spirit there is no matter, — all is Spirit, divine 3
Principle and its idea.

Question. — What is man?
Answer. — Man is not matter; he is not made up of 6
brain, blood, bones, and other material elements. The
Scriptures inform us that man is made in   Fleshly
the image and likeness of God. Matter is   factors unreal   9
not that likeness. The likeness of Spirit cannot be so
unlike Spirit. Man is spiritual and perfect; and because he is spiritual and perfect, he must be so under- 12
stood in Christian Science. Man is idea, the image, of
Love; he is not physique. He is the compound idea of
God, including all right ideas; the generic term for 15
all that reflects God's image and likeness; the conscious
identity of being as found in Science, in which man is
the reflection of God, or Mind, and therefore is eternal; 18
that which has no separate mind from God; that which
has not a single quality underived from Deity; that which
possesses no life, intelligence, nor creative power of his 21
own, but reflects spiritually all that belongs to his Maker.

And God said: "Let us make man in our image, after
our likeness; and let them have dominion over the fish 24
of the sea, and over the fowl of the air, and over the cattle,
and over all the earth, and over every creeping thing that
creepeth upon the earth."   27
Man is incapable of sin, sickness, and death. The
real man cannot depart from holiness, nor   Man
can God, by whom man is evolved, engender   unfallen   30
the capacity or freedom to sin. A mortal sinner is not

1 God's man. Mortals are the counterfeits of immortals.
They are the children of the wicked one, or the one evil,
3 which declares that man begins in dust or as a material
embryo. In divine Science, God and the real man are
inseparable as divine Principle and idea.

6 Error, urged to its final limits, is self-destroyed.
Error will cease to claim that soul is in body, that life
Mortals are and intelligence are in matter, and that
9 not immortals this matter is man. God is the Principle of
man, and man is the idea of God. Hence man is not
mortal nor material. Mortals will disappear, and im-
12 mortals, or the children of God, will appear as the only
and eternal verities of man. Mortals are not fallen children of God. They never had a perfect state of being,
15 which may subsequently be regained. They were, from
the beginning of mortal history, "conceived in sin and
brought forth in iniquity." Mortality is finally swallowed
18 up in immortality. Sin, sickness, and death must disappear to give place to the facts which belong to immortal
man.

21 Learn this, O mortal, and earnestly seek the spiritual
status of man, which is outside of all material selfhood.
Imperishable Remember that the Scriptures say of mortal
24 identity man: "As for man, his days are as grass: as
a flower of the field, so he flourisheth. For the wind
passeth over it, and it is gone; and the place thereof shall
27 know it no more."

When speaking of God's children, not the children of
men, Jesus said, "The kingdom of God is within you;"
30 The kingdom that is, Truth and Love reign in the real
within man, showing that man in God's image is
unfallen and eternal. Jesus beheld in Science the per-

fect man, who appeared to him where sinning mortal 1
man appears to mortals. In this perfect man the Saviour
saw God's own likeness, and this correct view of man 3
healed the sick. Thus Jesus taught that the kingdom
of God is intact, universal, and that man is pure and holy.
Man is not a material habitation for Soul; he is himself 6
spiritual. Soul, being Spirit, is seen in nothing imperfect
nor material.

Whatever is material is mortal. To the five corporeal 9
senses, man appears to be matter and mind united; but
Christian Science reveals man as the idea of
God, and declares the corporeal senses to be   Material
body never 12
God's idea
mortal and erring illusions. Divine Science
shows it to be impossible that a material body, though
interwoven with matter's highest stratum, misnamed 15
mind, should be man, — the genuine and perfect man,
the immortal idea of being, indestructible and eternal.
Were it otherwise, man would be annihilated.   18

Question. — What are body and Soul?

Answer. — Identity is the reflection of Spirit, the reflection in multifarious forms of the living Principle, 21
Love. Soul is the substance, Life, and intelli-   Reflection
gence of man, which is individualized, but not   of Spirit
in matter. Soul can never reflect anything inferior to 24
Spirit.

Man is the expression of Soul. The Indians caught
some glimpses of the underlying reality, when   Man 27
they called a certain beautiful lake "the smile   inseparable
from Spirit
of the Great Spirit." Separated from man,
who expresses Soul, Spirit would be a nonentity; man, 30
divorced from Spirit, would lose his entity. But there is,

1 there can be, no such division, for man is coexistent with
God.

3   What evidence of Soul or of immortality have you
within mortality?   Even according to the teachings of
     A vacant   natural science, man has never beheld Spirit
6   domicile   or Soul leaving a body or entering it. What
basis is there for the theory of indwelling spirit, except
the claim of mortal belief?   What would be thought of
9 the declaration that a house was inhabited, and by a certain class of persons, when no such persons were ever seen
to go into the house or to come out of it, nor were they
12 even visible through the windows?   Who can see a soul
in the body?

Question. — Does brain think, and do nerves feel, and
15 is there intelligence in matter?

Answer. — No, not if God is true and mortal man a
liar.   The assertion that there can be pain or pleasure
18   Harmonious   in matter is erroneous.   That body is most
     functions   harmonious in which the discharge of the nat-
ural functions is least noticeable.   How can intelligence
21 dwell in matter when matter is non-intelligent and
brain-lobes cannot think?   Matter cannot perform the
functions of Mind.   Error says, "I am man;" but this
24 belief is mortal and far from actual.   From beginning
to end, whatever is mortal is composed of material human beliefs and of nothing else.   That only is real which
27 reflects God.   St. Paul said, "But when it pleased God,
who separated me from my mother's womb, and called me
by His grace, . . . I conferred not with flesh and blood."
30   *Mortal man* is really a self-contradictory phrase, for
man is not mortal, "neither indeed can be;" man is im-

mortal. If a child is the offspring of physical sense and 1
not of Soul, the child must have a material, not a spiritual origin. With what truth, then, could the   Immortal   3
Scriptural rejoicing be uttered by any mother,   birthright
"I have gotten a man from the Lord"? On the contrary, if aught comes from God, it cannot be mortal and 6
material; it must be immortal and spiritual.

Matter is neither self-existent nor a product of Spirit.
An image of mortal thought, reflected on the retina, is 9
all that the eye beholds. Matter cannot see,   Matter's
feel, hear, taste, nor smell. It is not self-   supposed
                                    selfhood
cognizant, — cannot feel itself, see itself, nor   12
understand itself. Take away so-called mortal mind,
which constitutes matter's supposed selfhood, and matter
can take no cognizance of matter. Does that which we 15
call dead ever see, hear, feel, or use any of the physical
senses?

"In the beginning God created the heaven and the 18
earth. And the earth was without form, and void; and
darkness was upon the face of the deep."   Chaos and
(Genesis i. 1, 2.) In the vast forever, in the   darkness   21
Science and truth of being, the only facts are Spirit
and its innumerable creations. Darkness and chaos
are the imaginary opposites of light, understanding, 24
and eternal harmony, and they are the elements of
nothingness.

We admit that black is not a color, because it reflects 27
no light. So evil should be denied identity or power,
because it has none of the divine hues. Paul   Spiritual
says: "For the invisible things of Him, from   reflection   30
the creation of the world, are clearly seen, being understood by the things that are made." (Romans i. 20.)

1 When the substance of Spirit appears in Christian Science, the nothingness of matter is recognized. Where
3 the spirit of God is, and there is no place where God is not, evil becomes nothing, — the opposite of the something of Spirit. If there is no spiritual reflection, then
6 there remains only the darkness of vacuity and not a trace of heavenly tints.

Nerves are an element of the belief that there is sensa-
9 tion in matter, whereas matter is devoid of sensation.

Harmony from Spirit   Consciousness, as well as action, is governed by Mind, — is in God, the origin and gov-
12 ernor of all that Science reveals. Material sense has its realm apart from Science in the unreal. Harmonious action proceeds from Spirit, God. Inharmony has no
15 Principle; its action is erroneous and presupposes man to be in matter. Inharmony would make matter the cause as well as the effect of intelligence, or Soul, thus
18 attempting to separate Mind from God.

Man is not God, and God is not man. Again, God, or good, never made man capable of sin. It is the oppo-
21 Evil non-existent   site of good — that is, evil — which seems to make men capable of wrong-doing. Hence, evil is but an illusion, and it has no real basis. Evil is a
24 false belief. God is not its author. The supposititious parent of evil is a lie.

The Bible declares: "All things were made by Him
27 [the divine Word]; and without Him was not anything

Vapor and nothingness   made that was made." This is the eternal verity of divine Science. If sin, sickness, and
30 death were understood as nothingness, they would disappear. As vapor melts before the sun, so evil would vanish before the reality of good. One must hide the

other. How important, then, to choose good as the 1
reality! Man is tributary to God, Spirit, and to nothing
else. God's being is infinity, freedom, harmony, and 3
boundless bliss. "Where the Spirit of the Lord is,
there is liberty." Like the archpriests of yore, man is
free "to enter into the holiest," — the realm of God.   6
     Material sense never helps mortals to understand
Spirit, God. Through spiritual sense only, man comprehends and loves Deity. The various con-   The fruit   9
tradictions of the Science of Mind by the ma-   forbidden
terial senses do not change the unseen Truth, which remains forever intact. The forbidden fruit of knowledge, 12
against which wisdom warns man, is the testimony of
error, declaring existence to be at the mercy of death,
and good and evil to be capable of commingling. This 15
is the significance of the Scripture concerning this "tree
of the knowledge of good and evil," — this growth of
material belief, of which it is said: "In the day that thou 18
eatest thereof thou shalt surely die." Human hypotheses
first assume the reality of sickness, sin, and death, and
then assume the necessity of these evils because of their 21
admitted actuality. These human verdicts are the pro-
curers of all discord.
     If Soul sins, it must be mortal. Sin has the elements 24
of self-destruction. It cannot sustain itself. If sin is
supported, God must uphold it, and this is   Sense and
impossible, since Truth cannot support error.   pure Soul   27
Soul is the divine Principle of man and never sins, —
hence the immortality of Soul. In Science we learn that
it is material sense, not Soul, which sins; and it will be 30
found that it is the sense of sin which is lost, and not a
sinful soul. When reading the Scriptures, the substitu-

1 tion of the word *sense* for *soul* gives the exact meaning in
a majority of cases.

3   Human thought has adulterated the meaning of the
word *soul* through the hypothesis that soul is both an evil
      Soul   and a good intelligence, resident in matter.
6   defined   The proper use of the word *soul* can always
be gained by substituting the word *God,* where the deific
meaning is required. In other cases, use the word *sense,*
9 and you will have the scientific signification. As used
in Christian Science, Soul is properly the synonym of
Spirit, or God; but out of Science, soul is identical with
12 sense, with material sensation.

   Question. — Is it important to understand these explanations in order to heal the sick?
15   *Answer.* — It is, since Christ is "the way" and the
truth casting out all error. Jesus called himself "the
    Sonship   Son of man," but not the son of Joseph. As
18   of Jesus   woman is but a species of the genera, he was
literally the Son of Man. Jesus was the highest human
concept of the perfect man. He was inseparable from
21 Christ, the Messiah, — the divine idea of God outside
the flesh. This enabled Jesus to demonstrate his control over matter. Angels announced to the Wisemen of
24 old this dual appearing, and angels whisper it, through
faith, to the hungering heart in every age.

   Sickness is part of the error which Truth casts out.
27 Error will not expel error. Christian Science is the law
    Sickness   of Truth, which heals the sick on the basis
    erroneous   of the one Mind or God. It can heal in no
30 other way, since the human, mortal mind so-called is not
a healer, but causes the belief in disease.

Then comes the question, how do drugs, hygiene, and 1
animal magnetism heal? It may be affirmed that they
do not heal, but only relieve suffering tempo- *True healing* 3
rarily, exchanging one disease for another. *transcendent*
We classify disease as error, which nothing but Truth or
Mind can heal, and this Mind must be divine, not human. 6
Mind transcends all other power, and will ultimately supersede all other means in healing. In order to heal by
Science, you must not be ignorant of the moral and spir- 9
itual demands of Science nor disobey them. Moral ignorance or sin affects your demonstration, and hinders its
approach to the standard in Christian Science. 12

After the author's sacred discovery, she affixed the
name "Science" to Christianity, the name "error" to
corporeal sense, and the name "substance" to *Terms* 15
Mind. Science has called the world to battle *adopted by*
the author
over this issue and its demonstration, which
heals the sick, destroys error, and reveals the universal 18
harmony. To those natural Christian Scientists, the ancient worthies, and to Christ Jesus, God certainly revealed
the spirit of Christian Science, if not the absolute letter. 21

Because the Science of Mind seems to bring into dis-
honor the ordinary scientific schools, which wrestle with
material observations alone, this Science has *Science* 24
met with opposition; but if any system honors *the way*
God, it ought to receive aid, not opposition, from all thinking persons. And Christian Science does honor God as 27
no other theory honors Him, and it does this in the way
of His appointing, by doing many wonderful works
through the divine name and nature. One must fulfil 30
one's mission without timidity or dissimulation, for to be
well done, the work must be done unselfishly. Christianity

1 will never be based on a divine Principle and so found to
be unerring, until its absolute Science is reached. When
3 this is accomplished, neither pride, prejudice, bigotry,
nor envy can wash away its foundation, for it is built upon
the rock, Christ.

6   *Question.* — Does Christian Science, or metaphysical
healing, include medication, material hygiene, mesmerism, hypnotism, theosophy, or spiritualism?
9   *Answer.* — Not one of them is included in it. In divine Science, the supposed laws of matter yield to the
      Mindless   law of Mind. What are termed natural
12   methods   science and material laws are the objective
states of mortal mind. The physical universe expresses
the conscious and unconscious thoughts of mortals.
15 Physical force and mortal mind are one. Drugs and
hygiene oppose the supremacy of the divine Mind.
Drugs and inert matter are unconscious, mindless. Cer-
18 tain results, supposed to proceed from drugs, are really
caused by the faith in them which the false human consciousness is educated to feel.

21   Mesmerism is mortal, material illusion. Animal magnetism is the voluntary or involuntary action of error
      Animal   in all its forms; it is the human antipode
24 magnetism error of divine Science. Science must triumph
over material sense, and Truth over error, thus putting
an end to the hypotheses involved in all false theories
27 and practices.

Question. — Is materiality the concomitant of spirituality, and is material sense a necessary preliminary to
30 the understanding and expression of Spirit?

Answer. — If error is necessary to define or to reveal 1
Truth, the answer is yes; but not otherwise. *Material*
sense is an absurd phrase, for matter has no   Error only   3
sensation. Science declares that Mind, not   ephemeral
matter, sees, hears, feels, speaks. Whatever contradicts
this statement is the false sense, which ever betrays 6
mortals into sickness, sin, and death. If the unimpor-
tant and evil appear, only soon to disappear because
of their uselessness or their iniquity, then these ephem- 9
eral views of error ought to be obliterated by Truth.
Why malign Christian Science for instructing mortals how
to make sin, disease, and death appear more and more 12
unreal?

Emerge gently from matter into Spirit. Think not
to thwart the spiritual ultimate of all things, but come 15
naturally into Spirit through better health and   Scientific
morals and as the result of spiritual growth.   translations
Not death, but the understanding of Life, makes man im- 18
mortal. The belief that life can be in matter or soul in
body, and that man springs from dust or from an egg,
is the result of the mortal error which Christ, or Truth, 21
destroys by fulfilling the spiritual law of being, in which
man is perfect, even as the "Father which is in heaven
is perfect." If thought yields its dominion to other 24
powers, it cannot outline on the body its own beautiful
images, but it effaces them and delineates foreign agents,
called disease and sin.   27

The heathen gods of mythology controlled war and
agriculture as much as nerves control sensation or
muscles measure strength. To say that   Material   30
strength is in matter, is like saying that the   beliefs
power is in the lever. The notion of any life or intelli-

1 gence in matter is without foundation in fact, and you
can have no faith in falsehood when you have learned
3 falsehood's true nature.

Suppose one accident happens to the eye, another to
the ear, and so on, until every corporeal sense is quenched.
6 Sense versus   What is man's remedy? To die, that he may
   Soul   regain these senses? Even then he must gain
spiritual understanding and spiritual sense in order to
9 possess immortal consciousness. Earth's preparatory
school must be improved to the utmost. In reality man
never dies. The belief that he dies will not establish his
12 scientific harmony. Death is not the result of Truth but
of error, and one error will not correct another.

Jesus proved by the prints of the nails, that his body
15 was the same immediately after death as before. If death
   Death   restores sight, sound, and strength to man,
   an error   then death is not an enemy but a better friend
18 than Life. Alas for the blindness of belief, which makes
harmony conditional upon death and matter, and yet
supposes Mind unable to produce harmony! So long
21 as this error of belief remains, mortals will continue mortal in belief and subject to chance and change.

Sight, hearing, all the spiritual senses of man, are
24 eternal. They cannot be lost. Their reality and immor-
   Permanent   tality are in Spirit and understanding, not in
   sensibility matter, — hence their permanence. If this
27 were not so, man would be speedily annihilated. If the
five corporeal senses were the medium through which
to understand God, then palsy, blindness, and deafness
30 would place man in a terrible situation, where he would
be like those "having no hope, and without God in the
world;" but as a matter of fact, these calamities often

drive mortals to seek and to find a higher sense of happi- 1
ness and existence.

Life is deathless. Life is the origin and ultimate of 3
man, never attainable through death, but gained by walking in the pathway of Truth both before and

> Exercise
> of Mind- 6
> faculties

after that which is called death. There is more
Christianity in seeing and hearing spiritually
than materially. There is more Science in the perpetual
exercise of the Mind-faculties than in their loss. Lost 9
they cannot be, while Mind remains. The apprehension
of this gave sight to the blind and hearing to the deaf centuries ago, and it will repeat the wonder.   12

Question. — You speak of belief. Who or what is it
that believes?

Answer. — Spirit is all-knowing; this precludes the 15
need of believing. Matter cannot believe, and Mind
understands. The body cannot believe. The

> Understand-
> ing *versus* 18
> belief

believer and belief are one and are mortal.
Christian evidence is founded on Science or
demonstrable Truth, flowing from immortal Mind, and
there is in reality no such thing as *mortal* mind. Mere 21
belief is blindness without Principle from which to explain the reason of its hope. The belief that life is sentient and intelligent matter is erroneous.   24

The Apostle James said, "Show me thy faith without
thy works, and I will show thee my faith by my works."
The understanding that Life is God, Spirit, lengthens 27
our days by strengthening our trust in the deathless
reality of Life, its almightiness and immortality.

This faith relies upon an understood Principle. This 30
Principle makes whole the diseased, and brings out the

mind alone possess all faculties. 2

1 enduring and harmonious phases of things. The result
of our teachings is their sufficient confirmation. When,
3   Confirmation on the strength of these instructions, you are
by healing   able to banish a severe malady, the cure shows
that you understand this teaching, and therefore you re-
6 ceive the blessing of Truth.

The Hebrew and Greek words often translated *belief*
differ somewhat in meaning from that conveyed by the
9   Belief and English verb *believe;* they have more the sig-
firm trust   nificance of faith, understanding, trust, constancy, firmness. Hence the Scriptures often appear in
12 our common version to approve and endorse belief, when
they mean to enforce the necessity of understanding.

Question. — Do the five corporeal senses constitute
15 man?

Answer. — Christian Science sustains with immortal
proof the impossibility of any material sense, and defines
18   All faculties these so-called senses as *mortal beliefs,* the
from Mind   testimony of which cannot be true either of
man or of his Maker. The corporeal senses can take no
21 cognizance of spiritual reality and immortality. Nerves
have no more sensation, apart from what belief bestows upon them, than the fibres of a plant. Mind alone
24 possesses all faculties, perception, and comprehension.
Therefore mental endowments are not at the mercy of
organization and decomposition, — otherwise the very
27 worms could unfashion man. If it were possible for the
real senses of man to be injured, Soul could reproduce
them in all their perfection; but they cannot be dis-
30 turbed nor destroyed, since they exist in immortal Mind,
not in matter.

The less mind there is manifested in matter the better. 1
When the unthinking lobster loses its claw, the claw grows
again. If the Science of Life were understood, Possibilities 3
it would be found that the senses of Mind are of Life
never lost and that matter has no sensation. Then the
human limb would be replaced as readily as the lobster's 6
claw, — not with an artificial limb, but with the genuine
one. Any hypothesis which supposes life to be in matter
is an educated belief. In infancy this belief is not equal 9
to guiding the hand to the mouth; and as consciousness
develops, this belief goes out, — yields to the reality of
everlasting Life. 12

Corporeal sense defrauds and lies; it breaks all the
commands of the Mosaic Decalogue to meet its own demands. How then can this sense be the God- Decalogue 15
given channel to man of divine blessings or disregarded
understanding? How can man, reflecting God, be dependent on material means for knowing, hearing, seeing? 18
Who dares to say that the senses of man can be at one time
the medium for sinning against God, at another the medium for obeying God? An affirmative reply would con- 21
tradict the Scripture, for the same fountain sendeth not
forth sweet waters and bitter.

The corporeal senses are the only source of evil or 24
error. Christian Science shows them to be false, because matter has no sensation, and no organic Organic
construction can give it hearing and sight nor construction 27
make it the medium of Mind. Outside the valueless
material sense of things, all is harmony. A wrong sense
of God, man, and creation is *non-sense*, want of sense. 30
Mortal belief would have the material senses sometimes
good and sometimes bad. It assures mortals that there

1 is real pleasure in sin; but the grand truths of Christian
Science dispute this error.

3 Will-power is but a product of belief, and this belief
commits depredations on harmony. Human will is an
animal propensity, not a faculty of Soul.

Will-power
an animal
propensity

6 Hence it cannot govern man aright. Christian Science reveals Truth and Love as the
motive-powers of man. Will — blind, stubborn, and head-
9 long — cooperates with appetite and passion. From this
cooperation arises its evil. From this also comes its powerlessness, since all power belongs to God, good.

12 The Science of Mind needs to be understood. Until
it is understood, mortals are more or less deprived of
Truth. Human theories are helpless to make

Theories
helpless

15 man harmonious or immortal, since he is so
already, according to Christian Science. Our only need
is to know this and reduce to practice the real man's di-
18 vine Principle, Love.

"Quench not the Spirit. Despise not prophesyings."
Human belief — or knowledge gained from the so-called

True nature
and origin

21 material senses — would, by fair logic, annihilate man along with the dissolving elements
of clay. The scientifically Christian explanations of the
24 nature and origin of man destroy all material sense with
immortal testimony. This immortal testimony ushers
in the spiritual sense of being, which can be obtained
27 in no other way.

Sleep and mesmerism explain the mythical nature of
material sense. Sleep shows material sense as either

Sleep an
illusion

30 oblivion, nothingness, or an illusion or dream.
Under the mesmeric illusion of belief, a man
will think that he is freezing when he is warm, and that he

is swimming when he is on dry land. Needle-thrusts will 1
not hurt him. A delicious perfume will seem intolerable.
Animal magnetism thus uncovers material sense, and 3
shows it to be a belief without actual foundation or validity. Change the belief, and the sensation changes.
Destroy the belief, and the sensation disappears.   6

Material man is made up of involuntary and voluntary
error, of a negative right and a positive wrong, the latter
calling itself right. Man's spiritual individual- Man linked 9
ity is never wrong. It is the likeness of man's with Spirit
Maker. Matter cannot connect mortals with the true
origin and facts of being, in which all must end. It is only 12
by acknowledging the supremacy of Spirit, which annuls
the claims of matter, that mortals can lay off mortality and
find the indissoluble spiritual link which establishes man 15
forever in the divine likeness, inseparable from his creator.

The belief that matter and mind are one, — that matter is awake at one time and asleep at another, some- 18
times presenting no appearance of mind, — Material man
this belief culminates in another belief, that as a dream
man dies. Science reveals material man as never the real 21
being. The dream or belief goes on, whether our eyes are
closed or open. In sleep, memory and consciousness are
lost from the body, and they wander whither they will 24
apparently with their own separate embodiment. Personality is not the individuality of man. A wicked man
may have an attractive personality.   27

When we are awake, we dream of the pains and pleasures of matter. Who will say, even though he Spiritual
does not understand Christian Science, that existence the 30
this dream — rather than the dreamer — may one fact
not be mortal man? Who can rationally say otherwise,

1 when the dream leaves mortal man intact in body and
thought, although the so-called dreamer is unconscious?
3 For right reasoning there should be but one fact before
the thought, namely, spiritual existence. In reality there
is no other existence, since Life cannot be united to its
6 unlikeness, mortality.

Being is holiness, harmony, immortality. It is already
proved that a knowledge of this, even in small degree,
9 *Mind one* will uplift the physical and moral standard
and all of mortals, will increase longevity, will purify
and elevate character. Thus progress will finally destroy
12 all error, and bring immortality to light. We know that
a statement proved to be good must be correct. New
thoughts are constantly obtaining the floor. These two
15 contradictory theories — that matter is something, or
that all is Mind — will dispute the ground, until one is
acknowledged to be the victor. Discussing his cam-
18 paign, General Grant said: "I propose to fight it out on
this line, if it takes all summer." Science says: All is
Mind and Mind's idea. You must fight it out on this
21 line. Matter can afford you no aid.

The notion that mind and matter commingle in the
human illusion as to sin, sickness, and death must even-
24 *Scientific* tually submit to the Science of Mind, which
ultimatum denies this notion. *God is Mind, and God is
infinite; hence all is Mind.* On this statement rests the
27 Science of being, and the Principle of this Science is divine, demonstrating harmony and immortality.

The conservative theory, long believed, is that there
30 are two factors, matter and mind, uniting on some impossible basis. This theory would keep truth and error
always at war. Victory would perch on neither banner.

On the other hand, Christian Science speedily shows 1
Truth to be triumphant. To corporeal sense, the sun
appears to rise and set, and the earth to stand   Victory   3
still; but astronomical science contradicts this,   for Truth
and explains the solar system as working on a different plan. All the evidence of physical sense and all the 6
knowledge obtained from physical sense must yield to
Science, to the immortal truth of all things.

Question. — Will you explain sickness and show how it 9
is to be healed?
Answer. — The method of Christian Science Mind-healing is touched upon in a previous chapter entitled Christian 12
Science Practice. A full answer to the above   Mental
question involves teaching, which enables the   preparation
healer to demonstrate and prove for himself the Principle 15
and rule of Christian Science or metaphysical healing.
Mind must be found superior to all the beliefs of the
five corporeal senses, and able to destroy all ills. Sick- 18
ness is a belief, which must be annihilated by Mind destroys
the divine Mind. Disease is an experience of   all ills
so-called mortal mind. It is fear made manifest on the 21
body. Christian Science takes away this physical sense
of discord, just as it removes any other sense of moral or
mental inharmony. That man is material, and that mat- 24
ter suffers, — these propositions can only seem real and
natural in illusion. Any sense of soul in matter is not the
reality of being.   27
If Jesus awakened Lazarus from the dream, illusion, of
death, this proved that the Christ could improve on a false
sense. Who dares to doubt this consummate test of the 30
power and willingness of divine Mind to hold man forever

1 intact in his perfect state, and to govern man's entire
action? Jesus said: "Destroy this temple [body], and
3 in three days I [Mind] will raise it up;" and he did this
for tired humanity's reassurance.

Is it not a species of infidelity to believe that so great
6 a work as the Messiah's was done for himself or for God,

Inexhaustible who needed no help from Jesus' example to
divine Love preserve the eternal harmony? But mortals
9 did need this help, and Jesus pointed the way for them.
Divine Love always has met and always will meet every
human need. It is not well to imagine that Jesus demon-
12 strated the divine power to heal only for a select number
or for a limited period of time, since to all mankind and
in every hour, divine Love supplies all good.

15 The miracle of grace is no miracle to Love. Jesus
demonstrated the inability of corporeality, as well as the

Reason infinite ability of Spirit, thus helping erring
18 and Science human sense to flee from its own convictions
and seek safety in divine Science. Reason, rightly directed, serves to correct the errors of corporeal sense; but
21 sin, sickness, and death will seem real (even as the experiences of the sleeping dream seem real) until the Science of man's eternal harmony breaks their illusion with
24 the unbroken reality of scientific being.

Which of these two theories concerning man are you
ready to accept? One is the mortal testimony, changing,
27 dying, unreal. The other is the eternal and real evidence,
bearing Truth's signet, its lap piled high with immortal
fruits.

30 Our Master cast out devils (evils) and healed the sick.
It should be said of his followers also, that they cast fear
and all evil out of themselves and others and heal the sick.

God will heal the sick through man, whenever man is 1
governed by God. Truth casts out error now   Followers
as surely as it did nineteen centuries ago. All   of Jesus   3
of Truth is not understood; hence its healing power is not
fully demonstrated.

If sickness is true or the idea of Truth, you cannot 6
destroy sickness, and it would be absurd to try. Then
classify sickness and error as our Master did,   Destruction
when he spoke of the sick, "whom Satan hath   of all evil   9
bound," and find a sovereign antidote for error in the life-
giving power of Truth acting on human belief, a power
which opens the prison doors to such as are bound, and 12
sets the captive free physically and morally.

When the illusion of sickness or sin tempts you, cling
steadfastly to God and His idea. Allow nothing but His 15
likeness to abide in your thought. Let neither   Steadfast and
fear nor doubt overshadow your clear sense and   calm trust
calm trust, that the recognition of life harmonious — as 18
Life eternally is — can destroy any painful sense of, or
belief in, that which Life is not. Let Christian Science,
instead of corporeal sense, support your understanding of 21
being, and this understanding will supplant error with
Truth, replace mortality with immortality, and silence discord with harmony.   24

Question. — How can I progress most rapidly in the
understanding of Christian Science?

Answer. — Study thoroughly the letter and imbibe 27
the spirit. Adhere to the divine Principle of Christian Science and follow the behests of God,   Rudiments
abiding steadfastly in wisdom, Truth, and   and growth   30
Love. In the Science of Mind, you will soon ascertain

1 that error cannot destroy error. You will also learn
that in Science there is no transfer of evil suggestions
3 from one mortal to another, for there is but one Mind,
and this ever-present omnipotent Mind is reflected by
man and governs the entire universe. You will learn
6 that in Christian Science the first duty is to obey
God, to have one Mind, and to love another as
yourself.

9   We all must learn that Life is God. Ask yourself:
Am I living the life that approaches the supreme good?
Condition   Am I demonstrating the healing power of
12 of progress   Truth and Love? If so, then the way will
grow brighter "unto the perfect day." Your fruits
will prove what the understanding of God brings to man.
15 Hold perpetually this thought, — that it is the spiritual
idea, the Holy Ghost and Christ, which enables you to
demonstrate, with scientific certainty, the rule of healing,
18 based upon its divine Principle, Love, underlying, over-
lying, and encompassing all true being.

"The sting of death is sin; and the strength of sin is
21 the law," — the law of mortal belief, at war with the
Triumph   facts of immortal Life, even with the spiritual
over death   law which says to the grave, "Where is thy
24 victory?"   But "when this corruptible shall have put
on incorruption, and this mortal shall have put on immortality, then shall be brought to pass the saying that
27 is written, Death is swallowed up in victory."

Question. — Have Christian Scientists any religious
creed?
30   *Answer.* — They have not, if by that term is meant
doctrinal beliefs. The following is a brief exposition of

the important points, or religious tenets, of Christian 1
Science: —

1. As adherents of Truth, we take the inspired Word 3
of the Bible as our sufficient guide to eternal Life.

2. We acknowledge and adore one supreme and infinite God. We acknowledge His Son, one Christ; the 6
Holy Ghost or divine Comforter; and man in God's
image and likeness.

3. We acknowledge God's forgiveness of sin in the 9
destruction of sin and the spiritual understanding that
casts out evil as unreal. But the belief in sin is punished so long as the belief lasts. 12

4. We acknowledge Jesus' atonement as the evidence of divine, efficacious Love, unfolding man's unity
with God through Christ Jesus the Way-shower; and 15
we acknowledge that man is saved through Christ,
through Truth, Life, and Love as demonstrated by the
Galilean Prophet in healing the sick and overcoming 18
sin and death.

5. We acknowledge that the crucifixion of Jesus and
his resurrection served to uplift faith to understand eter- 21
nal Life, even the allness of Soul, Spirit, and the nothingness of matter.

6. And we solemnly promise to watch, and pray for 24
that Mind to be in us which was also in Christ Jesus; to
do unto others as we would have them do unto us; and
to be merciful, just, and pure. 27

KEY TO THE SCRIPTURES

These things saith He that is holy, He that is true, He that hath the key of David, He that openeth, and no man shutteth; and shutteth, and no man openeth; I know thy works: behold, I have set before thee an open door, and no man can shut it. — REVELATION.

CHAPTER XV

Genesis

And I appeared unto Abraham, unto Isaac, and unto Jacob by the name of God Almighty; but by My name Jehovah was I not known to them. — EXODUS.

All things were made by Him; and without Him was not anything made that was made. In Him was life; and the life was the light of men. — JOHN.

SCIENTIFIC interpretation of the Scriptures prop- 1
erly starts with the beginning of the Old Testament, chiefly because the spiritual import of   Spiritual   3
the Word, in its earliest articulations, often   interpretation
seems so smothered by the immediate context as to
require explication; whereas the New Testament narra- 6
tives are clearer and come nearer the heart. Jesus illumines them, showing the poverty of mortal existence,
but richly recompensing human want and woe with 9
spiritual gain. The incarnation of Truth, that amplifi-
cation of wonder and glory which angels could only
whisper and which God illustrated by light and har- 12
mony, is consonant with ever-present Love. So-called
mystery and miracle, which subserve the end of natural
good, are explained by that Love for whose rest the 15
weary ones sigh when needing something more native
to their immortal cravings than the history of perpetual
evil.   18

501

1   A second necessity for beginning with Genesis is that
the living and real prelude of the older Scriptures is so
3   **Spiritual**   brief that it would almost seem, from the
overture   preponderance of unreality in the entire narrative, as if reality did not predominate over unreality,
6 the light over the dark, the straight line of Spirit over
the mortal deviations and inverted images of the creator
and His creation.

9   Spiritually followed, the book of Genesis is the history
of the untrue image of God, named a sinful mortal. This
Deflection   deflection of being, rightly viewed, serves to
12   **of being**   suggest the proper reflection of God and the
spiritual actuality of man, as given in the first chapter
of Genesis. Even thus the crude forms of human thought
15 take on higher symbols and significations, when scientifically Christian views of the universe appear, illuminat-
ing time with the glory of eternity.

18   In the following exegesis, each text is followed by its
spiritual interpretation according to the teachings of Christian Science.

21   EXEGESIS

    Genesis i. i.   In the beginning God created the heaven
and the earth.

24   The infinite has no beginning. This word *beginning*
is employed to signify *the only*, — that is, the eternal ver-
Ideas and   ity and unity of God and man, including
27   **identities**   the universe. The creative Principle — Life,
Truth, and Love — is God. The universe reflects God.
There is but one creator and one creation. This crea-

tion consists of the unfolding of spiritual ideas and their 1
identities, which are embraced in the infinite Mind and
forever reflected. These ideas range from the infini- 3
tesimal to infinity, and the highest ideas are the sons
and daughters of God.

Genesis i. 2. And the earth was without form, and void; 6
and darkness was upon the face of the deep. And the
spirit of God moved upon the face of the waters.

The divine Principle and idea constitute spiritual har- 9
mony, — heaven and eternity. In the universe of Truth,
matter is unknown. No supposition of error   Spiritual
enters there. Divine Science, the Word of   harmony   12
God, saith to the darkness upon the face of error, "God
is All-in-all," and the light of ever-present Love illumines
the universe. Hence the eternal wonder, — that infinite 15
space is peopled with God's ideas, reflecting Him in
countless spiritual forms.

Genesis i. 3. And God said, Let there be light: and 18
there was light.

Immortal and divine Mind presents the idea of God:
first, in light; second, in reflection; third, in spiritual and 21
immortal forms of beauty and goodness. But   Mind's idea
this Mind creates no element nor symbol of   faultless
discord and decay. God creates neither erring thought, 24
mortal life, mutable truth, nor variable love.

Genesis i. 4. And God saw the light, that it was good:
and God divided the light from the darkness.   27

God, Spirit, dwelling in infinite light and harmony

1 from which emanates the true idea, is never reflected by
aught but the good.

3 *Genesis* i. 5. And God called the light Day, and the
darkness He called Night. And the evening and the morning were the first day.

6   All questions as to the divine creation being both
spiritual and material are answered in this passage, for
    Light preced- though solar beams are not yet included in
9   ing the sun   the record of creation, still there is light. This
light is not from the sun nor from volcanic flames, but it
is the revelation of Truth and of spiritual ideas. This
12 also shows that there is no place where God's light is not
seen, since Truth, Life, and Love fill immensity and are
ever-present. Was not this a revelation instead of a
15 creation?

    The successive appearing of God's ideas is represented
as taking place on so many *evenings* and *mornings*, —
18 Evenings and words which indicate, in the absence of solar
    mornings   time, spiritually clearer views of Him, views
which are not implied by material darkness and dawn.
21 Here we have the explanation of another passage of
Scripture, that "one day is with the Lord as a thousand
years." The rays of infinite Truth, when gathered into
24 the focus of ideas, bring light instantaneously, whereas
a thousand years of human doctrines, hypotheses, and
vague conjectures emit no such effulgence.

27   Did infinite Mind create matter, and call it *light?*
Spirit is light, and the contradiction of Spirit is matter,
    Spirit versus darkness, and darkness obscures light. Mate-
30   darkness   rial sense is nothing but a supposition of the
absence of Spirit. No solar rays nor planetary revolutions

form the day of Spirit. Immortal Mind makes its own 1
record, but mortal mind, sleep, dreams, sin, disease, and
death have no record in the first chapter of Genesis. 3

Genesis i. 6. And God said, Let there be a firmament in
the midst of the waters, and let it divide the waters from
the waters. 6

Spiritual understanding, by which human conception,
material sense, is separated from Truth, is the firmament.
The divine Mind, not matter, creates all iden- Spiritual 9
tities, and they are forms of Mind, the ideas of firmament
Spirit apparent only as Mind, never as mindless matter
nor the so-called material senses. 12

Genesis i. 7. And God made the firmament, and divided
the waters which were under the firmament from the waters
which were above the firmament: and it was so. 15

Spirit imparts the understanding which uplifts consciousness and leads into all truth. The Psalmist saith:
"The Lord on high is mightier than the noise Understanding 18
of many waters, yea, than the mighty waves of imparted
the sea." Spiritual sense is the discernment of spiritual
good. Understanding is the line of demarcation between 21
the real and unreal. Spiritual understanding unfolds
Mind, — Life, Truth, and Love, — and demonstrates the
divine sense, giving the spiritual proof of the universe in 24
Christian Science.

This understanding is not intellectual, is not the result
of scholarly attainments; it is the reality of all things 27
brought to light. God's ideas reflect the im- Original
mortal, unerring, and infinite. The mortal, reflected
erring, and finite are human beliefs, which apportion to 30

1 themselves a task impossible for them, that of distinguish-
ing between the false and the true. Objects utterly un-
3 like the original do not reflect that original. Therefore
matter, not being the reflection of Spirit, has no real entity. Understanding is a quality of God, a quality which
6 separates Christian Science from supposition and makes
Truth final.

> Genesis i. 8. And God called the firmament Heaven.
9 And the evening and the morning were the second day.

Through divine Science, Spirit, God, unites understanding to eternal harmony. The calm and exalted
12   Exalted   thought or spiritual apprehension is at peace.
     thought   Thus the dawn of ideas goes on, forming each
successive stage of progress.

15   Genesis i. 9. And God said, Let the waters under the
heaven be gathered together unto one place, and let the dry
land appear: and it was so.

18   Spirit, God, gathers unformed thoughts into their
   Unfolding   proper channels, and unfolds these thoughts,
   of thoughts   even as He opens the petals of a holy purpose
21 in order that the purpose may appear.

> Genesis i. 10. And God called the dry land Earth; and
the gathering together of the waters called He Seas: and
24 God saw that it was good.

Here the human concept and divine idea seem confused by the translator, but they are not so in the scien-
27   Spirit names   tifically Christian meaning of the text. Upon
   and blesses   Adam devolved the pleasurable task of finding names for all material things, but Adam has not yet

appeared in the narrative. In metaphor, the *dry land* 1
illustrates the absolute formations instituted by Mind,
while *water* symbolizes the elements of Mind. Spirit duly 3
feeds and clothes every object, as it appears in the line
of spiritual creation, thus tenderly expressing the fatherhood and motherhood of God. Spirit names and blesses 6
all. Without natures particularly defined, objects and
subjects would be obscure, and creation would be full of
nameless offspring, — wanderers from the parent Mind, 9
strangers in a tangled wilderness.

Genesis i. 11. And God said, Let the earth bring forth
grass, the herb yielding seed, and the fruit tree yielding 12
fruit after his kind, whose seed is in itself, upon the earth:
and it was so.

The universe of Spirit reflects the creative power of 15
the divine Principle, or Life, which reproduces the multitudinous forms of Mind and governs the mul-   Divine
tiplication of the compound idea man. The   propagation 18
tree and herb do not yield fruit because of any propagating power of their own, but because they reflect the Mind
which includes all. A material world implies a mortal 21
mind and man a creator. The scientific divine creation
declares immortal Mind and the universe created by God.
Infinite Mind creates and governs all, from the men- 24
tal molecule to infinity. This divine Principle of all
expresses Science and art throughout His Ever-appearing
creation, and the immortality of man and the   creation 27
universe. Creation is ever appearing, and must ever continue to appear from the nature of its inexhaustible source.
Mortal sense inverts this appearing and calls ideas mate- 30
rial. Thus misinterpreted, the divine idea seems to fall

1 to the level of a human or material belief, called mortal
man. But the seed is in itself, only as the divine Mind
3 is All and reproduces all — as Mind is the multiplier,
and Mind's infinite idea, man and the universe, is the
product. The only intelligence or substance of a thought,
6 a seed, or a flower is God, the creator of it. Mind is the
Soul of all. Mind is Life, Truth, and Love which governs all.

9 *Genesis* i. 12. And the earth brought forth grass, and
herb yielding seed after his kind, and the tree yielding
fruit, whose seed was in itself, after his kind: and God saw
12 that it was good.

God determines the gender of His own ideas. Gender is mental, not material. The seed within itself is
15 Mind's pure the pure thought emanating from divine
thought Mind. The feminine gender is not yet expressed in the text. *Gender* means simply *kind* or *sort,*
18 and does not necessarily refer either to masculinity or
femininity. The word is not confined to sexuality, and
grammars always recognize a neuter gender, neither
21 male nor female. The Mind or intelligence of production names the female gender last in the ascending order
of creation. The intelligent individual idea, be it male
24 or female, rising from the lesser to the greater, unfolds
the infinitude of Love.

Genesis i. 13. And the evening and the morning were
27 the third day.

The third stage in the order of Christian Science is an
important one to the human thought, letting in the light

of spiritual understanding. This period corresponds to 1
the resurrection, when Spirit is discerned to be the Life of
all, and the deathless Life, or Mind, dependent   Rising to   3
upon no material organization. Our Master   the light
reappeared to his students, — to their apprehension he
rose from the grave, — on the third day of his ascending 6
thought, and so presented to them the certain sense of
eternal Life.

Genesis i. 14. And God said, Let there be lights in the 9
firmament of the heaven, to divide the day from the night;
and let them be for signs, and for seasons, and for days,
and years.   12

Spirit creates no other than heavenly or celestial bodies,
but the stellar universe is no more celestial than our earth.
This text gives the idea of the rarefaction of   Rarefaction   15
thought as it ascends higher. God forms and   of thought
peoples the universe. The light of spiritual understanding gives gleams of the infinite only, even as nebulæ indi- 18
cate the immensity of space.

So-called mineral, vegetable, and animal substances
are no more contingent now on time or material struc- 21
ture than they were when "the morning stars Divine nature
sang together." Mind made the "plant of   appearing
the field before it was in the earth." The periods of 24
spiritual ascension are the days and seasons of Mind's
creation, in which beauty, sublimity, purity, and holiness
— yea, the divine nature — appear in man and the uni- 27
verse never to disappear.

Knowing the Science of creation, in which all is Mind
and its ideas, Jesus rebuked the material thought of his 30
fellow-countrymen: "Ye can discern the face of the

1 sky; but can ye not discern the signs of the times?"
How much more should we seek to apprehend the spirit-
3 Spiritual ideas ual ideas of God, than to dwell on the objects
apprehended of sense! To discern the rhythm of Spirit
and to be holy, thought must be purely spiritual.

6   *Genesis* i. 15. And let them be for lights in the firmament of the heaven, to give light upon the earth: and it
was so.

9   Truth and Love enlighten the understanding, in whose
"light shall we see light;" and this illumination is reflected spiritually by all who walk in the light and turn
12 away from a false material sense.

Genesis i. 16. And God made two great lights; the
greater light to rule the day, and the lesser light to rule the
15 night: He made the stars also.

The sun is a metaphorical representation of Soul outside the body, giving existence and intelligence to the
18   Geology   universe. Love alone can impart the limit-
a failure   less idea of infinite Mind. Geology has never
explained the earth's formations; it cannot explain them.
21 There is no Scriptural allusion to solar light until time has
been already divided into evening and morning; and the
allusion to fluids (Genesis i. 2) indicates a supposed for-
24 mation of matter by the resolving of fluids into solids,
analogous to the suppositional resolving of thoughts into
material things.
27 Light is a symbol of Mind, of Life, Truth, and Love,
Spiritual   and not a vitalizing property of matter. Sci-
subdivision ence reveals only one Mind, and this one shin-
30 ing by its own light and governing the universe, including

man, in perfect harmony. This Mind forms ideas, its 1
own images, subdivides and radiates their borrowed light,
intelligence, and so explains the Scripture phrase, "whose 3
seed is in itself." Thus God's ideas "multiply and replenish the earth." The divine Mind supports the sublimity, magnitude, and infinitude of spiritual creation. 6

Genesis i. 17, 18. And God set them in the firmament of
the heaven, to give light upon the earth, and to rule over
the day and over the night, and to divide the light from the 9
darkness: and God saw that it was good.

In divine Science, which is the seal of Deity and has
the impress of heaven, God is revealed as in-   Darkness   12
finite light. In the eternal Mind, no night is   scattered
there.

Genesis i. 19. And the evening and the morning were 15
the fourth day.

The changing glow and full effulgence of God's infinite ideas, images, mark the periods of progress.   18

Genesis i. 20. And God said, Let the waters bring forth
abundantly the moving creature that hath life, and fowl
that may fly above the earth in the open firmament of 21
heaven.

To mortal mind, the universe is liquid, solid, and aëri-
form. Spiritually interpreted, rocks and mountains stand 24
for solid and grand ideas. Animals and mor-   Soaring
tals metaphorically present the gradation of   aspirations
mortal thought, rising in the scale of intelligence, taking 27
form in masculine, feminine, or neuter gender. The
fowls, which fly above the earth in the open firmament

1 of heaven, correspond to aspirations soaring beyond and
above corporeality to the understanding of the incorporeal
3 and divine Principle, Love.

Genesis i. 21.   And God created great whales, and every
living creature that moveth, which the waters brought forth
6 abundantly, after their kind, and every winged fowl after
his kind: and God saw that it was good.

Spirit is symbolized by strength, presence, and power,
9 and also by holy thoughts, winged with Love. These an-

Seraphic   gels of His presence, which have the holiest
symbols   charge, abound in the spiritual atmosphere of
12 Mind, and consequently reproduce their own characteristics. Their individual forms we know not, but we do
know that their natures are allied to God's nature; and
15 spiritual blessings, thus typified, are the externalized, yet
subjective, states of faith and spiritual understanding.

Genesis i. 22.   And God blessed them, saying, Be fruit-
18 ful, and multiply, and fill the waters in the seas; and let
fowl multiply in the earth.

Spirit blesses the multiplication of its own pure and
21 perfect ideas. From the infinite elements of the one

Multiplication Mind emanate all form, color, quality, and
of pure ideas quantity, and these are mental, both primarily
24 and secondarily. Their spiritual nature is discerned only
through the spiritual senses. Mortal mind inverts the true
likeness, and confers animal names and natures upon its
27 own misconceptions. Ignorant of the origin and operations of mortal mind, — that is, ignorant of itself, — this
so-called mind puts forth its own qualities, and claims
30 God as their author; albeit God is ignorant of the ex-

istence of both this mortal mentality, so-called, and its 1
claim, for the claim usurps the deific prerogatives and is
an attempted infringement on infinity. 3

Genesis i. 23. And the evening and the morning were
the fifth day.

Advancing spiritual steps in the teeming universe of 6
Mind lead on to spiritual spheres and exalted beings. To
material sense, this divine universe is dim and   Spiritual
distant, gray in the sombre hues of twilight;   spheres   9
but anon the veil is lifted, and the scene shifts into light.
In the record, time is not yet measured by solar revolutions,
and the motions and reflections of deific power cannot be 12
apprehended until divine Science becomes the interpreter.

Genesis i. 24. And God said, Let the earth bring forth
the living creature after his kind, cattle, and creeping thing, 15
and beast of the earth after his kind: and it was so.

Spirit diversifies, classifies, and individualizes all
thoughts, which are as eternal as the Mind   Continuity   18
conceiving them; but the intelligence, exist-   of thoughts
ence, and continuity of all individuality remain in God,
who is the divinely creative Principle thereof. 21

Genesis i. 25. And God made the beast of the earth after
his kind, and cattle after their kind, and everything that
creepeth upon the earth after his kind: and God saw that 24
it was good.

God creates all forms of reality. His thoughts are
spiritual realities. So-called mortal mind — being non- 27
existent and consequently not within the range of im-

1 mortal existence — could not by simulating deific power
invert the divine creation, and afterwards recreate per-

3 God's   sons or things upon its own plane, since noth-
thoughts   ing exists beyond the range of all-inclusive
are spiritual
realities   infinity, in which and of which God is the
6 sole creator. Mind, joyous in strength, dwells in the
realm of Mind. Mind's infinite ideas run and dis-
port themselves. In humility they climb the heights of
9 holiness.

Moral courage is "the lion of the tribe of Juda," the
king of the mental realm. Free and fearless it roams in
12 Qualities   the forest. Undisturbed it lies in the open
of thought   field, or rests in "green pastures, . . . beside
the still waters." In the figurative transmission from the
15 divine thought to the human, diligence, promptness, and
perseverance are likened to "the cattle upon a thousand
hills." They carry the baggage of stern resolve, and
18 keep pace with highest purpose. Tenderness accompanies all the might imparted by Spirit. The individuality created by God is not carnivorous, as witness the
21 millennial estate pictured by Isaiah: —

The wolf also shall dwell with the lamb,
And the leopard shall lie down with the kid;
24   And the calf and the young lion, and the fatling together;
And a little child shall lead them.

Understanding the control which Love held over all,
27 Daniel felt safe in the lions' den, and Paul proved the
Creatures of viper to be harmless. All of God's creatures,
God useful   moving in the harmony of Science, are harm-
30 less, useful, indestructible. A realization of this grand
verity was a source of strength to the ancient worthies.

It supports Christian healing, and enables its possessor 1
to emulate the example of Jesus. "And God saw that
it was good."   3

Patience is symbolized by the tireless worm, creeping
over lofty summits, persevering in its intent. The serpent of God's creating is neither subtle nor   The serpent   6
poisonous, but is a wise idea, charming in its   harmless
adroitness, for Love's ideas are subject to the Mind which
forms them, — the power which changeth the serpent 9
into a staff.

Genesis i. 26. And God said, Let us make man in our
image, after our likeness; and let them have dominion over 12
the fish of the sea, and over the fowl of the air, and over
the cattle, and over all the earth, and over every creeping
thing that creepeth upon the earth.   15

The eternal Elohim includes the forever universe.
The name Elohim is in the plural, but this plurality of
Spirit does not imply more than one God, nor   Elohistic   18
does it imply three persons in one. It relates   plurality
to the oneness, the tri-unity of Life, Truth, and Love.
"Let *them* have dominion." Man is the family name 21
for all ideas, — the sons and daughters of God. All that
God imparts moves in accord with Him, reflecting good-
ness and power.   24

Your mirrored reflection is your own image or likeness. If you lift a weight, your reflection does this also.
If you speak, the lips of this likeness move in   Reflected   27
accord with yours. Now compare man before   likeness
the mirror to his divine Principle, God. Call the mirror
divine Science, and call man the reflection. Then note 30

1 how true, according to Christian Science, is the reflection
to its original. As the reflection of yourself appears in
3 the mirror, so you, being spiritual, are the reflection of
God. The substance, Life, intelligence, Truth, and Love,
which constitute Deity, are reflected by His creation;
6 and when we subordinate the false testimony of the
corporeal senses to the facts of Science, we shall see
this true likeness and reflection everywhere.
9   God fashions all things, after His own likeness. Life
is reflected in existence, Truth in truthfulness, God in
    Love imparts goodness, which impart their own peace and
12   beauty permanence. Love, redolent with unselfishness, bathes all in beauty and light. The grass beneath
our feet silently exclaims, "The meek shall inherit the
15 earth." The modest arbutus sends her sweet breath to
heaven. The great rock gives shadow and shelter. The
sunlight glints from the church-dome, glances into the
18 prison-cell, glides into the sick-chamber, brightens the
flower, beautifies the landscape, blesses the earth. Man,
made in His likeness, possesses and reflects God's domin-
21 ion over all the earth. Man and woman as coexistent
and eternal with God forever reflect, in glorified quality,
the infinite Father-Mother God.

24   *Genesis* i. 27. So God created man in His own image,
in the image of God created He him; male and female
created He them.

27   To emphasize this momentous thought, it is repeated
that God made man in His own image, to reflect the
    Ideal man divine Spirit. It follows that *man* is a generic
30   and woman term. Masculine, feminine, and neuter gen-
ders are human concepts. In one of the ancient lan-

guages the word for *man* is used also as the synonym of *mind*. This definition has been weakened by anthropomorphism, or a humanization of Deity. The word *anthropomorphic*, in such a phrase as "an anthropomorphic God," is derived from two Greek words, signifying *man* and *form*, and may be defined as a mortally mental attempt to reduce Deity to corporeality. The life-giving quality of Mind is Spirit, not matter. The ideal man corresponds to creation, to intelligence, and to Truth. The ideal woman corresponds to Life and to Love. In divine Science, we have not as much authority for considering God masculine, as we have for considering Him feminine, for Love imparts the clearest idea of Deity.

The world believes in many persons; but if God is personal, there is but one person, because there is but one God. His personality can only be reflected, not transmitted. God has countless ideas, and they all have one Principle and parentage. The only proper symbol of God as person is Mind's infinite ideal. What is this ideal? Who shall behold it? This ideal is God's own image, spiritual and infinite. Even eternity can never reveal the whole of God, since there is no limit to infinitude or to its reflections.

Divine personality

Genesis i. 28. And God blessed them, and God said unto them, Be fruitful, and multiply, and replenish the earth, and subdue it; and have dominion over the fish of the sea, and over the fowl of the air, and over every living thing that moveth upon the earth.

Divine Love blesses its own ideas, and causes them to multiply, — to manifest His power. Man is not made

1 to till the soil. His birthright is dominion, not sub-
  Birthright   jection. He is lord of the belief in earth
3 **of man**   and heaven, — himself subordinate alone to
his Maker. This is the Science of being.

Genesis i. 29, 30. And God said, Behold, I have given
6 you every herb bearing seed, which is upon the face of all
the earth, and every tree, in the which is the fruit of a tree
yielding seed; to you it shall be for meat. And to every
9 beast of the earth, and to every fowl of the air, and to
everything that creepeth upon the earth, wherein there is
life, I have given every green herb for meat: and it
12 was so.

God gives the lesser idea of Himself for a link to the
greater, and in return, the higher always protects the
15 **Assistance in** lower. The rich in spirit help the poor in
brotherhood one grand brotherhood, all having the same
Principle, or Father; and blessed is that man who seeth
18 his brother's need and supplieth it, seeking his own in
another's good. Love giveth to the least spiritual idea
might, immortality, and goodness, which shine through
21 all as the blossom shines through the bud. All the varied
expressions of God reflect health, holiness, immortality —
infinite Life, Truth, and Love.

24 *Genesis* i. 31. And God saw everything that He had
made, and, behold, it was very good. And the evening and
the morning were the sixth day.

27 The divine Principle, or Spirit, comprehends and expresses all, and all must therefore be as perfect as the
divine Principle is perfect. Nothing is new to Spirit.

Nothing can be novel to eternal Mind, the author of all 1
things, who from all eternity knoweth His own ideas.
Deity was satisfied with His work. How could Perfection 3
He be otherwise, since the spiritual creation of creation
was the outgrowth, the emanation, of His infinite self-
containment and immortal wisdom? 6

 Genesis ii. 1. Thus the heavens and the earth were
finished, and all the host of them.

 Thus the ideas of God in universal being are complete 9
and forever expressed, for Science reveals infinity and
the fatherhood and motherhood of Love. Hu- Infinity
man capacity is slow to discern and to grasp measureless 12
God's creation and the divine power and presence which
go with it, demonstrating its spiritual origin. Mortals
can never know the infinite, until they throw off the old 15
man and reach the spiritual image and likeness. What
can fathom infinity! How shall we declare Him, till,
in the language of the apostle, "we all come in the unity 18
of the faith, and of the knowledge of the Son of God, unto
a perfect man, unto the measure of the stature of the fulness of Christ"? 21

 Genesis ii. 2. And on the seventh day God ended His
work which He had made; and He rested on the seventh
day from all His work which He had made. 24

 God rests in action. Imparting has not impoverished,
can never impoverish, the divine Mind. No Resting in
exhaustion follows the action of this Mind, holy work 27
according to the apprehension of divine Science. The

1 highest and sweetest rest, even from a human standpoint,
is in holy work.

3   Unfathomable Mind is expressed. The depth, breadth,
height, might, majesty, and glory of infinite Love fill all

Love and man space. That is enough! Human language
6   *coexistent*   can repeat only an infinitesimal part of what
exists. The absolute ideal, man, is no more seen nor
comprehended by mortals, than is his infinite Principle,
9 Love. Principle and its idea, man, are coexistent and
eternal. The numerals of infinity, called *seven days*, can
never be reckoned according to the calendar of time.
12 These days will appear as mortality disappears, and they
will reveal eternity, newness of Life, in which all sense of
error forever disappears and thought accepts the divine
15 infinite calculus.

    Genesis ii. 4, 5. These are the generations of the heavens
and of the earth when they were created, in the day that the
18 Lord God [Jehovah] made the earth and the heavens, and
every plant of the field before it was in the earth, and every
herb of the field before it grew: for the Lord God [Jehovah]
21 had not caused it to rain upon the earth, and there was not
a man to till the ground.

    Here is the emphatic declaration that God creates all
24 through Mind, not through matter, — that the plant
Growth is   grows, not because of seed or soil, but because
from Mind   growth is the eternal mandate of Mind. Mor-
27 tal thought drops into the ground, but the immortal creating thought is from above, not from beneath. Because
Mind makes all, there is nothing left to be made by a
30 lower power. Spirit acts through the Science of Mind,
never causing man to till the ground, but making him

superior to the soil. Knowledge of this lifts man above 1
the sod, above earth and its environments, to conscious
spiritual harmony and eternal being.   3

Here the inspired record closes its narrative of being
that is without beginning or end. All that is made is
the work of God, and all is good. We leave   Spiritual   6
this brief, glorious history of spiritual creation   narrative
(as stated in the first chapter of Genesis) in the hands of
God, not of man, in the keeping of Spirit, not matter, — 9
joyfully acknowledging now and forever God's supremacy,
omnipotence, and omnipresence.

The harmony and immortality of man are intact. We 12
should look away from the opposite supposition that man
is created materially, and turn our gaze to the spiritual
record of creation, to that which should be engraved on 15
the understanding and heart "with the point of a diamond"
and the pen of an angel.

The reader will naturally ask if there is nothing more 18
about creation in the book of Genesis. Indeed there is,
but the continued account is mortal and material.

Genesis ii. 6. But there went up a mist from the earth, 21
and watered the whole face of the ground.

The Science and truth of the divine creation have been
presented in the verses already considered, and now the 24
opposite error, a material view of creation, is   The story
to be set forth. The second chapter of Gene-   of error
sis contains a statement of this material view of God and 27
the universe, a statement which is the exact opposite of
scientific truth as before recorded. The history of error
or matter, if veritable, would set aside the omnipotence 30

1 of Spirit; but it is the false history in contradistinction
to the true.

3   The Science of the first record proves the falsity of
the second. If one is true, the other is false, for they are
The two   antagonistic. The first record assigns all
6 records   might and government to God, and endows
man out of God's perfection and power. The second
record chronicles man as mutable and mortal, — as hav-
9 ing broken away from Deity and as revolving in an orbit
of his own. Existence, separate from divinity, Science
explains as impossible.

12   This second record unmistakably gives the history of
error in its externalized forms, called life and intelligence in matter. It records pantheism, opposed to the
15 supremacy of divine Spirit; but this state of things is
declared to be temporary and this man to be mortal, —
dust returning to dust.

18   In this erroneous theory, matter takes the place of Spirit.
Matter is represented as the life-giving principle of the
Erroneous   earth. Spirit is represented as entering mat-
21 represen-   ter in order to create man. God's glowing
tation
denunciations of man when not found in His
image, the likeness of Spirit, convince reason and coincide
24 with revelation in declaring this material creation false.

This latter part of the second chapter of Genesis, which
portrays Spirit as supposedly cooperating with matter in
27 Hypothetical constructing the universe, is based on some
reversal   hypothesis of error, for the Scripture just pre-
ceding declares God's work to be finished. Does Life,
30 Truth, and Love produce death, error, and hatred? Does
the creator condemn His own creation? Does the unerring Principle of divine law change or repent? It can-

not be so. Yet one might so judge from an unintelligent 1
perusal of the Scriptural account now under comment.

Because of its false basis, the mist of obscurity evolved 3
by error deepens the false claim, and finally declares that
God knows error and that error can improve   *Mist, or*
His creation. Although presenting the exact   *false claim*   6
opposite of Truth, the lie claims to be truth. The creations of matter arise from a mist or false claim, or from
mystification, and not from the firmament, or under- 9
standing, which God erects between the true and false.
In error everything comes from beneath, not from above.
All is material myth, instead of the reflection of 12
Spirit.

It may be worth while here to remark that, according
to the best scholars, there are clear evidences of two dis- 15
tinct documents in the early part of the book of   *Distinct*
Genesis. One is called the Elohistic, because   *documents*
the Supreme Being is therein called Elohim. The other 18
document is called the Jehovistic, because Deity therein is
always called Jehovah, — or Lord God, as our common
version translates it.   21

Throughout the first chapter of Genesis and in three
verses of the second, — in what we understand to be the
spiritually scientific account of creation, — it is   *Jehovah*   24
Elohim (God) who creates. From the fourth   *or Elohim*
verse of chapter two to chapter five, the creator is called
Jehovah, or the Lord. The different accounts become 27
more and more closely intertwined to the end of chapter
twelve, after which the distinction is not definitely trace-
able. In the historic parts of the Old Testament, it is 30
usually Jehovah, peculiarly the divine sovereign of the
Hebrew people, who is referred to.

1   The idolatry which followed this material mythology is
seen in the Phœnician worship of Baal, in the Moabitish
3   Gods of the   god Chemosh, in the Moloch of the Amorites,
  heathen   in the Hindoo Vishnu, in the Greek Aphro-
dite, and in a thousand other so-called deities.
6   It was also found among the Israelites, who constantly
went after "strange gods." They called the Supreme
  Jehovah a   Being by the national name of Jehovah. In
9   tribal deity   that name of Jehovah, the true idea of God
seems almost lost. God becomes "a man of war," a
tribal god to be worshipped, rather than Love, the divine
12 Principle to be lived and loved.

Genesis ii. 7. And the Lord God [Jehovah] formed man
of the dust of the ground, and breathed into his nostrils
15 the breath of life; and man became a living soul.

Did the divine and infinite Principle become a finite
deity, that He should now be called Jehovah? With
18   Creation   a single command, Mind had made man,
  reversed   both male and female. How then could a
material organization become the basis of man? How
21 could the non-intelligent become the medium of Mind,
and error be the enunciator of Truth? Matter is not
the reflection of Spirit, yet God is reflected in all His
24 creation. Is this addition to His creation real or unreal? Is it the truth, or is it a lie concerning man and
God?
27   It must be a lie, for God presently curses the ground.
Could Spirit evolve its opposite, matter, and give matter
ability to sin and suffer? Is Spirit, God, injected into
30 dust, and eventually ejected at the demand of matter?
Does Spirit enter dust, and lose therein the divine nature

and omnipotence? Does Mind, God, enter matter to be- 1
come there a mortal sinner, animated by the breath of
God? In this narrative, the validity of matter is opposed, 3
not the validity of Spirit or Spirit's creations. Man reflects God; *mankind* represents the Adamic race, and is
a human, not a divine, creation.   6

The following are some of the equivalents of the term
man in different languages. In the Saxon, *mankind, a*
woman, any one; in the Welsh, *that which rises*   Definitions 9
up, — the primary sense being *image, form;* in   of man
the Hcbrcw, *image, similitude;* in the Icelandic, *mind.*
The following translation is from the Icelandic: —   12

And God said, Let us make man after our mind and
our likeness; and God shaped man after His mind; after
God's mind shaped He him; and He shaped them male and 15
female.

In the Gospel of John, it is declared that all things were
made through the Word of God, "and without Him [the 18
logos, or *word*] was not anything made that   No baneful
was made." Everything good or worthy, God   creation
made. Whatever is valueless or baneful, He did not 21
make, — hence its unreality. In the Science of Genesis
we read that He saw everything which He had made,
"and, behold, it was very good." The corporeal scnscs 24
declare otherwise; and if we give the same heed to the
history of error as to the records of truth, the Scriptural
record of sin and death favors the false conclusion of the 27
material senses. Sin, sickness, and death must be deemed
as devoid of reality as they are of good, God.

Genesis ii. 9. And out of the ground made the Lord God 30
[Jehovah] to grow every tree that is pleasant to the sight,

1 and good for food; the tree of life also, in the midst of the garden, and the tree of knowledge of good and evil.

3 The previous and more scientific record of creation declares that God made "every plant of the field be-
Contradicting first creation fore it was in the earth." This opposite
6 declaration, this statement that life issues from matter, contradicts the teaching of the first chapter, — namely, that all Life is God. Belief is less than
9 understanding. Belief involves theories of material hearing, sight, touch, taste, and smell, termed the five senses. The appetites and passions, sin, sickness, and death,
12 follow in the train of this error of a belief in intelligent matter.

The first mention of evil is in the legendary Scriptural
15 text in the second chapter of Genesis. God pronounced
Record of error good all that He created, and the Scriptures declare that He created all. The "tree of
18 life" stands for the idea of Truth, and the sword which guards it is the type of divine Science. The "tree of knowledge" stands for the erroneous doctrine that the
21 knowledge of evil is as real, hence as God-bestowed, as the knowledge of good. Was evil instituted through God, Love? Did He create this fruit-bearer of sin in contra-
24 diction of the first creation? This second biblical account is a picture of error throughout.

Genesis ii. 15. And the Lord God [Jehovah] took the
27 man, and put him into the garden of Eden, to dress it and to keep it.

The name Eden, according to Cruden, means *pleasure,*
30 *delight.* In this text Eden stands for the mortal, mate-

rial body. God could not put Mind into matter nor in- 1
finite Spirit into finite form to dress it and *Garden of*
keep it, — to make it beautiful or to cause it *Eden* 3
to live and grow. Man is God's reflection, needing no
cultivation, but ever beautiful and complete.

Genesis ii. 16, 17. And the Lord God [Jehovah] com- 6
manded the man, saying, Of every tree of the garden thou
mayest freely eat: but of the tree of the knowledge of good
and evil, thou shalt not eat of it: for in the day that thou 9
eatest thereof thou shalt surely die.

Here the metaphor represents God, Love, as tempting
man, but the Apostle James says: "God cannot be 12
tempted with evil, neither tempteth He any *No*
man." It is true that a knowledge of evil would *temptation*
from God
make man mortal. It is plain also that mate- 15
rial perception, gathered from the corporeal senses, constitutes evil and mortal knowledge. But is it true that God,
good, made "the tree of life" to be the tree of death to His 18
own creation? Has evil the reality of good? Evil is unreal because it is a lie, — false in every statement.

Genesis ii. 19. And out of the ground the Lord God 21
[Jehovah] formed every beast of the field, and every fowl
of the air; and brought them unto Adam to see what he
would call them: and whatsoever Adam called every living 24
creature, that was the name thereof.

Here the lie represents God as repeating creation, but
doing so materially, not spiritually, and ask- *Creation's* 27
ing a prospective sinner to help Him. Is the *counterfeit*
Supreme Being retrograding, and is man giving up his
dignity? Was it requisite for the formation of man 30

1 that dust should become sentient, when all being is the
reflection of the eternal Mind, and the record declares
3 that God has already created man, both male and
female? That Adam gave the name and nature of
animals, is solely mythological and material. It can-
6 not be true that man was ordered to create man anew
in partnership with God; this supposition was a dream,
a myth.

9   *Genesis* ii. 21, 22. And the Lord God [Jehovah, Yawah]
caused a deep sleep to fall upon Adam, and he slept: and
He took one of his ribs, and closed up the flesh instead
12 thereof; and the rib, which the Lord God [Jehovah] had
taken from man, made He a woman, and brought her unto
the man.

15   Here falsity, error, credits Truth, God, with inducing
a sleep or hypnotic state in Adam in order to perform a

Hypnotic   surgical operation on him and thereby create
18 surgery   woman. This is the first record of magnetism. Beginning creation with darkness instead of light,
— materially rather than spiritually, — error now simu-
21 lates the work of Truth, mocking Love and declaring what great things error has done. Beholding the
creations of his own dream and calling them real and
24 God-given, Adam — *alias* error — gives them names.
Afterwards he is supposed to become the basis of the
creation of woman and of his own kind, calling them
27 *mankind,* — that is, a kind of man.

But according to this narrative, surgery was first per-

Mental   formed mentally and without instruments;
30 midwifery   and this may be a useful hint to the medical
faculty. Later in human history, when the forbidden

fruit was bringing forth fruit of its own kind, there 1
came a suggestion of change in the *modus operandi*, —
that man should be born of woman, not woman again 3
taken from man. It came about, also, that instruments
were needed to assist the birth of mortals. The first
system of suggestive obstetrics has changed. Another 6
change will come as to the nature and origin of man,
and this revelation will destroy the *dream* of existence,
reinstate reality, usher in Science and the glorious fact 9
of creation, that both man and woman proceed from
God and are His eternal children, belonging to no lesser
parent. 12

Genesis iii. 1–3. Now the serpent was more subtle than
any beast of the field which the Lord God [Jehovah] had
made. And he said unto the woman, Yea, hath God said, 15
Ye shall not eat of every tree of the garden? And the
woman said unto the serpent, We may eat of the fruit of
the trees of the garden: but of the fruit of the tree which is 18
in the midst of the garden, God hath said, Ye shall not eat
of it, neither shall ye touch it, lest ye die.

Whence comes a talking, lying serpent to tempt the 21
children of divine Love? The serpent enters into the
metaphor only as evil. We have nothing in the   Mythical
animal kingdom which represents the species   serpent   24
described, — a talking serpent, — and should rejoice that
evil, by whatever figure presented, contradicts itself and
has neither origin nor support in Truth and good. Seeing 27
this, we should have faith to fight all claims of evil, because we know that they are worthless and unreal.

Adam, the synonym for error, stands for a belief of 30
material mind. He begins his reign over man some-

1 what mildly, but he increases in falsehood and his days
Error or become shorter. In this development, the im-
3 Adam mortal, spiritual law of Truth is made manifest
as forever opposed to mortal, material sense.

In divine Science, man is sustained by God, the divine
6 Principle of being. The earth, at God's command, brings
Divine forth food for man's use. Knowing this, Jesus
providence once said, "Take no thought for your life,
9 what ye shall eat, or what ye shall drink," — presuming
not on the prerogative of his creator, but recognizing God,
the Father and Mother of all, as able to feed and clothe
12 man as He doth the lilies.

Genesis iii. 4, 5. And the serpent said unto the woman,
Ye shall not surely die: for God doth know that in the day
15 ye eat thereof, then your eyes shall be opened; and ye shall
be as gods, knowing good and evil.

This myth represents error as always asserting its su-
18 periority over truth, giving the lie to divine Science and
Error's saying, through the material senses: "I can
assumption open your eyes. I can do what God has not
21 done for you. Bow down to me and have another god.
Only admit that I am real, that sin and sense are more
pleasant to the eyes than spiritual Life, more to be de-
24 sired than Truth, and I shall know you, and you will be
mine." Thus Spirit and flesh war.

The history of error is a dream-narrative. The dream
27 has no reality, no intelligence, no mind; therefore the
Scriptural dreamer and dream are one, for neither is
allegory true nor real. *First,* this narrative supposes
30 that something springs from nothing, that matter precedes mind. *Second,* it supposes that mind enters matter,

and matter becomes living, substantial, and intelligent. 1
The order of this allegory — the belief that everything
springs from dust instead of from Deity — has been main- 3
tained in all the subsequent forms of belief. This is the
error, — that mortal man starts materially, that non-
intelligence becomes intelligence, that mind and soul are 6
both right and wrong.

It is well that the upper portions of the brain represent
the higher moral sentiments, as if hope were ever prophe- 9
sying thus: The human mind will sometime   Higher
rise above all material and physical sense, ex-   hope
changing it for spiritual perception, and exchanging hu- 12
man concepts for the divine consciousness. Then man
will recognize his God-given dominion and being.

If, in the beginning, man's body originated in non- 15
intelligent dust, and mind was afterwards put into body
by the creator, why is not this divine order   Biological
still maintained by God in perpetuating the   inventions 18
species? Who will say that minerals, vegetables, and
animals have a propagating property of their own?
Who dares to say either that God is in matter or that 21
matter exists without God? Has man sought out other
creative inventions, and so changed the method of his
Maker? 24

Which institutes Life, — matter or Mind? Does Life
begin with Mind or with matter? Is Life sustained by
matter or by Spirit? Certainly not by both, since flesh 27
wars against Spirit and the corporeal senses can take no
cognizance of Spirit. The mythologic theory of material life at no point resembles the scientifically Christian 30
record of man as created by Mind in the image and likeness of God and having dominion over all the earth. Did

1 God at first create one man unaided, — that is, Adam, —
but afterwards require the union of the two sexes in order
3 to create the rest of the human family? No! |God makes
and governs all.|

All human knowledge and material sense must be
6 gained from the five corporeal senses. Is this knowledge
Progeny
cursed safe, when eating its first fruits brought death?
"In the day that thou eatest thereof thou shalt
9 surely die," was the prediction in the story under consideration. Adam and his progeny were cursed, not blessed;
and this indicates that the divine Spirit, or Father, con-
12 demns material man and remands him to dust.

Genesis iii. 9, 10. And the Lord God [Jehovah] called
unto Adam, and said unto him, Where art thou? And he
15 said, I heard Thy voice in the garden, and I was afraid,
because I was naked; and I hid myself.

Knowledge and pleasure, evolved through material
18 sense, produced the immediate fruits of fear and shame.
Shame the
effect of sin Ashamed before Truth, error shrank abashed
from the divine voice calling out to the cor-
21 poreal senses. Its summons may be thus paraphrased:
"Where art thou, man? Is Mind in matter? Is Mind
capable of error as well as of truth, of evil as well as of
24 good, when God is All and He is Mind and there is but
one God, hence one Mind?"

Fear was the first manifestation of the error of mate-
27 rial sense. Thus error began and will end the dream of
Fear comes
of error matter. In the allegory the body had been
naked, and Adam knew it not; but now error
30 demands that *mind* shall see and feel through matter, the
five senses. The first impression material man had of

himself was one of nakedness and shame. Had he lost 1
man's rich inheritance and God's behest, dominion over
all the earth? No! This had never been bestowed on 3
Adam.

Genesis iii. 11, 12. And He said, Who told thee that
thou wast naked? Hast thou eaten of the tree, whereof I 6
commanded thee that thou shouldst not eat? And the man
said, The woman whom Thou gavest to be with me, she gave
me of the tree, and I did eat. 9

Here there is an attempt to trace all human errors
directly or indirectly to God, or good, as if He were the
creator of evil. The allegory shows that the *The beguiling* 12
snake-talker utters the first voluble lie, which *first lie*
beguiles the woman and demoralizes the man. Adam,
alias mortal error, charges God and woman with his own 15
dereliction, saying, "The woman, whom Thou gavest
me, is responsible." According to this belief, the rib taken
from Adam's side has grown into an evil mind, named 18
woman, who aids man to make sinners more rapidly than
he can alone. Is this an help meet for man?
Materiality, so obnoxious to God, is already found in the 21
rapid deterioration of the bone and flesh which came from
Adam to form Eve. The belief in material life and intelligence is growing worse at every step, but error has its 24
suppositional day and multiplies until the end thereof.
Truth, cross-questioning man as to his knowledge of
error, finds woman the first to confess her fault. She 27
says, "The serpent beguiled me, and I did *False*
eat;" as much as to say in meek penitence, *womanhood*
"Neither man nor God shall father my fault." She has 30
already learned that corporeal sense is the serpent. Hence

1 she is first to abandon the belief in the material origin of
man and to discern spiritual creation. This hereafter
3 enabled woman to be the mother of Jesus and to behold
at the sepulchre the risen Saviour, who was soon to manifest the deathless man of God's creating. This enabled
6 woman to be first to interpret the Scriptures in their true
sense, which reveals the spiritual origin of man.

Genesis iii. 14, 15. And the Lord God [Jehovah] said
9 unto the serpent, . . . I will put enmity between thee and
the woman, and between thy seed and her seed; it shall
bruise thy head, and thou shalt bruise his heel.

12   This prophecy has been fulfilled. The Son of the Virgin-
mother unfolded the remedy for Adam, or error; and the

Spirit and   Apostle Paul explains this warfare between the

flesh
15   idea of divine power, which Jesus presented,
and mythological material intelligence called *energy* and
opposed to Spirit.

18   Paul says in his epistle to the Romans: "The carnal
mind is enmity against God; for it is not subject to the
law of God, neither indeed can be. So then they that
21 are in the flesh cannot please God. But ye are not in the
flesh, but in the Spirit, if so be that the spirit of God dwell
in you."

24   There will be greater mental opposition to the spiritual, scientific meaning of the Scriptures than there has

Bruising   ever been since the Christian era began. The

sin's head
27   serpent, material sense, will bite the heel of
the woman, — will struggle to destroy the spiritual idea
of Love; and the woman, this idea, will bruise the head
30 of lust. The spiritual idea has given the understanding

a foothold in Christian Science. The seed of Truth and 1
the seed of error, of belief and of understanding, — yea,
the seed of Spirit and the seed of matter, — are the wheat 3
and tares which time will separate, the one to be burned,
the other to be garnered into heavenly places.

Genesis iii. 16. Unto the woman He said, I will greatly 6
multiply thy sorrow and thy conception: in sorrow thou
shalt bring forth children; and thy desire shall be to thy
husband, and he shall rule over thee.   9

Divine Science deals its chief blow at the supposed material foundations of life and intelligence. It dooms idolatry. A belief in other gods, other creators, Judgment 12
and other creations must go down before Chris- on error
tian Science. It unveils the results of sin as shown in
sickness and death. When will man pass through the 15
open gate of Christian Science into the heaven of Soul,
into the heritage of the first born among men? Truth is
indeed "the way."   18

Genesis iii. 17–19. And unto Adam He said, Because
thou hast hearkened unto the voice of thy wife, and hast
eaten of the tree of which I commanded thee, saying, Thou 21
shalt not eat of it: cursed is the ground for thy sake; in
sorrow shalt thou eat of it all the days of thy life: thorns
also and thistles shall it bring forth to thee; and thou shalt 24
eat the herb of the field: in the sweat of thy face shalt thou
eat bread, till thou return unto the ground; for out of it
wast thou taken: for dust thou art, and unto dust shalt 27
thou return.

In the first chapter of Genesis we read: "And God
called the dry land Earth; and the gathering together 30

1 of the waters called He Seas." In the Apocalypse it is
written: "And I saw a new heaven and a new earth: for
3   the first heaven and the first earth were passed
New earth
and no more away; and there was no more sea." In St.
sea
        John's vision, heaven and earth stand for spir-
6 itual ideas, and the sea, as a symbol of tempest-tossed
human concepts advancing and receding, is represented
as having passed away. The divine understanding reigns,
9 is all, and there is no other consciousness.

The way of error is awful to contemplate. The illusion of sin is without hope or God. If man's spiritual
12   The fall   gravitation and attraction to one Father, in
of error   whom we "live, and move, and have our being," should be lost, and if man should be governed by
15 corporeality instead of divine Principle, by body instead
of by Soul, man would be annihilated. Created by flesh
instead of by Spirit, starting from matter instead of from
18 God, mortal man would be governed by himself. The
blind leading the blind, both would fall.

Passions and appetites must end in pain. They are
21 "of few days, and full of trouble." Their supposed joys
are cheats. Their narrow limits belittle their gratifica-
tions, and hedge about their achievements with thorns.
24 Mortal mind accepts the erroneous, material conception of life and joy, but the true idea is gained from the
True   immortal side. Through toil, struggle, and sor-
27 attainment row, what do mortals attain? They give up
their belief in perishable life and happiness; the mortal
and material return to dust, and the immortal is reached.

30   *Genesis* iii. 22–24. And the Lord God [Jehovah] said,
Behold, the man is become as one of us, to know good

and evil: and now, lest he put forth his hand, and take 1
also of the tree of life, and eat, and live forever; therefore
the Lord God [Jehovah] sent him forth from the garden 3
of Eden, to till the ground from whence he was taken.
So He drove out the man: and He placed at the east
of the garden of Eden Cherubims, and a flaming sword 6
which turned every way, to keep the way of the tree of
life.

A knowledge of evil was never the essence of divin- 9
ity or manhood. In the first chapter of Genesis, evil
has no local habitation nor name. Crea- *Justice and*
tion is there represented as spiritual, entire, *recompense* 12
and good. "Whatsoever a man soweth, that shall he
also reap." Error excludes itself from harmony. Sin
is its own punishment. Truth guards the gateway 15
to harmony. Error tills its own barren soil and buries
itself in the ground, since ground and dust stand for
nothingness. 18

No one can reasonably doubt that the purpose of this
allegory — this second account in Genesis — is to depict
the falsity of error and the effects of error. 21
Subsequent Bible revelation is coordinate *Inspired*
interpreta-
with the Science of creation recorded in the *tion*
first chapter of Genesis. Inspired writers interpret the 24
Word spiritually, while the ordinary historian interprets
it literally. Literally taken, the text is made to appear
contradictory in some places, and divine Love, which 27
blessed the earth and gave it to man for a possession, is
represented as changeable. The literal meaning would
imply that God withheld from man the opportunity to 30
reform, lest man should improve it and become better;
but this is not the nature of God, who is Love always, —

1 Love infinitely wise and altogether lovely, who "seeketh
not her own."

3   Truth should, and does, drive error out of all selfhood.
Truth is a two-edged sword, guarding and guiding.
Spiritual   Truth places the cherub wisdom at the gate
6   gateway   of understanding to note the proper guests.
Radiant with mercy and justice, the sword of Truth
gleams afar and indicates the infinite distance between
9 Truth and error, between the material and spiritual, —
the unreal and the real.

The sun, giving light and heat to the earth, is a figure
12 of divine Life and Love, enlightening and sustaining the
Contrasted   universe. The "tree of life" is significant of
testimony   eternal reality or being. The "tree of knowl-
15 edge" typifies unreality. The testimony of the serpent is
significant of the illusion of error, of the false claims that
misrepresent God, good. Sin, sickness, and death have
18 no record in the Elohistic introduction of Genesis, in which
God creates the heavens, earth, and man. Until that
which contradicts the truth of being enters into the arena,
21 evil has no history, and evil is brought into view only as
the unreal in contradistinction to the real and eternal.

Genesis iv. 1. And Adam knew Eve his wife; and she
24 conceived, and bare Cain, and said, I have gotten a man
from the Lord [Jehovah].

This account is given, not of immortal man, but of mor-
27 tal man, and of sin which is temporal. As both mortal
Erroneous   man and sin have a beginning, they must
conception   consequently have an end, while the sinless,
30 real man is eternal. Eve's declaration, "I have gotten
a man from the Lord," supposes God to be the author

of sin and sin's progeny. This false sense of existence 1
is fratricidal. In the words of Jesus, it (evil, devil) is
"a murderer from the beginning." Error begins by 3
reckoning life as separate from Spirit, thus sapping the
foundations of immortality, as if life and immortality
were something which matter can both give and take 6
away.

What can be the standard of good, of Spirit, of Life,
or of Truth, if they produce their opposites, such as evil, 9
matter, error, and death? God could never   Only one
impart an element of evil, and man possesses   standard
nothing which he has not derived from God. How then 12
has man a basis for wrong-doing? Whence does he
obtain the propensity or power to do evil? Has Spirit
resigned to matter the government of the universe?   15

The Scriptures declare that God condemned this lie as
to man's origin and character by condemning its symbol,
the serpent, to grovel beneath all the beasts   A type of   18
of the field. It is false to say that Truth and   falsehood
error commingle in creation. In parable and argument,
this falsity is exposed by our Master as self-evidently 21
wrong. Disputing these points with the Pharisees and
arguing for the Science of creation, Jesus said: "Do men
gather grapes of thorns?" Paul asked: "What com- 24
munion hath light with darkness? And what concord
hath Christ with Belial?"

The divine origin of Jesus gave him more than human 27
power to expound the facts of creation, and demonstrate
the one Mind which makes and governs man   Scientific
and the universe. The Science of creation,   offspring   30
so conspicuous in the birth of Jesus, inspired his wisest
and least-understood sayings, and was the basis of his

1 marvellous demonstrations. Christ is the offspring of
Spirit, and spiritual existence shows that Spirit creates
3 neither a wicked nor a mortal man, lapsing into sin, sickness, and death.

In Isaiah we read: "I make peace, and create evil. I
6 the Lord do all these things;" but the prophet referred to
Cleansing   divine law as stirring up the belief in evil to its
upheaval   utmost, when bringing it to the surface and re-
9 ducing it to its common denominator, nothingness. The
muddy river-bed must be stirred in order to purify the
stream. In moral chemicalization, when the symptoms
12 of evil, illusion, are aggravated, we may think in our ignorance that the Lord hath wrought an evil; but we ought
to know that God's law uncovers so-called sin and its
15 effects, only that Truth may annihilate all sense of evil
and all power to sin.

Science renders "unto Cæsar the things which are
18 Cæsar's; and unto God the things that are God's." It
Allegiance   saith to the human sense of sin, sickness, and
to Spirit   death, "God never made you, and you are a
21 false sense which hath no knowledge of God." The purpose of the Hebrew allegory, representing error as assum-
ing a divine character, is to teach mortals never to believe
24 a lie.

Genesis iv. 3, 4. Cain brought of the fruit of the ground
an offering unto the Lord [Jehovah]. And Abel, he also
27 brought of the firstlings of his flock, and of the fat thereof.

Cain is the type of mortal and material man, conceived
Spiritual and   in sin and "shapen in iniquity;" he is not the
30 material   type of Truth and Love. Material in origin
and sense, he brings a material offering to God. Abel

1 record of a material creation which followed the spiritual,
— a creation so wholly apart from God's, that Spirit
3   Material   had no participation in it. In God's creation
    inception   ideas became productive, obedient to Mind.
There was no rain and "not a man to till the ground."
6 Mind, instead of matter, being the producer, Life was
self-sustained. Birth, decay, and death arise from the
material sense of things, not from the spiritual, for in
9 the latter Life consisteth not of the things which a man
eateth. Matter cannot change the eternal fact that
man exists because God exists. Nothing is new to the
12 infinite Mind.

In Science, Mind neither produces matter nor does
matter produce mind. No mortal mind has the might
15   First evil   or right or wisdom to create or to destroy.
     suggestion   All is under the control of the one Mind,
even God. The first statement about evil, — the first
18 suggestion of more than the one Mind, — is in the fable
of the serpent. The facts of creation, as previously recorded, include nothing of the kind.

21   The serpent is supposed to say, "Ye shall be as gods,"
but these gods must be evolved from materiality and be
     Material   the very antipodes of immortal and spiritual
24   personality   being. Man is the likeness of Spirit, but a
material personality is not this likeness. Therefore man,
in this allegory, is neither a lesser god nor the image and
27 likeness of the one God.

Material, erroneous belief reverses understanding and
truth. It declares mind to be in and of matter, so-called
30 mortal life to be Life, infinity to enter man's nostrils
so that matter becomes spiritual. Error begins with
corporeality as the producer instead of divine Prin-

ciple, and explains Deity through mortal and finite con- 1
ceptions.

"Behold, the man is become as one of us." This could 3
not be the utterance of Truth or Science, for according
to the record, material man was fast degenerating and
never had been divinely conceived. 6

The condemnation of mortals to till the ground means
this, — that mortals should so improve material belief
by thought tending spiritually upward as to   Mental   9
destroy materiality. Man, created by God,   tillage
was given dominion over the whole earth. The notion
of a material universe is utterly opposed to the theory 12
of man as evolved from Mind. Such fundamental errors
send falsity into all human doctrines and conclusions,
and do not accord infinity to Deity. Error tills the 15
whole ground in this material theory, which is entirely a
false view, destructive to existence and happiness. Outside of Christian Science all is vague and hypothetical, the 18
opposite of Truth; yet this opposite, in its false view of
God and man, impudently demands a blessing.

The translators of this record of scientific creation 21
entertained a false sense of being. They believed in
the existence of matter, its propagation and   Erroneous
power. From that standpoint of error, they   standpoint   24
could not apprehend the nature and operation of Spirit.
Hence the seeming contradiction in that Scripture, which
is so glorious in its spiritual signification. Truth has 27
but one reply to all error, — to sin, sickness, and death:
"Dust [nothingness] thou art, and unto dust [nothingness]
shalt thou return." 30

"As in Adam [error] all die, even so in Christ [Truth]
shall all be made alive." The mortality of man is a

authenticate all the others. A simple statement of Chris- 1
tian Science, if demonstrated by healing, contains the
proof of all here said of Christian Science. If Proof given 3
one of the statements in this book is true, every in healing
one must be true, for not one departs from the stated system and rule. You can prove for yourself, dear reader, 6
the Science of healing, and so ascertain if the author has
given you the correct interpretation of Scripture.

The late Louis Agassiz, by his microscopic examination 9
of a vulture's ovum, strengthens the thinker's conclusions
as to the scientific theory of creation. Agassiz Embryonic
was able to see in the egg the earth's atmos- evolution 12
phere, the gathering clouds, the moon and stars, while the
germinating speck of so-called embryonic life seemed a
small sun. In its history of mortality, Darwin's theory 15
of evolution from a material basis is more consistent than
most theories. Briefly, this is Darwin's theory, — that
Mind produces its opposite, matter, and endues matter 18
with power to recreate the universe, including man. Material evolution implies that the great First Cause must
become material, and afterwards must either return to 21
Mind or go down into dust and nothingness.

The Scriptures are very sacred. Our aim must be to
have them understood spiritually, for only by this under- 24
standing can truth be gained. The true the- True theory
ory of the universe, including man, is not in of the
material history but in spiritual development. universe 27
Inspired thought relinquishes a material, sensual, and
mortal theory of the universe, and adopts the spiritual and
immortal. 30

It is this spiritual perception of Scripture, which lifts
humanity out of disease and death and inspires faith.

1 "The Spirit and the bride say, Come! . . . and whosoever will, let him take the water of life freely." Christian

3 Scriptural   Science separates error from truth, and breathes
perception   through the sacred pages the spiritual sense of
life, substance, and intelligence. In this Science, we dis-
6 cover man in the image and likeness of God. We see that
man has never lost his spiritual estate and his eternal
harmony.

9 How little light or heat reach our earth when clouds
cover the sun's face! So Christian Science can be seen
The clouds only as the clouds of corporeal sense roll away.
12 dissolving   Earth has little light or joy for mortals before
Life is spiritually learned. Every agony of mortal error
helps error to destroy error, and so aids the apprehension
15 of immortal Truth. This is the new birth going on
hourly, by which men may entertain angels, the true
ideas of God, the spiritual sense of being.

18 Speaking of the origin of mortals, a famous naturalist
says: "It is very possible that many general statements
Prediction of now current, about birth and generation, will
21 a naturalist be changed with the progress of information."
Had the naturalist, through his tireless researches, gained
the diviner side in Christian Science, — so far apart from
24 his material sense of animal growth and organization, —
he would have blessed the human race more abundantly.

Natural history is richly endowed by the labors and
27 genius of great men. Modern discoveries have brought
Methods of to light important facts in regard to so-called
reproduction embryonic life. Agassiz declares ("Methods
30 of Study in Natural History," page 275): "Certain animals, besides the ordinary process of generation, also
increase their numbers naturally and constantly by self-

division." This discovery is corroborative of the Science 1
of Mind, for this discovery shows that the multiplication
of certain animals takes place apart from sexual condi- 3
tions. The supposition that life germinates in eggs and
must decay after it has grown to maturity, if not before,
is shown by divine metaphysics to be a mistake, — a 6
blunder which will finally give place to higher theories
and demonstrations.

Creatures of lower forms of organism are supposed 9
to have, as classes, three different methods of reproduction and to multiply their species sometimes The three
through eggs, sometimes through buds, and processes 12
sometimes through self-division. According to recent
lore, successive generations do not begin with the *birth* of
new individuals, or personalities, but with the formation 15
of the nucleus, or egg, from which one or more individualities subsequently emerge; and we must therefore look
upon the simple ovum as the germ, the starting-point, of 18
the most complicated corporeal structures, including those
which we call human. Here these material researches
culminate in such vague hypotheses as must necessarily 21
attend false systems, which rely upon physics and are devoid of metaphysics.

In one instance a celebrated naturalist, Agassiz, dis- 24
covers the pathway leading to divine Science, and beards
the lion of materialism in its den. At that Deference to
point, however, even this great observer mis- material law 27
takes nature, forsakes Spirit as the divine origin of
creative Truth, and allows matter and material law to
usurp the prerogatives of omnipotence. He absolutely 30
drops from his summit, coming down to a belief in the
material origin of man, for he virtually affirms that

1 the germ of humanity is in a circumscribed and non-
intelligent egg.

3   If this be so, whence cometh Life, or Mind, to the
human race? Matter surely does not possess Mind.

Deep-reaching interrogations God is the Life, or intelligence, which forms
6 and preserves the individuality and identity
of animals as well as of men. God cannot
become finite, and be limited within material bounds.
9 Spirit cannot become matter, nor can Spirit be developed
through its opposite. Of what avail is it to investigate
what is miscalled material life, which ends, even as it be-
12 gins, in nameless nothingness? The true sense of being
and its eternal perfection should appear now, even as it
will hereafter.

15   Error of thought is reflected in error of action. The
continual contemplation of existence as material and cor-

Stages of existence poreal — as beginning and ending, and with
18 birth, decay, and dissolution as its component
stages — hides the true and spiritual Life, and causes
our standard to trail in the dust. If Life has any starting-
21 point whatsoever, then the great I AM is a myth. If Life
is God, as the Scriptures imply, then Life is not embryonic, it is infinite. An egg is an impossible enclosure for
24 Deity.

Embryology supplies no instance of one species producing its opposite. A serpent never begets a bird, nor
27 does a lion bring forth a lamb. Amalgamation is deemed
monstrous and is seldom fruitful, but it is not so hideous
and absurd as the supposition that Spirit — the pure and
30 holy, the immutable and immortal — can originate the
impure and mortal and dwell in it. As Christian Science
repudiates self-evident impossibilities, the material senses

must father these absurdities, for both the material senses 1
and their reports are unnatural, impossible, and unreal.
Either Mind produces, or it is produced. If Mind is 3
first, it cannot produce its opposite in quality and quantity,
called matter. If matter is first, it cannot pro- The real
duce Mind. Like produces like. In natural producer 6
history, the bird is not the product of a beast. In spiritual
history, matter is not the progenitor of Mind.

One distinguished naturalist argues that mortals spring 9
from eggs and in races. Mr. Darwin admits this, but he
adds that mankind has ascended through all The ascent
the lower grades of existence. Evolution de- of species 12
scribes the gradations of human belief, but it does not
acknowledge the method of divine Mind, nor see that material methods are impossible in divine Science and that 15
all Science is of God, not of man.

Naturalists ask: "What can there be, of a material
nature, transmitted through these bodies called eggs, — 18
themselves composed of the simplest material Transmitted
elements, — by which all peculiarities of an- peculiarities
cestry, belonging to either sex, are brought down from 21
generation to generation?" The question of the naturalist amounts to this: How can matter originate or transmit mind? We answer that it cannot. Darkness and 24
doubt encompass thought, so long as it bases creation on
materiality. From a material standpoint, "Canst thou
by searching find out God?" All must be Mind, or 27
else all must be matter. Neither can produce the other.
Mind is immortal; but error declares that the material
seed must decay in order to propagate its species, and 30
the resulting germ is doomed to the same routine.

The ancient and hypothetical question, Which is first,

1 the egg or the bird? is answered, if the egg produces the
parent. But we cannot stop here. Another question

3   Causation not follows: Who or what produces the parent of
     in matter   the egg? That the earth was hatched from the
"egg of night" was once an accepted theory. Heathen

6 philosophy, modern geology, and all other material hypotheses deal with causation as contingent on matter
and as necessarily apparent to the corporeal senses, even

9 where the proof requisite to sustain this assumption is un-
discovered. Mortal theories make friends of sin, sickness,
and death; whereas the spiritual scientific facts of exist-

12 ence include no member of this dolorous and fatal triad.

Human experience in mortal life, which starts from an
egg, corresponds with that of Job, when he says, "Man

15   Emergence that is born of a woman is of few days, and
   of mortals   full of trouble." Mortals must emerge from
this notion of material life as all-in-all. They must peck

18 open their shells with Christian Science, and look outward
and upward. But thought, loosened from a material
basis but not yet instructed by Science, may become wild

21 with freedom and so be self-contradictory.

From a material source flows no remedy for sorrow,
sin, and death, for the redeeming power, from the ills

24   Persistence they occasion, is not in egg nor in dust. The
   of species   blending tints of leaf and flower show the
order of matter to be the order of mortal mind. The

27 intermixture of different species, urged to its utmost
limits, results in a return to the original species. Thus
it is learned that matter is a manifestation of mortal

30 mind, and that matter always surrenders its claims when
the perfect and eternal Mind is understood.

Naturalists describe the origin of mortal and material

existence in the various forms of embryology, and ac- 1
company their descriptions with important observations,
which should awaken thought to a higher and 3
purer contemplation of man's origin. This *Better basis than embryology*
clearer consciousness must precede an under-
standing of the harmony of being. Mortal thought must 6
obtain a better basis, get nearer the truth of being, or
health will never be universal, and harmony will never
become the standard of man. 9

One of our ablest naturalists has said: "We have no
right to assume that individuals have grown or been
formed under circumstances which made material con- 12
ditions essential to their maintenance and reproduction,
or important to their origin and first introduction."
Why, then, is the naturalist's basis so materialistic, 15
and why are his deductions generally material?

Adam was created before Eve. In this instance, it is
seen that the maternal egg never brought forth Adam. 18
Eve was formed from Adam's rib, not from a *All nativity in thought*
foetal ovum. Whatever theory may be adopted
by general mortal thought to account for human origin, 21
that theory is sure to become the signal for the appearance of its method in finite forms and operations. If con-
sentaneous human belief agrees upon an ovum as the 24
point of emergence for the human race, this potent belief
will immediately supersede the more ancient superstition about the creation from dust or from the rib of our 27
primeval father.

You may say that mortals are formed before they
think or know aught of their origin, and you *Being is immortal* 30
may also ask how belief can affect a result
which precedes the development of that belief. It can

1 only be replied, that Christian Science reveals what "eye
hath not seen," — even the cause of all that exists, — for
3 the universe, inclusive of man, is as eternal as God, who
is its divine immortal Principle. There is no such thing
as mortality, nor are there properly any mortal beings,
6 because being is immortal, like Deity, — or, rather, being
and Deity are inseparable.

Error is always error. It is *no thing.* Any statement
9 of life, following from a misconception of life, is errone-

Our conscious   ous, because it is destitute of any knowledge
development   of the so-called selfhood of life, destitute of
12 any knowledge of its origin or existence. The mortal
is unconscious of his fœtal and infantile existence; but
as he grows up into another false claim, that of self-con-
15 scious matter, he learns to say, "I am somebody; but
who made me?" Error replies, "God made you." The
first effort of error has been and is to impute to God the
18 creation of whatever is sinful and mortal; but infinite
Mind sets at naught such a mistaken belief.

Jesus defined this opposite of God and His creation
21 better than we can, when he said, "He is a liar, and the

Mendacity   father of it." Jesus also said, "Have not I
of error   chosen you twelve, and one of you is a devil?"
24 This he said of Judas, one of Adam's race. Jesus never
intimated that God made a devil, but he did say, "Ye
are of your father, the devil." All these sayings were to
27 show that mind in matter is the author of itself, and is
simply a falsity and illusion.

It is the general belief that the lower animals are less
30   Ailments   sickly than those possessing higher organiza-
of animals   tions, especially those of the human form.
This would indicate that there is less disease in propor-

repeated this operation daily, until the child could remain 1
under water twenty minutes, moving and playing without harm, like a fish.   Parents should remember this, 3
and learn how to develop their children properly on dry
land.

Mind controls the birth-throes in the lower realms of 6
nature, where parturition is without suffering.   Vegetables, minerals, and many animals suffer no   The curse
pain in multiplying; but human propagation   removed   9
has its suffering because it is a false belief. Christian Science reveals harmony as proportionately increasing as the
line of creation rises towards spiritual man, — towards 12
enlarged understanding and intelligence; but in the line
of the corporeal senses, the less a mortal knows of sin,
disease, and mortality, the better for him, — the less pain 15
and sorrow are his.   When the mist of mortal mind evaporates, the curse will be removed which says to woman,
"In sorrow thou shalt bring forth children."   Divine 18
Science rolls back the clouds of error with the light of
Truth, and lifts the curtain on man as never born and as
never dying, but as coexistent with his creator.   21

Popular theology takes up the history of man as if he
began materially right, but immediately fell into mental
sin; whereas revealed religion proclaims the Science of 24
Mind and its formations as being in accordance with
the first chapter of the Old Testament, when God, Mind,
spake and it was done.   27

CHAPTER XVI

The Apocalypse

Blessed is he that readeth, and they that hear the words of this prophecy, and keep those things which are written therein: for the time is at hand. — REVELATION.

Great is the Lord, and greatly to be praised in the city of our God, in the mountain of His holiness. — PSALMS.

1 ST. JOHN writes, in the tenth chapter of his book of Revelation: —

3 And I saw another mighty angel come down from heaven, clothed with a cloud: and a rainbow was upon his head, and his face was as it were the sun, and his feet as pillars of 6 fire: and he had in his hand a little book open: and he set his right foot upon the sea, and his left foot on the earth.

9 This angel or message which comes from God, clothed with a cloud, prefigures divine Science. To mortal sense
The new Science seems at first obscure, abstract, and
12 Evangel dark; but a bright promise crowns its brow. When understood, it is Truth's prism and praise. When you look it fairly in the face, you can heal by its means, 15 and it has for you a light above the sun, for God "is the light thereof." Its feet are pillars of fire, foundations of Truth and Love. It brings the baptism of the Holy 18 Ghost, whose flames of Truth were prophetically described by John the Baptist as consuming error.

This angel had in his hand "a little book," open for 1
all to read and understand. Did this same book contain
the revelation of divine Science, the "right   Truth's   3
foot" or dominant power of which was upon   volume
the sea, — upon elementary, latent error, the source of
all error's visible forms? The angel's left foot was upon 6
the earth; that is, a secondary power was exercised upon
visible error and audible sin. The "still, small voice"
of scientific thought reaches over continent and ocean 9
to the globe's remotest bound. The inaudible voice of
Truth is, to the human mind, "as when a lion roareth."
It is heard in the desert and in dark places of fear. It 12
arouses the "seven thunders" of evil, and stirs their latent
forces to utter the full diapason of secret tones. Then is
the power of Truth demonstrated, — made manifest in 15
the destruction of error. Then will a voice from harmony
cry: "Go and take the little book. . . . Take it, and eat
it up; and it shall make thy belly bitter, but it shall be in 18
thy mouth sweet as honey." Mortals, obey the heavenly
evangel. Take divine Science. Read this book from
beginning to end. Study it, ponder it. It will be indeed 21
sweet at its first taste, when it heals you; but murmur not
over Truth, if you find its digestion bitter. When you
approach nearer and nearer to this divine Principle, when 24
you eat the divine body of this Principle, — thus partaking of the nature, or primal elements, of Truth and Love,
— do not be surprised nor discontented because you must 27
share the hemlock cup and eat the bitter herbs; for the
Israelites of old at the Paschal meal thus prefigured this
perilous passage out of bondage into the El Dorado of faith 30
and hope.

The twelfth chapter of the Apocalypse, or Revela-

1 tion of St. John, has a special suggestiveness in connection with the nineteenth century. In the opening of the
3 To-day's   sixth seal, typical of six thousand years since
   lesson   Adam, the distinctive feature has reference
to the present age.

6 *Revelation* xii. 1. And there appeared a great wonder in
heaven; a woman clothed with the sun, and the moon
under her feet, and upon her head a crown of twelve
9 stars.

Heaven represents harmony, and divine Science interprets the Principle of heavenly harmony. The great
12   miracle, to human sense, is divine Love, and
   True estimate
   of God's   the grand necessity of existence is to gain the
   messenger true idea of what constitutes the kingdom of
15 heaven in man. This goal is never reached while we
hate our neighbor or entertain a false estimate of anyone whom God has appointed to voice His Word. Again,
18 without a correct sense of its highest visible idea, we can
never understand the divine Principle. The botanist must
know the genus and species of a plant in order to classify
21 it correctly. As it is with things, so is it with persons.
Abuse of the motives and religion of St. Paul hid from
view the apostle's character, which made him equal to
24 Persecution his great mission. Persecution of all who have
   harmful   spoken something new and better of God has
not only obscured the light of the ages, but has been fatal
27 to the persecutors. Why? Because it has hid from
them the true idea which has been presented. To misunderstand Paul, was to be ignorant of the divine idea he
30 taught. Ignorance of the divine idea betrays at once a
greater ignorance of the divine Principle of the idea — igno-

rance of Truth and Love. The understanding of Truth 1
and Love, the Principle which works out the ends of eternal
good and destroys both faith in evil and the practice of 3
evil, leads to the discernment of the divine idea.

Agassiz, through his microscope, saw the sun in an
egg at a point of so-called embryonic life. Because of 6
his more spiritual vision, St. John saw an *Espousals*
"angel standing in the sun." The Revelator *supernal*
beheld the spiritual idea from the mount of vision. 9
Purity was the symbol of Life and Love. The Revelator
saw also the spiritual ideal as a woman clothed in light, a
bride coming down from heaven, wedded to the Lamb 12
of Love. To John, "the bride" and "the Lamb" represented the correlation of divine Principle and spiritual idea,
God and His Christ, bringing harmony to earth. 15

John saw the human and divine coincidence, shown in
the man Jesus, as divinity embracing humanity in Life
and its demonstration, — reducing to human *Divinity and* 18
perception and understanding the Life which *humanity*
is God. In divine revelation, material and corporeal selfhood disappear, and the spiritual idea is understood. 21

The woman in the Apocalypse symbolizes generic man,
the spiritual idea of God; she illustrates the coincidence
of God and man as the divine Principle and *Spiritual* 24
divine idea. The Revelator symbolizes Spirit *sunlight*
by the sun. The spiritual idea is clad with the radiance
of spiritual Truth, and matter is put under her feet. The 27
light portrayed is really neither solar nor lunar, but spiritual Life, which is "the light of men." In the first chapter
of the Fourth Gospel it is written, "There was a man sent 30
from God . . . to bear witness of that Light."

John the Baptist prophesied the coming of the im-

1 maculate Jesus, and John saw in those days the spiritual
idea as the Messiah, who would baptize with the Holy
3 Spiritual idea Ghost, — divine Science. As Elias presented
revealed the idea of the fatherhood of God, which Jesus
afterwards manifested, so the Revelator completed this
6 figure with woman, typifying the spiritual idea of God's
motherhood. The moon is under her feet. This idea
reveals the universe as secondary and tributary to Spirit,
9 from which the universe borrows its reflected light, substance, life, and intelligence.

The spiritual idea is crowned with twelve stars. The
12 twelve tribes of Israel with all mortals, — separated by
Spiritual idea belief from man's divine origin and the true
crowned idea, — will through much tribulation yield to
15 the activities of the divine Principle of man in the harmony of Science. These are the stars in the crown of
rejoicing. They are the lamps in the spiritual heavens
18 of the age, which show the workings of the spiritual idea
by healing the sick and the sinning, and by manifesting
the light which shines "unto the perfect day" as the night
21 of materialism wanes.

Revelation xii. 2. And she being with child cried, travail-
ing in birth, and pained to be delivered.

24 Also the spiritual idea is typified by a woman in travail, waiting to be delivered of her sweet promise, but re-
Travail membering no more her sorrow for joy that
27 and joy the birth goes on; for great is the idea, and the
travail portentous.

Revelation xii. 3. And there appeared another wonder in
30 heaven; and behold a great red dragon, having seven heads
and ten horns, and seven crowns upon his heads.

Human sense may well marvel at discord, while, to a 1
diviner sense, harmony is the real and discord the unreal.
We may well be astonished at sin, sickness, and   The dragon   3
death. We may well be perplexed at human   as a type
fear; and still more astounded at hatred, which lifts
its hydra head, showing its horns in the many inventions 6
of evil. But why should we stand aghast at nothingness?
The great red dragon symbolizes a lie, — the belief
that substance, life, and intelligence can be material. 9
This dragon stands for the sum total of human error.
The ten horns of the dragon typify the belief that matter has power of its own, and that by means of an 12
evil mind in matter the Ten Commandments can be
broken.

The Revelator lifts the veil from this embodiment of 15
all evil, and beholds its awful character; but he also
sees the nothingness of evil and the allness of   The sting of
God. The Revelator sees that old serpent,   the serpent   18
whose name is devil or evil, holding untiring watch, that
he may bite the heel of truth and seemingly impede the
offspring of the spiritual idea, which is prolific in health, 21
holiness, and immortality.

Revelation xii. 4. And his tail drew the third part of the
stars of heaven, and did cast them to the earth: and the 24
dragon stood before the woman which was ready to be
delivered, for to devour her child as soon as it was born.

The serpentine form stands for subtlety, winding its 27
way amidst all evil, but doing this in the name of good.
Its sting is spoken of by Paul, when he refers   Animal
to "spiritual wickedness in high places." It   tendency   30
is the animal instinct in mortals, which would impel

1 them to devour each other and cast out devils through
Beelzebub.

3   As of old, evil still charges the spiritual idea with error's
own nature and methods. This malicious animal instinct, of which the dragon is the type, incites mortals to
6 kill morally and physically even their fellow-mortals, and
worse still, to charge the innocent with the crime. This
last infirmity of sin will sink its perpetrator into a night
9 without a star.

The author is convinced that the accusations against
Jesus of Nazareth and even his crucifixion were instigated
12   Malicious   by the criminal instinct here described. The
barbarity   Revelator speaks of Jesus as the Lamb of God
and of the dragon as warring against innocence. Since Jesus
15 must have been tempted in all points, he, the immaculate,
met and conquered sin in every form. The brutal barbarity of his foes could emanate from no source except the
18 highest degree of human depravity. Jesus "*opened not
his mouth.*" Until the majesty of Truth should be demonstrated in divine Science, the spiritual idea was arraigned
21 before the tribunal of so-called mortal mind, which was
unloosed in order that the false claim of mind in matter
might uncover its own crime of defying immortal Mind.
24   From Genesis to the Apocalypse, sin, sickness, and
death, envy, hatred, and revenge, — all evil, — are typi-
    Doom of   fied by a serpent, or animal subtlety. Jesus
27   the dragon   said, quoting a line from the Psalms, "They
hated me without a cause." The serpent is perpetually
close upon the heel of harmony. From the beginning
30 to the end, the serpent pursues with hatred the spiritual
idea. In Genesis, this allegorical, talking serpent typifies mortal mind, "more subtle than any beast of the

field." In the Apocalypse, when nearing its doom, this 1
evil increases and becomes the great red dragon, swollen
with sin, inflamed with war against spirituality, and ripe 3
for destruction. It is full of lust and hate, loathing the
brightness of divine glory.

Revelation xii. 5. And she brought forth a man child, 6
who was to rule all nations with a rod of iron: and her
child was caught up unto God, and to His throne.

Led on by the grossest element of mortal mind, Herod 9
decreed the death of every male child in order that the
man Jesus, the masculine representative of the *The conflict*
spiritual idea, might never hold sway and de- *with purity* 12
prive Herod of his crown. The impersonation of the
spiritual idea had a brief history in the earthly life of our
Master; but "of his kingdom there shall be no end," 15
for Christ, God's idea, will eventually rule all nations
and peoples — imperatively, absolutely, finally — with divine Science. This immaculate idea, represented first 18
by man and, according to the Revelator, last by woman,
will baptize with fire; and the fiery baptism will burn up
the chaff of error with the fervent heat of Truth and Love, 21
melting and purifying even the gold of human character.
After the stars sang together and all was primeval harmony, the material lie made war upon the spiritual idea; 24
but this only impelled the idea to rise to the zenith of
demonstration, destroying sin, sickness, and death, and
to be caught up unto God, — to be found in its divine 27
Principle.

Revelation xii. 6. And the woman fled into the wilderness, where she hath a place prepared of God.   30

1   As the children of Israel were guided triumphantly
through the Red Sea, the dark ebbing and flowing tides
3   Spiritual   of human fear, — as they were led through the
    guidance   wilderness, walking wearily through the great
desert of human hopes, and anticipating the promised
6 joy, — so shall the spiritual idea guide all right desires
in their passage from sense to Soul, from a material sense
of existence to the spiritual, up to the glory prepared for
9 them who love God. Stately Science pauses not, but
moves before them, a pillar of cloud by day and of fire
by night, leading to divine heights.

12   If we remember the beautiful description which Sir
Walter Scott puts into the mouth of Rebecca the Jewess
in the story of Ivanhoe, —

15   When Israel, of the Lord beloved,
            Out of the land of bondage came,
            Her fathers' God before her moved,
18   An awful guide, in smoke and flame, —

we may also offer the prayer which concludes the same
hymn, —

21   And oh, when stoops on Judah's path
            In shade and storm the frequent night,
            Be Thou, longsuffering, slow to wrath,
24   A burning and a shining light!

Revelation xii. 7, 8. And there was war in heaven:
Michael and his angels fought against the dragon; and the
27 dragon fought, and his angels, and prevailed not; neither
was their place found any more in heaven.

The Old Testament assigns to the angels, God's divine
30   Angelic   messages, different offices. Michael's charac-
    offices   teristic is spiritual strength. He leads the
hosts of heaven against the power of sin, Satan, and

fights the holy wars. Gabriel has the more quiet task 1
of imparting a sense of the ever-presence of ministering
Love. These angels deliver us from the depths. Truth 3
and Love come nearer in the hour of woe, when strong
faith or spiritual strength wrestles and prevails through
the understanding of God. The Gabriel of His presence 6
has no contests. To infinite, ever-present Love, all is
Love, and there is no error, no sin, sickness, nor death.
Against Love, the dragon warreth not long, for he is 9
killed by the divine Principle. Truth and Love prevail
against the dragon because the dragon cannot war with
them. Thus endeth the conflict between the flesh and 12
Spirit.

Revelation xii. 9. And the great dragon was cast out,
that old serpent, called the devil, and Satan, which deceiv- 15
eth the whole world: he was cast out into the earth, and his
angels were cast out with him.

That false claim — that ancient belief, that old serpent 18
whose name is devil (evil), claiming that there is intelligence in matter either to benefit or to injure
men — is pure delusion, the red dragon; and Dragon 21
it is cast out by Christ, Truth, the spiritual cast down to earth
idea, and so proved to be powerless. The words "cast
unto the earth" show the dragon to be nothingness, dust 24
to dust; and therefore, in his pretence of being a talker,
he must be a lie from the beginning. His angels, or messages, are cast out with their author. The beast and the 27
false prophets are lust and hypocrisy. These wolves in
sheep's clothing are detected and killed by innocence, the
Lamb of Love. 30
Divine Science shows how the Lamb slays the wolf.

1 Innocence and Truth overcome guilt and error. Ever since the foundation of the world, ever since error would

3 **Warfare with error** establish material belief, evil has tried to slay the Lamb; but Science is able to destroy this lie, called evil. The twelfth chapter of the Apocalypse

6 typifies the divine method of warfare in Science, and the glorious results of this warfare. The following chapters depict the fatal effects of trying to meet error with error.

9 The narrative follows the order used in Genesis. In Genesis, first the true method of creation is set forth and then the false. Here, also, the Revelator first exhibits

12 the true warfare and then the false.

Revelation xii. 10–12. And I heard a loud voice saying in heaven, Now is come salvation, and strength, and the

15 kingdom of our God, and the power of His Christ: for the accuser of our brethren is cast down, which accused them before our God day and night. And they overcame him by

18 the blood of the Lamb, and by the word of their testimony; and they loved not their lives unto the death. Therefore rejoice, ye heavens, and ye that dwell in them. Woe to the

21 inhabiters of the earth and of the sea! for the devil is come down unto you, having great wrath, because he knoweth that he hath but a short time.

24 For victory over a single sin, we give thanks and magnify the Lord of Hosts. What shall we say of the mighty

Pæan of jubilee conquest over all sin? A louder song, sweeter

27 than has ever before reached high heaven, now rises clearer and nearer to the great heart of Christ; for the accuser is not there, and Love sends forth her

30 primal and everlasting strain. Self-abnegation, by which we lay down all for Truth, or Christ, in our warfare against error, is a rule in Christian Science. This rule clearly

interprets God as divine Principle, — as Life, represented 1
by the Father; as Truth, represented by the Son; as Love,
represented by the Mother.   Every mortal at some period, 3
here or hereafter, must grapple with and overcome the
mortal belief in a power opposed to God.

The Scripture, "Thou hast been faithful over a few 6
things, I will make thee ruler over many," is literally fulfilled, when we are conscious of the supremacy   The robe
of Truth, by which the nothingness of error   of Science   9
is seen; and we know that the nothingness of error is in
proportion to its wickedness.   He that touches the hem
of Christ's robe and masters his mortal beliefs, animality, 12
and hate, rejoices in the proof of healing, — in a sweet
and certain sense that God is Love.   Alas for those who
break faith with divine Science and fail to strangle the 15
serpent of sin as well as of sickness!   They are dwellers
still in the deep darkness of belief.   They are in the surg-
ing sea of error, not struggling to lift their heads above the 18
drowning wave.

What must the end be?   They must eventually expi-
ate their sin through suffering.   The sin, which one has 21
made his bosom companion, comes back to him   Expiation by
at last with accelerated force, for the devil   suffering
knoweth his time is short.   Here the Scriptures declare 24
that evil is temporal, not eternal.   The dragon is at last
stung to death by his own malice; but how many periods
of torture it may take to remove all sin, must depend upon 27
sin's obduracy.

Revelation xii. 13.   And when the dragon saw that he
was cast unto the earth, he persecuted the woman which 30
brought forth the man child.

1 The march of mind and of honest investigation will
bring the hour when the people will chain, with fetters of
3 Apathy to   some sort, the growing occultism of this period.
occultism   The present apathy as to the tendency of
certain active yet unseen mental agencies will finally be
6 shocked into another extreme mortal mood, — into human
indignation; for one extreme follows another.

Revelation xii. 15, 16. And the serpent cast out of his
9 mouth water as a flood, after the woman, that he might
cause her to be carried away of the flood. And the earth
helped the woman, and the earth opened her mouth, and
12 swallowed up the flood which the dragon cast out of his
mouth.

Millions of unprejudiced minds — simple seekers for
15 Truth, weary wanderers, athirst in the desert — are wait-
Receptive   ing and watching for rest and drink. Give
hearts   them a cup of cold water in Christ's name,
18 and never fear the consequences. What if the old dragon
should send forth a new flood to drown the Christ-idea?
He can neither drown your voice with its roar, nor again
21 sink the world into the deep waters of chaos and old night.
In this age the earth will help the woman; the spiritual
idea will be understood. Those ready for the blessing
24 you impart will give thanks. The waters will be paci-
fied, and Christ will command the wave.

When God heals the sick or the sinning, they should
27 know the great benefit which Mind has wrought. They
Hidden ways   should also know the great delusion of mor-
of iniquity   tal mind, when it makes them sick or sinful.
30 Many are willing to open the eyes of the people to the
power of good resident in divine Mind, but they are

not so willing to point out the evil in human thought, 1
and expose evil's hidden mental ways of accomplishing
iniquity. 3
Why this backwardness, since exposure is necessary
to ensure the avoidance of the evil? Because people like
you better when you tell them their virtues *Christly* 6
than when you tell them their vices. It re- *warning*
quires the spirit of our blessed Master to tell a man his
faults, and so risk human displeasure for the sake of doing 9
right and benefiting our race. Who is telling mankind
of the foe in ambush? Is the informer one who sees the
foe? If so, listen and be wise. Escape from evil, and 12
designate those as unfaithful stewards who have seen the
danger and yet have given no warning.
At all times and under all circumstances, overcome 15
evil with good. Know thyself, and God will supply
the wisdom and the occasion for a victory *The armor*
over evil. Clad in the panoply of Love, *of divinity* 18
human hatred cannot reach you. The cement of a
higher humanity will unite all interests in the one
divinity. 21
Through trope and metaphor, the Revelator, immortal
scribe of Spirit and of a true idealism, furnishes the
mirror in which mortals may see their own *Pure religion* 24
image. In significant figures he depicts the *enthroned*
thoughts which he beholds in mortal mind. Thus he
rebukes the conceit of sin, and foreshadows its doom. 27
With his spiritual strength, he has opened wide the gates
of glory, and illumined the night of paganism with the
sublime grandeur of divine Science, outshining sin, sorcery, 30
lust, and hypocrisy. He takes away mitre and sceptre.
He enthrones pure and undefiled religion, and lifts on

1 high only those who have washed their robes white in
obedience and suffering.

3   Thus we see, in both the first and last books of the
Bible, — in Genesis and in the Apocalypse, — that sin

Native noth- is to be Christianly and scientifically reduced
6 *ingness of sin* to its native nothingness. "Love one another" (I John, iii. 23), is the most simple and profound
counsel of the inspired writer. In Science we are chil-
9 dren of God; but whatever is of material sense, or mortal, belongs not to His children, for materiality is the
inverted image of spirituality.

12   Love fulfils the law of Christian Science, and nothing
short of this divine Principle, understood and demon-

Fulfilment strated, can ever furnish the vision of the
15 *of the Law* Apocalypse, open the seven seals of error with
Truth, or uncover the myriad illusions of sin, sickness,
and death. Under the supremacy of Spirit, it will be seen
18 and acknowledged that matter must disappear.

In Revelation xxi. 1 we read: —

And I saw a new heaven and a new earth: for the first
21 heaven and the first earth were passed away; and there was
no more sea.

The Revelator had not yet passed the transitional
24 stage in human experience called death, but he already

Man's present saw a new heaven and a new earth. Through
possibilities what sense came this vision to St. John? Not
27 through the material visual organs for seeing, for optics
are inadequate to take in so wonderful a scene. Were this
new heaven and new earth terrestrial or celestial, mate-

rial or spiritual? They could not be the former, for the 1
human sense of space is unable to grasp such a view.
The Revelator was on our plane of existence, while yet 3
beholding what the eye cannot see, — that which is invisible to the uninspired thought. This testimony of Holy
Writ sustains the fact in Science, that the heavens and 6
earth to one human consciousness, that consciousness
which God bestows, are spiritual, while to another, the
unillumined human mind, the vision is material. This 9
shows unmistakably that what the human mind terms
matter and spirit indicates states and stages of consciousness. 12

Accompanying this scientific consciousness was another revelation, even the declaration from heaven, supreme harmony, that God, the divine Principle   Nearness 15
of harmony, is ever with men, and they are   of Deity
His people. Thus man was no longer regarded as a miserable sinner, but as the blessed child of God. Why? 18
Because St. John's corporeal sense of the heavens and
earth had vanished, and in place of this false sense was
the spiritual sense, the subjective state by which he could 21
see the new heaven and new earth, which involve the
spiritual idea and consciousness of reality. This is Scriptural authority for concluding that such a recognition of 24
being is, and has been, possible to men in this present
state of existence, — that we can become conscious,
here and now, of a cessation of death, sorrow, and pain. 27
This is indeed a foretaste of absolute Christian Science.
Take heart, dear sufferer, for this reality of being will
surely appear sometime and in some way. There will 30
be no more pain, and all tears will be wiped away. When
you read this, remember Jesus' words, "The kingdom of

1 God is within you." This spiritual consciousness is
therefore a present possibility.

3   The Revelator also takes in another view, adapted to
console the weary pilgrim, journeying "uphill all the way."

He writes, in Revelation xxi. 9: —

6   And there came unto me one of the seven angels which
had the seven vials full of the seven last plagues, and talked
with me, saying, Come hither, I will show thee the bride,
9 the Lamb's wife.

This ministry of Truth, this message from divine Love,
carried John away in spirit. It exalted him till he be-
12 came conscious of the spiritual facts of being
and the "New Jerusalem, coming down from
God, out of heaven," — the spiritual outpour-
15 ing of bliss and glory, which he describes as the city
which "lieth foursquare." The beauty of this text is,
that the sum total of human misery, represented by
18 the seven angelic vials full of seven plagues, has full
compensation in the law of Love. Note this, — that the
very message, or swift-winged thought, which poured
21 forth hatred and torment, brought also the experience
which at last lifted the seer to behold the great city, the
four equal sides of which were heaven-bestowed and
24 heaven-bestowing.

Vials of wrath and consolation

Think of this, dear reader, for it will lift the sack-
cloth from your eyes, and you will behold the soft-
27 winged dove descending upon you. The very
circumstance, which your suffering sense
deems wrathful and afflictive, Love can make an angel
30 entertained unawares. Then thought gently whispers:

Spiritual wedlock

"Come hither! Arise from your false consciousness 1
into the true sense of Love, and behold the Lamb's
wife, — Love wedded to its own spiritual idea." Then 3
cometh the marriage feast, for this revelation will destroy forever the physical plagues imposed by material
sense. 6

This sacred city, described in the Apocalypse (xxi. 16)
as one that "lieth foursquare" and cometh "down from
God, out of heaven," represents the light and   The city 9
glory of divine Science. The builder and   foursquare
maker of this New Jerusalem is God, as we read in the
book of Hebrews; and it is "a city which hath founda- 12
tions." The description is metaphoric. Spiritual teaching must always be by symbols. Did not Jesus illustrate
the truths he taught by the mustard-seed and the prodi- 15
gal? Taken in its allegorical sense, the description of
the city as foursquare has a profound meaning. The
four sides of our city are the Word, Christ, Christianity, 18
and divine Science; "and the gates of it shall not be shut
at all by day: for there shall be no night there." This
city is wholly spiritual, as its four sides indicate. 21

As the Psalmist saith, "Beautiful for situation, the
joy of the whole earth, is mount Zion, on the sides of
the north, the city of the great King." It is   The royally 24
indeed a city of the Spirit, fair, royal, and   divine gates
square. Northward, its gates open to the North Star,
the Word, the polar magnet of Revelation; eastward, 27
to the star seen by the Wisemen of the Orient, who followed it to the manger of Jesus; southward, to the
genial tropics, with the Southern Cross in the skies, 30
— the Cross of Calvary, which binds human society
into solemn union; westward, to the grand realization

1 of the Golden Shore of Love and the Peaceful Sea of
Harmony.

3   This heavenly city, lighted by the Sun of Righteousness, — this New Jerusalem, this infinite All, which to
     Revelation's   us seems hidden in the mist of remoteness, —
6   pure zenith   reached St. John's vision while yet he taber-
nacled with mortals.

In Revelation xxi. 22, further describing this holy city,
9 the beloved Disciple writes: —

And I saw no temple therein: for the Lord God Almighty
and the Lamb are the temple of it.

12   There was no temple, — that is, no material structure
in which to worship God, for He must be worshipped
     The shrine   in spirit and in love. The word *temple* also
15   celestial   means *body*. The Revelator was familiar
with Jesus' use of this word, as when Jesus spoke of his
material body as the temple to be temporarily rebuilt
18 (John ii. 21). What further indication need we of the
real man's incorporeality than this, that John saw
heaven and earth with "no temple [body] therein"?
21 This kingdom of God "is within you," — is within
reach of man's consciousness here, and the spiritual
idea reveals it. In divine Science, man possesses this
24 recognition of harmony consciously in proportion to his
understanding of God.

The term Lord, as used in our version of the Old
27 Testament, is often synonymous with Jehovah, and ex-
     Divine sense   presses the Jewish concept, not yet elevated
     of Deity   to deific apprehension through spiritual trans-
30 figuration. Yet the word gradually approaches a higher
meaning. This human sense of Deity yields to the divine

sense, even as the material sense of personality yields 1
to the incorporeal sense of God and man as the infinite
Principle and infinite idea, — as one Father with His uni- 3
versal family, held in the gospel of Love. The Lamb's
wife presents the unity of male and female as no longer
two wedded individuals, but as two individual natures 6
in one; and this compounded spiritual individuality reflects God as Father-Mother, not as a corporeal being.
In this divinely united spiritual consciousness, there is no 9
impediment to eternal bliss, — to the perfectibility of
God's creation.

This spiritual, holy habitation has no boundary 12
nor limit, but its four cardinal points are: first, the
Word of Life, Truth, and Love; second, The city of
the Christ, the spiritual idea of God; third,   our God   15
Christianity, which is the outcome of the divine Principle of the Christ-idea in Christian history; fourth,
Christian Science, which to-day and forever interprets 18
this great example and the great Exemplar. This city
of our God has no need of sun or satellite, for Love
is the light of it, and divine Mind is its own interpreter. 21
All who are saved must walk in this light. Mighty
potentates and dynasties will lay down their honors ·
within the heavenly city. Its gates open towards light 24
and glory both within and without, for all is good, and
nothing can enter that city, which "defileth, . . . or
maketh a lie." 27

The writer's present feeble sense of Christian Science
closes with St. John's Revelation as recorded by the
great apostle, for his vision is the acme of this Science 30
as the Bible reveals it.

In the following Psalm one word shows, though faintly,

1 the light which Christian Science throws on the Scriptures
by substituting for the corporeal sense, the incorporeal
3 or spiritual sense of Deity: —

PSALM XXIII

[DIVINE LOVE] is my shepherd; I shall not want.
6   [LOVE] maketh me to lie down in green pastures:
[LOVE] leadeth me beside the still waters.

[LOVE] restoreth my soul [spiritual sense]: [LOVE] lead-
9 eth me in the paths of righteousness for His name's sake.

Yea, though I walk through the valley of the shadow of
death, I will fear no evil: for [LOVE] is with me; [LOVE'S]
12 rod and [LOVE'S] staff they comfort me.

[LOVE] prepareth a table before me in the presence of
mine enemies: [LOVE] anointeth my head with oil; my cup
15 runneth over.

Surely goodness and mercy shall follow me all the days of
my life; and I will dwell in the house [the consciousness]
18 of [LOVE] for ever.

CHAPTER XVII

Glossary

These things saith He that is holy, He that is true, He that hath the key of David, He that openeth, and no man shutteth; and shutteth, and no man openeth; I know thy works: behold, I have set before thee an open door, and no man can shut it. — REVELATION.

IN Christian Science we learn that the substitution of 1
the spiritual for the material definition of a Scriptural word often elucidates the meaning of the inspired 3
writer. On this account this chapter is added. It contains the metaphysical interpretation of Bible terms, giving their spiritual sense, which is also their original 6
meaning.

ABEL. Watchfulness; self-offering; surrendering to the creator the early fruits of experience. 9

ABRAHAM. Fidelity; faith in the divine Life and in the eternal Principle of being.
This patriarch illustrated the purpose of Love to create 12
trust in good, and showed the life-preserving power of spiritual understanding.

ADAM. Error; a falsity; the belief in "original sin," 15
sickness, and death; evil; the opposite of good, — of God and His creation; a curse; a belief in intelligent matter,

1 finiteness, and mortality; "dust to dust;" red sand-
stone; nothingness; the first god of mythology; not
3 God's man, who represents the one God and is His own
image and likeness; the opposite of Spirit and His creations; that which is not the image and likeness of good,
6 but a material belief, opposed to the one Mind, or Spirit;
a so-called finite mind, producing other minds, thus making "gods many and lords many" (I Corinthians viii. 5);
9 a product of nothing as the mimicry of something; an
unreality as opposed to the great reality of spiritual existence and creation; a so-called man, whose origin,
12 substance, and mind are found to be the antipode of
God, or Spirit; an inverted image of Spirit; the image
and likeness of what God has not created, namely, mat-
15 ter, sin, sickness, and death; the opposer of Truth,
termed error; Life's counterfeit, which ultimates in
death; the opposite of Love, called hate; the usurper
18 of Spirit's creation, called self-creative matter; immortality's opposite, mortality; that of which wisdom saith,
"Thou shalt surely die."

21   The name Adam represents the false supposition that
Life is not eternal, but has beginning and end; that the
infinite enters the finite, that intelligence passes into non-
24 intelligence, and that Soul dwells in material sense; that
immortal Mind results in matter, and matter in mortal
mind; that the one God and creator entered what He cre-
27 ated, and then disappeared in the atheism of matter.

ADVERSARY. An adversary is one who opposes, denies,
disputes, not one who constructs and sustains reality and
30 Truth. Jesus said of the devil, "He was a murderer from
the beginning, . . . he is a liar and the father of it."

This view of Satan is confirmed by the name often con- 1
ferred upon him in Scripture, the "adversary."

ALMIGHTY. All-power; infinity; omnipotence. 3

ANGELS. God's thoughts passing to man; spiritual
intuitions, pure and perfect; the inspiration of goodness,
purity, and immortality, counteracting all evil, sensuality, 6
and mortality.

ARK. Safety; the idea, or reflection, of Truth, proved
to be as immortal as its Principle; the understanding of 9
Spirit, destroying belief in matter.
    God and man coexistent and eternal; Science show-
ing that the spiritual realities of all things are created 12
by Him and exist forever. The ark indicates temptation
overcome and followed by exaltation.

ASHER (Jacob's son). Hope and faith; spiritual com- 15
pensation; the ills of the flesh rebuked.

BABEL. Self-destroying error; a kingdom divided
against itself, which cannot stand; material knowledge. 18
    The higher false knowledge builds on the basis of evi-
dence obtained from the five corporeal senses, the more
confusion ensues, and the more certain is the downfall 21
of its structure.

BAPTISM. Purification by Spirit; submergence in
Spirit. 24
    We are "willing rather to be absent from the body,
and to be present with the Lord." (II Corinthians v. 8.)

1 BELIEVING. Firmness and constancy; not a faltering
nor a blind faith, but the perception of spiritual Truth.
3 Mortal thoughts, illusion.

BENJAMIN (Jacob's son). A physical belief as to life,
substance, and mind; human knowledge, or so-called
6 mortal mind, devoted to matter; pride; envy; fame;
illusion; a false belief; error masquerading as the possessor of life, strength, animation, and power to act.
9 Renewal of affections; self-offering; an improved
state of mortal mind; the introduction of a more spiritual
origin; a gleam of the infinite idea of the infinite Prin-
12 ciple; a spiritual type; that which comforts, consoles,
and supports.

BRIDE. Purity and innocence, conceiving man in the
15 idea of God; a sense of Soul, which has spiritual bliss
and enjoys but cannot suffer.

BRIDEGROOM. Spiritual understanding; the pure con-
18 sciousness that God, the divine Principle, creates man
as His own spiritual idea, and that God is the only creative power.

21 BURIAL. Corporeality and physical sense put out of
sight and hearing; annihilation. Submergence in Spirit;
immortality brought to light.

24 CANAAN (the son of Ham). A sensuous belief; the
testimony of what is termed material sense; the error
which would make man mortal and would make mortal
27 mind a slave to the body.

CHILDREN. The spiritual thoughts and representatives of Life, Truth, and Love.

Sensual and mortal beliefs; counterfeits of creation, 1 whose better originals are God's thoughts, not in embryo, but in maturity; material suppositions of life, sub- 3 stance, and intelligence, opposed to the Science of being.

CHILDREN OF ISRAEL. The representatives of Soul, not corporeal sense; the offspring of Spirit, who, having 6 wrestled with error, sin, and sense, are governed by divine Science; some of the ideas of God beheld as men, casting out error and healing the sick; Christ's offspring. 9

CHRIST. The divine manifestation of God, which comes to the flesh to destroy incarnate error.

CHURCH. The structure of Truth and Love; what- 12 ever rests upon and proceeds from divine Principle.

The Church is that institution, which affords proof of its utility and is found elevating the race, rousing the 15 dormant understanding from material beliefs to the apprehension of spiritual ideas and the demonstration of divine Science, thereby casting out devils, or error, and 18 healing the sick.

CREATOR. Spirit; Mind; intelligence; the animating divine Principle of all that is real and good; self-existent 21 Life, Truth, and Love; that which is perfect and eternal; the opposite of matter and evil, which have no Principle; God, who made all that was made and could not 24 create an atom or an element the opposite of Himself.

DAN (Jacob's son). Animal magnetism; so-called mortal mind controlling mortal mind; error, working out 27 the designs of error; one belief preying upon another.

1 DAY. The irradiance of Life; light, the spiritual idea
of Truth and Love.

3 "And the evening and the morning were the first day."
(Genesis i. 5.) The objects of time and sense disappear
in the illumination of spiritual understanding, and Mind
6 measures time according to the good that is unfolded.
This unfolding is God's day, and "there shall be no night
there."

9 DEATH. An illusion, the lie of life in matter; the unreal and untrue; the opposite of Life.

Matter has no life, hence it has no real existence. Mind
12 is immortal. The flesh, warring against Spirit; that
which frets itself free from one belief only to be fettered
by another, until every belief of life where Life is not
15 yields to eternal Life. Any material evidence of death is
false, for it contradicts the spiritual facts of being.

DEVIL. Evil; a lie; error; neither corporeality nor
18 mind; the opposite of Truth; a belief in sin, sickness,
and death; animal magnetism or hypnotism; the lust of
the flesh, which saith: "I am life and intelligence in
21 matter. There is more than one mind, for I am mind, —
a wicked mind, self-made or created by a tribal god and
put into the opposite of mind, termed matter, thence to
24 reproduce a mortal universe, including man, not after the
image and likeness of Spirit, but after its own image."

DOVE. A symbol of divine Science; purity and peace;
27 hope and faith.

DUST. Nothingness; the absence of substance, life, or
intelligence.

EARS. Not organs of the so-called corporeal senses, 1 but spiritual understanding.

Jesus said, referring to spiritual perception, "Having 3 ears, hear ye not?" (Mark viii. 18.)

EARTH. A sphere; a type of eternity and immortality, which are likewise without beginning or end.   6

To material sense, earth is matter; to spiritual sense, it is a compound idea.

ELIAS. Prophecy; spiritual evidence opposed to mate- 9 rial sense; Christian Science, with which can be discerned the spiritual fact of whatever the material senses behold; the basis of immortality.   12

"Elias truly shall first come and restore all things." (Matthew xvii. 11.)

ERROR. See chapter on Recapitulation, page 472.   15

EUPHRATES (river). Divine Science encompassing the universe and man; the true idea of God; a type of the glory which is to come; metaphysics taking the 18 place of physics; the reign of righteousness. The atmosphere of human belief before it accepts sin, sickness, or death; a state of mortal thought, the only error of which 21 is limitation; finity; the opposite of infinity.

EVE. A beginning; mortality; that which does not last forever; a finite belief concerning life, substance, 24 and intelligence in matter; error; the belief that the human race originated materially instead of spiritually, — that man started first from dust, second from a rib, and 27 third from an egg.

1　EVENING. Mistiness of mortal thought; weariness of mortal mind; obscured views; peace and rest.

3　EYES. Spiritual discernment, — not material but mental.

　　Jesus said, thinking of the outward vision, "Having 6 eyes, see ye not?" (Mark viii. 18.)

　　FAN. Separator of fable from fact; that which gives action to thought.

9　FATHER. Eternal Life; the one Mind; the divine Principle, commonly called God.

　　FEAR. Heat; inflammation; anxiety; ignorance; error; 12 desire; caution.

　　FIRE. Fear; remorse; lust; hatred; destruction; affliction purifying and elevating man.

15　FIRMAMENT. Spiritual understanding; the scientific line of demarcation between Truth and error, between Spirit and so-called matter.

18　FLESH. An error of physical belief; a supposition that life, substance, and intelligence are in matter; an illusion; a belief that matter has sensation.

21　GAD (Jacob's son). Science; spiritual being understood; haste towards harmony.

　　GETHSEMANE. Patient woe; the human yielding to 24 the divine; love meeting no response, but still remaining love.

GHOST. An illusion; a belief that mind is outlined and limited; a supposition that spirit is finite.

GIHON (river). The rights of woman acknowledged morally, civilly, and socially.

GOD. The great I AM; the all-knowing, all-seeing, all-acting, all-wise, all-loving, and eternal; Principle; Mind; Soul; Spirit; Life; Truth; Love; all substance; intelligence.

GODS. Mythology; a belief that life, substance, and intelligence are both mental and material; a supposition of sentient physicality; the belief that infinite Mind is in finite forms; the various theories that hold mind to be a material sense, existing in brain, nerve, matter; suppositious minds, or souls, going in and out of matter, erring and mortal; the serpents of error, which say, "Ye shall be as gods."

God is one God, infinite and perfect, and cannot become finite and imperfect.

GOOD. God; Spirit; omnipotence; omniscience; omnipresence; omni-action.

HAM (Noah's son). Corporeal belief; sensuality; slavery; tyranny.

HEART. Mortal feelings, motives, affections, joys, and sorrows.

HEAVEN. Harmony; the reign of Spirit; government by divine Principle; spirituality; bliss; the atmosphere of Soul.

1 HELL. Mortal belief; error; lust; remorse; hatred;
revenge; sin; sickness; death; suffering and self-de-
3 struction; self-imposed agony; effects of sin; that which
"worketh abomination or maketh a lie."

HIDDEKEL (river). Divine Science understood and
6 acknowledged. *omniscience*

HOLY GHOST. Divine Science; the development of
eternal Life, Truth, and Love.

9 I, or EGO. Divine Principle; Spirit; Soul; incorporeal, unerring, immortal, and eternal Mind.
There is but one I, or Us, but one divine Principle, or
12 Mind, governing all existence; man and woman unchanged forever in their individual characters, even as
numbers which never blend with each other, though they
15 are governed by one Principle. All the objects of God's
creation reflect one Mind, and whatever reflects not this
one Mind, is false and erroneous, even the belief that
18 life, substance, and intelligence are both mental and
material.

I AM. God; incorporeal and eternal Mind; divine
21 Principle; the only Ego.

IN. A term obsolete in Science if used with reference
to Spirit, or Deity.

24 INTELLIGENCE. Substance; self-existent and eternal
Mind; that which is never unconscious nor limited.
See chapter on Recapitulation, page 469.

ISSACHAR (Jacob's son). A corporeal belief; the ₁
offspring of error; envy; hatred; selfishness; self-will;
lust.   3

JACOB. A corporeal mortal embracing duplicity, repentance, sensualism. Inspiration; the revelation of
Science, in which the so-called material senses yield to 6
the spiritual sense of Life and Love.

JAPHET (Noah's son). A type of spiritual peace, flowing from the understanding that God is the divine Prin- 9
ciple of all existence, and that man is His idea, the child
of His care.

JERUSALEM. Mortal belief and knowledge obtained 12
from the five corporeal senses; the pride of power and
the power of pride; sensuality; envy; oppression; tyranny. Home, heaven.   15

JESUS. The highest human corporeal concept of the
divine idea, rebuking and destroying error and bringing
to light man's immortality.   18

JOSEPH. A corporeal mortal; a higher sense of Truth
rebuking mortal belief, or error, and showing the immortality and supremacy of Truth; pure affection blessing 21
its enemies.

JUDAH. A corporeal material belief progressing and
disappearing; the spiritual understanding of God and 24
man appearing.

1 KINGDOM OF HEAVEN. The reign of harmony in divine
Science; the realm of unerring, eternal, and omnipotent
3 Mind; the atmosphere of Spirit, where Soul is supreme.

KNOWLEDGE. Evidence obtained from the five corporeal senses; mortality; beliefs and opinions; human
6 theories, doctrines, hypotheses; that which is not divine
and is the origin of sin, sickness, and death; the opposite of spiritual Truth and understanding.

9 LAMB OF GOD. The spiritual idea of Love; self-immolation; innocence and purity; sacrifice.

LEVI (Jacob's son). A corporeal and sensual belief;
12 mortal man; denial of the fulness of God's creation;
ecclesiastical despotism.

LIFE. See chapter on Recapitulation, page 468.

15 LORD. In the Hebrew, this term is sometimes employed as a title, which has the inferior sense of master,
or ruler. In the Greek, the word *kurios* almost always
18 has this lower sense, unless specially coupled with the
name God. Its higher signification is Supreme Ruler.

LORD GOD. Jehovah.
21 This double term is not used in the first chapter of
Genesis, the record of spiritual creation. It is introduced in the second and following chapters, when the
24 spiritual sense of God and of infinity is disappearing
from the recorder's thought, — when the true scientific
statements of the Scriptures become clouded through a

physical sense of God as finite and corporeal. From this
follow idolatry and mythology, — belief in many gods, o
material intelligences, as the opposite of the one Spir , 3
or intelligence, named Elohim, or God.

MAN. The compound idea of infinite Spirit; the sr rit-
ual image and likeness of God; the full representat' n of 6
Mind.

MATTER. Mythology; mortality; another r me for
mortal mind; illusion; intelligence, substanc and life 9
in non-intelligence and mortality; life resultin n death,
and death in life; sensation in the sensatior ss; mind
originating in matter; the opposite of Trut the oppo- 12
site of Spirit; the opposite of God; that of wh h immortal
Mind takes no cognizance; that which mortal mind sees,
feels, hears, tastes, and smells only in belief. 15

MIND. The only I, or Us; the only Spirit, Soul, divine
Principle, substance, Life, Truth, Love; the one God;
not that which is *in* man, but the divine Principle, or God, 18
of whom man is the full and perfect expression; Deity,
which outlines but is not outlined.

MIRACLE. That which is divinely natural, but must 21
be learned humanly; a phenomenon of Science.

MORNING. Light; symbol of Truth; revelation and
progress. 24

MORTAL MIND. Nothing claiming to be something,
for Mind is immortal; mythology; error creating other
errors; a suppositional material sense, *alias* the belief 27

1 that sensation is in matter, which is sensationless; a belief that life, substance, and intelligence are in and of
3 matter; the opposite of Spirit, and therefore the opposite of God, or good; the belief that life has a beginning and therefore an end; the belief that man is the off-
6 spring of mortals; the belief that there can be more than one creator; idolatry; the subjective states of error; material senses; that which neither exists in Science nor
9 can be recognized by the spiritual sense; sin; sickness; death.

MOSES. A corporeal mortal; moral courage; a type
12 of moral law and the demonstration thereof; the proof that, without the gospel, — the union of justice and affection, — there is something spiritually lacking, since justice
15 demands penalties under the law.

MOTHER. God; divine and eternal Principle; Life, Truth, and Love.

18 NEW JERUSALEM. Divine Science; the spiritual facts and harmony of the universe; the kingdom of heaven, or reign of harmony.

21 NIGHT. Darkness; doubt; fear.

NOAH. A corporeal mortal; knowledge of the nothingness of material things and of the immortality of all
24 that is spiritual.

OIL. Consecration; charity; gentleness; prayer; heavenly inspiration.

27 PHARISEE. Corporeal and sensuous belief; self-righteousness; vanity; hypocrisy.

PISON (river). The love of the good and beautiful, and 1
their immortality. *omnipresence*

PRINCIPLE. See chapter on Recapitulation, page 465. 3

PROPHET. A spiritual seer; disappearance of material sense before the conscious facts of spiritual Truth.

PURSE. Laying up treasures in matter; error. 6

RED DRAGON. Error; fear; inflammation; sensuality; subtlety; animal magnetism; envy; revenge.

RESURRECTION. Spiritualization of thought; a new 9
and higher idea of immortality, or spiritual existence; material belief yielding to spiritual understanding.

REUBEN (Jacob's son). Corporeality; sensuality; de- 12
lusion; mortality; error.

RIVER. Channel of thought.
When smooth and unobstructed, it typifies the course 15
of Truth; but muddy, foaming, and dashing, it is a type of error.

ROCK. Spiritual foundation; Truth. Coldness and 18
stubbornness.

SALVATION. Life, Truth, and Love understood and demonstrated as supreme over all; sin, sickness, and 21
death destroyed.

SEAL. The signet of error revealed by Truth.

1 SERPENT (*ophis*, in Greek; *nacash*, in Hebrew).
Subtlety; a lie; the opposite of Truth, named error;
3 the first statement of mythology and idolatry; the belief
in more than one God; animal magnetism; the first lie
of limitation; finity; the first claim that there is an oppo-
6 site of Spirit, or good, termed matter, or evil; the first
delusion that error exists as fact; the first claim that sin,
sickness, and death are the realities of life. The first
9 audible claim that God was not omnipotent and that
there was another power, named *evil*, which was as real
and eternal as God, good.

12 SHEEP. Innocence; inoffensiveness; those who follow
their leader.

SHEM (Noah's son). A corporeal mortal; kindly affec-
15 tion; love rebuking error; reproof of sensualism.

SON. The Son of God, the Messiah or Christ. The
son of man, the offspring of the flesh. "Son of a year."

18 SOULS. See chapter on Recapitulation, page 466.

SPIRIT. Divine substance; Mind; divine Principle;
all that is good; God; that only which is perfect, ever-
21 lasting, omnipresent, omnipotent, infinite.

SPIRITS. Mortal beliefs; corporeality; evil minds;
supposed intelligences, or gods; the opposites of God;
24 errors; hallucinations. (See page 466.)

SUBSTANCE. See chapter on Recapitulation, page
468.

SUN. The symbol of Soul governing man, — of 1
Truth, Life, and Love.

SWORD. The idea of Truth; justice. Revenge; 3
anger.

TARES. Mortality; error; sin; sickness; disease;
death. 6

TEMPLE. Body; the idea of Life, substance, and intelligence; the superstructure of Truth; the shrine of
Love; a material superstructure, where mortals congre- 9
gate for worship.

THUMMIM. Perfection; the eternal demand of divine
Science. 12
The Urim and Thummim, which were to be on Aaron's
breast when he went before Jehovah, were holiness and
purification of thought and deed, which alone can fit us 15
for the office of spiritual teaching.

TIME. Mortal measurements; limits, in which are
summed up all human acts, thoughts, beliefs, opinions, 18
knowledge; matter; error; that which begins before,
and continues after, what is termed death, until the mortal
disappears and spiritual perfection appears. 21

TITHE. Contribution; tenth part; homage; gratitude.
A sacrifice to the gods.

UNCLEANLINESS. Impure thoughts; error; sin; dirt. 24

UNGODLINESS. Opposition to the divine Principle and
its spiritual idea.

1 UNKNOWN. That which spiritual sense alone comprehends, and which is unknown to the material senses.

3 Paganism and agnosticism may define Deity as "the
great unknowable;" but Christian Science brings God
much nearer to man, and makes Him better known as
6 the All-in-all, forever near.

Paul saw in Athens an altar dedicated "to the unknown
God." Referring to it, he said to the Athenians: "Whom
9 therefore ye ignorantly worship, Him declare I unto you."
(Acts xvii. 23.)

URIM. Light.

12 The rabbins believed that the stones in the breast-
plate of the high-priest had supernatural illumination,
but Christian Science reveals Spirit, not matter, as the
15 illuminator of all. The illuminations of Science give us
a sense of the nothingness of error, and they show the
spiritual inspiration of Love and Truth to be the only fit
18 preparation for admission to the presence and power of
the Most High.

VALLEY. Depression; meekness; darkness.

21 "Though I walk through the valley of the shadow of
death, I will fear no evil." (Psalm xxiii. 4.)

Though the way is dark in mortal sense, divine Life
24 and Love illumine it, destroy the unrest of mortal thought,
the fear of death, and the supposed reality of error. Christian Science, contradicting sense, maketh the valley to bud
27 and blossom as the rose.

VEIL. A cover; concealment; hiding; hypocrisy.
The Jewish women wore veils over their faces in token

of reverence and submission and in accordance with 1
Pharisaical notions.

The Judaic religion consisted mostly of rites and cere- 3
monies. The motives and affections of a man were of
little value, if only he appeared unto men to fast. The
great Nazarene, as meek as he was mighty, rebuked the 6
hypocrisy, which offered long petitions for blessings upon
material methods, but cloaked the crime, latent in thought,
which was ready to spring into action and crucify God's 9
anointed. The martyrdom of Jesus was the culminating
sin of Pharisaism. It rent the veil of the temple. It revealed the false foundations and superstructures of super- 12
ficial religion, tore from bigotry and superstition their
coverings, and opened the sepulchre with divine Science,
— immortality and Love.   15

WILDERNESS. Loneliness; doubt; darkness. Spon-
taneity of thought and idea; the vestibule in which a
material sense of things disappears, and spiritual sense 18
unfolds the great facts of existence.

WILL. The motive-power of error; mortal belief; animal power. The might and wisdom of God.   21
"For this is the will of God." (I Thessalonians
iv. 3.)
Will, as a quality of so-called mortal mind, is a wrong- 24
doer; hence it should not be confounded with the term
as applied to Mind or to one of God's qualities.

WIND. That which indicates the might of omnipo- 27
tence and the movements of God's spiritual government,
encompassing all things. Destruction; anger; mortal
passions.   30

1 The Greek word for *wind* (*pneuma*) is used also for
spirit, as in the passage in John's Gospel, the third chap-
3 ter, where we read: "The wind [*pneuma*] bloweth where
it listeth. . . . So is every one that is born of the Spirit
[*pneuma*]." Here the original word is the same in both
6 cases, yet it has received different translations, as in other
passages in this same chapter and elsewhere in the New
Testament. This shows how our Master had constantly
9 to employ words of material significance in order to unfold
spiritual thoughts. In the record of Jesus' supposed
death, we read: "He bowed his head, and gave up the
12 ghost;" but this word *ghost* is *pneuma*. It might be translated *wind* or *air,* and the phrase is equivalent to our
common statement, "He breathed his last." What
15 Jesus gave up was indeed air, an etherealized form of
matter, for never did he give up Spirit, or Soul.

WINE. Inspiration; understanding. Error; fornica-
18 tion; temptation; passion.

YEAR. A solar measurement of time; mortality;
space for repentance.
21 "One day is with the Lord as a thousand years."
(II Peter iii. 8.)
One moment of divine consciousness, or the spiritual
24 understanding of Life and Love, is a foretaste of eternity.
This exalted view, obtained and retained when the Science of being is understood, would bridge over with life
27 discerned spiritually the interval of death, and man
would be in the full consciousness of his immortality and
eternal harmony, where sin, sickness, and death are un-
30 known. Time is a mortal thought, the divisor of which

is the solar year. Eternity is God's measurement of Soul- 1
filled years.

YOU. As applied to corporeality, a mortal; finity. 3

ZEAL. The reflected animation of Life, Truth, and
Love. Blind enthusiasm; mortal will.

ZION. Spiritual foundation and superstructure; in- 6
spiration; spiritual strength. Emptiness; unfaithful-
ness; desolation.

CHAPTER XVIII

Fruitage

Wherefore by their fruits ye shall know them. — JESUS.

That ye might walk worthy of the Lord unto all pleasing, being fruitful in every good work, and increasing in the knowledge of God. — PAUL.

Let us get up early to the vineyards; let us see if the vine flourish, whether the tender grape appear, and the pomegranates bud forth. — SOLOMON'S SONG.

THOUSANDS of letters could be presented in testimony of the healing efficacy of Christian Science and particularly concerning the vast number of people who have been reformed and healed through the perusal or study of this book.

For the assurance and encouragement of the reader, a few of these letters are here republished from THE CHRISTIAN SCIENCE JOURNAL and CHRISTIAN SCIENCE SENTINEL. The originals are in the possession of the Editor, who can authenticate the testimonials which follow.

RHEUMATISM HEALED

I was a great sufferer from a serious form of rheumatic trouble, my hands being affected to such an extent that it was impossible for me even to dress without assistance. The trouble finally reached the knees, and I became very lame and had to be assisted in and out of bed. I went to the different health resorts for the benefit I hoped to derive from the baths and waters that were prescribed by physicians, but found no permanent relief. I was placed under an X-ray examination, and was told that the joints were becoming ossified. I then consulted a celebrated specialist, who after a thorough examination said my condition would continue to grow worse and that I would become completely helpless. At that time a copy of "Science and Health with Key to the Scriptures" by Mrs. Eddy was loaned me. I read it more from curiosity than with the thought of any physical benefit. As the truth was unfolded to me, I realized that the mental condition was what needed correcting, and that the Spirit of truth which inspired this book was my physician. My healing is complete, and the liberation in thought is manifest in a life of active usefulness rather than the bondage of helpless invalidism and suffering. I owe to our beloved Leader, Mrs. Eddy, gratitude which words cannot express. Her revelation of the practical rather than the merely theoretical application of Jesus' words, "Ye shall know the truth, and the truth shall make you free," proved to be my redeemer. I did not even have to apply to a practitioner, but am most grateful for the helpful words of loving friends. — E. B. B., Pasadena, Cal.

ASTIGMATISM AND HERNIA HEALED

It is nearly five years since I bought my first copy of Science and Health, the reading of which cured me of chronic constipation, nervous headache, astigmatism, and hernia, in less than four months.

Where would I be now, had not this blessed truth been brought to me by much persuasion of a very dear friend?

I certainly should have been deep in the slough of despond, if not in the grave. Am I truly thankful for all the good that has come to me and mine? I try to let my works testify of that; but to those whom I do not meet in person, I can truly say, Yes; I am indeed more thankful than words can express for the glorious healing that has come to me, both physical, mental, and moral, and I also convey herein, my song of gratitude to the dear Leader who has through her fidelity to Truth enabled me to touch at least the hem of Christ's garment. — B. S. J., Sioux City, Iowa.

SUBSTANCE OF LUNGS RESTORED

It was about fifteen years ago that Christian Science first came to my notice. At that time I had been a chronic invalid for a good many years. I had acute bowel trouble, bronchitis, and a number of other troubles. One physician had told me that my lungs were like wet paper, ready to tear at any time, and I was filled with fear, as my mother, two brothers, and a sister had been victims of consumption. I tried many physicians and every material remedy that promised help, but no help came until I found a copy of Mrs. Eddy's book, Science and Health. The book was placed in my hands by one who did not then appreciate it, and I was told that it would be hard for me to understand it. I commenced reading it with this thought, but I caught beautiful glimpses of Truth, which took away my fear and healed me of all those diseases, and they have never returned.

I would also like to tell how I was healed of a sprained

ankle. The accident occurred in the morning, and all that day and during the night I gave myself Christian Science treatment, as best I could. The next morning it seemed to be no better, being very sore, badly swollen, and much discolored. Feeling that I had done all I could, I decided to stop thinking about it. I took my copy of Science and Health and began reading. Very soon I became so absorbed in the book that I forgot all about my ankle; it went entirely out of my thought, for I had a glimpse of all God's creation as spiritual, and for the time being lost sight of my material selfhood. After two hours I laid the book down and walked into another room. When next I thought of my ankle, I found it was not hurting me. The swelling had gone down, the black and blue appearance had nearly vanished, and it was perfectly well. It was healed while I was "absent from the body" and "present with the Lord." This experience was worth a great deal to me, for it showed me how the healing is done. — C. H., Portland, Ore.

FIBROID TUMOR HEALED IN A FEW DAYS

My gratitude for Christian Science is boundless. I was afflicted with a fibroid tumor which weighed not less than fifty pounds, attended by a continuous hemorrhage for eleven years. The tumor was a growth of eighteen years.

I lived in Fort Worth, Tex., and I had never heard of Christian Science before leaving there for Chicago in the year 1887. I had tried to live near to God, and I feel sure He guided me in all my steps to this healing and saving truth. After being there several weeks

I received letters from a Texas lady who had herself been healed, and who wrote urging me to try Christian Science.

Changing my boarding-place, I met a lady who owned a copy of Science and Health, and in speaking to her of having seen the book, she informed me she had one, and she got it and told me I could read it. The revelation was marvellous and brought a great spiritual awakening. This awakened sense never left me, and one day when walking alone it came to me very suddenly that I was healed, and I walked the faster declaring every step that I was healed. When I reached my boarding-place, I found my hostess and told her I was healed. She looked the picture of amazement. The tumor began to disappear at once, the hemorrhage ceased, and perfect strength was manifest.

There was no joy ever greater than mine for this Christ-cure, for I was very weary and heavy laden. I thought very little of either sleeping or eating, and my heart was filled with gratitude, since I knew I had touched the hem of his garment.

I must add that the reading of Science and Health, and that alone, healed me, and it was the second copy I ever saw. — S. L., Fort Worth, Tex.

SPINAL TROUBLE AND INDIGESTION HEALED

For many years I have relied wholly upon Christian Science for healing; and I am glad to acknowledge the spiritual help and many other benefits received from following its teachings. I have great cause to be grateful to God and to our revered Leader, Mrs. Eddy, for these blessings, which her discovery and love for humanity made possible. I had read but a few pages in our textbook, "Science and Health with Key to the Scriptures," when I saw that it was the truth, and that it contained something I had thought could never be found in this existence. Proofs of healing came immediately, and I was able to do much useful work without a sense of burden or fatigue.

As time went on I learned the nothingness of discouragement, and understood in a measure that God is my Life and that all action is in divine Mind. I was healed of spinal trouble; and nervousness and weakness faded away and were replaced by health and strength. A larger sense of joy and gratitude did much towards overcoming indigestion, which had caused suffering for a number of years. A sprained ankle was cured in a few hours by applying what I understood of Christian Science, and by holding steadfastly to the statement our Leader makes on page 384 of Science and Health, that "God never punishes man for doing right, for honest labor, or for deeds of kindness." The following day I walked two miles with no sense of discomfort. Beliefs of heredity and lack have been overcome, and self-will, self-love, and pride are less in evidence. — Miss G. W., Brookline, Mass.

A CASE OF MENTAL SURGERY

I have felt for some time I should give my experience in mental surgery. In May, 1902, going home for lunch, on a bicycle, and while riding down a hill at a rapid gait, I was thrown from the wheel, and falling on my left side with my arm under my head, the bone was broken about half-way between the shoulder and elbow. While the pain was intense, I lay still in the dust, declaring the truth and denying that there could be a break or accident in the realm of divine Love, until a gentleman came to assist me, saying, he thought I had been stunned. I was only two and a half blocks from home, so I mounted my wheel again and managed to reach it. On arriving there I lay down and asked my little boy to bring me our text-book. He immediately brought Science and Health, which I read for about ten minutes, when all pain left.

I said nothing to my family of the accident, but attended to some duties and was about half an hour late in returning to the office, this being my only loss of time from work. My friends claimed that the arm had not been broken, as it would have been impossible for me to continue my work without having it set, and carrying it in a sling until the bone knit together. Their insistence almost persuaded me that I might have been mistaken, until one of my friends invited me to visit a physician's office where they were experimenting with an X-ray machine. The physician was asked to examine my left arm to see if it differed from the ordinary. On looking through it, he said, "Yes, it has been broken, but whoever set it made a perfect job of it, and you will never have any further trouble from that break." My friend then asked the doctor to show how he could tell where the break had been. The doctor pointed out the place as being slightly thicker at that part, like a piece of steel that had been welded. This was the first of several cases of mental surgery that have come under my notice, and it made a deep impression on me.

For the benefit of others who may have something similar to meet, I will say that I have overcome almost constant attacks of sick headaches, extending back to my earliest recollection. — L. C. S., Salt Lake City, Utah.

CATARACT QUICKLY CURED

I wish to add my testimony to those of others, and hope that it may be the means of bringing some poor sufferer to health, to happiness, and to God. I was healed through simply reading this wonderful book, Science and Health. I had been troubled periodically for many years with sore eyes, and had been to many doctors, who called the disease iritis and cataract. They told me that my eyes would always give me trouble, and that I would eventually lose my sight if I remained in an office, and advised me to go under an operation. Later on I had to wear glasses at my work, also out of doors as I could not bear the winds, and my eyes were gradually becoming worse. I could not read for longer than a few minutes at a time, otherwise they would smart severely. I had to rest my eyes each evening to enable me to use them the next day; in fact gas-light was getting unbearable because of the pain, and I made home miserable. A dear brother told me about Christian Science, and said that if I would read Science and Health it would help me. He procured for me the loan of the book. The first night I read it, it so interested me I quite forgot all about my eyes until my wife remarked that it was eleven o'clock. I found that I had been reading this book for nearly four hours, and I remarked immediately after, "I believe my eyes are cured," which was really the case. The next day, on looking at my eyes, my wife noticed that the cataract had disappeared. I put away my outdoor glasses, which I have not required since, and through the understanding gained by studying Christian Science I have been able to do away with my indoor glasses also, and have had no return of pain in my eyes since. This is now a year and a half ago. — G. F. S., Liverpool, England.

VALVULAR HEART DISEASE HEALED

Fourteen years ago my heart awoke to gratitude to God and the dear Leader at the same time. After a patient and persistent effort of three months' duration, to procure a copy of Science and Health (during which time I had visited every bookstore, and many of the second-hand bookstores in the city of St. Paul), and had failed to find it, I at last remembered that the stranger who told me I might be healed, had mentioned a name, and McVicker's Theatre Building in Chicago as being in some way connected with the work. I sent there for information regarding a book called Health and Science, and the return mail brought me the book, Science and Health, and in it I at once found sure promise of deliverance from valvular heart disease, with all the accompaniments, such as extreme nervousness, weakness, dyspepsia, and insomnia. I had suffered from these all my life, finding no permanent relief, even, in material remedies, and no hope of cure at any time. Only those who have been held in such bondage and have been liberated by the same means, can know the eager joy of the first perusal of that wonderful book.

the way to holiness and health. I read on, thinking only of the spiritual enlightenment, content to wait until I should be led to some person who would heal me; but old things had passed away, and all things had become new. I was completely healed before I had met a Scientist, or one who knew anything about Christian Science, and before I had read a line of any other Christian Science literature except one leaf of a tract; so it is absolutely certain that the healing was entirely impersonal, as was also the teaching, which enabled me to begin at once demonstrating the power of Truth to destroy all forms of error. — E. J. W., North Yakima, Wash.

THE TRUE PHYSICIAN FOUND

It is with a deep sense of gratitude that I send the particulars of my healing through Christian Science. While visiting friends in the southwestern part of Ontario, about three years ago, my attention was called to Christian Science and the wonderful healing it was doing. I had lived in New York for twenty-five years, but had never heard of Christian Science before, to my recollection.

Up to that time, for seventeen years, I had suffered with indigestion and gastritis in the worst form, often being overcome from a seeming pressure against the heart. I had asthma for four years, also had worn glasses for four years. It seemed to me that I had swallowed every known medicine to relieve my indigestion, but they only gave me temporary benefit. I purchased a copy of Science and Health, and simply from the reading of that grand book I was completely healed of all my physical ailments in two weeks' time. I have used no medicine from that day to this, and with God's help, and the wonderful light revealed to me through the reading of Mrs. Eddy's book, I never expect to again. I used to smoke eight or ten cigars a day, and also took an occasional drink, but the desire for these has gone, — I feel forever. I travel on the road, and am constantly being invited to indulge, but it is no effort to abstain, and in many instances I find that my refusal helps others.

While I fully appreciate the release from my physical troubles, this pales into insignificance in comparison with the spiritual uplifting Christian Science has brought me. I had not been inside a church for more than ten years, to attend regular services, until I entered a Christian Science church. What I saw and realized there, seemed so genuine that I loved Christian Science from the very start. I have never taken a treatment, — every inch of the way has been through study and practical demonstration, and I know that all can do the same thing if they will try.

Since I have been in Science I have overcome a case of ulcerated tooth in one night through the reading of Science and Health; also a severe attack of grip in thirty-six hours by obeying the Scripture saying, "Physician, heal thyself." — B. H. N., New York, N. Y.

CANCER AND CONSUMPTION HEALED

I was a great sufferer for many years from internal cancer and consumption. I was treated by the best of physicians in New York, Minneapolis, and Duluth, and was finally given up as incurable, when I heard of Christian Science. A neighbor who had been healed of consumption, kindly loaned me Science and Health by Mrs. Eddy, which I read and became interested in. In three months' time, I was healed, the truth conveyed to me by this book being the healer, and not only of these diseases, but I was made whole mentally as well. I have not been in bed one day since, or rather in eleven years. I have had many good demonstrations during this time, have passed through many a "fiery trial," but this blessed truth has caused me to stand, at times seemingly alone, and God was with me.

I will mention a demonstration of painless childbirth which I have had since coming to Idaho. Perhaps it may help some sister who is looking through the *Journal* for a demonstration of this kind, as I was before my baby came. Good help being scarce here, I did my housework up to the time I was confined, and was in perfect health. I awoke my husband one morning at five o'clock, and at half past five baby was born, no one being present but my husband and myself. It was quite a surprise to the rest of the family to see me sitting by the fire with a new baby on my lap. My son got the breakfast, of which I ate heartily; at noon I joined the family in the dining-room. I was out on the porch the second day, around the yard the third day, and have been perfectly well ever since, which has been now over three years. To one who had previously passed through agony untold, with a physician in attendance, this seemed wonderful. I hope this will interest some one who is seeking the truth, and I wish to express my sincere love for our beloved

Leader, who has given us the "Key to the Scriptures." —
E. C. C., Lewiston, Idaho.

A REMARKABLE CASE

Nine years ago my only child was hovering between
life and death. Some of the best physicians in Boston
had pronounced his case incurable, saying that if he
lived he would always be an invalid and a cripple. One
of the diseases was gastric catarrh. He was allowed
to eat but very few things, and even after taking every
precaution, he suffered to the extent that he would
lie in spasms for half a day. He also had rickets; physicians saying that there was not a natural bone in his
body.

It was while he was in what seemed to be his greatest
agony, and when I was in the darkest despair, that I
first heard of Christian Science. The bearer of the joyful
tidings could only tell me to come and hear of the wonderful things that Christian Science was doing. I accepted
the invitation, for I was willing to try anything to save
my child, and the following Friday evening I attended
my first meeting, which was in The Mother Church of
Christ, Scientist. Long before the service began every
seat was filled, which was amazing to me, being an ordinary weekly meeting, and that night I realized from the
testimonies given that Christian Science was the religion
for which I had been searching for years. The next
day I went to find a practitioner, but was unable to get
the one who had been recommended, he being too busy.
On my way home I thought of some of the testimonies
which I had heard the night before, — of people being

healed by simply reading Science and Health. I resolved at once to borrow a copy, and not dreaming of the sacrifice that my friend would make by conferring such a favor, I went and asked her for a loan of Science and Health. I never saw any one part so reluctantly with a book as my friend did with her copy of the textbook.

I read it silently and audibly, day and night, in my home, and although I could not seem to understand it, yet the healing commenced to take place at once. The little mouth which had been twisted by spasms grew natural and the child was soon able to be up, playing and romping about the house as any child should. About this time we decided to move to the far West.

I was young in Science at the time, and my husband greatly feared that the journey would cause a relapse for the child, but instead, he continued to improve. I constantly read the Bible, Science and Health, and Miscellaneous Writings, the two weeks we traveled, and we were the only ones in our car who, throughout the journey, did not get train sick. The child's limbs grew perfectly straight, he ate anything he wanted, and for years he has been a natural, healthy child in every way. He has passed through some of the worst forms of contagion untouched and unharmed.

I had been reading Science and Health several months, before I gave any thought to myself and my numerous complaints. I had never been very strong, and some of my ailments were supposed to be hereditary and chronic, hence I dragged through many tedious years with a belief in medical laws and hereditary laws resting upon me.

Just before I commenced reading Science and Health I spent a half day in having my eyes examined by one of the leading oculists in Boston. His verdict was that my eyes were in a dreadful condition, and that I would always need to wear glasses. In the meantime I commenced to read Science and Health, and when I thought of my eyes, I had no need for glasses. The years that I have been in Science I have used my eyes incessantly, night as well as day, doing all kinds of trying work and without requiring the aid of glasses. I was healed of all my complaints whilst seeking the truth for my child, and many of them have never returned. Those that appeared simply came to the surface to be destroyed. Teeth have been restored and facial blemishes removed, unconsciously, simply by reading Science and Health. All of this is, however, nothing to compare with the spiritual uplifting which I have received, and I have everything to be thankful for. — M. T. W., Los Angeles, Cal.

INTENSE SUFFERING OVERCOME

For about five years I was afflicted with sciatic rheumatism, in such a severe form that my body was drawn out of shape. When able to be around, I walked with the assistance of a cane. The attacks were periodical, recurring every few months; any exposure to rain or dampness would bring one. At one time I was in bed eleven weeks, suffering intensely all the time except when relieved by hypodermic injections. When I had these attacks, my regular physician was always in attendance. My daughter consulted another physician, who said there would have to be an operation which would include the exposing and scraping of the sciatic nerve. There was also another physician who, knowing of the case, examined my heart and claimed that it was weak and that I was liable to pass on at any time from heart trouble.

After suffering three years I heard of Christian Science, but did not avail myself of it for two years, when I decided to give up all other means and rely wholly upon it. It was not convenient to call a practitioner, so I took Science and Health and applied its teachings as best I could. In three days the trouble completely left me and there has never been the slightest return. My health has been good ever since, and I am at present in perfect physical health. I have been benefited in every way by Christian Science, physically, mentally, and spiritually, and would not be without my understanding of it for anything. — Mrs. E. A. K., Billings, Mont.

HEALED OF RHEUMATISM AND BRIGHT'S DISEASE

I am very thankful to God for what He has done for me. I was suddenly left alone, with many troubles and trials, and I took up the study of the Bible. I was trying to understand it, prior to joining some church, as it seemed to me this would be expected. I had attended all sorts of churches from my childhood up, but never could find any that met my need. As time passed on, my condition became very alarming. Sciatic rheumatism, that had troubled me for some years, became so severe I could scarcely do anything.

Then there appeared some complications, so distressing that I was unable to walk far, and had to sit down frequently by the way. I thought I had Bright's disease, — such excruciating pains, no tongue could tell my sufferings. With all these things upon me, death seemed very near. I had never joined any church, and I thought it now too late, as I would have to wait six months on probation, and I would be dead before that.

About this time I made some inquiries of my sister in reference to Christian Science, as she had already turned to that faith, and I soon found that it was just what I had been looking for. I saw at once that it declared the truth and nothing but the truth. I commenced reading Science and Health, also the New Testament. I wanted to find out what Jesus said, as I did not expect then to live long. I did not go to the meetings, nor did I read Science and Health to be cured, — not thinking of that, — but to be saved from an everlasting hell hereafter. My sister urged me to have a practitioner, but I kept on reading, and praying to God in silence, and what happened? Where had the diseases gone? I persisted in reading Science and Health, together with the Bible, with the knowledge that God as revealed by Christ Jesus can do everything, that He made everything that was made, that He can and does heal the afflicted. He has healed me, thanks to His most holy name. — G. J. H., Charleston, Ill.

GRATEFUL FOR MANY BLESSINGS

In the year 1901, Christian Science found me a hopeless invalid. I had suffered for seven years previous with a very painful back, the result of an operation. I could get no rest or sleep at night, as I could not lie down, but had to sit propped in a chair with pillows around me. Only those who have suffered as I did can know the full misery of it. I had come to the end of material means and never hoped to get well. One day, however, while out walking, it was my good fortune to come to a Christian Scientist's house, and there the teaching was explained to me. I was advised to buy Science and Health, which I did, and the study of this book has healed my back entirely. Christian Science has also cured me of long-standing catarrh of the throat, and neuralgia with which I had been afflicted from childhood. Before coming into Science I had doctored with three of the best physicians in Seattle, but none could give me relief.

I am no longer a sufferer, but rejoice exceedingly in Christian Science. God's promise has been fulfilled to me, "But unto you that fear my name shall the Sun of righteousness arise with healing in his wings." — E. O., Georgetown, Wash.

FREED FROM NEURASTHENIC AND OTHER TROUBLES

Christian Science found in me a minister's son who had failed to profit by continuous teaching in the old thought. Some years ago I was pronounced by a professor of *materia medica,* whose works are in general use, a neurasthenic. I had been in this condition more or less for eight years, and up to two years ago, when Christian Science was first brought to my attention (thanks to Almighty God) through a kind friend, I was almost constantly taking medicine and had in all eleven physicians who undoubtedly did their best, but without avail, notwithstanding almost all known drugs were prescribed, and further I had tried very many patent medicines. I was also put through forms of hygienic treatment and other things that offered inducements. At the time of coming into Science I was taking three times daily forty minims of cod-liver oil and three of creosote, also three drops of Fowler's solution of arsenic, and on the month or so previous had bought eighteen dollars' worth of patent medicine. I was restricted to the simplest means of diet, — all stews, fries, sweets, berries, and tomatoes I had not touched for two years.

I started to read Science and Health, and before I had half finished the book once I was eating everything that any one does. I read the book eleven times straight ahead and many times skipping about. The book has done the work and I am a well man. — C. E. M., Philadelphia, Pa.

MANY ILLS OVERCOME

I have received much help, spiritually and physically, through Christian Science. I had what the doctors diagnosed as muscular rheumatism, dropsy, and constipation of thirty years' standing. A dear friend whom I had known as an invalid had been healed by Christian Science and advised me to read Science and Health. I did so, having a desire to know the truth. One of my troubles was that I could not sleep. I began reading the Bible and the Christian Science textbook, and troubles of every kind disappeared before I had read Science and Health through. The thought came, What about the old remedies? but truth prevailed, and I took all the material remedies I had and threw them away. That was seven years ago, and I have not had any use for them since. My husband was healed of the tobacco habit of fifty years' standing, also of kidney trouble, by reading Science and Health. I have not words to express the gratitude I feel to-day for the many blessings that have come to our home. — Mrs. M. K. O., Seattle, Wash.

A HELPFUL HEALING

I became interested in Christian Science about eleven years ago, and was healed of neuralgia of the stomach, from which I had suffered from a child. As I grew older, the spells became more frequent and more severe; the only relief physicians could give me was by hypodermic injections of morphine. Finally, after each spell, I would be prostrated for a day or two with the after-effect of the morphine. I was entirely healed of this trouble through the study of Science and Health. I think I never realized what fear meant until I began to try and put into practice my understanding of Christian Science for my children. I have proved, however, many times, that fear can neither help nor hinder in our demonstration of truth. The first time I realized this was in the overcoming of a severe case of croup for my little boy. I was awakened one night by the sound that seems to bring terror to every mother's heart, and found the little fellow sitting up in bed, gasping for breath. I got up, took him in my arms, and went into the next room. My first thought was, "O if only there was another Christian Scientist in town!" But there was not, and the work must be done and done quickly. I tried to treat him, but was so frightened I could not think; so I picked up Science and Health, which lay on the table beside me, and began reading aloud. I had read but a few lines when these words came to me as though a voice spoke, "The word of God is quick, and powerful, and sharper than any two-edged sword." Almost immediately after, the little one said, "Mamma, sing 'Shepherd,' " — our Leader's hymn, that both the big and the little children love. I began singing, and commencing with the second line, the little voice joined me. I shall never forget the feeling of joy and peace that came over me, when I realized how quickly God's word, through Science and Health and the beautiful hymn, had accomplished the healing work. This is only one of many instances in which the power of God's word to heal has been demonstrated in our home. — A. J. G., Riverside, Cal.

RELIEF FROM MANY ILLS

Paul said, "Be ye transformed by the renewing of your mind." In my own case deafness has been overcome by an enlarged understanding of God's word, as explained by Mrs. Eddy in Science and Health. Many times I have been enabled to turn to God, to know it was His will to help in trouble, and obtained the needed benefit. Catarrh has disappeared; tonsilitis, which very frequently laid me aside from duties in the schoolroom and home, is no longer manifest. When temptation comes (for Christian Science is both preventive and curative), I turn to that wonderful book, Science and Health, and my precious Bible, grown dearer since read in the new light of spiritual understanding, until I know that my mind is renewed, because the action is changed and the inflammation has abated.

Thus in my experience in Christian Science, I have seen the transformation begun, and Truth is able to perfect that which is begun in me so gloriously. — Mrs. C. A. McL., Brooklyn, Nova Scotia.

HEALTH AND PEACE ATTAINED

For fifteen years I was a great sufferer physically and mentally. Eminent physicians treated me for hereditary consumption, torpid liver, and many other diseases. I sought relief at famous springs, the ozone of Florida, and the pure air of Colorado, but in vain. My life was one ceaseless torture.

During all this time, however, I was an earnest seeker after Truth. I examined every religious teaching with a calm and unprejudiced attention. From an orthodox Protestant I became a skeptic, and a follower of Voltaire, Tom Paine, and Ingersoll; yet all the while I retained faith in a supreme intelligent Being who made all. Sick, weary, doubting, and despairing, I accidentally went into a Christian Science church in New York City, on a Wednesday evening, not knowing what kind of a place it was. Seeing a large number of people going into the building, I followed, supposing that a marriage ceremony had attracted the crowd. Being informed it was their regular Wednesday evening service, I inquired as to the denomination. I concluded that it was another new fad, but after investigation I procured a copy of Science and Health, promising I would read it carefully. I began reading the book on Tuesday and finished on Friday of the same week. I was still in the dark. I laid the book down, involuntarily closed my eyes, and silently prayed to God.

I remained in that attitude a few moments, when I felt like the mariner who had been tossed for days upon a boisterous sea, the clouds bending low, the billows rolling high, all nature wrapped in darkness; in his despair he kneels and commits his soul to God, when he suddenly beholds the North Star breaking through the clouds, enabling him to guide his ship to the shores of safety. Many things were made plain to me. I saw that there is one Fatherhood of God and one brotherhood of man; that though "once I was blind, now I see;" that there was no more pain, nor aches, no fear, nor indigestion. I slept that night like a babe and awoke next morning refreshed. There are now no traces whatever of my former complaint and I feel like a new being. — L. P., New York, N. Y.

HEALTH AND PEACE GAINED

About nine years ago I was drawn to Christian Science by a relative whose many afflictions had given place to health and harmony, and whose loving gratitude was reflected in every word and deed. The thought came to me, God indeed healeth all our diseases.

My first reading of Science and Health was without understanding. I was full of darkness and gloom, and it was laid aside for a time. The good seed had been sown, however, and erelong the reading was resumed, and with such interest that my afflictions disappeared "like mist before the morning sun." Asthma (thought to be hereditary), neuralgia in an aggravated form, and besides these, the tobacco and liquor habit of many years' standing left me. Bless the Lord, "He sent his word" and healed me, — for the reading of Science and Health brought to my consciousness the truth that makes free. — S., Shellman, Ga.

CONSUMPTION QUICKLY CURED

I became interested in Christian Science nearly five years ago through the healing of my wife of what the doctors called consumption in its last stages. I had tried everything that I could get in the way of *materia medica*, and every doctor would tell me nearly the same story about the case. At last they recommended for her only a higher, drier climate, and when she would be at her worst to give her something to quiet her.

I tried different climates, but she was no better, indeed worse. At last she struggled along until the first of March, 1899. She had taken to her bed again. For two days and nights she suffered, and I called a physician. He came and diagnosed the case, and said that he could do nothing for her but give her some morphine tablets to make her rest. I gave her two of them according to direction, and just before the time to give her the third, she called me to her bed-side, and said, "Don't give me any more of that stuff, for it does me more harm than good," so I turned and placed them in the fire, though I did not then know anything about Christian Science. We had heard of it, but that was all. I gave her the last tablet at eight o'clock that night, and about nine o'clock the next day a lady who had been healed in Christian Science visited her, and introduced her to this great truth. She accepted it and thought she would try it. The lady loaned her Science and Health. She got the book about ten o'clock that day and read it until dinner was called. She ate a hearty dinner, the first in about three days, and that same evening she dressed herself, walked into the dining-room, ate a hearty supper and enjoyed it. She slept well that night. She borrowed this lady's copy of Science and Health two hours each day for eight days, and was healed. The first day that she read Science and Health she weighed about ninety-five pounds. Three months later she weighed one hundred and thirty-five pounds. — A. J. D., Houston, Tex.

A PROFITABLE STUDY

It may help others to know that some one was really healed of severe illness through Christian Science. It is over nine years since we first became interested in the Science, and it would be hard to find a healthier person than I am now. I can go all day, from morning till night, upheld by the thought that "they that wait upon the Lord shall renew their strength." I can truly say that I scarcely know what physical weariness is any more. Before I came into Science the physicians said that one lung was gone, and that the other was affected with tuberculosis; so, from their standpoint, there was little left for me to hope for. We had tried every remedy that they had suggested. I had gone to the mountains, but could not stay there on account of the altitude; and when they did not know what else to do, they said we would better go to England — that the ocean air would be beneficial. So we spent three months in the British Isles, and when I came back I seemed much better, but this only lasted a short time. In little more than a month I was worse than ever, and my mother was told that I had but a few weeks, or at most months, to live.

At that time, a lady, a stranger to us, suggested that we try Christian Science. There was no prejudice against it, as we did not even know what it was. We knew of no Scientists in the Western town where we were living, and when we were told that we could send to Kansas City for absent treatment, we thought it was absurd. We were then told that many people had been healed through the reading of the Christian Science textbook, Science and Health, and to us this seemed a little worse than the absent treatment, but as we had tried everything we had heard of up to that time, my mother sent for the book.

It came in the middle of October and we began to read it together. It seemed to me from the first that it was something I had always believed, but did not know how to express — it seemed such a natural thing. My improvement was very gradual, but I felt I was recovering. After the Christmas holidays I started in at school and went the whole term without missing a day, — something I had never done before. I finished my school course without missing a day — in fact, I have not spent a day in bed since that time. I feel absolutely certain that I have two sound, healthy lungs now. The hollows in my chest have filled out, and I breathe perfectly on both sides; rarely have a cold to meet, and have not a sign of a cough.

People sometimes say, "Oh, well, maybe you never had consumption." Well, I had all the symptoms, and they are every one gone through the reading of Science and Health. — E. L. B., Chicago, Ill.

HEALED OF INFIDELITY AND MANY PHYSICAL ILLS

I feel compelled to write my testimony and hope that I may be accepted as one more witness to the Truth as contained in Science and Health with Key to the Scriptures.

In the year 1883 I first heard of Christian Science. I was sitting in a saloon in Leadville, Col., reading a daily paper of that place. My eyes lighted upon an article which spoke of some peculiar people in Boston who claimed to have discovered how to heal as Jesus healed. I do not remember much of the article, but those words stayed with me.

I had drifted out to Colorado from New York City (my home), where I had been under the treatment of many leading physicians. The last one, who was too honest to take my money knowing that he could not cure me, advised me to keep away from doctors and quit taking medicine, as nothing but death could cure me. My trouble was pronounced by some to be Bright's disease, by others gravel on the kidneys with very acute inflammation of the bladder and prostate gland.

In the spring of 1888 my wife and myself were spending the evening at the house of a gentleman whose wife had been healed in the East by Christian Science. The gentleman took a book from its bookcase saying, "Here is a work on Christian Science." It proved to be Science and Health. I knew as soon as I had read the title-page that this was the very book we wanted. We immediately sent for the book, and when it arrived we obeyed the angel and feasted on it. I was very much prejudiced against the Bible, and my first demonstration over self was to consent to read the four Gospels. My wife bought me a New Testament and I began to read it. What a change came over me! All my prejudice was gone in an instant! When I read the Master's words, I caught his meaning and the lesson he tried to convey. It was not difficult for me to accept the whole Bible, for I could not help myself, I was just captured. The disease with which I had been troubled for years tormented me worse than ever for about six months, as if trying to turn me aside; but I lost all fear of it.

I kept up my study of Science and Health and the disease disappeared. I can honestly say that Science and Health was my only healer, and it has been my only teacher. — R. A. C., Los Angeles, Cal.

DISEASED EYES CURED

Christian Science came to me when I was a wreck, my body being completely covered with sores. My eyes were very bad, so that I sat in a darkened room for weeks together, most of the time in bed under opiates. The home doctor and a specialist said the disease of the eyes could not be cured, though they might help me for a while. I had one operation, and the doctor said if I took cold I would become totally blind. My suffering was beyond telling.

A clergyman called almost every day, and sat by my bed and wept, and my good, kind doctor shed tears many times. Finally, after a year of this terrible suffering, I was sent to Indiana, to a sister who had been healed of lung trouble by Christian Science. The first day I was there she read to me from the Bible and from "Science and Health with Key to the Scriptures" by Mrs. Eddy, and I was healed. I knew that God was no respecter of persons, and when I saw what had been done for my sister, who was changed from being a mere frame to a strong, robust, healthy, rosy-cheeked woman, the cough all gone, I said, "God has as much for me, if I will accept it." I was healed instantaneously by Christian Science, and am thankful to God for giving us this understanding through Mrs. Eddy, our beloved Leader. I am now in perfect health. — Mrs. F. S., Laurel, Miss.

THE TEXTBOOK HEALED ME

For twelve years previous to the fall of 1897 I had been under the care of a physician much of the time. Different opinions were given by them, as to the nature of the trouble, some diagnosing it as an abnormal growth, etc. I was healed through reading "Science and Health with Key to the Scriptures" by Mrs. Eddy. It was a clear case of transformation of the body by the renewal of the mind. I am perfectly well at the present time. — J. M. H., Omaha, Neb.

OBSTINATE STOMACH TROUBLE HEALED

There is no doubt that by far the greater number come to Christian Science by the way of physical healing, but there are those to whom this does not particularly appeal. In the hope that it may be of benefit to some such, and in gratitude for help received, I submit my own experience. Three years ago I knew nothing of Christian Science, aside from the knowledge gathered from the daily papers and current literature. When I thought of the subject at all, it was to class Christian Science with various human theories with which I could not be in sympathy, for they seemed to rely upon both good and evil. I had never known of a case of healing, had never read the textbook or heard of the *Journal* or *Sentinel,* but I would sometimes see people going into the Christian Science church. I was tired of trying to find anything satisfactory in religious belief, for it seemed as if God either could not or would not bring into harmony the terrible conditions existing in human society. I had quit using any form of prayer except the Lord's Prayer, and even then omitted the words "lead us not into temptation." How I longed to know just a little of the "why?" and "wherefore?" of it all.

Here is where Christian Science found me. I was thrown in contact with a dear friend of whom I had seen very little for a year or more, a thoroughly educated woman and a thinker. She told me she had taken some treatments in Christian Science for a physical trouble, and had become very much interested in the study of "Science and Health with Key to the Scriptures" by Mrs. Eddy. She asked me if I would like to look at the book, and I said I would be glad to do so. The first chapter, "Prayer," appealed to me from the first, and when I came to Mrs. Eddy's spiritual sense of the Lord's Prayer (Science and Health, p. 17), my interest was fully aroused. I knew that in a dim way I was learning what it means to "pray without ceasing." Very soon I bought a book of my own, and with the help of our Lesson-Sermons, as given in the *Quarterly*, I began in earnest the study of Science and Health, in connection with the Bible.

I stood very much in need of physical healing at this time, having suffered for several years from an obstinate form of stomach trouble. So far as I know, I gave no thought to the benefits I might derive physically from the study, but I did believe this Science held the truth of things, and I was so absorbed in getting an understanding of the Principle that I thought very little of myself. After about three or four months' study I realized that the stomach trouble was gone, and with it went other physical troubles, which have never returned. This healing was brought about by the earnest, conscientious seeking for the truth, as contained in the Bible and interpreted by our Leader in our textbook, Science and Health. I have since learned more of the Science of healing and have been able in a small way to help others in need. I have also learned that in living and loving is healing realized, and in reflecting divine Love I have the "signs following."

When we think of the pure, loving, unselfish life Mrs. Eddy must have lived in order to become conscious of this truth and give it to us, words are a poor medium through which to express the gratitude which her followers feel for her. It is best expressed by obediently following her, even as she is following Christ. — H. T., Omaha, Neb.

DYSPEPSIA QUICKLY HEALED

It has occurred to me that I have had ample time to meditate on the many blessings which I have received through Christian Science, as it is now more than six years since I was entirely healed of dyspepsia as well as constipation in its worst form by the reading of Science and Health. So aggravated were the conditions that for three years or more I was unable to drink a glass of cold water. Everything that I drank had to be hot, and my only means of relief from the bowel trouble was hot water injections, for a period of more than three years.

I can truthfully say that I was permanently, and I might say instantly, healed of those two ailments by reading Science and Health as before stated, and in fact I do not think I had read more than thirty pages of this book when I ignored entirely the most rigid kind of diet. I ate and drank everything I wished without a single harmful effect from that time to this date, and there has not been a drop of medicine in our home for more than six years, in a family of five.

I have also seen the power of Truth manifested in our home by having our youngest child relieved of the most excruciating pain, and changed to his most playful mood, immediately upon notifying one of the faithful practitioners of this city. For all this I am endeavoring to be thankful to God and to our faithful Leader, Mrs. Eddy, whose pure and undefiled life enabled her to discover this precious truth for the benefit of all mankind. — M. C. McK., Denver, Col.

AFTER TWENTY YEARS' SUFFERING

From early girlhood I was considered an invalid, having been injured by a hard fall while playing. The pain was intense for some time and for several hours I was unable to walk or stand alone. Later, a growing weakness of the back accompanied with sharp pains alarmed my parents, who called a physician, and he pronounced it spinal trouble. Then followed nearly twenty years of increased suffering, at times very severe. As years went by and I became a wife and mother, my suffering increased. Everything that medical skill could do was done, but finding no lasting benefit from anything, I lost hope of recovery.

When Christian Science found me I was under the doctor's sentence that if I lived the week through I would become entirely helpless, not able to move hand or foot. My husband was a travelling man, and being urgently called home, he met an old friend on the train who asked why we did not try Christian Science. The reply, We know nothing of it, was followed by a brief explanation of its healing power and the benefit his family had received. This inspired my husband with new hope, and on his arrival at home he called on a practitioner, who recommended our getting Science and Health, which we did, but ignorance and the prejudice of old education produced such fear that I hid the book under the covers of the bed whenever the children came into the room, fearing that it was not of God and would injure them. God's dear love was, however, more potent than these foolish fears, and the first day I read from its sacred pages I was convinced its teachings were the same truths as Jesus Christ had taught centuries ago. When I had read a few pages, I reached out and threw my medicine from the open window at the head of my bed. I then turned back to the book and began reading again, when, lo, the Christ-idea dawned upon me, and I was healed instantaneously.

I first noticed the spot in my back cooling, and soon I got out of bed. I continued to read eagerly; I felt as if I wanted to devour the healing truth, and drank it in as a thirsty plant does the gentle rain. When dinner was prepared, I walked out and ate a hearty meal with the family, to the amazement of all. We shall never forget what a joyful meal this was. How we did thank God for Christian Science!

As year after year has gone by, till twenty years have passed and the healing has remained perfect, I have grown to thank God with deeper sincerity that one brave woman was found pure enough to bring forth this Christ-healing again, to remain forever among men and to save suffering humanity from all disease and sin. — Mrs. P. L. H., Fairmont, Minn.

FROM DESPAIR TO HOPE AND JOY

I have often had a desire to make public what Christian Science has done for me, but I never could tell of all my blessings, they are so many. From childhood I was always sick, never knew one hour of rest, and was under the doctor's care most of the time. I was living in the East at that time, and was advised to try change of climate, which I did. I came West with my family in the spring of the year, but instead of growing better I grew steadily worse, until at last I was obliged to keep my bed for nearly three years, — a great sufferer. My ailments were, it seemed, all that flesh is heir to, and were called incurable by the doctors; viz., Bright's disease, and many others, — in the last stages. My case was known among physicians, many of whom were prominent specialists, as a most extreme one. Many, upon looking at me, would turn away with a wise shake of the head and say, "What keeps her alive?" My physicians, who were exceedingly kind and did all that lay within their power for me, gave me up and the death sentence was pronounced on me by all who attended me.

It was then I realized that "man's extremity is God's opportunity." The "little book" was handed me at this hour of great need. I read it, not thinking it would heal me, but, like a drowning man, I grasped at it. I read it, read it again, and soon found myself growing stronger; then I kept on reading and was perfectly healed of all the supposedly incurable diseases. — L. B., Austin, Minn.

TRUTH MAKES FREE

As the son of a physician, a graduate in pharmacy, and an ex-druggist, I had a perfect contempt for what I thought Christian Science to be. About six and a half years ago, however, having exhausted all material means at my command, — *materia medica*, electricity, gymnastics, cycling, and so on, — and being in a hopeless state, the study of Christian Science was taken up. I had been a sufferer from catarrh and sore throat for over thirty years, and in the last five were added several others, including dyspepsia, and bronchitis, and a loss in flesh of sixty pounds. I was completely healed, and regained health, strength, and flesh through the spiritual understanding of Christian Science, the result of about six weeks' study. This good and perfect gift came to me through the careful and prayerful study of Christian Science, as revealed to the world to-day through Science and Health. The promise of Christ Jesus, "the truth shall make you free," was fulfilled, and the past six years of health and harmony have been spent in striving to "hold fast that which is good."

While most grateful for the physical healing, my gratitude for the mental and spiritual regeneration is beyond expression. When I learned that Jesus' mission of healing sickness as well as sin did not end with his short stay upon earth, but is practical in all ages, my joy was unbounded. Having spent thousands in the old way, it seemed wonderful to be healed at such small cost as the price of the "little book" and a few weeks' study. Every thought of prejudice immediately vanished before the proofs that Christian Science is indeed the elucidation and practical application of Jesus' teachings, which are demonstrable truth, "The same yesterday, and to-day, and forever." — C. N. C., Memphis, Tenn.

DEAF EARS UNSTOPPED

As a mother of a family my heart goes out in love and gratitude to that good woman we are privileged to call our Leader, for all she has done through her book for me and mine.

Ten years ago I was healed of hereditary deafness and catarrh of the head, simply through reading the book, Science and Health. For years previous I had consulted and taken treatment from some of the best specialists for the ear and throat, both in England and America, but grew worse all the time. I was then urged by a lady who had been healed through Christian Science to buy this book and study it. I did so very reluctantly, but had not read fifty pages before I felt I had indeed found the truth which makes free, and can truly say, from that time I have never had a return of the ailment.

That for which I am, however, most grateful, is the daily help it is to me in my household of young children. I am sure if mothers only knew what Christian Science truly means they would give all they possess to know it. We have seen croup, measles, fever, and various other children's complaints, so-called, disappear like dew before the morning sun, through the application of Christian Science, — the understanding of God as ever-present and omnipotent. It has been proven to me without a doubt that God is a very present help in trouble, and what a blessed help this wonderful truth is in the training of our children, and how quickly the child grasps it.

Some time ago my little girl, then three years old, dislocated her shoulder. I was alone in the house at the time. The pain was so intense that she became faint. I treated her the best I knew how, but kept holding the thought that just as soon as some one came I would run for help. She seemed to grow worse and cried very much. I undressed her and tried to twist the arm into place, but it caused such suffering that I began to get afraid. Then like a flash came the thought, What would you do if you were out of the reach of a practitioner? Now is your time to prove God's power and presence. With these thoughts came such a sense of calm and trustfulness that I lost all fear. I then asked the child if I should read to her; she said "Yes, mamma, read the truth-book." I began reading aloud to her from Science and Health. In about half an hour I noticed she tried to lift the arm but screamed and became very pale. I continued to read aloud and again she made an effort to put some candy into her mouth. This time I noticed with joy that she almost reached her mouth before she felt the pain. I kept reading aloud to her until my sister and two boys came in, when she jumped off her bed, so delighted to see her brothers that she forgot her arm. She then began to tell her aunt that she had broken her arm and mamma treated it with the truth-book. When this happened, it was about 10.30 A. M. and by 3 P. M. she was playing out doors as though nothing had ever happened. — Mrs. M. G., Winnipeg, Man.

SAVED FROM INSANITY AND SUICIDE

A few years ago, while under a sense of darkness and despair caused by ill health and an unhappy home, Science and Health was loaned me with a request that I should read it.

At that time my daughter was given up by *materia medica* to die of lingering consumption, supposed to have been inherited. My own condition seemed even more alarming, as insanity was being manifested, and rather than go to an insane asylum, it seemed to me the only thing to do was to commit suicide. Heart trouble, kidney complaint, and continual headaches caused from female trouble were some of the many ailments I had to contend with. My doctor tried to persuade me to undergo an operation as a means of relief, but I had submitted to a severe operation ten years previous, and found only additional suffering as a result, so I would not consent.

When I began with Science and Health, I read the chapter on "Prayer" first, and at that time did not suppose it possible for me to remember anything I read, but felt a sweet sense of God's protection and power, and a hope that I should at last find Him to be what I so much needed, — a present help in time of trouble. Before that chapter on "Prayer" was finished, my daughter was downstairs eating three meals a day, and daily growing stronger. Before I had finished reading the textbook she was well, but never having heard that the reading of Science and Health healed any one, it was several months before I gave God the glory.

One by one my many ailments left me, all but the headaches; they were less frequent, until at the end of three years the fear of them was entirely overcome.

Neither myself nor my daughter have ever received treatments, but the study of the Bible and Science and Health, the Christian Science textbook by Mrs. Eddy, has healed us and keeps us well.

While Christian Science was very new to me, I attended an experience meeting in First Church of Christ, Scientist, Chicago. A gentleman told of an unhappy woman who was about to separate from her husband. This gentleman had asked her if she did not love her husband. She replied, "No; when I married him I did, but not now." He told her God made man in His image and likeness, and that He is perfect. He said to her, "Go home and see only God's perfect man; you don't need to love a sinful mortal such as you have been looking upon." The lady followed his advice, as he told her there is no separation in divine Mind. In a short time peace and harmony were in her home, and both husband and wife became members of a Christian Science church.

This testimony was like a message from heaven to me. I had received many benefits from the study of Science and Health, but it had never dawned upon my darkened consciousness till then how wonderful our God is. I knew what had taken place in that home could take place in my unhappy home where there was neither rest nor peace.

I hopefully took up my cross, and step by step my burden grew lighter, as I journeyed along, realizing the presence of the Christ, Truth, that indeed makes us free. Not all at once did any outward change appear, but at the end of three years all was peace, all the members of the family attending church together and realizing that there is but one Mind. — E. J. B., Superior, Wis.

STOMACH TROUBLE HEALED

I was healed of stomach trouble of many years' standing by reading Science and Health. My condition had reached the stage in which I had periodical attacks, that came on with greater frequency. I was a travelling salesman, and it was a common occurrence for me to have to call a physician to my hotel to administer morphine for an acute form of this disease. This became a regular thing at certain places, and these attacks always left me worse than before. As a result of the last one I lost a great deal in weight. I had tried many physicians and most of the usual remedies during these years of suffering, without any good result. Finally, as a last resort, I decided to try Christian Science, and I was healed by reading "Science and Health with Key to the Scriptures" by Mrs. Eddy.

My health has been of the best since I was healed, now six years ago. In the family we have depended entirely on Christian Science for our healing, and have ever found it efficacious. We consider the physical healing, however, only incidental to the understanding of God and His goodness. This, together with our increased love for the Bible, is proving most valuable to us. We are humbly trying to live the lives that will prove our gratitude to God, and to our beloved Leader, Mrs. Eddy. — Charles E. Peck, St. Johnsbury, Vt.

FREED FROM MANY YEARS OF SUFFERING

In the spring of 1880 I was taken down with a severe attack of stomach trouble, was bedfast for three months, and not able to drive out for nearly six months. During this time I had three good doctors treating me. I gained a little in strength, but had very little relief from the stomach trouble. I was recommended to try mineral springs and did so, but with the same disappointment. I went to a sanitarium, but yet the stomach trouble prevailed. I had some friends who recommended patent medicines, but no healing came.

I worried along in this way for several years. Finally I read medicine nearly two years with a good doctor friend, especially for my own benefit, and during this time I had a severe attack of bladder trouble, and for fifteen years I suffered so severely at times that I thought life was not really worth living. In connection with these troubles I suffered every winter with rheumatism and the grip. I also had a growth coming on both eyes called cataract, which caused my eyes to be inflamed nearly all the time, and this growth had made such progress that it was causing my vision to be very dim when reading. Corns were not forgotten, as I was reminded of them very frequently, and for all these troubles I had tried every remedy I heard of that I was able to get, specialists included, without relief.

Thanks to a friend who took me in this hopeless, discouraged condition and led me to the light that never knows darkness, I got a copy of Science and Health by Mrs. Eddy and was healed in a short time by reading this work. — D. W. L., Anderson, Ind.

RELIEF FROM INTENSE SUFFERING

I became interested in Christian Science in 1901. For four or five years I had suffered with severe attacks which nothing but an opiate seemed to relieve. After one which I think was the worst I ever had, I consulted our family physician, who diagnosed my case as a dangerous kidney disease and said that no medicine could help me but that I must undergo a surgical operation. I continued to grow worse and went to see the physician again, and he advised me to consult a doctor who was connected with the city hospital of Augusta. This doctor made an examination and diagnosed the difficulty as something different but quite as serious. Meanwhile a friend offered me a copy of Science and Health. I said I did not care to read the book, but she was so urgent that I finally promised to do so. I received the book on Saturday, and on Sunday morning I sat down to read it. When I reached the place where Mrs. Eddy says she found this truth in the Bible, I began comparing the two books. I read passages which looked very reasonable to me, and said to myself, This is nearer to the truth than anything I have ever seen. I continued to read all day, stopping only long enough to eat my dinner. As I read on, everything became clearer to me, and I felt that I was healed. During the evening a neighbor came in, and I said, "I am healed, and that book has healed me." I read on and was certainly healed. Eight days after my healing I did my own washing. This occurred in February, 1901. About six weeks after, I was called to care for my mother, who was under the care of my former physician. I again let him examine my side, as he wished to see if the trouble was still there. He said, "It is certainly gone." I said to him, "Doctor, you told me I would never be a well woman unless I was operated upon; what has healed me?" He replied, "God has healed you." — S. H. L., North Pittston, Me.

GRATEFUL FOR MANY BLESSINGS

It is with sincere gratitude for the many blessings Christian Science has brought me, that I give this testimony. I first heard of Christian Science about fifteen years ago. A friend of mine was taking treatment for physical troubles, and was reading the textbook of Christian Science, Science and Health with Key to the Scriptures. The title of the book appealed to me very strongly. I said to my friend, "If that is a Key to the Scriptures, I must have it."

I had long been a member of a Bible class in an orthodox Sabbath school, but I never felt satisfied with that which was taught; there was something lacking, I did not understand then what it was. I purchased a copy of Science and Health and began to study it. I wish I could express in words what that book brought me. It illumined the Bible with a glorious light and I began to understand some of the Master's sayings, and tried to apply them.

I had had a longing to live a better Christian life for many years, and often wondered why I failed so utterly to understand the Bible. Now I knew; it was lack of spiritual apprehension.

I did not know at first that people were healed of disease and sin by simply reading Science and Health, but found after a while that such was the case. At that time I had many physical troubles, and one after another of these ills simply disappeared and I found that I had no disease, — I was perfectly free. The spiritual uplifting was glorious, too, and as I go on in the study of this blessed Science, I find I am gaining surely an understanding that helps me to overcome both sin and disease in myself and in others. My faith in good is increased and I know I am losing my belief in evil as a power equal to good. The pathway is not wearisome, because each victory over self gives stronger faith and a more earnest desire to press on. — E. J. R., Toledo, Ohio.

GRATEFUL FOR MORAL AND SPIRITUAL AWAKENING

About four years ago, after I had tried different ways and means to be relieved from bodily suffering, a faithful friend called my attention to the teaching of Christian Science. After some opposition, I decided to investigate it, with the thought that if this teaching would be helpful, it was meant for me as well as for others; if it did not afford any help, I could put it aside again, but that I would find out and be convinced.

After I had read Mrs. Eddy's work, Science and Health, a few days, I found that my ailments had disappeared, and a rest had come to me which I had never before known. I had smoked almost incessantly, although I had often determined to use my will power and never smoke again, but had always failed. This desire as well as the desire for drink simply disappeared, and I wish to say here, that I received all these benefits before I had gained much understanding of what I was reading. Like a prisoner, who had been in chains for years, I was suddenly set free. I did not then know how the chain had been removed, but I had to acknowledge that it came through the reading of this book. I then felt an ardent desire to read more, and to know what this power was that had freed me in a few days of that which I had been trying for years to shake off and had failed. It then became clear to me that this was the truth which Jesus Christ taught and preached to free humanity almost two thousand years ago. It did not, however, occur to me to apply it in my business affairs; on the contrary, I first thought that if I continued in my study I would have to retire from business.

This did not happen, however, for I gradually found that the little understanding of this wonderful teaching which I had acquired became a great help to me in my business. I became more friendly, more honest, more loving to my fellow-men; and I also acquired better judgment and was able to do the right thing at the right time. As a natural result my business improved. Before I knew anything of Christian Science my business had often been a burden to me, fear and worry deprived me of my rest. How different it is now! Through the study of the Bible, which now possesses unmeasurable treasures for me, and of our textbook, Science and Health, and the other works of our Leader, I receive peace and confidence in God and that insight into character which is necessary for the correct management of any business. — W. H. H., Bloomfield, Neb.

HEREDITARY DISEASE OF THE LUNGS CURED

For a long time I have been impelled to contribute a testimony of the healing power of Truth. As I read other testimonies and rejoice in them, some one may rejoice in mine. I was healed by reading Science and Health. By applying it, I found it to be the truth that Jesus taught, — the truth that sets free.

From childhood I had never known a well day. I was healed of lung trouble of long standing. Consumption was hereditary in our family, my mother and three brothers having passed on with it. The law of *materia medica* said that in a short time I must follow them. I also had severe stomach trouble of over eight years' standing, during which time I always retired without supper, as the fear of suffering from my food was so great that I denied myself food when hungry. For over twenty years I had ovarian trouble, which was almost unbearable at times. It dated from the birth of my first child, and at one time necessitated an operation. I suffered with about all the ills that flesh is heir to: I had trouble with my eyes from a child; wore glasses for fourteen years, several oculists saying I would go blind, one declaring I would be blind in less than a year if I did not submit to an operation, which I refused to do.

But thanks be to God whose Truth reached me through the study of our textbook. Words fail to express what Christian Science has done for me in various ways, for my children, my home, my all. The physical healing is but a small part; the spiritual unfolding and uplifting is the "pearl of great price," the half that has never been told. — Mrs. J. P. M., Kansas City, Mo.

TEXTBOOK APPRECIATED

It has been my privilege to have interviews with representatives of more than sixty per cent of the nations of this earth, under their own vine and fig-tree. I had never heard a principle understandingly advanced that would enable mankind to obey the apostolic command, "prove all things," until Science and Health with Key to the Scriptures was placed in my hands. I believe that the honest study of this book in connection with the Bible will enable one to "prove all things."

I make this unqualified statement because of what my eyes have seen and my ears heard from my fellow-men of unquestioned integrity, and the positive proofs I have gained by the study of these books. Many supposed material laws that had been rooted and grounded in my mentality from youth have been overcome. It required some time for me to wake up to our Leader's words in Miscellaneous Writings, p. 206: "The advancing stages of Christian Science are gained through growth, not accretion." I had many disappointments and falls before I was willing to do the scientific work required to prove this statement; yet notwithstanding the cost to ourselves, I am convinced that we cannot do much credit to the cause we profess to love until we place ourselves in a position to prove God as He really is to us individually, and our relation to Him, by scientific work.

I wish to express loving gratitude to our Leader for the new edition of Science and Health. In studying this new edition one cannot help seeing the wisdom, love, and careful and prayerful thought expressed in the revision. Often the changing of a single word in a sentence makes the scientific thought not only more lucid to him who is familiar with the book, but also to those just coming into the blessed light. All honor to that God-loving, God-fearing woman, Mary Baker G. Eddy, whose only work is the work of love in the helping of mankind to help themselves; who has placed before her fellow-men understandingly, what man's divine rights are, and what God really is. — H. W. B., Hartford, Conn.

RUPTURE AND OTHER SERIOUS ILLS HEALED

When I took up the study of Christian Science nearly three years ago, I was suffering from a very bad rupture of thirty-two years' standing. Sometimes the pain was so severe that it seemed as if I could not endure it. These spells would last four or five hours, and while everything was done for me that could be done, no permanent relief came to me until I commenced reading Science and Health with Key to the Scriptures. After I had once looked into it I wanted to read all the time. I was so absorbed in the study of the "little book" that I hardly realized when the healing came, but I was healed, not only of the rupture, but also of other troubles, — inflammatory rheumatism, catarrh, corns, and bunions.

I would never part with the book if I could not get another. I am seventy-seven years old, and am enjoying very good health. — Mrs. M. E. P., St. Johnsbury, Vt.

MOTHER AND DAUGHTER HEALED

When Christian Science came to me, I had been taking medicine every day for twenty years, on account of constipation. I had been treated by doctors and specialists; had taken magnetic treatments and osteopathy; had tried change of climate; had an operation in a hospital, and when I came out was worse than before. I was so discouraged, after I had tried everything I ever heard of, and was no better but rather grew worse, that it seemed as though I must give up trying to get well, when a friend suggested that I try Christian Science. I had heard that Christian Scientists healed by prayer, and I thought this must be the way Jesus had healed. I felt that this was all there was left for me to try. I sent for the book, Science and Health, and commenced to read it out of curiosity, not thinking or knowing that I could be helped by the reading, but thinking I must still take medicine and that I must also have treatment by a Scientist. I,

it is high time I put the candle in the candlestick where all who will may see. My earliest recollection was a day of suffering, — a physical inheritance from my mother, which gave simple interest for a time until years advanced and compound interest was added. My father was a physician, and material remedies were used for my mother without avail, consequently his confidence in them for me was shaken, — in fact he often told me it was better to suffer without medicine than become a chronic doser, without pain.

I began teaching in early life and continued for more than twenty years, and during that time not a day passed without pain, or fear of pain, and only for my innate love of life it would have become an intolerable burden. For five years oatmeal was my chief food and I became almost as attached to it as Kaspar Hauser to his crust. I was early taught to have faith in God, and many times was relieved of pain only to have it appear again in an aggravated form.

At last my heart cried out for the living God, and the answer came by one of His messengers, who told me of Christian Science. I replied that I believed God could heal, but that I had no faith in the healing of Christian Science, but would like to investigate its theology, as it might aid in giving me some clue to the meaning of life. For three years I had searched the works of the most scientific writers to find the origin of life; many times I would think I had traced it to the beginning, but it would elude my grasp every time. One day in talking with my friend, she said she would like to loan me the textbook, Science and Health, which I very willingly accepted. Not long afterward I felt a severe attack of suffering. I opened the book for the first time and found a paragraph near the middle which attracted my attention. I read the same paragraph over and over for nearly two hours. When the tea bell rang I closed the book and I shall never forget my perception of the new heaven and the new earth, — everything in nature that I could see seemed to have been washed and made clean. The flowers that I have always loved so much, and that from childhood had told me such sweet stories, now spoke to me of the All-in-all, the hearts of my friends seemed kinder, — I had touched the hem of the garment of healing.

I ate my supper that evening forgetful of the preparations I had made for suffering, and when the next day began I was more zealous of good work than ever before. Since closing Science and Health at my first reading I have never been able to find the paragraph which I had read so many times over, the words seemed to have slipped away from me, but my joy knew no bounds at having found the pearl of great price. By the continued reading of the book I was entirely healed, and for fourteen years I have not seen a day of physical suffering. — Miss L. M., Rome, N. Y.

DEAFNESS AND DROPSY HEALED

I had been deaf from childhood. I suffered intensely after eating, and dropsy was another of my complaints. This, with consumption, caused one doctor to say, "It puzzles me; I have never seen such a case before as yours."

I met a friend who had been cured in Christian

Science, and she said, "Try Christian Science." I got a copy of Science and Health and in three weeks I was entirely cured. I felt uplifted. It seemed as if God's arms were around and about me. I felt as if heaven had come down to earth for me. After five years of suffering can any one wonder at my unspeakable gratitude? — A. B., Pittsburgh, Pa.

GRATEFUL FOR MANY BLESSINGS

In 1894 I began the study of Christian Science. At that time I was greatly in need of its healing truth. For a number of years previous I had been a semi-invalid with no hope of ever being well and strong again. Several years before this time I had undergone an operation which resulted in peritonitis. For three years previous to my study of Science and Health by Mrs. Eddy, I was scarcely ever free from headache caused by the weakened and diseased condition of the internal organs. At the time I began the study of Christian Science I was taking five kinds of medicine.

I began to read Science and Health, and did not take treatment, for I thought, "If this is truth, I shall be healed; if it is not, I shall be able to detect it, and will have nothing to do with it." I became a devoted student and gradually my bodily diseases left me, — I was free, and since that time, nearly ten years ago, neither my two children nor myself have taken any medicine; and our understanding of truth has been able to meet and overcome any suggestion of illness.

I was a devoted member of an orthodox church,

but as I grew older I began to question my beliefs, and to my questions I could find no satisfactory answer. I became dissatisfied and finally ceased attending church. I could not accept the idea of God taught there, and at last my friends looked sadly upon me as an atheist. There I stood until I learned to know God as revealed in Science and Health, and then all my questionings were answered. In my girlhood I had always prayed to the God I held in mind, and when the shadows of sickness, pain, and death came to my family, I prayed as only those can who know that if He helps not, there is none; but my prayers were unanswered. Then I closed my Bible, saying, "There is a mistake somewhere, perhaps some time I may know."

Only those who know the attitude of mind that I was in can understand the joy that came to me as I began to learn of God in Christian Science, and of my relation to Him.

Many proofs of the healing power of Truth and of His protecting care throng my thoughts. Seven years ago, when we were in a far distant country, where Christian Science was then unknown, my little daughter came in one morning from her school, saying, "Mother, I have measles; twenty of the girls are sick in bed and I am afraid they will put me there also." Her face, hands, and chest were covered with a deep red rash, throat sore, and eyes inflamed. We began immediately to do our work in Science and at night, when I left her at the door of the college, her face was clear, her eyes bright, and all fear destroyed. That was the end of the disease. — F. M. P., Boston, Mass.

A JOYFUL EXPERIENCE

In love and gratitude to God, and to Mrs. Eddy, the interpreter of Jesus' beautiful teachings, I wish to tell of some of the benefits which I have received from Christian Science. It is a little over a year since Science found me in a deplorable condition, physically as well as mentally. I had ailments of many years' standing, — chronic stomach trouble, severe eye trouble, made almost unbearable from the constant fear of losing my sight (a fate which had befallen my mother), also a painful rupture of twenty-five years' standing. These ailments, combined with unhappy conditions in my home, made me very despondent. I had entirely lost my belief in an all-merciful God, and I did not know where to turn for help. At that time Christian Science was brought to my notice, and I shall never forget the sublime moment when I perceived that an all-loving Father is always with me. Forgotten was all sorrow and worry, and after four weeks' reading in Science and Health all my ailments had disappeared. I am to-day a healthy, contented woman.

All this has come to pass in one short year, and my earnest desire is to be more and more worthy to be called a child of God. This is in loving gratitude for an understanding of this glorious truth. — Mrs. R. J., Chicago, Ill.

AN EVER-PRESENT HELP

It is a year since I began to read Science and Health, and I will now try to outline what a knowledge of its teachings has done for me.

My condition was then very trying; my eyes, which had caused me much trouble since childhood, were very painful. For these I had been treated by some of the best specialists in my native land, and after coming to the United States I had been doctored much and had worn glasses for four years. I also had catarrh, for which I had taken much medicine without being relieved. In addition to this I was an excessive smoker, using tobacco in some form almost constantly. I had contracted a smoker's heart, and used liquors freely.

The one who brought to me that which I now prize so highly, was a book agent. I told him that I should be forced to leave my trade on account of my eyes. He then told me of having been healed of a cancer, through Christian Science treatment. He showed me a copy of Science and Health, which had the signs of much use, and after being assured that if I did my part I would be healed of all my diseases, I sent for a copy of the book.

My recovery was very rapid, for after reading the book only three weeks I was completely healed of the tobacco habit. I will say, in regard to this healing, that it did not require even as much as a resolution on my part. I was smoking a cigar, while reading Science and Health, when all the desire to continue smoking left me, and I have never had a desire to use tobacco in any form since then. My eyes were the next to manifest the influence of the new knowledge gained, and had soon so far recovered that I could go about my work with ease, and I have had no more use for glasses. To-day my heart is normal, the catarrh has totally disappeared, and I am not addicted to the use of liquor.

Christian Science has proved to be an ever-present help, not only in overcoming physical ailments, but in business and daily life. It has also overcome a great sense of fear. The Bible, which I regarded with suspicion, has become my guide, and Christianity has become a sweet reality, because the Christian Science textbook has indeed been a "Key to the Scriptures" and has breathed through the Gospel pages a sweet sense of harmony. — A. F., Sioux City, Iowa.

SEVERE EYE TROUBLE OVERCOME

After hearing Christian Science lightly spoken of, from a Christian pulpit, I decided to go to one of the services and hear for myself. From infancy I had been devoted to my church, and as soon as I was old enough I was ever active in the work. Feeling it to be my duty to attend every service held in my own church, I took advantage of the Wednesday evening meetings. My first visit was not my last, I am thankful to say, for I saw immediately that these people not only preached Christianity, but practised and lived it. At that time I was wearing glasses and had worn them for sixteen years. At times I suffered the most intense pain, and for this phase of the trouble, one specialist after another had been consulted. All gave me very much the same advice; each one urged extreme carefulness and gave me glasses that seemed to relieve for a time. None of them held out any hope that my sight would ever be restored, saying that the defect had existed since infancy, and that in time I should be blind.

The thought of blindness was very distressing to me, but I tried to bear it with Christian resignation, since I thought that God had seen fit to afflict me; but since I have learned that He is a loving Father, who gives only good, I regret that I ever charged Him with my affliction. I had no treatment, but I read Science and Health, and my eyes were healed and glasses laid aside. I can never find words to express my thanks to our dear Leader, through whose teachings my sight has been regained. I can truthfully say that "whereas I was blind, now I see" — through an understanding of Truth I have found my sight perfect as God gave it. — Miss B. S., Wilmington, N. C.

A TESTIMONY FROM IRELAND

It is with a heart full of love and gratitude to God, and to our dear Leader, that I send this testimony to the Field. I had never been a strong girl; had always been subject to colds and chills, and suffered all my life from a delicate throat. Seven years ago I had a very severe attack of rheumatic fever and subsequently two less severe ones. These left all sorts of evils behind them, — debility, chronic constipation, and several others, so that with these ills my life was often a burden to me and I used to think I never should receive relief or health. I had also lost all love for God and faith in Him. I could not accept a God who, as I then believed, visited sickness and sorrow upon His children as a means for drawing them to Him.

I was in this state of mind and body when Christian Science found me. A dear friend, seeing my suffering, presented the truth to me, and though at first I did not believe that there could be healing for me, the Christian Scientists' God seemed to be the one I had been looking for all my life. I began to read Science and Health, and shall never forget my joy at finding that I could love and trust God. I took to studying the Bible, and read nothing but Science and Health and other Christian Science literature for a year. After studying the "little book" for about six weeks, I one day realized that I was a well woman, that I had taken no medicine for three weeks, and that my body was perfectly harmonious. The reading of Science and Health had healed me. The wonderful joy and spiritual uplifting which came to me then no words of mine can describe. I had also suffered from astigmatism and had for several years been obliged to use special glasses when reading or working, and could never use my eyes for more than half an hour; but from the first reading of Science and Health I found that I could read in any light and for any length of time without the slightest discomfort. I am not only grateful for the physical healing but for the mental regeneration. I rejoice that I am now able to help others who are sick and sorrowing. — E. E. L., Curragh Camp, County Kildare, Ireland.

THE TEXTBOOK MAKES OPERATION UNNECESSARY

In the early part of the year 1895 my physician said I must undergo a surgical operation in order ever to be well.

While in great fear, and dreading the operation, a kind neighbor called, and after telling me of Christian Science gave me a copy of Science and Health. She said I must put aside all medicine, and by reading faithfully she knew I could be healed. The book became my constant companion, and in a short time I was healed. Besides the relief from an operation, I was completely healed of severe headaches and stomach trouble. Physicians could give me no help for either of these ailments. For ten years I have not used medicine of any kind, and have not missed a Christian Science service on account of sickness during this period. I am perfectly well. To say that I am grateful to God for all this does not express my feelings. The physical healing was wonderful, but the understanding given me of God, and the ability to help others outweigh all else. I also love our dear Leader. — Mrs. V. I. B., Concord, N. H.

KIDNEY DISEASE AND EYE TROUBLE HEALED

Early in 1904 I was teaching in a private boarding-school. I was a very unhappy, discontented woman; I had kidney disease, besides sore eyes, and my general health was very bad. The doctor said that the climate did not suit me, and that I certainly should have a change. The best thing, he said, was to go back to France (my own country); but I did not like to leave the school, so I struggled on until July, when we went travelling for a month, but I came home worse than ever. I had a lot of worry, one disappointment after another, and I often thought that life was not worth living. In September, 1904, we heard for the first time of Christian Science through a girl who was attending our boarding-school, and who was healed through Christian Science treatment. We bought the textbook, "Science and Health with Key to the Scriptures" by Mrs. Eddy, and what a revelation it was and is to us; it is indeed the fountain of Truth. I had read Science and Health but a very short time when I took off my glasses, began to sleep well, and soon found myself well in mind and body. Besides this, it has brought harmony into our school, where there had been discord, and everything is changed for the better. I cannot describe the happiness that has come to me through Christian Science; I can only exclaim with the psalmist: "Bless the Lord, O my soul;" and may God bless Mrs. Eddy.

My one aim now is to live Christian Science, not in words only, but in deeds; loving God more and my neighbor as myself, and following meekly and obediently all our Leader's teachings. Words cannot express my gratitude to Mrs. Eddy for Christian Science. — S. A. K., Vancouver, B. C.

DISEASE OF BOWELS HEALED

When I first heard of Christian Science I had been afflicted for nine years with a very painful disease of the bowels, which four physicians failed even to diagnose, all giving different causes for the dreadful sufferings I endured. The last physician advised me to take no more medicine for these attacks, as drugs would not reach the cause, or do any good. About this time I heard of Christian Science, and had the opportunity of reading "Science and Health with Key to the Scriptures" by Mrs. Eddy, a few minutes every day for about a week, and I was thereby healed. In looking back I found I had not suffered in the least from the time I began reading this book. It has been nearly seventeen years since this wonderful healing, and I have had no return of the disease. My gratitude is endless and can be best expressed by striving mightily to walk in the path our Leader has so lovingly shown us in Science and Health. — Mrs. J. W. C., Scranton, Pa.

HEALED BY READING THE TEXTBOOK

After doctoring about a year, I was obliged to give up school and was under medical care for two years; but grew worse instead of better. I was then taken to specialists, who pronounced my case incurable, saying I was in the last stages of kidney disease and could live only a short time. Shortly afterward my uncle gave me a copy of "Science and Health with Key to the Scriptures," and asked me to study it. After studying a short time I was able to walk a distance of several miles, which I had not been able to do for three years. I also laid aside glasses which I had worn seven years, having been told I would become blind if my eyes did not receive proper care. It is over a year since I received God's blessing, and I am now enjoying perfect health and happiness. I have never had my glasses on since I first began reading Science and Health, and I have not used any medicine. — L. R., Spring Valley, Minn.

A TESTIMONY FROM SCOTLAND

I came to Christian Science purely for physical healing. I was very ill and unhappy; very cynical and disbelieving in regard to what I heard of God and religion.

I tried to live my life in my own way and put religion aside. I was a great believer in fate and in will-power, and thought to put them in the place of God, with the consequence that I was led to do many rash and foolish things. I am now thankful to say that my outlook on life is entirely changed; I have proved God's wisdom and goodness so often that I am willing and thankful to know my future is in His hands and that all things must work out for the best. I have found a God whom I can love and worship with my whole heart, and I now read my Bible with interest and understanding.

I was healed of very bad rheumatism simply by reading Science and Health. I had tried many medicines, also massage, with no result, and the doctors told me that I would always suffer from this disease, as it was inherited, and also because I had rheumatic fever when a child. I suffered day and night, and nothing relieved me until Science proved to me the falseness of this belief by removing it. I gave up all the medicines I was taking and have never touched any since, and that is more than two years ago. Before this I had often tried to do without a medicine that I had taken every day for ten years, but was always ill and had to return to it, until I found out that one Mind is the only medicine, and then I was freed from the suffering.

I had also suffered constantly from bilious attacks, colds, and a weak chest, and had been warned not to be out in wet weather, etc., but now, I am glad to say, I am quite free from all those material laws and go out in all sorts of weather. — R. D. F., Edinburgh, Scotland.

CURING BETTER THAN ENDURING

For eight years I was a great sufferer from weak lungs and after being treated by ten different physicians, in the States of Illinois, Missouri, and Colorado, I was told there was no hope of my recovery from what they pronounced tuberculosis, which was hereditary, my father having been afflicted with it. I was greatly emaciated and hardly able to be about. My general condition was aggravated by what the doctors said was paralysis of the bowels. Three physicians so diagnosed it at different times, and assured my husband that I could never get more than temporary relief. This indeed I found difficult to obtain, in spite of my almost frantic efforts. At times I was nearly insane from suffering, and after eight years of doctoring I found myself steadily growing worse. For four years I did not have a normal action of the bowels, and it was only by extreme effort and by resort to powerful drugs or mechanical means, with resultant suffering, that any action whatever could be brought about.

I had heard nothing of the curative power of Christian Science, and only to oblige a friend I went one night, about three years ago, to one of their mid-week testimonial meetings, in Boulder, Colorado. I was much impressed by what I heard there, and determined at once to investigate this strange religion, in the hope that it might have something good for me. I bought the text-book, Science and Health, and from the first I found myself growing stronger and better, both physically and mentally, as I acquired a better understanding and endeavored to put into practice what I learned. In one week

I was able to get along better without drugs than I had for years with them, and before three months had passed I was better than I had been any time in my life, for I had always suffered more or less from bowel trouble. Since that time I have taken no medicine whatever, and rely wholly upon Christian Science. My lungs are now sound, my bowels normally active, my general health excellent, and I am able to endure without fatigue tasks that before would have prostrated me. The study of our textbook was the sole means of my healing. — L. M. St. C., Matachin, Canal Zone, Panama.

SEVERE ECZEMA DESTROYED

It is only two years since I came from darkness into the light of Christian Science, and to me the spiritual uplifting has been wonderful, to say nothing of the physical healing. Words cannot express my gratitude for benefits I have received in that time. For five years I suffered with that dreaded disease, eczema, all over my body. Five doctors said there was no help for me. The suffering seemed as terrible as the hell fire that I had been taught to believe in. When Christian Science came to me two years ago through a dear friend, she gave me a copy of Science and Health and asked me to read it. I told her that I would, for I was like a drowning man grasping at a straw. I had been a Bible student for twenty-eight years, but when I commenced reading Science and Health with the Bible I was healed in less than a week. I never had a treatment. A case of measles was also destroyed in twenty-four hours after it appeared. — Mrs. M. B. G., Vermilion, Ohio.

SCIENCE AND HEALTH A PRICELESS BOON

I am a willing witness to the healing power of Christian Science, having had a lifetime's battle with disease and medical experiments. Various doctors finally admitted that they had exhausted their resources, and could only offer me palliatives, saying that a cure was impossible. I had paralysis of the bowels, frequent sick headaches with unutterable agony, and my mortal career was nearly brought to an end by a malignant type of yellow fever. Many were the attending evils of this physical inharmony, but God confounds the wisdom of men, for while studying Science and Health two years ago, the veil of ignorance was lifted and perfect health was shown to me to be my real condition, and to such there is no relapse. The constant use of glasses, which were apparently a necessity to me for years, was proven needless, and they were laid aside. Mrs. Eddy has made Scripture reading a never-failing well of comfort to me. By her interpretation "the way of the Lord" is made straight to me and mine. It aids us in our daily overcoming of the tyranny of the flesh and its rebellion against the blessed leading of Christ, Truth. The daily study of the Bible and our textbook is bringing more and more into our consciousness the power of God unto salvation. — J. C., Manatee, Fla.

A CRITIC CONVINCED

With gratitude to God I acknowledge my lifelong debt to Christian Science. In 1895 I attended my first

Christian Science meeting, and was deeply impressed with the earnestness of the people and the love reflected, but as for the spiritual healing of the physical body, I did not believe such a thing to be possible. I bought Science and Health and studied it to be able to dispute intelligently with the supposedly deluded followers of Christian Science. I pursued the study carefully and thoroughly, and I have had abundant reason since to be glad that I did, for through this study, and the resultant understanding of my relation to God, I was healed of a disease with which I had been afflicted since childhood and for which there was no known remedy. Surely my experience has been the fulfilling in part of the Scripture: "He sent His Word and healed them, and delivered them from their destructions." I believe that Science and Health reveals the Word referred to by David. — C. A. B. B., Kansas City, Mo.

BORN AGAIN

It was in April, 1904, that I first heard the "still, small voice" of the Christ and received healing through Christian Science; and the blessings have been so many since, that it would take too much space to name them. Reared from childhood in an intellectual atmosphere, my paternal grandfather having been an orthodox minister of the old school for forty years, and my father a deep student, ever seeking for the truth of all things, I began early to ponder and to study into the meaning of life, and came to the conclusion before I was twenty that though God probably existed in some remote place, still it was impossible to connect Him with my present living. My highest creed, therefore, became, "Do right because it *is* right and not for fear of being punished." Then began the suffering. Sorrow after sorrow followed each other in rapid succession; for ten long years there was no rest, the road was indeed long and hard and had no turning, until finally the one thing that had stood by me all through the trials, namely, my health, gave way, and with that went my last hope. But the last hour of the night had come, the dawn of day was at hand; a dear friend left Science and Health upon my piano one day, saying that I would gain much good by reading it.

Glad to get away from my own poor thoughts, I opened the "little book" and began to read. I had read only a short time when such a wonderful transformation took place! I was renewed; born again. Mere words cannot tell the story of the mighty uplifting that carried me to the very gates of heaven. When I began to read the book, life was a burden, but before I had finished reading it the first time, I was doing all my housework and doing it easily; and since that glorious day I have been a well woman. My health is splendid, and I am striving to let my light so shine that others may be led to the truth. There have been some mighty struggles with error, and I have learned that we cannot reach heaven with one long stride or easily drift inside the gate, but that the "asking" and the "seeking" and the "knocking" must be earnest and persistent.

For a long time I was always looking back to see if

the error had gone, until one day when I realized that to catch a glimpse of what spiritual sense means I must put corporeal sense behind me. I then set to work in earnest to find the true way. I opened Science and Health and these words were before me, "If God were understood, instead of being merely believed, this understanding would establish health" (p. 203). I saw that I must get the right understanding of God! I closed the book and with head bowed in prayer I waited with longing intensity for some answer. How long I waited I do not know, but suddenly, like a wonderful burst of sunlight after a storm, came clearly this thought, "Be still, and know that I am God." I held my breath — deep into my hungering thought sank the infinite meaning of that "I." All self-conceit, egotism, selfishness, everything that constitutes the mortal "I," sank abashed out of sight. I trod, as it were, on holy ground. Words are inadequate to convey the fulness of that spiritual uplifting, but others who have had similar experiences will understand.

From that hour I have had an intelligent consciousness of the ever-presence of an infinite God who is only good. — C. B. G., Hudson, Mass.

A RESTLESS SENSE OF EXISTENCE DESTROYED

Through reading Science and Health and the illumination which followed, I was healed of ulceration of the stomach and kindred troubles, a restless sense of existence, agnosticism, etc. The torture I endured with the stomach trouble I will not attempt to describe. The attending physician declared that I could live but a short time, and I felt there would be a limit to my endurance of the torture, but the disease was dissipated into nothingness through Christian Science, which brought me peace.

Like many others I had been seemingly lost in the sea of error, without a compass, yet earnestly and honestly seeking a haven. I had investigated all kinds of religions and philosophies that came under my notice, with the exception of Christian Science, which was not then deemed worthy of inquiry, and yet it held the very truth I was searching for — the light which "shineth in the darkness; and the darkness comprehended it not." Three years of stubborn resistance to Truth, with increasing suffering, followed — then the light came, and with it a new experience. Now, after nine years of Christian Science experience, under severe tests, it can be truthfully said that it has not failed me in any hour of need. — J. F. J., Cincinnati, Ohio.

MORALLY AND PHYSICALLY HEALED

I did not accept Christian Science on account of any healing of my own, but after seeing my mother, who was fast drifting toward helplessness with rheumatism, restored to perfect health with only a few treatments in Christian Science, I thought surely this must be the truth as Jesus taught and practised it, and if so it was what I had been longing for.

This was about ten years ago and was the first I had ever heard of Christian Science. We soon got a copy of Science and Health and I began in the right way to see if Christian Science were the truth. I had no thought of studying it for bodily healing; in fact, I did not think I needed it for that, but my soul cried out for something I had not yet found. This book was indeed a key to the Scriptures.

It was not long after I began reading before I discovered that my eyes were good and strong, I could read as much as I wished, and at any time, which was something I could not do before, as my eyes had always been weak. The doctors said they never would be very strong, and that if I did not wear glasses, I might lose my sight altogether. I never gave up to wearing glasses, and now, thanks to Christian Science, I do not need them, my work for the past two years as a railway mail clerk being a good test. At the same time my eyes were healed, I also noticed that I was entirely healed of another ailment which had been with me all my life, and which was believed to be inherited. Since that time my growth has seemed to me slow, yet when I look back and view myself as I was before Christian Science found me, and compare it with my life as it now is, I can only close my eyes to the picture and rejoice that I have been "born again" and that I have daily been putting off "the old man with his deeds," and putting on "the new man."

Some of the many things that have been overcome through the study of Science and Health, and through realizing and practising the truth it teaches, are profanity, the use of tobacco, a very quick temper, which made both myself and those around me at times very miserable, and such thoughts as malice, revenge, etc. — O. L. R., Fort Worth, Tex.

HEALTH AND UNDERSTANDING GAINED

Most of my boyhood days were spent in the hands of physicians. From birth I was considered a very weakly child, but my mother was brave, and being much devoted to me did everything within her knowledge and power for my comfort. Sickness and medicine were continually before me, and by the time I reached my teens I thought I knew a material remedy for every ill. I continued in my delusion, because I was never told the real cause of my trouble. Besides being under a leading specialist for two years, I was also an outdoor patient at a noted hospital, but I was not healed. It is wonderful how the "little ones" are cared for in the face of all these seeming difficulties. I always used the prayers that I had been taught, and as I grew older I began to ask for wisdom. Little by little I gained a desire for freedom, and my prayers finally led me to the truth. The first week that I heard of Christian Science, I visited the home of dear Christian Science friends, and was at once refreshed by their purity of thought and example. I bought a copy of Science and Health, and, after studying it a little while with the Bible, I saw that if the Bible was true, Science and Health must also be true. I began to demonstrate over my physical and mental condition, and as soon as the fear and pain began to leave me I felt encouraged to go on. I was healed, and stopped complaining. I kept on studying our textbook, and when I got an understanding in a small degree of the Science of Mind, my first thought was to help others. I was guided where I could progress in Science, and was no longer "carried about with every wind of doctrine," but held to Principle as closely as possible. From the time the healing came into my consciousness, the desire for material remedies left me, because Christian Science at once pointed out the way to get at the cause of discord and disease. All that I had to give up were the false beliefs of mortal mind. Christian Science then taught me to love the church, and to appreciate what it had already done for mankind. I often thought of the old adage, "Charity begins at home," and after three years' preparation I felt able to take Christian Science to my home, where it found, in due time, ready acceptance and willing disciples. This gave me even greater joy than my own healing. The more good I saw accomplished, the more love I had for the truth. Christian Science changed my course from the first, and gave me a nobler aim and purpose in life. I was not so easily influenced by other people's shortcomings, when I learned that evil has neither personality nor place. I was not so ready to take offence, when I found out the way to work unselfishly for the upbuilding of the Cause. — A. E. J., Toledo, Ohio.

AN EVER-PRESENT HELP FOUND

On the 23rd of March, 1900, I received from one of my daughters a copy of Science and Health on my seventy-first birthday. Although a constant reader of all kinds of papers and books, I had never heard anything of Christian Science, except a short notice that spring in a San Francisco newspaper, from an orthodox clergyman, referring to the Christian Science people in not very complimentary style.

In Mrs. Eddy's book I came across a great deal of thought that was not readily understood at the first reading, but by continued and careful study, and a good deal of help from my knowledge of chemistry and natural philosophy, I soon shook off the belief of sensation in matter, — the so-called elementary substance. One afternoon I put the belt on my circular saw to cut blocks of firewood and also to split a small stick of frame timber. In doing this the stick closed and pinched the saw. I picked up a small wooden wedge and tried to drive it into the saw kerf, but a bit of ice let the stick on to the back of the saw and instantly it flew, with heavy force, into my face, and bouncing off my left cheek fell about twenty feet off on the snow. The blood spattered on the snow next the saw table, and on feeling with my hand there were two wounds, one on the lock of the jaw and another forward, as big as a dollar, on the cheek bone. "Now," I thought to myself, "there is a case of surgery for you," and without further ceremony, I began to treat the case to the best of my knowledge, with the result that the bleeding stopped almost instantly, and so did a thumping pain, which had commenced. I paid no more attention to the matter, but finished my work, and then went to supper. When I washed my face, I felt a big lump on the jawbone where the block of wood struck, but after my usual reading I went to bed and slept all night until near daylight, when a pain on the right side awoke me. On feeling with my hand there was another big lump on the right side, but I treated it and went to sleep again. I never lost an hour from the hurt, although I found out that my jaw was broken. There is no scar, only a little red spot on the cheek, and the lumps on the bone have long since disappeared.

In summing up the benefits I have received from the reading of Science and Health, I can but refer to a condition of sickness dating back to the war (1862), when chronic and malignant diarrhœa came near making an end of my material existence. My hearing, also, was seriously impaired from the effect of cannon firing at Shiloh, but it has come back to me, and where I formerly dared not eat an orange, or grapes, I can now eat anything without being hurt. My peace of mind is giving me a rest which I never experienced before during my life, and I have ceased to look away off for the divine presence that was always near, though I did not know it. — L. B., Baldy, N. M.

MANY PHYSICAL AND MENTAL TROUBLES OVERCOME

Less than a year ago, when nothing but trouble seemed to encompass me, I was led to Christian Science. My mother's copy of Science and Health was always lying on the table, but I scarcely ever read it. One day, however, the mental conflict was so great I commenced reading in the hope of obtaining peace. Every day since then my companions have been the Bible and Science and Health. At that time I had a very serious eruption on my face, which had been there two years. We had consulted several physicians, and used every remedy suggested to eradicate it, but they proved useless. I had given up all hopes of its ever being healed, as the physician we last consulted pronounced it tuberculosis of the skin and incurable. A few weeks after I commenced reading, I was amazed to see it almost healed over, and to-day my cheek is perfectly smooth, while the scar is disappearing.

In April my baby was born with only the practitioner and a woman friend present. I suffered little pain, and the third day I went down-stairs. I am able to nurse him, — a privilege of which I was deprived with my first child. He is a picture of health, having never been sick a day since he was born. — K. E. W. L., Mt. Dora, Fla.

A NEW LIFE GAINED

Leaving home when a young man, I carried with me a protection against the temptation of a great city, — a mother's prayers and a small Bible. For a time I read the Bible and prayed, but without understanding. This did not suffice, and evil seemed to gain the victory. I soon omitted to read my Bible; forgot to go to God in prayer for guidance and help, and looked to the world for that which it never has and never can give, — health, peace, and joy.

Thus, years later, when Christian Science came into my home, it found me prayerless, churchless, godless; a home discordant, and with no thought or knowledge of spiritual things. Up to this time, my wife had for years been seeking health through the physicians, but without success, and as a last resort had been sent to Christian Science. The help received was so wonderful that I commenced the study of Science and Health. The first effect which I realized from the reading of our textbook, was a great love for the Bible and a desire to read it, something which I had not done for years. I went in silent prayer to God, that I might see the light and truth which would enable me to become a better man. "Ye must be born again." Thus again, and as a child, was I taught to pray "the effectual fervent prayer" which "availeth much." In a few weeks' study of Science and Health together with the Bible, and without other help, I was healed of a desire for liquor, of years' standing, and of the use of tobacco. Ten years have passed and these appetites have never returned. I have never used either liquor or tobacco in any form from that time to the present. Surely this Scripture is fulfilled in our home: "Old things are passed away; behold, all things are become new." How can we estimate the value of a book, the study of which brings such transformation and regeneration? Only as we endeavor to live, and strive to practise what it teaches, can we begin to pay our debt to God, and to her whom He has sent to make plain to human understanding the life and teaching of Christ Jesus. — W. H. P., Boston, Mass.

A VOICE FROM ENGLAND

For a number of years I was a weary woman, not ill enough in health to be called an invalid, but suffering more than could be told with fatigue and weakness. Feeling that this was God's will, I did not ask to be healed, although I was constantly doctoring. I suffered with dyspepsia, congestion of the liver, and many other things, including weak eyesight. With all the medicine, and with different changes for rest, I never regained health, and thought I never should, so I prayed for grace to bear my cross patiently for others' sake. One day, while lying on my couch exhausted, which had become a frequent experience, the words came to me, "Whatsoever ye shall ask in prayer, believing, ye shall receive." I rose, knelt down and said, O God, make me well. I was telling a friend this and she kindly gave me a *Sentinel*. Imagine my joy when I saw the testimonies of healing! I believed them, remembering our Lord's words, "Blessed are they that have not seen, and yet have believed." I obtained a copy of Science and Health and before a week had passed I realized that if God was my all I needed no glasses. My eyes were healed in a few days, and since then I have never thought of glasses. I was also cured of dyspepsia, and nothing that I have eaten has hurt me since then. The belief in health laws was next destroyed, by knowing that our heavenly Father did not make them, and from this has come the beautiful experience of the overcoming of fatigue.

For this alone I can never be thankful enough. True indeed are the words, "They shall run, and not be weary." This was more than a year ago, and I can say that not once have I felt inclined to lie on the couch, nor have I had a headache, although I am doing more work than ever before. Fear has also been overcome in many ways. — A. L., Chelmsford, England.

DEPRAVED APPETITES OVERCOME

When Christian Science first came to me, or rather, when I first came to Christian Science, I did not have a very bad opinion of myself. I thought I was a pretty good fellow. I had no religious views. I seemed to be getting along as well as, if not better than, some who professed Christianity. So I drifted along until I was led to investigate Christian Science.

As I progressed in the understanding as gained from the study of both Science and Health and the Bible, and commenced to know myself, I found that a great change had been wrought in me. For fifteen years I had used tobacco, both chewing and smoking; for ten years I had been a victim of the drink habit, sometimes to excess; I was also addicted to profanity. Christian Science removed these appetites. A stomach trouble and other lesser ills, such as headache, a bad temper, an inordinate love of money, etc., disappeared under the same benign influence. Those things that seemed to be pleasure do not give me pleasure now. They were not real pleasure. I have lost nothing, I have sacrificed nothing; but I have gained everything, and not yet the whole, for I can see plenty yet to be done.

The condition of mind before investigating and after is as different as black and white. As Mrs. Eddy says, "Not matter, but Mind, satisfieth." — G. B. P., Henry, S. D.

CATARRH OF THE STOMACH HEALED

I should like to express my gratitude for the many benefits I have received through Christian Science, and to mention the great joy brought to me in the thought that man is not the helpless victim of sin, disease, and death. Through its teachings I have been able to overcome many errors.

When Christian Science found me, one year ago last April, in Chicago, I was suffering from catarrh of the stomach, which had been very persistent, and I had been a slave to the cigarette habit for eighteen years. Pain and weakness had robbed me of all that one holds dear. The first symptoms of the disease appeared about five years ago in the form of severe cramps of the stomach, which finally developed into other symptoms of that painful disease. I doctored continually, my diet daily becoming more rigid, until three slices of toast became my daily allowance of food.

In this condition I left the East for my home in Chicago, hoping that a change of climate might benefit me. After spending six weeks there and finding no relief, I concluded to return East. The Sunday morning before leaving I picked up a Sunday paper, and glancing through the religious items my eyes fell on the notices of Christian Science church services. Curiosity led me to a service and I shall never forget that morning or the surprise and joy it gave me to find that beautiful church, and to know that so great a number actually believed that God does heal the sick to-day. This brought a first ray of hope. The evening service found me there again. Among the notices read was that of a reading room, giving the location and time of opening. Monday morning found me there promptly, and the first book I picked up was Science and Health which opened a new world to me.

I had dieted so long and suffered so much that I had a morbid fear of food. When I had reached and read "neither food nor the stomach, without the consent of mortal mind, can make one suffer" (Science and Health, p. 221), I left the reading room for something to eat. I found a bakery near by, and bought a bag of cakes which I ate, and shortly after I had a hearty dinner without the least complaint from my stomach.

From that time until now I have eaten anything that I wished, and the craving for cigarettes, which I had for many years, has entirely vanished. The understanding of Truth, which entirely relieved the diseased stomach, healed also the morbid appetite for smoking. After coming back East, I bought a copy of Science and Health, which I have read daily, and find it a continual help in all the affairs of life.

In my home and at work I find this Science a comfort and source of strength. I have had many difficulties in the way, but it has helped me out of them all. — W. E. B., New Britain, Conn.

SPINAL DISEASE HEALED

When I first heard of Christian Science, seven years ago, I supposed that it was some old fad under a new name. In the little Texas town where we then lived there were two or three Christian Scientists who met at the home of one of their number to read the Lesson-Sermon. Meeting one of them one day, I asked if unbelievers could come to their meetings. She said that they could if they wanted to. I went, expecting them to do something that I could laugh at when telling my friends about it. How surprised I was to find out that they did n't do anything but read the Bible and another book which they called Science and Health. I still thought it all foolishness, but resolved to go to their meetings until I found out all they believed. I continued to go until I began to understand a little of what they knew, not what they believed; and instead of spending my time telling others what a silly thing Christian Science is, I am now trying to find words to tell what a great and wonderful thing it is. I have been healed of so-called incurable spinal disease of ten years' standing by studying the Bible and Science and Health. Science and Health has been my only teacher, and I wish to send my thanks to our dear Leader.

There are no other Scientists near where we now live, but I have the *Quarterly* and study the lessons by myself. I have five small children, and Christian Science is invaluable to me in controlling them, and in overcoming their common ills. They often help themselves and each other to destroy their little hurts and fears. — Mrs. M. H., Oleta, Okla.

MANY TROUBLES OVERCOME

In the second chapter of First Peter, ninth verse, I read "that ye should show forth the praises of him who hath called you out of darkness into his marvellous light." The periodicals so wisely established by our Leader give us one means of showing forth the praises of Truth.

From the darkness of physical pain and weariness into the light of wholeness and joyousness in work and living, — from the darkness of a clouded sight into the light of clearer vision, — from the darkness of doubt and discord into the marvellous light of the reality of good, — this is what a reading of the Christian Science textbook has done for me.

At the time the book was lent to me, I was teaching in the public schools of Chicago, and absences from my work on account of illness were of frequent occurrence. For five weeks I had been under the care of a specialist for an organic trouble, and he said I would have to come as many more months before a cure could be effected. At this time, Science and Health was brought to my notice. I never thought of such a thing as being healed by the reading of the book, but my thought was so changed that I was healed, not only of the organic trouble, but of blurred eyesight, fatigue, and a train of other discordant manifestations. I did not go back to the physician until four months later to pay my bill (which, by the way, was more than five times the price of the Science and Health I had purchased). From the time I read the book I taught steadily without losing time from my work. I was helped, too, with my work in many other ways.

Through reading the textbook I learned that God has given us strength to do all we have to do, and that it is the things we do not have to do (the envying, strife, emulating, vainglorying, and so on) that leave in their wake fatigue and discord.

Gratitude to our beloved Leader, Mrs. Eddy, and to her faithful students, with whom I afterwards became associated, can be expressed only by daily efforts to put into practice what has been taught. — T. H. A., Madison, Wis.

PREJUDICE OVERCOME

I became interested in Christian Science somewhat over three years ago when in much need of help. I had never been strong, and as I grew older I grew weaker and at last became so ill that life was a burden to me. Science and Health by Mrs. Eddy was sent to me, in answer to prayer, as I thought. I was a little afraid of all these new fads, as I thought them, but I had not read far before I felt that I had found the truth which makes us free. I was healed of stomach trouble, inward weakness, and bilious attacks.

One physician said I might have to undergo an operation before I could get well, but, thanks to this Truth, I have found that the only operation needed was the regeneration of this so-called human mind by learning to know God. In many cases I have been able to help myself and others.

Words cannot express my thanks to Mrs. Eddy, and to all who are bringing these great truths to the help of the whole world. — E. E. M., Huntington, W. Va.

A CONVINCING TESTIMONY

I became interested in Christian Science some five years ago, the practical nature of its statements appealing to me, and I must say, at the outset, that with my little experience I have found it all and more than I ever dreamt of realizing on this plane of existence. I am satisfied that I have found Truth. God is indeed to me an ever-present help.

My little girl, some ten months old, was afflicted with constipation. It was so severe I dreaded to go out anywhere with her, as I knew not when she would be taken with a convulsion. I had tried all the usual remedies in such cases, but it seemed to grow more obstinate. There was a Christian Scientist living in the same house with us, a Scientist who let her light shine, and while she said little, I felt the reflection of Love. I had no knowledge of the teachings of Christian Science, save that God was the physician at all times. In my own way I believed He was all-powerful, and I said to my husband one day, "I am through with medicine for baby. I am just going to leave her in God's care and see what He will do. I have done all I can." I did as I said, laid my burden at God's feet, and did not pick it up again. In two days the child was perfectly natural, and has since been free from the trouble. She is now six years of age. Some months later a second test came. She woke up at nine o'clock at night crying and holding her ear. There was to sense a gathering. I was alone. I took up my Science and Health and Bible, but the more I worked the louder she screamed. Error kept suggesting material remedies, but I said firmly: "No; I shall not go back to error. God will help me." Just then I thought of my own fear, how excessive it was, and a conversation I had with the Scientist who first voiced the truth to me, came to mind. She said she always found it helpful to treat herself and cast out her own fear before treating a patient. I put baby down and again took up my Science and Health, and these were the words I read: —

"Every trial of our faith in God makes us stronger. The more difficult seems the material condition to be overcome by Spirit, the stronger should be our faith and the purer our love. The Apostle John says: 'There is no fear in Love, but perfect Love casteth out fear'" (Science and Health, p. 410). I looked up, the crying had ceased, the child was smiling, and in a few minutes asked to be put to bed. There has been no further trouble of that kind.

I have since seen the power of Truth overcome error of many forms, including croup, whooping-cough, tonsilitis, etc. I am thankful for all these proofs, but far more grateful am I for the spiritual teaching to love, to forgive, to curb my tongue, and cease my criticism. — M. A. H., Brockton, Mass.

HEALED PHYSICALLY AND SPIRITUALLY

I had been taking medicine continually for many years. Finally I was taken suddenly ill and could not leave my room for about two months, then I went away for three months, thinking that I should come back and be able to continue my work. I improved very much, but the fear of quick consumption was with my doctor and my family and friends, and I was warned about the coming winter. Only too soon the fear manifested itself. I had worked just three weeks when all the pains and aches returned, and I had to go to bed as soon as I got home, so there was no pleasure in living. My employer advised me to see my physician, and said perhaps I should not work that winter. I then and there turned to Christian Science. I could not afford to give up work and live away from home, neither did I want to depend on doctors and medicine any longer. I took the book and read it on my way to work, and at noon I lay down on a couch instead of going out for luncheon and fell asleep. When I awoke I was a different person, all pains and aches had gone, and I was free. I was so happy I could hardly contain myself; to material sense it was wonderful. As I walked I kept saying, "Wonderful, wonderful, wonderful," and tried to understand "the scientific statement of being" by repeating portions at a time, then pondering over them. I read the book four times in succession, and every time I found more and more to aid in the understanding.

This healing was in October, 1901, with no other help than Science and Health, and soon I was relieved of other chronic ailments. In February I was able to put away eyeglasses, which I had worn ten years and a half for astigmatism. Oculists told me I would always have to wear them. A month later my father asked me to help him, as he was suffering so much from constipation, dyspepsia, and neuralgia. He had been subsisting on bran, nearly starving himself until he was most miserable, and his limbs seemed so cold that they were kept wrapped in blankets. I felt very humble as he asked me, and told him I would have a practitioner help him, as I had never treated any one; but he would not consent to have any one but myself, and I finally told him I would try, but that he must not hold Science responsible if he were not benefited, for my lack of understanding, and not Science, would be at fault. At my request he read Science and Health, ate whatever he wanted, and used no medicine in any form. After two treatments I received word from him that he was healed of that bondage of thirty years' standing. In view of all these signs which followed my acceptance of Christian Science, I knew it must be true. — R. L. A., Chicago, Ill.

A VOICE FROM THE SOUTH

I was delicate from childhood, and my parents did not think it was possible for me to live more than a few years. I lived, however, although there was not much improvement in my health. Travel and change of climate brought only temporary relief, and the physicians gave me no hope that I would ever be well.

As a last resort I began the study of Science and Health, and before I had finished reading the book I realized that its author was divinely commissioned to bring this spiritual message to a waiting world. Through this reading my health was restored, and I was healed of one disease that has been called incurable by all physicians.

For this, together with the greater and higher blessing of having the spiritual fact of being unfolded to me, I am most grateful.

What shall be rendered for such benefits received and made possible by the consecrated life of our revered Leader? Only by following the teachings of our textbook, and by loving obedience to her gentle and timely admonitions can we show our true sense of gratitude. — F. H. D., De Funiak Springs, Fla.

HEALED AFTER MUCH SUFFERING

A testimony given in the *Journal* led me to investigate Christian Science, and I hope in return to be the means of leading some one else to see the beauty of this saving truth, and to learn to know God aright and man's relationship to Him. I know from experience that it is prejudice and misapprehension of what Christian Science is, that keeps many from enjoying the blessings it bestows.

I had been taking patent medicines for several years, and had been to one of the best sanitariums in this country, but was not healed, although I received some benefit, for which I shall always feel grateful, for I know the physicians did all they could for me. I sometimes thought I had exhausted all remedies, but did not give up, for I felt there must be something to heal me if I could find it.

When in this state of mind Christian Science came to my notice, and after reading several *Journals*, I purchased a copy of Science and Health. I read for several days at odd times. I commenced to improve, and in about a week I was healed of most of my ills, among which were dyspepsia and nervous debility.

Although I had heard about Christian Science before, I had never heard that the reading of the Christian Science textbook had ever effected the healing of anybody. I commenced reading to find out what Christian Science was, but was surprised to find myself improving, and was soon assured that it was the theology of Science and Health that healed me, just as it was the theology of Jesus that healed the sick.

It has also proved to me that there can be no Christian Science Church that does not heal the sick and sinful, for healing follows as the natural result of the teaching of Christian Science. The Bible has become a new revelation to me, and I can read it much more understandingly by the light received through the reading of Science and Health. — A. F. M., Fairmont, Minn.

THROUGH GREAT TRIBULATIONS

When I attempt to make plain what Christian Science has done for me, words fail me. For twenty years I was a constant sufferer, my spine having been injured when I was very young. As a little child I suffered so much that I would look up to the stars and beg God, who I thought might be up there somewhere, to take me away from the earth, — I was so tired. A great wall of pain seemed to separate me from the pleasures enjoyed by others, and I could not explain how I felt, because no one could understand. Years passed, and I saw my earthly happiness swept away; my heart was broken and I did not know what to do. I cried for help, day after day and night after night, although I was not sure what God was, nor where He was. I only knew that I suffered, and was in need of help, and that there was no earthly help for either mind or body. I loved purity, truth, and right always, and this made evil seem a most terrible reality. I was unable to cope with it, and so found myself in despair. This was my condition when I commenced reading Science and Health. I was ready for its message, and in about ten days there came a wonderful insight into the truth which heals the sick and binds up the broken-hearted. All pain left me, I had a glimpse of the new heavens and the new earth, and was beginning to be fed by Love divine.

I had suffered for years with insomnia. That night I rested like a child, and awoke the next morning well and happy. A flood of light daily illumined the pages of the "little book," and the revelation it holds for all came to my waiting heart. "The peace which passeth all understanding" rested upon me, and joy too deep for words transformed my life. My prayers were answered, for I had found God in Christian Science.

The Bible, which I knew very little about, became my constant study, my joy, and my guide. The copy which I bought at the time of my healing is marked from Genesis to Revelation. It was so constantly in my hands for three years that the cover became worn and the leaves loose, so it has been laid away for a new one. Two and three o'clock in the morning often found me poring over its pages, which grew more and more sacred to me every day, and the help I received therefrom was wonderful, for which I can find no words to express my gratitude. — I. L., Los Angeles, Cal.

A HELPFUL TESTIMONY

Words cannot express my gratitude to God for Christian Science. When I first read Science and Health, I had tried every remedy I had ever heard of. I felt no change in mind or body that I was conscious of until I read page 16 of the chapter on "Prayer," in Science and Health. The first words of the "spiritual sense of the Lord's Prayer," telling of our Father-Mother God, gave me a glimpse of heavenly light. I stopped and reasoned, and remembered the teachings of Jesus. The truth of man's spiritual being dawned on my consciousness. I realized I was not subject to mortal laws, as I had been taught all my life. I could not explain how I knew this, but I knew it. Through Christian Science, Mrs. Eddy had given me what

I had longed for all my life, — a Mother, a perfect "Father-Mother God." I had known there was a great lack, and at that time I believe the orthodox world had but half of the truth which Jesus came to establish. When I read, "Give us this day our daily bread," and its spiritual interpretation, my tears began to flow; all the years of bitterness, hate, and fear melted away. I knew then, as I know now, that nothing satisfies but Love. That day began the outward and inward conscious healing, — mental and physical. There never came a doubt! I absolutely knew that Christian Science was and is the truth. Money, friends, materiality, are nothing beside the conscious knowledge of God, man, and the universe.

I did not need treatment from any one, — Science and Health was so clear and beautiful. I could not understand the Bible before, but I found it illumined now that I had a little understanding of Christian Science. For ten years I have not had to lie down in the daytime from any sickness. I am now, and have been all these years, the picture of perfect health. When I first read Science and Health I weighed one hundred and four pounds; I now weigh over one hundred and sixty. This physical health is not to be compared to my happiness, — my harmony that nothing can take away, — because it is the gift of God. Nothing has shown me the perversity of the human mind more than in its conclusions in regard to my healing. Even when I felt and knew that I was healed, people constantly said, because I was thin and delicate looking, "You are not well, any one could look at you and know it." Now that I am fleshy, they say, "You don't look as if you ever had a pain in all your life. You could not have had consumption."

When I think what my life was before I had Christian Science, of the six years of colds, suffering, and coughing, not to mention the unhappiness, I want to "work, watch, and pray" for the Mind of Christ, that I may work rightly in God's vineyard, and to know that in truth, what belongs to one belongs to all, — that one God, one Life, Truth, and Love is all. — A. C. L., Kansas City, Kans.

DESIRE FOR LIQUOR AND TOBACCO DISAPPEARED

I first heard of Christian Science four years ago. At that time drinking and smoking were my comforters. I had no other companionship. I had lived almost constantly from childhood in an evil atmosphere. Though I was far from being satisfied with my condition, I failed to see how to better it until I read Science and Health. I used occasionally to listen to a sermon, but sermons did not give me any more comfort than I derived from my pipe, hence I concluded that church-going could not satisfy me and I preferred drinking and smoking. When I began to read Science and Health, I saw it offered something substantial. After a few months' study all desire for drinking and smoking disappeared. I did not give them up; I made no sacrifices, I simply found something better. I might mention that I had smoked ever since I can remember. I used to smoke years before I left school, and, like most Englishmen, loved my pipe, and would almost prefer to miss a meal rather than to go without my smoke. I used to think it gave me comfort. During my four years' study of Christian Science I have not spent a cent for doctors or medicine, neither have I lost a day from my work on account of sickness, which compares wonderfully with the previous four years. I take a great interest and pleasure in reading the Bible and studying the lessons in the *Quarterly*. The Bible used to be a most mysterious book to me, but Science and Health makes it a most precious book, making its meaning clearer, plainer, and simpler.

I take this opportunity to express my gratitude to Mrs. Eddy and to the friend who invited me to attend the service held in the Auditorium years ago. I also wish to acknowledge the benefit I have had from the *Journal* and the *Sentinel*. They have helped me wonderfully. If the value of Science and Health and these publications were measured as business men value things, by the results or benefits they bring, they certainly would be priceless to me. It would be impossible to measure their value, as I have got something from Science and Health that all the money in the world could not buy. — H. P. H., Chicago, Ill.

AN EXPRESSION OF LOVING GRATITUDE

In the spring of 1893, while studying for the ministry, Science and Health was placed in my hands, and the truth contained therein at once became to me the pearl of great price. I literally devoured the book, reading it about eighteen hours a day. Its originality was startling, upsetting my preconceived opinions of God, man, and creation. Two sentences especially appealed to me: "The foundation of mortal discord is a false sense of man's origin" (p. 262), and, "For right reasoning, there should be but one fact before the thought, namely, spiritual existence" (p. 492). I had found the keynote to the Science of being as taught in this marvellous book, and persevered until a glimpse of the new heavens and new earth came, for the old were passing away. With this spiritual uplifting came also physical health.

All my life had been spent in semi-invalidism, and I seemed destined to a life of suffering. In three weeks after beginning Science and Health, to my joyful surprise I found myself a well man, sound physically, and uplifted spiritually. Life was being lived from a new basis, the old things of personal sense were passing away and all things becoming new. I learned that the infinite good is the one Friend upon whom we can call at all times, an all-powerful, ever-present help in every time of trouble; that His children are really governed in peace and harmony by spiritual law, and as the right understanding of it is gained, the other things soon follow, bringing a peace the human concept can never know.

For the last twelve years my whole time has been devoted to Christian Science practice, and I have seen nearly every so-called incurable disease healed by its beneficent influence. God bless our dear Leader! She has set before us an open door, which no man can shut, and it is but a question of time when the world will know her better and love her more. — E. E. N., Washington, D. C.

HEALED OF BRIGHT'S DISEASE

August 18, 1902, I was taken down with what three doctors pronounced Bright's disease, and they stated that I would not live a year, or if I did succeed in living longer, I would be mentally unbalanced. On December 6, 1902, my wife presented me with Science and Health as a birthday gift, and it was indeed the best present I ever received. Since that time I have been reading it and attending Second Church here. I have not used any medicine since, nor has any one in our home. I am in the finest of health and have lost all my bad habits. This truth has brought a great spiritual uplifting to all of us, and words cannot express my gratitude to Mrs. Eddy and to all who have helped me to the same. — T. V., Chicago, Ill.

FIBROID TUMOR DESTROYED

When quite young I was impressed that the Bible was not properly interpreted by the preachers, for I could not conceive of a God of wrath who was unjust enough to allow His little ones to suffer pain, misery, and death. I had hope, however, that some day the truth would be revealed to an awakening world, but little did I dream that even then there was one of God's noble women who reflected sufficient purity and holiness to entertain the "angel of his presence," and commune with the true God.

I was believed to be predisposed to scrofula, so that I was not a strong or attractive child, and my girlhood and womanhood were scarcely ever free from dread of the laws of matter and lack of strength. The climax was reached when a physician informed me, after weeks of treatment, that I had a fibroid tumor, which required an operation. The conditions were most trying and I was heartsick and discouraged when, in January, 1893, I heard of Christian Science through a letter from a dear sister who had been greatly benefited thereby, and I resolved to go at once to a practitioner, for I believed it to be the long-lost truth that would make me free. It meant a great effort and sacrifice for me to go to Chicago at that time, but divine Love opened the way and I reached there in March. I had been in my sister's home but a few days, reading Science and Health almost constantly, when I asked her if I had not better have treatment for the tumor, which had given me so much trouble. She said to me, "You feel well, do you not?" I assured her that I never had felt so well as I had since reaching there. "Well," she said with decision, "your tumor is gone, for God never made it," and her statements were true, for it has never been heard of from that day. Since then I have been healed of chronic sore throat, hay fever, and other troubles, and I know that Christian Science is the truth. — B. W. S., Coldwater, Mich.

LIGHT OUT OF DARKNESS

I have received so much benefit from the testimonies in the *Sentinel* and *Journal* that I send mine, hoping it may cheer some struggling heart. I was reared by kind and loving Christian parents and was a member of an orthodox church for over twenty years, but I was never satisfied. I was filled with fear and bound down by the false gods of this world, — sin, disease, and poverty; consequently every way I turned, and in everything I attempted to do, I was met with disappointment and failure; but God was leading me into a different life.

My interest was first awakened to Christian Science about thirteen years ago, and I have been a willing disciple ever since. Through the reading of Science and Health I was healed of chronic catarrh and laryngitis, and it also enabled me to lay off my glasses. Christian Science has not only helped me mentally, morally, and physically, but the greatest blessing of all is the spiritual uplifting which enabled me to know that God is both able and willing to care for His children, if we are but willing to do our part and bear the cross which, though it seems heavy at times, always brings a sure reward. Christian Science has not only helped me, but it has enabled me to help others.

The Bible is a new book to me. I now see what Jesus meant when he said, "Come unto me, all ye that labor and are heavy laden, and I will give you rest."

My heart goes out in gratitude to Mrs. Eddy for the work she has done and is still doing for the world, and to God I am most grateful that He has guided me into the truth, that I may have life, and have it more abundantly. — Mrs. M. M., Chicago, Ill.

A GRATEFUL TESTIMONY

"Thy word is a lamp unto my feet, and a light unto my path."

This has been proven to me in every way. When Christian Science came to me, I was a wreck, physically, mentally, and financially; but since the reading of Science and Health turned my thought toward the light, I have found that, as far as I am willing to receive the word and live it, all comforts are supplied me. I am especially grateful for the spiritual help. I know that things which I did and thought last year I would not do or think this year, and am satisfied. Through the careful and prayerful study of Science and Health I have been lifted from sickness to health, from sorrow to peace, from lack to plenty, and, the most beautiful of all, from darkness to light. — Mrs. H. S. C., Seattle, Wash.

HEALED OF CONSUMPTION AND ASTHMA

It is a pleasure to acknowledge the great benefits which have come to me through Christian Science. It is nearly ten years since I began the investigation of the subject by borrowing a copy of Science and Health. I had become a hopeless sufferer from asthma, — the disease being so aggravated at times as to make breathing almost impossible. I was also a victim of that dread disease, consumption. It was hereditary, nearly all my family on both sides having passed away with it. I took up Christian Science very much as a drowning man catches at a straw. However, I was much interested as soon as I began to understand it, and having read the book nearly all my waking hours for a few weeks, I became so much better and so convinced of its truth, that myself and wife destroyed all the medicines in the home, and have never since used any remedy except Christian Science. I continued to study and to put into practice the teaching as best I knew, and was restored to health in a few months.

Prior to my investigation of Christian Science I had been from boyhood an outspoken infidel, had read that class of literature extensively, and had no desire for anything of a religious nature, — the orthodox teaching never having appealed to me as a rational exposition of an all-wise God. I now have no more doubt of the truth of the teaching of the great Way-shower, Jesus of Nazareth, than I doubt the correctness of the basic law of mathematics or music. I have no doubt whatever that Christian Science saved me from the grave, and thus proved a most practicable and efficient help in time of greatest need. However great my physical suffering has been, I can but feel glad that through it the door of consciousness was opened to let in the light of Truth. Thus I have progressed a little way in the knowledge of God, good, as revealed in Christian Science. — C. B., Webb City, Mo.